Chapter-wise
Topical Objective
Study *for* Package

CBSE 2022 Class 12 Term I

Physics

Corporate Office

DISHA PUBLICATION

45, 2nd Floor, Maharishi Dayanand Marg,
Corner Market, Malviya Nagar, New Delhi - 110017
Tel : 49842349 / 49842350

Typeset by Disha DTP Team

www.dishapublication.com
Books & ebooks for School & Competitive Exams

www.mylearninggraph.com
Etests for Competitive Exams

Write to us at **feedback_disha@aiets.co.in**

Contents

1. ELECTRIC CHARGES AND FIELDS — 1-44

2. ELECTROSTATIC POTENTIAL AND CAPACITANCE — 45-90

3. CURRENT ELECTRICITY — 91-134

4. MOVING CHARGES AND MAGNETISM — 135-176

5. MAGNETISM AND MATTER — 177-200

6. ELECTROMAGNETIC INDUCTION — 201-236

7. ALTERNATING CURRENT — 237-276

1

Electric Charges and Fields

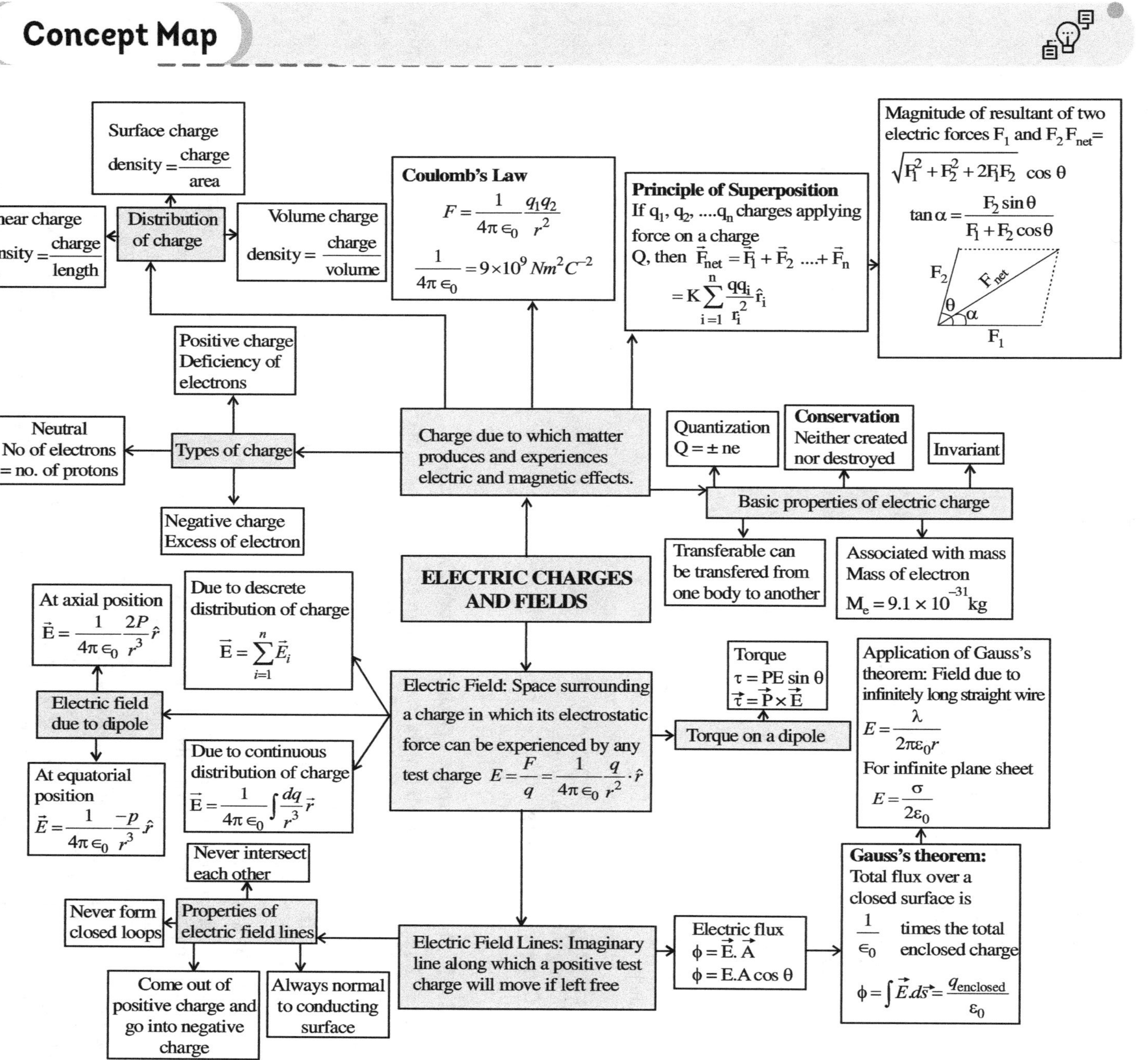

Topic 1 — **Electric Charges & its Basic Properties, Conductors & Insulators, Methods of Charging, Coulomb's Law, Forces between Multiple Charges and Continuous Charge Distribution** 

ELECTRIC CHARGE

Charge is something associated with matter due to which it produces and experiences electric and magnetic effects.

The study of charges is called electricity. The study of charges at rest is called **static electricity** or **electrostatics** while the study of charges in motion is called **current electricity**. There are two types of electric charge :

(i) *Positive charge* and (ii) *Negative charge*

The magnitude of elementary positive or negative charge is same and is equal to 1.6×10^{-19} C.

On a neutral body the net charge is equal to zero i.e. the sum of $+$ (ve) charges is equal to the sum of $-$ (ve) charges. The charges are produced by transfer of atomic electrons from one body to another.

The $+$ (ve) charge means the deficiency of electrons while $-$ (ve) charge means excess of electrons. Charge is a scalar quantity and its **SI unit** is ampere second or **coulomb** (C).

Basic Properties of Electric Charge

(i) *Similar charges repel and opposite charges attract.*

(ii) *A charged body attracts light uncharged bodies.*

(iii) *Accelerated charge radiates energy.*

Charge at rest, $v = 0$	Charge moving at constant speed, $v = $ const.	Charge moving with variable speed, $v \neq$ const.
produces $\vec{E}$ not $\vec{B}$ and radiation	produces $\vec{E}$ and $\vec{B}$ but no radiation	produces $\vec{E}$ and $\vec{B}$ and radiates energy.

(iv) *The charge resides on the outer surface of a conductor. In insulators, it remains where placed i.e. may reside inside the body.*

In case of irregular conducting bodies charge density is not uniform. It is maximum where the radius of curvature is minimum and vice–versa. (as $\sigma \propto 1/R$). *This is why the charge leaks from sharp points.*

(v) *The charge is relativistically invariant.* This means the charge is unaffected by motion.

i.e., charge (q) *at rest* = charge (q) *in motion.*

(vi) *Charge is associated with mass.*

(vii) **Conservation of charge :** *Charge is conserved* i.e., the charge can neither be created nor be destroyed but it may simply be transferred from one body to other.

(viii) *Charge is transferable.*

Quantization of Electric Charge or Principle of Atomicity of Charge

Just as a substance is formed of atoms, a charge is formed of small units of charges, each unit being known as fundamental or elementary charge, which is equal to e = 1.6×10^{-19} coulomb. The principle of quantisation of charge states that *any physically existing charge (q) is integral multiple of elementary charge (e).*

i.e., $q = \pm ne,$ where 'n' is an integer.

One coulomb charge means deficiency of 6.25×10^{18} electrons from a neutral body *i.e., the total number of electrons in one coulomb of charge is 6.25×10^{18} .*

CONDUCTORS AND INSULATORS

The materials which allow electric charge (or electricity) to flow freely through them are called **conductors**. Metals are very good conductors of electric charge. Silver, copper and aluminium are some of the best conductors of electricity. Our skin is also a conductor of electricity. Graphite is the only non-metal which is a conductor of electricity.

All metals, alloys and graphite have '*free electrons*', which can move freely throughout the conductor. These free electrons make metals, alloys and graphite good conductor of electricity.

Aqueous solutions of electrolytes are also conductors.

The materials which do not allow electric charge to flow through them are called **nonconductors** *or* **insulators**.

For example, most plastics, rubber, non-metals (except graphite), dry wood, wax, mica, porcelain, dry air etc., are insulators.

Insulators can be charged but do not conduct electric charge. Insulators do not have '*free electrons*' that is why insulators do not conduct electricity.

METHODS OF CHARGING

A body can be charged by following methods.

(a) **By friction :** By rubbing two bodies together, both positive and negative charges in equal amounts appear simultaneously due to transfer of electrons from one body to the other. When a glass rod is rubbed with silk, the rod becomes positively charged while the silk becomes negatively charged. The decrease in the mass of glass rod is equal to the total mass of electrons lost by it. A comb moving through dry hair gets electrically charged. It starts attracting small bits of paper.

(b) **By electrostatic induction :** If a charged body is brought near a neutral body, the charged body will attract opposite charge and repel similar charge present in the neutral body. As a result of this one side of neutral body becomes (+ ve) while the other (–ve). This process is called "electrostatic induction".

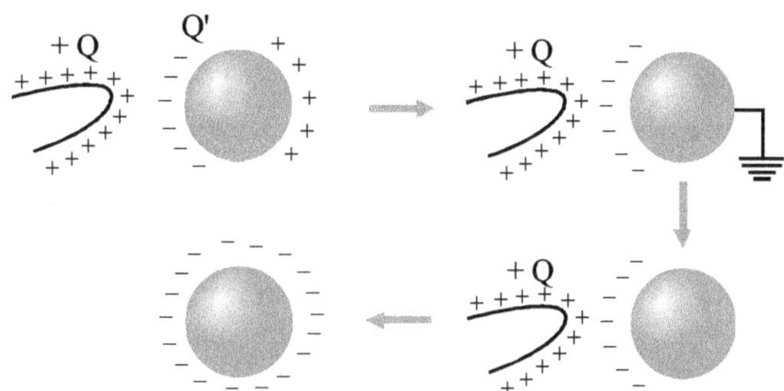

Induced charge can be lesser or equal to inducing charge (but never greater) and its max. value is given by $Q' = -Q(1 - 1/k)$, where 'Q' is inducing charge and 'K' is the dielectric const. of the material of the uncharged body.
For metals $k = \infty \Rightarrow Q' = -Q$.

(c) **By conduction :** Take two conductors, one charged and other uncharged. Bring the conductors in contact with each other. The charge (whether – ve or + ve) under its own repulsion will spread over both the conductors. Thus the conductors will be charged with the same sign. This is called as charging by conduction (through contact).

Charge can be **detected** and **measured** with the help of *gold leaf electroscope, electrometer, voltmeter* or *ballastic galvanometer.*

If a charged body is brought near a charged electroscope the leaves will further diverge if the charge on the body is similar to that on the electroscope and will usually converge if opposite.

COULOMB'S LAW - ELECTROSTATIC FORCE BETWEEN TWO POINT CHARGES

According to coulomb's law *force between two point charges (interaction force) is directly proportional to the product of magnitude of charges (q_1 and q_2) and is inversely proportional to the square of the distance(r) between them.*

i.e., $F \propto \dfrac{q_1 q_2}{r^2}$ or, $F = k \dfrac{q_1 q_2}{r^2}$ where k is a constant

$k = \dfrac{1}{4\pi\varepsilon_0\varepsilon_r}$ $[k = 9 \times 10^9 \text{ N-m}^2\text{C}^{-2}$ in vacuum]

ε_0 = permittivity of free space $= 8.85 \times 10^{-12}$ N-m^2/C^2,

ε_r = relative permittivity (dielectric constant of medium)

This force is conservative in nature. This is also called **inverse square law**. The direction of force is always along the line joining the point charges.

This law is valid for large as well as small distance (up to 10^{-15} m). At a distance less than 10^{-15} m the nuclear force dominates over the coulomb force.

It is valid only for stationary charges not for moving charges.

Coulomb's law in vector form

Suppose the position vectors of two charges q_1 and q_2 are $\vec{r_1}$ and $\vec{r_2}$, then, electric force on charge q_1 due to charge q_2 is,

$$\vec{F}_{12} = \frac{1}{4\pi\varepsilon_0} \frac{q_1 q_2}{|\vec{r_1} - \vec{r_2}|^3}(\vec{r_1} - \vec{r_2})$$

Similarly, electric force on q_2 due to charge q_1 is

$$\vec{F}_{21} = \frac{1}{4\pi\varepsilon_0} \frac{q_1 q_2}{|\vec{r}_2 - \vec{r}_1|^3} (\vec{r}_2 - \vec{r}_1)$$

Here q_1 and q_2 are to be substituted with sign.

Position vector of charges q_1 and q_2 are $\vec{r}_1 = x_1\hat{i} + y_1\hat{j} + z_1\hat{k}$

and $\vec{r}_2 = x_2\hat{i} + y_2\hat{j} + z_2\hat{k}$ respectively.

Where (x_1, y_1, z_1) and (x_2, y_2, z_2) are

the co-ordinates of charges q_1 and q_2 respectively

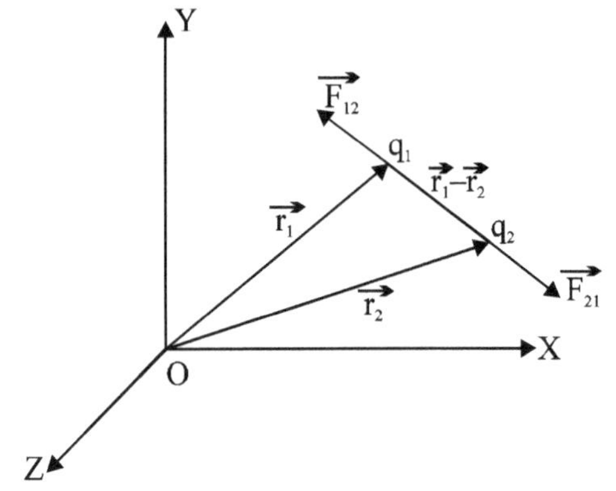

SUPERPOSITION PRINCIPLE – FORCES BETWEEN MULTIPLE CHARGES

Forces between multiple charges – Forces between multiple charges is obtained by what is called the "principle of superposition". Consider a system of n stationary charges $q_1, q_2, q_3, ..., q_n$ in vacuum. What is the force on q_1 due to $q_2, q_3, ..., q_n$? Coulomb's law is not enough to answer this question. Recall that forces of mechanical origin add according to the parallelogram law of addition. Experimentally it is verified that force on any charge due to a number of other charges is the vector sum of all the forces on that charge due to the other charges, taken one at a time. The individual forces are unaffected due to the presence of other charges. This is termed as the principle of superposition. To better understand the concept, consider a system of three charges q_1, q_2 and q_3, as shown in Fig. The force on one charge, say q_1, due to two other charges q_2, q_3 can therefore be obtained by performing a vector addition of the forces due to each one of these charges. Thus, if the force on q_1 due to q_2 is denoted by F_{12} and even though other charges are present F_{12} is given by Eq.

$$F_{12} = \frac{1}{4\pi\varepsilon_0} \frac{q_1 q_2}{r_{12}^2} \hat{r}_{12}$$

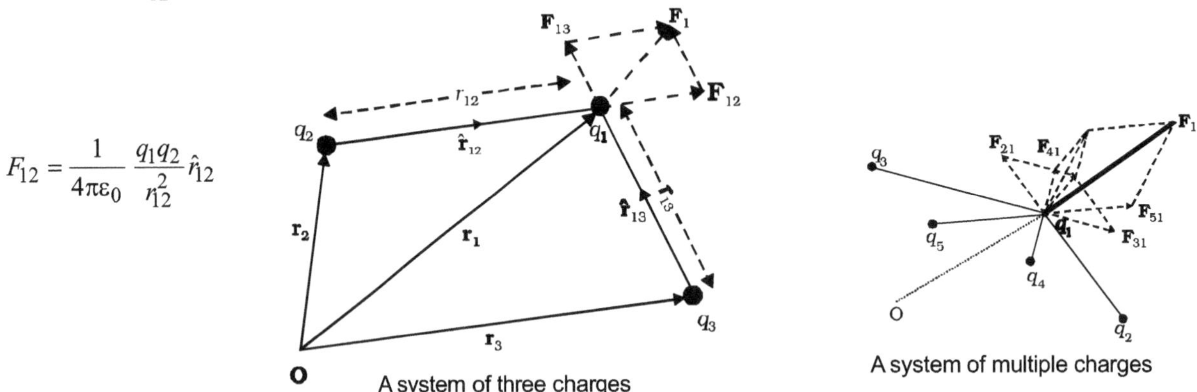

A system of three charges

A system of multiple charges

In the same way, the force on q_1 due to q_3, denoted by F_{13}, is given by $F_{13} = \dfrac{1}{4\pi\varepsilon_0} \dfrac{q_1 q_3}{r_{13}^2} \hat{r}_{13}$ which again is the Coulomb force on

q_1 due to q_3, even though other charge q_2 is present. Thus the total force F_1 on q_1 due to the two charges q_2 and q_3 is given as

$$F_1 = F_{12} + F_{13} = \frac{1}{4\pi\varepsilon_0} \frac{q_1 q_2}{r_{12}^2} \hat{r}_{12} + \frac{1}{4\pi\varepsilon_0} \hat{r}_{13}$$

The above calculation of force can be generalised to a system of charges more than three, as shown in Fig. The principle of superposition says that in a system of charges $q_1, q_2, ... q_n$, the force on q_1 due to q_2 is the same as given by Coulomb's law, i.e., it is unaffected by the presence of the other charges $q, q_4, ... q_n$. The total force F_1 on the charge q_1, due to all other charges $(q_2, ... q_n)$, is then given by the vector sum of the forces $F_{12}, F_{13}, ... F_{1n}$:

$$F_1 = F_{12} + F_{13} + ... + F_{1n} = \frac{1}{4\pi\varepsilon_0}\left[\frac{q_1 q_2}{r_{12}^2}\hat{r}_{12} + \frac{q_1 q_2}{r_{12}^2}\hat{r}_{13} + ... + \frac{q_1 q_n}{r_{1n}^2}\hat{r}_{1n}\right] = \frac{q_1}{4\pi\varepsilon_0}\sum_{i=2}^{n} \frac{q_1}{r_{1i}^2}\hat{r}_{1i}$$

Illustration 1 :

What is the force between two small charged spheres having charges of 4×10^{-7} C and 6×10^{-7} C placed 30 cm apart in air ?

Sol. According to Coulomb's law, $F = \dfrac{1}{4\pi\varepsilon_0} \dfrac{q_1 q_2}{r^2}$

$\Rightarrow \quad F = \dfrac{9\times10^9 \times 4\times10^{-7} \times 6\times10^{-7}}{(30\times10^{-2})^2}$ or, $F = 2.4 \times 10^{-2}\,\text{N}$ repulsive in nature as the two charges are like charges.

CONTINUOUS CHARGE DISTRIBUTION

Continuous distribution of charge : An amount of charge distributes uniformly or non-uniformly on a body. It is of following three types

(a) **Linear charge distribution (λ) :** Charge on a line e.g. charged straight wire, circular charged ring etc.

$$\lambda = \dfrac{\text{Charge}}{\text{Length}} = \text{Linear charge density}$$

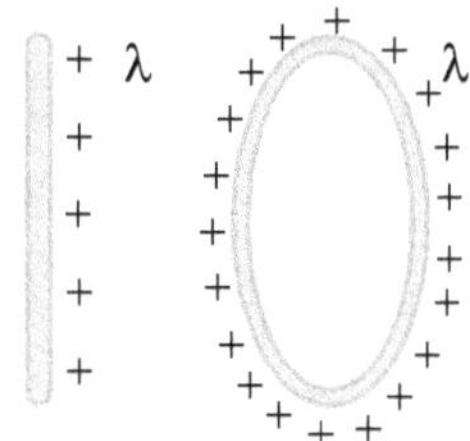

(b) **Surface charge distribution (σ) :** Charge distributed on a surface e.g. plane sheet of charge, conducting sphere, conducting cylinder etc.

$$\sigma = \dfrac{\text{Charge}}{\text{Area}} = \text{Surface charge density}$$

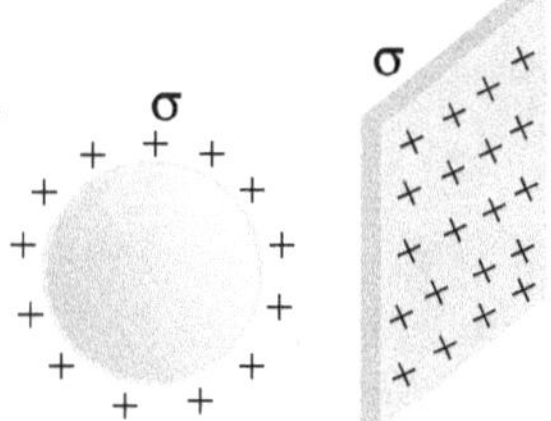

(c) **Volume charge distribution (ρ) :** Charge distributes throughout the volume of the body e.g. charge on a dielectric sphere etc.

$$\rho = \dfrac{\text{Charge}}{\text{Volume}} = \text{Volume charge density}$$

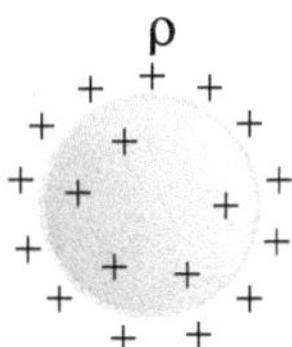

Discrete distribution of charge : A system consisting of ultimate individual charges.

Q_1 Q_2 Q_3 Q_4

Illustration 2 :

A spherical conducting shell of inner radius r_1 and outer radius r_2 has a charge Q. A charge q is placed at the centre of the shell. What is the surface charge density of the inner and outer surfaces of the shell?

Sol. When charge Q is given to the conducting shell, it will be on the outer surface. When charge q is placed at the centre of the shell, it must induce charge $-q$ on the inner surface and $+q$ on the outer surface of the shell. There will be electric field inside the conducting shell. There is charge $-q$ on the inner surface and $(Q + q)$ on the outer surface of the shell,

Charge density of the inner surface, $\sigma_1 = \dfrac{-q}{4\pi r_1^2}$

Charge density of the outer surface, $\sigma_2 = \dfrac{Q+q}{4\pi r_2^2}$

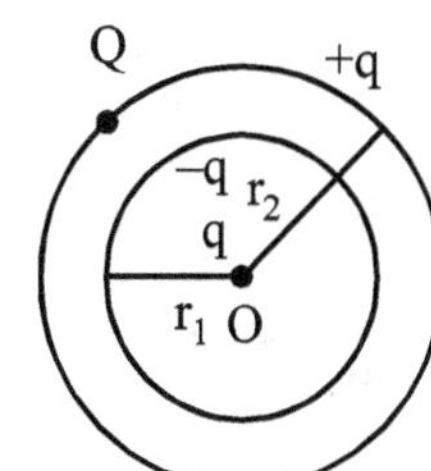

Practice Exercise-1

Multiple Choice Questions

1. Two small spheres each having the charge $+Q$ are suspended by insulating threads of length L from a hook. This arrangement is taken in space where there is no gravitational effect, then the angle ______ between the two suspensions and the tension is ________ in each thread.

(a) $180°, \dfrac{1}{4\pi\varepsilon_0}\dfrac{Q^2}{(2L)^2}$

(b) $90°, \dfrac{1}{4\pi\varepsilon_0}\dfrac{Q^2}{L^2}$

(c) $180°, \dfrac{1}{4\pi\varepsilon_0}\dfrac{Q^2}{2L^2}$

(d) $180°, \dfrac{1}{4\pi\varepsilon_0}\dfrac{Q^2}{L^2}$

2. Two equal point charges each of $3\mu C$ are separated by a certain distance in metres. If they are located at $(\hat{i} + \hat{j} + \hat{k})$ and $(2\hat{i} + 3\hat{j} + \hat{k})$, then the electrostatic force between them is

(a) $9 \times 10^3\,N$

(b) $16 \times 10^{-3}\,N$

(c) $10^{-3}\,N$

(d) $9 \times 10^{-2}\,N$

3. A body is positively charged, it implies that

(a) there is only positive charge in the body

(b) there is positive as well as negative charge in the body but the positive charge is more than negative charge

(c) there is equal positive and negative charge in the body but the positive charge lies in the outer regions

(d) negative charge is displaced from its position

4. On rubbing, when one body gets positively charged and other negatively charged, the electrons transferred from positively charged body to negatively charged body are

(a) valence electrons only

(b) electrons of inner shells

(c) both valence electrons and electrons of inner shell

(d) yet to be established

5. Three charges $+q$, $+2q$ and $+4q$ are connected by strings as shown in the figure. What is ratio of tensions in the strings AB and BC?

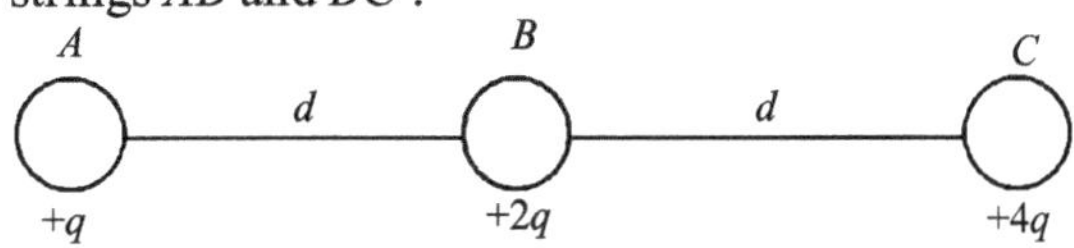

(a) $1:2$ (b) $1:3$ (c) $2:1$ (d) $3:1$

6. Two charge q and $-3q$ are placed fixed on x–axis separated by distance d. Where should a third charge $2q$ be placed such that it will not experience any force?

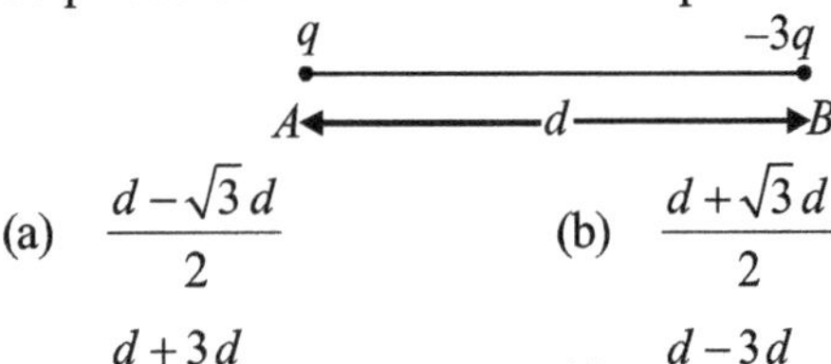

(a) $\dfrac{d - \sqrt{3}\,d}{2}$

(b) $\dfrac{d + \sqrt{3}\,d}{2}$

(c) $\dfrac{d + 3d}{2}$

(d) $\dfrac{d - 3d}{2}$

7. Two positive ions, each carrying a charge q, are separated by a distance d. If F is the force of repulsion between the ions, the number of electrons missing from each ion will be (e being the charge of an electron)

(a) $\dfrac{4\pi\varepsilon_0\,Fd^2}{e^2}$

(b) $\sqrt{\dfrac{4\pi\varepsilon_0\,Fe^2}{d^2}}$

(c) $\sqrt{\dfrac{4\pi\varepsilon_0\,Fd^2}{e^2}}$

(d) $\dfrac{4\pi\varepsilon_0\,Fd^2}{q^2}$

8. A large nonconducting sheet M is given a uniform charge density. Two uncharged small metal rods A and B are placed near the sheet as shown in figure. Then

(a) M attracts A

(b) M attracts B

(c) A attracts B

(d) All of these

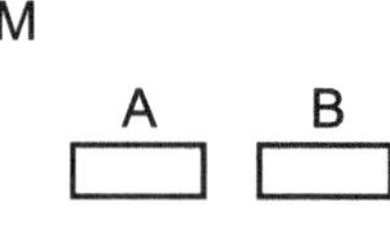

9. Three charges $-q_1$, $+q_2$ and $-q_3$ are place as shown in the figure. The x - component of the force on $-q_1$ is proportional to

(a) $\dfrac{q_2}{b^2} - \dfrac{q_3}{a^2}\cos\theta$

(b) $\dfrac{q_2}{b^2} + \dfrac{q_3}{a^2}\sin\theta$

(c) $\dfrac{q_2}{b^2} + \dfrac{q_3}{a^2}\cos\theta$

(d) $\dfrac{q_2}{b^2} - \dfrac{q_3}{a^2}\sin\theta$

10. A total charge Q is broken in two parts Q_1 and Q_2 and they are placed at a distance R from each other. The maximum force of repulsion between them will occur. when

(a) $Q_2 = \dfrac{Q}{R}, Q_1 = Q - \dfrac{Q}{R}$

(b) $Q_2 = \dfrac{Q}{4}, Q_1 = Q - \dfrac{2Q}{3}$

(c) $Q_2 = \dfrac{Q}{4}, Q_1 = \dfrac{3Q}{4}$

(d) $Q_1 = \dfrac{Q}{2}, Q_2 = \dfrac{Q}{2}$

Assertion & Reason Questions

DIRECTIONS (Qs. 11-14): *Each of these questions contains an assertion followed by reason. Read them carefully and answer the question on the basis of following options. You have to select the one that best describes the two statements.*

(a) If both Assertion and Reason are correct and the Reason is a correct explanation of the Assertion.

(b) If both Assertion and Reason are correct but Reason is not a correct explanation of the Assertion.

(c) If the Assertion is correct but Reason is incorrect.

(d) If the Assertion is incorrect but the Reason is correct.

11. **Assertion :** When bodies are charged through friction, there is a transfer of electric charge from one body to another, but no creation or destruction of charge.

Reason : This follows from conservation of electric charges.

12. **Assertion :** Coulomb force and gravitational force follow the same inverse-square law.

    Reason : Both laws are same in all aspects.

13. **Assertion :** The property that the force with which two charges attract or repel each other are not affected by the presence of a third charge.

    Reason : Force on any charge due to a number of other charge is the vector sum of all the forces on that charge due to other charges, taken one at a time.

14. **Assertion :** Consider two identical charges placed distance 2d apart, along x-axis.

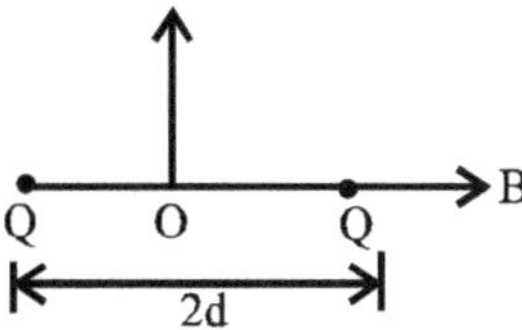

    The equilibrium of a positive test charge placed at the point O midway between them is stable for displacements along the x-axis.

    Reason: Force on test charge is zero.

Case / Passage Based Questions

A body can be charged by following methods.

(a) **By friction :** By rubbing two bodies together, both positive and negative charges in equal amounts appear simultaneously due to transfer of electrons from one body to the other.

(b) **By electrostatic induction :** If a charged body is brought near a neutral body, the charged body will attract opposite charge and repel similar charge present in the neutral body. As a result of this one side of neutral body becomes (+ ve) while the other (–ve). This process is called "electrostatic induction".

(c) **By conduction :** Take two conductors, one charged and other uncharged. Bring the conductors in contact with each other. The charge (whether – ve or + ve) under its own repulsion will spread over both the conductors. Thus the conductors will be charged with the same sign.

15. When a body is charged by induction, then the body
    (a) becomes neutral
    (b) does not lose any charge
    (c) loses whole of the charge on it
    (d) loses part of the charge on it

16. On charging by conduction, mass of a body may
    (a) increase   (b) decreases
    (c) increase or decrease (d) None of these

17. If a body is positively charged, then it has
    (a) excess of electrons
    (b) excess of protons
    (c) deficiency of electrons
    (d) deficiency of neutrons

18. A clyindrical conductor is placed near another positively charged conductor. The net charge acquired by the cylindrical conductor will be
    (a) positive only   (b) negative only
    (c) zero   (d) either positive or negative

19. A positive point charge Q is brought near an isolated metal cube then
    (a) the cube becomes negatively charged.
    (b) the cube becomes positively charged.
    (c) the interior becomes positively charged and the surface becomes negatively charged.
    (d) the interior remains charge free and the surface gets nonuniform charge distribution.

Very Short Answer Questions

20. Force between two point electric charges kept at a distance r apart in air in F. If these charges are kept at the same distance in water, how does the force between them change?

21. What does $q_1 + q_2 = 0$ signify in electrostatics ?

22. In a medium the force of attraction between two point electric charges, distance d apart is F. What distance apart should these be kept in the same medium so that the force between them becomes (i) 3F and (ii) F/3?

23. Calculate the charge carried by 12.5×10^{18} electrons.

24. What is the value of ϵ_0 in S.I system.

Short Answer Questions

25. Two point electric charges of values q and 2q are kept at a distance d apart from each other in air. A third charge Q is to be kept along the same line in such a way that the net force acting on q and 2q is zero. Calculate the position of charge Q in terms of of q and d.

26. Two point charges Q and q are placed at a distance of x and x/2 respectively from a third point charge 4q, all charges are on the same straight line. Calculate the magnitude and nature of charge Q, such that the net force experienced by the charge q is zero.

27. A polythene piece rubbed with wool is found to have a negative charge of 3.2×10^{-7} C. Calculate the no. of electrons transferred.

28. The electrostatic force of repulsion between two equal charged ions is 3.7×10^{-9} N, when they are separated by a distance of 5 Å . How many electrons are numbering from each ion.

29. Two point charges each of 1C separated by 1m distance experience a force of 9×10^9 N. How much force is experienced by them if they are immersed in water, keeping the distance of separator between them same? Given dielectric const. of water = 80

Topic 2 | **Electric Field, Electric Field due to a Point Charge, Electric**  **Field Lines, Electric Dipole, Dipole Moment, Torque on a Dipole, Electric Field due to a Dipole**

ELECTRIC FIELD

The physical field where a charged particle, irrespective of the fact whether it is in motion or at rest, experiences force is called an electric field. The concept of electric field was given by Michael Faraday.

Electric field intensity at a point is equal to the electrostatic force experienced by a unit positive point charge, both in magnitude and direction.

If a test charge q_0 is placed at a point in an electric field and experiences a force $\vec{F}$ due to some charges (called source charges), the electric field intensity at that point due to source charges is given by

$$\vec{E} = \frac{\vec{F}}{q_0}.$$

The presence of the charge q_0 will generally change the original distribution of the other charges, particularly if the charges are on conductors. However, we may choose q_0 to be small enough so that its effect on the original charge distribution is negligible.

$$\vec{E} = \lim_{q_0 \to 0} \frac{F}{q_0}$$

ELECTRIC FIELD DUE TO A POINT CHARGE

The electric field produced by a point charge q can be obtained in general terms from Coulomb's law. First, note that the magnitude of the force exerted by the charge q on a test charge q_0 is $F = kqq_0/r^2$. Then, divide this value by q_0 to obtain the magnitude of the field. Since q_0 is eliminated algebraically from the result, the electric field does not depend on the test charge.

Electric field due to a point charge q : $E = \dfrac{kq}{r^2}$

If (x, y, z) are the co-ordinates of the observation point P, then

$$\vec{r} = x\hat{i} + y\hat{j} + z\hat{k}$$

Also, $r = (x^2 + y^2 + z^2)^{1/2}$ and $r^3 = (x^2 + y^2 + z^2)^{3/2}$

Now, $\vec{E}(\vec{r}) = \dfrac{1}{4\pi\varepsilon_0} \dfrac{q}{r^3} \vec{r} = \dfrac{1}{4\pi\varepsilon_0} \dfrac{q}{(x^2 + y^2 + z^2)^{3/2}} (x\hat{i} + y\hat{j} + z\hat{k})$

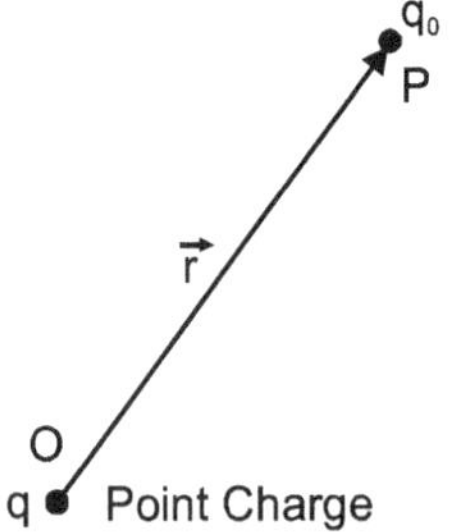

The three rectangular components of $\vec{E}(\vec{r})$ are as follows :

$$E_x(\vec{r}) = \frac{1}{4\pi\varepsilon_0} \frac{q}{(x^2 + y^2 + z^2)^{3/2}} x, \ E_y(\vec{r}) = \frac{1}{4\pi\varepsilon_0} \frac{q}{(x^2 + y^2 + z^2)^{3/2}} y \ \text{and} \ E_z(\vec{r}) = \frac{1}{4\pi\varepsilon_0} \frac{q}{(x^2 + y^2 + z^2)^{3/2}} z$$

Electric Field due to Discrete Distribution of Charge

Point charges placed at different position, use vector approach (superposition rule)

$$\vec{E} = \vec{E_1} + \vec{E_2} + \dots = \sum_{i=1}^{n} \vec{E_i} \quad \text{with} \quad \vec{E_i} = \frac{1}{4\pi\varepsilon_0} \frac{q_i}{r_i^3} \vec{r_i}$$

ELECTRIC FIELD LINES

The magnitude of electric field strength at any point is measured by the number of electric lines of force passing per unit small area around that point normally and the direction of field at any point is given by the tangent to the line of force at the point.

Also, an electric line of force is that imaginary smooth curve drawn in an electric field along which a free isolated unit positive charge (initially at rest) moves.

Properties of Electric Lines of Force

(i) The lines of force diverge out radially from a +ve charge and converge at a – ve charge. More correctly the lines of force are always directed from higher to lower potential.

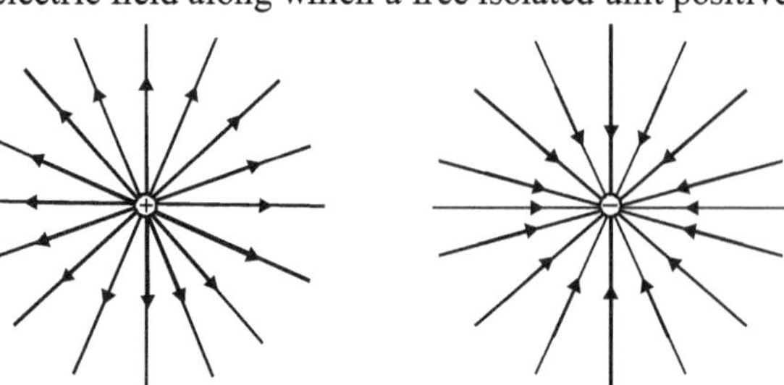

(ii) The tangent drawn at any point on line of force gives the direction of force acting on a positive charge placed at that point.

(iii) Two lines of force never intersect. If they are assumed to intersect, there will be two directions of electric field at the point of intersection, which is impossible.

(iv) These lines have a tendency to contract in tension like a stretched elastic string. This actually explains attraction between opposite charges.

These lines have a tendency to separate from each other in the direction perpendicular to their length. This explains repulsion between like charges.

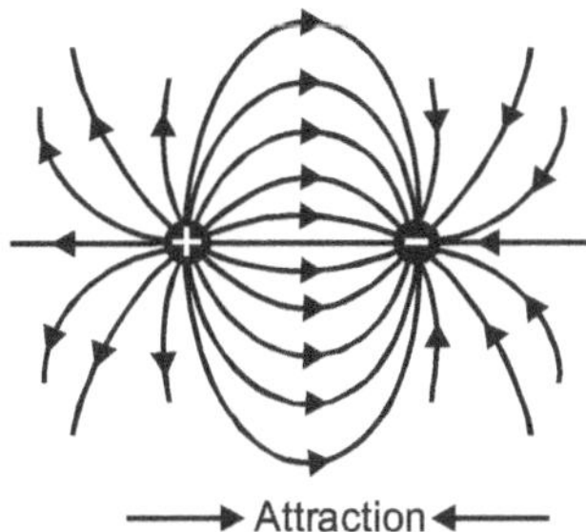
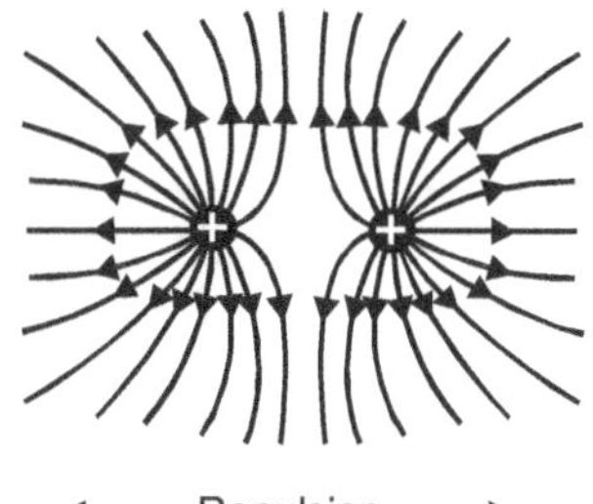

(v) The number of lines originating or terminating on a charge is proportional to the magnitude of charge. In rationalised MKS system $(1/\varepsilon_0)$ electric lines are associated with unit charge. So if a body encloses a charge q total lines of force associated with it (called flux) will be $\dfrac{q}{\varepsilon_0}$.

ELECTRIC DIPOLE, DIPOLE MOMENT AND TORQUE ON A DIPOLE

Electric dipole is a pair of equal and opposite point charges separated by a small distance.

Dipole moment is the product of the magnitude of either charge and the distance between them,

Dipole moment $= \left|\overrightarrow{p}\right| = q \times 2a$

It is directed from negative to positive charge.

The S.I. unit of dipole moment is coulomb - metre (Cm)

Torque on a Dipole in a uniform external field : There is a force qE on q and a force –qE on –q. The net force on the dipole is zero, since **E** is uniform. However, the charges are separated, so the forces act at different points, resulting in a torque on the dipole. When the net force is zero, the torque (couple) is independent of the origin. Its magnitude equals the magnitude of each force multiplied by the arm of the couple (perpendicular distance between the two antiparallel forces).

Magnitude of torque $= q\mathbf{E} \times 2\,a \sin\theta = 2\,q\,a\,E \sin\theta$

Its direction is normal to the plane of the paper, coming out of it. The magnitude of $\vec{p} \times \vec{E}$ is also $p\,E \sin\theta$ and its direction is normal to the paper, coming out of it.

Thus, $\vec{\tau} = \vec{p} \times \vec{E}$

ELECTRIC FIELD DUE TO A DIPOLE

Electric Field at an Axial Point of a Dipole

Electric field at P due to negative charge $\overrightarrow{E}_1 = \dfrac{1}{4\pi\varepsilon_0} \dfrac{q}{\left(r+\dfrac{d}{2}\right)^2}(-\hat{r})$

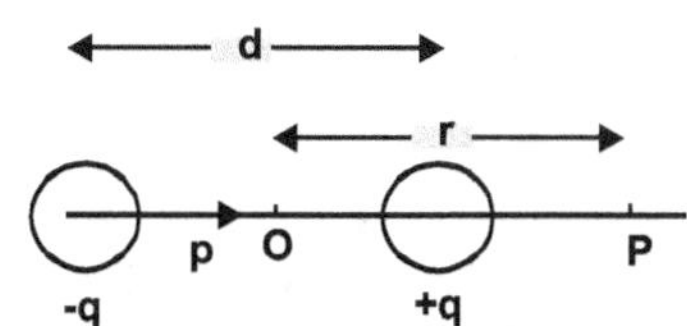

Electric field at P due to positive charge $\overrightarrow{E}_2 = \dfrac{1}{4\pi\varepsilon_0} \dfrac{q}{\left(r-\dfrac{d}{2}\right)^2}(+\hat{r})$

Total electric field at axial point P is $\vec{E}_a = \vec{E}_1 + \vec{E}_2$

$$\vec{E}_a = \frac{q}{4\pi\varepsilon_0}\left(\frac{1}{(r-d/2)^2} - \frac{1}{(r+d/2)^2}\right)\hat{r} \quad\text{or}\quad \vec{E}_a = \frac{q}{4\pi\varepsilon_0}\frac{2.r.d}{(r^2-d^2/4)^2}\hat{r} = \frac{2pr}{4\pi\varepsilon_0(r^2-d^2/4)^2}\hat{r}$$

When $r \gg d$, $\vec{E}_a = \dfrac{1}{4\pi\varepsilon_0}\dfrac{2p}{r^3}\hat{r}$, The axial field is parallel to dipole moment.

Electric Field at an Equatorial Point of Dipole

Electric field at P due to negative charge, $E_1 = \dfrac{1}{4\pi\varepsilon_0}\dfrac{q}{(r^2+d^2/4)}$

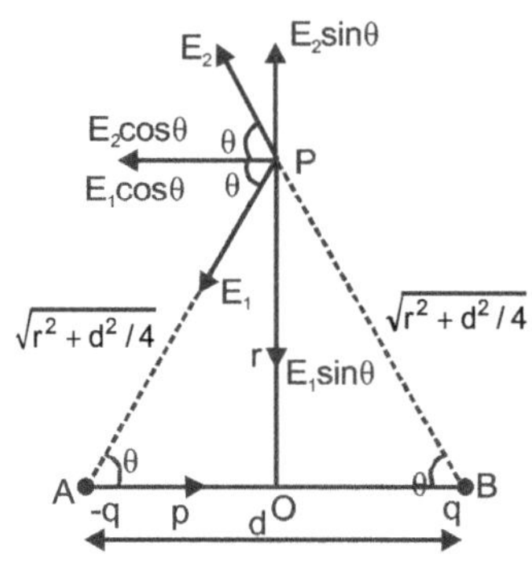

Electric field at P due to positive charge, $E_2 = \dfrac{1}{4\pi\varepsilon_0}\left(\dfrac{q}{r^2+d^2/4}\right)$

Fields E_1 and E_2 are equal in magnitude

Resolving E_1 and E_2 into two components one along OP and other perpendicular to OP

We find, $E_1\sin\theta = E_2\sin\theta$

Total field $E_\perp = E_1\cos\theta + E_2\cos\theta = 2E_1\cos\theta = 2E_2\cos\theta$

$$E_\perp = 2\frac{q}{4\pi\varepsilon_0}\frac{1}{(r^2+d^2/4)}\frac{d/2}{\sqrt{r^2+d^2/4}} = \frac{q.d}{4\pi\varepsilon_0(r^2+d^2/4)^{3/2}} = \frac{p}{4\pi\varepsilon_0(r^2+d^2/4)^{3/2}}$$

If $r \gg d$ $\;\vec{E}_\perp = \dfrac{1}{4\pi\varepsilon_0}\dfrac{p}{r^3}(-\hat{r})$ i.e. field at equatorial point is antiparallel to dipole moment.

From this it is clear that :

(i) Intensity due to a dipole varies as $(1/r^3)$ and can never be zero unless $r \to \infty$ or $p \to 0$.

(ii) E will be maximum when $\cos^2\theta = \max = 1$, i.e., $\theta = 0$, *for end on, axial or tan A position E is maximum*

$$E_{max} = \frac{1}{4\pi\varepsilon_0}\frac{2p}{r^3}$$

(iii) E will be minimum when $\cos^2\theta = \min = 1$ i.e. $\theta = 90°$ i.e., *for broad on, equatorial or tan B position E is minimum*

$$E_{min} = \frac{1}{4\pi\varepsilon_0}\frac{p}{r^3}$$

(iv) The electric field at axial point is parallel to dipole moment vector and electric field at equatorial point is antiparallel to dipole moment vector.

(v) The ratio of field at axial point to field at equatorial point is $E_a : E_\perp = 2 : 1$.

Illustration 3 :

Two point charges $q_1 = 3\,\mu C$ and $q_2 = -3\,\mu C$ are located 20 cm apart in vacuum. What is the electric field at the mid point of the line joining the two charges? If a charge of -1.5×10^{-9} C is placed at the mid point, what is the force experienced by that charge?

Sol. Field at O due to $q_1 = \dfrac{kq_1}{AO^2} = \dfrac{9\times10^9 \times 3\times10^{-6}}{(0.1)^2} = 2.7\times10^6$ N/C along OB

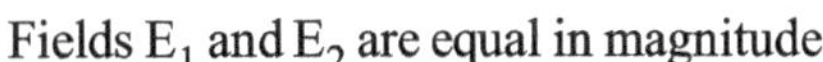

Field at O due to $q_2 = \dfrac{kq_2}{OB^2} = \dfrac{9\times10^9 \times 3\times10^{-6}}{(0.1)^2} = 2.7\times10^6$ N/C along OB

$\therefore$ Total field at O $= E_1 + E_2 = 2 \times 2.7 \times 10^6 = 5.4 \times 10^6$ N/C

Force on the charge $(-1.5\times10^{-9}$ C) at O $= F = q_E = 1.5\times10^{-9}\times5.4\times10^6 = 8.1\times10^{-3}$ N along OA

Illustration 4 :

Two charges of $+10\,\mu C$ and $+40\,\mu C$ respectively are placed 12 cm apart. Find the position of the point where the electric field is zero.

Sol. At O, Electric field is $E_1 = E_2$

$$\Rightarrow \frac{kq_1}{x^2} = \frac{kq_2}{(r-x)^2} \Rightarrow \frac{10\times10^{-6}}{x^2} = \frac{40\times10^{-6}}{(r-x)^2}$$

$$(r-x)^2 = 4x^2$$

or $\pm\,(r-x) = 2x \Rightarrow r = 3x$

$$x = \frac{r}{3} = \frac{0.12}{3} = 0.04\,\text{m}.$$

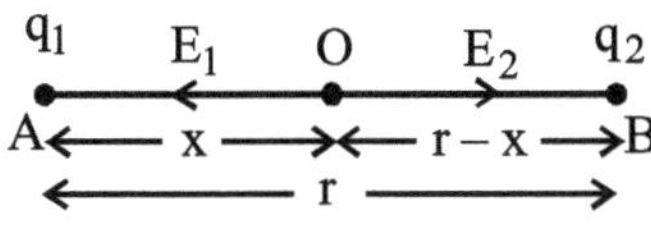

$\therefore$ Electric field intensity will be zero at a distance of 0.04 m from $10\,\mu C$ charge

Illustration 5 :

A spherical conductor of radius 12 cm has a charge of 1.6×10^{-7} C distributed uniformly on its surface. What is the electric field (a) inside the sphere (b) just outside the sphere?

Sol. (a) Inside the sphere (hollow) $E = 0$

(b) Just outside the sphere $E = \dfrac{kq}{R^2} = \dfrac{9\times10^9 \times 1.6\times10^{-7}}{(0.12)^2} = 10^5\,\text{N/C}$.

Practice Exercise-2

Multiple Choice Questions

1. Figure shows the electric lines of force emerging from a charged body. If the electric field at A and B are E_A and E_B respectively and if the displacement between A and B is r then

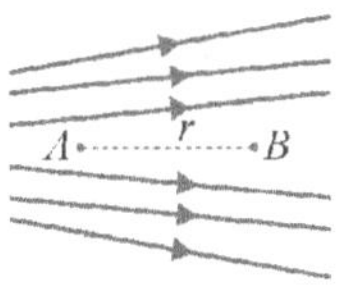

   (a) $E_A > E_B$

   (b) $E_A < E_B$

   (c) $E_A = \dfrac{E_B}{r}$

   (d) $E_A = \dfrac{E_B}{r^2}$

2. An electric dipole with dipole moment 4×10^{-9} cm is aligned at $30°$ with the direction of a uniform electric field of magnitude 5×10^4 NC^{-1}. The torque acting on the dipole is

   (a) 1×10^{-4} Nm   (b) 5×10^{-8} Nm

   (c) 11×10^{-12} Nm   (d) 25×10^{-19} Nm

3. The electric field at a point on equatorial line of a dipole _______ to direction of the dipole moment.

   (a) will be parallel

   (b) will be in opposite direction

   (c) will be perpendicular

   (d) are not related

4. The electric field intensity just sufficient to balance the earth's gravitational attraction on an electron will be: (given mass and charge of an electron respectively are 9.1×10^{-31} kg and 1.6×10^{-19} C.)

   (a) -5.6×10^{-11} N/C   (b) -4.8×10^{-15} N/C

   (c) -1.6×10^{-19} N/C   (d) -3.2×10^{-19} N/C

5. Which one of the following is not a property of field lines

   (a) Field lines are continuous curves without any breaks.

   (b) Two field lines cannot cross each other.

   (c) Field lines start at positive charge and end at negative charge

   (d) They form closed loop

6. If a dipole of dipole moment $\vec{p}$ is placed in a uniform electric field $\vec{E}$, then torque acting on it is given by

   (a) $\vec{\tau} = \vec{p}.\vec{E}$ (b) $\vec{\tau} = \vec{p}\times\vec{E}$

   (c) $\vec{\tau} = \vec{p}+\vec{E}$ (d) $\vec{\tau} = \vec{p}-\vec{E}$

7. If E_a be the electric field strength of a short dipole at a point on its axial line and E_e that on the equatorial line at the same distance, then

   (a) $E_e = 2E_a$ (b) $E_a = 2E_e$

   (c) $E_a = E_e$ (d) None of these

8. Which of the following graphs shows the correct variation in magnitude of torque on an electric dipole rotated in a uniform electric field from stable equillibrium to unstable equillibrium?

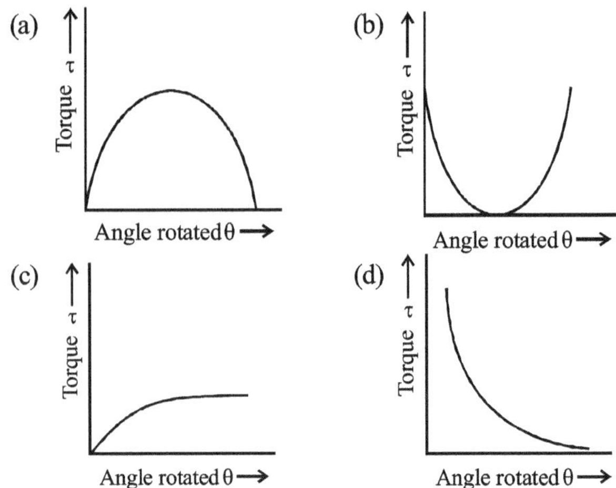

9. The electric intensity due to a dipole of length 10 cm and having a charge of 500 μC, at a point on the axis at a distance 20 cm from one of the charges in air, is
   (a) 6.25×10^7 N/C   (b) 9.28×10^7 N/C
   (c) 13.1×10^{11} N/C   (d) 20.5×10^7 N/C

Assertion & Reason Questions

DIRECTIONS (Qs. 10-14) : *Each of these questions contains an assertion followed by reason. Read them carefully and answer the question on the basis of following options. You have to select the one that best describes the two statements.*
(a) If both Assertion and Reason are correct and the Reason is a correct explanation of the Assertion.
(b) If both Assertion and Reason are correct but Reason is not a correct explanation of the Assertion.
(c) If the Assertion is correct but Reason is incorrect.
(d) If the Assertion is incorrect but the Reason is correct.

10. **Assertion :** If a proton and an electron are placed in the same uniform electric field. They experience different acceleration.
    Reason : Electric force on a test charge is dependent of its mass.
11. **Assertion :** A metallic shield in form of a hollow shell may be built to block an electric field.
    Reason : In a hollow spherical shield, the electric field inside it is zero at every point.
12. **Assertion :** A point charge is brought in an electric field, the field at a nearby point will increase or decrease, depending on the nature of charge.
    Reason : The electric field is independent of the nature of charge.
13. **Assertion :** On disturbing an electric dipole in stable equillibrium in an electric field, it returns back to its stable equillibrium orientation.
    Reason : A restoring torque acts on the dipole on being disturbed from its stable equillibrium.
14. **Assertion :** On going away from a point charge or a small electric dipole, electric field decreases at the same rate in both the cases.
    Reason : Electric field is inversely proportional to square of distance from the charge or an electric dipole.

Electric dipole is a pair of equal and opposite point charges separated by a small distance.

Dipole moment is the product of the magnitude of either charge and the distance between them,

Dipole moment $= \left| \vec{p} \right| = q \times 2a$

It is directed from negative to positive charge.

Dipole in a uniform external field : There is a force qE on q and a force –qE on –q. The net force on the dipole is zero, since **E** is uniform. However, the charges are separated, so the forces act at different points, resulting in a torque on the dipole. When the net force is zero, the torque (couple) is independent of the origin.

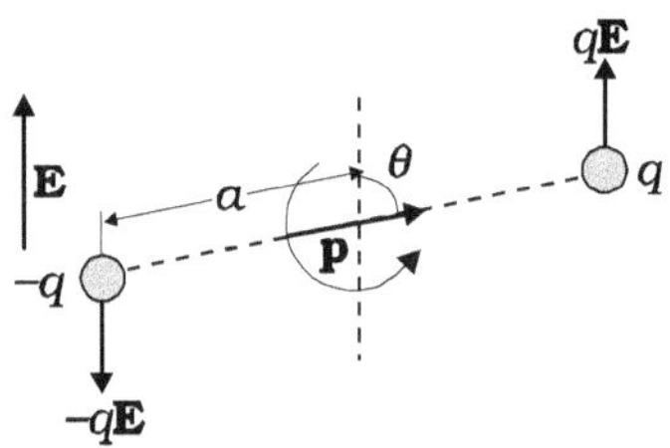

15. An electric dipole has a pair of equal and opposite point charges q and $-q$ separated by a distance $2x$. The axis of the dipole is
    (a) from positive charge to negative charge
    (b) from negative charge to positive charge
    (c) perpendicular to the line joining the two charges drawn at the centre and pointing upward direction
    (d) perpendicular to the line joining the two charges drawn at the centre and pointing downward direction
16. The electric field at a point on equatorial line of a dipole and direction of the dipole moment
    (a) will be parallel
    (b) will be in opposite direction
    (c) will be perpendicular
    (d) are not related
17. An electric dipole is placed at an angle of 30° to a non-uniform electric field. The dipole will experience
    (a) a translational force only in the direction of the field
    (b) a translational force only in the direction normal to the direction of the field
    (c) a torque as well as a translational force
    (d) a torque only
18. Intensity of an electric field (E) depends on distance r, due to a dipole, is related as
    (a) $E \propto \dfrac{1}{r}$ (b) $E \propto \dfrac{1}{r^2}$ (c) $E \propto \dfrac{1}{r^3}$ (d) $E \propto \dfrac{1}{r^4}$
19. On decreasing the distance between the two charges of a dipole which is perpendicular to electric field and decreasing the angle between the dipole and electric field, the torque on the dipole
    (a) increases   (b) decreases
    (c) remains same   (d) cannot be predicted

Very Short Answer Questions

20. Sketch the lines of force due to two equal positive point charges placed near each other.

21. What orientation of an electric dipole in a uniform electric field corresponds to its stable equilibrium?

22. If an oil drop of weight 3.2×10^{-13} N is moving in an electric field of 5×10^5 V/m, find the charge on oil drop.

23. A given charge situated at a distance from an electric dipole in the end on position, experiences a force F. If the distance of charge is doubled, what will the force acting on the charge?

24. The electric field strength at a distance r from a point charge Q is E. What will be electric field strength if the distance of the observation point is increased by 2r?

Short Answer Questions

25. Derive an expression for electric field due to a single point charge.

26. Derive an expression for the electric field intensity due to an electric dipole at a point on its axial line.

27. Derive an expression for the electric field intensity at an equatorial point of an electric dipole.

28. An electric dipole is held in a uniform electric field.

   (i)   Show that no translatory force acts on it.

   (ii) Derive an expression for the torque acting on it.

29. Two point electric charges of unknown magnitude and sign are placed at a distance 'd' apart. The electric field intensity is zero at a point, not between the charges but on the line joining them. Write two essential conditions for this to happen.

30. An electric dipole is placed at rest in a uniform electric field, and released. How will it move?

31. Define the electric field at the point P due to the system of three point charges, shown.

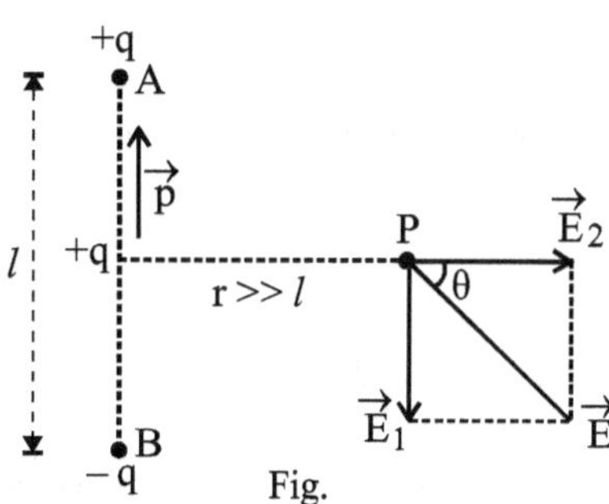

32. If an electron, moving with a finite velocity, enters a transverse electric field, then which path will the electron be take?

33. Two point charges $q_1 = +0.2$ C and $q_2 = +0.4$ C are placed 0.1 m apart. Calculate the electric field at

  (i)   mid point between the charges.

  (ii) a point on the line joining q_1 and q_2 so that it is 0.05 m away from q_2 and 0.15 m away from q_1.

34. Three charges $-\sqrt{2}$ μC, $2\sqrt{2}$ μC and $-\sqrt{2}$ μC are arranged along a straight line as shown in the figure. Calculate the total electric field intensity due to all these charges at the point P.

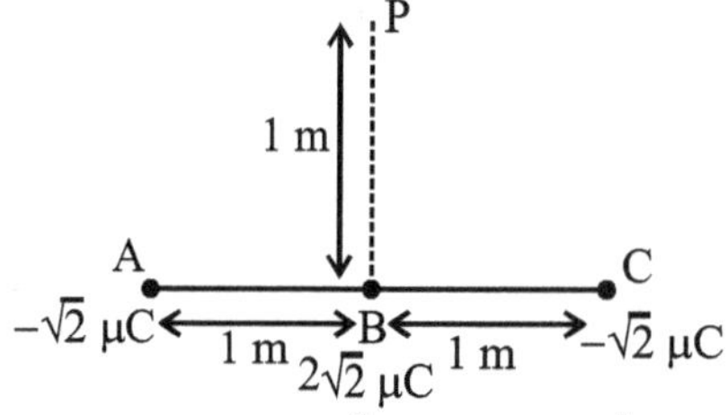

35. Two point charges 2×10^{-7} C and 1×10^{-7} C are 1 cm apart. What is the magnitude of the field produced by either charge at the site of the other?

36. Calculate the electric field due to a dipole of length 10 cm and consisting of ± 100 μC charges at a point 20 cm from each charge (equatorial point).

37. An electric dipole consists of the two particles, having the opposite charges $+2 \times 10^{-6}$ C and -2×10^{-6} C and separated by a distance of 10^{-2} m. What is the electric dipole moment of the dipole? Calculate the electric field at a point P on the axis of dipole at a distance of 1 m from it's mid point. Also, calculate the electric field at a point P on the equator of dipole at a distance of 1 m from its mid point.

Topic 3   Electric Flux, Gauss's Theorem and its Applications 

ELECTRIC FLUX

Electric flux over an area in an electric field is the total number of electric lines of force crossing this area.

It is measured by the product of surface area and the corresponding component of electric field normal to the area.

$$\phi = \oint \overline{E} . d\overline{s}$$

It is a scalar quantity. Its SI unit is volt metre (Vm) or Nm^2/C. Dimensions : $[ML^3T^{-3}A^{-1}]$

GAUSS'S THEOREM

The surface integral of electrostatic field $\vec{E}$ produced by any source over any closed surface S in vacuum or the total electric flux over the closed surface in vacuum is $\dfrac{1}{\varepsilon_0}$ times the total charge contained inside the surface S.

Mathematically, $\phi_E = \oint \vec{E}.\vec{dS} = \dfrac{Q}{\varepsilon_0}$

Proof of Gauss's Theorem for Spherically Symmetric Surface

Electric flux though a surface element dS is

$$d\phi = E.dS = \frac{1}{4\pi\varepsilon_0}\frac{q}{r^2}\hat{r}(dS\hat{n}) \implies d\phi = \frac{1}{4\pi\varepsilon_0}\frac{qdS}{r^2}\hat{r}.\hat{n}$$

Here, $\hat{r}.\hat{n} = 1.1\cos 0° = 1$

$\therefore \qquad d\phi = \dfrac{1}{4\pi\varepsilon_0}.\dfrac{q.dS}{r^2}$

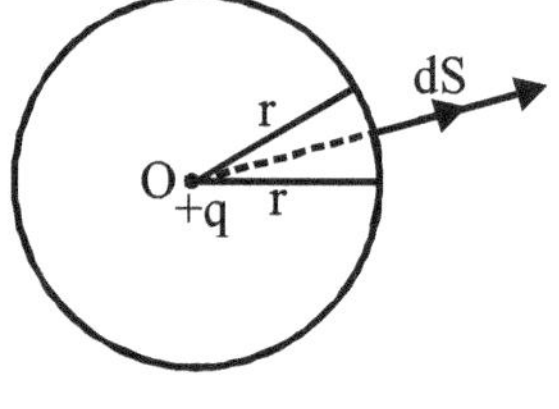

Total electric flux through the spherical surface is

$$\phi_E = \oint_S d\phi = \frac{1}{4\pi\varepsilon_0}.\frac{q}{r^2}\oint_S dS = \frac{1}{\phi\pi\varepsilon_0}.\frac{q}{r^2}.4\pi r^2 = \frac{q}{\varepsilon_0}$$

This law is valid for symmetrical charge distribution and for all vector fields obeying inverse square law.

Application of Gauss's Theorem

Gauss's law is used to calculate electric flux, electric field intensity etc.

Electric Field Due to a line Charge or Infinitely Long Straight Wire

Consider an infinite line which has a linear charge density λ. Using Gauss's law, let us find the electric field at a distance 'r' from the line charge.

The cylindrical symmetry tells us that the field strength will be the same at all points at a fixed distance r from the line. Thus, the field lines are directed radially outwards, perpendicular to the line charge.

The appropriate choice of Gaussian surface is a cylinder of radius r and length L. On the flat end faces, S_2 and S_3, $\vec{E}$ is perpendicular $\vec{dS}$, which means flux is zero on them.

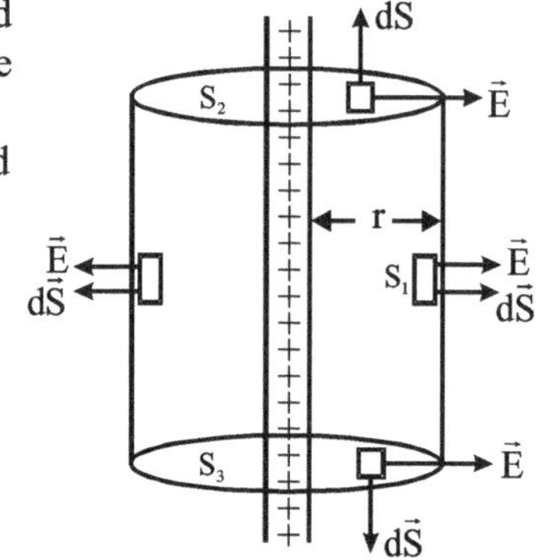

On the curved surface S_1, $\vec{E}$ is parallel to $\vec{dS}$, so that $\vec{E}.\vec{dS} = EdS$.

The charge enclosed by the cylinder is $Q = \lambda L$.

Applying Gauss's law to the curved surface, we have

$$E\oint dS = E(2\pi rL) = \frac{\lambda L}{\varepsilon_0} \quad \text{or,} \quad E = \frac{\lambda}{2\pi\varepsilon_0 r}$$

Electric Field Due to Uniformly Charged Infinite Plane Sheet

To find electric field due to infinite plane sheet of charge at any point P at distant r from it, choose a cylinder of area of cross-section A through the point P as the Gaussian surface.

The flux due to the electric field of the plane sheet of charge passes only through the two circular caps of the cylinder.

Let surface charge density $= \sigma$

According to Gauss's law

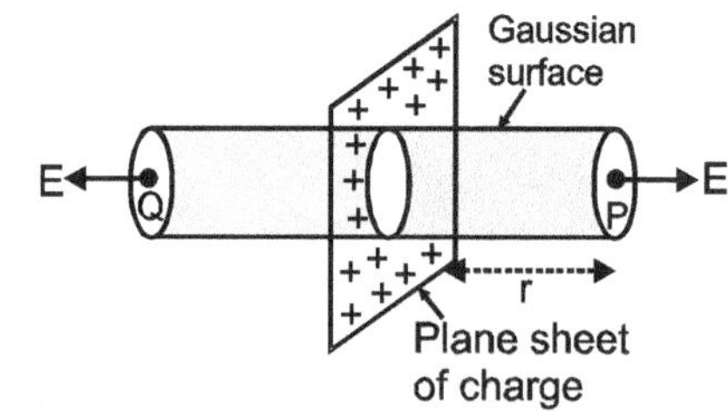

$$\oint \vec{E}.\vec{dS} = q_{in}/\varepsilon_0$$

$$\underbrace{\int E\,ds\cos\theta}_{\text{I circular surface}} + \underbrace{\int E\,ds\cos\theta}_{\text{II circular surface}} + \underbrace{\int E\,ds\cos\theta}_{\text{cylindrical surface}} = \frac{\sigma A}{\varepsilon_0}$$

$$\text{or,} \quad EA + EA + 0 = \frac{\sigma A}{\varepsilon_0} \quad \text{or} \quad E = \frac{\sigma}{2\varepsilon_0}$$

Illustration 6 :

The electric field in a region is given by $\vec{E} = E_0 \dfrac{x}{\ell}\hat{i}$. Find the charge contained inside a cubical volume bounded by the surfaces $x = 0$, $x = \ell$ $y = 0$, $y = \ell$, $z = 0$ and $z = \ell$.

Sol. At $x = 0$, $E = 0$ and $x = \ell$, $\vec{E} = E_0\hat{i}$.

The direction of the field is along the x-axis, so it will cross the yz – face of the cube. The flux of this field

$$f = \phi_{left\ face} + \phi_{right\ face} = 0 + E_0\ell^2 = E_0\ell^2$$

By Gauss's law, $\phi = \dfrac{q}{\epsilon_0}$

$\therefore\ q = \epsilon_0\,\phi = \epsilon_0\,E_0\ell^2$.

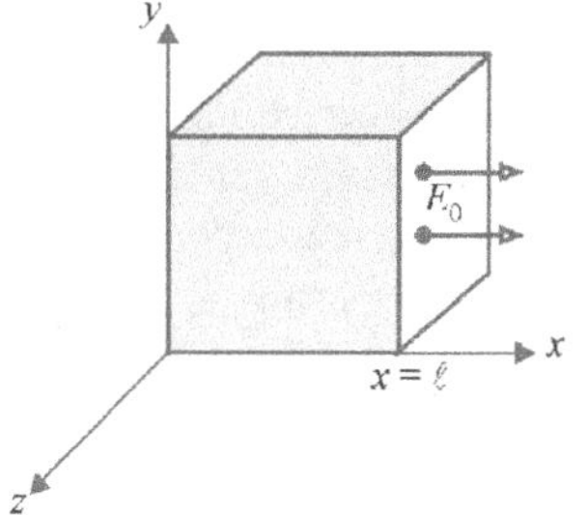

Practice Exercise-3

Multiple Choice Questions

1. A rod of length 2.4 m and radius 4.6 mm carries a negative charge of 4.2×10^{-7} C spread uniformly over it surface. The electric field near the mid–point of the rod, at a point on its surface is
   (a) -8.6×10^5 N C^{-1} (b) 8.6×10^4 N C^{-1}
   (c) -6.7×10^5 N C^{-1} (d) 6.7×10^4 N C^{-1}

2. The total electric flux emanating from a closed surface enclosing an α-particle is (e-electronic charge)
   (a) $\dfrac{2e}{\varepsilon_0}$ (b) $\dfrac{e}{\varepsilon_0}$ (c) $e\varepsilon_0$ (d) $\dfrac{\varepsilon_0 e}{4}$

3. A square surface of side L meter in the plane of the paper is placed in a uniform electric field E (volt/m) acting along the same plane at an angle θ with the horizontal side of the square as shown in Figure. The electric flux linked to the surface, in units of volt. m, is
   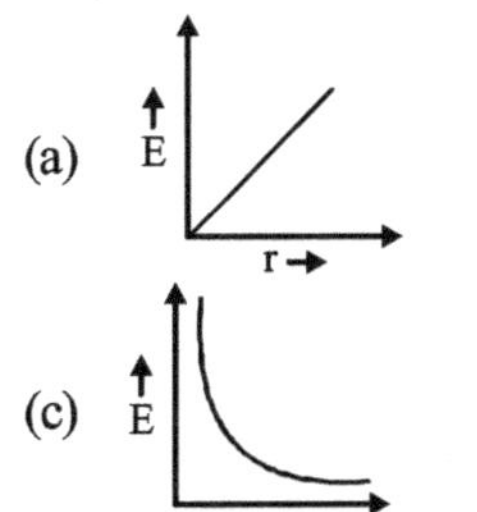
   (a) EL^2
   (b) $EL^2 \cos\theta$
   (c) $EL^2 \sin\theta$
   (d) zero

4. The E-r curve for an infinite linear charge distribution will be
   (a) 
   (b)
   (c)
   (d)

5. At the centre of a cubical box $+ Q$ charge is placed. The value of total flux that is coming out a wall is
   (a) Q/ε_o (b) $Q/3\varepsilon_o$ (c) $Q/4\varepsilon_o$ (d) $Q/6\varepsilon_o$

6. The Gaussian surface
   (a) can pass through a continuous charge distribution.
   (b) cannot pass through a continuous charge distribution.
   (c) can pass through any system of discrete charges.
   (d) can pass through a continuous charge distribution as well as any system of discrete charges.

7. In a region, the intensity of an electric field is given by $\vec{E} = 2\hat{i} + 3\hat{j} + \hat{k}$ in NC^{-1}. The electric flux through a surface $\vec{S} = 10\hat{i}$ m^2 in the region is
   (a) $5\,\text{Nm}^2\text{C}^{-1}$ (b) $10\,\text{Nm}^2\text{C}^{-1}$
   (c) $15\,\text{Nm}^2\text{C}^{-1}$ (d) $20\,\text{Nm}^2\text{C}^{-1}$

8. In the figure the net electric flux through the area A is $\phi = \vec{E}\cdot\vec{A}$ when the system is in air. On immersing the system in water the net electric flux through the area
   (a) becomes zero
   (b) remains same
   (c) increases
   (d) decreases

9. A charge q is placed at the centre of the open end of a cylindrical vessel. The flux of the electric field through the surface of the vessel is
   (a) zero
   (b) q/ε_o
   (c) $q/2\varepsilon_o$
   (d) $2q/\varepsilon_o$

10. If the electric flux entering and leaving an enclosed surface respectively is ϕ_1 and ϕ_2, the electric charge inside the surface will be
    (a) $(\phi_2 + \phi_2) \times \varepsilon_o$ (b) $(\phi_2 - \phi_2) \times \varepsilon_o$
    (c) $(\phi_1 + \phi_2) \times \varepsilon_o$ (d) $(\phi_2 - \phi_1) \times \varepsilon_o$

Assertion & Reason Questions

DIRECTIONS (Qs. 11) : *Each of these questions contains an assertion followed by reason. Read them carefully and answer the question on the basis of following options. You have to select the one that best describes the two statements.*
(a) If both Assertion and Reason are correct and the Reason is a correct explanation of the Assertion.
(b) If both Assertion and Reason are correct but Reason is not a correct explanation of the Assertion.
(c) If the Assertion is correct but Reason is incorrect.
(d) If the Assertion is incorrect but the Reason is correct.

11. **Assertion :** Four point charges q_1, q_2, q_3 and q_4 are as shown in figure. The flux over the shown Gaussian surface depends only on charges q_3 and q_4.

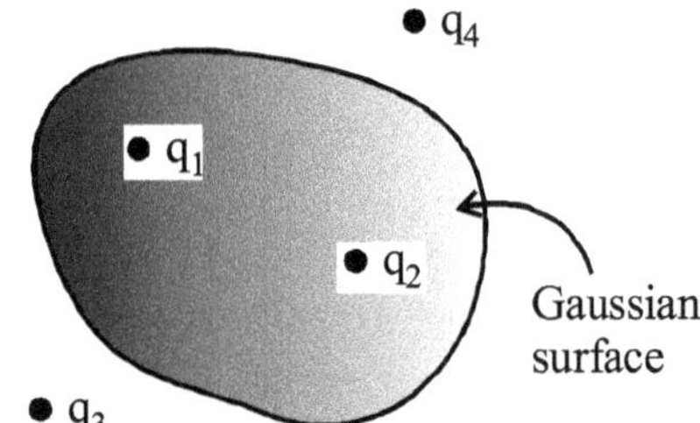

Reason : Electric field at all points on Gaussian surface depends only on charges q_1 and q_2.

Case / Passage Based Questions

Electric flux over an area in an electric field is the total number of electric lines of force crossing this area.

It is measured by the product of surface area and the corresponding component of electric field normal to the area.

$$\phi = \oint \vec{E}.d\vec{s}$$

It is a scalar quantity. Its SI unit is volt metre (Vm) or Nm^2/C. Dimensions : $[ML^3T^{-3}A^{-1}]$

12. For a given surface the Gauss's law is stated as $\oint \vec{E}.d\vec{A} = 0$. From this we can conclude that
(a) E is necessarily zero on the surface
(b) E is perpendicular to the surface at every point
(c) the total flux through the surface is zero
(d) the flux is only going out of the surface

13. In a region of space having a uniform electric field E, a hemispherical bowl of radius r is placed. The electric flux ϕ through the bowl is
(a) $2\pi RE$ (b) $4\pi R^2E$ (c) $2\pi R^2E$ (d) πR^2E

14. A cylinder of radius R and length ℓ is placed in a uniform electric field E parallel to the axis of the cylinder. The total flux over the curved surface of the cylinder is
(a) zero   (b) πR^2E (c) $2\pi R^2E$ (d) $E/\pi R^2$

15. Electric flux over a surface in an electric field may be
(a) positive   (b) negative
(c) zero   (d) All of these

16. Electric charges are distributed in a small volume. The flux of the electric field through a spherical surface of radius 1 m surrounding the total charge is 100 V-m. The flux over the concentric sphere of radius 2 m will be
(a) 25 V-m   (b) 50 V-m
(c) 100 V-m   (d) 200 V-m

Very Short Answer Questions

17. Figure shows three point charges, $+2q$, $-q$ and $+3q$. Two charges $+2q$ and $-q$ are enclosed within a surface S. What is the electric flux due to this configuration through the surface S?

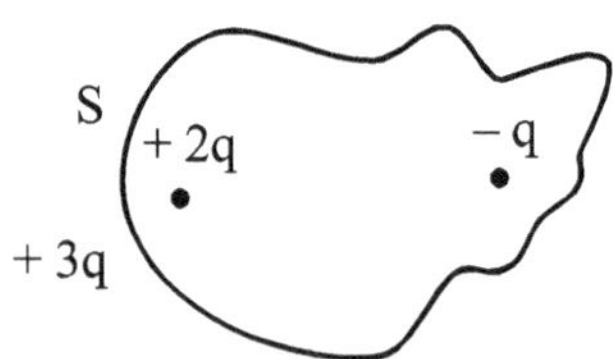

18. What is the electric flux through a cube of side 1cm which enclosed an electric dipole?

19. How does the electric flux due to a point charge enclosed by a spherical Gaussian surface get affected when its radius is increased?

Short Answer Questions

20. The electrostatic field due to a point charge depends on the distance r as $\left(\dfrac{1}{r^2}\right)$, similarly indicate how each of the following quantities depends on r.
(a) Electric field due to infinitely long straight wire.
(b) Electric field intensity due to a uniformly charged spherical shell.

21. A cylinder of radius R and length L is placed in a uniform electric field $\vec{E}$, parallel to it's axis, as shown. Calculate the total electric flux through the surface of cylinder.

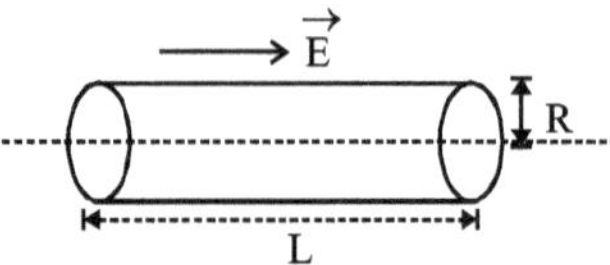

22. A hemispherical surface of radius R is so placed in the uniform electric field $\vec{E}$ that $\vec{E}$ is parallel to the axis of circular plane. What will the outcoming electric flux?

Important Tips & Formulae

- No point charge produces electric field at its own location.

- Electric field intensity at a point on the axial line of electric dipole is double the electric field intensity at a point on the equatorial line of electric dipole *i.e.*, $E_{axial} = 2E_{equatorial}$.

- Electric field always directs from higher potential to lower potential.

- The ratio of electric force and gravitational force between a proton and an electron is $\dfrac{ke^2}{Gm_e m_p} \cong 2.4 \times 10^{39}$

- A positive charge in electric field always moves from higher potential to lower potential while a negative charge moves from lower potential to higher potential.

- Coulomb's law is valid for point charges and at a distance greater than 10^{-15} m.

- Electric field intensity inside a hollow conducting body is zero.

- If two charge sphere having same radii carries charge Q_1 and Q_2 are made to touch each other, then charge on each sphere will be $q = \dfrac{Q_1 + Q_2}{2}$.

- Electric field is different at different points on the surface of an irregularly shaped charged conductor.

- It is a false that the path traced by a positive test charge is a field line but actually the path traced by a unit positive test charge represents a field line only when it moves along a straight line.

- Electric field at the centre of a charged ring of radius r is zero. Its value is maximum at a distance $\dfrac{r}{\sqrt{2}}$ on the axis of charged ring.

- The electric field at any point on the surface of a conductor is directly proportional to the surface charge density at that point *i.e*, $E \propto \sigma$.

- Electric field due to dipole $E \propto \dfrac{1}{r^3}$ decreases much rapidly as compared to the field due to point charge $\left(E \propto \dfrac{1}{r^2} \right)$.

- Let an electron of mass m and charge e is moving in a circular path of radius r about infinitely positively charged wire (charge density λ) then the velocity of electron in dynamic equilibrium is given by $v = \sqrt{\dfrac{e\lambda}{2\pi\varepsilon_0 m}}$.

- An infinite number of charges, each equal to q are placed along x-axis at $x = 1$, $x = 2$, $x = 4$, $x = 8$ --------- and so on. Electric field at the point $x = 0$ due to this set of charges

$$\vec{E} = \dfrac{q}{3\pi\varepsilon_0}$$

If electric field in the above set up, the consecutive charges have opposite sign $\vec{E} = \dfrac{q}{5\pi\varepsilon_0}$.

- Electric field between two oppositely charged infinite plates having charges equal in magnitude is

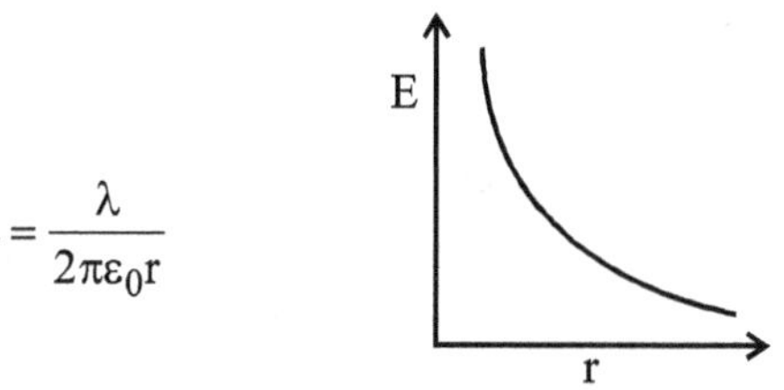

$$E = \dfrac{Q}{\varepsilon_0}$$

- If charge on two parallel plates are equal in sign and magnitude then electric field between the plates is zero.

- Electric field due to long infinite line charge varies with distance as follows.

$$E = \dfrac{\lambda}{2\pi\varepsilon_0 r}$$

- Electric field(E) versus distance (r) graph for a charged conducting sphere or cell of charge.

$$E_{in} = 0 \text{ and } V_{in} = \text{constant} = V_s$$

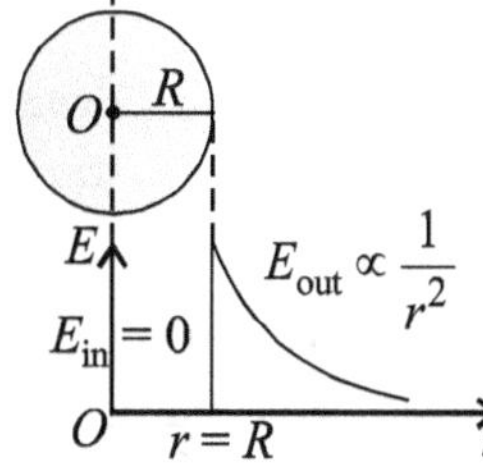

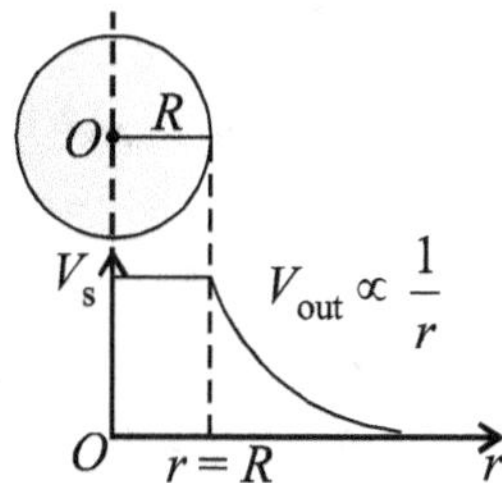

NCERT Questions

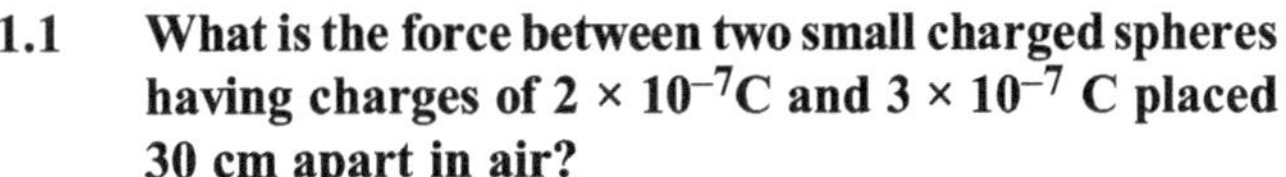

1.1 What is the force between two small charged spheres having charges of 2×10^{-7}C and 3×10^{-7} C placed 30 cm apart in air?

Sol. Given, $q_1 = 2 \times 10^{-7}$C, $q_2 = 3 \times 10^{-7}$C, $r = 30$ cm $= 0.3$ m, $F = ?$

By formula, $F = \dfrac{1}{4\pi\varepsilon_0} \dfrac{q_1 q_2}{r^2}$

$$= \dfrac{9 \times 10^9 \times 2 \times 10^{-7} \times 3 \times 10^{-7}}{(0.3)^2}$$

$$= 6 \times 10^{-3} \text{ N (repulsive)}$$

1.2 The electrostatic force on a small sphere of charge 0.4 μC due to another small sphere of charge -0.8 μC in air is 0.2 N.

(a) What is the distance between the two spheres?

(b) What is the force on the second sphere due to the first?

Sol. Given, $q_1 = 0.4$ μC, $q_2 = -0.8$ μC,

$F_{12} = 0.2$ N, (a) $r = ?$, (b) $F_{21} = ?$

(a) We know $|F| = \dfrac{1}{4\pi\varepsilon_0} \dfrac{q_1 q_2}{r^2}$

$\Rightarrow r^2 = \dfrac{1}{4\pi\varepsilon_0} \dfrac{q_1 q_2}{F}$

$$= \dfrac{9 \times 10^9 \times 0.4 \times 10^{-6} \times 0.8 \times 10^{-6}}{0.2}$$

$$= 144 \times 10^{-4}$$

$\therefore \quad r = 12 \times 10^{-2}$ m $= 12$ cm

(b) The force is mutual. The same force of 0.2 N acts on the second sphere due to the first.

1.3 Check that the ratio $ke^2/G\,m_e\,m_p$ is dimensionless. Look up a Table of Physical Constants and determine the value of this ratio. What does the ratio signify?

Sol. An electron and a proton have charges of 1.6×10^{-19} C each and their masses are 9.1×10^{-31} kg and 1.6×10^{-27} kg respectively.

Universal Gravitational Constant

$$G = 6.7 \times 10^{-11} \text{ Nm}^2/\text{kg}^2$$

and $k = \dfrac{1}{4\pi\varepsilon_0} = 9 \times 10^9$ Nm^2/C^2

Electrostatic force between electron and proton,

$$F_e = \dfrac{1}{4\pi\varepsilon_0} \dfrac{e.e}{r^2}$$

where r is the distance between their centres. Gravitational force between electron and proton,

$$F_g = \dfrac{G.m_e m_p}{r^2}$$

Dividing we get, $\dfrac{F_e}{F_g} = \dfrac{e^2}{4\pi\varepsilon_0 G m_e m_p} \approx 2.4 \times 10^{39}$.

The ratio is quite huge. This shows that electrostatic forces are much stronger than gravitational forces. A common example is the lifting of a piece of a paper by charged comb against the force of entire earth on that paper.

1.4 (a) Explain the meaning of the statement 'electric charge of a body is quantised'.

(b) Why can one ignore quantisation of electric charge when dealing with macroscopic i.e., large scale charge?

Sol. (a) *Quantization of electric charge.* It is now a well known fact that all charges occurring in nature are positive or negative integral multiples of a basic unit of electric charge which we take as the magnitude of the charge on an electron. We use symbol e for the amount of charge on an electron. Hence charge on an electron is $-$ e and that on a proton happens to be $+$ e, while charge on a neutron is zero. Any charged body will have $\pm$ ne charge, where n is an integer. This fact is called the quantization of electric charge.

(b) At the macroscopic level one deals with charges that are enormous compared to the magnitude of charge e. Since e $= 1.6 \times 10^{-19}$ C, a charge of magnitude, say, 1 μC contains something like 10^{13} times the electronic charge. At this scale, the fact that charge can increase or decrease only in units of e is not very different from saying that charge can take continuous values. Thus, at the macroscopic level, the quantisation of charge has no practical consequence and can be ignored.

1.5 When a glass rod is rubbed with a silk cloth, charges appear on both. A similar phenomenon is observed with many other pairs of bodies. Explain how this observation is consistent with the law of conservation of charge.

Sol. Charge is neither created nor destroyed. It is merely transferred from one body to another. Electrons are transferred from glass to silk, so glass has positive charge and silk has negative charge.

1.6 Four point charges $q_A = 2$ μC, $q_B = -5$ μC, $q_C = 2\,\mu$C, and $q_D = -5$ μC are located at the corners of a square ABCD of side 10 cm. What is the force on a charge of 1 μC placed at the centre of the square?

Sol. The center O of the square is at equal distance of $\sqrt{2}$ cm from each corner. Since opposite corners have equal charges, forces along both diagonals will be balanced.

Resultant force on 1 μC charge at the centre of the square ABCD will be zero.

1.7 (a) **An electrostatic field line is a continuous curve. That is, a field line cannot have sudden breaks. Why not?**

(b) **Explain why two field lines never cross each other at any point?**

Sol. (a) They start from a positive charge and end at a negative charge. They are continuous, because force is continuous. They do not have sudden breaks, otherwise a moving test charge will have to take jumps.

(b) Two lines of force do not intersect each other. If they intersect at a point, there will be two directions of field at that point. Since it is impossible, hence they don't intersect.

1.8 **Two point charges $q_A = 3$ μC and $q_B = -3$ μC are located 20 cm apart in vacuum.**

(a) **What is the electric field at the midpoint O of the line AB joining the two charges?**

(b) **If a negative test charge of magnitude 1.5×10^{-9} C is placed at this point, what is the force experienced by the test charge?**

Sol. Given, $q_A = 3$ μC $= 3 \times 10^{-6}$C,

$$q_B = -3 \ \mu C = -3 \times 10^{-6}C,$$

$$r_A = 10 \ cm = 0.1 \ m, \ r_B = 10 \ cm = 0.1 \ m,$$

(a) $E_O = ?,$

$q_O = 1.5 \times 10^{-9}$ C, $F_O = ?$

E at O due to charge at A,

0.2 m

A •————————•————————• B
+3μC   O   −3μC

$$E_A = \frac{1}{4\pi\varepsilon_0} \frac{q_A}{r_A^2} = \frac{9 \times 10^9 \times 3 \times 10^{-6}}{(0.1)^2}$$

$$= 27 \times 10^5 NC^{-1} \text{ along OB}$$

Also, E at O due to charge at B,

$E_B = 27 \times 10^5$ NC^{-1} along OB

Resultant E at O,

$$E_O = E_A + E_B = 27 \times 10^5 + 27 \times 10^5$$

$$= 54 \times 10^5 \ NC^{-1} \text{ along OB}$$

(b) For point O, E $= 54 \times 10^5$ NC^{-1},

$$q_0 = 1.5 \times 10^{-9} \ C$$

By relation, $F = q_0 \ E$

$$F = 1.5 \times 10^{-9} \times 54 \times 10^5 = 8.1 \times 10^{-4}$$

$$= 8.0 \times 10^{-3} \text{ N along OA.}$$

1.9 **A system has two charges $q_A = 2.5 \times 10^{-7}$ C and $q_B = -2.5 \times 10^{-7}$ C located at points A (0, 0, −15 cm) and B (0, 0, + 15 cm), respectively. What are the total charge and electric dipole moment of the system?**

Sol. The system is an electric dipole of charge strength
$q = (2.5 \times 10^{-7} - 2.5 \times 10^{-7})C =$ zero
Electric dipole moment,

$$p = qa = 2.5 \times 10^{-7} \times 0.3$$

$$= 7.5 \times 10^{-8} \text{ C-m along Z-axis.}$$

1.10 **An electric dipole with dipole moment 4×10^{-9} C-m is aligned at 30° with the direction of a uniform electric field of magnitude 5×10^4 NC^{-1}. Calculate the magnitude of the torque acting on the dipole.**

Sol. Given, $p = 4 \times 10^{-9}$ C-m,

$$E = 5 \times 10^4 \ N \ C^{-1} \ \&$$

$$\theta = 30° \text{ i.e. } \sin \theta = 0.5, \ \tau = ?$$

By formula,

$$\tau = pE \sin \theta = 4 \times 10^{-9} \times 5 \times 10^4 \times 0.5$$

$$= 10^{-4} \text{ J (or Nm)}$$

1.11 **A polythene piece rubbed with wool is found to have a negative charge of 3.2×10^{-7} C.**

(a) **Estimate the number of electrons transferred (from which to which?)**

(b) **Is there a transfer of mass from wool to polythene?**

Sol. (a) Given, $q = -3.2 \times 10^{-7}$ C,

$$e = -1.6 \times 10^{-19} \ C, \ n = ?$$

By relation, $q = ne$

or $\quad n = q/e = \dfrac{-3.2 \times 10^{-7}}{-1.6 \times 10^{-19}} = 2 \times 10^{12}$

These electrons are transferred from *wool* to *polythene*.

(b) Since electrons have a definite mass (9.1×10^{-31} kg), the transfer of electrons may result in mass transfer by amount nm $= 2 \times 10^{12} \times 9.1 \times 10^{-31} = 18.2 \times 10^{-19}$ kg which is negligible.

1.12 (a) **Two insulated charged copper spheres A and B have their centres separated by a distance of 50 cm. What is the mutual force of electrostatic repulsion if the charge on each is 6.5×10^{-7} C? The radii of A and B are negligible compared to the distance of separation.**

(b) **What is the force of repulsion if each sphere is charged double the above amount, and the distance between them is halved?**

Sol. (a) Given, $q_1 = 6.5 \times 10^{-7}$ C,

$$q_2 = 6.5 \times 10^{-7} \ C,$$

$$r = 50 \ cm = 0.5 \ m, \ F = ?$$

By formula, $\quad F = \dfrac{1}{4\pi\varepsilon_0}\dfrac{q_1 q_2}{r^2}$

$$= \dfrac{9\times10^9 \times 6.5\times10^{-7} \times 6.5\times10^{-7}}{(0.5)^2}$$

$$= 1.521 \times 10^{-2} \text{ N}$$

(b) Doubling charge on each sphere increases the force four times. Making the distance half, further increases the force four times.

So new force becomes 16 times.

Now $F = 1.521 \times 10^{-2} \times 16 = 24.34 \times 10^{-2}$

$$= 0.2434 \text{ N}$$

1.13 Suppose the spheres A and B in question 1.12 have identical sizes. A third sphere of the same size but uncharged is brought in contact with the first, then brought in contact with the second, and finally removed from both. What is the new force of repulsion between A and B?

Sol. Before contact, sphere A has charge 6.5×10^{-7} C, while C has no charge. On contact, A and C both have equal charge, i.e. 3.25×10^{-7} C each.

Then sphere C (with charge 3.25×10^{-7} C) comes in contact with sphere B having charge 6.5×10^{-7} C. Both share the total charge equally.

Then B has a charge $\dfrac{3.25 + 6.5}{2}\times10^{-7}$

$$= 4.875 \times 10^{-7}\text{C}$$

Now, $q_1 = 3.25 \times 10^{-7}$ C; $q_2 = 4.875 \times 10^{-7}$C

$\therefore \quad F = \dfrac{1}{4\pi\varepsilon_0}\dfrac{q_1 q_2}{r^2}$

$$= \dfrac{9\times10^9 \times 3.25\times10^{-7} \times 4.875\times10^{-7}}{(0.5)^2}$$

$$= 0.5625 \times 10^{-2} \text{ N.}$$

1.14 Figure shows tracks of three charged particles in a uniform electrostatic field. Give the signs of the three charges. Which particle has the highest charge to mass ratio?

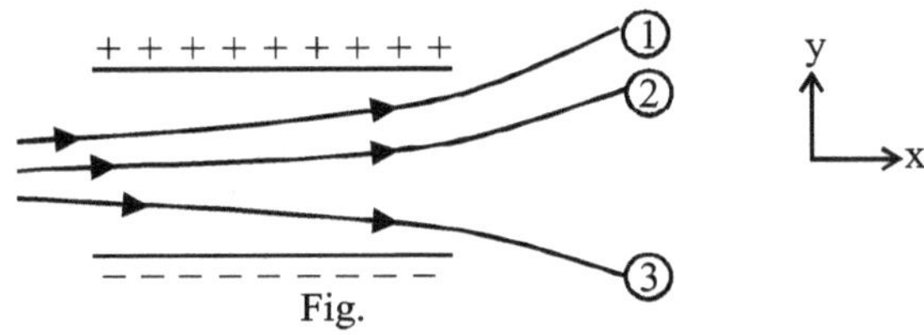

Fig.

Sol. Particle 1 and 2 have negative charge.

Particle 3 has positive charge.

Particle 3 has highest charge to mass ratio, because its path is more curved.

1.15 Consider a uniform electric field

$$\mathbf{E} = 3 \times 10^3 \ \hat{\mathbf{i}} \text{ N/C.}$$

(a) **What is the flux of this field through a square of 10 cm on a side whose plane is parallel to the *yz*-plane?**

(b) **What is the flux through the same square if the normal to its plane makes a 60° angle with the *x*-axis?**

Sol. Given, $\vec{E} = 3\times10^3\,\hat{i}\,\text{N C}^{-1}$,

$$A = 10 \times 10 = 100 \text{ cm}^2 = 10^{-2}\text{m}^2$$

Since surface lies in Y–Z plane, normal to the surface

is along X-axis, $\vec{A} = 10^{-2}\hat{i}\,\text{m}^2$

(a) $\theta = 0°$, $\phi = ?$ (b) $\theta = 60°$, $\phi = ?$

By relation $\phi = \vec{E}.\vec{A} = EA \cos\theta$

Substituting the values, we get,

(a) $\phi = 3 \times 10^3 \times 10^{-2} \times 1 = 30 \text{ Nm}^2/\text{C}$

(b) $\phi = 3 \times 10^3 \times 10^{-2} \times 0.5 = 15 \text{ Nm}^2/\text{C}$

1.16 What is the net flux of the uniform electric field of question 1.15 through a cube of side 20 cm oriented so that its faces are parallel to the coordinate planes?

Sol. Zero. The number of lines entering the cube is the same as the number of lines leaving the cube.

1.17 Careful measurement of the electric field at the surface of a black box indicates that the net outward flux through the surface of the box is 8.0×10^3 Nm²/C.

(a) **What is the net charge inside the box?**

(b) **If the net outward flux through the surface of the box were zero, could you conclude that there were no charges inside the box? Why or why not?**

Sol. (a) Given, Electric flux $= \phi = 8.0 \times 10^3\text{Nm}^2\text{C}^{-1}$,

$\varepsilon_0 = 8.854 \times 10^{-12}$ C²N⁻¹m⁻²(taken), q = ?

By Gauss's law

Flux $\phi = q/\varepsilon_0$ or $q = \phi\varepsilon_0$

$$= 8 \times 10^3 \times 8.854 \times 10^{-12} = 7.1 \times 10^{-8}\text{C.}$$

(b) In case, net outward flux through the surface is zero. The conclusion is if any charges are present inside the cube, their algebraic sum is zero.

1.18 A point charge +10 μC is at a distance 5 cm directly above the centre of a square of side 10 cm, as shown in Fig. What is the magnitude of the electric flux through the square? (Hint: Think of the square as one face of a cube with edge 10 cm.)

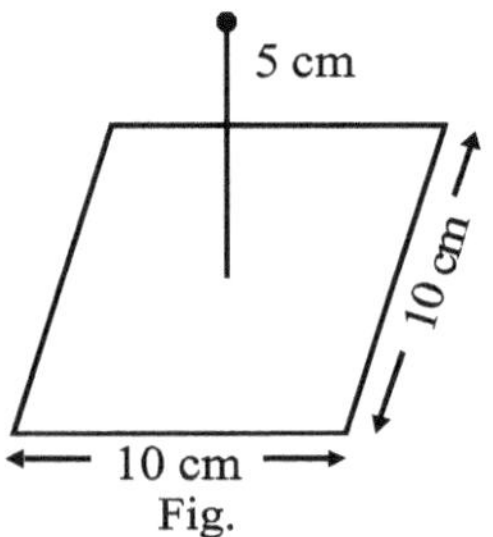

Fig.

Sol. The situation is shown in figure.

The square can be considered as one of the faces of a cube of each side 10 cm, enclosing the point charge inside it. The cube surface will act as Gaussian surface.

Given, $q = 10\,\mu C = 10 \times 10^{-6} C$,

$$\varepsilon_0 = 8.854 \times 10^{-12} C^2 N^{-1} m^2 \text{ (taken)}$$

By Gauss's law for whole closed surface,

$$\phi = q/\varepsilon_0 = \frac{10 \times 10^{-6}}{8.854 \times 10^{-12}}$$

$$= 1.13 \times 10^6 \, Nm^2/C$$

As one face area is *one-sixth* of total surface area of the cube,

$$\text{Flux through one face} = \frac{\phi}{6} = \frac{1.13 \times 10^6}{6}$$

$$= 1.88 \times 10^5 \, Nm^2/C$$

1.19 **A point charge of 2.0 μC is at the centre of a cubic Gaussian surface 9.0 cm on edge. What is the net electric flux through the surface?**

Sol. Given, $q = 2\,\mu C = 2 \times 10^{-6} C$,

$\varepsilon_0 = 8.854 \times 10^{-12} C^2 N^{-1} m^{-1}$ (taken), $\phi = ?$

By Gauss's law $\quad \phi = q/\varepsilon_0$

$= (2 \times 10^{-6}) / (8.854 \times 10^{-12})$

$= 2.26 \times 10^5 \, Nm^2/C^{-1}$

1.20 **A point charge causes an electric flux of $-1.0 \times 10^3 \, Nm^2/C$ to pass through a spherical Gaussian surface of 10.0 cm radius centred on the charge. (a) If the radius of the Gaussian surface were doubled, how much flux would pass through the surface? (b) What is the value of the point charge?**

Sol. Given, Flux $= \phi = -1.0 \times 10^3 \, Nm^2 C^{-1}$,

$\varepsilon_0 = 8.854 \times 10^{-12} C^2 N^{-1} m^{-2}$ (taken), $q = ?$

(a) By Gauss's law, electric flux $\phi = q/\varepsilon_0$

It is independent of dimensions and shape of the Gaussian surface.

So, $\quad \phi = -1.0 \times 10^3 \, Nm^2 C^{-1}$

(b) We have,

$$q = \phi\varepsilon_0 = -10^3 \times 8.854 \times 10^{-12}$$

$$= -8.854 \times 10^{-9} \, C.$$

1.21 **A conducting sphere of radius 10 cm has an unknown charge. If the electric field 20 cm from the centre of the sphere is 1.5×10^3 N/C and points radially inward, what is the net charge on the sphere?**

Sol. Given, $E = -1.5 \times 10^3 \, N C^{-1}$ (E is taken negative because it points inwardly opposite to r)

$$r = 20cm = 0.2m, \ q = ?$$

For outside point, the charge on the conducting sphere behaves as a point charge situated at the centre of the sphere.

By formula, $E = \dfrac{1}{4\pi\varepsilon_0} \dfrac{q}{r^2}$

or $\quad q = E \times 4\pi\varepsilon_0 r^2$

$$= -\frac{1.5 \times 10^3 \times (0.2)^2}{9 \times 10^9} = -\frac{6}{9} \times 10^{-9}$$

$$= -6.67 \times 10^{-8} \, C.$$

1.22 **A uniformly charged conduction sphere of 2.4 m diameter has a surface charge density of 80.0 μC/m². (a) Find the charge on the sphere. (b) What is the total electric flux leaving the surface of the sphere?**

Sol. Given, $r = 1.2$ m,

$$\sigma = 80.0\mu Cm^{-2} = 80 \times 10^{-6} Cm^{-2},$$

$$\varepsilon_0 = 8.854 \times 10^{12} C^2 N^{-1} m^{-2} \text{ (taken)}$$

(a) $q = ?$ (b) $\phi = ?$

(a) By relation,

$$q = \sigma A = \sigma 4\pi r^2$$

$$= 80 \times 10^{-6} \times 4 \times 3.14 \times (1.2)^2$$

$$= 8 \times 12.56 \times 1.44 \times 10^{-5}$$

$$= 144.7 \times 10^{-5} = 1.447 \times 10^{-3} C$$

(b) For outside space, the charge on the conducting sphere behaves as a point charge situated at the centre of the sphere.

By Gauss's theorem, $\phi = q/\varepsilon_0$

$$= \frac{1.44 \times 10^{-3}}{8.854 \times 10^{-12}} = 1.63 \times 10^8 Nm^2/C$$

1.23 **An infinite line charge produces a field of 9×10^4 N/C at a distance of 2 cm. Calculate the linear charge density.**

Sol. Given, $E = 9 \times 10^4 \, N C^{-1}$,

$$r = 2 \text{ cm} = 2 \times 10^{-2} m, \ \lambda = ?$$

By formula, $E = \dfrac{\lambda}{2\pi\varepsilon_0 r}$ or $\lambda = 2\pi\varepsilon_0 rE$

$$= \frac{2 \times 10^{-2} \times 9 \times 10^4}{2 \times 9 \times 10^9} = 10^{-7} Cm^{-1}.$$

1.24 Two large, thin metal plates are parallel and close to each other. On their inner faces, the plates have surface charge densities of opposite signs and of magnitude 17.0×10^{-22} C/m². What is E: (a) in the outer region of the first plate, (b) in the outer region of the second plate, and (c) between the plates?

Sol. Given, $\sigma_1 = +17.0 \times 10^{-22} \, Cm^{-2}$,

$$\sigma_2 = -17.0 \times 10^{-22} \, Cm^{-2},$$

$$\varepsilon_0 = 8.854 \times 10^{-12} \, C^2 N^{-1} m^{-2} \, \text{(taken)}$$

(a) $E_P = ?$ (b) $E_Q = ?$ (c) $E_R = ?$

The situation is shown in figure.

$$\vec{E}_P = \vec{E}_1 + \vec{E}_2$$

I Region σ_1

I Sheet

II Region σ_1

$$\vec{E}_Q = \vec{E}_2 - \vec{E}_1$$

II Sheet σ_2

III Region σ_2

$$\vec{E}_R = \vec{E}_1 - \vec{E}_2$$

By formula,

$$E = \frac{\sigma}{2\varepsilon_0} \, \& \, E_1 = \frac{\sigma_1}{2\varepsilon_0}, \quad E_2 = \frac{\sigma_2}{2\varepsilon_0};$$

$$E_P = E_1 + E_2$$

$$E_R = -E_1 - E_2 = -(E_1 + E_2); \quad E_Q = E_2 - E_1$$

Take $\sigma_1 = \sigma, \sigma_2 = -\sigma$

(a) $E_P = \dfrac{\sigma_1}{2\varepsilon_0} + \dfrac{\sigma_2}{2\varepsilon_0}$

$$= \frac{17 \times 10^{-22} - 17 \times 10^{-22}}{2\varepsilon_0} = \text{zero}$$

(b) $E_R = -\left(\dfrac{\sigma_1}{2\varepsilon_0} + \dfrac{\sigma_2}{2\varepsilon_0} \right)$

$$= -\frac{17 \times 10^{-22} - 17 \times 10^{-22}}{2\varepsilon_0} = \text{zero}$$

(c) $E_Q = \dfrac{\sigma_2}{2\varepsilon_0} - \dfrac{\sigma_1}{2\varepsilon_0}$

$$= \frac{-17 \times 10^{-22} - 17 \times 10^{-22}}{2\varepsilon_0}$$

$$= \frac{34 \times 10^{-22}}{2 \times 8.854 \times 10^{-12}} = -1.92 \times 10^{-10} \, NC^{-1}.$$

ADDITIONAL EXERCISES

1.25 An oil drop of 12 excess electrons is held stationary under a constant electric field of 2.55×10^4 NC⁻¹ in Millikan's oil drop experiment. The density of the oil is 1.26 g cm⁻³. Estimate the radius of the drop ($g = 9.81$ ms⁻²; $e = 1.60 \times 10^{-19}$ C).

Sol. Given, n = 12, e = 1.6×10^{-9} C,

$E = 2.55 \times 10^4$ Vm⁻¹,

$\sigma = 1.26$g cm⁻³ = 1.26×10^3 kg m⁻³,

    g = 9.81 m s⁻²,

Radius of drop, r = ?

Now, downward force of gravity on drop

= upward force due to electric field

i.e.   mg = neE   or, (4/3) $\pi r^3 \sigma g$ = ne E

or, $r = \left(\dfrac{3 \, neE}{4 \pi \sigma g} \right)^{1/3}$

$$= \left(\frac{3 \times 12 \times 1.6 \times 10^{-19} \times 2.55 \times 10^4}{4 \times 3.14 \times 1.26 \times 10^3 \times 9.81} \right)^{1/3}$$

$$= 9.8175 \times 10^{-7} m = 9.8175 \times 10^{-4} mm$$

1.26 Which among the curves shown in Fig. cannot possibly represent electrostatic field lines?

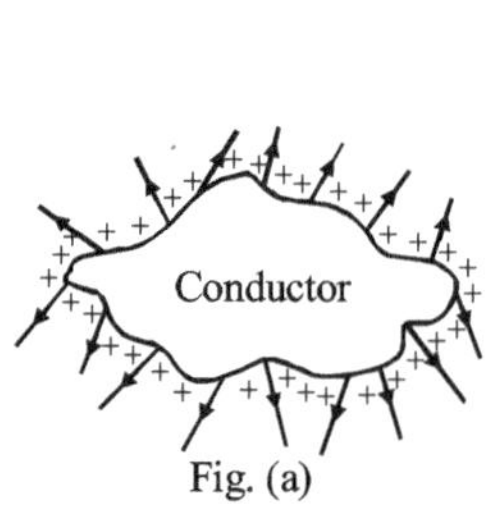

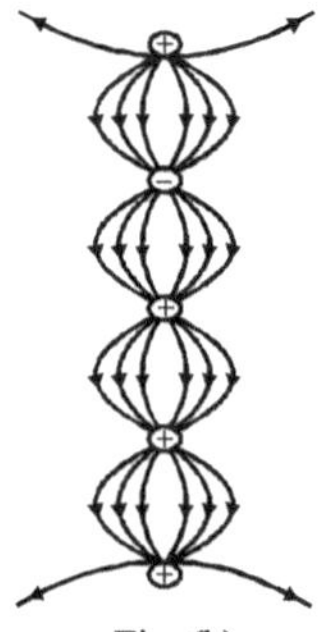

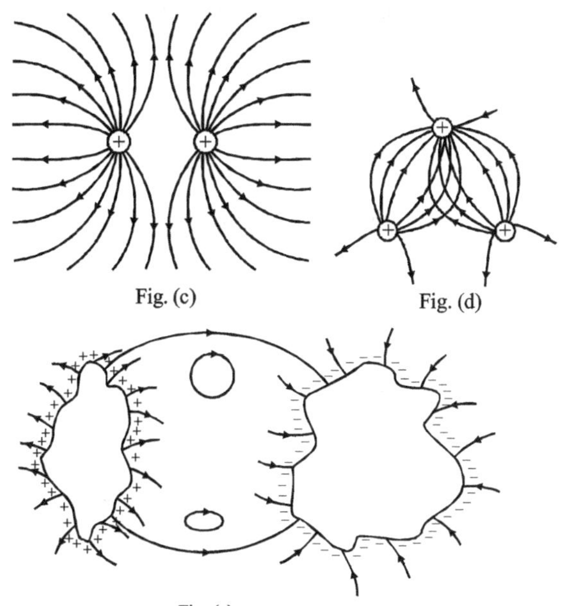

Fig. (c)   Fig. (d)

Fig. (e)

Sol. Only (c) is right; the rest cannot represent electrostatic field lines, because field lines

- must be normal to a conductor
- cannot start from a negative charge,
- cannot intersect each other,
- must be parallel to a conductor.

1.27 In a certain region of space, electric field is along the Z-direction throughout. The magnitude of electric field is however, not constant but increases uniformly along the positive Z-direction, at the rate of 10^5 NC^{-1} per metre. What are the force and torque experienced by a system having a total dipole moment equal to 10^{-7} cm in the negative Z-direction ?

Sol. $qx = 10^{-7}$ NC^{-1}/m (given) ... (1)

Let E = Electric field at A

$\therefore$ $E + x \times 10^5$ = Electric field at B

[$\because$ E is increasing at the rate of 10^5 NC^{-1}m^{-1}]

+q F_A F_B –q +Z →
A   B
|← x →|
E   (E + x × 10^5)

$\therefore$ F_A = electric force on $(+ q) = qE$ ... (2)

F_B = electric force on $(-q)$

$= q (E + x \times 10^5)$ ... (3)

As these two forces are acting without any perpendicular distance between their direction, hence torque on the dipole will be zero

Further, net force on the dipole

$= F_B - F_A$ (along BA)

$= q(E + 10^5 x) - qE = 10^5$

$qx = 10^5 \times 10^{-7}$ [from eq. (1)]

$= 10^{-2}$ N, along $(-Z)$ direction.

1.28 (a) A conductor A with a cavity as shown in Fig. (a) is given a charge must appear on the outer surface of the conductor.

(b) Another conductor B with charge q is inserted into the cavity keeping B insulated from A. Show that the total charge on the outside surface of A is $Q + q$ [Fig. (b)].

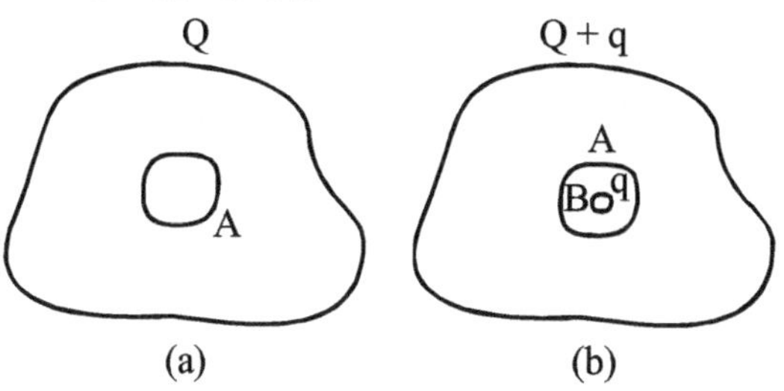

(a)   (b)

Fig.

(c) A sensitive instrument is to be shielded from the strong electrostatic field in its environment. Suggest a possible way.

Sol. (a) Taking a close Gaussian surface just inside touching the outer surface of the conductor (A). Since electric field inside the Gaussian surface is zero.

$\therefore$ $\oint \vec{E}.\vec{ds} = \dfrac{Q}{\varepsilon_0} = 0$

Hence there is no charge inside the Gaussian surface and whole charge Q lies on the outer surface of conductor A.

(b) Charge $+ Q$ appears on conductor A forming cavity. Induced charge $+ q$ appears on outer surface of A. Therefore, total charge $(Q + q)$ appears on outer surface of A.

(c) The instrument should be enclosed inside a metallic case to make its environment field free.

1.29 A hollow charged conductor has a tiny hole cut into its surface. Show that the electric field in the hole is $(\sigma/2\varepsilon_0)\hat{n}$, where $\hat{n}$ is the unit vector in the outward normal direction, and σ is the surface charge density near the hole.

Sol. E_1 = Field at A & B (which are 2 points just out-side & within the cavity as shown) due to the entire shell except that material which originally was there at the place of the cavity.

E_2 = field at A & B because of that material which were there originally in place of cavity.

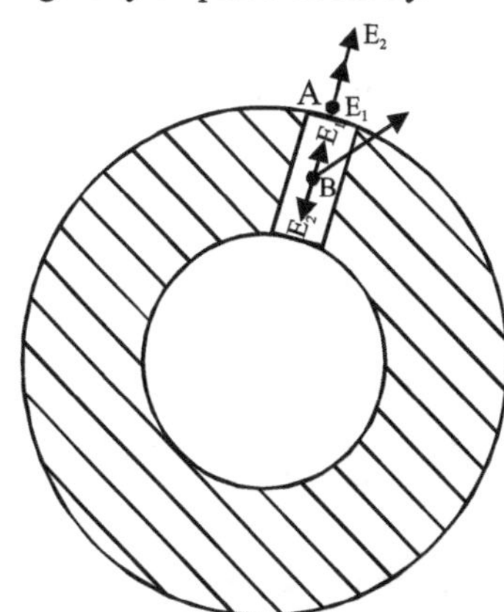

$\therefore$ If there were no cavity, the total field at point A

would be $= \dfrac{\sigma}{\varepsilon_0}$

i.e. $E_1 + E_2 = \dfrac{\sigma}{\varepsilon_0}$ ...(1)

And at point B would be zero (because inside a charged conductor electric field is always zero)

i.e. $E_1 - E_2 = 0$ ...(2)

$\therefore$ $E_1 = E_2$

By putting it in eq. (1), we get

$E_1 = \dfrac{\sigma}{2\varepsilon_0}$

The direction will be radially outward because of symmetry.

1.30 **Obtain the formula for the electric field due to a long thin wire of uniform linear charge density λ without using Gauss's law. [Hint: Use Coulomb's law directly and evaluate the necessary integral.]**

Sol. Let AB be a thin wire having charge density (linear) λ. D is any point at normal distance r from a point C, in the middle of the wire.

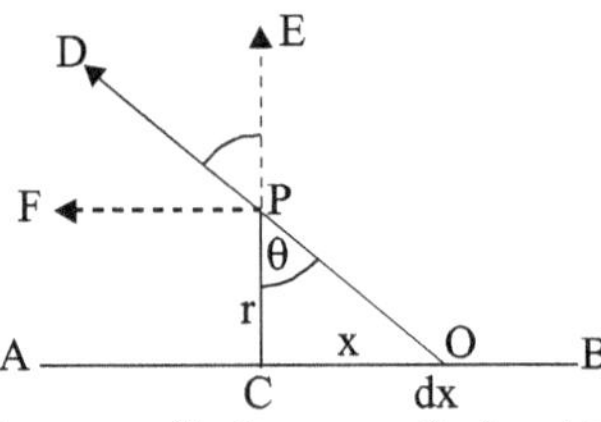

Let 'dx' be a small element of wire AB & at a distance

$\sqrt{r^2 + x^2}$ from point D.

Now, electric intensity at D due to charge on the element dx only

$E_{DF} = \dfrac{1}{4\pi\varepsilon_0} \cdot \dfrac{\lambda dx}{r^2 + x^2}$ along DF

Component along DG,

$E_{DG} = \dfrac{1}{4\pi\varepsilon_0} \cdot \dfrac{\lambda dx}{r^2 + x^2} \cos\theta$ and

$E_{DH} = \dfrac{1}{4\pi\varepsilon_0} \cdot \dfrac{\lambda dx}{(r^2 + x^2)} \sin\theta$

The parallel component E_{DH} will be cancelled by the parallel component of the field of the charge by a similar element dx on the other half. The radial components gets added.

Radial component of electric intensity due to charge on element dx.

$dE = \dfrac{1}{4\pi\varepsilon_0} \cdot \dfrac{\lambda dx}{(r^2 + x^2)} \cos\theta$ ...(i)

From the fig.

$x = r \tan\theta$

$dx = r \sec^2\theta \, d\theta$ ...(ii)

$\Rightarrow$ $(r^2 + x^2) = \tan^2\theta = r^2(1 + \tan^2\theta)$

$(r^2 + x^2) = r^2 \sec^2\theta$ ...(iii)

Putting equation (ii) & (iii) in equation (i), we have

$dE = \dfrac{\lambda}{4\pi\varepsilon_0} \cdot \dfrac{r \sec^2\theta.d\theta}{r^2 \sec^2\theta} \cos\theta = \dfrac{\lambda}{4\pi\varepsilon_0 r} \cos\theta \, d\theta$

Since, wire has infinite length, its end A and B are quite away.

Hence 'θ' varies from $-\pi/2$ to $+\pi/2$

$\Rightarrow \displaystyle\int_{-\pi/2}^{+\pi/2} \dfrac{\lambda}{4\pi\varepsilon_0 r} \cos\theta \, d\theta$

$= \dfrac{\lambda}{4\pi\varepsilon_0 r}[\sin\theta]_{-\pi/2}^{\pi/2} \Rightarrow E = \dfrac{\lambda}{2\pi\varepsilon_0 r}$

1.31 **It is now believed that protons and neutrons (which constitute nuclei of ordinary matter) are themselves built out of more elementary units called quarks. A proton and a neutron consist of three quarks each. Two types of quarks, the so called 'up' quark (denoted by u) of charge + (2/3) e, and the 'down' quark (denoted by d) of charge (–1/3) e, together with electrons build up ordinary matter. (Quarks of other types have also been found which give rise to different unusual varieties of matter.) Suggest a possible quark composition of a proton and neutron.**

Sol. Proton, $p = 2u + 1d = 2 \times \dfrac{2}{3}e - \dfrac{e}{3} = e$

Neutron, $n = 1u + 2d = 1 \times \dfrac{2}{3}e + 2 \times \left(-\dfrac{e}{3}\right) = 0$

1.32 **(a)** **Consider an arbitrary electrostatic field configuration. A small test charge is placed at a null point (i.e., where E = 0) of the configuration. Show that the equilibrium of the test charge is necessarily unstable.**

(b) **Verify this result for the simple configuration of two charges of the same magnitude and sign placed a certain distance apart.**

Sol. **(a)** Proving it by contradiction. Suppose the equilibrium is stable; then the test charge displaced slightly in any direction will experience a restoring force towards the null-point. That is, all field lines near the null point should be directed inwards towards the null point. That is, there is a net inward flux of electric field through a closed surface around the null-point. But by Gauss's law, the flux of electric field through a surface, not enclosing any charge, must be zero. Hence, the equilibrium cannot be stable.

(b) The mid-point of the line joining the two charges is a null-point. Displace a test charge from the null-point slightly along the line. There is a restoring force. But displace it, say, normal to the line. You will see that the net force takes it away from the null-point. Remember, stability of equilibrium needs restoring force in all directions.

1.33 A particle of mass m and charge $(-q)$ enters the region between the two charged plates initially moving along x-axis with speed v_x. The length of plate is L and an uniform electric field E is maintained between the plates. Show that the vertical deflction of the particle at the far edge of the plate is $qEL^2 / \left(2mv_x^2\right)$.

Sol. Let the point at which the charged particle enters the electric field, be origin $O\,(0, 0)$, then after travelling a horizontal displacement L, it gets deflected by displacement y in vertical direction as it comes out of electric field. So, co-ordinates of its initial position are $x_1 = 0$ and $y_1 = 0$ and of final position on coming out of electric field are

$$x_2 = L \text{ and } y_2 = y$$

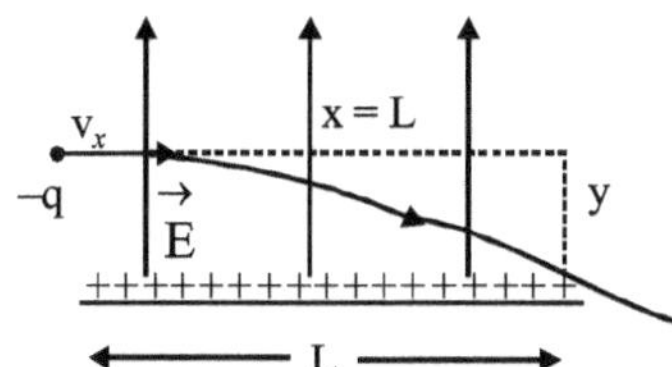

Components of its acceleration are $a_x = 0$

and $a_y = \dfrac{F}{m} = \dfrac{qE}{m}$ and of initial velocity are

$$u_x = v_x \text{ and } u_y = 0$$

So, by 2nd equation of motion in horizontal direction,

$$y_2 - y_1 = u_x t + \frac{1}{2}a_x t^2 \text{ or } L - 0 = u_x t + 0'$$

$$\Rightarrow\ t = \frac{L}{v_x} \qquad\qquad \text{...(i)}$$

and by 2nd equation of motion in vertical direction,

$$y_2 - y_1 = u_y t + \frac{1}{2}a_y t^2$$

or $y - 0 = 0 + \dfrac{1}{2} \cdot \dfrac{qE}{m} \cdot \left(\dfrac{L}{v_x}\right)^2 \qquad \text{...(ii)}$

or $y = \dfrac{qEL^2}{2mv_x^2}$

This gives the vertical deflection of the particle at the far edge of the plate.

1.34 Suppose that the particle in Q.1.33 is an electron projected with velocity $v_x = 2.0 \times 10^6$ ms^{-1}. If E between the plates separated by 0.5 cm is 9.1×10^2 N/C, where will the electron strike the upper plate? Charge of electron, $e = 1.6 \times 10^{-19}$ C and mass of electron, $m_e = 9.1 \times 10^{-31}$ kg.

Sol. If the electron is released just near the negatively charged plate, then $y = 0.5$ cm and hence

$$y = \frac{qEL^2}{2mv_x^2} \quad \text{or} \quad L^2 = \frac{2mv_x^2 y}{qE}$$

$$L^2 = \frac{2 \times 9.1 \times 10^{-31}\text{kg} \times \left(2 \times 10^6 \text{ms}^{-1}\right)^2 \times 0.5 \times 10^{-2}\text{ m}}{1.6 \times 10^{-19}\text{ C} \times 9.1 \times 10^2\text{ N/C}}$$

$$= 2.5 \times 10^{-4}$$

or $L = 1.6 \times 10^{-2}$ m $= 1.6$ cm

Past year Exercise

Multiple Choice Question

1. If the net electric flux through a closed surface is zero, then we can infer

(a) no net charge is enclosed by the surface.

(b) uniform electric field exists within the surface.

(c) electric potential varies from point to point inside the surface.

(d) charge is present inside the surface.

Very Short Answer Questions

2. Two point charges having equal charges separated by 1 m distance experience a force of 8 N. What will be the force experienced by them, if they are held in water, at the same distance? (Given K$_{water}$ = 80)

3. A proton is placed in a uniform electric field directed along the position X-axis. In which direction will it tend to move?

4. In which orientation, a dipole placed in a uniform electric field is in (a) stable, (b) unstable equilibrium?

5. Distinguish between a dielectric and a conductor?

6. Why most electrostatic field be normal to the surface at every point of a charged conductor.

7. What is the amount of work done in moving a point charge around a circle of radius r at the centre of which another point charge is located?

8. Two charges of magnitudes +4Q and –Q are located at point (a, 0) and (–3a, 0) respectively. What is the electric flux due to these charges through a sphere of radius '2a' with its centre at the origin?

9. Why do the electrostatic field lines not form closed loops?

10. Why do the electric field lines never cross each other?

11. Two identical conducting balls A and B have charges-Q and +3Q respectively. They are brought in contact with each other and then separated by a distance d apart. Find the nature of the Coulomb force between them.

OR

A metallic spherical shell has an inner radius R$_1$ and outer radius R$_2$. A charge Q is placed at the centre of the shell. What will be the surface charge density on the (i) inner surface, and (ii) outer surface of the shell?

Short Answer Questions

12. A spherical conducting shell of inner radius R_1 and outer radius R_2 has a charge Q. A charge q is placed at the centre of the shell.

    (i) What is the surface charge density on the (1) Inner surface, (2) Outer surface of the shell?

    (ii) Write the expression for the electric field at a point $X > R_2$ from the centre of the shell.

13. Two uniformly large parallel thin plates having charge densities $+\sigma$ and $-\sigma$ are kept in the X-Z plane at a distance d apart. Sketch an equipotential surface due to electric field between the plates. If a particle of mass m and charge $-q$ remains stationary between the plates. What is the magnitude and direction of this field?

14. Two charged conducting spheres of radii r_1 and r_2 connected to each other by a wire. Find the ratio of electric fields at the surfaces of the two spheres.

15. Two identical metallic spherical shells A and B having charges $+4Q$ and $-10Q$ are kept a certain distance apart. A third identical uncharged sphere C is first placed in contact with sphere A and then with sphere B, then spheres A and B are brought in contact and then separated. Find the charge on the spheres A and B.

16. Plot a graph showing the variation of Coulomb's force (F) versus $1/r^2$, where r is the distance between the two charges of each pair of charges: $(1\ \mu C, 2\ \mu C)$ and $(1\mu C, -3\mu C)$. Interpret the graphs obtained.

17. Using Gauss's law obtain the expression for the electric field due to uniformly charged spherical shell of radius R at a point outside the shell. Draw a graph showing the variation of electric field with r, for $r > R$ and $r < R$.

18. State Guass's law in electrostatics. A cube with each side a is kept is an electric field is given by E = Cx. (as is shown in the figure) where, C is a positive dimensional constant. Find out :

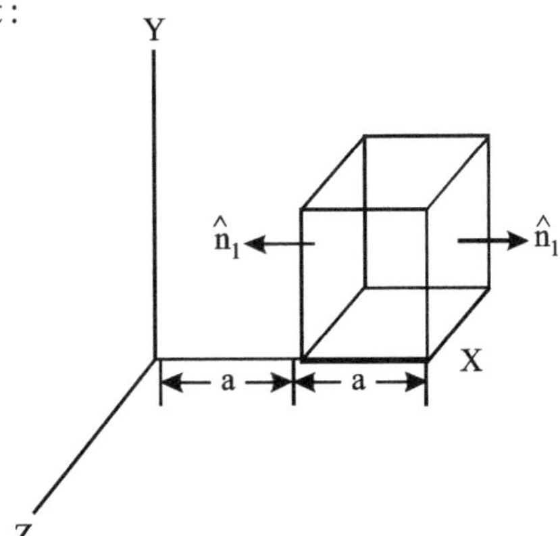

    (i) The electric flux through the cube, and

    (ii) The net charge inside the cube.

19. Draw a plot showing the variation of

    (i) electric field (E) and

    (ii) electric potential (V) with distance r due to a point charge Q.

20. (a) Define electric flux. Write its SI unit.

    (b) Consider a uniform electric field $\vec{E} = 5' \ 10^3 \hat{i}$ NC^{-1}. Calculate the flux of this field through a square surface of area 12 cm^2 when :

    (i) its plane is parallel to the y-z plane, and

    (ii) the normal to its plane makes a $60°$ angle with the x-axis.

21. A hollow cylindrical box of length 0.5 m and area of cross-section 20 cm^2 is placed in a three dimensional coordinate system as shown in the figure. The electric field in the region is given by $\vec{E} = 20x\ \hat{i}$, where E is NC^{-1} and x is in metres. Find :

    (i) Net flux through the cylinder

    (ii) Charge enclosed in the cylinder

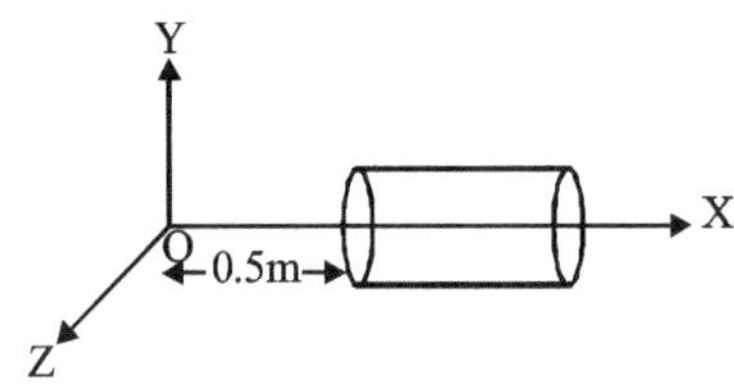

22. Given a uniform electric field $\vec{E} = 2 \times 10^3 \hat{i}$ N/C, find the flux of this field through a square of side 20 cm, whose plane is parallel to the y–z plane. What would be the flux through the same square, if the plane makes an angle of $30°$ with the x-axis ?

23. Apply Gauss's law to show that for a charged spherical shell, the electric field outside the shell is, as if the entire charge were concentrated at the centre.

OR

Two large parallel plane sheets have uniform charge densities $+\sigma$ and $-\sigma$. Determine the electric field (i) between the sheets, and (ii) outside the sheets.

NCERT Exemplar

Multiple Choice Questions

1. In figure two positive charges q_2 and q_3 fixed along the y-axis, exert a net electric force in the $+$ x-direction on a charge q_1 fixed along the x-axis. If a positive charge Q is added at $(x, 0)$, the force on q_1

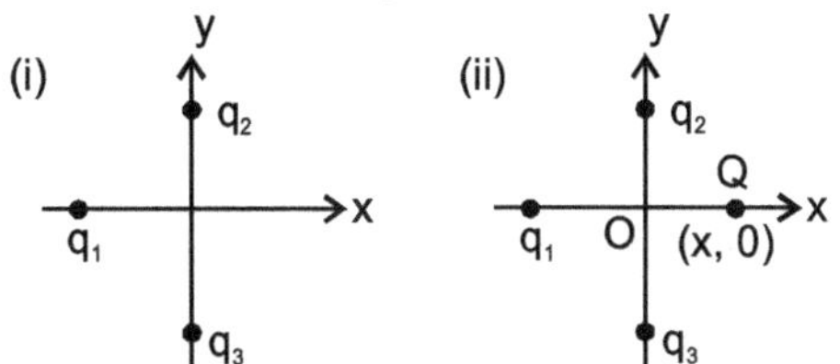

   (a) shall increase along the positive x-axis
   (b) shall decrease along the positive x-axis
   (c) shall point along the negative x-axis
   (d) shall increase but the direction changes because of the intersection of Q with q_2 and q_3

2. A point positive charge is brought near an isolated conducting sphere (figure). The electric field is best given by

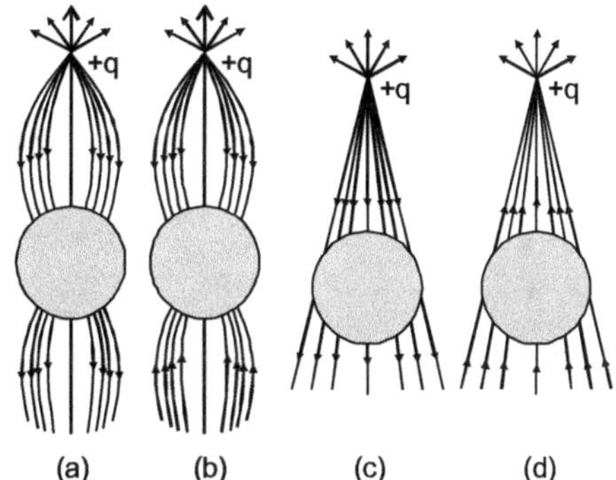

   (a)   (b)   (c)   (d)

3. The electric flux through the surface

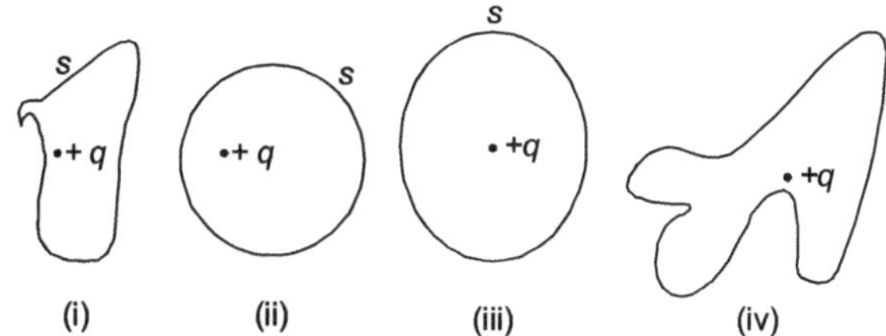

   (i)   (ii)   (iii)   (iv)

   (a) in Fig. (iv) is the largest
   (b) in Fig. (iii) is the least
   (c) in Fig. (ii) is same as Fig. (iii) but is smaller than Fig. (iv)
   (d) is the same for all the figures

4. Five charges q_1, q_2, q_3, q_4, and q_5 are fixed at their positions as shown in Figure, S is a Gaussian surface. The Gauss' law is given by $\int_s E.dS = \dfrac{q}{\varepsilon_0}$. Which of the following statements is correct?

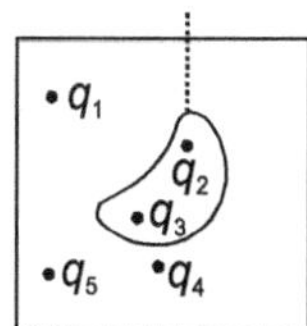

   (a) E on the LHS of the above equation will have a contribution from q_1, q_5 and q_1, q_5 and q_3 while q on the RHS will have a contribution from q_2 and q_4 only
   (b) E on the LHS of the above equation will have a contribution from all charges while q on the RHS will have a contribution from q_2 and q_4 only
   (c) E on the LHS of the above equation will have a contribution from all charges while q on the RHS will have a contribution from q_1, q_3 and q_5.
   (d) Both E on the LHS and q on the RHS will have contributions from q_2 and q_4 only

5. Figure shows electric field lines in which an electric dipole P is placed as shown. Which of the following statements is correct?

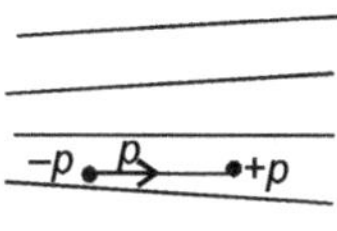

   (a) The dipole will not experience any force
   (b) The dipole will experience a force towards right
   (c) The dipole will experience a force towards left
   (d) The dipole will experience a force upwards

6. A point charge $+ q$ is placed at a distance d from an isolated conducting plane. The field at a point P on the other side of the plane is
   (a) directed perpendicular to the plane and away from the plane
   (b) directed perpendicular to the plane but towards the plane
   (c) directed radially away from the point charge
   (d) directed radially towards the point charge.

7. A hemisphere is uniformly charged positively. The electric field at a point on a diameter away from the centre is directed
   (a) perpendicular to the diameter
   (b) parallel to the diameter
   (c) at an angle tilted towards the diameter
   (d) at an angle tilted away from the diameter

Very Short Answer Questions

8. If the total charge enclosed by a surface is zero, does it imply that the electric field everywhere on the surface is zero? Conversely, if the electric field everywhere on a surface is zero, does it imply that net charge inside is zero.

9. What will be the total flux through the faces of the cube with side of length a if a charge q is placed at

    (a) A: a corner of the cube.

    (b) B: mid-point of an edge of the cube.

    (c) C: centre of a face of the cube.

    (d) D: mid-point of B and C.

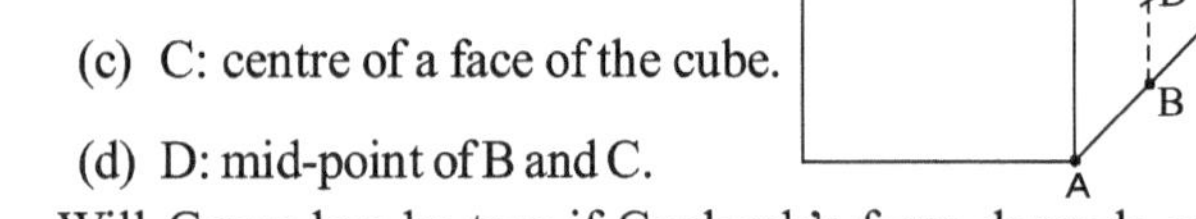

10. Will Gauss law be true if Coulomb's force depends on $\dfrac{1}{r^3}$ instead of $\dfrac{1}{r^2}$?

Short Answer Questions

11. Fig. shows the electric field lines around three point charges A, B and C.

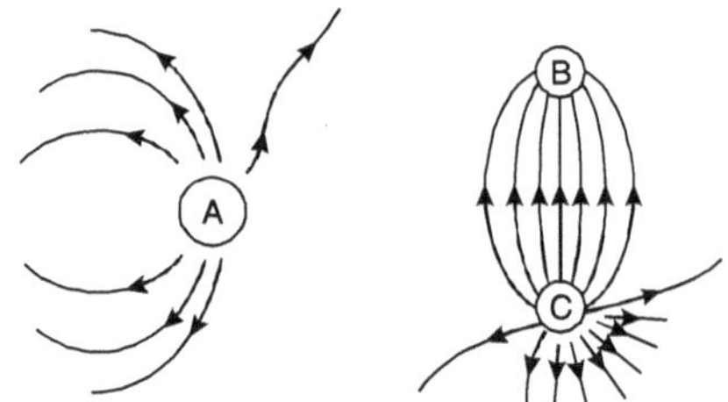

    (a) Which charges are positive?
    (b) Which charge has the largest magnitude? Why?

    (c) In which region or regions of the picture could the electric field be zero? Justify your answer.
    (i) near A, (ii) near B, (iii) near C, (iv) nowhere.

12. Two uniformly charged large plane sheets S_1 and S_2 having charge densities σ_1 and σ_2 ($\sigma_1 > \sigma_2$) are placed at a distance d parallel to each other. A charge q_0 is moved along a line of length $a(a < d)$ at an angle $45°$ with the normal to S_1. Calculate the work done by the electric field.

13. The following data was obtained for the dependence of the magnitude of electric field, with distance, from a reference point O, within the charge distribution in the shaded region.

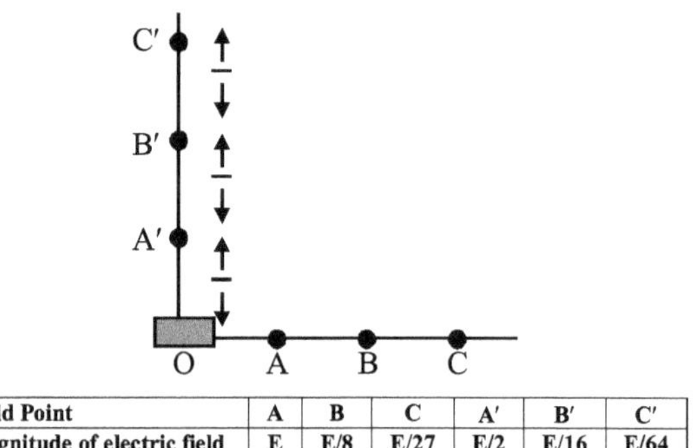

Field Point	A	B	C	A′	B′	C′
Magnitude of electric field	E	E/8	E/27	E/2	E/16	E/64

    (i) Identify the charge distribution and justify your answer.

    (ii) If the potential due to this charge distribution, has a value V at the point A, what is its value at the point?

Objectiue Practice Exercise

Multiple Choice Questions

DIRECTIONS : *This section contains multiple choice questions. Each question has four choices (a), (b), (c) and (d) out of which only one is correct.*

1. When a body is charged by induction, then the body
    (a) becomes neutral
    (b) does not lose any charge
    (c) loses whole of the charge on it
    (d) loses part of the charge on it

2. Quantisation of charge implies
    (a) charge cannot be destroyed
    (b) charge exists on particles
    (c) there is a minimum permissible charge on a particle
    (d) charge, which is a fraction of a coulomb is not possible.

3. For an isolated system, it is possible to create or destroy charged particle, but it is not possible to create or destroy.
    (a) net charge of the system
    (b) charge on each particle
    (c) charge distribution of system
    (d) None of these

4. When some charge is transferred to ...*A*... it readily gets distributed over the entire surface of ... *A*... If some charge is put on ... *B*..., it stays at the same place.
    Here, A and B refer to
    (a) insulator, conductor
    (b) conductor, insulator
    (c) insulator, insulator
    (d) conductor, conductor

5. A positively charged rod is brought near an uncharged conductor. If the rod is then suddenly withdrawn, the charge left on the conductor will be
    (a) positive
    (b) negative
    (c) zero
    (d) cannot say

6. Two spheres A and B of exactly same mass are given equal positive and negative charges respectively. Their masses after charging
    (a) remains unaffected
    (b) mass of A > mass of B
    (c) mass of A < mass of B
    (d) Nothing can be said

7. Coulomb's law is true for
    (a) atomic distances ($= 10^{-11}$ m)
    (b) nuclear distances ($= 10^{-15}$ m)
    (c) charged as well as uncharged particles
    (d) all the distances

8. In annihilation process, in which an electron and a positron transform into two gamma rays, which property of electric charge is displayed?
   (a) Additivity of charge
   (b) Quantisation of charge
   (c) Conservation of charge
   (d) Attraction and repulsion

9. Which of the following statements is incorrect?
   (a) The charge q on a body is always given by $q = ne$, where n is any integer, positive or negative.
   (b) By convention, the charge on an electron is taken to be negative.
   (c) The fact that electric charge is always an integral multiple of e is termed as quantisation of charge.
   (d) The quatisation of charge was experimentally demonstrated by Newton in 1912.

10. Which of the following statements is incorrect? Study of charges, by scientists, concludes that
    (a) there are two kinds of electric charges.
    (b) bodies like plastic, fur acquire elecrtic charge on rubbing.
    (c) like charges attract, unlike charges repel each other.
    (d) the property which differentiates two kinds of charges is called the polarity of the charge.

11. What happens when some charge is placed on a soap bubble?
    (a) Its radius decreases   (b) Its radius increases
    (c) The bubble collapses   (d) None of these

12. Consider a neutral conducting sphere. A positive point charge is placed outside the sphere. The net charge on the sphere is then
    (a) negative and distributed uniformly over the surface of the sphere
    (b) negative and appears only at the point on the sphere closest to the point charge
    (c) negative and distributed non-uniformly over the entire surface of the sphere
    (d) zero

13. A charged particle is free to move in an electric field. It will travel
    (a) always along a line of force
    (b) along a line of force, if its initial velocity is zero
    (c) along a line of force, if it has some initial velocity in the direction of an acute angle with the line of force
    (d) none of the above

14. If one penetrates a uniformly charged spherical cloud, electric field strength
    (a) decreases directly as the distance from the centre
    (b) increases directly as the distance from the centre
    (c) remains constant
    (d) None of these

15. Electric lines of force about a negative point charge are
    (a) circular anticlockwise   (b) circular clockwise
    (c) radial, inwards   (d) radial, outwards

16. Electric lines of force
    (a) exist everywhere
    (b) exist only in the immediate vicinity of electric charges
    (c) exist only when both positive and negative charges are near one another
    (d) are imaginary

17. A region surrounding a stationary electric dipoles has
    (a) magnetic field only
    (b) electric field only
    (c) both electric and magnetic fields
    (d) no electric and magnetic fields

18. The electric field at a point on equatorial line of a dipole and direction of the dipole moment
    (a) will be parallel
    (b) will be in opposite direction
    (c) will be perpendicular
    (d) are not related

19. An electric dipole is placed at an angle of 30° to a non-uniform electric field. The dipole will experience
    (a) a translational force only in the direction of the field
    (b) a translational force only in the direction normal to the direction of the field
    (c) a torque as well as a translational force
    (d) a torque only

20. The spatial distribution of electric field due to charges (A, B) is shown in figure. Which one of the following statements is correct ?

    (a) A is +ve and B −ve, |A| > |B|
    (b) A is −ve and B +ve, |A| = |B|
    (c) Both are +ve but A > B
    (d) Both are −ve but A > B

21. In the figure, charge q is placed at origin O. When the charge q is displaced from its position the electric field at point P changes

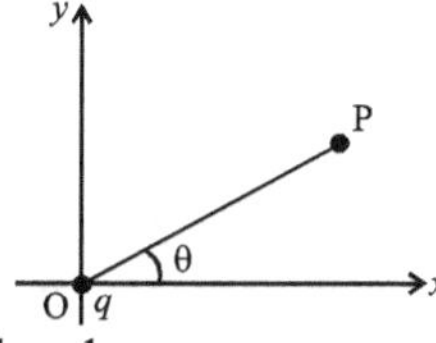

    (a) at the same time when q is displaced.
    (b) at a time after $\dfrac{OP}{c}$ where c is the speed of light.
    (c) at a time after $\dfrac{OP\cos\theta}{c}$.
    (d) at a time after $\dfrac{OP\sin\theta}{c}$

22. An electric dipole is placed in a uniform electric field. The dipole will experience
    (a) a force that will displace it in the direction of the field
    (b) a force that will displace it in a direction opposite to the field.
    (c) a torque which will rotate it without displacement
    (d) a torque which will rotate it and a force that will displace it

23. On decreasing the distance between the two charges of a dipole which is perpendicular to electric field and decreasing the angle between the dipole and electric field, the torque on the dipole
    (a) increases   (b) decreases
    (c) remains same   (d) cannot be predicted.

24. A sphere of radius R has uniform distribution of electric charge in its volume. At a distance x from its centre for x <R, the electric field is directly proportional to
    (a) $1/x^2$ (b) $1/x$ (c) x (d) x^2

25. In a medium of dielectric constant K, the electric field is $\vec{E}$. If ϵ_0 is permittivity of the free space, the electric displacement vector is
    (a) $\dfrac{K\vec{E}}{\epsilon_0}$ (b) $\dfrac{\vec{E}}{K\epsilon_0}$ (c) $\dfrac{\epsilon_0 \vec{E}}{K}$ (d) $K\epsilon_0 \vec{E}$

26. Positive electric flux indicates that electric lines of force are directed
    (a) outwards   (b) inwards
    (c) either (a) or (b)   (d) None of these

27. If the flux of the electric field through a closed surface is zero, then
    (a) the electric field must be zero everywhere on the surface
    (b) the electric field may not be zero everywhere on the surface
    (c) the charge inside the surface must be zero
    (d) the charge in the vicinity of the surface must be zero

28. If the electric flux entering and leaving an enclosed surface respectively is ϕ_1 and ϕ_2, the electric charge inside the surface will be
    (a) $(\phi_2 + \phi_2) \times \varepsilon_o$ (b) $(\phi_2 - \phi_2) \times \varepsilon_o$
    (c) $(\phi_1 + \phi_2) \times \varepsilon_o$ (d) $(\phi_2 - \phi_1) \times \varepsilon_o$

29. The Gaussian surface
    (a) can pass through a continuous charge distribution.
    (b) cannot pass through a continuous charge distribution.
    (c) can pass through any system of discrete charges.
    (d) can pass through a continuous charge distribution as well as any system of discrete charges.

30. Gauss's law is true only if force due to a charge varies as
    (a) r^{-1} (b) r^{-2} (c) r^{-3} (d) r^{-4}

31. For a given surface the Gauss's law is stated as $\oint \vec{E}.d\vec{A} = 0$. From this we can conclude that
    (a) E is necessarily zero on the surface
    (b) E is perpendicular to the surface at every point
    (c) the total flux through the surface is zero
    (d) the flux is only going out of the surface

32. Total electric flux coming out of a unit positive charge put in air is
    (a) ε_0 (b) ε_0^{-1} (c) $[4\pi\varepsilon_0]^{-1}$ (d) $4\pi\varepsilon_0$

33. Gauss's law is valid for
    (a) any closed surface
    (b) only regular close surfaces
    (c) any open surface
    (d) only irregular open surfaces

34. A point charge +q is placed at mid point of a cube of side 'L'. The electric flux emerging from the cube is
    (a) $\dfrac{q}{\varepsilon_0}$ (b) $\dfrac{6qL^2}{\varepsilon_0}$ (c) $\dfrac{q}{6L^2\varepsilon_0}$ (d) zero

35. It is not convenient to use a spherical Gaussian surface to find the electric field due to an electric dipole using Gauss's theorem because
    (a) Gauss's law fails in this case
    (b) This problem does not have spherical symmetry
    (c) Coulomb's law is more fundamental than Gauss's law
    (d) Spherical Gaussian surface will alter the dipole moment

36. An electric dipole is put in north-south direction in a sphere filled with water. Which statement is correct?
    (a) Electric flux is coming towards sphere
    (b) Electric flux is coming out of sphere
    (c) Electric flux entering into sphere and leaving the sphere are same
    (d) Water does not permit electric flux to enter into sphere

37. The electric field near a conducting surface having a uniform surface charge density is given by
    (a) $\dfrac{\sigma}{\varepsilon_0}$ and is parallel to the surface
    (b) $\dfrac{2\sigma}{\varepsilon_0}$ and is parallel to the surface
    (c) $\dfrac{\sigma}{\varepsilon_0}$ and is normal to the surface
    (d) $\dfrac{2\sigma}{\varepsilon_0}$ and is normal to the surface

38. Select the correct statements from the following.
    (a) The electric field due to a charge outside the Gaussian surface contributes zero net flux through the surface.
    (b) The electgric flux of the electric field $\oint \vec{E} \cdot d\vec{A}$ is zero. The electric field is zero everywhere on the surface.
    (c) Total flux linked with a closed body, not enclosing any charge will be zero.
    (d) Total electric flux, if a dipole is enclosed by a surface is zero.

39. The number of electric lines of force that radiate outwards from one coulomb of charge in vacuum is
    (a) 1.13×10^{11} (b) 1.13×10^{10}
    (c) 0.61×10^{11} (d) 0.61×10^9

40. In figure + Q charge is located at one of the edge of the cube, then electric flux through cube due to + Q charge is
    (a) $\dfrac{+Q}{\epsilon_0}$ (b) $\dfrac{+Q}{2\epsilon_0}$
    (c) $\dfrac{+Q}{4\epsilon_0}$ (d) $\dfrac{+Q}{8\epsilon_0}$

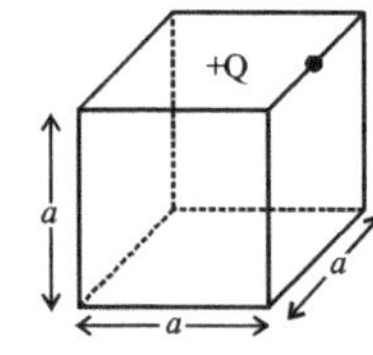

41. A square frame of edge l cm is placed with its positive normal making an angle of $60°$ with a uniform electric field E. The flux of the electric field through the surface bounded by the frame is
    (a) $El^2/2$ (b) $El^2/\sqrt{3}$ (c) $El^2/3$ (d) $2El^2$

Chapter Test

Time : *30 minutes*   **Max. Marks : 15**

Direction:

Each question number **1-15** carry **1 mark** each.

1. Among two discs A and B, first have radius 10 cm and charge 10^{-6} μC and second have radius 30 cm and charge 10^{-5} C. When they are touched, charge on both q_A and q_B respectively will, be

   (a) $q_A = 2.75$ μC, $q_B = 3.15$ μC
   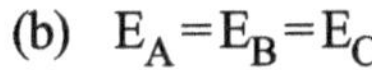
   (b) $q_A = 1.09$ μC, $q_B = 1.53$ μC
   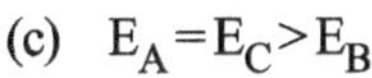
   (c) $q_A = q_B = 5.5$ μC
   (d) None of these

2. Figure shows some of the electric field lines corresponding to an electric field. The figure suggests that
   (a) $E_A > E_B > E_C$
   (b) $E_A = E_B = E_C$
   (c) $E_A = E_C > E_B$
   (d) $E_A = E_C < E_B$

3. The surface density on the copper sphere is σ. The electric field strength on the surface of the sphere is
   (a) σ   (b) σ/2   (c) $\sigma/2\varepsilon_o$ (d) Q/ε_o

DIRECTIONS (Qs. 4-6) : *Each of these questions contains an assertion followed by reason. Read them carefully and answer the question on the basis of following options. You have to select the one that best describes the two statements.*

(a) If both Assertion and Reason are correct and the Reason is a correct explanation of the Assertion.

(b) If both Assertion and Reason are correct but Reason is not a correct explanation of the Assertion.

(c) If the Assertion is correct but Reason is incorrect.

(d) If the Assertion is incorrect but the Reason is correct.

4. **Assertion :** A uniformly charged disc has a pin hole at its centre. The electric field at the centre of the disc is zero.

   Reason : Disc can be supposed to be made up of many rings. Also electric field at the centre of uniformly charged ring is zero.

5. **Assertion :** On bringing a positively charged rod near the uncharged conductor, the conductor gets attracted towards the rod.

   Reason : The electric field lines of the charged rod are perpendicular to the surface of conductor.

6. **Assertion :** The property that the force with which two charges attract or repel each other are not affected by the presence of a third charge.

   Reason : Force on any charge due to a number of other charge is the vector sum of all the forces on that charge due to other charges, taken one at a time.

DIRECTIONS : (Qs. 7-11) *are case based questions.*

Figure shows five charged lumps of plastic. The cross-section of Gaussian surface S is indicated. Assuming $q_1 = q_4 = 3.1$ nC, $q_2 = q_5 = -5.9$ nC, and $q_3 = -3.1$ nC.

7. Find the net electric flux through the surface is

   (a) -670 Nm^2/C

   (b) $+670$ Nm^2/C

   (c) -360 Nm^2/C
   (d) $+360$ Nm^2/C

8. Electric field at point A depends on __________ charge.
   (a) q_1
   (b) q_2
   (c) both q_1 and q_2
   (d) None of these

   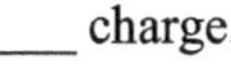

9. The surface density on the copper sphere is σ. The electric field strength on the surface of the sphere is
   (a) σ   (b) σ/2   (c) $\sigma/2\varepsilon_o$ (d) σ/ε_o

10. A charge q is placed at the centre of the open end of a cylindrical vessel. The flux of the electric field through the surface of the vessel is
    (a) zero
    (b) q/ε_o
    (c) $q/2\varepsilon_o$
    (d) $2q/\varepsilon_o$

11. At the centre of a cubical box $+ Q$ charge is placed. The value of total flux that is coming out a wall is
    (a) Q/ε_o (b) $Q/3\varepsilon_o$ (c) $Q/4\varepsilon_o$ (d) $Q/6\varepsilon_o$

Very Short Answer Type Questions

12. What is the angle between the directions of electric field at any (i) axial point and (ii) equatorial point due to an electric dipole?

13. In a medium the force of attraction between two point electric charges, distance 'd' apart is F. What distance apart should these be kept in the same medium so that the force between them becomes 3F?

14. An electric dipole, when held at 30° with respect to a uniform electric field of 10^4 N/C, experience a torque of 9×10^{-26} Nm. Calculate the dipole moment of the dipole.

15. Define intensity of electric field at a point. At what points is the electric dipole field intensity parallel to the line joining the charges?

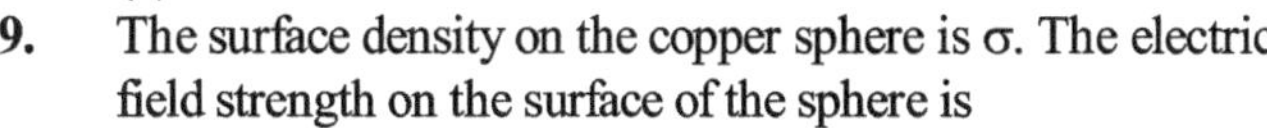

Solutions

Practice Exercise-1

1. **(a)** In the absence of gravitational force, the only force acts on the spheres is electrostatic repulsion and so the angle between two suspension becomes 180°. So force between the sphere

$$F = \frac{1}{4\pi\,\epsilon_0}\frac{Q^2}{(2L)^2}$$

2. **(b)** Here, $r_1 = \hat{i} + \hat{j} + \hat{k} \Rightarrow r_2 = 2\hat{i} + 3\hat{j} + \hat{k}$

$\therefore \quad \vec{r} = \vec{r_2} - \vec{r_1} = (2\hat{i} + 3\hat{j} + \hat{k}) - (\hat{i} + \hat{j} + \hat{k}) = \hat{i} + 2\hat{j}$

$|\vec{r}| = \sqrt{(1)^2 + (2)^2} = \sqrt{5}$

By Coulomb's law,

$$F = \frac{1}{4\pi\varepsilon_0}\frac{q_1 q_2}{r^2} = \frac{9\times10^9 \times 3\times10^{-6} \times 3\times10^{-6}}{(\sqrt{5})^2}$$

$$= \frac{81}{5}\times10^{-3}\,\text{N, Nearest answer is } 16\times10^{-3}\,\text{N}.$$

3. **(b)** When we say that a body is charged, we always mean that the body is having excess of electrons (negatively charged) or is of deficient of electrons (positively charged).

4. **(a)** Valence electrons are outermost electrons these can get transferred on rubbing.

5. **(b)** $T_{AB} = \dfrac{kq\cdot 2q}{d^2} + \dfrac{kq\cdot 4q}{(2d)^2} = \dfrac{3kq^2}{d}$

$$T_{BC} = \frac{k\cdot 4q\cdot 2q}{d^2} + \frac{kq\cdot 4q}{(2d)^2} = \frac{9kq^2}{d^2}$$

6. **(b)**

$$\overset{2q}{\underset{P}{\bullet}} \quad\quad \overset{q}{\underset{A}{\bullet}} \quad \overset{-3q}{\underset{B}{\bullet}}$$
$$|\!\!\leftarrow\!\!-\ell\!-\!\!\rightarrow\!\!|\!\!\leftarrow\!\!-d\!-\!\!\rightarrow\!\!|$$

Let a charge $2q$ be placed at P, at a distance I from A where charge q is placed, as shown in figure.

The charge $2q$ will not experience any force, when force, when force of repulsion on it due to q is balanced by force of attraction on it due to $-3q$ at B where AB $= d$

or $\quad \dfrac{(2q)(q)}{4\pi\varepsilon_0\ell^2} = \dfrac{(2q)(-3q)}{4\pi\varepsilon_0(\ell+d)^2}$

$(\ell + d)^2 = 3\ell^2 \quad$ or $\quad 2\ell^2 - 2\ell d - d^2 = 0$

$\therefore \quad \ell = \dfrac{2d \pm \sqrt{4d^2 + 2d^2}}{4} = \dfrac{d}{2} \pm \dfrac{\sqrt{3}d}{2}$

$\ell = \dfrac{d + \sqrt{3}d}{2}$

7. **(c)** Let n be the number of electrons missing.

$$F = \frac{1}{4\pi\varepsilon_0}\cdot\frac{q^2}{d^2} \Rightarrow q = \sqrt{4\pi\varepsilon_0 d^2 F} = ne$$

$$\therefore \quad n = \sqrt{\frac{4\pi\varepsilon_0 F d^2}{e^2}}$$

8. **(d)**

9. **(b)** Force on charge q_1 due to q_2 is

$$F_{12} = k\frac{q_1 q_2}{b^2}$$

Force on charge q_1 due to q_3 is

$$F_{13} = k\frac{q_1 q_3}{a^2}$$

The X - component of the force (F_x) on q_1 is $F_{12} + F_{13}\sin\theta$

$$\therefore \quad F_x = k\frac{q_1 q_2}{b^2} + k\frac{q_1 q_2}{a^2}\sin\theta$$

$$\therefore \quad F_x \propto \frac{q_2}{b^2} + \frac{q_3}{a^2}\sin\theta$$

10. **(d)** $Q_1 + Q_2 = Q \dots$ (i) and $F = k\dfrac{Q_1 Q_2}{r^2} \quad \dots$ (ii)

From (i) and (ii) $F = \dfrac{kQ_1(Q - Q_1)}{r^2}$

For F to be maximum $\dfrac{dF}{dQ_1} = 0 \Rightarrow Q_1 = Q_2 = \dfrac{Q}{2}$

11. **(a)** Conservation of electric charge states that the total charge of an isolated system remains unchanged with time.

12. **(c)** Coulomb force and gravitational force follow the same inverse-square law. But gravitational force is always attractive force, while coulomb force can be of both force attractive and repulsive.

13. **(b)** The individual force are unaffected due to presence of other charges. This is the principal of superposition of charges. Force on any charge due to a number of other charges is the vector sum of all the forces on that charge due to the other charges, taken one at a time.

14. **(b)** If +ve charge is displaced along x-axis, then net force will always act in a direction opposite to that of displacement and the test charge will always come back to its original position.

15. **(b)** Charging by induction involves transfer of charges from one part to the other of the body. No loss of charge is involved.

16. **(c)** On charging by conduction, body may gain mass, if it acquires negative charge. It may lose mass, if it acquires positive charge.

17. **(c)** Positive charge is due to deficiency of electrons.

18. **(c)** Net charge acquired by induction is zero, as there is only transfer of electrons from one part of body to the other.

19. **(a)**

20. $F = \dfrac{kq_1 q_2}{r^2}$ and $F_w = \dfrac{k'q_1 q_2}{r^2} \Rightarrow \dfrac{F_w}{F} = \dfrac{k'}{k} = 1/80$ (the dielectric constant of water is 80)

$\therefore$ Force will reduce 80 times.

21. In electrostatics, $q_1 + q_2 = 0$ signify $q_1 = -q_2$

22. (i) $F = \dfrac{kq_1q_2}{d^2}$ $\quad \therefore F \propto \dfrac{1}{d^2}$

$\dfrac{3F}{F} = \dfrac{d^2}{d'^2}$ $\quad \therefore \dfrac{d}{d'} = \sqrt{3}$

$\therefore d' = \dfrac{d}{\sqrt{3}}$

(ii) $\dfrac{F/3}{F} = \dfrac{d^2}{d'^2}$ $\quad \therefore \dfrac{d}{d'} = \dfrac{1}{\sqrt{3}}$

$\therefore d' = \sqrt{3}d.$

23. $1e = 1.6 \times 10^{-19} C$

$\therefore$ Charge carried by 12.5×10^{18} electrons
$= 12.5 \times 10^{18} \times 1.6 \times 10^{-19} = 2C$

24. $8.854 \times 10^{-12} C^2 N^{-1} m^{-2}$

25. Force between the charges q and 2q $= \dfrac{kq \times 2q}{d^2}$

For the net force on q and 2q to be zero, Q must be placed between q and 2q and it must be of negative sign.

$\therefore \dfrac{kq.Q}{x^2} = \dfrac{kQ.2q}{(d-x)^2} \Rightarrow \dfrac{(d-x)^2}{x^2} = 2$

$\therefore x = \dfrac{d}{1+\sqrt{2}}$ and $d - x = \dfrac{\sqrt{2}d}{1+\sqrt{2}}$

26.

Force on q due to 4q charge, $F_A = \dfrac{k\,4q.q}{(x/2)^2} = \dfrac{k\,4q^2}{(x/2)^2}$

Force on q due to Q, $F_B = \dfrac{k.Qq}{(x/2)^2}$

Net force on q = 0 if $F_B = F_A$

i.e. $\dfrac{k\,Qq}{(x/2)^2} = \dfrac{k\,4q^2}{(x/2)^2} \Rightarrow Q = 4q$

27. $e = -1.6 \times 10^{-19} C, Q = -3.2 \times 10^{-7} C; \quad Q = ne$

$\therefore n = \dfrac{Q}{e} = 2 \times 10^{12}$

28. $F = \dfrac{kq_1q_2}{r^2} = \dfrac{k(ne)^2}{r^2}$

$\Rightarrow 3.7 \times 10^{-9} = \dfrac{9 \times 10^9 \times (n \times 1.6 \times 10^{-19})^2}{(5 \times 10^{-10})^2} \quad \therefore n = 2$

29. $\varepsilon_r = \dfrac{F}{F_m} \therefore F_m = \dfrac{F}{k} = \dfrac{9 \times 10^9}{80}$

$= 1.125 \times 10^8 N$

Practice Exercise-2

1. (a) Figure indicates the presence of some positive charge to the left of A.

$\therefore E_A > E_B \;(\because r_A < r_B)$

2. (a) Given,

Dipole moment, $p = 4 \times 10^{-9}$ Cm

Electric field, $E = 5 \times 10^4 NC^{-1}$

Torque is given by

$\tau = p.E \sin\theta$
$= 4 \times 10^{-9} \times 5 \times 10^4 \times \sin 30° = 1 \times 10^{-4}$ Nm

3. (b) The direction of electric field at equatorial point A or B will be in opposite direction, as that of direction of dipole moment.

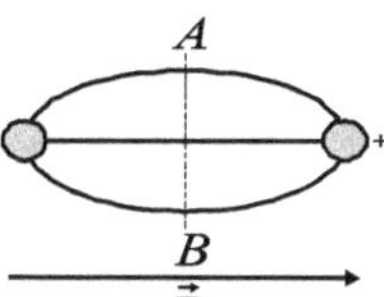

4. (a) $-eE = mg$

$\overrightarrow{E} = -\dfrac{9.1 \times 10^{-31} \times 10}{1.6 \times 10^{-19}} = -5.6 \times 10^{-11} N/C$

5. (d) Electric field lines do not form closed loop. This follows from the conservative nature of electric field.

6. (b) Given : Dipole moment of the dipole $= \vec{p}$ and uniform electric field $= \vec{E}$. We know that dipole moment (p) = q.a (where q is the charge and a is dipole length). And when a dipole of dipole moment $\vec{p}$ is placed in uniform electric field $\vec{E}$, then Torque $(\tau) =$ Either force $\times$ perpendicular distance between the two forces = qa E $\sin\theta$ or $\tau = pE \sin\theta$ or

$\vec{\tau} = \vec{p} \times \vec{E}$ (vector form)

7. (b) We have $E_a = \dfrac{2kp}{r^3}$ and $E_e = \dfrac{kp}{r^3}$; $\therefore E_a = 2E_e$

8. (a)

9. (a) Given : Length of the dipole $(2l) = 10$cm $= 0.1$m or $l = 0.05$ m

Charge on the dipole (q) = 500 μC = 500 $\times 10^{-6}$ C and distance of the point on the axis from the mid-point of the dipole $(r) = 20 + 5 = 25$ cm = 0.25 m.

We know that the electric field intensity due to dipole on the given point (E)

$= \dfrac{1}{4\pi\varepsilon_0} \times \dfrac{2(q.2l)r}{(r^2 - l^2)^2}$

$= 9 \times 10^9 \times \dfrac{2(500 \times 10^{-6} \times 0.1) \times 0.25}{[(0.25)^2 - (0.05)^2]^2}$

$= 6.25 \times 10^7 \; N/C$ (k = 1 for air)

10. (c) Electron and proton have same amount of charge so they have same coulomb force. They have different acceleration because they have different masses.

11. (a) The electrostatic shielding is possible by metallic conductor.

12. **(c)** The electric field will increase if positive charge is brought in an electric field.

13. **(a)** The restoring torque brings it back to its stable equillibrium.

14. **(d)** The rate of decrease of electric field is different in the two cases. In case of a point charge, it decreases as $1/r^2$ but in the case of electric dipole it decreases more rapidly, as $E \propto 1/r^3$.

15. **(b)**

16. **(b)** The direction of electric field at equatorial point A or B will be in opposite direction, as that of direction of dipole moment.

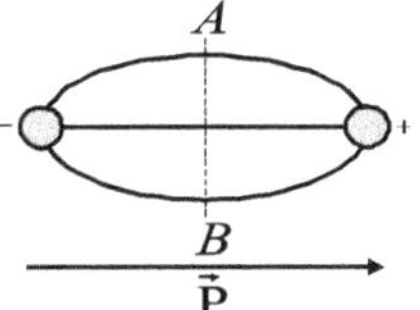

17. **(c)**

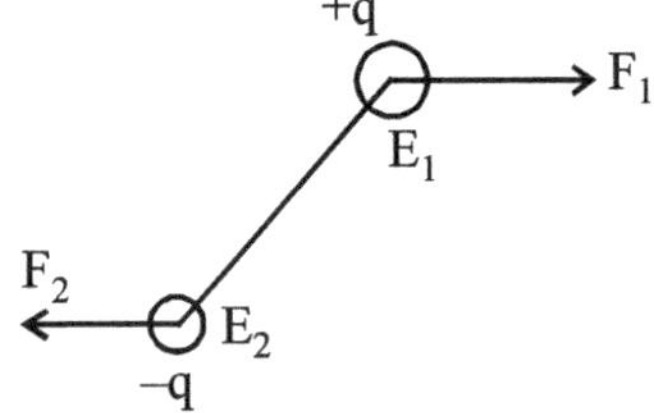

The electric field will be different at the location of force on the two charges. Therefore the two charges will be unequal. This will result in a force as well as torque.

18. **(c)** Intensity of electric field due to a Dipole

$$E = \frac{p}{4\pi\varepsilon_0 r^3} \sqrt{3\cos^2\theta + 1} \Rightarrow E \propto \frac{1}{r^3}$$

19. **(b)** Since $\tau = pE\sin\theta$ on decreasing the distance between the two charges, and on decreasing angle θ between the dipole and electric field, $\sin\theta$ decreases therefore torque decreases.

20. Lines of force due to two equal positive point charges

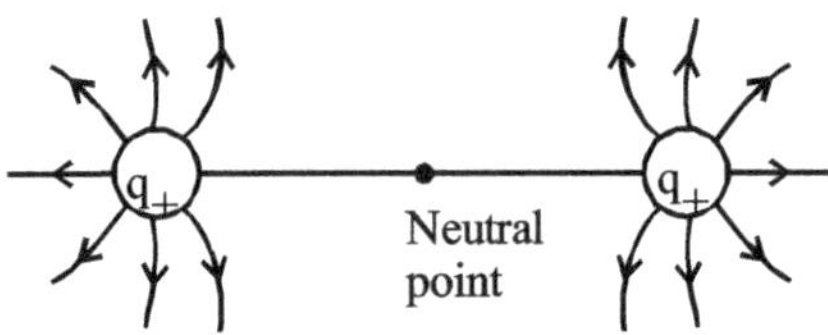

21. If the dipole is placed along the direction of the field, its equilibrium is stable $(\theta = 0°)$.

22. $qE = mg \Rightarrow q = \dfrac{mg}{E} = \dfrac{3.2\times10^{-13}}{5\times10^5} \Rightarrow q = 0.64\times10^{-18}\,C$

23. For an electric dipole, $F \propto \dfrac{1}{r^3}$

$$\therefore \quad \text{New force, } F^1 = \frac{F}{2^3} = \frac{F}{8}.$$

24. Electric field $E \propto \dfrac{1}{r^2}$.

So when distance becomes 3r, E becomes $\dfrac{E}{9}$.

25. Let a single point charge is situated at the origin O of the coordinate system XYZ. Consider a test charge q_0 (unit +ve charge) at point P (x, y, z)

Force exerted on q_0 by q = $\overline{F} = \dfrac{kqq_0}{r^2}\hat{r}$

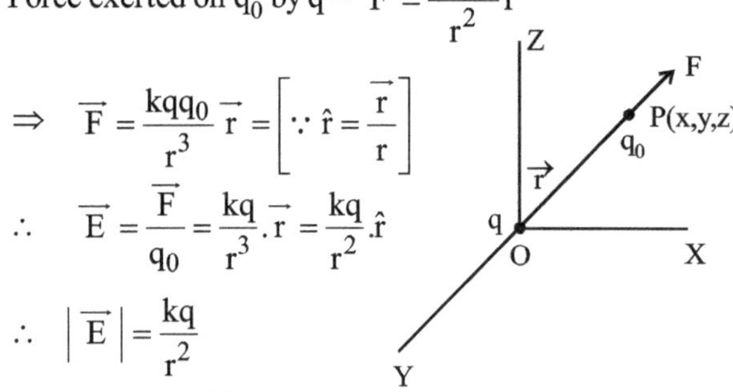

$$\Rightarrow \overline{F} = \frac{kqq_0}{r^3}\overrightarrow{r} = \left[\because \hat{r} = \frac{\overrightarrow{r}}{r}\right]$$

$$\therefore \quad \overline{E} = \frac{\overline{F}}{q_0} = \frac{kq}{r^3}\overrightarrow{r} = \frac{kq}{r^2}\hat{r}$$

$$\therefore \quad \left|\overline{E}\right| = \frac{kq}{r^2}$$

If $q > 0$, then $\overrightarrow{E}$ is directed radially onwards at every point in electric field. If $q < 0$, then $\overrightarrow{E}$ is directed inwards.

$$\therefore \quad \overrightarrow{r} = x\hat{i} + y\hat{j} + z\hat{k} \text{ and}$$

$$\left|\overrightarrow{r}\right| = \sqrt{x^2 + y^2 + z^2}$$

$$\therefore \quad \overline{E} = \frac{kq}{(x^2 + y^2 + z^2)^{3/2}}(x\hat{i} + y\hat{j} + z\hat{k})$$

$$\therefore \quad E_x = \frac{kq}{(x^2 + y^2 + z^2)^{3/2}}x,$$

$$E_y = \frac{kq}{(x^2 + y^2 + z^2)^{3/2}}y \text{ and}$$

$$E_z = \frac{kq}{(x^2 + y^2 + z^2)^{3/2}}z$$

26.

Electric field intensity at P due to charge,

$$-q = \left|\overrightarrow{E_1}\right| = \frac{kq}{AP^2} = \frac{kq}{(r+a)^2} \text{ along } \overrightarrow{PA}$$

Electric field intensity at P due to charge +q

$$\left|\overrightarrow{E_2}\right| = \frac{kq}{BP^2} = \frac{kq}{(r-a)^2} \text{ along } \overrightarrow{BP} \quad \because \left|\overrightarrow{E_2}\right| > \left|\overrightarrow{E_1}\right|$$

$$\therefore \quad \text{Resultant intensity at P} = \overrightarrow{E} = \overrightarrow{E_2} - \overrightarrow{E_1}$$

along $\overrightarrow{BP}$

$$\left|\overrightarrow{E}\right| = \frac{kq}{(r-a)^2} - \frac{kq}{(r+a)^2}$$

$$= kq\left[\frac{1}{(r-a)^2} - \frac{1}{(r+a)^2}\right]$$

$$= kq\left[\frac{(r+a)^2 - (r-a)^2}{(r^2-a^2)^2}\right] = \frac{kq\times4ar}{(r^2-a^2)^2}$$

$$= \frac{k(2aq)2r}{(r^2-a^2)^2} = \frac{k\left|\overrightarrow{p}\right|.2r}{(r^2-a^2)^2}$$

where $\left|\overrightarrow{p}\right| = $ dipole moment $= 2aq$

If the dipole is short, $2a \ll r$ $\therefore |\overrightarrow{E}| = \dfrac{2k|\overrightarrow{p}|}{r^3}$

27.

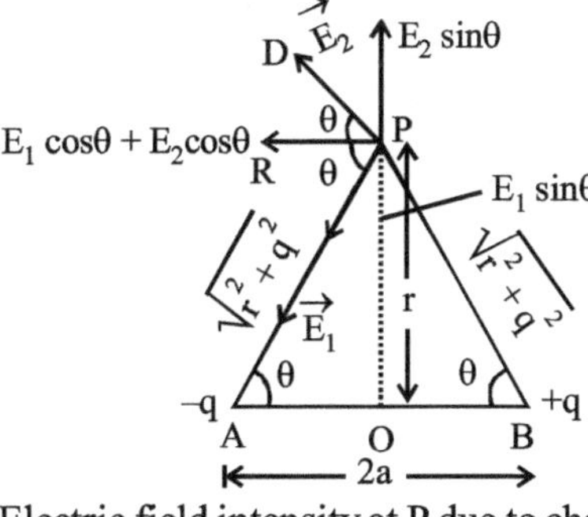

Electric field intensity at P due to charge, $-q$ at

$$A = |\overrightarrow{E_1}| = \frac{kq}{AP^2} = \frac{kq}{(r^2+a^2)} \text{ along } \overrightarrow{PA}$$

Electric field intensity at P due to charge, $+q$ at

$$B = |\overrightarrow{E_2}| = \frac{kq}{BP^2} = \frac{kq}{(r^2+a^2)} \text{ along } \overrightarrow{PD}$$

$$\because \quad |\overrightarrow{E_2}| = |\overrightarrow{E_1}|$$

$\therefore \quad E_1 \sin\theta$ and $E_2 \sin\theta$ are equal and opposite and will cancel each other.

$\therefore$ Resultant intensity at $P = |\overrightarrow{E}| = E_1 \cos\theta + E_2 \cos\theta$

$= 2E_1 \cos\theta$

$$= \frac{kq}{(r^2+a^2)} \cdot \frac{OB}{BP} = \frac{kq}{(r^2+a^2)} \cdot \frac{a}{\sqrt{r^2+a^2}}$$

$$= \frac{|\overrightarrow{p}|}{(r^2+a^2)^{3/2}} \quad \text{where } |\overrightarrow{p}| = 3qa \text{ along } \overrightarrow{PR} \,||\, \overrightarrow{BA}$$

For a short dipole $2a \ll r$

$$\therefore \quad |\overrightarrow{E}| = \frac{k|\overrightarrow{p}|}{r^3}$$

28.

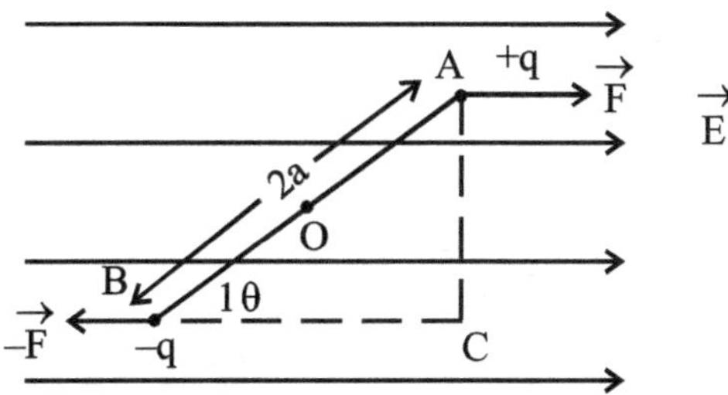

(i) Let the dipole AB is held in the uniform electric field $\overrightarrow{E}$ at an angle θ.

Force on $+q = q\overrightarrow{E}$ along $\overrightarrow{E}$.

and force on $-q = -q\overrightarrow{E}$ opposite to $\overrightarrow{E}$.

$\therefore$ Net force on the dipole $= q\overrightarrow{E} - q\overrightarrow{E} = 0$

(ii) Two equal and parallel forces from a couple which will rotate the dipole in clockwise direction and tends to align it along the direction of the field.

$\therefore$ Torque = force × perpendicular distance between the forces

$$\tau = F \times AC = qE \times AB \sin\theta$$
$$= qE \times 2a \sin\theta$$
$$\tau = pE \sin\theta, \text{ where } p = q \times 2a$$

$$\therefore \quad \overrightarrow{\tau} = \overrightarrow{p} \times \overrightarrow{E}$$

29. (a) The two charges are of opposite sign so that force will be attractive in nature.
(b) The two charges have different magnitudes – the charge of smaller magnitude will be nearer to the point where the total field intensity is zero.

30. A torque will develop and it will align the dipole in the direction of electric field. The dipole shall not move as net force on it is zero.

31. The electric field $\overrightarrow{E_1}$ at the point P due to point charges $+q$ and $-q$ at the point A and B, respectively, forming an electric dipole, is of magnitude

$$E_1 = \left(\frac{1}{4\pi\varepsilon_0}\right)\left(\frac{p}{r^3}\right) = \left(\frac{1}{4\pi\varepsilon_0}\right)\left(\frac{ql}{r^3}\right)$$

and direction opposite to the electric dipole moment $\overrightarrow{p}$, as shown. The electric field $\overrightarrow{E_2}$ at the point P due to the point $+q$ at the point O is of magnitude

$$E_2 = \left(\frac{1}{4\pi\varepsilon_0}\right)\left(\frac{qr}{r^3}\right)$$

and direction along OP, as shown. since the two electric fields $\overrightarrow{E_1}$ and $\overrightarrow{E_2}$ are mutually perpendicular and hence, the resultant electric field at the point P has the magnitude.

$$E = \sqrt{E_1^2 + E_2^2}$$

$$= \left(\frac{1}{4\pi\varepsilon_0 r^3}\right)\sqrt{(q^2 l^2 + q^2 r^2)}$$

$$= \left(\frac{q}{4\pi\varepsilon_0 r^3}\right)\sqrt{(l^2 + r^2)}$$

and direction making an θ with OP, i.e.,

$$\theta = \tan^{-1}\left(\frac{E_1}{E_2}\right) = \tan^{-1}\left(\frac{l}{r}\right)$$

32. If an electron, moving with a finite velocity v in the $+x$ direction, enters a transverse electric field $\overrightarrow{E}$ in the $-y$ direction, as shown, it has no acceleration in the x direction but an acceleration $\overrightarrow{a}$ in the $+y$ direction.

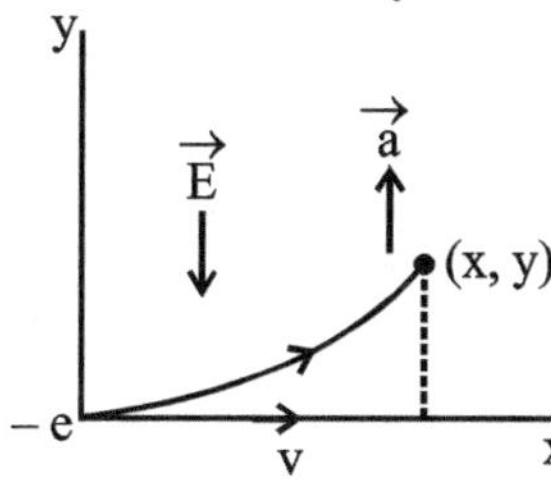

The displacements in the time t in the x and y directions are

$$x = vt$$

$$y = \frac{1}{2}at^2 = \frac{1}{2}\left(\frac{eE}{m}\right)t^2 = \left(\frac{eE}{2mv^2}\right)x^2$$

which means that the path of electron is parabolic.

33. (i) $q_1 = 0.2\,C$, $q_2 = 0.4\,C$

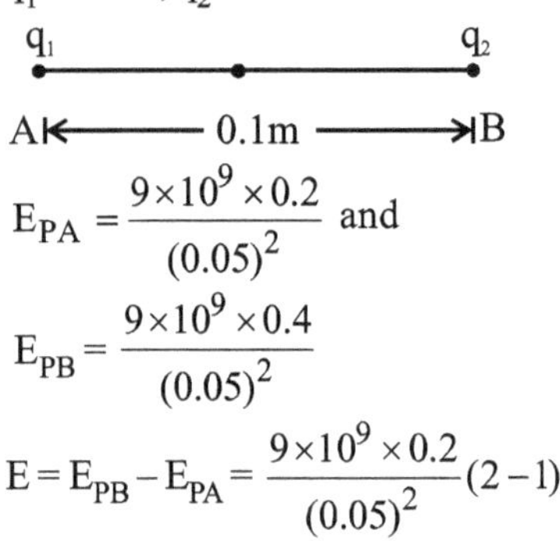

$$E_{PA} = \frac{9\times10^9 \times 0.2}{(0.05)^2} \text{ and}$$

$$E_{PB} = \frac{9\times10^9 \times 0.4}{(0.05)^2}$$

$$E = E_{PB} - E_{PA} = \frac{9\times10^9 \times 0.2}{(0.05)^2}(2-1)$$

$$\Rightarrow \quad E = 7.2 \times 10^{11}\,\text{N/C}$$

(ii) $E = E_{PA} + E_{PB}$

$$= \frac{9\times10^9 \times 0.2}{(0.15)^2} + \frac{9\times10^9 \times 0.4}{(0.05)^2}$$

$$E = 1.52 \times 10^{12}\,\text{N/C}.$$

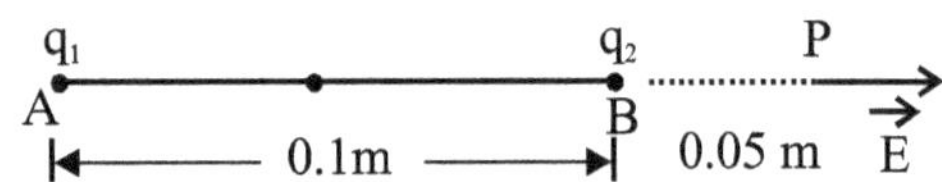

34. $E_{PA} = \dfrac{kq_A}{AP^2} = \dfrac{9\times10^9 \times \sqrt{2}\times10^{-6}}{\left(\sqrt{2}\right)^2}$

$$= 6.36 \times 10^3\,\text{N/C}$$

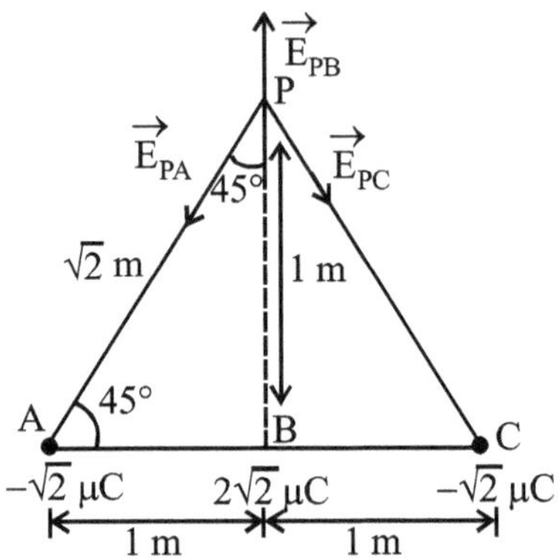

$$E_{PC} = E_{PA}$$

$$E_{PB} = \frac{9\times10^9 \times 2\sqrt{2}\times10^{-6}}{1^2} = 25.45 \times 10^3\,\text{N/C}$$

Resultant of E_{PA} and E_{PC} along $\overrightarrow{PB} = 2E_{PA}\cos45°$

$$= 2 \times 6.36 \times 10^3 \times \frac{1}{\sqrt{2}} = 9 \times 10^3\,\text{N/C}$$

∴ Net electric field at P is $E = 25.45 \times 10^3 - 9 \times 10^3 = 16.45 \times 10^3$ N/C along BP.

35.

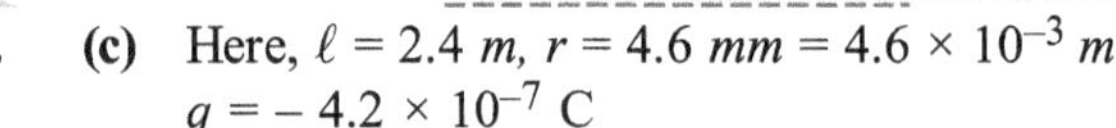

$$q_1 = 2\times10^{-7}\,C \qquad q_2 = 1\times10^{-7}\,C$$

Electric field due to q_1 at the site of $q_2 = E_1$

$$= \frac{kq_1}{r^2} = \frac{9\times10^9 \times 2\times10^{-7}}{(10^{-2})^2} = 1.8\times10^7\,\text{N/C}$$

Electric field due to q_2 at the site of

$$q_1 = E_2 = \frac{kq_2}{r^2} = \frac{9\times10^9 \times 2\times10^{-7}}{(10^{-2})^2}$$

$$= 9\times10^6\,\text{N/C}.$$

36. $E = \dfrac{kp}{(r^2 + a^2)^{3/2}}$

$$= \frac{9\times10^9 \times 100\times10^{-6} \times 0.1}{(0.2)^3}$$

$$= 1.125 \times 10^7\,\text{N/C}.$$

37. The electric dipole moment of dipole has the magnitude

$$p = ql = 2 \times 10^{-6} \times 10^{-2} = 2 \times 10^{-8}\,\text{C-m}$$

The electric field at the point P on the axis of dipole has the magnitude

$$E = \left(\frac{1}{4\pi\varepsilon_0}\right)\left(\frac{2p}{r^3}\right) = (9\times10^9)\left(\frac{2\times2\times10^{-8}}{1^3}\right) = 360\,\text{N/C}$$

The electric field at the point P on the equator of dipole has the magnitude

$$E = \left(\frac{1}{4\pi\varepsilon_0}\right)\left(\frac{p}{r^3}\right) = (9\times10^9)\left(\frac{2\times10^{-8}}{1^3}\right) = 180\,\text{N/C}$$

Practice Exercise-3

1. **(c)** Here, $\ell = 2.4\ m$, $r = 4.6\ mm = 4.6 \times 10^{-3}\ m$

$$q = -4.2 \times 10^{-7}\ C$$

Linear charge density, $\lambda = \dfrac{q}{\ell}$

$$= \frac{-4.2\times10^{-7}}{2.4} = -1.75 \times10^{-7}\ C\ m^{-1}$$

Electric field, $E = \dfrac{\lambda}{2\pi\varepsilon_0 r}$

$$= \frac{-1.75\times10^{-7}}{2\times3.14\times8.854\times10^{-12} \times 4.6\times10^{-3}}$$

$$= -6.7 \times 10^5\ N\ C^{-1}$$

2. **(a)** According to Gauss's law total electric flux through a closed surface is $\dfrac{1}{\varepsilon_0}$ times the total charge inside that surface.

Electric flux, $\phi_E = \dfrac{q}{\varepsilon_0}$

Charge on α-particle $= 2e$ ∴ $\phi_E = \dfrac{2e}{\varepsilon_0}$

3. **(d)** Electric flux, $\phi = EA\cos\theta$, where θ = angle between E and normal to the surface.

Here $\theta = \dfrac{\pi}{2} \Rightarrow \phi = 0$

4. (c) The field due to infinite linear charge distribution

$$E = \frac{1}{4\pi\varepsilon_0}\int\frac{dq}{r} \Rightarrow E \propto \frac{1}{r}$$

So curve is hyperbolic.

5. (d) According to Gauss' Law

$$\oint E.ds = \frac{Q_{\text{enclosed by closed surface}}}{\varepsilon_o} = \text{flux}$$

so total flux = Q/ε_o

Since cube has six face, so flux coming out through one wall or one face is $Q/6\varepsilon_o$.

6. (a) Gaussian surface cannot pass through any discrete charge because electric field due to a system of discrete charges is not well defined at the location of the charges. But the Gaussian surface can pass through a continuous charge distribution.

7. (d) Here, $\vec{E} = 2\hat{i}+3\hat{j}+\hat{k}\ NC^{-1}, \vec{S}=10\hat{i}\ m^2$

Electric flux, $\phi = \vec{E}.\vec{S}$

$$= (2\hat{i}+3\hat{j}+\hat{k}\ NC^{-1}).(10\hat{i}\ m^2)$$
$$= 20\ Nm^2C^{-1}$$

8. (d) Since electric field $\vec{E}$ decreases inside water, therefore flux $\phi = \vec{E}\cdot\vec{A}$ also decreases.

9. (a) The flux is zero according to Gauss' Law because it is a open surface which enclosed a charge q.

10. (d)

11. (d) Electric field at any point depends on presence of all charges.

12. (c) $\oint\vec{E}\cdot d\vec{A}=0$, represents charge inside close surface is zero. Electric field as any point on the surface may be zero.

13. (c) $\phi = E(ds)\cos\theta = E(2\pi r^2)\cos 0° = 2\pi r^2 E$.

14. (a) For the curved surface, $\theta = 90°$

$$\therefore\ \ \phi = E\ ds\cos 90° = 0.$$

15. (d)

16. (c) Flux does not depend on the size and shape of the close surface, and so, it remains same.

17. By Gauss's theorem

Electric flux through the closed surface S is

$$\phi_s = \frac{\Sigma q}{\varepsilon_0} = \frac{+2q-q}{\varepsilon_0} = \frac{q}{\varepsilon_0}$$

18. According to the Gauss's law of electrostatics, electric flux through a closed surface is given by

$$\phi_E = \oint\vec{E}.\overrightarrow{ds} = \frac{Q}{\varepsilon_0}\ ....(i)$$

Here,

E = electrostatic field

Q = total charge enclosed by the surface

ε_0 = absolute electric permittivity of free space

In the given case, cube encloses an electric dipole. Therefore the total charge enclosed by the cube is zero. i.e. Q = 0

Therefore, from (i), we have

$$\phi_E = \oint\vec{E}.\overrightarrow{ds} = \frac{0}{\varepsilon_o} = 0$$

19. According to Gauss's law, flux through a closed surface is given by $\phi = \dfrac{q}{\varepsilon_0}$

Here, q is the charge enclosed by the Gaussian surface. Since, on increasing the radius of the Gaussian surface, charge through the spherical Gaussian surface will not be affected when its radius is increased.

20. (a) Electric field, $E = \dfrac{\lambda}{2\pi\varepsilon_0 r}$

i.e., $E\propto\dfrac{1}{r}$.

(b) Electric field outside the shell,

$$E = \frac{q}{4\pi\in_0 r^2}\ \text{i.e., } E\propto\frac{1}{r^2}$$

21. The cylinder is simply placed in the uniform electric field $\vec{E}$ which may otherwise be in any direction, and it does not have any charge enclosed inside of it. Therefore, according to the Gauss's law, the total electric flux through the surface of cylinder must be zero.

22. The outward electric flux through the curved surface is equal to the inward electric flux through the circular plane, i.e., it is

$$\phi_E = (\pi R^2)E$$

Past year Exercise

1. (a) According to Gauss's theorem

$$\phi = \frac{\Sigma q_{en}}{\varepsilon_0}$$

So, net charge enclosed by the surface is zero if the net electric flux through a closed surface is zero.

2. Force acting between two point charges

$$F = \frac{1}{K}\frac{q_1 q_2}{r^2}$$

$$\therefore\ \ F\propto\frac{1}{K}\ \ [\because q_1, q_2 \text{ and } r \text{ are same}]$$

$$\Rightarrow\ \text{So, } \frac{F_{air}}{F_{medium}} = \frac{K_{medium}}{K_{air}}$$

$$\Rightarrow\ \frac{8}{F_{Water}} = \frac{80}{1} \Rightarrow F_{water} = \frac{8}{80} = \frac{1}{10}N$$

3. Proton will move in the direction of uniform electric field.

4. (i) For stable equilibrium angle between p and E is $0°$.

(ii) For unstable equilibrium, angle between p and E is $180°$.

5. Dielectrics are non-conductor and does not have free electrons at all. While conductor has free electrons which makes it able to pass the electricity through it.

6. The electric lines of forces exerts lateral pressure on each other leads to repulsion between like charges. Thus in order to stable spacing, the lines are normal to the surface.

7. Zero.

8. It is clear that the sphere of radius 2a encloses the charge +4Q only

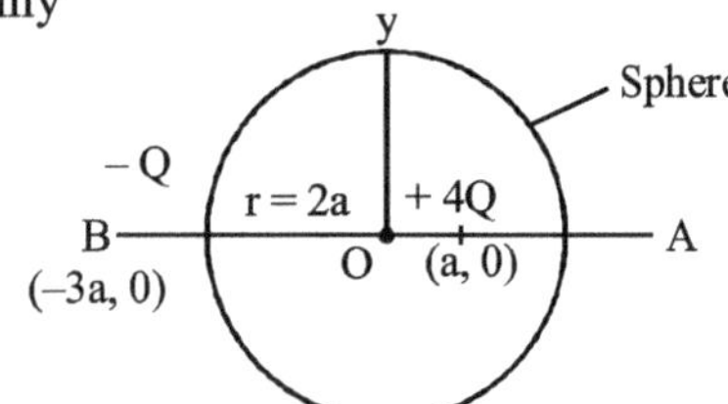

Therefore, electric flux

$$\phi = \oint \vec{E} \cdot \overrightarrow{ds} = \frac{1}{\in_0} \cdot 4Q = \frac{4Q}{\in_0}$$

9. Electric field lines form a closed loop, then work done by electric force should be zero in closed loop but we do not find any zero value. Hence, electric field lines do not form any closed loop.

10. Electric field lines do not cross each other because the tangent to a line of electric field at any point gives the direction of the electric field at that point. If any two lines of electric field cross each other, then at the intersection point, there would be two tangents and hence two directions for electric field, which is not possible.

11. When balls A and B are brought in contact with each other, then charge on each ball = $(-Q + 3Q)/2 = +Q$

Again two balls are separated by a distance 'd' then force

between them $F = \dfrac{KQ_1 Q_2}{d^2}$

And charge of both the balls is of same nature, positive hence coulomb force is of repulsive nature.

OR

When charge Q is placed at the centre of the shell, − Q charge induced on the inner surface and +Q charge induced on the outer surface, so charge density on the

(i) inner surface of the shell $\sigma_{inner} = \dfrac{charge}{area} = \dfrac{-Q}{\pi R_1^2}$ and

(ii) outer surface of the shell $\sigma_{outer} = \dfrac{charge}{area} = \dfrac{+Q}{\pi R_2^2}$

12. Here two points are important

(i) Charge resides on the outer surface of spherical conductor

(ii) Equal charge of opposite nature induces in the surface of conductor nearer to source charge.

(i) (1) Charge produced on inner surface due to induction = −q

∴ Surface charge density of inner surface

$$= \frac{-q}{4\pi R_1^2}$$

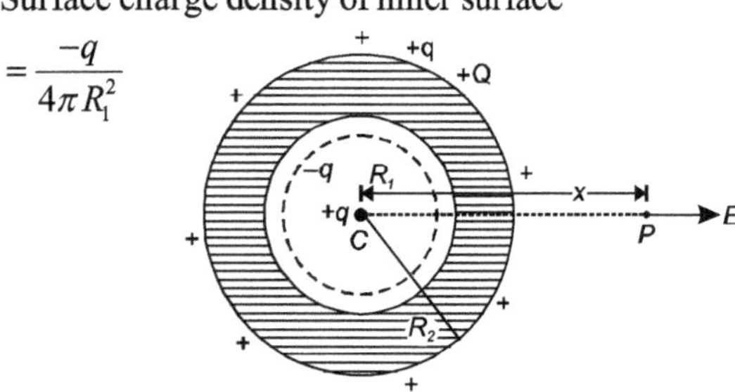

When charge −q is induced on inner walls then equal charge +q is produced at outer surface.

(2) ∴ Charge on outer surface

$$= q + Q$$

∴ Surface charge density of outer surface

$$= \frac{q + Q}{4\pi R_2^2}$$

(ii) Electric field intensity at P separated by a distance $x \, (x > R_2)$

$$E = \frac{1}{4\pi\varepsilon_0} \frac{(q + Q)}{x^2}$$

[along CP and away from spherical shell]

13.

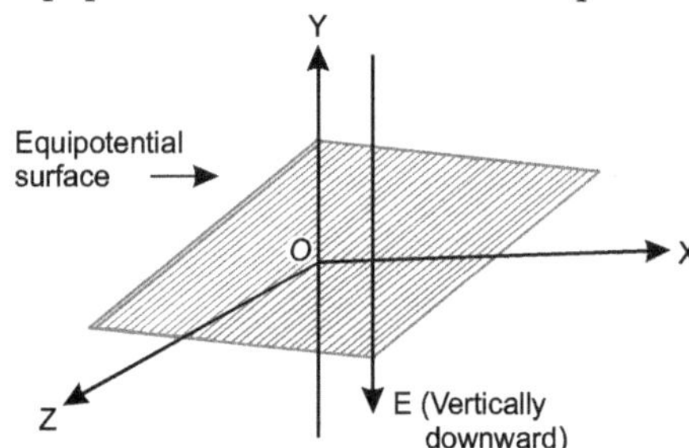

Negative q charge experiences force in a direction opposite to the direction of electric field.

∴ Negative q charge balances when

$$qE = mg$$

$$E = \frac{mg}{q}$$

The direction of electric field is along vertically downward direction.

The equipotential surface between the plates is:

14. Electric potential on the surface of connected charged conducting sphere would be equal.

i.e, $V_1 = V_2$

$$\frac{1}{4\pi\varepsilon_0} \frac{q_1}{r_1} = \frac{1}{4\pi\varepsilon_0} \frac{q_2}{r_2}$$

[Assuming q_1 and q_2 are charges on the spheres connected to each other and r_1, r_2 are their radii.]

$$\frac{q_1}{r_1} = \frac{q_2}{r_2}$$

or, $\dfrac{q_1}{q_2} = \dfrac{r_1}{r_2}$ ...(i)

Now, ratio of electric field intensities.

$$\frac{E_1}{E_2} = \frac{\dfrac{1}{4\pi\varepsilon_0} \cdot \dfrac{q_1}{r_1^2}}{\dfrac{1}{4\pi\varepsilon_0} \cdot \dfrac{q_2}{r_2^2}} = \frac{q_1}{q_2} \times \frac{r_2^2}{r_1^2}$$

$$\frac{E_1}{E_2} = \frac{r_1}{r_2} \times \frac{r_2^2}{r_1^2} \quad \text{[From Eq. (i)]}$$

$$\frac{E_1}{E_2} = \frac{r_2}{r_1}$$

15. When C and A are placed in contact, charge of A equally divides in two spheres. Therefore charge on each A and C $= +2Q$

Now, C is placed in contact with B, then charge on each B and C becomes

$$\frac{2Q + (-10Q)}{2} = -4Q$$

When A and B are placed in contact then charge on each, A and B becomes

$$\frac{2Q + (-4Q)}{2} = -Q$$

16. According to Coulomb's law, magnitude of force acting between two stationary point charges is given by

$$F = \left(\frac{q_1 q_2}{4\pi\varepsilon_0}\right)\left(\frac{1}{r^2}\right)$$

For given, $q_1 q_2$, $F \propto \left(\dfrac{1}{r^2}\right)$

Higher the magnitude of product of charges $q_1 q_2$, higher the slope.

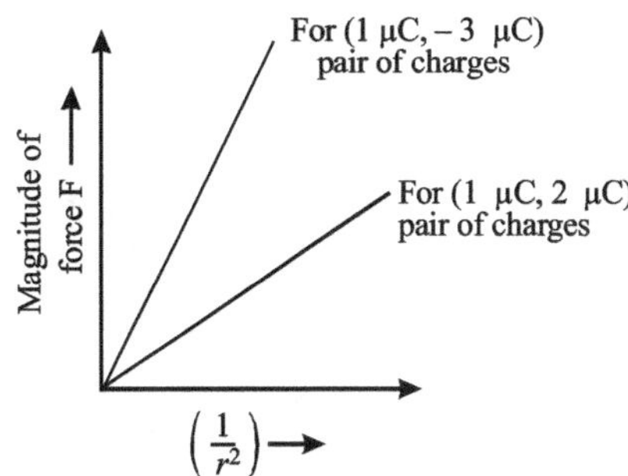

17. Let us consider charge $+q$ is uniformly distributed over a spherical shell of radius R. Let electric field is to be obtained at P lies outside of spherical shell.

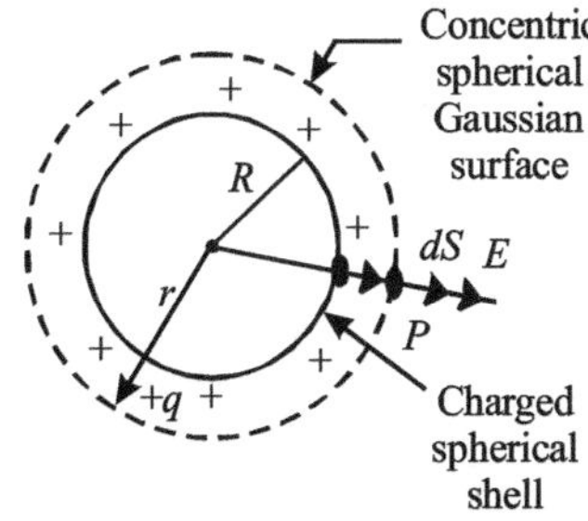

E at any point is radially outward and has same magnitude at all points which lies at the same distance (r) from centre of spherical shell. Therefore, consider a Gaussian surface of radius r such that r > R.

Gaussian surface enclosed charge q inside it.

By Gauss's theorem,

$$\oint E.dS = \frac{q}{\varepsilon_0}$$

$$\oint E.dS \cos 0° = \frac{q}{\varepsilon_0} \quad [\because E \text{ and } dS \text{ are along the same direction}]$$

$$E \oint dS = \frac{q}{\varepsilon_0}$$

$$E \times 4\pi r^2 = \frac{q}{\varepsilon_0}$$

$$E = \frac{1}{4\pi\varepsilon_0}\cdot\frac{q}{r^2}$$

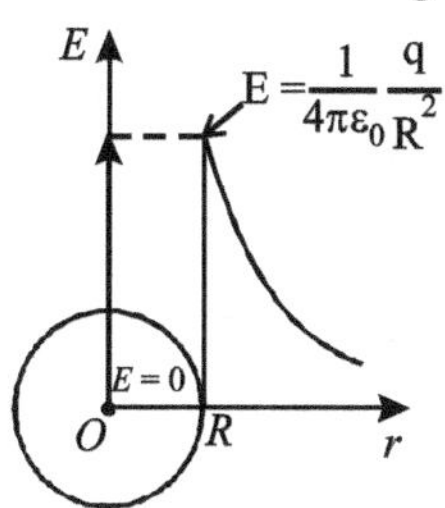

Variation of E with r for a charged spherical shell.

18. Gauss's law states that the total electric flux through a closed surface is equal to $\dfrac{1}{\varepsilon_0}$ times the charge enclosed by it.

i.e., $\phi = \dfrac{q}{\varepsilon_0}$

Now, the electric field $E = Cx\hat{i}$ is in X-direction only. So faces with surface vector perpendicular to this field would give zero electric flux i.e., $\phi = E\ ds \cos 90° = 0$,

So, flux would be due to only two surfaces,

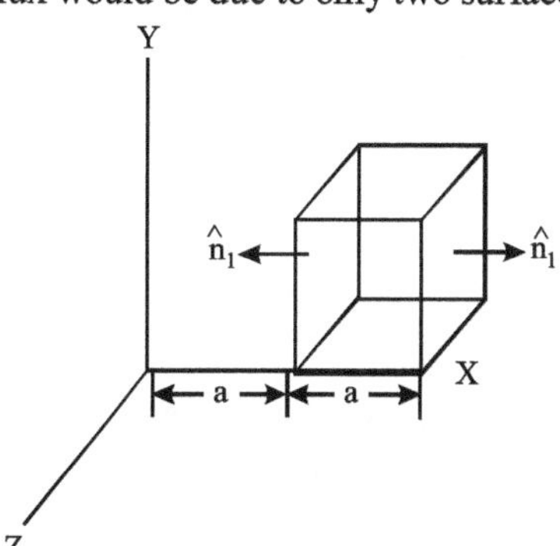

Magnitude of E at left face

$$E_L = Cx = Ca \qquad [x = a \text{ at left face}]$$

Magnitude of E at right face

$$E_R = Cx = C2a = 2aC \quad [x = 2\ a \text{ at right face}]$$

Thus,

$$\phi_L = E_L \cdot dS$$
$$= -aC \times a^2 = -a^3 C \qquad [\text{As } \theta = 180°]$$
$$\phi_R = E_R \cdot dS = 2aC\ dS \cos\theta$$
$$= 2aCa^2 = 2a^3 C$$

(i) Net flux through cube is
$$= \phi_L + \phi_R$$
$$= -a^3 C + 2a^3 C$$
$$= a^3 C\ N\text{-}m^2 C^{-1}$$

(ii) Net charge inside the cube

By Gauss's law

$$\phi = \frac{q}{\varepsilon_0}$$
$$q = a^3 C\varepsilon_0$$

19. The plot showing the variation of (i) electric field and (ii) electric potential with distance r due to a point charge q is shown below.

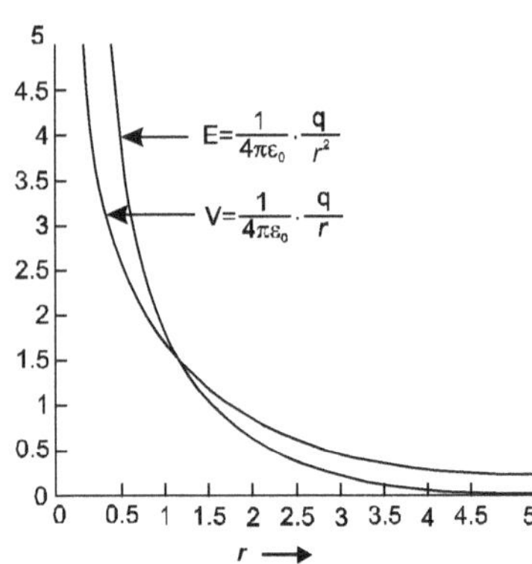

Potential will be maximum where r will be minimum (not zero) also the electric field will be maximum when squared distance will be minimum (not zero)

20. (a) Electric flux is defined as the number of electric field lines crossing a unit area perpendicular to the area. Its SI unit is $N\,m^2\,C^{-1}$

(b) Given: $\vec{E} = 5 \times 10^3\,\hat{i}\,NC^{-1}$,
$A = 12\,cm^2 = 12 \times 10^{-4}\,m^2$

(i) The plane of surface area being parallel to YZ plane, Electric flux of the field

$$\phi = \vec{E}.\vec{A} = (5 \times 10^3\,\hat{i}).\,12 \times 10^{-4}\,\hat{i}) = 6\,NC^{-1}m^2$$

(ii) When normal to the plane of surface area makes an angle of 60° with the X-axis, then flux
$$\phi = EA\cos\theta = 5 \times 10^3 \times 12 \times 10^{-4} \times 0.5 = 0.25\,NC^{-1}m^2$$

21. (i) Given: $\vec{E} = 20x\,\hat{i}$
$A = 20\,cm^2 = 20 \times 10^{-4}\,m^2$

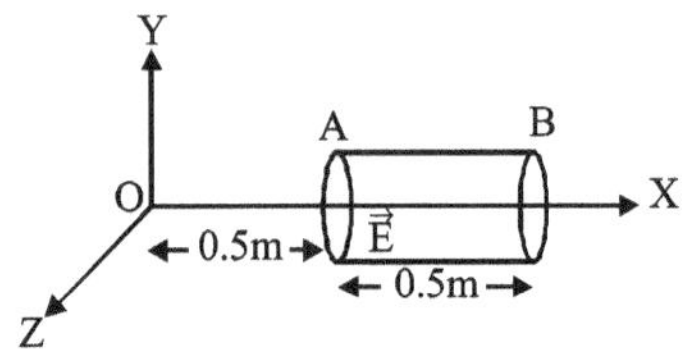

Since the electric field $\vec{E} = 20x\,\hat{i}$ is directed along the x-axis, there is no any flux across curved surface.

Flux through the face A of the cylinder

$$\phi_1 = \oint \vec{E}.\vec{ds}$$
$$= Es\cos 180°$$
$$= 20 \times 0.5 \times (-1) \times 20 \times 10^{-4}$$
$$= -200 \times 10^{-4} = -2 \times 10^{-2}\,NC^{-1}\,m^2$$

Flux through the face B of the cylinder

$$\phi_2 = \oint \vec{E}.\vec{ds}$$
$$= EA\cos\theta$$
$$= 20 \times 20 \times 10^{-4} \times 1$$
$$= 400 \times 10^{-4}\,NC^{-1}\,m^2$$
$$= 4 \times 10^{-2}\,NC^{-1}\,m^2$$

Therefore net flux through the cylinder
$$\phi = \phi_1 + \phi_2$$
$$= 4 \times 10^{-2} - 2 \times 10^{-2}$$
$$= 2 \times 10^{-2}\,NC^{-1}\,m^2$$

(ii) According to Gauss's theorem

$$\phi = \int \vec{E}.\vec{ds} = \frac{Q}{\epsilon_0}$$

or, $2 \times 10^{-2} = \dfrac{Q}{\epsilon_0}$

or, $Q = 2 \times 10^{-2} \times 8.854 \times 10^{-12} = 1.7708 \times 10^{-3}\,C$

Hence the charge enclosed by the cylinder is $1.7708 \times 10^{-13}\,C$

22. When the plane is parallel to the *y-z* plane:

$$\phi = \vec{E}.\vec{A}$$

Here: $\vec{E} = 2 \times 10^3\,\hat{i}\,N/C$
$\vec{A} = (20\,cm)^2\,\hat{i} = 4 \times 10^{-2}\,\hat{i}\,m^2$

$\therefore \quad \phi = (2 \times 10^3\,\hat{i}).(4 \times 10^{-2}\,\hat{i})$

$\Rightarrow \quad \phi = 80\,Weber$

When the plane makes a 30° angle with the *x*-axis, the area vector makes a 60° angle with the *x*-axis.

$$\phi = \vec{E}\cdot\vec{A}$$
$\Rightarrow \quad \phi = EA\cos\theta$
$\Rightarrow \quad \phi = (2 \times 10^3)(4 \times 10^{-2})\cos 60°$
$\Rightarrow \quad \phi = 80/2$
$\Rightarrow \quad \phi = 40\,Weber$

23. We consider a thin shell of radius R carrying a charge Q on its surface. **At a point P_0 outside the shell (r>R)** According to Gauss's law,

$$\oint_{S_1} \vec{E}_0.\vec{dS} = \frac{Q}{\varepsilon_0}\ or\ E_0(4\pi r^2) = \frac{Q}{\varepsilon_0}$$

or, $E_0 = \dfrac{Q}{4\pi\varepsilon_0 r^2} = \dfrac{\sigma}{\varepsilon_0}\dfrac{R^2}{r^2}$

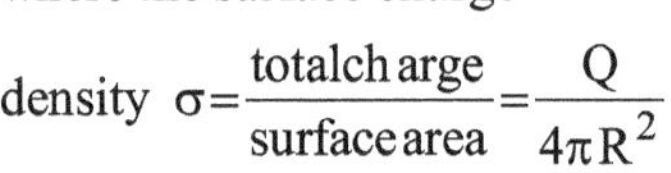

where the surface charge

density $\sigma = \dfrac{total\ charge}{surface\ area} = \dfrac{Q}{4\pi R^2}$

The electric field at any point outside the shell is same as if the entire charge is concentrated at centre of shell.

OR

Let us consider two positively charged thin parallel sheets A and B with uniform surface densities of charge σ_1 and σ_2 respectively.

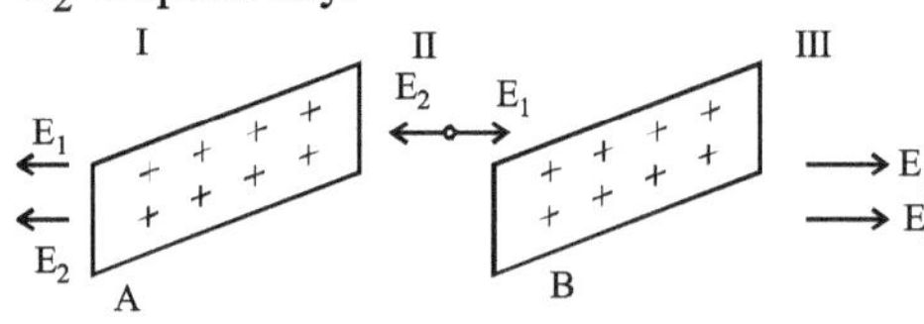

Let $\sigma_1 > \sigma_2 > 0$

In region I, $E_I = -E_1 - E_2 = \dfrac{-\sigma_1}{2\varepsilon_0} - \dfrac{\sigma_2}{2\varepsilon_0}$

$\Rightarrow \quad E_I = -\dfrac{1}{2\varepsilon_0}(\sigma_1 + \sigma_2)$

In region II, $E_{II} = E_1 - E_2$

$$= \frac{\sigma_1}{2\varepsilon_0} - \frac{\sigma_2}{2\varepsilon_0} = \frac{\sigma_1 - \sigma_2}{2\varepsilon_0}$$

In region III, $E_{III} = E_1 + E_2$

$$= \frac{\sigma_1}{2\varepsilon_0} + \frac{\sigma_2}{2\varepsilon_0} = \frac{\sigma_1 + \sigma_2}{2\varepsilon_0}$$

In $\sigma_1 = \sigma$ and $\sigma_2 = -\sigma$ then $E_I = 0$, $E_{III} = 0$

$$E_{II} = \frac{2\sigma}{2\varepsilon_0} = \frac{\sigma}{\varepsilon_0} = \text{constant}$$

Clearly, field (i) between the sheets

$$E_{II} = \frac{\sigma}{\varepsilon_0} = \text{constant and}$$

(ii) outside the sheets $E_I = E_{III} = 0$

NCERT Exemplar 

1. **(a)** The force on q_1 depend on the force acting between q_1 and q_2 and q_1 and q_3 so that the net force acting on q_1 by q_2 and q_1 by q_3 is along the $+$ x-direction, so the force acting between q_1, q_2 and q_1, q_3 is attractive force as shown in figure :

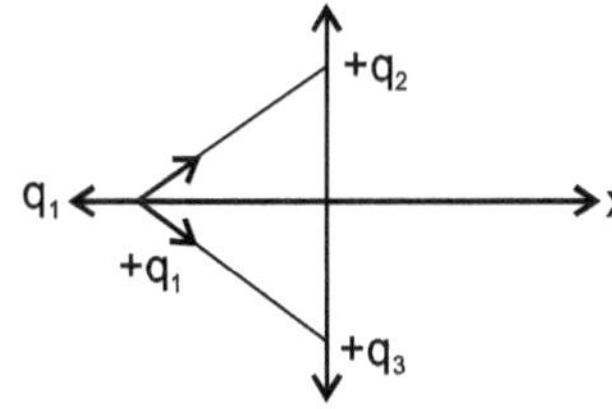

The attractive force between these charges states that q_1 is a negative charge (since, q_2 and q_3 are positive).

Then the force acting between q_1 and charge Q (positive) is also know as attractive force and then the net force on q_1 by q_2, q_3 and Q are along the same direction as shown in the figure.

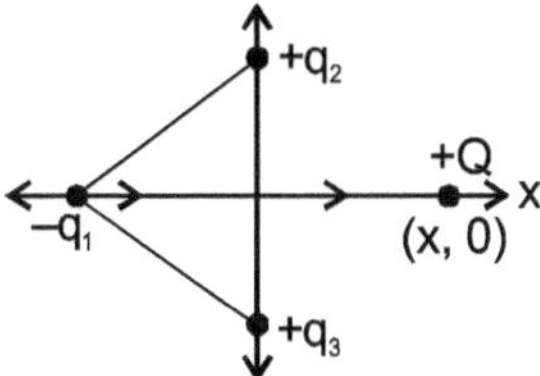

The figure shows that the force on q_1 shall increase along the positive x-axis due to the positive charge Q.

2. **(a)** If a positive point charge is brought near an isolated conducting sphere without touching the sphere, then the free electrons in the sphere are attracted towards the positive Charge and electric field passes through a charged body. This leaves an excess of positive charge on the (right) surface of sphere due to the induction process.

Both type of charges are bound in the (isolated conducting) sphere and cannot escape. They, therefore, reside on the surface.

Thus, the left surface of sphere has an excess of negative charge and the right surface of sphere has an excess of positive charge as shown in figure.

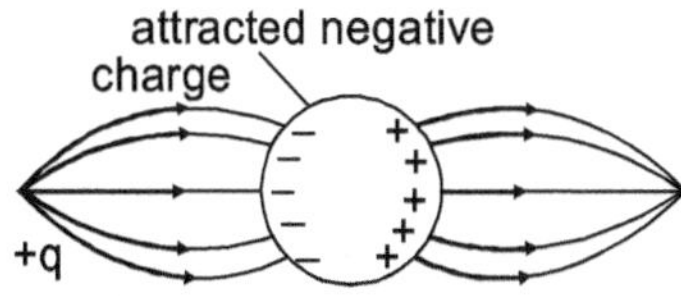

An electric field lines start from positive charge and ends at negative charge.

Also, electric field line emerges from a positive charge, in case of single charge and ends at infinity shown in figure (a).

3. **(d)** **By Gauss's law :** The total of the electric flux out of a closed surface is equal to the charge enclosed devided by the permittivity i.e., $\phi = \dfrac{Q}{\varepsilon_0}$.

Thus, electric flux through a surface doesn't depend on the shape, size or area of a surface but it depends on the number of charges enclosed by the surface. So all the given figures have same electric flux as all of them also has same single positive charge.

4. **(b)** Gauss's law states that total electric flux of an enclosed surface is given by, $\oint_s E.dS = \dfrac{q}{\varepsilon_0}$, includes the sum of all charges enclosed by the surface.

The charges may be located anywhere inside the surface, and out side the surface. Then, the electric field on the left side of equation is due to all the charges, both inside and outside S.

So, E on LHS of the above equation will have a contribution from all charges while q on the RHS will have a contribution from q_2 and q_4 only.

5. **(c)** The electric field lines, are directed away from positively charged source and directed toward negatively charged source. In electric field force are directly proportional to the electric field strength hence, higher the electric field strength greater the force and vice-versa.

The space between the electric field lines is increasing, from left to right so strength of electric field decreases with the increase in the space between electric field lines. Then the force on charges also decreases from left to right.

Thus, the force on charge $-q$ is greater than force on charge $+q$ in turn dipole will experience a force towards left.

6. **(a)** When a positive point charge $+q$ is placed near an isolated conducting plane, some negative charge develops on the surface of the plane towards the charge and an equal positive charge develops on opposite side of the plane. This is called induction process and the electric field on a isolated conducting plane at point is directly projected in a plane perpendicular to the field and away from the plane.

7. **(a)** Consider a point on diameter away from the centre of hemisphere uniformly positively charged, then the electric field is perpendicular to the diameter and the component of electric intensity parallel to the diameter cancel out.

8. No. the field may be normal. However, the converse is true.

9. (a) $\dfrac{q}{8\varepsilon_0}$ (b) $\dfrac{q}{4\varepsilon_0}$ (c) $\dfrac{q}{2\varepsilon_0}$ (d) $\dfrac{q}{2\varepsilon_0}$

10. No, Gauss law will not be true because Gauss's law is based on the inverse square dependence on distance contained in the coulomb's law.

11. (a) Charges A and C are positive since lines of force emanate from them.

    (b) Charge C has the largest magnitude since maximum number of field lines are associated with it.

    (c) (i) near A. There is no neutral point between a positive and a negative charge. A neutral point may exist between two like charges. From the figure we see that a neutral point exists between charges A and C. Also between two like charges the neutral point is closer to the charge with smaller magnitude. Thus, electric field is zero near charge A.

12. $E_1 = \dfrac{\sigma_1}{\varepsilon_0}$; $E_2 = \dfrac{\sigma_2}{\varepsilon_0}$

    $E = E_1 - E_2 = \dfrac{\sigma_1 - \sigma_2}{\varepsilon_0}$

    $W = q_0 E \times \dfrac{a}{\sqrt{2}}$

    $\therefore \ W = \dfrac{q_0(\sigma_1 - \sigma_2)a}{\sqrt{2}\varepsilon_0}$

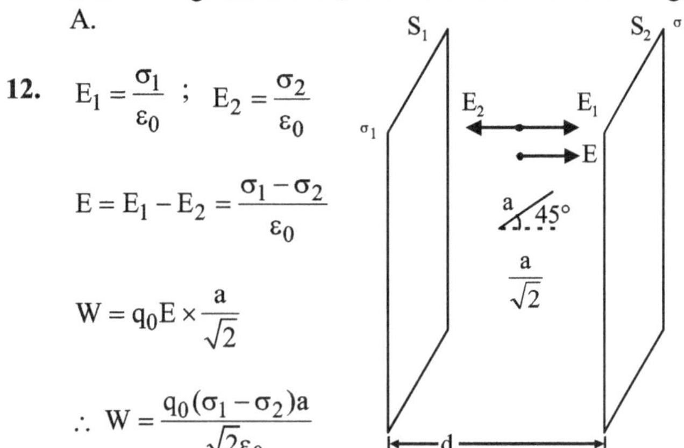

13. (i) When the charge is distributed along a line, straight or curved, it is called linear charge distribution.

    (ii) $\because$ The potential at any point A is given by,

    $$V = \dfrac{1}{4\pi\epsilon_0} \int_L \dfrac{\lambda dl}{|\vec{l} - \vec{l'}|}$$

    Where $\vec{l}$ is the location of the electrostatic potential and $\vec{l'}$ is the position vector of the elementary portion dl.

1. **(b)**   2. **(d)**

3. **(a)** The charge of an isolated system is conserved.

4. **(b)** When some charge is given to conductor it spreads on its surface. When some charge is given to insulator, it remains there, it do not spread, Free charges in conductor interact with added charge, so added charge spreads on surface to be in equilibrium.

5. **(c)**   6. **(c)**   7. **(d)**

8. **(c)** Electron having a charge of -1.6×10^{-19}C undergoes annihilation with it's antiparticle positron having a charge of $+1.6 \times 10^{-19}$C as $e^- + e^+ \rightarrow \gamma + \gamma$

    Net charge before annihilation

    $= -1.6 \times 10^{-19}C + 1.6 \times 10^{-19}C = 0$

    Net charge after annihilation $= 0 + 0 = 0$

    i.e., net charge remains same.

9. **(d)** Milikan demonstrated the quantisation of charge experimentally. Charge on electron $= -e = -1.6 \times 100^{-19}$C. Addition of charge can occur in integral multiples of e.

10. **(c)** Like charges repel $\longleftarrow \oplus \ \oplus \longrightarrow$

    Unlike charges attract $\oplus \longrightarrow \ \longleftarrow \ominus$

    To specify particular charge on body, term used is polarity.

    On rubbing, plastic rod acquires negative charge, cat's fur acquires positive charge. There are only two kinds of charges: +, –.

11. **(b)**

12. **(d)** When a positive point charge is placed outside a conducting sphere, a rearrangement of charge takes place on the surface. But the total charge on the sphere is zero as no charge has left or entered the sphere.

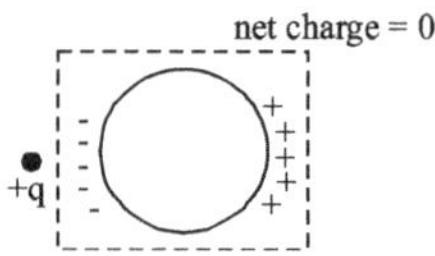

13. **(b)** If charge particle is put at rest in electric field, then it will move along line of force.

14. **(a)**   15. **(c)**   16. **(d)**   17. **(b)**

18. **(b)** The direction of electric field at equatorial point A or B will be in opposite direction, as that of direction of dipole moment.

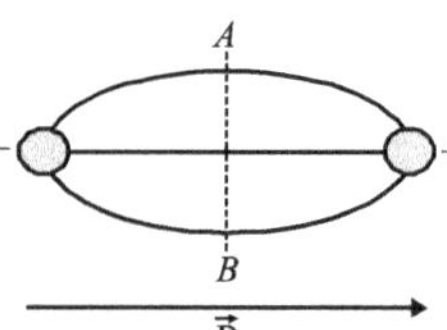

19. **(c)** The electric field will be different at the location of force on the two charges. Therefore the two charges will be unequal. This will result in a force as well as torque.

20. **(a)** Since lines of force starts from A and ends at B, so A is +ve and B is –ve. Lines of forces are more crowded near A, so A > B.

21. **(b)** The electric field around a charge propagates with the speed of light away from the charge. Therefore the

    required time $= \dfrac{\text{distance}}{\text{speed}} = \dfrac{OP}{c}$.

22. **(c)** When a dipole is placed in a uniform electric field, two equal and opposite forces act on it. Therefore, a torque acts which rotates the dipole.

23. **(b)** Since $\tau = pE \sin\theta$ on decreasing the distance between the two charges, and on decreasing angle θ between the dipole and electric field, $\sin\theta$ decreases therefore torque decreases.

24. **(c)** Since $x < R$, that is the point is inside the sphere electric field $E \propto x$. as $E = \dfrac{kq}{R^3}x$

25. **(d)** Electric displacement vector, $\vec{D} = \varepsilon\vec{E}$

As, $\varepsilon = \varepsilon_0 K$ $\therefore$ $\vec{D} = \varepsilon_0 K\vec{E}$

26. **(a)**   **27.** **(c)**   **28.** **(d)**

29. **(a)** Gaussian surface cannot pass through any discrete charge because electric field due to a system of discrete charges is not well defined at the location of the charges. But the Gaussian surface can pass through a continuous charge distribution.

30. **(b)**

31. **(c)** $\oint \vec{E}.d\vec{A} = 0$, represents charge inside close surface is zero. Electric field as any point on the surface may be zero.

32. **(b)** Total flux coming out from unit charge

$$\phi = \vec{E}.\overrightarrow{ds} = \frac{1}{\varepsilon_0} \times 1 = \varepsilon_0^{-1}$$

33. **(a)**

34. **(a)** By Gauss theorem

$$\text{Total electric flux} = \frac{\text{Total charge inside cube}}{\varepsilon_0} = \frac{q}{\varepsilon_0}$$

35. **(b)**

36. **(c)** If electric dipole, the flux coming out from positive charge is equal to the flux coming in at negative charge *i.e.* total charge on sphere = 0. From Gauss law, total flux passing through the sphere = 0.

37. **(c)** Electric field near the conductor surface is given by $\dfrac{\sigma}{\varepsilon_0}$ and it is perpendicular to surface.

38. **(d)**

39. **(a)** Here, $q = 1$ C, $\varepsilon_0 = 8.85 \times 10^{-12}$ $C^2 N^{-1} m^{-2}$

Number of lines of force = Electric force

$$= \frac{q}{\varepsilon_0} = \frac{1}{8.85 \times 10^{-12}} = 1.13 \times 10^{11}$$

40. **(c)**

41. **(a)** $\text{Flux}(\phi) = \vec{E}\cdot\Delta\vec{A} = E\Delta A\cos 60° = El^2/2$

Chapter Test

1. **(c)** The charge on disc A is 10^{-6} μC. The charge on disc B is 10×10^{-6} μC. The total charge on both $= 11$ μC. When touched, this charge will be distributed equally *i.e.*, 5.5 μC on each disc.

2. **(c)**

3. **(d)** According to Gauss's theorem,

$$E\oint ds = \frac{q}{\epsilon_0}\left[\text{Here}\oint ds = 4\pi R^2\right]$$

$$\therefore E = \frac{q/4\pi R^2}{\epsilon_0} \quad [\because q/4\pi R^2 = \sigma]$$

or $E = \sigma/\varepsilon_0$

4. **(a)** The electric field due to disc is superposition of electric field due to its constituent ring as given in Reason.

5. **(b)** Though the net charge on the conductor is still zero but due to induction negatively charged region is nearer to the rod as compared to the positively charged region. That is why the conductor gets attracted towards the rod.

6. **(b)** Force on any charge due to a number of other charges is the vector sum of all the forces on that charge due to the other charges, taken one at a time. The individual force are unaffected due to the presence of other charges. This is the principle of superposition of charges.

7. **(a)** $\phi = \dfrac{\Sigma q}{\epsilon_0} = \dfrac{-5.9 \times 10^{-9}}{8.85 \times 10^{-12}} = -670\, \text{Nm}^2/\text{C}$

8. **(c)** Electric field at any point depends on all the charges.

9. **(d)** According to Gauss's theorem,

$$E\oint ds = \frac{q}{\epsilon_0}\left[\text{Here}\oint ds = 4\pi R^2\right]$$

$$\therefore E = \frac{q/4\pi R^2}{\epsilon_0} \quad [\because q/4\pi R^2 = \sigma]$$

or $E = \sigma/\varepsilon_0$

10. **(a)** The flux is zero according to Gauss' Law because it is a open surface which enclosed a charge q.

11. **(d)** According to Gauss' Law

$$\oint E.ds = \frac{Q_{\text{enclosed by closed surface}}}{\varepsilon_0} = \text{flux}$$

so total flux $= Q/\varepsilon_0$

Since cube has six face, so flux coming out through one wall or one face is $Q/6\varepsilon_0$.

12. The angle between the directions of electric field at any

(i) axial point is 0°.

(ii) equatorial point is 90°.

13. According to Coulombs law, the force between two point charges is inversely proportional to the square of the distance between the charges.

$$\therefore \quad \frac{F_1}{F_2} = \frac{r_2^2}{r_1^2} \Rightarrow \frac{F}{3F} = \frac{r_2^2}{d^2} \qquad \text{or } r_2 = \frac{d}{\sqrt{3}}$$

14. The torque acting on a dipole placed in a uniform electric field is given by Torque, $\tau = p \times E = pE\sin\theta$.

Here $\theta = 30°$.

$$E = 10^4 \, \text{N/C and } \tau = 9 \times 10^{-26} \, \text{Nm}.$$

So, dipole moment

$$p = \frac{\tau}{E\sin\theta} = \frac{9 \times 10^{-26}}{10^4 \times (1/2)} = 18 \times 10^{-30} \, \text{C-m}.$$

15. The intensity of electric field at a point is defined as the force that a unit positive charge would experience if placed at that point.

i.e., $\quad E = \underset{q \to 0}{\text{lt}} \left(\dfrac{F}{q} \right)$

At all points on the equatorial line, the dipole field intensity is parallel to the line joining the two charges.

Electrostatic Potential and Capacitance

2

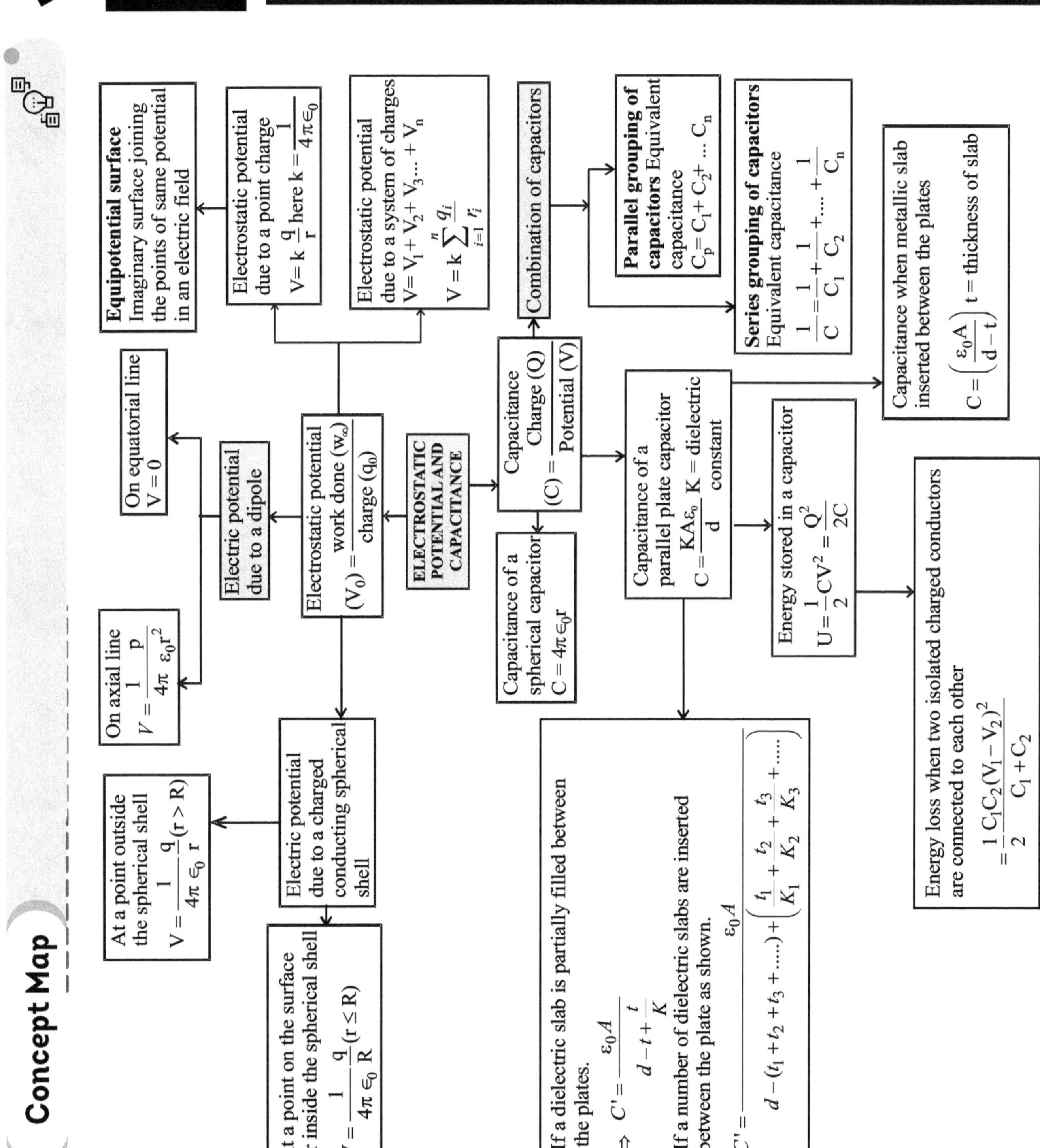

Topic 1 — **Electrostatic Potential, Electrostatic Potential Difference, Electrostatic Potential due to a Point Charge, A Dipole, A System of Charges and Equipotential Surfaces** 

ELECTROSTATIC POTENTIAL

Electrostatic potential at a point in an electric field is *the minimum work done by an external agent in moving a unit positive charge from infinity or a reference point to that point against the electrical force of the field.*

Electrostatic potential at a point in electric field is numerically equal but opposite in sign to the work performed by electrical force to bring unit positive charge from infinity to that point.

If W is the work done by external agent in bringing a positive test charge q_0 from infinity to a point then the potential V at that point

$$\text{Electriostatic potential } V = \frac{W_{ext}}{q_0} - \frac{W_E \,(\text{work done by electric field})}{q_0 \,(\text{test charge})}$$

Its **S.I. unit:** volt or joule coulomb^{-1}; It is a scalar quantity.

ELECTROSTATIC POTENTIAL DIFFERENCE

Electrostatic potential deference between two points is equal to the minimum work done in moving a unit positive test charge from one point to the other.

$$V_B - V_A = \frac{W_{AB}}{q_0} \Rightarrow W_{AB} = q_0 \,(V_B - V_A)$$

W_E is the work done by the electric field then ;

$$-(V_B - V_A) = \frac{W_E}{q_0} \Rightarrow W_E = -q_0 \,(V_B - V_A)$$

$$W_{ext.} = -W_E$$

Relation between Electric Potential and field :

$$dV = -E_x dx \quad \text{or} \quad E_x = -\left(\frac{dV}{dx}\right)_{y,\,z\,\text{constant}}$$

ELECTROSTATIC POTENTIAL DUE TO A POINT CHARGE

To calculate the potential at point P, due to the point charge, calculate the potential difference between the point P and infinity which automatically will be the potential of the point.

Let any point lies between P and infinity at a distance x from the given point charge. Potential difference across dx

$$dV = -Edx \cos 0° \quad \text{or,} \quad dV = -Edx$$

$$dV = -\frac{1}{4\pi\varepsilon_0} \cdot \frac{q}{x^2} \, dx \; ; \quad \int_{V_p}^{0} dV = -\frac{1}{4\pi\varepsilon_0} \cdot q \int_{r}^{\infty} \frac{dx}{x^2} \quad \text{or,} \quad V_P = \frac{1}{4\pi\varepsilon_0} \cdot \frac{q}{r}$$

ELECTROSTATIC POTENTIAL DUE TO A DIPOLE

(i) **End on or axial or tan-A position**

$$V_{max.} = \frac{1}{4\pi\varepsilon_0} \cdot \frac{p}{r^2} \quad \text{and} \quad E_{max.} = \frac{1}{4\pi\varepsilon_0} \cdot \frac{2p}{r^3}$$

(ii) Broad on or equatorial or tan-B position

$$V_{min.} = 0 \quad \text{and} \quad E_{min.} = \frac{1}{4\pi\varepsilon_0} \cdot \frac{p}{r^3}$$

Potential due to a dipole varies with distance, as $V \propto (1/r^2)$ and field $E \propto (1/r^3)$

$$V_{max.} = \frac{kp}{r^2} \ (\theta = 0°), \ V_{min.} = \frac{kp}{r^3} \ (\theta = 90°),$$

$$E_{max.} = \frac{2kp}{r^3} \ (\theta = 0°), \ E_{min.} = \frac{kp}{r^3} \ (\theta = 90°)$$

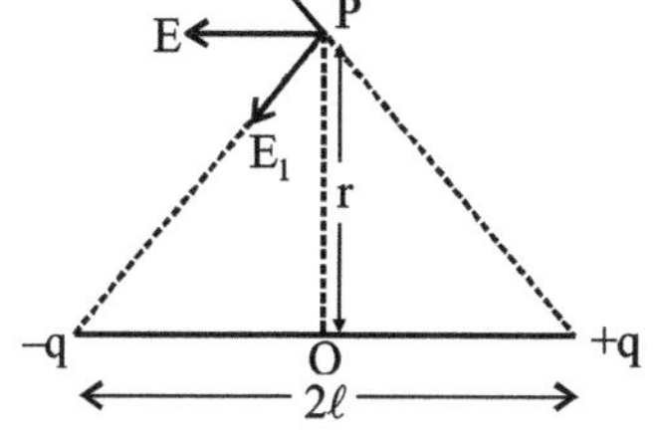

If the point 'P' lies on the line making an angle 'θ' with the axis of the dipole, then intensity at point P

$$E = \frac{p}{4\pi\varepsilon_0 r^3}\sqrt{(3\cos^2\theta + 1)}$$

ELECTROSTATIC POTENTIAL DUE TO A SYSTEM OF CHARGES

Consider a system of charges $q_1, q_2, \ldots q_n$ with position vectors $\mathbf{r_1, r_2, \ldots r_n}$ relative to some origin. By the **superposition principle**, the potential V at P due to the total charge configuration is the algebraic sum of the potentials due to the individual charges

i.e; $V = V_1 + V_2 + \ldots + V_n$

$$= \frac{1}{4\pi\varepsilon_0}\left(\frac{q_1}{r_{1P}} + \frac{q_2}{r_{2P}} + \ldots + \frac{q_n}{r_{nP}} \right)$$

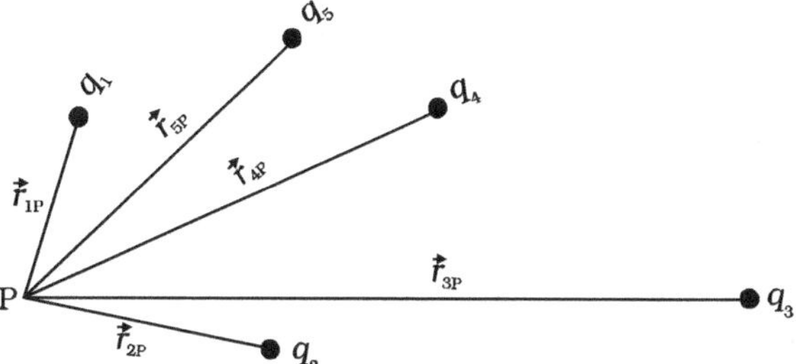

Electric Potential Gradient

The maximum rate of change of potential at right angles to an equipotential surface EPS is an electric field is defined as potential gradient i.e., $\vec{E}_r = -\frac{\partial V}{\partial r}\hat{r}$.

Illustration 1 :

Calculate the potential due to a thin charged rod of length ℓ at the points along and perpendicular to the length. Charge per unit length on the rod is λ.

Sol. Electric potential due to small element of length dx

$$dV = \frac{kdq}{(b^2 + x^2)^{1/2}} = \frac{k\lambda dx}{(b^2 + x^2)^{1/2}}$$

Therefore electric potential due to complete rod

$$V = \int_a^{a+\ell} \frac{k\lambda dx}{(b^2 + x^2)^{1/2}} = k\lambda \int_a^{a+\ell} \frac{dx}{(b^2 + x^2)^{1/2}} \ ; \qquad V = k\lambda \ln\left| \frac{(a + \ell) + \sqrt{b^2 + (\ell + a)^2}}{a + \sqrt{b^2 + a^2}} \right|$$

EQUIPOTENTIAL SURFACES

An equipotential surface is that at every point of which electric potential is same.

No work is done in moving a test charge on an equipotential surface. Equipotential surface is always perpendicular to the electric field lines.

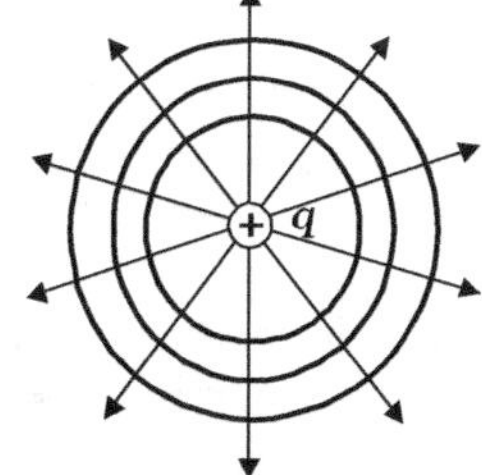

For a single charge q
equipotential surfaces are spherical
surfaces centred at the charge

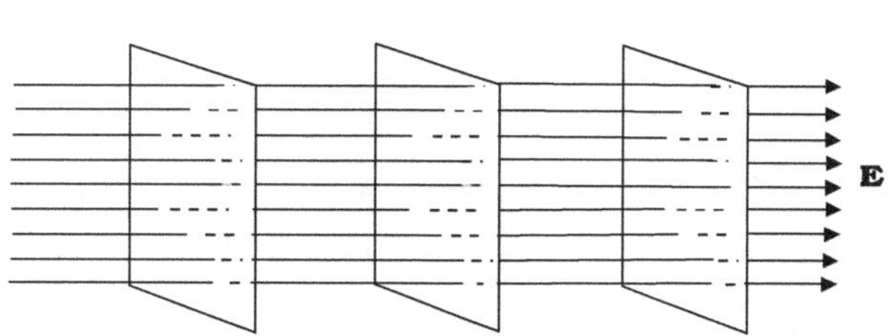

Equipotential surfaces for a uniform electric field.

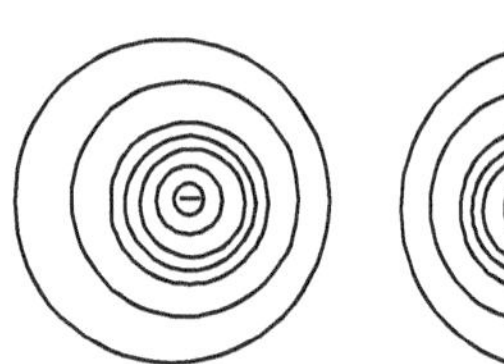
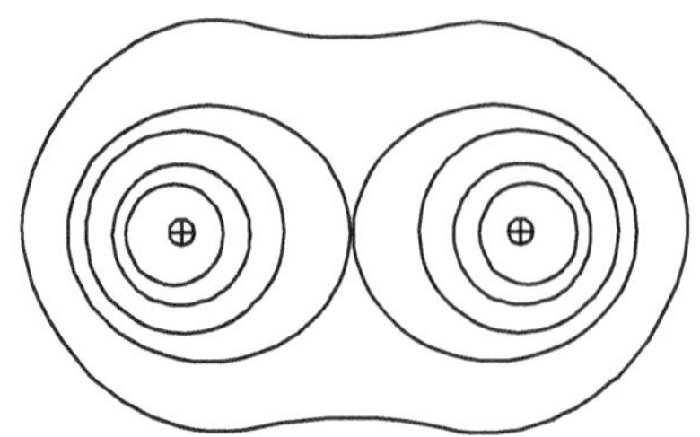

Equipotential surfaces for (a) a dipole   (b) two identical positive charges.

(i)   EPS can never cross each other (otherwise potential at a point will have two values)

(ii) EPS are always $\perp$ to ELF (electric line of force)

(iii) If a charge is moved from one point to other over an EPS work–done will be zero, as

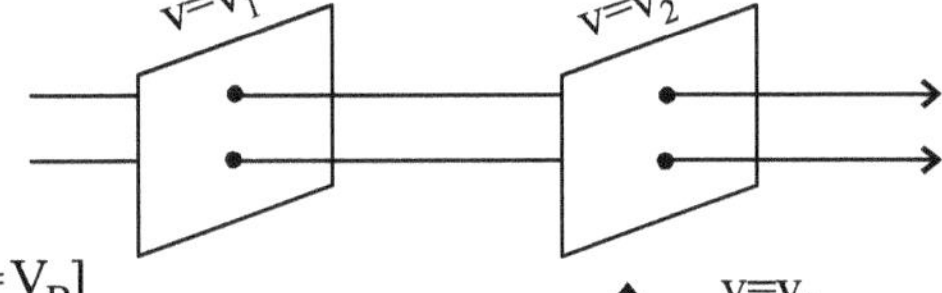

$$W_{AB} = -V_{AB} = q(V_B - V_A) = 0 \qquad [\because V_A = V_B]$$

(iv) Shape of EPS in an uniform electric field is planar.

(v)   Equipotential surface due to an isolated point charge is spherical.

(vi) Equipotential surface due to a line charge is cylindrical.

(vii) The intensity of electric field along an EPS is always zero.

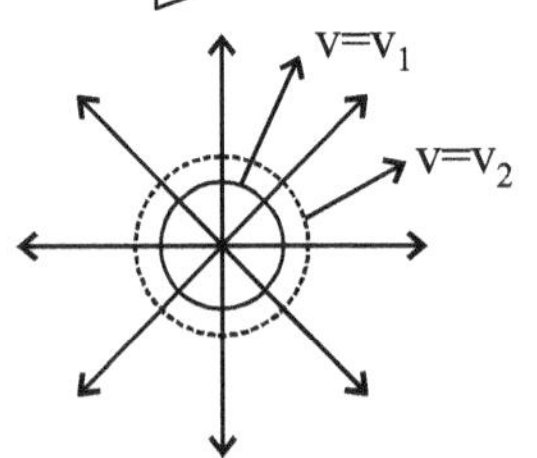

Practice Exercise-1

Multiple Choice Questions

1. A hollow metal sphere of radius 5 cm is charged such that the potential on its surface is 10 V. The potential at a distance of 2 cm from the centre of the sphere is

(a) zero   (b) 10 V   (c) 4 V   (d) 10/3 V

2. Four point charges $-Q$, $-q$, $2q$ and $2Q$ are placed, one at each corner of the square. The relation between Q and q for which the potential at the centre of the square is zero is

(a) $Q = -q$ (b) $Q = -\dfrac{1}{q}$ (c) $Q = q$ (d) $Q = \dfrac{1}{q}$

3. A plastic disc is charged on one side with a uniform surface charge density σ and then three quadrant of the disk are removed. The remaining quadrant is shown in figure, with $V = 0$ at infinity, the potential due to the remaining quadrant at point P is

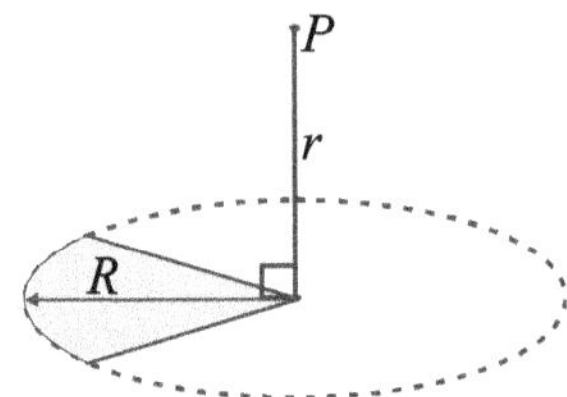

(a) $\dfrac{\sigma}{2\,\epsilon_0}[(r^2 + R)^{1/2} - r]$ (b) $\dfrac{\sigma}{2\,\epsilon_0}[R - r]$

(c) $\dfrac{\sigma}{8\,\epsilon_0}[(r^2 + R^2)^{1/2} - r]$ (d) None of these

4. Consider the following statements and select the true/false.

  I.   Electric field lines are always perpendicular to equipotential surface.

  II. No two equipotential surfaces can intersect each other.

  III. Electric field lines are in the direction of tangent to an equipotential surface.

(a) T, F, F   (b) F, T, F

(c) T, T, F   (d) T, T, T

5. The electric potential _______ inside a conducting sphere

(a) increases from centre to surface.

(b) decreases from centre to surface

(c) remains constant from centre to surface

(d) is zero at every point inside

6. Figure shows two hollow charged conductors A and B having same positive surface charge densities. B is placed inside A and does not touches it. On connecting them with a conductor

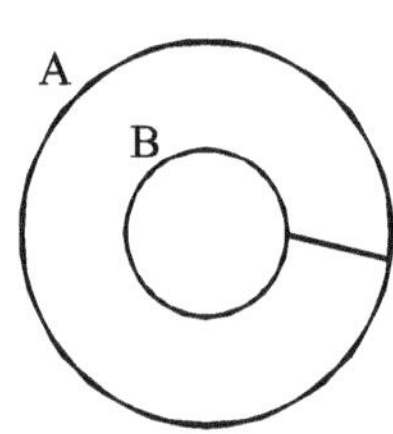

(a) charge will flow from A to B

(b) charge will flow from B to A

(c) charge oscillates between A and B

(d) no charge will flow.

7. Two equally charged spheres of radii a and b are connected together. What will be the ratio of electric field intensity on their surfaces?

(a) $\dfrac{a}{b}$ (b) $\dfrac{a^2}{b^2}$ (c) $\dfrac{b}{a}$ (d) $\dfrac{b^2}{a^2}$

8. Four points a, b, c and d are set at equal distance from the centre of a dipole as shown in figure. The electrostatic potential V_a, V_b, V_c, and V_d would satisfy the following relation:

    (a) $V_a > V_b > V_c > V_d$

    (b) $V_a > V_b = V_d > V_c$

    (c) $V_a > V_c = V_b = V_d$

    (d) $V_b = V_d > V_a > V_c$

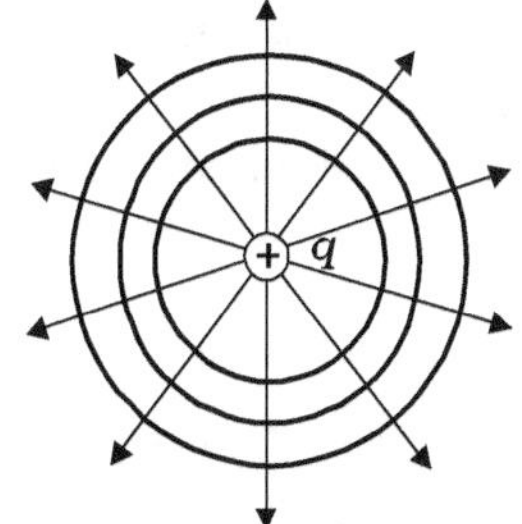

9. The electric potential at a point (x, y) in the x – y plane is given by $V = -kxy$. The field intensity at a distance r from the origin varies as

    (a) r^2 (b) r (c) $\dfrac{1}{r}$ (d) $\dfrac{1}{r^2}$

10. In a hollow spherical shell, potential (V) changes with respect to distance (s) from centre as

    (a) 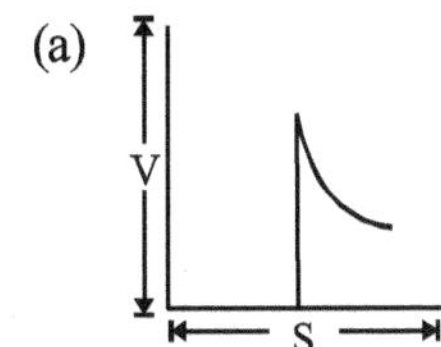   (b) 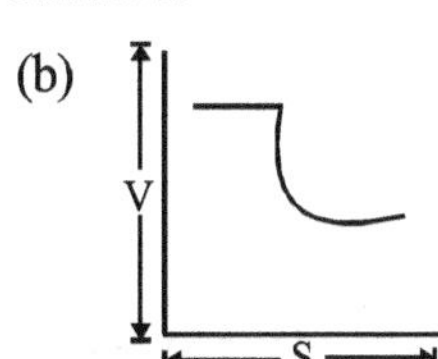

    (c) 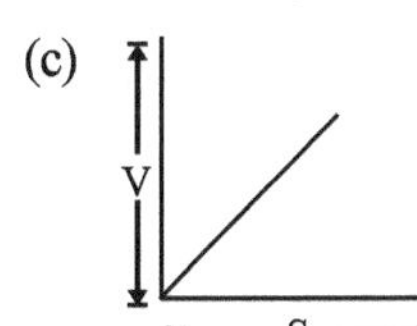   (d) 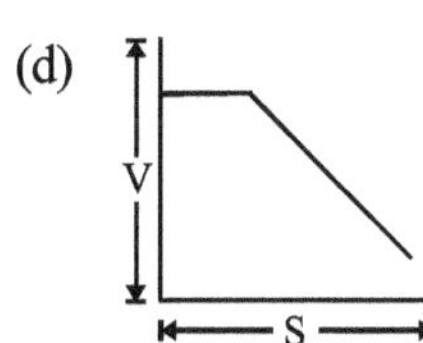

Assertion & Reason Questions

DIRECTIONS (Qs. 11-12) : *Each of these questions contains an assertion followed by reason. Read them carefully and answer the question on the basis of following options. You have to select the one that best describes the two statements.*

(a) If both Assertion and Reason are correct and the Reason is a correct explanation of the Assertion.

(b) If both Assertion and Reason are correct but Reason is not a correct explanation of the Assertion.

(c) If the Assertion is correct but Reason is incorrect.

(d) If the Assertion is incorrect but the Reason is correct.

11. **Assertion :** Electric potential due to dipole $\propto \dfrac{1}{r}$.

    Reason : Electric potential due to a point charge $\propto \dfrac{1}{r^2}$.

12. **Assertion :** For a non-uniformly charged thin circular ring with net charge is zero, the electric field at any point on axis of the ring is zero.

    Reason : For a non-uniformly charged thin circular ring with net charge zero, the electric potential at each point on axis of the ring is maximum.

Case/Passage Based Questions

An equipotential surface is that at every point of which electric potential is same.

No work is done in moving a test charge on an equipotential surface. Equipotential surface is always perpendicular to the electric field lines.

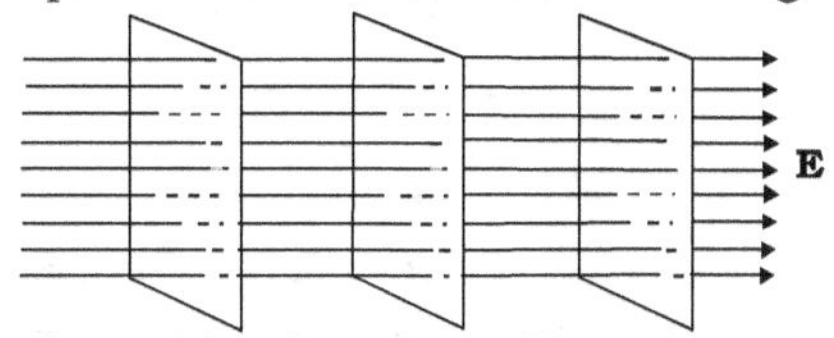

For a single charge q equipotential surfaces are spherical surfaces centred at the charge

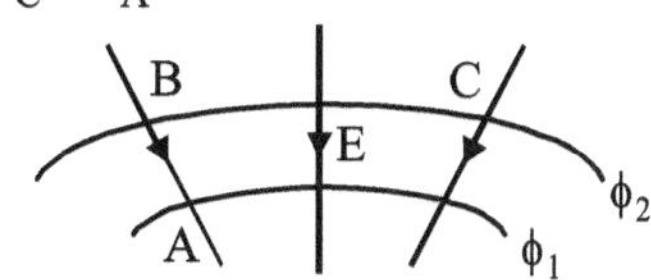

Equipotential surfaces for a uniform electric field.

13. A unit charge moves on an equipotential surface from a point A to point B, then

    (a) $V_A - V_B = + ve$ (b) $V_A - V_B = 0$

    (c) $V_A - V_B = - ve$ (d) it is stationary

14. In moving from A to B along an electric field line, the work done by the electric field on an electron is 6.4×10^{-19} J. If ϕ_1 and ϕ_2 are equipotential surfaces, then the potential difference $V_C - V_A$ is

    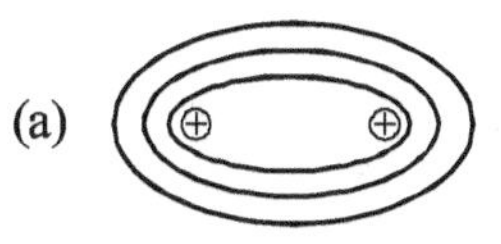

    (a) -4 V   (b) 4 V   (c) zero   (d) 6.4 V

15. Which of the following figure shows the correct equipotential surfaces of a system of two positive charges?

    (a)    (b) 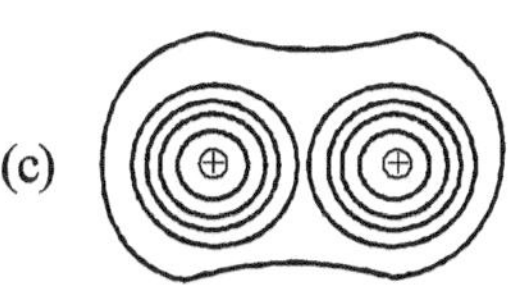

    (c) 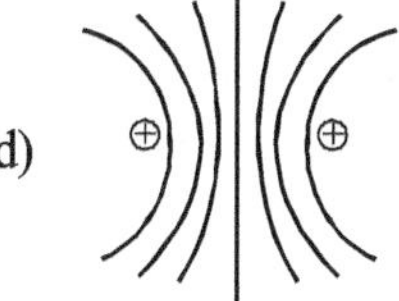   (d)

16. From a point charge, there is a fixed point A. At A, there is an electric field of 500 V/m and potential difference of 3000 V. Distance between point charge and A will be

    (a) 6m   (b) 12m   (c) 16m   (d) 24m

17. A unit charge moves on an equipotential surface from a point A to point B, then

    (a) $V_A - V_B = + ve$ (b) $V_A - V_B = 0$

    (c) $V_A - V_B = - ve$ (d) it is stationary

| **Very Short Answer Questions** | **Short Answer Questions** |

18. Is electrostatic potential necessarily zero at a point where electric field strength is zero.

19. Write down the relation between electric field and potential at a point.

20. Draw an equipotential surface in a uniform electric field.

21. What is an equipotential surface? Show that the electric field is always directed perpendicular to an equipotential surface.

22. Calculate the electric potential at the surface of a gold nucleus. Given, the radius of the nucleus $= 6.6 \times 10^{-15}$ m and atomic number of gold $= 79$.

Topic 2 — Electrostatic Potential Energy, Electrostatic Potential Energy of a System of Charges, Electrostatics of Conductors and Dielectrics and Electric Polarisation

ELECTROSTATIC POTENTIAL ENERGY

Electrostatic potential energy of a system of point charges is the total amount of work done in bringing various charges to their respective positions from infinitely large mutual separations.

$$\text{Electrostatic Potential energy} = \frac{kq_1q_2}{r}.$$

The SI unit of electrostatic potential energy is joule. One joule is the energy stored in moving a charge of 1C through a potential of 1 volt.

Electron Volt:– One electron volt (e.v.) is the kinetic energy gained or lost by an electron in moving through a potential difference of 1 volt.

$$1\,eV = 1.6 \times 10^{-19}\,J.$$

$$1\,meV = 10^{-3}\,eV,\ 1\,keV = 10^{3}\,eV,\ 1\,MeV = 10^{6}\,eV.$$

Electrostatic Potential Energy of a System of Charges

Electrostatic potential energy of a system of point charges is defined as the total amount of work done in bringing the different charges to their respective positions from infinitely large mutual separations.

Electrostatic Potential Energy of a System of Two Point Charges: Consider two point charges q_1 and q_2 lying at points A and B, whose locations are r_1 and r_2 respectively.

To find the electric potential energy of this two charge system, we must mentally build the system, starting with both charges infinitely far away and at rest. First, the charge q_1 is brought from infinity to the point r_1. There is no external field against which work needs to be done, so work done in bringing q_1 from infinity to r_1 is zero.

V is potential that has been set up by q_1 at the point B, where q_2 is to be placed.

$$\therefore \quad V = \frac{1}{4\pi\varepsilon_0} \cdot \frac{q_1}{r_{AB}}$$

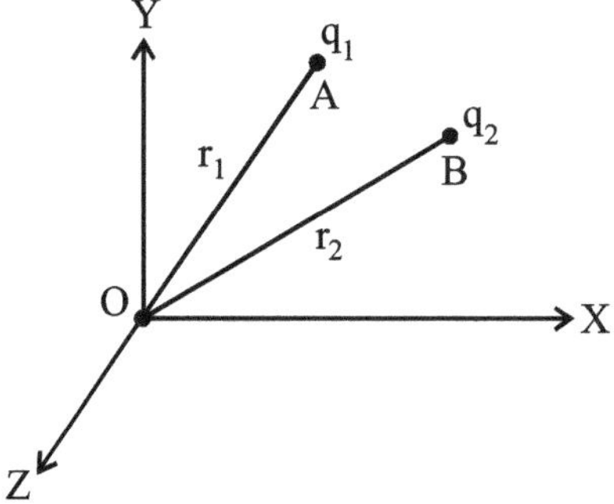

where, r_{AB} is the distance between points A and B.

By definition, work done in carryin charge q_2 from ∞ to B.

$$W = \text{Potential} \times \text{Charge}$$

$$W = \frac{1}{4\pi\varepsilon_0} \frac{q_1}{r_{AB}} \cdot q_2 = \frac{1}{4\pi\varepsilon_0} \frac{q_1 q_2}{r_{AB}}$$

The work is stored in the systems of two point charges q_1 and q_2 in the form of electrostatic potential energy U of the system.

$$\text{Thus,} \quad U = W = \frac{1}{4\pi\varepsilon_0} \cdot \frac{q_1 q_2}{r_{AB}}$$

Electrostatic potential energy is a scalar quantity. In the above formula, the values of q_1 and q_2 must be with proper signs.

- If $q_1, q_2 > 0$, potential energy is positive. It means that two charges are of same sign i.e., they repel each other. Then, in bringing closer, work is done against the force of repulsion, so that the electrostatic potential energy of the system increases. Conversely, in separating them, work is obtained from the system, so the potential energy of the system decreases.

- If $q_1, q_2 > 0$, potential energy is negative. It means that two charges are of opposite sign i.e., they attract each other. In this case, potential energy of the system decreases in bringing them closer and increases in separating them further.

Torque and work done Potential Energy in rotating an Electric Dipole in a Field

When an electric dipole is placed in an uniform electric field, a torque acts on it which subjects the dipole to rotatory motion.

$$\vec{F}_{net} = [q\,\vec{E} + (-q\,\vec{E})] = 0$$

Torque $\vec{\tau} = q\vec{E} \times 2\vec{\ell}\,\sin\theta \Rightarrow \vec{\tau} = \vec{p} \times \vec{E}$

There is no net force acting on the dipole in a uniform electric field.

Work done in rotating an electric dipole from θ_1 to θ_2 (uniform field)

$$dW = \tau d\theta \Rightarrow w = \int dW = \int \tau\, d\theta$$

$$\Rightarrow \quad W = \int_{\theta_1}^{\theta_2} PE\sin\theta\, d\theta = PE\,(\cos\theta_1 - \cos\theta_2)$$

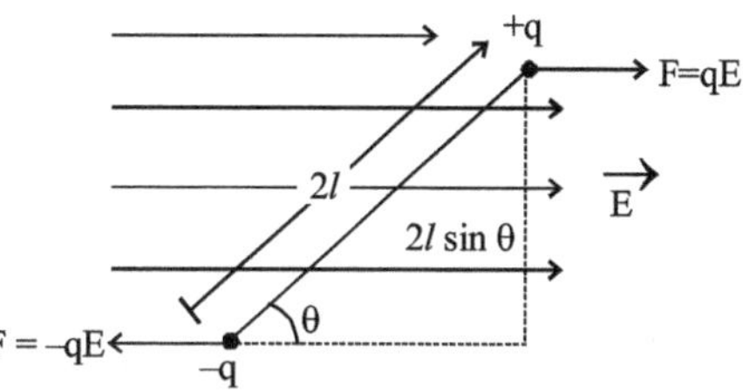

An external torque (τ_{ext}) is applied to the dipole so that it, rotates from angle θ_0 to θ_1 with respect to the electric field (E). Work done by the external torque (τ_{ext})

$$W = \int_{\theta_0}^{\theta_1} \tau_{ext}(\theta)d\theta = \int_{\theta_0}^{\theta_1} PE\sin\theta d\theta = PE\left[-\cos\theta\right]_{\theta_0}^{\theta_1}$$

$$W = PE\,(\cos\theta_0 - \cos\theta_1)$$

e.g. $W_{\theta \to 180°} = PE\,(1 - (-1)) = 2PE$

$$W_{\theta \to 90°} = PE\,(1 - 0) = PE$$

If a dipole is rotated from field direction ($\theta = 0$) to θ, then $W = PE\,(1 - \cos\theta)$

$\tau = \min = 0$ $\tau = \max. = PE$ $\tau = \min = 0$

$W = \min = 0$ $W = PE$ $W = \max. = 2PE$

This work done W is stored as the potential energy of the system i.e., dipole placed in external electric field E,

$U(\theta) = PE\,(\cos\theta_0 - \cos\theta_1)$

Illustration 2 :

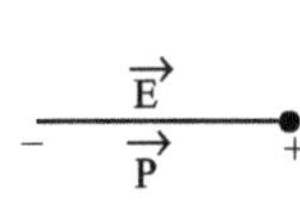

In nuclear fission, a Uranium-235 nucleus captures a neutron and splits apart into two lighter nuclei. Sometimes the two fission products are a barium nucleus (charge 56e) and a krypton nucleus (charge 36e). Assume that these nuclei are positive point charges separated by $r = 14.6 \times 10^{-15}$ m. Calculate the potential energy of this two charge system in electron volts.

Sol. The potential energy for two point charges separated by a distance r is $U = kq_1q_2/r$.

To find this energy in electron volts we calculate the potential due to one of the charges kq_1/r in volts and multiply by the other charge.

The potential energy of the two charges

$$U = \frac{kq_1q_2}{r} = \frac{k(56e)(36e)}{r}$$

Factor out e and substitute the given values :

$$U = \frac{k(56e)(36e)}{r} = e\frac{ke(56)(36)}{r}$$

$$U = e\frac{(8.99 \times 10^9\,\text{N.m}^2/\text{C}^2)(1.6 \times 10^{-19}\,\text{C})(56)(36)}{14.6 \times 10^{-15}\,\text{m}}$$

$$U = e\,(1.99 \times 10^8\,\text{V}) = 199\,\text{MeV}.$$

ELECTROSTATICS OF CONDUCTORS

Let us note important results regarding electrostatics of conductors.

(i)   Inside a conductor, electrostatic field is zero.

(ii)   At the surface of a charged conductor, electrostatic field must be normal to the surface at every point.

(iii)   The interior of a conductor can have no excess charge in the static situation.

(iv)   Electrostatic potential is constant throughout the volume of the conductor and has the same value (as inside) on its surface.

(v)   Electric field at the surface of a charged conductor $E = \dfrac{\sigma}{\varepsilon_0}\,\hat{n}$, where σ is the surface charge density and $\hat{n}$ is a unit vector normal to the surface in the outward direction.

DIELECTRICS AND ELECTRIC POLARISATION

Dielectrics are non-conducting substances. In contrast to conductors, they have no (or negligible number of) charge carriers.

A dielectric with polar molecules also develops a net dipole moment in an external field, but for a different reason. In the absence of any external field, the different permanent dipoles are oriented randomly due to thermal agitation; so the total dipole moment $\vec{P}$ is zero. When an external field is applied, the individual dipole moments tend to align with the field. When summed over all the molecules, there is then a net dipole moment in the direction of the external field, i.e., the dielectric is polarised. The extent of polarisation depends on the relative strength of two mutually opposite factors: the dipole potential energy in the external field tending to align the dipoles with the field and thermal energy tending to disrupt the alignment. There may be, in addition, the 'induced dipole moment' effect as for non-polar molecules, but generally the alignment effect is more important for polar molecules.

Non-polar molecules
Polar molecules

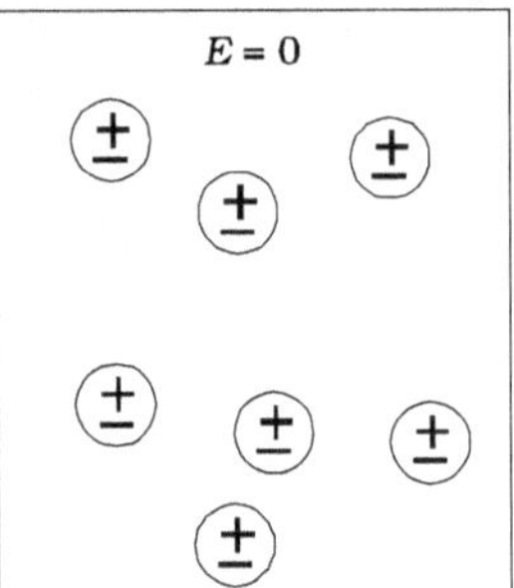

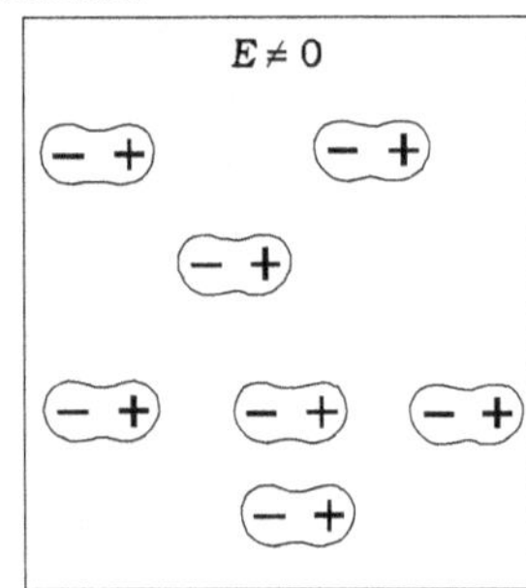

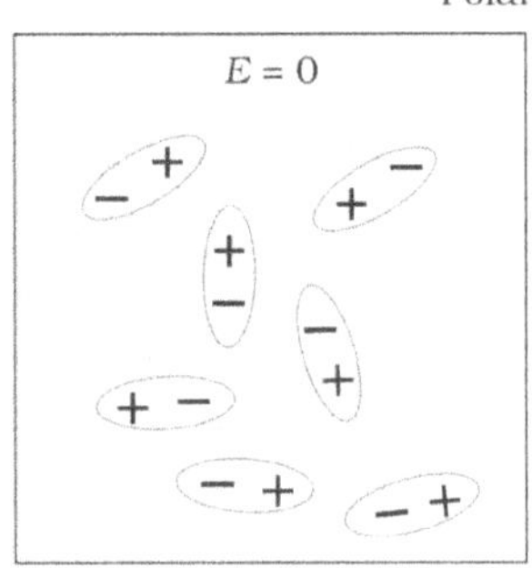

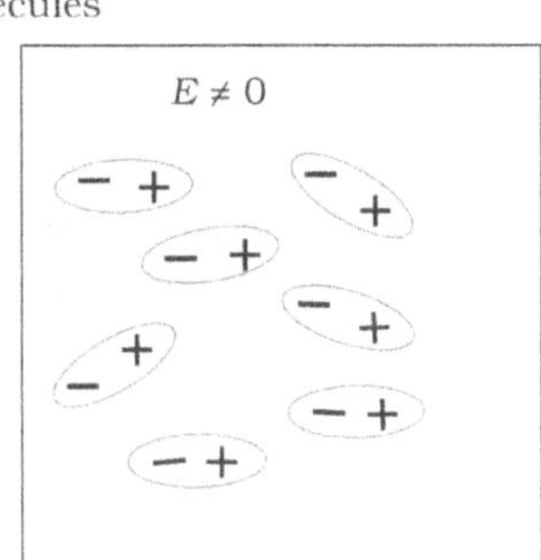

Electric Susceptibility (χ) The polarisation density of dielectric is directly proportional to the reduced value of the electric field

i.e., $P \propto \varepsilon_0 E$ or, $P = \chi \varepsilon_0 E$

Here, χ is called electric susceptibility.

Electric susceptibility (χ) is different for different dielectrics.

For vacuum $\chi = 0$

Electric susceptibility (χ) related with dielectric constant (k) as

$k = 1 + \chi$

Practice Exercise-2

Multiple Choice Questions

1.   A charge q is projected into a uniform electric field E, work done when it moves a distance y is,

     (a) qEy (b) qy/E (c) qE/y (d) y/qE

2.   Consider the following statements and select the true/false statements

     I.   In an external electric field, the positive and negative charges of a non–polar molecule are displaced in opposite directions.

     II.   In non –polar molecules displacement stops when the external force on the constituent charges of the molecule is balanced by the restoring force.

     III.   The non–polar molecule develops an induced dipole moment.

     (a)   T, T, F   (b)   F, T, T   (c)   T, F, T   (d)   T, T, T

3.   An electric dipole of moment $\vec{p}$ is placed normal to the lines of force of electric intensity $\overline{E}$, then the work done in deflecting it through an angle of $180°$ is

     (a) pE (b) $+2pE$ (c) $-2pE$ (d) zero

4. Match the entries of Column I and Column II

Column I	Column II
(A) Inside a conductor placed in an external electric field.	(1) Potential energy = 0
(B) At the centre of a dipole	(2) Electric field = 0
(C) Dipole in stable equilibrium	(3) Electric potential = 0
(D) Electric dipole perpendicular to uniform electric field.	(4) Torque = 0

   (a) $(A) \rightarrow (2); (B) \rightarrow (4); (C) \rightarrow (3); (D) \rightarrow (1)$
   (b) $(A) \rightarrow (2); (B) \rightarrow (3); (C) \rightarrow (4); (D) \rightarrow (1)$
   (c) $(A) \rightarrow (2); (B) \rightarrow (3); (C) \rightarrow (1); (D) \rightarrow (4)$
   (d) $(A) \rightarrow (1); (B) \rightarrow (3); (C) \rightarrow (4); (D) \rightarrow (2)$

5. Which of the following about potential difference between any two points, are true/false.
   I.   It depends only on the initial and final position.
   II. It is the work done per unit positive charge in moving from one point to other.
   III. It is more for a positive charge of two units as compared to a positive charge of one unit.
   (a) T, F, F   (b) F, T, F   (c) T, T, F   (d) T, T, T

Assertion & Reason Questions

DIRECTIONS (Qs. 6-9) : *Each of these questions contains an assertion followed by reason. Read them carefully and answer the question on the basis of following options. You have to select the one that best describes the two statements.*
(a) If both Assertion and Reason are correct and the Reason is a correct explanation of the Assertion.
(b) If both Assertion and Reason are correct but Reason is not a correct explanation of the Assertion.
(c) If the Assertion is correct but Reason is incorrect.
(d) If the Assertion is incorrect but the Reason is correct.

6. **Assertion:** The potential difference between any two points in an electric field depends only on initial and final position.
   Reason: Electric field is a conservative field so the work done per unit positive charge does not depend on path followed.
7. **Assertion :** Polar molecules have permanent dipole moment.
   Reason : In polar molecules, the centres of positive and negative charges coincide even when there is no external field.
8. **Assertion :** Dielectric polarisation means formation of positive and negative charges inside the dielectric.
   Reason: Free electrons are formed in this process.
9. **Assertion :** In the absence of an external electric field, the dipole moment per unit volume of a polar dielectric is zero.
   Reason : The dipoles of a polar dielectric are randomly oriented.

Case/Passage Based Questions

Electrostatic potential energy of a system of point charges is the total amount of work done in bringing various charges to their respective positions from infinitely large mutual separations.

If two charges having charge q_1 and q_2 are placed at a distance r from each other, then the potential energy of the system is given by

$$U = \frac{1}{4\pi\varepsilon_0} \frac{q_1 q_2}{r}$$

The above potential energy is formed due to work done in bringing any one of the charge at the distance r of other charge from infinity so. $W = U = \dfrac{1}{4\pi\varepsilon_0} \dfrac{q_1 q_2}{r}$

10. The potential energy of a system of two charges is negative when
   (a) both the charges are positive
   (b) both the charges are negative
   (c) one charge is positive and other is negative
   (d) both the charges are separated by infinite distance
11. The electric potential at point A is 1 V and at another point B is 5V. A charge 3 μC is released from B. What will be the kinetic energy of the charge as it passes through A ?
   (a) 8×10^{-6} J   (b) 12×10^{-6} J
   (c) 12×10^{-9} J   (d) 4×10^{-6} J
12. A square of side 'a' has charge Q at its centre and charge 'q' at one of the corners. The work required to be done in moving the charge 'q' from the corner to the diagonally opposite corner is
   (a) zero   (b) $\dfrac{Qq}{4\pi \in_0 a}$
   (c) $\dfrac{Qq\sqrt{2}}{4\pi \in_0 a}$ (d) $\dfrac{Qq}{2\pi \in_0 a}$
13. When a positive charge q is taken from lower potential to a higher potential point, then its potential energy will
   (a) increase   (b) decrease
   (c) remain unchanged   (d) become zero
14. If a unit charge is taken from one point to another over an equipotential surface, then
   (a) work is done on the charge
   (b) work is done by the charge
   (c) work done on the charge is constant
   (d) no work is done

Very Short Answer Questions

15. What would be the workdone if a point charge +q, is taken from a point A to the point B on the circumference of a circle drawn with another point charge +q at the centre?
16. If a point charge + q, is taken first from A to C, then from C to B of a circle drawn with another point charge +q at centre, then along which path more work will be done?

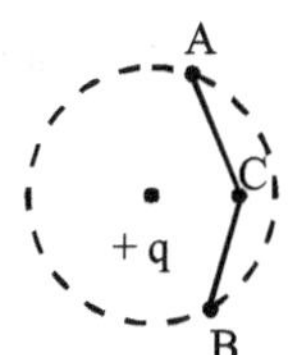

Short Answer Questions

17. A point charge of $+2\ \mu C$ is kept fixed at the origin. Another point charge of $+4\ \mu C$ is brought from a far off point to a point distant 50 cm from the origin. Calculate the electrostatic potential energy of this two charge system. Another charge of $+1\ \mu C$ is brought to a point distant 100 cm from each of these two charges (assumed to be kept fixed). What is work done?

18. Two identical plane metallic surfaces A and B are kept parallel to each other in air, separated by a distance of 1 cm as shown in the figure. A is given a positive potential of 10 V and the outer surface of B is earthed.

(i) What is the magnitude and direction of the uniform electric field between Y and Z?

(ii) What is the workdone in moving a charge of $20\ \mu C$ from X to Y?

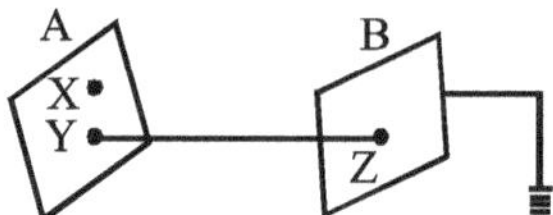

<table>
<tr><td>**Topic 3**</td><td>**Capacitors and Capacitance, Capacitance of a Parallel Plate Capacitor With and Without Dielectric Medium Combination of Capacitors, Energy Stored in a Capacitor**</td><td></td></tr>
</table>

CAPACITORS AND CAPACITANCE

Two large metal plates separated by certain distance constitute a capacitor.

The charge storing capacity of the capacitor is called its capacitance.

If Q is the charge on each metal plate and V is the potential difference between them, then

$$Q \propto V \Rightarrow Q = CV \Rightarrow C = \frac{Q}{V}\,,\ \text{C is a constant called the capacitance of the capacitor.}$$

The **S.I. unit** of capacitance is farad.

1 farad = 1 coulomb/1 volt; $1\mu F = 10^{-6} F$ and $1\,pF = 10^{-12}\,F$.

CAPACITANCE OF A PARALLEL PLATE CAPACITOR WITH AND WITHOUT DIELECTRIC MEDIUM

The parallel plate capacitor has two parallel metallic plates of any shape each of surface area A. Both these plates are separated by a distance d apart. Plate 1 is given a positive charge so that equal negative charge is induced on the plate 2 which is earthed from outside. This earthing reduces the potential difference between the plates, as a result capacitor can store more charge and hence its capacity C increases.

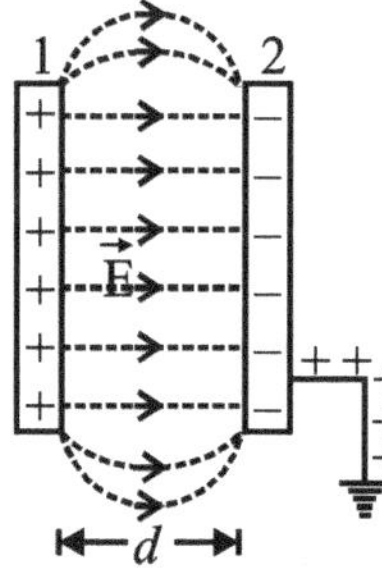

The capacitance is given by, $C = \dfrac{K\varepsilon_0 A}{d}$

where K is the dielectric constant of the medium in between the plates.

Special cases :

(i) When medium between the plates is air (K=1) Capacitance, $C = \dfrac{\varepsilon_0 A}{d}$

(ii) **When the space between the capacitor is partly filled with the dielectric,**

$$C = \frac{\varepsilon_0 A}{d - t + \dfrac{t}{K}} = \frac{\varepsilon_0 A}{d - t\left(1 - \dfrac{1}{K}\right)}$$

where t is the thickness of dielectric medium between the plates. The induced charge on the dielectric faces is q', which is given as

$$q' = -\left(1 - \frac{1}{K}\right)q$$

(iii) **When a metallic sheet of thickness t (t < d) is introduced between the plates, then**

$$C = \frac{\varepsilon_0 A}{d - t}$$

(iv) When the space between the plates is filled with a dielectric medium which linearly varies as such its value near one plate is K_1, and that near the other plate is K_2, then

$$C = \frac{\varepsilon_0 A(K_2 - K_1)}{\log_e(K_2 / K_1)}$$

(v) If the space between the plates of a parallel plate capacitor is filled with two dielectric medium of thicknesses d_1 and d_2 $(d = d_1 + d_2)$ having dielectric constants K_1 and K_2 then

the capacitance will be, $C = \dfrac{\varepsilon_0 A}{\dfrac{d_1}{K_1} + \dfrac{d_2}{K_2}}$

Spherical Capacitor

A spherical capacitor consists of two concentric spherical conductors of radii R_1 and R_2.

Case I : When outer sphere is earthed : $C = \dfrac{Q}{V} = 4\pi\varepsilon_0 \dfrac{R_1 R_2}{R_2 - R_1}$ *(in air or vacuum)*

In presence of medium between plates: $C = 4\pi\varepsilon_r\,\varepsilon_0 \dfrac{R_1 R_2}{R_2 - R_1}$

Case II : When inner sphere is earthed : $C = \dfrac{4\pi\varepsilon_0 R_2^2}{R_2 - R_1}$

COMBINATION OF CAPACITORS

Series Combination of Capacitors

In series combination of capacitors, charge Q through each capacitor $C_1, C_2, C_3, \dots\, C_n$ remains same but potential difference is different having values say, $V_1, V_2, V_3 \dots\, V_n$ respectively.

Let C_s be the equivalent capacitance then, $V = \dfrac{Q}{C_s}$

$V = V_1 + V_2 + V_3 + \dots + V_n$

$\dfrac{Q}{C_s} = \dfrac{Q}{C_1} + \dfrac{Q}{C_2} + \dfrac{Q}{C_3} + \dots + \dfrac{Q}{C_n}$

Equivalent capacitance, $\dfrac{1}{C_s} = \dfrac{1}{C_1} + \dfrac{1}{C_2} + \dfrac{1}{C_3} + \dots + \dfrac{1}{C_n}$

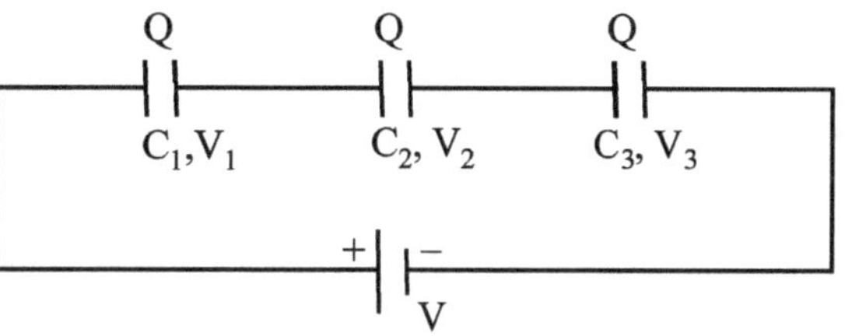

Parallel Combination of Capacitors

In parallel combination of capacitors, charge in each capacitor $C_1, C_2, C_3, \dots\, C_n$ is different $Q_1, Q_2, Q_3, \dots Q_n$ but potential difference is same V.

If Q is the total charge on the parallel network, then

$Q = Q_1 + Q_2 + Q_3 + \dots + Q_n$

Let C_p be the equivalent capacitance, then

$C_p V = C_1 V + C_2 V + C_3 V + \dots + C_n V$

$\therefore$ Equivalent capacitance, $C_p = C_1 + C_2 + C_3 \dots + C_n$

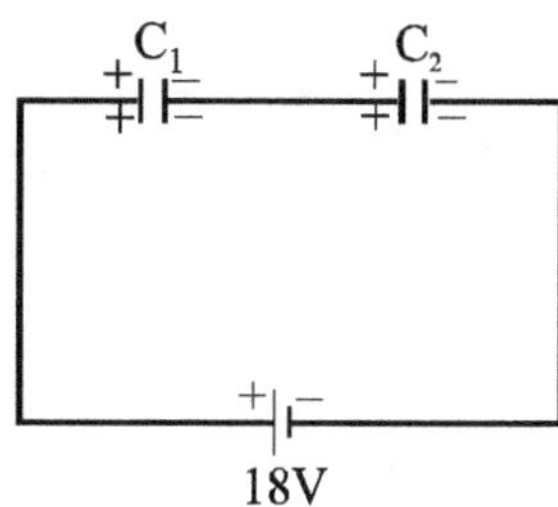

Illustration 3 :

Two capacitors of capacitance $C_1 = 6\,\mu F$ and $C_2 = 3\,\mu F$ are connected in series across a cell of emf 18 V. Calculate :
(a) the equivalent capacitance (b) the potential difference across each capacitor (c) the charge on each capacitor.

Sol. (a) As two capacitors are connected in series, $\therefore \dfrac{1}{C} = \dfrac{1}{C_1} + \dfrac{1}{C_2}$

$\Rightarrow C = \dfrac{C_1 C_2}{C_1 + C_2} = \dfrac{6 \times 3}{6 + 3} = 2\mu F$

(b) Potential difference across capacitor C_1,

$V_1 = \dfrac{C_2}{C_1 + C_2} V = \dfrac{3}{6 + 3} \times 18 = 6$ Volts

Potential difference across capacitor C_2,

$$V_2 = \frac{C_1}{C_1 + C_2} V = \frac{6}{6+3} \times 18 = 12 \text{ Volts}$$

Note that the smaller capacitor C_2 has a larger potential difference across it.

(c) $Q_1 = Q_2 = C_1 V_1 = C_2 V_2 = CV [V = V_1 + V_2]$

Charge on each capacitor $= C_{eq} V = 2\mu F \times 18 \text{ volts} = 36\mu C$

Illustration 4 :

Calculate the equivalent capacitance between points A and B.

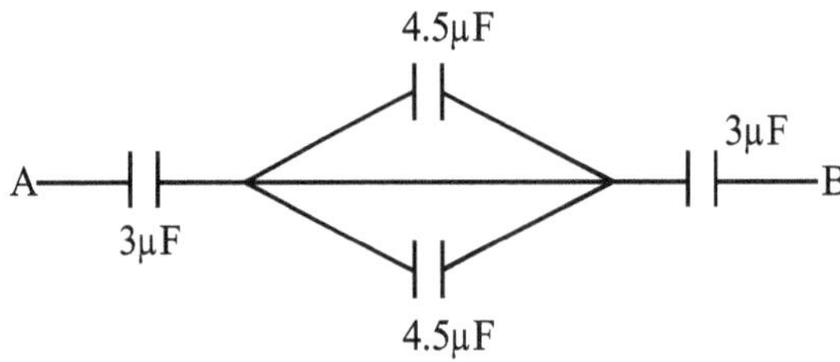

Sol. Capacitances 4.5 μF and 4.5 μF are in parallel and in parallel comination $C_p = C_1 + C_2 = 4.5 + 4.5 = 9 \text{ nF}$

3 nF , 9 nF and 3 nF are in series. $\dfrac{1}{C_s} = \dfrac{1}{3} + \dfrac{1}{9} + \dfrac{1}{3} = \dfrac{2}{3} + \dfrac{1}{9} = \dfrac{6+1}{9} = \dfrac{7}{9}$

$$C_s = \frac{9}{7} = 1.29 \text{ nF} .$$

ENERGY STORED IN A CAPACITOR

The work done to store charge in a capacitor against the potential difference is stored as the potential energy of the capacitor. When an additional small charge (dq) is transferred from one plate to another plate, the small work done is given by

$$dW = Vdq = \frac{q}{C} dq$$

[Let charge on plate when dq charge is transferred be q]
The total work done in transferring charge (Q) is given by

$$W = \int_0^Q \frac{q}{C} dq = \frac{1}{C} \int_0^Q q\, dq = \frac{1}{C} \left[\frac{(q)^2}{2} \right]_0^Q = \frac{Q^2}{2C}$$

$$U = \frac{1}{2} CV^2 = \frac{1}{2} QV = \frac{Q^2}{2C}, \quad U = \frac{\varepsilon_0 E^2}{2} \times \text{(Volume between the plates)}$$

Energy density, $U = \dfrac{1}{2} \varepsilon_0 E^2$

Illustration 5 :

How much energy will be stored in a capacitor of 470 μF capacity, when charged by a battery of 20 V?

Sol. Given : $C = 470 \mu F = 470 \times 10^{-6} F, V = 20 V$

Energy stored in a capacitor, $E = \dfrac{1}{2} CV^2 = \dfrac{1}{2} \times 470 \times 10^{-6} \times 20^2 = 9.4 \times 10^{-2} J$

Practice Exercise-3

Multiple Choice Questions

1. On decreasing the distance between the plates of a parallel plate capacitor, its capacitance
   (a) remains unaffected
   (b) decreases
   (c) first increases then decreases.
   (d) increases

2. In the given circuit diagram, both capacitors are initially uncharged. The capacitance $C_1 = 2F$ and $C_2 = 4F$ emf of battery A and B are 2V and 4V respectively.

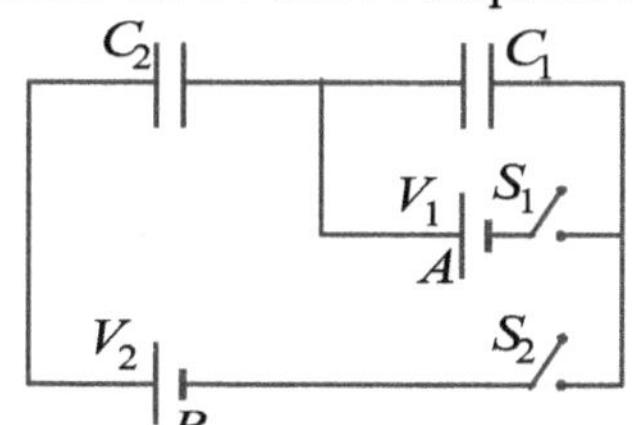

Column I	Column II
(A) On closing switch S_1 with S_2 open work done by battery A is	(1) $\dfrac{64}{3}$
(B) Switch S_1 is open and S_2 is closed, work done by battery B is	(2) 4
(C) Charge on capacitor C_2 is (after S_1 open and S_2 closed)	(3) 8
(D) Charge on C_1 when both are closed	(4) $\dfrac{16}{3}$

   (a) (A) → (1); (B) → (2); (C) → (2); (D) → (4)
   (b) (A) → (4); (B) → (3); (C) → (3); (D) → (1)
   (c) (A) → (2); (B) → (3); (C) → (2); (D) → (1)
   (d) (A) → (3); (B) → (1); (C) → (4); (D) → (2)

3. The potential energy of a charged parallel plate capacitor is U_0. If a slab of dielectric constant k is inserted between the plates, then the new potential energy will be
   (a) U_0/k (b) $U_0 k^2$ (c) U_0/k^2 (d) U_0^2

4. Three capacitors each of capacitance C and break down voltage V are joined in series. The capacitance of the combination will be _______ and break down voltage of the combination will be _______.
   (a) $\dfrac{C}{3}, \dfrac{V}{3}$ (b) $3C, \dfrac{V}{3}$ (c) $\dfrac{C}{3}, 3V$ (d) $3C, 3V$

5. A capacitor is charged by using a battery which is then disconnected. A dielectric slab of dielectric k is then inserted between the plates, which results in
   (a) Reduction of charge on the plates and increase of potential difference across the plates.
   (b) Increase in the potential difference across the plate, reduction in stored energy, but no change in the charge on the plates.
   (c) Decrease in the potential difference across the plates, reduction in the stored energy, but no change in the charge on the plates.
   (d) None of these

6. Find the capacitance between P and Q (Fig). Each Capacitor has capacitance C.
   (a) 2C
   (b) 3C
   (c) 8C
   (d) 6C

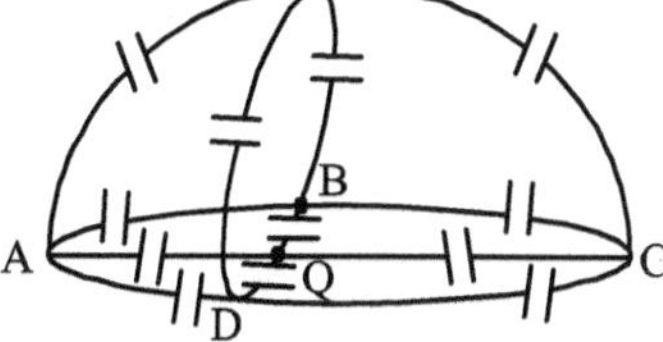

Assertion & Reason Questions

DIRECTIONS (Qs. 7-10) : *Each of these questions contains an assertion followed by reason. Read them carefully and answer the question on the basis of following options. You have to select the one that best describes the two statements.*
   (a) If both Assertion and Reason are correct and the Reason is a correct explanation of the Assertion.
   (b) If both Assertion and Reason are correct but Reason is not a correct explanation of the Assertion.
   (c) If the Assertion is correct but Reason is incorrect.
   (d) If the Assertion is incorrect but the Reason is correct.

7. **Assertion :** A parallel plate capacitor is connected across battery through a key. A dielectric slab of dielectric constant k is introduced between the plates. The energy stored becomes k times.
   Reason : The surface density of charge on the plate remains constant.

8. **Assertion :** If two metal plates having charges $Q, -Q$ face each other at some separation are dipped into an oil tank, then electric field between the plates decreases.
   Reason : Electric field between the plates, $E_{med} = \dfrac{E_{air}}{\kappa}$ due to polarization of dielectrical materials.

9. **Assertion :** A dielectric is inserted between the plates of a battery connected capacitor. The potential difference between the plates remains constant.
   Reason : As the battery remains connected maintaining the same potential difference.

10. Assertion : Charges are given to plates of two plane parallel plate capacitors C_1 and C_2 (such that $C_2 = 2C_1$) as shown in figure. Then the key K is pressed to complete the circuit. Finally the net charge on upper plate and net charge on lower plate of capacitor C_1 is negative.

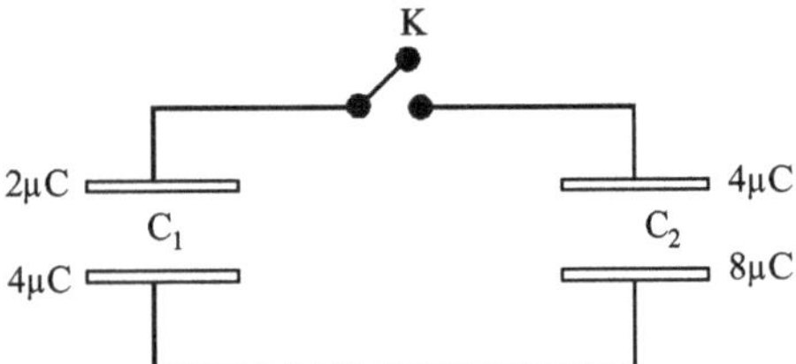

Reason : In a parallel plate capacitor both plates always carry equal and positive charge.

Case/Passage Based Questions

Two capacitors of capacity 6 μF and 3 μF are charged to 100 V and 50 V separately and connected as shown in figure. Now all the three switches S_1, S_2 and S_3 are closed.

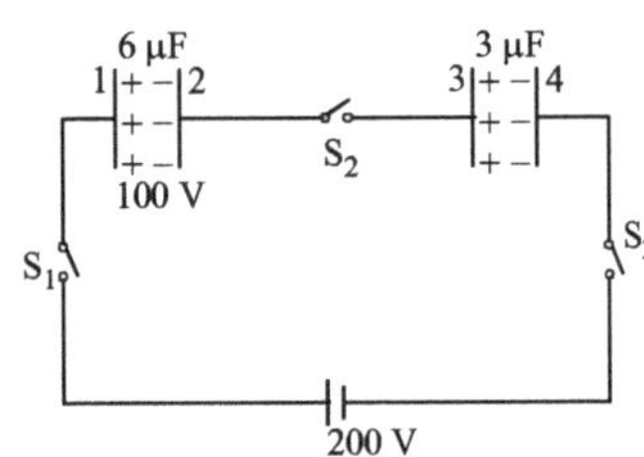

11. Which plates form an isolated system?
   (a) plate 1 and plate 4 separately
   (b) plate 2 and plate 3 separately
   (c) plate 2 and plate 3 jointly
   (d) none of these
12. Charge on the 6 μF capacitor in steady state will be
   (a) 400 μC   (b) 700 μC   (c) 800 μC   (d) 250 μC
13. Charge on the 3 μF capacitor in steady state will be
   (a) 400 μC   (b) 700 μC   (c) 800 μC   (d) 250 μC
14. Suppose q_1, q_2 and q_3 be the magnitudes of charges flowing from charges S_1, S_2 and S_3 after they are closed. Then

   (a) $q_1 = q_3$ and $q_2 = 0$ (b) $q_1 = q_3 = \dfrac{q_2}{2}$

   (c) $q_1 = q_3 = 2q_2$ (d) $q_1 = q_2 = q_3$
15. A 2 μF capacitor is charged to 100 V and then its plates are connected by a conducting wire. The heat produced is
   (a) 0.001 J   (b) 0.01 J   (c) 0.1 J   (d) 1J

Very Short Answer Questions

16. In a parallel plate capacitor the potential difference of 10^2 V is maintained between the plates. What will be the electric field at points A and B?
17. How much energy will be stored by a capacitor of 470 μF when charged by a battery of 20 V?
18. Write the physical quantity which has its unit coulomb/volt? Is it a vector or a scalar quantity?

Short Answer Questions

19. Calculate the capacitance of the capacitor C in the figure if the equivalent capacitance of the combination between A and B is 15 μF.

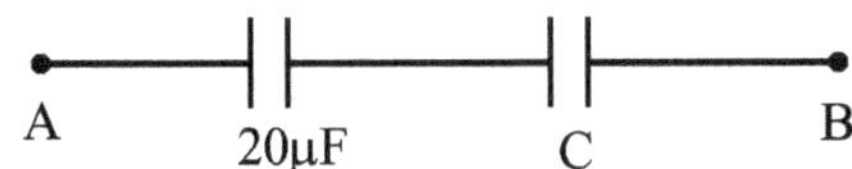

20. The equivalent capacitance of the combination between A and B in the given figure is 15 μF. Calculate the capacitance of capacitor C.

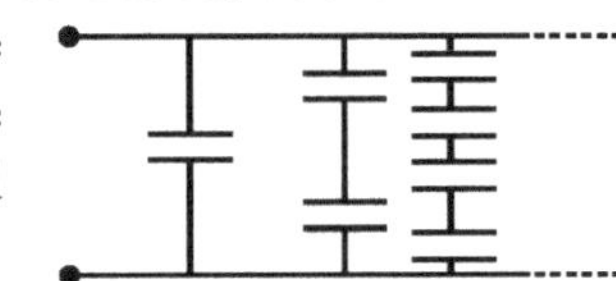

21. n small drops of same size are charged to V volt each. They coelesce to form a bigger drop. Calculate the capacity.
22. An infinite number of the identical capacitors, each of the capacitance 1 μF, are connected, as shown. Then, what is the equivalent capacitance between the points A and B?
23. Is it possible for a metal sphere of 1 cm radius to hold a charge of 1C?
24. A parallel plate capacitor with air has a capacitance of 10 pF. If the distance between the plates is reduced to half and the space between them is filled with a material of dielectric constant 10, find the new capacitance.
25. Calculate the equivalent capacitance between points A and B in the following combination.

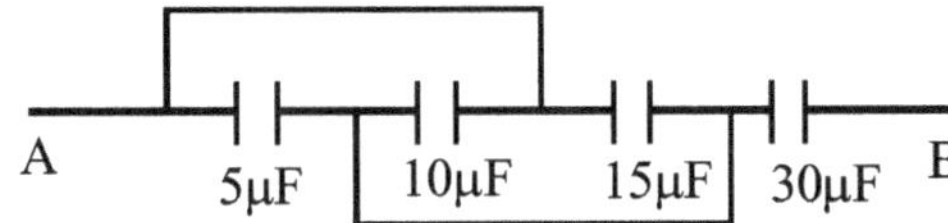

Important Tips & Formulae

- The value of electric potential at the centre of the line joining two equal and opposite charge is zero. But, at the centre of the line joining two equal and similar charge, potential is not zero.

- The relation between electric field and potential is given by $E = -\dfrac{dv}{dr}$. This equation suggest that electric potential can exist at a point where the electric field is zero and its vice versa.

- No work is done in moving a charge over any equipotential surface. But work will be done if a charge moves from one equipotential surface to other.

- Capacitance of a parallel plate capacitor does not depend upon the charge given, potential raised or nature of metals and thickness of plates.

- If plates of a parallel plate capacitor (initial seperation d) is moved away with some velocity. Then the rate of change of capacitance with time is proportional to $\dfrac{1}{d^2}$.

- Force of attraction between the plates of a parallel plate capacitor is independent of separation between the plates but varies inversely with area of plates.

- Electrostatic force between the metal plates of an isolated parallel plate capacitor $F_{\text{plate}} = \dfrac{Q^2}{2A\varepsilon_0}$

- Spherical conductor is equivalent to a spherical capacitor if its outer sphere has infinite radius.

- A spherical capacitor behaves as a parallel plate capacitor if its spherical surfaces have large radii and are close to each other.

- Electric field intensity is a vector quantity. Therefore, vector algebra is used for finding resultant electric field intensity. But, electric potential and electric potential energy both are scalar quantity. Therefore, they should be added algebraically only.

- If two spheres having radii R_1 and R_2 and charges Q_1 and Q_2 are joined by a wire, then

- In a polar molecule, the centre of positive and negative charges coincide. The molecule then has no permanent dipole moment. Polar molecule is one in which the centre of positive and negative charges are separated. They have permanent dipole moment.

  - Common potential $V = \dfrac{Q_1 + Q_2}{4\pi\varepsilon_0 (R_1 + R_2)}$

  - Charges on each sphere are

    $Q_1' = \dfrac{(Q_1 + Q_2)R_1}{(R_1 + R_2)}$ and $Q_2' = \dfrac{(Q_1 + Q_2)R_2}{(R_1 + R_2)}$

- If n identical capacitors, each of capacitance C are connected in parallel which are charged to a potential V. If these are separated and connected in series then potential difference of combination will be nV.

- Let n charged drops, each of capacitance C and charge q is charged to potential V. If they coalesce to form a single drop, then, Total charge $= nq$, Total capacity $= n^{1/3}C$

- A capacitor of capacity C_1 charged to potential V_1 is connected to another capacitor of capacity C_2 and potential V_2. Now if batteries are connected to each other with reverse polarity i.e., positive plate of a capacitor connected to negative plate of other. Then common potential is given by
  For numerical calculation we may assume as

  $$V = \frac{Q_1 + Q_2}{C_1 + C_2} = \frac{C_1 V_1 - C_2 V_2}{C_1 + C_2}$$

- Two plates having unequal area can form capacitor. But, in this case effective overlapping area should be considered.

- When a dielectric is placed between the plates of a parallel plate capacitor then its capacitance increases but potential difference decreases. To maintain the same capacitance and potential difference of capacitor, separation between the plates has to be increased say by d'. In such case

  $$K = \frac{t}{t - d'}$$

- Magnitude of force between two plates of a capacitor is

  $$F = \frac{\theta^2}{2A\varepsilon_0}$$

NCERT Questions

2.1   **Two charges 5×10^{-8}C and -3×10^{-8}C are located 16 cm apart. At what point (s) on the line joining the two charges is the electric potential zero? Take the potential at infinity to be zero.**

Sol.   Let the point be at distance x m from first charge, and its distance from second charge becomes $(0.16 - x)$ m.

Now, $q_1 = 5 \times 10^{-8}$C, $q_2 = -3 \times 10^{-8}$C,

$\qquad r_1 = x$ m, $r_2 = (0.16 - x)$ m

$V_1 + V_2 = 0$, $x = ?$

By formula,

$$V_1 + V_2 = \frac{1}{4\pi\varepsilon_0}\frac{q_1}{r_1} + \frac{1}{4\pi\varepsilon_0}\frac{q_2}{r_2} = 0$$

$$\Rightarrow \quad \frac{1}{4\pi\varepsilon_0}\left(\frac{q_1}{r_1} + \frac{q_2}{r_2}\right) = 0$$

$$\Rightarrow \quad \frac{q_2}{r_2} = -\frac{q_1}{r_1}, \frac{r_1}{r_2} = -\frac{q_1}{q_2}$$

Substituting the values, we get,

$$\frac{x}{(0.16 - x)} = -\frac{5 \times 10^{-8}}{-3 \times 10^{-8}} = \frac{5}{3}$$

$$3x = 0.8 - 5x \Rightarrow 8x = 0.8$$

or, $x = 0.1$ m $= 10$ cm.

The required point is at distance 10 cm from first (5×10^{-8}C) charge.

2.2   **A regular hexagon of side 10 cm has a charge 5 μC at each of its vertices. Calculate the potential at the centre of the hexagon.**

Sol.   Geometrically each vertex is at a distance of 10 cm (length of side) from centre of the hexagon.

So, for all charges,

$\qquad r = 10$ cm $= 0.1$ m,

$\qquad q = 5\mu$C $= 5 \times 10^{-6}$ C, n $= 6$, V $= ?$

By formula, $V = \dfrac{1}{4\pi\varepsilon_0}\dfrac{nq}{r}$

$$V = \frac{9 \times 10^9 \times 6 \times 5 \times 10^{-6}}{0.1} = 2.7 \times 10^6 \text{ V}.$$

2.3   **Two charges 2 μC and -2 μC are placed at points A and B 6 cm apart.**
     (a)   Identify an equipotential surface of the system.
     (b)   What is the direction of the electric field at every point on this surface?

Sol.   (a)   The system represents an electric dipole of charge strength 2 μC, electric dipole length 0.06 m and electric dipole moment

$\qquad\qquad = 0.12 \times 10^{-6}$ C-m.

By formula, $V = \dfrac{1}{4\pi\varepsilon_0}\dfrac{p\cos\theta}{r^2}$

     (i)   For points on axial line, $\theta = 0°$, $\cos\theta = 1$.

$\qquad\qquad V \propto 1/r^2$.

The equipotential surfaces are spherical with centre at the centre of the dipole.

     (ii)   For points on equatorial line,

$\qquad\qquad \theta = 90°$, $\cos\theta = $ zero.

The equatorial plane is plane of zero potential.

     (b)   Direction of electric field at every point of the equipotential surface is normal to the surface.

2.4   **A spherical conductor of radius 12cm has a charge of 1.6×10^{-7}C distributed uniformly on its surface. What is the electric field**
     (a)   inside the sphere
     (b)   just outside the sphere
     (c)   at a point 18 cm from the centre of the sphere?

Sol.   Given, R $= 12$ cm $= 0.12$ m, q $= 1.6 \times 10^{-7}$ C
     (a)   r < 12 cm, E $= ?$
     (b)   r $=$ R $= 12$ cm, E $= ?$
     (c)   r $= 18$ cm, E $= ?$
     (a)   For a point inside the spherical conductor, electric field, E $=$ zero
     (b)   For point just on the surface of the conductor, E $= \dfrac{1}{4\pi\varepsilon_0}\dfrac{q}{R^2}$

$$= \frac{9 \times 10^9 \times 1.6 \times 10^{-7}}{(0.12)^2} = \frac{9 \times 1.6 \times 10^2}{144 \times 10^{-4}}$$

$$= 10^5 \text{ NC}^{-1}.$$

     (c)   For point outside the conductor,

$$E = \frac{1}{4\pi\varepsilon_0}\cdot\frac{q}{r^2} = \frac{9 \times 10^9 \times 1.6 \times 10^{-7}}{(0.18)^2}$$

$$= \frac{9 \times 1.6 \times 10^2}{324 \times 10^{-4}} = 4.4 \times 10^4 \text{NC}^{-1}.$$

2.5   **A parallel plate capacitor with air between the plates has a capacitance of 8 pF (1 pF $= 10^{-12}$ F). What will be the capacitance if the distance between the plates is reduced by half, and the space between them is filled with a substance of the dielectric constant 6?**

Sol.   Given, $C_0 = 8$ pF $= 8 \times 10^{-12}$F, $d_2 = d_1/2$,

$\qquad\qquad$ K $= 6$, $C_K = ?$

By formula, $C = \dfrac{K\varepsilon_0 A}{d}$

In first case, $C_0 = \dfrac{\varepsilon_0 A}{d}$

In second case, $C_K = \dfrac{K\varepsilon_0 A}{d/2} = \dfrac{2K\varepsilon_0 A}{d}$

Dividing, we get, $\dfrac{C_K}{C_0} = \dfrac{2K\varepsilon_0 A}{d} \times \dfrac{d}{\varepsilon_0 A} = 2K$

or $C_K = 2KC_0 = 2 \times 6 \times 8 \times 10^{-12}$

$\qquad\qquad = 96 \times 10^{-12} = 96$ pF.

2.6 Three capacitors each of capacitance 9 pF are connected in series.
(a) What is the total capacitance of the combination?
(b) What is the potential difference across each capacitor if the combination is connected to a 120V supply?

Sol. Given, $C = 9$ pF $= 9 \times 10^{-12}$ F, $n = 3$,
(a) $C_s = ?$, (b) $V = 120$ V, $V_1 = ?$, $V_2 = ?$, $V_3 = ?$

By formula, $C_s = \dfrac{C}{n} = \dfrac{9 \times 10^{-12}}{3} = 3 \times 10^{-12} = 3$pF.

(b) Since in series, charge q is same on each capacitor,
$C_1 V_1 = C_2 V_2 = C_3 V_3$
As $C_1 = C_2 = C_3$,
We have, $V_1 = V_2 = V_3 = V_c$ (say)
Since $V_1 + V_2 + V_3 = V$
$3V_c = 120 \Rightarrow V_c = 40$V
∴ Potential difference across each capacitor is 40 V.

2.7 Three capacitors of capacitances 2 pF, 3 pF and 4 pF are connected in parallel.
(a) What is the total capacitance of the combination?
(b) Determine the charge on each capacitance if the combination is connected to a 100 V supply.

Sol. Given, $C_1 = 2$ pF, $C_2 = 3$ pF, $C_3 = 4$ pF,
(a) $C_p = ?$, (b) $V = 100$V, $q_1 = ?$, $q_2 = ?$, $q_3 = ?$
(a) By formula, in parallel combination,
$C_p = C_1 + C_2 + C_3 = 2 + 3 + 4 = 9$ pF
(b) In parallel combination, potential difference is same across each capacitor.
By relation, $q = CV$. Substituting the values,
we get, $q_1 = 2 \times 100 = 200$pC $= 200 \times 10^{-12}$C
$q_2 = 3 \times 100 = 300$pC $= 300 \times 10^{-12}$C
$q_3 = 4 \times 100 = 400$pC $= 400 \times 10^{-12}$C.

2.8 In a parallel plate capacitor with air between the plates, each plate has an area of 6×10^{-3} m^2 and the distance between the plates is 3 mm. Calculate the capacitance of the capacitor. If this capacitor is connected to a 100 V supply, what is the charge on each plate of the capacitor?

Sol. Given, $A = 6 \times 10^{-3}$m^2, $d = 3$ mm
$= 3 \times 10^{-3}$m, $\varepsilon_0 = 8.854 \times 10^{-12}$C^2 N^{-1} m^{-2}
$V = 100$V, $C = ?$, $q = ?$

By formula, $C = \dfrac{\varepsilon_0 A}{d} = \dfrac{8.854 \times 10^{-12} \times 6 \times 10^{-3}}{3 \times 10^{-3}}$
$= 17.718 \times 10^{-12}$ F $= 17.7$ pF.
And by relation, $q = CV = 17.7 \times 10^{-12} \times 100$
$= 17.7 \times 10^{-10}$C.

2.9 Explain what would happen if in the capacitor given in question 2.8, a 3 mm thick mica sheet (of dielectric constant = 6) were inserted between the plates,
(a) while the voltage supply remained connected and,
(b) after the supply was disconnected.

Sol. Given, $C_0 = 17.7$ pF, $C_K = KC_0 = 6\,C_0$.
(a) While the supply remained connected; voltage will remain constant
$q_K = C_K V = 6\,C_0 V = 6 \times 17.7 \times 10^{-10}$ C
$= 1.06 \times 10^{-8}$C.

Charge on capacitor becomes six times.

(b) When supply is disconnected; Charge will remain constant
$q = C_K V_K$

$V_K = \dfrac{q}{C_k} = \dfrac{q}{KC_0} = 16.7$ V

Potential difference between plates becomes one-sixth.

2.10 A 12pF capacitor is connected to a 50V battery. How much electrostatic energy is stored in the capacitor?

Sol. Given, $C = 12$ pF $= 12 \times 10^{-12}$ F,
$V = 50$V, $E = ?$

By formula, electrostatic energy $E = \dfrac{1}{2} CV^2$

$= \dfrac{1}{2} \times 12 \times 10^{-12} \times (50)^2 = 1.5 \times 10^{-8}$ J.

2.11 A 600pF capacitor is charged by a 200V supply. It is then disconnected from the supply and is connected to another uncharged 600 pF capacitor. How much electrostatic energy is lost in the process?

Sol. Given, $C_1 = 600$ pF $= 600 \times 10^{-12}$
F $= 6 \times 10^{-10}$F, $C_2 = 6 \times 10^{-10}$ F,
$V_1 = 200$ V, $V_2 = 0$,
Loss of energy, $\Delta E = ?$

By formula, $\Delta E = \dfrac{C_1 C_2 (V_1 - V_2)^2}{2(C_1 + C_2)}$

$= \dfrac{6 \times 10^{-10} \times 6 \times 10^{-10}(200 - 0)^2}{2(6 \times 10^{-10} + 6 \times 10^{-10})}$

$= \dfrac{36 \times 10^{-20} \times 200 \times 200}{2 \times 12 \times 10^{-10}} = 6 \times 10^{-6}$J.

ADDITIONAL EXERCISES

2.12 A charge of 8 mC is located at the origin. Calculate the work done in taking a small charge of -2×10^{-9} C from a point P(0, 0, 3cm) to a point Q(0, 4cm, 0) via a point R (0, 6 cm, 9 cm).

Sol. Let $\vec{r_1}$ and $\vec{r_2}$ are the position vectors for points P and Q then

$\vec{r_1} = 3\,\hat{k}$ and $r_1 = 3$ cm $= 0.03$ m
$\vec{r_2} = 4\,\hat{j}$ and $r_2 = 4$ cm $= 0.04$ m

Position of point R does not affect the result.
Also q $= 8$ mC $= 8 \times 10^{-3}$ C.

By formula, $V = \dfrac{1}{4\pi\varepsilon_0}\dfrac{q}{r}$

For point P,

$V_1 = \dfrac{9\times10^9 \times 8\times10^{-3}}{0.03} = 24\times10^8\,V$

For point Q,

$V_2 = \dfrac{9\times10^9 \times 8\times10^{-3}}{0.04} = 18\times10^8\,V$

Potential difference, $(V_2 - V_1)$
$= 18 \times 10^8 - 24 \times 10^8 = -6 \times 10^8\,V$
Work done W = charged moved × potential difference,
$= (-2 \times 10^{-9})(-6 \times 10^8) = 1.2\,J$

2.13 **A cube of side b has a charge q at each of its vertices. Determine the potential and electric field due to this charge array at the centre of the cube.**

Sol. Geometrically, distance of centre of the cube from each

vertex $= \dfrac{\sqrt{3}}{2}b$.

Potential at centre due to charge at one vertex

$= \dfrac{1}{4\pi\varepsilon_0}\dfrac{q}{\sqrt{3}b/2} = \dfrac{q}{2\sqrt{3}\pi\varepsilon_0 b}$

Potential at centre due to charge at eight vertices,

$V = \dfrac{8q}{2\sqrt{3}\pi\varepsilon_0 b} = \dfrac{4q}{\sqrt{3}\pi\varepsilon_0 b}$

Electric field = zero.
It is due to symmetry of charge about the point.

2.14 **Two tiny spheres carrying charges 1.5 μC and 2.5 μC are located 30 cm apart. Find the potential and electric field:**

(a) **at the mid-point of the line joining the two charges, and**

(b) **at a point 10 cm from this midpoint in a plane normal to the line and passing through the mid-point.**

Sol. The situation is shown in figure.

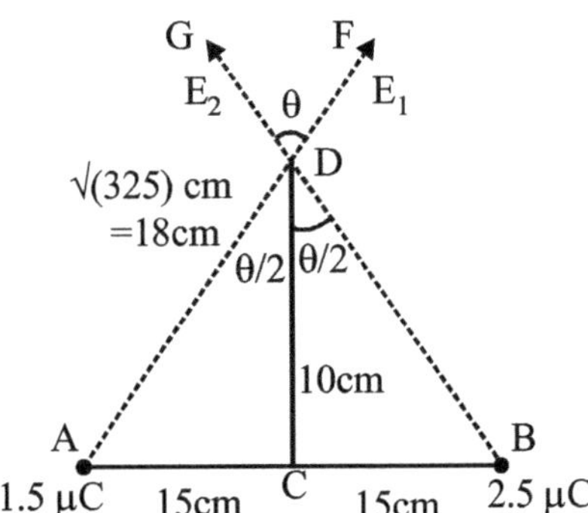

(a) Potential at C due to charge at A

$= \dfrac{1}{4\pi\varepsilon_0}\cdot\dfrac{1.5\times10^{-6}}{0.15} = 9 \times 10^9 \times 10^{-5}\,V$

Potential at C due to charge at B

$= \dfrac{1}{4\pi\varepsilon_0}\dfrac{2.5\times10^{-6}}{0.15} = 15\times10^4\,V$

Total potential at C = $9 \times 10^4 + 15 \times 10^4$
$= 24 \times 10^4$ V.
Intensity of electric field at C due to charge at A

$= \dfrac{1}{4\pi\varepsilon_0}\cdot\dfrac{1.5\times10^{-6}}{(0.15)^2}$ along CB

$= 9\times10^9 \times \dfrac{15\times10^{-7}}{225\times10^{-4}} = 6\times10^5\,NC^{-1}$

Intensity of electric field at C due to charge at B

$= \dfrac{1}{4\pi\varepsilon_0}\cdot\dfrac{2.5\times10^{-6}}{(0.15)^2}$ along CA

$= 9\times10^9 \times \dfrac{25\times10^{-7}}{225\times10^{-4}} = 10\times10^5\,NC^{-1}$

Resultant intensity of electric field at C
$= 10 \times 10^5 - 6 \times 10^5 = 4 \times 10^5\,NC^{-1}$ from
2.5 μC to 1.5 μC.

(b) Potential at D due to charge at A

$= \dfrac{1}{4\pi\varepsilon_0}\cdot\dfrac{1.5\times10^{-6}}{0.18}$

$= 9\times10^9 \times \dfrac{15\times10^{-7}}{18\times10^{-2}} = 7.5\times10^4\,V$

Potential at D due to charge at B

$= \dfrac{1}{4\pi\varepsilon_0}\cdot\dfrac{1.5\times10^{-6}}{0.18}$

$= 9\times10^9 \times \dfrac{25\times10^{-7}}{18\times10^{-2}} = 12.5\times10^4\,V$

Total potential at D
$= 7.5 \times 10^4 + 12.5 \times 10^4 = 20 \times 10^4$ V
Intensity of electric field at D due to charge at A

$= \dfrac{1}{4\pi\varepsilon_0}\cdot\dfrac{1.5\times10^{-6}}{0.0324}$ along DF

$= 9\times10^9 \times \dfrac{15\times10^{-7}}{324\times10^{-4}} = 5/12\times10^6\,NC^{-1}$

Intensity of electric field at D due to charge at B

$= \dfrac{1}{4\pi\varepsilon_0}\cdot\dfrac{2.5\times10^6}{0.0324}$ along DG

$= 9\times10^9 \times \dfrac{25\times10^{-7}}{324\times10^{-4}} = 25/36\times10^6\,NC^{-1}$

Angle GDF $= \theta = 2 \times \theta/2 = 2\tan^{-1}(1.5)$
$= 2 \times 56°18' = 112°36'$
$\cos\theta = -0.3843$, $\sin\theta = 0.9232$

Resultant intensity of electric field at D

$$= \left[\left(\frac{5}{12} \times 10^6 \right)^2 + \left(\frac{25}{36} \times 10^6 \right)^2 + 2 \left(\frac{5}{12} \times 10^6 \right) \right.$$

$$\left. \left(\frac{25}{36} \times 10^6 \right) (-0.3843) \right]^{1/2}$$

$$= \left[\frac{25}{144} + \frac{625}{1296} - \frac{250 \times 0.3843}{432} \right]^{1/2} \times 10^6$$

$$= \left[\frac{225 + 625 - 288.225}{1296} \right]^{1/2} \times 10^6$$

$$= \left[\frac{561.775}{1296} \right]^{1/2} \times 10^6 = \frac{23.7}{36} \times 10^6$$

$$= 0.66 \times 10^6 = 6.6 \times 10^5 \text{ NC}^{-1}$$

For direction, for angle α with DF,

$$\tan \alpha = \frac{\dfrac{25}{36} \times 10^6 \times \sin \theta}{\dfrac{5}{12} \times 10^6 + \dfrac{25}{36} \times 10^6 \times \cos \theta}$$

$$= \frac{\dfrac{25}{36} \times 10^6 \times 0.9232}{\dfrac{5}{12} \times 10^6 + \dfrac{25}{36} \times 10^6 \times (-0.3843)}$$

$$= \frac{25 \times 10^6 \times 0.9232}{15 \times 10^6 + 25 \times 10^6 \times (-0.3843)}$$

$$= \frac{25 \times 0.9232}{15 - 25 \times 0.3843}$$

$$= \frac{23.0800}{15 - 9.6075} = \frac{23.08}{5.3925} = 4.2798$$

$\alpha = 76°51'$ along DF.

Note: In the Fig. since,

$$\angle ADC = \frac{\theta}{2} = 65°18'.$$

$$\angle DAC = 90° - (56°18') = 33°42'.$$

Since direction of electric field is $76°51'$ with DF, it will be at an angle

$$= 180° - [(76°51') + (33°42')] = 180° - 110°33' = 69°27'.$$

with line AB, joining the two charges.

2.15 **A spherical conducting shell of inner radius r_1 and outer radius r_2 has a charge Q.**

(a) **A charge q is placed at the centre of the shell. What is the surface charge density on the inner and outer surfaces of the shell?**

(b) **Is the electric field inside a cavity with no charge, zero even if the shell is not spherical, but has any irregular shape? Explain.**

Sol. (a) Surface charge density on the inner and outer shell. Taking a Gaussian surface of radius $r > r_1$ but $r < r_2$. Since the Gaussian surface is inside the conductor, therefore electric field is zero everywhere.

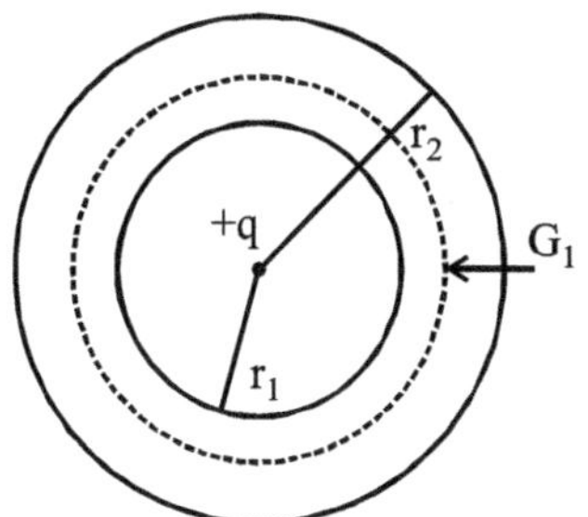

$$\oint E.dA = \frac{q_{enclosed}}{\varepsilon_0} = \frac{q' + q}{\varepsilon_0}$$

where q' be the charge on the inner shell surface.

$$\Rightarrow \oint E.dA = 0 \ [\because E = 0]$$

$$\Rightarrow \frac{q' + q}{\varepsilon_0} = 0 \quad \Rightarrow q' = -q$$

The conducting shell has no net charge, yet its inner shell has $-q$ surface charge. Because the net charge on the shell is zero and no charge can be internal to the conductor, there must be $+q$ charge on the outer surface of the conductor, other than $+Q$.

$\therefore$ Surface charge density of inner surface

$$= \frac{-q}{4\pi r_1^2}$$

And surface charge density of outer surface

$$= \frac{+Q + q}{4\pi r_2^2}.$$

(b) By Gauss's law, the net charge on the inner surface enclosing the cavity (not having any charge) must be zero. For a cavity of arbitrary shape, this is not enough to claim that the electric field inside must be zero. The cavity may have positive and negative charges with total charge zero. To dispose of this possibility, take a closed loop, part of which is inside the cavity along a field line and the rest gives a net work done by the field in carrying a test charge over a closed loop. We know this is impossible for an electrostatic field. Hence there are no field lines inside the cavity i.e., no field, and no charge on the inner surface of the conductor, whatever be its shape.

2.16 (a) **Show that the normal component of electrostatic field has a discontinuity from one side of a charged surface to another given by $(\hat{E}_2 - \hat{E}_1) \cdot \hat{n} = \dfrac{\sigma}{\varepsilon_0}$**

where $\hat{n}$ is a unit vector normal to the surface at a point and σ is the surface charge density at that point. (The direction of $\hat{n}$ is from side 1 to side 2.) Hence show that just outside a conductor, the electric field is $\sigma \hat{n} / \varepsilon_0$.

(b) Show that the tangential component of electrostatic field is continuous from one side of a charged surface to another.

Sol. **(a)** For a plane elementary area ds having surface charge density σ, $q = \sigma ds$

By applying Gauss's theorem,

$$\vec{E}.\hat{n}\,ds = \frac{q}{\varepsilon_0} = \frac{\sigma ds}{\varepsilon_0} \Rightarrow \vec{E}.\hat{n} = \frac{\sigma}{\varepsilon_0}.$$

For (b), use the fact that work done by electrostatic field on a closed loop is zero.

2.17 A long charged cylinder of linear charged density λ is surrounded by a hollow co-axial conducting cylinder. What is the electric field in the space between the two cylinders?

Sol. The charge $+q$ spreads uniformly on the outer surface of A and $-q$ uniformly spreads on the inner surface of B. An electric field $\vec{E}$ is produced between the two shells which will be directed radially outwards as shown in Fig.

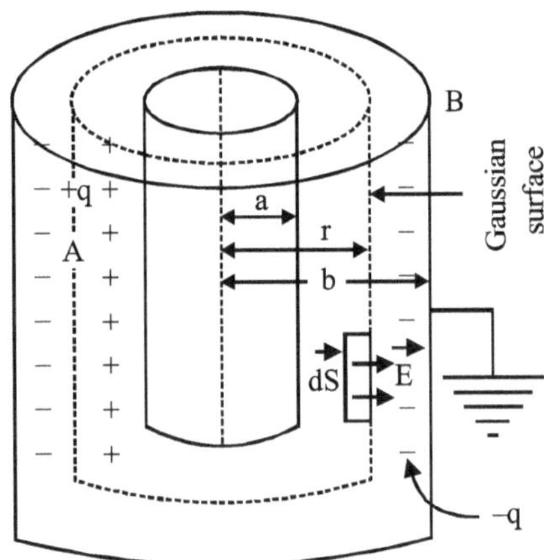

Let us consider a coaxial cylindrical Gaussian surface of radius r. The electric flux through this cylindrical Gaussian surface is given by

$$\phi_E = \int \vec{E}.\vec{ds} = \int EdS\cos 0°$$

$$= E\int dS = E(2\pi r\ell)$$

The flux through the end faces of the Gaussian cylinder is zero because $\vec{E}$ is parallel to them. Hence ϕ_E is the flux through whole of the Gaussian surface.

Applying Gauss's law, $E \times 2\pi r\ell = \dfrac{q}{\varepsilon_0}$

or $\quad E = \dfrac{1}{2\pi\varepsilon_0\ell}.\dfrac{q}{r}$ ...(1)

or $\quad E = \dfrac{1}{2\pi\varepsilon_0 r}.\dfrac{q}{\ell} = \dfrac{1}{2\pi\varepsilon_0 r}.\lambda$

2.18 In a hydrogen atom, the electron and proton are bound at a distance of about 0.53Å.

(a) Estimate the potential energy of the system in eV, taking the zero of the potential energy at infinite separation of the electron from proton.

(b) What is the minimum work required to free the electron, given that its kinetic energy in the orbit is half the magnitude of potential energy obtained in (a)?

(c) What are the answers to (a) and (b) above if the zero of potential energy is taken at 1.06 Å separation?

Sol. **(a)** Given, $q_1 = +1.6 \times 10^{-19}$ C,

$q_2 = -1.6 \times 10^{-19}$ C,

$r = 0.53$ Å $= 0.53 \times 10^{-10}$ m

By formula, potential energy,

$$U = \frac{1}{4\pi\varepsilon_0}.\frac{q_1 q_2}{r}$$

$$= \frac{9\times10^9 \times (1.6\times10^{-19})\times(-1.6\times10^{-19})}{0.53\times10^{-10}}$$

$$= -\frac{144}{53} = -27.17 \text{ eV.}$$

(b) Kinetic energy of electron

$$= +\frac{27.17}{2} = 13.585 \text{ eV.}$$

Total energy of electron
$$= -27.17 + 13.585 = -13.585 \text{ eV.}$$

When electron is free, energy becomes zero.
Then Work done = increase in energy of electron
$$= 0 - (-13.585) = 13.835 \text{ eV.}$$

(c) Potential energy,

$$U = \frac{1}{4\pi\varepsilon_0}.q_1 q_2\left(\frac{1}{r_1} - \frac{1}{r_2}\right)$$

$$= 9 \times 10^9 \times (1.6 \times 10^{-19}) \times (-1.6 \times 10^{-19})$$

$$\left(\frac{1}{0.53\times10^{-10}} - \frac{1}{1.06\times10^{-10}}\right)J = -13.585 \text{ eV.}$$

Kinetic energy of electron $= +13.585$ eV.

2.19 If one of the two electrons of a H_2 molecule is removed, we get a hydrogen molecular ion H_2^+. In the ground state of an H_2^+, the two protons are separated by roughly 1.5 Å, and the electron is roughly 1 Å from each proton. Determine the potential energy of the system. Specify your choice of the zero of potential energy.

Sol. By formula, potential energy of the system
U = P.E. of first proton and electron system + P.E. of second proton and electron system + P.E. of proton and proton system

Applying values, we get

$$U = 9 \times 10^9 \times \frac{(1.6 \times 10^{-19}) \times (-1.6 \times 10^{-19})}{1 \times 10^{-10} \times 1.6 \times 10^{-19}}$$

$$+ 9 \times 10^9 \times \frac{(1.6 \times 10^{-19}) \times (-1.6 \times 10^{-19})}{1 \times 10^{-10} \times 1.6 \times 10^{-19}}$$

$$+ 9 \times 10^9 \times \frac{(1.6 \times 10^{-19})^2}{1.5 \times 10^{-10} \times 1.6 \times 10^{-19}}$$

$$9 \times 10^9 \times \frac{1.6 \times 10^{-19}}{10^{-10}} \left(-\frac{1}{1} - \frac{1}{1} + \frac{1}{1.5} \right) = -19.2 \text{ eV.}$$

(zero of potential energy is taken to be at infinite)

2.20 **Two charged conducting spheres of radii a and b are connected to each other by a wire. What is the ratio of electric fields at the surfaces of the two spheres? Use the result obtained to explain why charge density on the sharp and pointed ends of a conductor is higher than that of its flatter portions.**

Sol. The two spheres in contact will have same electric potential.

Let σ_1 and σ_2 be the surface densities of charge (charge density) on the two spheres respectively.

Then, charge on first sphere, $q_1 = 4\pi a^2 \sigma_1$

charge on second sphere, $q_2 = 4\pi b^2 \sigma_2$

Potential of first sphere, $V_1 = \frac{q_1}{a} = 4\pi a \sigma_1$

Potential of second sphere, $V_2 = \frac{q_2}{b} = 4\pi b \sigma_2$

Electric field of first sphere on the surface,

$$E_1 = \frac{q_1}{a^2} = 4\pi \sigma_1$$

Electric field of second sphere on the surface,

$$E_2 = \frac{q_2}{b^2} = 4\pi \sigma_2$$

Since, $V_1 = V_2$, $4\pi a \sigma_1 = 4\pi b \sigma_2$, i.e. $\dfrac{a}{b} = \dfrac{\sigma_2}{\sigma_1}$

And also $\dfrac{E_1}{E_2} = \dfrac{\sigma_1}{\sigma_2} = \dfrac{b}{a}$.

The ratio of electric field is inverse of the ratio of the radii of the two spheres, since, ratio of charge densities is inverse of the ratio of the radii of the charged surfaces.

For a sharp pointed end, $a = 0$, $\sigma = $ infinite

For flat portion, $a = \infty$, $\sigma = 0$. This explains accumulation of charge at the pointed region of a charged conductor.

2.21 **Two charges –q and +q are located at points (0, 0, – a) and (0, 0, a), respectively.**

(a) **Why is the electrostatic potential at the points (0, 0, z) and (x, y, 0)?**

(b) **Obtain the dependence of potential on the distance r of a point from the origin when r/a >> 1.**

(c) **How much work is done in moving a small test charge from the point (5, 0, 0) to (–7, 0, 0) along the x-axis? Does the answer change if the path of the test charge between the same points is not along the x-axis?**

Sol. **(a)** Distance between points (0, 0, –a) and (0, 0, z) = z + a

Distance between points (0, 0, a) and (0, 0, z) = z – a

Potential due to charge – q at point

$$(0, 0, z) = \frac{1}{4\pi\varepsilon_0} \frac{-q}{z + a}$$

Potential due to charge + q at point

$$(0, 0, z) = \frac{1}{4\pi\varepsilon_0} \frac{q}{z - a}$$

Total potential at point

$$(0, 0, z) = -\frac{q}{4\pi\varepsilon_0 (z + a)} + \frac{q}{4\pi\varepsilon_0 (z - a)}$$

$$= \frac{q}{4\pi\varepsilon_0} \left[\frac{1}{(z - a)} - \frac{1}{(z + a)} \right]$$

$$= \frac{q}{4\pi\varepsilon_0} \times \frac{2a}{z^2 - a^2} = \frac{1}{4\pi\varepsilon_0} \cdot \frac{p}{z^2 - a^2}$$

where $p = q.2a = $ dipole moment of charge system.

Distance between points (0, 0, –a) and

$$(x, y, 0) = \sqrt{x^2 + y^2 + a^2}$$

Distance between points (0, 0, a) and

$$(x, y, 0) = \sqrt{x^2 + y^2 + a^2}$$

Since the two distances are equal and charges are equal and opposite, total potential at point (x, y, 0) = zero.

(b) The dependence on r is $1/r^2$ type

(c) Zero; no, because work done by electrostatic field between two points is independent of the path connecting the two points.

2.22 **Figure shows a charge array known as an electric quadrupole. For a point on the axis of the quadrupole, obtain the dependence of potential on r for r/a >> 1, and contrast your results with that due to an electric dipole, and an electric monopole (i.e., a single charge),**

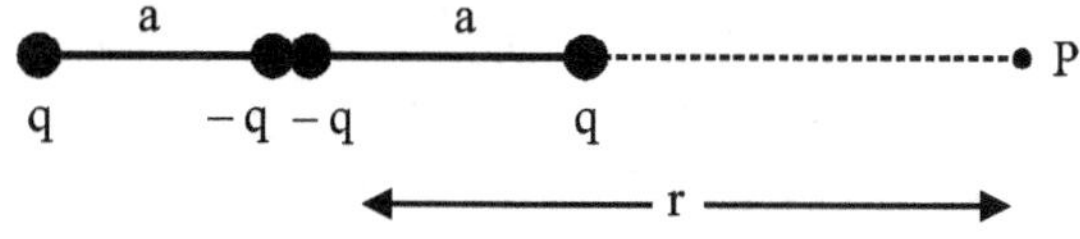

Sol. Situation is shown in following figure.

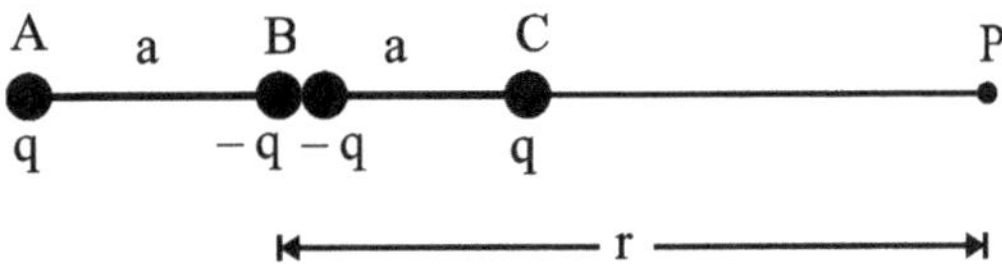

Potential at P due to charge $+q$ at A

$$= \frac{1}{4\pi\varepsilon_0}\cdot\frac{q}{r+a}$$

Potential at P due to charge $-2q$ at B

$$= \frac{1}{4\pi\varepsilon_0}\cdot\frac{-2q}{r}$$

Potential at P due to charge $+q$ at C

$$= \frac{1}{4\pi\varepsilon_0}\cdot\frac{q}{r-a}$$

Total potential at P

$$= \frac{1}{4\pi\varepsilon_0}\left(\frac{q}{r+a}-\frac{2q}{r}+\frac{q}{r-a}\right)$$

$$= \frac{q}{4\pi\varepsilon_0}\left[\frac{r(r-a)-2(r^2-a^2)+r(r+a)}{r(r+a)(r-a)}\right]$$

$$= \frac{q}{4\pi\varepsilon_0}\left(\frac{r^2-ar-2r^2+2a^2+r^2+ar}{r(r^2-a^2)}\right)$$

$$= \frac{q}{4\pi\varepsilon_0}\cdot\frac{2a^2}{r(r^2-a^2)}$$

As $\dfrac{r}{a} \gg 1$ i.e., $r^2 \gg a^2 \Rightarrow r^2-a^2 \to r^2$

Hence $V = \dfrac{2a^2 q}{4\pi\varepsilon_0}\cdot\dfrac{1}{r^3}$ i.e., $V \propto \dfrac{1}{r^3}$ for quadrupole. But

$V \propto \dfrac{1}{r^2}$ for dipole and $V \propto \dfrac{1}{r}$ for monopole.

2.23 **An electrical technician requires a capacitance of 2 μF in a circuit across a potential difference of 1 kV. A large number of 1 μF capacitors are available to him each of which can withstand a potential difference of not more than 400 V. Suggest a possible arrangement that requires the minimum number of capacitors.**

Sol. Since each capacitor can withstand a potential difference of 400 V, at least three must be used in series to share 1 kV potential difference, 3 in series will have capacitance $= (1/3)\,\mu\text{F}$.

To have $2\,\mu\text{F}$ combination, we must connect six such series combinations, in parallel.

Total capacitors required $=$ 3 in series $\times$ 6 in parallel $= 18$

2.24 **What is the area of the plates of a 2 F parallel plate capacitor, given that the separation between the plates is 0.5 cm? [You will realise from your answer why ordinary capacitors are in the range of μF or less. However, electrolytic capacitors do have a much larger capacitance (0.1 F) because of very minute separation between the conductors.]**

Sol. Given, $C = 2\text{F}$, $d = 0.5$ cm $= 0.5 \times 10^{-2}$ m,

$$\varepsilon_0 = \frac{1}{4\pi \times 9 \times 10^9}, \quad A = ?$$

By formula, capacitance, $C = \dfrac{\varepsilon_0 A}{d}$

and $A = \dfrac{Cd}{\varepsilon_0} = 2 \times 0.5 \times 10^{-2} \times 4 \times 3.14 \times 9 \times 10^9$

$\qquad = 113.04 \times 10^7 \text{ m}^2 = 1130.4 \text{ km}^2$

2.25 **Obtain the equivalent capacitance of the network in Fig. For a 300 V supply, determine the charge and voltage across each capacitor.**

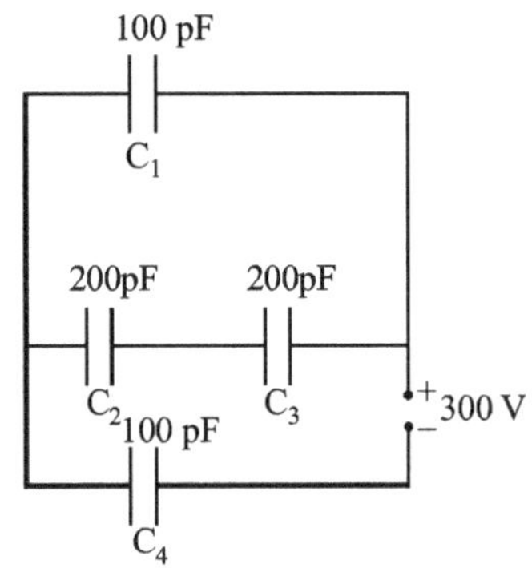

Sol. Figure shows equivalent circuit

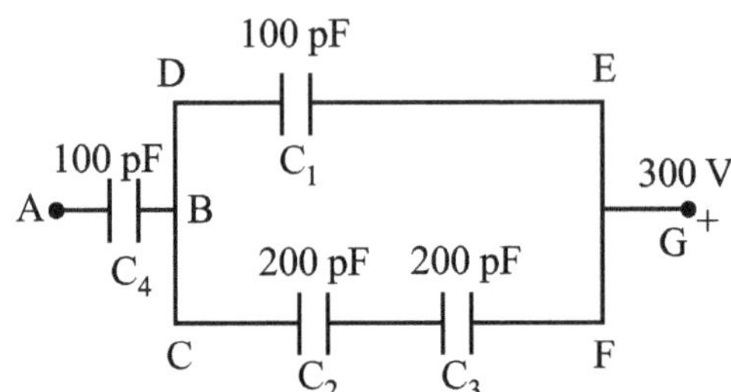

Capacitance between C and F (C_2, C_3 in series) $= 200/2 = 100$ pF

Capacitance between B and G (in parallel)
$\qquad = 100 + 100 = 200$ pF

Capacitance between A and G (in series)
$\qquad = (100 \times 200)/(100 + 200) = (200/3)$ pF

Potential difference of 300 V between A and G divided between points A and B and points B and G, in the inverse ratio of the capacitance between them. Thus,

Potential difference between A and B $= 200$V

Potential difference between B and G $= 100$V

Hence, $V_4 = 200$ V and $q_4 = C_4 V_4$
$\qquad\qquad = 2 \times 10^{-8}$ C

$V_1 = 100$ V and $q_1 = C_1 V_1 = 10^{-8}$ C

$V_2 = V_3 = 50$ V and $q_2 = q_3 = C_2 V_2 = C_3 V_3$
$\qquad = 10^{-8}$ C.

2.26 The plates of a parallel plate capacitor have an area of 90 cm² each and area separated by 2.5 mm. The capacitor is charged by connecting it to a 400 V supply.
    (a) How much electrostatic energy is stored by the capacitor?
    (b) View this energy as stored in the electrostatic field between the plates, and obtain the energy per unit volume u, Hence arrive at a relation between u and the magnitude of electric field E between the plates.

Sol. (a) Given, $A = 90$ cm² $= 90 \times 10^{-4}$ m²,
    $d = 2.5$ mm $= 2.5 \times 10^{-3}$ m, $V = 400$ V, $C = ?$
    By formula, capacitance

$$C = \frac{\varepsilon_0 A}{d} = \frac{1 \times 90 \times 10^{-4}}{4\pi \times 9 \times 10^9 \times 2.5 \times 10^{-3}}$$

$$= \frac{10^{-8}}{4 \times 3.14 \times 25} = \frac{1}{3.14} \times 10^{-10} \text{ F} \text{ and}$$

$$E = \frac{1}{2} CV^2 = \frac{1}{2} \times \frac{1}{3.14} \times 10^{-10} \times 400 \times 400$$

$$= \frac{8}{3.14} \times 10^{-6} = 2.55 \times 10^{-6} \text{ J}.$$

    (b) Volume of medium between parallel plates,
    $V = A \times d = 90 \times 10^{-4} \times 2.5 \times 10^{-3}$
       $= 225 \times 10^{-7}$ m³
    Hence, energy per unit volume,

$$u = \frac{2.55 \times 10^{-6}}{225 \times 10^{-7}} = 0.113 \text{ Jm}^{-3}.$$

2.27 A 4μF capacitor is charged by a 200 V supply. It is then disconnected from the supply, and is connected to another uncharged 2μF capacitor. How much electrostatic energy of the first capacitor is lost in the form of heat and electromagnetic radiation?

Sol. Given, $C_1 = 4\mu F = 4 \times 10^{-6}$ F, $C_2 = 2\mu F = 2 \times 10^{-6}$ F,
    $V_1 = 200$ V, $V_2 = 0$,
    Loss of energy, $\Delta E = ?$
    By formula,

$$\Delta E = \frac{C_1 C_2 (V_1 - V_2)^2}{2(C_1 + C_2)}$$

$$= \frac{4 \times 10^{-6} \times 2 \times 10^{-6} (200 - 0)^2}{2(4 + 2) \times 10^{-6}} = \frac{8}{3} \times 10^{-2} \text{ J}$$

Hence, energy converted into heat and electromagnetic radiation = 2.67×10^{-2} J.

2.28 Show that the force on each plate of parallel plate capacitor has a magnitude equal to (1/2) QE, where Q is the charge on the capacitor, and E is the magnitude of electric field between the plates. Explain the origin of the factor 1/2.

Sol. Suppose we increase the separation of the plates by Δx. Work done by external agency = $F\Delta x$. This goes to increase the potential energy of the capacitor by u and Δx where u is energy density.
$F = ua$ which is easily seen to be (1/2) QE, using u $= (1/2)\varepsilon_0 E^2$. The physical origin of the factor 1/2 in the force formula lies in the fact that just outside the conductor, field is E, and inside it is zero. So the average value E/2 contributes to the force.

2.29 A spherical capacitor consists of two concentric spherical conductors, held in position by suitable insulating supports Fig.

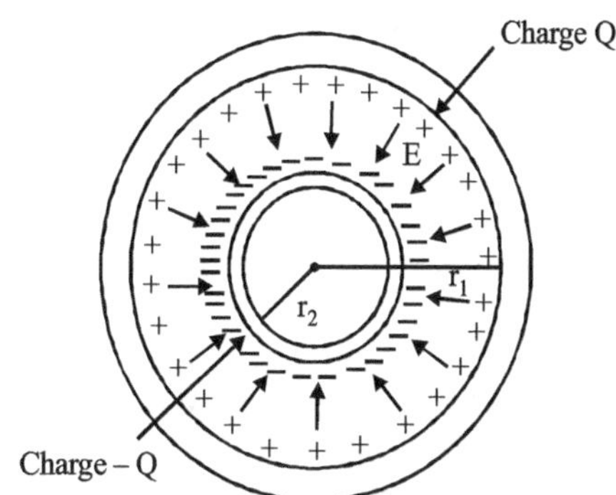

Show that the capacitance of a spherical capacitor is given by, $C = \dfrac{4\pi\varepsilon_0 r_1 r_2}{r_1 - r_2}$

where r_1 and r_2 are the radii of outer and inner spheres, respectively.

Sol. Let r_1 is the radius of the outer sphere B. r_2 is the radius of the inner sphere A.

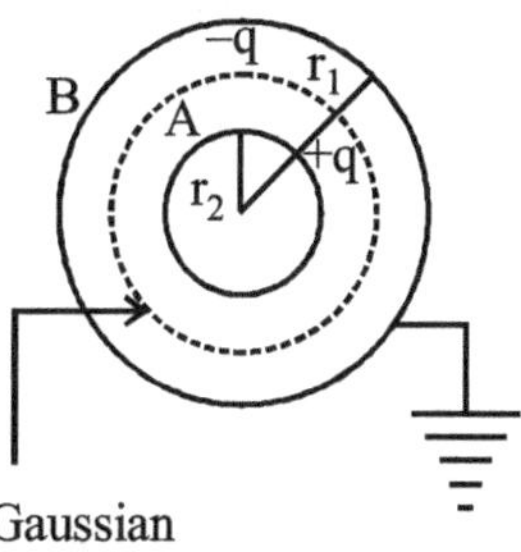

+ q is the charge given to A.
– q is the charge induced to the inner surface of B.
+ q is the charge induced to the outer surface of B which will flow to the earth as B is earthed.
V is the potential difference between A and B.

$\therefore$ Capacitance $C = \dfrac{q}{V}$

The electric field is non uniform in between the two spheres

So, $E = \dfrac{dV}{dr} \Rightarrow dV = Edr$

$\therefore V = \displaystyle\int_A^B dV = \int_{r_2}^{r_1} Edr$

Electric field E at any point on the gaussian surface is radially outwards

By Gauss's theorem, $E = \dfrac{kq}{r^2}$

$$\therefore \quad V = \int_{r_2}^{r_1} \frac{kq}{r^2}.dr = kq\int_{r_2}^{r_1} \frac{dr}{r^2} = kq\left[-\frac{1}{r}\right]_{r_2}^{r_1}$$

$$= kq\left[\frac{1}{r_2}-\frac{1}{r_1}\right] = kq\left[\frac{r_1-r_2}{r_1 r_2}\right]$$

$$C = \frac{q}{V} = \frac{q}{kq\dfrac{r_1-r_2}{r_1 r_2}} = \frac{4\pi\varepsilon_0 r_1 r_2}{r_1-r_2}$$

$$\left[\because \quad k = \frac{1}{4\pi\varepsilon_0}\right]$$

2.30 A spherical capacitor has an inner sphere of radius 12 cm and an outer sphere of radius 13 cm. The outer sphere is earthed and the inner sphere is given a charge of 2.5 μC. The space between the concentric spheres is filled with a liquid of dielectric constant 32.
   (a) Determine the capacitance of the capacitor.
   (b) What is the potential of the inner sphere?
   (c) Compare the capacitance of this capacitor with latter is much smaller.

Sol. Given, $r_1 = 12$ cm $= 12 \times 10^{-2}$ m, $r_2 = 13$ cm $= 13 \times 10^{-2}$ m, $q = 2.5$ μC $= 2.5 \times 10^{-6}$ C, K $= 32$
   (a) By formula, capacitance C

$$= K.4\pi\varepsilon_0 \frac{r_2 r_1}{r_2 - r_1} = \frac{32\times13\times10^{-2}\times12\times10^{-2}}{9\times10^9(13\times10^{-2}-12\times10^{-2})}$$

$$= \frac{1664}{3}\times10^{-11} = 5.55 \times 10^{-9}\text{ F.}$$

   (b) Potential of inner sphere, $V = q/C$

$$= \frac{2.5\times10^{-6}\times3}{1664\times10^{-11}} = 4.5\times10^2\,\text{V.}$$

   (c) Capacitance of sphere, C

$$= 4\pi\varepsilon_0 = \frac{12\times10^{-2}}{9\times10^9} = 1.33\times10^{-11}\text{F.}$$

It is small because it forms no capacitor.

2.31 **Answer carefully:**
   (a) Two large conducting spheres carrying charges Q_1 and Q_2 are brought close to each other. Is the magnitude of electrostatic force between them exactly given by $Q_1 Q_2/4\pi\varepsilon_0 r^2$, where r is the distance between their centres?
   (b) If Coulomb's law involved $1/r^1$ dependence (instead of $1/r^2$), would Gauss's law be still true ?
   (c) A small test charge is released at rest at a point in an electrostatic field configuration. Will it travel along the field line passing through that point?
   (d) What is the work done by the field of a nucleus in a complete circular orbit of the electron? What if the orbit is elliptical?
   (e) We know that electric field is discontinuous across the surface of a charged conductor. Is electric potential also discontinuous there?
   (f) What meaning would you give to the capacitance of a single conductor?
   (g) What meaning would you give to the capacitance of a single conductor?

Sol. (a) No, because charge distributions on the spheres will not be uniform.
   (b) No.
   (c) Not necessarily. (True only if the field line is a straight line.) The field line gives the direction of acceleration, not that of velocity, in general.
   (d) Zero, no matter what the shape of the complete orbit is.
   (e) No, potential is continuous.
   (f) A single conductor is a capacitor with one of the 'plates' at infinity.
   (g) A water molecule has permanent dipole moment. However, detailed explanation of the value of dielectric constant requires microscopic theory and is beyond the scope of the book.

2.32 A cylindrical capacitor has two co-axial cylinders of length 15 cm and radii 1.5 cm and 1.4 cm. The outer cylinder is earthed and the inner cylinder is given a charge of 3.5 μC. Determine the capacitance of the system and the potential of the inner cylinder. Neglect end effects (i.e., bending of field lines at the ends).

Sol. Given, $\ell = 15$ cm $= 15 \times 10^{-2}$ m, $r_1 = 1.4$ cm $= 1.4 \times 10^{-2}$ m, $r_2 = 1.5$ cm $= 1.5 \times 10^{-2}$ m, $q = 3.5$ μC $= 3.5 \times 10^{-6}$ C

By formula, capacitance C

$$= 2\pi\varepsilon_0\ell\,/\log_e\frac{r_2}{r_1} = 2\pi\varepsilon_0\ell\,/2.3026\log_{10}\frac{r_2}{r_1}$$

$$= \frac{1}{2\times9\times10^9}\times\frac{15\times10^{-2}}{2.3026\times0.02996} = 1.2\times10^{-10}\text{ F.}$$

By relation, $V = q/C = \dfrac{3.5\times10^{-6}}{1.2\times10^{-10}} = 2.92\times10^4$ V.

2.33 A parallel plate capacitor is to be designed with a voltage rating 1 kV, using a material of dielectric constant 3 and dielectric strength about 10^7 Vm^{-1}. (Dielectric strength is the maximum electric field a material can tolerate without breakdown, i.e., without starting to conduct electricity through partial ionisation.) For safety, we should like the field never to exceed, say 10% of the dielectric strength. What minimum area of the plates is required to have a capacitance of 50 pF?

Sol. The capacitor must have a tolerance of 10 kV ($\because$ 1 kV is 10% of 10 kV).
Hence minimum dielectric slab thickness,
$d = V/E = 10^4/10^7 = 10^{-3}$ m.
A will be minimum when d is minimum

Now $d = 10^{-3}$ m, $C = 50$ pF $= 50 \times 10^{-12}$ F, $K = 3$, $A = ?$

By formula, capacitance, $C = \dfrac{K\varepsilon_0 A}{d}$

or $A = \dfrac{Cd}{K\varepsilon_0} = \dfrac{50 \times 10^{-12} \times 10^{-3}}{3} \times (4 \times \pi \times 9 \times 10^9)$

$\qquad = 2 \times \pi \times 3 \times 10^{-4} = 18.84 \times 10^{-4} \text{ m}^2 = 18.84 \text{ cm}^2.$

2.34 **Describe schematically the equipotential surfaces corresponding to**

   (a) **a constant electric field in the Z-direction,**

   (b) **a field that uniformly increases in magnitude but remains in a constant (say, Z) direction,**

   (c) **a single positive charge at the origin, and**

   (d) **a uniform grid consisting of long equally spaced parallel charged wires in a plane.**

Sol. **(a)** Planes parallel to X–Y plane

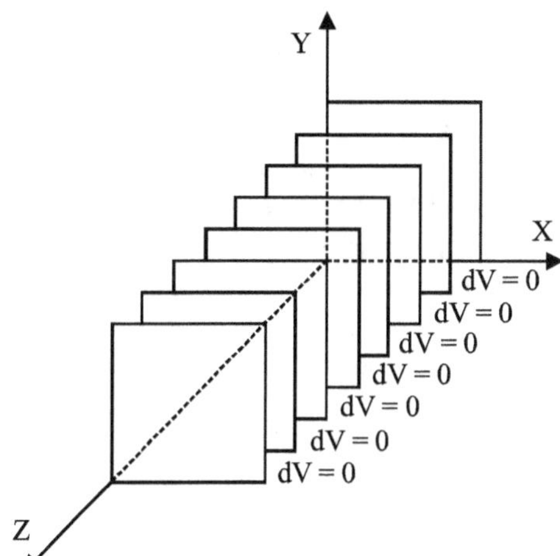

Equipotential surfaces corresponding to a constant electric field in the Z-direction (dV = p.d between successive equipotential surfaces which is zero in this case)

(b) Same as in (a), except that planes differing by a fixed potential get closer as field increases.

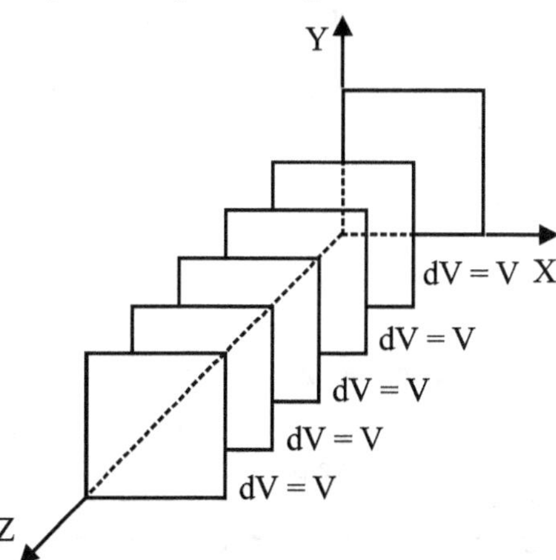

Equipotential surfaces corresponding to a uniformly increasing electric field in the Z-direction

(c) Concentric spheres centered at the origin.

(d) A periodically varying shape near the grid which gradually reaches the shape of planes parallel to the grid at far distances.

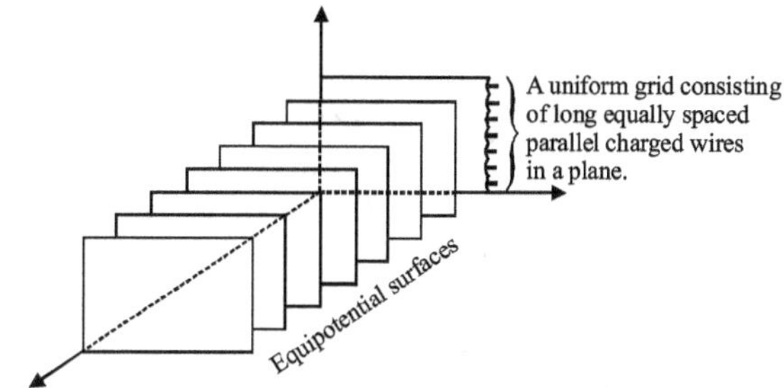

2.35 **In a Van De Graaff generator, a spherical metal shell is to be a 15×10^6 V electrode. The dielectric strength of the gas surrounding the electrode is 5×10^{-7} V/m. What is the minimum radius of the spherical shell required? (You will learn from this exercise why one cannot build an electrostatic generator using a very small shell which requires a small charge to acquire a high potential.)**

Sol. Given, $V = 15 \times 10^6$ V

Dielectric strength of the surrounding gas,

$E = 5 \times 10^7$ V m^{-1}

Radius of spherical shell, $r = ?$

For a spherical shell, $V = \dfrac{1}{4\pi\varepsilon_0} \dfrac{q}{r}$

If σ be surface density of charge, then

$q = 4\pi r^2 \sigma \qquad \therefore \quad V = \dfrac{4\pi r^2 \sigma}{4\pi\varepsilon_0 r} = r\dfrac{\sigma}{\varepsilon_0} = rE$

$\left[\because E = \dfrac{\sigma}{\varepsilon_0}\right]$ we have, $r = V/E$

$\qquad = \dfrac{15 \times 10^6}{5 \times 10^7} = 0.3$ m $= 30$ cm

2.36 **A small sphere of radius r_1 and charge q_1 is enclosed by a spherical shell of radius r_2 and charge q_2. Show that if q_1 is positive, charge will necessarily flow from the sphere to the shell (when the two are connected by a wire) no matter what the charge q_2 on the shell is.**

Sol. Potential of inner sphere due to its own charge $=$

$\dfrac{1}{4\pi\varepsilon_0}\dfrac{q_1}{r_1}$

Potential of inner sphere due to its presence inside the

shell $= \dfrac{1}{4\pi\varepsilon_0}\dfrac{q_2}{r_2}$

Total potential of the sphere $= \dfrac{1}{4\pi\varepsilon_0}\left(\dfrac{q_1}{r_1} + \dfrac{q_2}{r_2}\right)$

Potential of the shell $= \dfrac{1}{4\pi\varepsilon_0}\dfrac{q_2}{r_2}$

Potential difference between sphere and shell

$$= \dfrac{1}{4\pi\varepsilon_0}\left(\dfrac{q_1}{r_1}+\dfrac{q_2}{r_2}\right)-\dfrac{1}{4\pi\varepsilon_0}\dfrac{q_2}{r_2} \;=\; \dfrac{1}{4\pi\varepsilon_0}\dfrac{q_1}{r_1}$$

It is independent of the charge q_2 on the shell. Since q_1 is positive, potential difference between sphere and shell is positive. Charge (if positive) will always flow from sphere to shell.

2.37 **Answer the following:**

(a) The top of the atmosphere is at about 400 kV with respect to the surface of the earth, corresponding to an electric field that decreases with altitude. Near the surface of the earth, the field is about $100\ \text{Vm}^{-1}$. Why then do we not get an electric shock as we step out of our house into the open? (Assume the house to be a steel cage so there is no field inside!)

(b) A man fixes outside his house one evening a two metre high insulating slab carrying on its top a large aluminium sheet of area $1\ \text{m}^2$. Will he get an electric shock if he touches the metal sheet next morning?

(c) The discharging current in the atmosphere due to the small conductivity of air is known to be 1800 A on an average over the globe. Why then does the atmosphere not discharge itself completely in due course and become electrically neutral? In other words, what keeps the atmosphere charged?

(d) What are the forms of energy into which the electrical energy of the atmosphere is dissipated during a lightning? (Hint: The earth has an electric field of about $100\ \text{Vm}^{-1}$ at its surface in the downward direction, corresponding to a surface charge density $=-10^{-9}\ \text{C m}^{-2}$. Due to the slight conductivity of the atmosphere up to about 50 km (beyond which it is good conductor), about $+1800$ C is pumped every second into the earth as a whole. The earth, however, does not get discharged since thunderstorms and lightning occurring continually all over the globe pump an equal amount of negative charge on the earth.)

Sol. (a) Our body and the ground form an equipotential surface. As we step out into the open, the original equipotential surfaces of open, the original equipotential surfaces of open air change, keeping our head and the ground at the same potential.

(b) Yes. The steady discharging current in the atmosphere charges up the aluminium sheet gradually and raises its voltage to an extent depending on the capacitance of the capacitor (formed by the sheet, slab and the ground).

(c) The atmosphere is continually being charged by thunderstorms and lightning all over the globe and discharged through regions of ordinary weather. The two opposing currents are, on an average, in equilibrium.

(d) Light energy involving in lightning; heat and sound energy in the accompanying thunder.

Past year Exercise

Multiple Choice Question

1. An electric dipole consisting of charges $+q$ and $-q$ separated by a distance L is in stable equilibrium in a uniform electric field $\vec{E}$. The electrostatic potential energy of the dipole is

   (a) qLE (b) zero   (c) $-qLE$ (d) $-2\,qEL$

Very Short Answer Questions

2. Name the physical quantity whose SI unit is J/C. Is it a scalar or a vector quantity?

3. A hollow metal sphere of radius 5 cm is charged such that potential on its surface is 10 V. What is the potential at the centre of the sphere?

4. Draw equipotential surface due to a single point charge.

5. Why is electrostatic potential is constant throughout the volume of the conductor and has the same value as on its surface?

6. Write the expression for the work done on an electric dipole of dipole moment $\vec{p}$ in turning it from its position of stable equilibrium to a position of unstable equilibrium in a uniform electric field $\vec{E}$.

7. Two charges of 5μC and -5μC are placed at points A and B 2 cm apart. Depict an equipotential surface of the system.

8. "For any charge configuration, equipotential surface through a point is normal to the electric field." Justify.

9. A point charge $+Q$ is placed at point O as shown in the figure. Is the potential difference $V_A - V_B$ positive, negative or zero?

10. What is the geometrical shape of equipotential surfaces due to single isolated charge?

Short Answer Questions

11. (i) Depict the equipotential surfaces for a system of two identical positive point charges placed a distance d apart.

   (ii) Deduce the expression for the potential energy of a system of two point charges q_1 and q_2 brought from infinity to the points with positions r_1 and r_2 respectively in presence of external electric field E.

12. Net capacitance of three identical capacitors in series is 1 μF. What will be their net capacitance if connected in parallel?
    Find the ratio of energy stored in the two configurations if they are both connected to the same source.

13. Figure shows two identical capacitors C_1 and C_2, each of 2 μF capacitance, connected to a battery of 5V. Initially switch 'S' is closed. After some time S is left open and dielectric slabs of dielectric constant $K = 5$ are inserted to fill completely the space between the plates of the two capacitors. How will the (i) charge and (ii) potential difference between the plates of the capacitors be affected after the slabs are inserted?

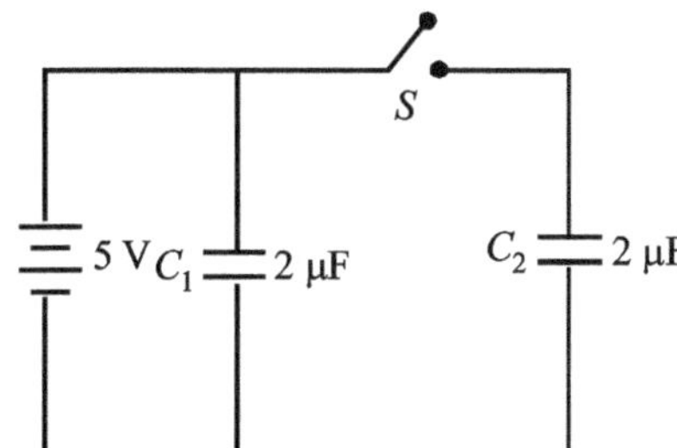

14. Two point charges 3 μC and -3 μC are placed at points A and B, 5 cm apart.
    (i) Draw the equipotential surface of the system.
    (ii) Why do equipotential surfaces get close to each other near the point charge?

15. A test charge, q is moved without acceleration from A to C along the path from A to B and then from B to C in electric field E as shown in the figure. (i) Calculate the potential difference between A and C. (ii) At which point (of the two) is the electric potential more and why?

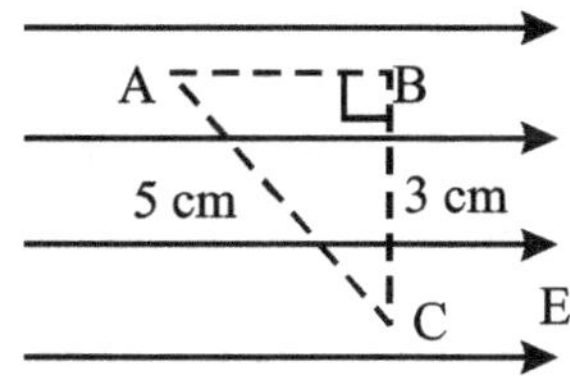

16. A capacitor of unknown capacitance is connected across a battery of V volts. The charge stored in it is 300 μC. When potential across the capacitor is reduced by 100 V, the charge stored in it becomes 100 μC. Calculate the potential V and the unknown capacitance. What will be the charge stored in the capacitor if the voltage applied had increased by 100 V?

17. A slab of material of dielectric constant K has the same area as that of the plates of a parallel plate capacitor but has the thickness 2d/3, where d is the separation between the plates. Find out the expression for its capacitance when the slab is inserted between the plates of the capacitor.

18. A parallel plate capacitor of capacitance C is charged to a potential V. It is then connected to another uncharged capacitor having the same capacitance. Find out the ratio of the energy stored in the combined system to that stored initially in the single capacitor.

19. A capacitor 'C', a variable resistor 'R' and a bulb 'B' are connected in series to the ac mains in circuit as shown. The bulb glows with some brightness. How will the glow of the bulb change if (i) a dielectric slab is introduced between the plates of the capacitor, keeping resistance R to be the same; (ii) the resistance R is increased keeping the same capacitance?

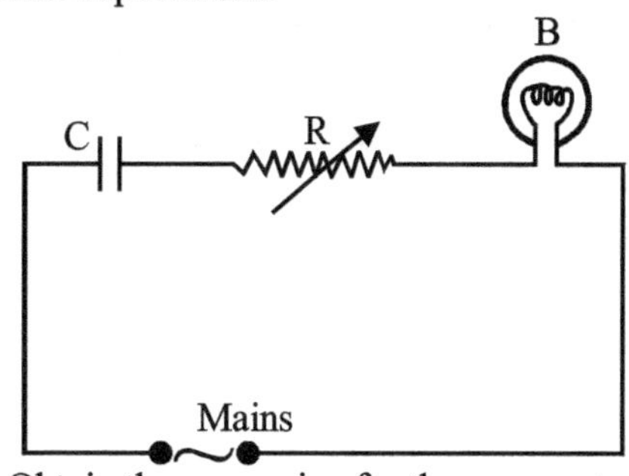

20. (a) Obtain the expression for the energy stored per unit volume in a charged parallel plate capacitor.
    (b) The electric field inside a parallel plate capacitor is E. Find the amount of work done in moving a charge q over a closed loop a b c d a.

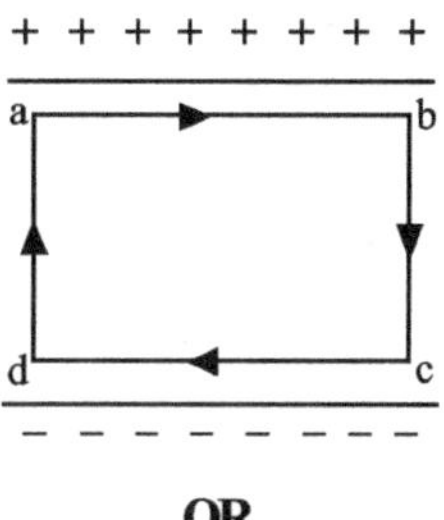

OR

(a) Derive the expression for the capacitance of a parallel plate capacitor having plate area A and plate separation d.
(b) Two charged spherical conductors of radii R_1 and R_2 when connected by a conducting wire acquire charges q_1 and q_2 respectively. Find the ratio of their surface charge densities in terms of their radii.

21. Define an equipotential surface. Draw equipotential surfaces :
    (i) in the case of a single point charge and
    (ii) in a constant electric field in Z-direction.
    Why the equipotential surfaces about a single charge are not equidistant ?
    (iii) Can electric field exist tangential to an equipotential surface ? Give reason.

22. The space between the plates of a parallel plate capacitor is completely filled in two ways. In the first case, it is filled with a slab of dielectric constant K. In the second case, it is filled with two slabs of equal thickness and dielectric constants K_1 and K_2 respectively as shown in the figure. The capacitance of the capacitor is same in the two cases. Obtain the relationship between K, K_1 and K_2.

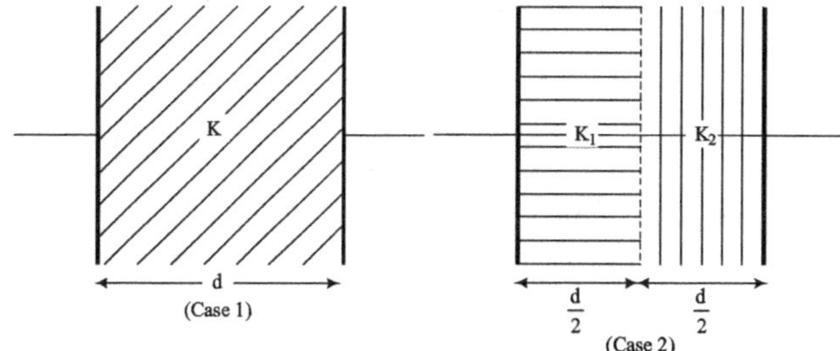

23. A parallel plate capacitor of plate area A each and separation d, is being charged by an ac source. Show that the displacement current inside the capacitor is the same as the current charging the capacitor.

24. Four point charges Q, q, Q and q are placed at the corners of a square of side 'a' as shown in the figure.

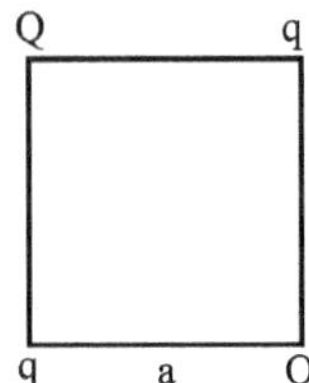

Find the
(a) resultant electric force on a charge Q, and
(b) potential energy of this system.

OR

(a) Three point charges q, – 4q and 2q are placed at the vertices of an equilateral triangle ABC of side 'ℓ' as shown in the figure. Obtain the expression for the magnitude of the resultant electric force acting on the charge q.

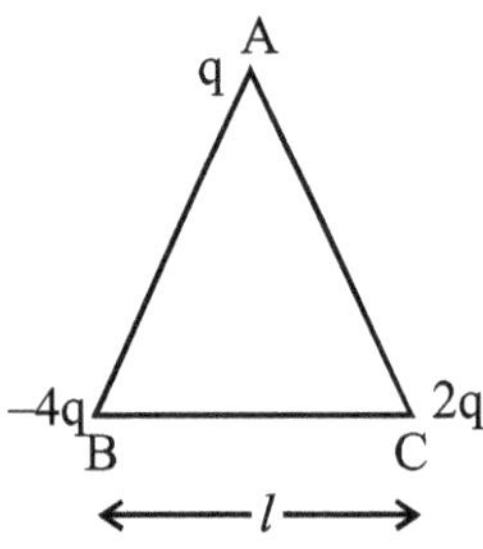

(b) Find out the amount of the work done to separate the charges at infinite distance.

25. Two identical parallel plate capacitors A and B are connected to a battery of V volts with the switch S closed. The switch is now opened and the free space between the plates of the capacitors is filed with a dielectric of dielectric constant K. Find the ratio of the total electrostatic energy stored in both capacitors before and after the introduction of the dielectric.

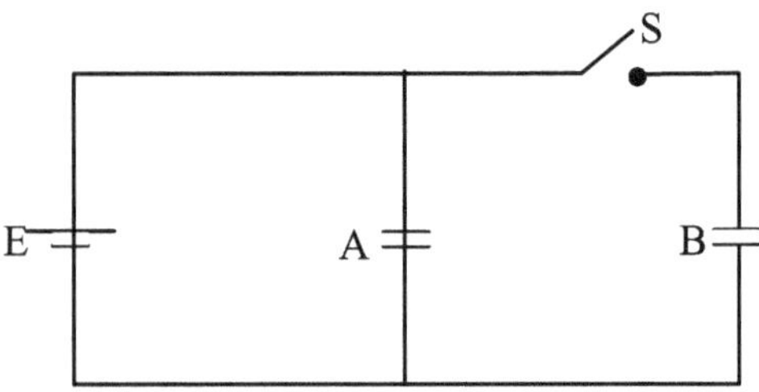

26. An electric dipole of length 4 cm, when placed with its axis making an angle of 60° with a uniform electric field, experiences a torque of $4\sqrt{3}$ Nm. Calculate the potential energy of the dipole, if it has charge ± 8 nC.

NCERT Exemplar

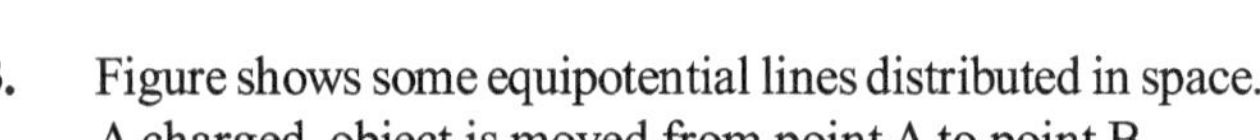

Multiple Choice Questions

1. A capacitor of 4 µF is connected as shown in the circuit. The internal resistance of the battery is 0.5Ω. The amount of charge on the capacitor plates will be

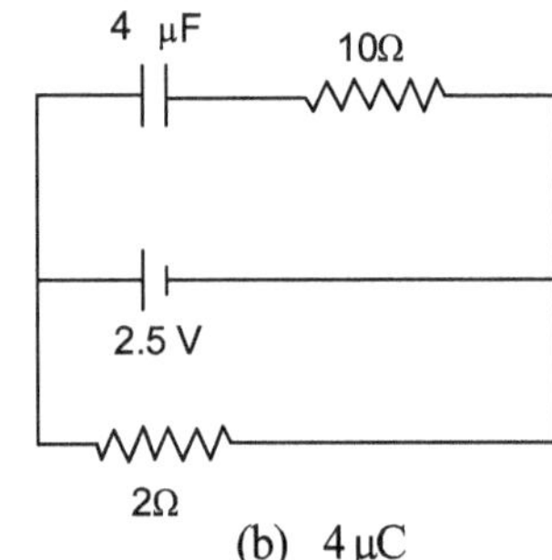

(a) 0 µC   (b) 4 µC
(c) 16 µC   (d) 8 µC

2. A positively charged particle is released from rest in an uniform electric field. The electric potential energy of the charge
(a) remains a constant because the electric field is uniform
(b) increases because the charge moves along the electric field
(c) decreases because the charge moves along the electric field
(d) decreases because the charge moves opposite to the electric field

3. Figure shows some equipotential lines distributed in space. A charged object is moved from point A to point B.
(a) The work done in Fig. (i) is the greatest
(b) The work done in Fig. (ii) is least
(c) The work done is the same in Fig. (i), Fig.(ii) and Fig. (iii)
(d) The work done in Fig. (iii) is greater than Fig. (ii) but equal to that in

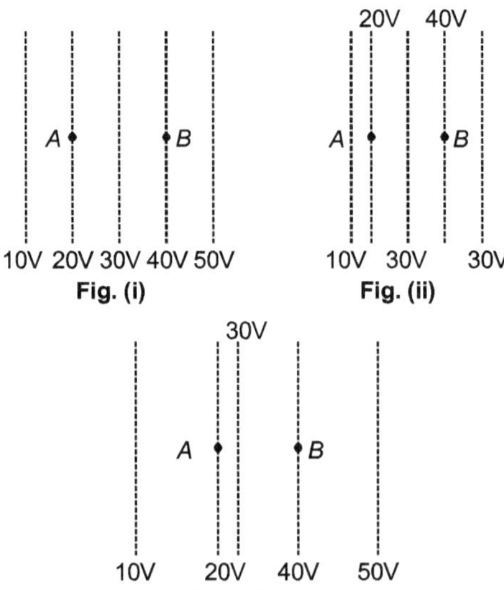

4. The electrostatic potential on the surface of a charged conducting sphere is 100V. Two statements are made in this regard S_1 at any point inside the sphere, electric intensity is zero. S_2 at any point inside the sphere, the electrostatic potential is 100V. Which of the following is a correct statement?
   (a) S_1 is true but S_2 is false
   (b) Both S_1 and S_2 are false
   (c) S_1 is true, S_2 is also true and S_1 is the cause of S_2
   (d) S_1 is true, S_2 is also true but the statements are independant

5. Equipotentials at a great distance from a collection of charges whose total sum is not zero are approximately
   (a) spheres   (b) planes
   (c) paraboloids   (d) ellipsoids

6. A parallel plate capacitor is made of two dielectric blocks in series. One of the blocks has thickness d_1 and dielectric constant K_1 and the other has thickness d_2 and dielectric constant K_2 as shown in figure. This arrangement can be thought as a dielectric slab of thickness d $(= d_1 + d_2)$ and effective dielectric constant K. The K is

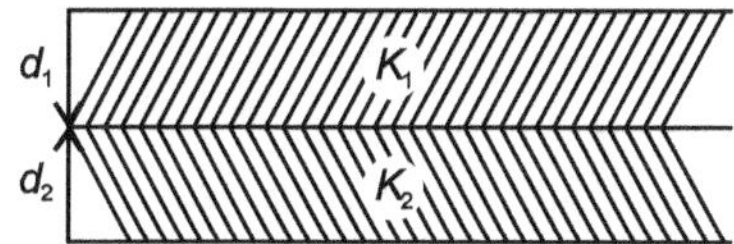

   (a) $\dfrac{K_1 d_1 + K_2 d_2}{d_1 + d_2}$ (b) $\dfrac{K_1 d_1 + K_2 d_2}{K_1 + K_2}$

   (c) $\dfrac{K_1 K_2 (d_1 + d_2)}{(K_1 d_2 + K_2 d_1)}$ (d) $\dfrac{2K_1 K_2}{K_1 + K_2}$

Very Short Answer Questions

7. Consider two conducting spheres of radii R_1 and R_2 with $R_1 > R_2$. If the two are at the same potential, the larger sphere has more charge than the smaller sphere. State whether the charge density of the smaller sphere is more or less than that of the larger one.

8. A test charge q is made to move in the electric field of a point charge Q along two different closed paths (Fig.) First path has sections along the perpendicular to lines of electric field. Second path is a rectangular loop of the same area as the first loop. How does the work done compare in the two cases?

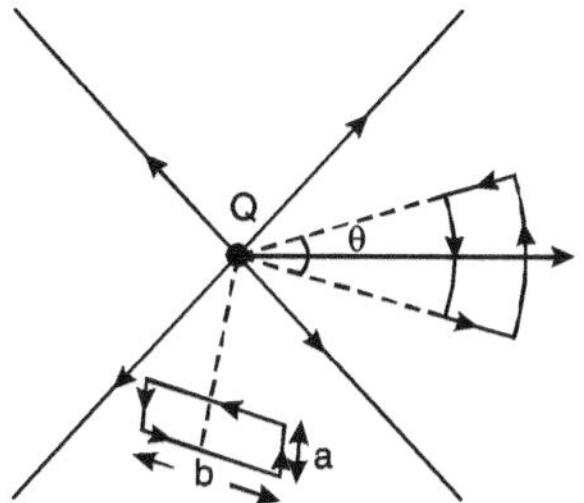

9. Prove that a closed equipotential surface with no charge within itself must enclose an equipotential volume.

10. Three charged particles are initially in position 1. They are free to move and they come in position 2 after some time. Let U_1 and U_2 be the electrostatic potential energies in position 1 and 2. Which is greater U_1 or U_2 and why?

11. When a car is moved into a painting chamber, a mist of paint is sprayed around it. When the body of the car is given a sudden electric charge and the mist of paint is attracted to it, presto—the car is quickly and uniformly painted. What does the phenomenon of polarization have to do with this?

Short Answer Questions

12. Calculate potential energy of a point charge $-q$ placed along the axis due to a charge $+Q$ uniformly distributed along a ring of radius R. Sketch P.E. as a function of axial distance z from the centre of the ring. Looking at graph, can you see what would happen if $-q$ is displaced slightly from the centre of the ring (along the axis)?

13. A solid conducting sphere having a charge Q is surrounded by an uncharged concentric conducting hollow spherical shell. Let the potential difference between the surface of the solid sphere and that of the outer surface of the hollow shell be V. If the shell is now given a charge of $-3Q$, what will be the new potential difference between the same two surfaces?

14. A hollow sphere of radius 2R is charged to V volts and another smaller sphere of radius R is charged to V/2 volts. Now the smaller sphere is placed inside the bigger sphere without changing the net charge on each sphere. What would be the potential difference between the two spheres?

Objective Practice Exercise

Multiple Choice Questions

DIRECTIONS : *This section contains multiple choice questions. Each question has four choices (a), (b), (c) and (d) out of which only one is correct.*

1. The electric potential inside a conducting sphere
   (a) increases from centre to surface
   (b) decreases from centre to surface
   (c) remains constant from centre to surface
   (d) is zero at every point inside

2. In a region of constant potential
   (a) the electric field is uniform
   (b) the electric field is zero
   (c) the electric field shall necessarily change if a charge is placed outside the region
   (d) None of these

3. It becomes possible to define potential at a point in an electric field because electric field
   (a) is a conservative field
   (b) is a non-conservative field
   (c) is a vector field
   (d) obeys principle of superposition

4. Which of the following about potential at a point due to a given point charge is true ?
   The potential at a point P due to a given point charge
   (a) is a function of distance from the point charge.
   (b) varies inversely as the square of distance from the point charge.
   (c) is a vector quantity
   (d) is directly proportional to the square of distance from the point charge.

5. A cube of a metal is given a positive charge Q. For this system, which of the following statements is true?
   (a) Electric potential at the surface of the cube is zero
   (b) Electric potential within the cube is zero
   (c) Electric field is normal to the surface of the cube
   (d) Electric field varies within the cube

6. There are two metallic spheres of same radii but one is solid and the other is hollow, then
   (a) solid sphere can be given more charge
   (b) hollow sphere can be given more charge
   (c) they can be charged equally (maximum)
   (d) None of the above

7. The electric potential due to the pair of charges ($+ 10\mu c$ and $+ 20\ \mu c$ the middle of the line joing them is [if sepration is 2 cm]
   (a) $27\,MV$ (b) $35\,MV$ (c) $37\,MV$ (d) $40\,MV$

8. Potential due to electric dipole along equatorial line is.
   (a) maximum   (b) increasing
   (c) zero   (d) None of these

9. Figure below shows a hollow conducting body placed in an electric field. Which of the quantities are zero inside the body?
   (a) Electric field and potential
   (b) Electric field and charge density
   (c) Electric potential and charge density.
   (d) Electric field, potential and charge density.

10. The positive terminal of 12 V battery is connected to the ground. Then the negative terminal will be at
    (a) $-6\,V$ (b) $+12\,V$ (c) zero   (d) $-12\,V$

11. Let V be the electric potential at a given point. Then the electric field E_x along x-direction at that point is given by
    (a) $\int_0^\infty V dx$ (b) $\dfrac{dV}{dx}$ (c) $-\dfrac{dV}{dx}$ (d) $-V\dfrac{dV}{dx}$

12. The electric field is along the direction in which the potential
    (a) increases at max^m rate   (b) decreases at max^m rate
    (c) increases at min^m rate   (d) None of these

13. Potential at any point inside a charged hollow sphere
    (a) increases with distance
    (b) is a constant
    (c) decreases with distance from centre
    (d) is zero

14. A solid sphere of radius R has uniform volume charge density. The electric potential at a points (r <R) is
    (a) due to the charge inside a sphere of radius r only
    (b) due to the entire charge of the sphere
    (c) due to the charge in the spherical sheel of inner and outer radii r and R, only
    (d) independent of r

15. A, B and C are three points in a uniform electric field. The electric potential is
    (a) maximum at B
    (b) maximum at C
    (c) same at all the three points A, B and C
    (d) maximum at A

16. Identify the false statement.
    (a) Inside a charged or neutral conductor, electrostatic field is zero
    (b) The electrostatic field at the surface of the charged conductor must be tangential to the surface at any point
    (c) There is no net charge at any point inside the conductor
    (d) Electrostatic potential is constant throughout the volume of the conductor

17. Three charges 2 q, – q and – q are located at the vertices of an equilateral triangle. At the centre of the triangle
    (a) the field is zero but potential is non-zero
    (b) the field is non-zero, but potential is zero
    (c) both field and potential are zero
    (d) both field and potential are non-zero

18. The electrostatic potential energy of a system of two charges is negative when
    (a) both the charges are positive
    (b) both the charges are negative
    (c) one charge is positive and other is negative
    (d) both the charges are separated by infinite distance

19. Two conducting spheres of radii R_1 and R_2 having charges Q_1 and Q_2 respectively are connected to each other. There is
    (a) no change in the energy of the system
    (b) an increase in the energy of the system
    (c) always a decrease in the energy of the system
    (d) a decrease in the energy of the system unless $Q_1 R_2 = Q_2 R_1$

20. A ball of mass 1 g carrying a charge 10^{-8} C moves from a point A at potential 600 V to a point B at zero potential. The change in its K.E. is
    (a) -6×10^{-6} erg   (b) -6×10^{-6} J
    (c) 6×10^{-6} J   (d) 6×10^{-6} erg

21. On moving a charge of 20 coulomb by 2 cm, 2 J of work is done, then the potential difference between the points is
    (a) $0.1\,V$ (b) $8\,V$ (c) $2\,V$ (d) $0.5\,V.$

22. Two points P and Q are maintained at the potentials of 10 V and – 4 V, respectively. The work done in moving 100 electrons from P to Q is:
    (a) 9.60×10^{-17} J   (b) -2.24×10^{-16} J
    (c) 2.24×10^{-16} J   (d) -9.60×10^{-17} J

23. A and B are two points in an electric field. If the work done in carrying 4.0C of electric charge from A to B is 16.0 J, the potential difference between A and B is
    (a) zero   (b) $2.0\,V$ (c) $4.0\,V$ (d) $16.0\,V$

24. A system of three positive charges placed at the vertices of an equilateral triangle. To decrease the potential energy of the system,

(a) a positive charge should be placed at centroid
(b) a negative charge should be placed at centroid.
(c) distance between the charges should be decreased.
(d) it should be rotated by an angle of $\dfrac{\pi}{2}$ radian.

25. The work done in carrying a charge q once around a circle of radius r with a charge Q placed at the centre will be
(a) $Qq(4\pi\varepsilon_0 r^2)$
(b) $Qq/(4\pi\varepsilon_0 r)$
(c) zero
(d) $Qq^2/(4\pi\varepsilon_0 r)$

26. On decreasing the distance between the plates of a parallel plate capacitor, its capacitance
(a) remains unaffected
(b) decreases
(c) first increases then decreases.
(d) increases

27. A sheet of aluminium foil of negligible thickness is introduced between the plates of a capacitor. The capacitance of the capacitor
(a) decreases   (b) remains unchanged
(c) becomes infinite   (d) increases

28. The potential gradient at which the dielectric of a condenser just gets punctured is called
(a) dielectric constant   (b) dielectric strength
(c) dielectric resistance   (d) dielectric number

29. When air in a capacitor is replaced by a medium of dielectric constant K, the capacity
(a) decreases K times   (b) increases K times
(c) increases K^2 times   (d) remains constant

30. Capacitors are used in electrical circuits where appliances need more
(a) voltage   (b) current
(c) resistance   (d) power

31. A parallel plate capacitor is charged by connecting it to a battery. Now the distance between the plates of the capacitor is increased. Which of the following remains constant ?
(a) Capacitance
(b) Charge on each plate of the capacitor.
(c) Potential difference between the plates of capacitor
(d) Energy stored in the capacitor.

32. A parallel plate condenser is immersed in an oil of dielectric constant 2. The field between the plates is
(a) increased, proportional to 2
(b) decreased, proportional to $\dfrac{1}{2}$
(c) increased, proportional to -2
(d) decreased, proportional to $-\dfrac{1}{2}$

33. Capacitance (in F) of a spherical conductor with radius 1 m is
(a) 1.1×10^{-10} (b) 10^6
(c) 9×10^{-9} (d) 10^{-3}

34. A parallel plate capacitor is charged to a certain voltage. Now, if the dielectric material (with dielectric constant k) is removed then the

(a) capacitance increases by a factor of k
(b) electric field reduces by a factor k
(c) voltage across the capacitor decreases by a factor k
(d) None of these.

35. A dielectric slab is inserted between the plates of an isolated charged capacitor. Which of the following quantities remain unchanged ?
(a) The charge on the capacitor
(b) The stored energy in the Capacitor
(c) The potential difference between the plates
(d) The electric field in the capacitor

36. The capacitors of capacity C_1 and C_2 are connected in parallel, then the equivalent capacitance is
(a) $C_1 + C_2$ (b) $\dfrac{C_1 C_2}{C_1 + C_2}$ (c) $\dfrac{C_1}{C_2}$ (d) $\dfrac{C_2}{C_1}$

37. A conductor carries a certain charge. When it is connected to another uncharged conductor of finite capacity, then the energy of the combined system is
(a) more than that of the first conductor
(b) less than that of the first conductor
(c) equal to that of the first conductor
(d) uncertain

38. In a charged capacitor, the energy resides
(a) in the positive charges.
(b) in both the positive and negative charges.
(c) in the field between the plates.
(d) around the edges of the capacitor plates.

39. To obtain 3 µF capacity from three capacitors of 2 µF each, they will be arranged.
(a) all the three in series
(b) all the three in parallel
(c) two capacitors in series and the third in parallel with the combinatioin of first two
(d) two capacitors in parallel and the third in series with the combinatioin of first two

40. Three capacitors each of capacitance C and of breakdown voltage V are joined in series. The capacitance and breakdown voltage of the combination will be
(a) $3C, \dfrac{V}{3}$ (b) $\dfrac{C}{3}, 3V$ (c) $3C, 3V$ (d) $\dfrac{C}{3}, \dfrac{V}{3}$

41. A 5.0 µF capacitor is charged to a potential difference of 800 V and discharged through a conductor. The energy given to the conductor during the discharge is
(a) 1.6×10^{-2} joule   (b) 3.2 joule
(c) 1.6 joule   (d) 4.2 joule

42. In the given figure, the charge on 3 µF capacitor is
(a) 10µC
(b) 15µ
(c) 30µC
(d) 5µC

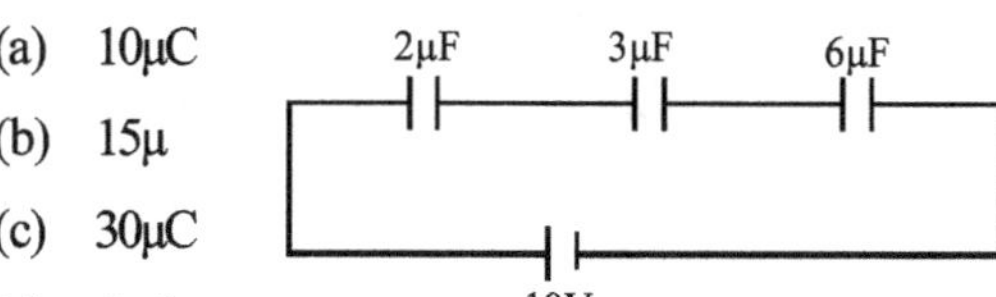

43. An electric dipole consisting of charges $+q$ and $-q$ separated by a distance L is in stable equilibrium in a uniform electric field $\vec{E}$. The electrostatic potential energy of the dipole is **[CBSE 2020]**

(a) qLE (b) zero   (c) $-qLE$ (d) $-2\,qEL$

44. A capacitor of 4 μF is connected as shown in the circuit. The internal resistance of the battery is 0.5Ω. The amount of charge on the capacitor plates will be

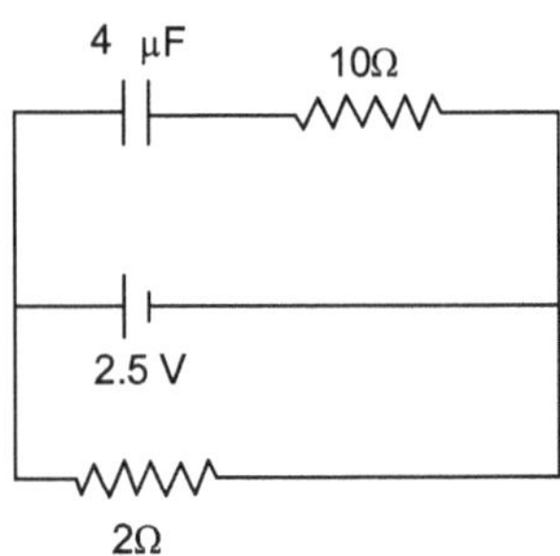

(a) $0\ \mu C$ (b) $4\ \mu C$ (c) $16\ \mu C$ (d) $8\ \mu C$

45. A positively charged particle is released from rest in an uniform electric field. The electric potential energy of the charge

(a) remains a constant because the electric field is uniform

(b) increases because the charge moves along the electric field

(c) decreases because the charge moves along the electric field

(d) decreases because the charge moves opposite to the electric field

46. Figure shows some equipotential lines distributed in space. A charged object is moved from point A to point B.

(a) The work done in Fig. (i) is the greatest

(b) The work done in Fig. (ii) is least

(c) The work done is the same in Fig. (i), Fig.(ii) and Fig. (iii)

(d) The work done in Fig. (iii) is greater than Fig. (ii) but equal to that in

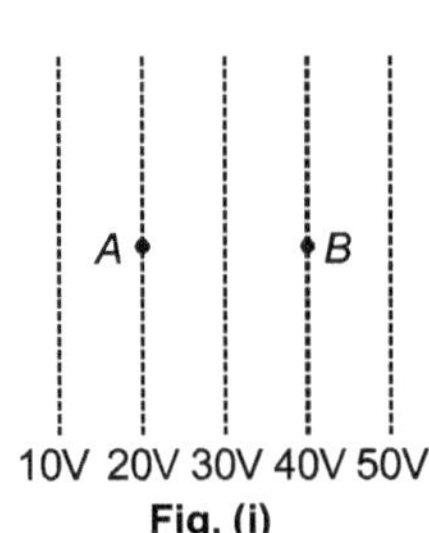

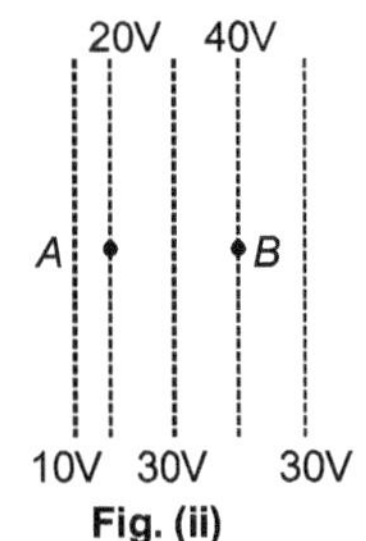

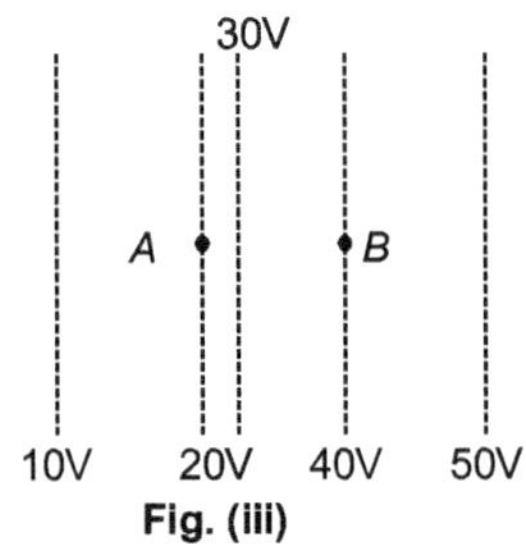

47. The electrostatic potential on the surface of a charged conducting sphere is 100V. Two statements are made in this regard S_1 at any point inside the sphere, electric intensity is zero. S_2 at any point inside the sphere, the electrostatic potential is 100V. Which of the following is a correct statement?

(a) S_1 is true but S_2 is false

(b) Both S_1 and S_2 are false

(c) S_1 is true, S_2 is also true and S_1 is the cause of S_2

(d) S_1 is true, S_2 is also true but the statements are independant

48. A parallel plate capacitor is made of two dielectric blocks in series. One of the blocks has thickness d_1 and dielectric constant K_1 and the other has thickness d_2 and dielectric constant K_2 as shown in figure. This arrangement can be thought as a dielectric slab of thickness d $(= d_1 + d_2)$ and effective dielectric constant K. The K is

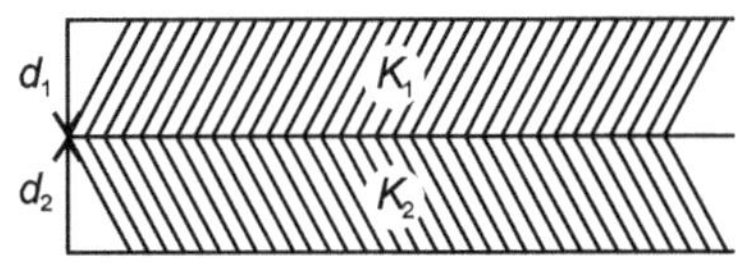

(a) $\dfrac{K_1 d_1 + K_2 d_2}{d_1 + d_2}$ (b) $\dfrac{K_1 d_1 + K_2 d_2}{K_1 + K_2}$

(c) $\dfrac{K_1 K_2 (d_1 + d_2)}{(K_1 d_2 + K_2 d_1)}$ (d) $\dfrac{2K_1 K_2}{K_1 + K_2}$

49. Charges are placed on the vertices of a square as shown. Let $\vec{E}$ be the electric field and V the potential at the centre. If the charges on A and B are interchanged with those on D and C respectively, then

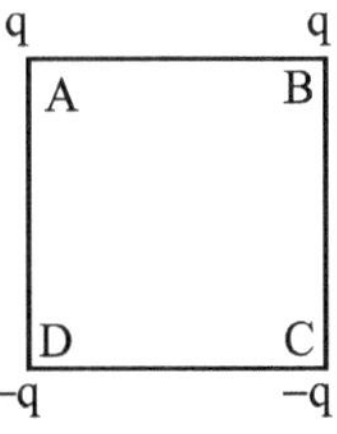

(a) $\vec{E}$ changes, V remains unchanged

(b) $\vec{E}$ remains unchanged, V changes

(c) both $\vec{E}$ and V change

(d) $\vec{E}$ and V remain unchanged

50. Two conducting spheres of radii R_1 and R_2 having charges Q_1 and Q_2 respectively are connected to each other. There is

(a) no change in the energy of the system

(b) an increase in the energy of the system

(c) always a decrease in the energy of the system

(d) a decrease in the energy of the system unless $Q_1 R_2 = Q_2 R_1$

Chapter Test

Time : 30 minutes   **Max. Marks : 15**

Direction :

Each question number **1-15** carry **1 mark** each.

1. Charges are placed on the vertices of a square as shown. Let $\vec{E}$ be the electric field and V the potential at the centre. If the charges on A and B are interchanged with those on D and C respectively, then

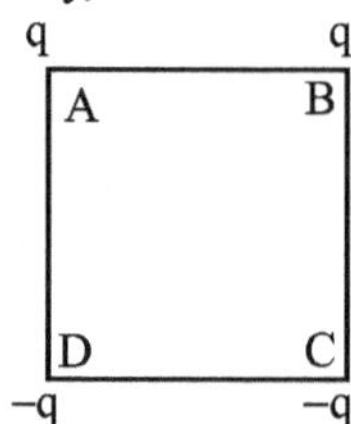

   (a) $\vec{E}$ changes, V remains unchanged
   (b) $\vec{E}$ remains unchanged, V changes
   (c) both $\vec{E}$ and V change
   (d) $\vec{E}$ and V remain unchanged

2. Two conducting spheres of radii R_1 and R_2 having charges Q_1 and Q_2 respectively are connected to each other. There is
   (a) no change in the energy of the system
   (b) an increase in the energy of the system
   (c) always a decrease in the energy of the system
   (d) a decrease in the energy of the system unless $Q_1R_2 = Q_2R_1$

3. Three capacitors are connected in the arms of a triangle ABC as shown in figure 5 V is applied between A and B. The voltage between B and C is

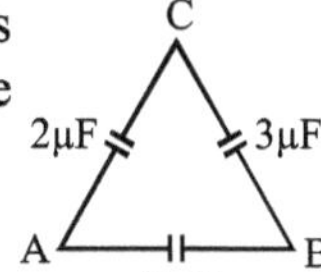

   (a) 2V   (b) 1V
   (c) 3V   (d) 1.5V

4. The electric potential V is given as a function of distance $\times$ (metre) by
   $V = (5 x^2 + 10 x - 4)$ volt. Value of electric field at x = 1 m is
   (a) -23 V/m   (b) 11 V/m
   (c) 6 V/m   (d) -20 V/m

DIRECTIONS (Qs. 5-6) : Each of these questions contains an assertion followed by reason. Read them carefully and answer the question on the basis of following options. You have to select the one that best describes the two statements.
   (a) If both Assertion and Reason are correct and the Reason is a correct explanation of the Assertion.
   (b) If both Assertion and Reason are correct but Reason is not a correct explanation of the Assertion.
   (c) If the Assertion is correct but Reason is incorrect.
   (d) If the Assertion is incorrect but the Reason is correct.

5. **Assertion :** Rate of change of potential is maximum at right angles to an equipotential surface.
   Reason : There is no net force is acting on the dipole in a uniform electric field.

6. **Assertion :** A dielectric is inserted between the plates of a battery connected capacitor. The potential difference between the plates remains constant.
   Reason : As the battery remains connected maintaining the same potential difference.

DIRECTIONS : (Qs. 7-11) *are case based questions.*

Combination of capacitors in series

Equivalent capacitance of capacitors

$$\frac{1}{C_S} = \frac{1}{C_1} + \frac{1}{C_2} + \frac{1}{C_3} + ... + \frac{1}{C_n}$$

Combination of capacitors in parallel

Equivalent capacitance of capacitors,
$$C_P = C_1 + C_2 + C_3 + ... + C_n$$

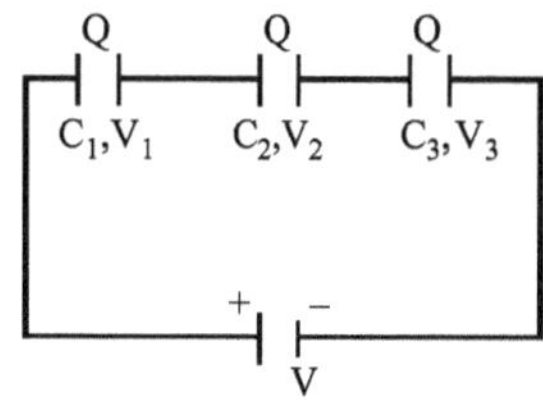

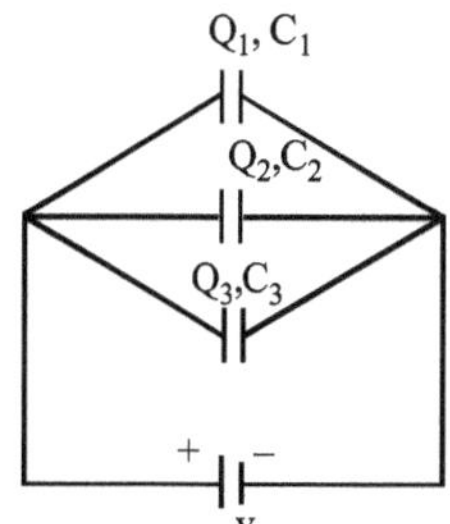

7. The capacitor, whose capacitance is 6, 6 and $3\mu F$ respectively are connected in series with 20 volt line. Find the charge on $3\mu F$.

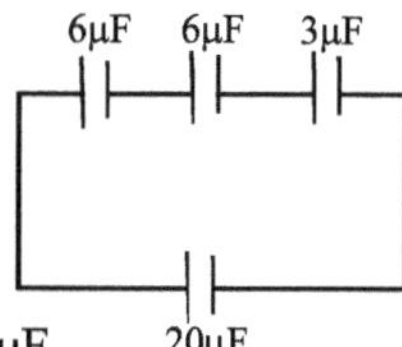

   (a) $30\ \mu c$ (b) $60\ \mu F$
   (c) $15\ \mu F$ (d) $90\ \mu F$

8. Three condensor each of capacitance 2F are put in series. The resultant capacitance is
   (a) 6 F (b) 3/2 F (c) 2/3 F (d) 5 F

9. To obtain $3\,\mu F$ capacity from three capacitors of $2\,\mu F$ each, they will be arranged.
   (a) all the three in series
   (b) all the three in parallel
   (c) two capacitors in series and the third in parallel with the combinatioin of first two
   (d) two capacitors in parallel and the third in series with the combinatioin of first two

10. A combination of parallel plate capacitors is maintained at a certain potential difference.

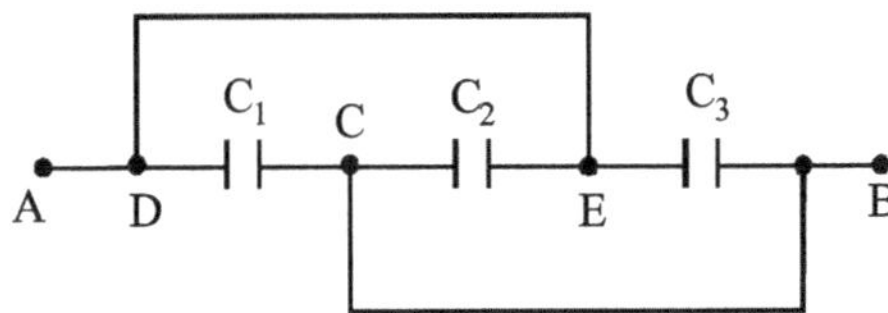

   When a 3 mm thick slab is introduced between all the plates, in order to maintain the same potential difference, the distance between the plates is increased by 2.4 mm. Find the dielectric constant of the slab.
   (a) 3 (b) 4 (c) 5 (d) 6

11. Two capacitors of capacitances $3\mu F$ and $6\mu F$ are charged to a potential of 12V each. They are now connected to each other, with the positive plate of each joined to the negative plate of the other. The potential difference across each will be
   (a) zero (b) 4 *V*
   (c) 6 *V* (d) 12 *V*

Very Short Answer Type Questions

12. Two spherical conductors A and B of radii r_A and r_B ($r_A > r_B$) are given equal amounts of charge. In which direction will the charge flow when these spheres are brought in contact?
    Give reason for your answer.

13. Two capacitors $3\,\mu F$ and $6\,\mu F$ are connected in series with a 6 V battery. Across which of the capacitors will there be larger potential difference?

14. Three identical capacitors C_1, C_2 and C_3 are joined to a battery of e.m.f e as shown in the figure. Let V_1, V_2 and V_3 be the potential differences across C_1, C_2 and C_3 respectively. How are V_1, V_2 and V_3 related to one another and with E.

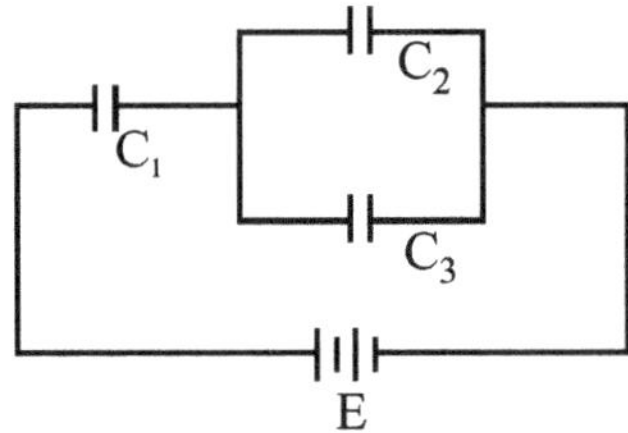

15. A sheet of aluminium foil of negligible thickness is introduced between the plates of a capacitor. The capacitance of the capacitor.

Solutions 

Practice Exercise-1 

1. **(b)** Potential at any point inside the sphere = potential at the surface of the sphere = 10V.

2. **(a)** Let the side length of square be 'a' then potential at centre O is

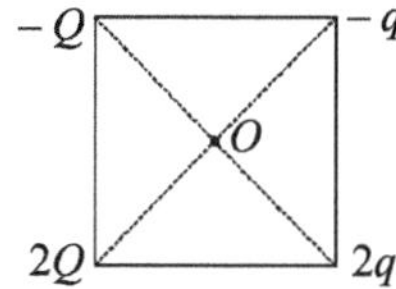

$$V = \frac{k(-Q)}{\left(\dfrac{a}{\sqrt{2}}\right)} + \frac{k(-q)}{\dfrac{a}{\sqrt{2}}} + \frac{k(2q)}{\dfrac{a}{\sqrt{2}}} + \frac{k(2Q)}{\dfrac{a}{\sqrt{2}}} = 0 \text{ (Given)}$$

$$= -Q - q + 2q + 2Q = 0 = Q + q = 0 \Rightarrow Q = -q$$

3. **(c)** The potential at P due to whole disc is

$$V = \frac{\sigma}{2\,\epsilon_0}\left[\sqrt{R^2 + r^2} - r\right]$$

Now potential due to quarter disc,

$$V = \frac{V}{4} = \frac{\sigma}{8\,\epsilon_0}\left[\sqrt{R^2 + r^2} - r\right]$$

4. **(c)** Electric field lines are always perpendicular to equipotential surface so, they cannot be in a direction of tangent to an equipotential surface.

5. **(c)** Electric potential inside a conductor is constant and it is equal to that on the surface of the conductor.

6. **(b)** Irrespective of the charges on the inner and outer conductors, the inner conductor is always at a higher potential as long as the charge on inner conductor is not zero. Therefore charge flows from B to A. When the whole charge of B flows to A and charge on B becomes zero then A and B are at same potential.

7. **(c)**

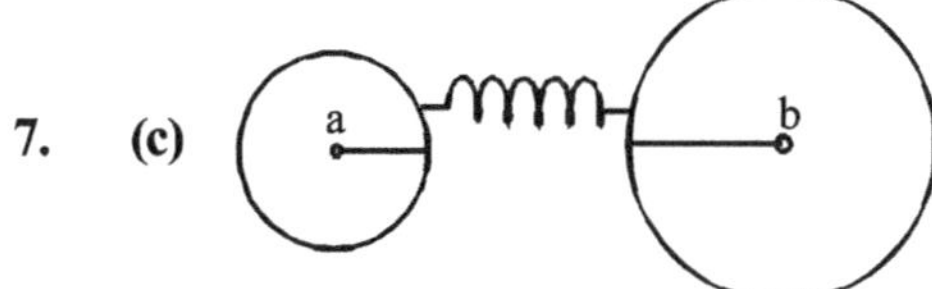

Let charge on each sphere $= q$
when they are connected together their potential will be equal.
Now let charge on a $= q_1$ and on b $= 2q - q_1$

$$\Rightarrow V_a = V_b \text{ or } \frac{1}{4\pi\varepsilon_0}\frac{q_1}{a} = \frac{1}{4\pi\varepsilon_0}\frac{2q - q_1}{b}$$

$$\Rightarrow \frac{q_1}{2q - q_1} = \frac{a}{b}$$

$$\frac{E_a}{E_b} = \frac{\dfrac{1}{4\pi\varepsilon_0}\dfrac{q_1}{a^2}}{\dfrac{1}{4\pi\varepsilon_0}\dfrac{q_2}{b^2}} = \left(\frac{q_1}{2q - q_1}\right)\frac{b^2}{a^2}$$

$$= \frac{a}{b}\cdot\frac{b^2}{a^2} = \frac{b}{a} = b : a$$

8. **(b)**

9. **(b)** $\vec{E} = \dfrac{\partial v}{\partial x}\hat{i} + \dfrac{\partial v}{\partial y}\hat{j}$ $\quad \therefore |\vec{E}| = k(\sqrt{x^2 + y^2}) = kr$

Given $v = -kxy$ $\quad E \propto r$

$$\therefore \vec{E} = ky\hat{i} + kx\hat{j}$$

10. **(b)** In shell, q charge is uniformly distributed over its surface, it behaves as a conductor.

$V=$ potential at surface $= \dfrac{q}{4\pi\varepsilon_0 R}$

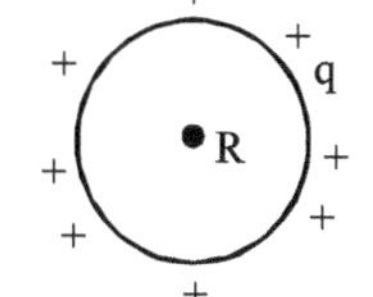

and inside $V = \dfrac{q}{4\pi\varepsilon_0 R}$

Because of this it behaves as an equipotential surface.

11. **(d)** $V_{\text{point charge}} = \dfrac{Kq}{r}$ and $V_{\text{dipole}} = \dfrac{KP}{r^2}$

12. **(d)**   **13.** **(b)**

14. **(b)** $W_{\text{el.}} = q(V_i - V_f)$

or $\quad 6.4 \times 10^{-19} = -1.6 \times 10^{-19}(V_A - V_B)$

or $\quad V_A - V_B = -4V$

or $\quad V_A - V_C = -4V \qquad (\because V_B = V_C)$

or $\quad V_C - V_A = 4V$

15. **(c)** Equipotential surfaces are normal to the electric field lines. The following figure shows the equipotential surfaces along with electric field lines for a system of two positive charges.

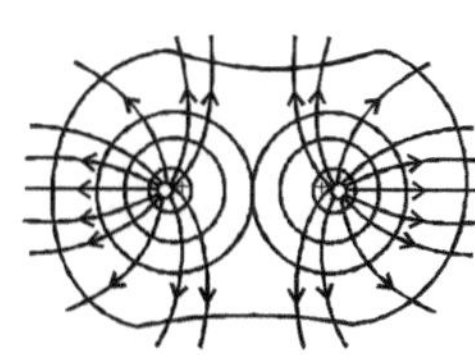

16. **(a)** $E = 500\,\text{V/m} \qquad\qquad V = 3000\,\text{V}.$

We know that electric field $(E) = 500 = \dfrac{V}{d}$

or $d = \dfrac{3000}{500} = 6\,\text{m}$

17. **(b)** At. equipotential surface, the potential is same at any point i.e., $V_A = V_B$ as shown in figure. Hence no work is required to move unit change from one point to another i.e.,

$$V_A - V_B = \frac{W}{\text{unit charge}} = 0 \Rightarrow W = 0$$

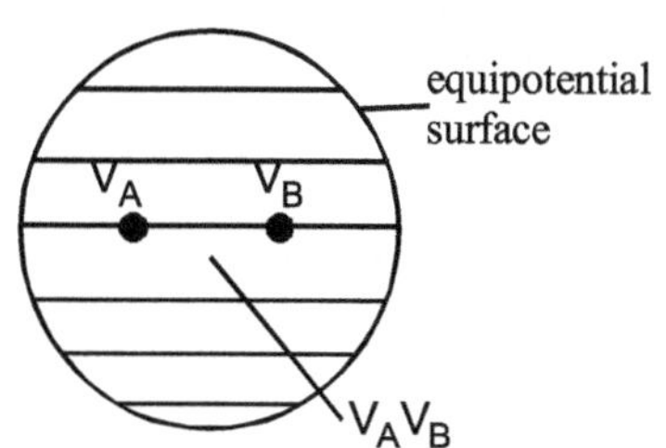

18. No, it is not necessary.

$\because \quad E = -\dfrac{dV}{dr}$

$\therefore$ If V is constant, E will be zero.

Ex: The electric field inside a hollow spherical conductor is zero but potential is not zero.

19. Electric field, $E = -\dfrac{dV}{dr}$

i.e. electric field at a point is the negative of the electric potential gradient at that point.

20. It is a plane surface perpendicular to the electric field.

21. An equipotential surface is that at every point of which electric potential is same. Consider two points A and B on the equipotential surface.

By definition, potential difference between two points A and B = work done in carrying a unit positive charge from A to B.

$\Rightarrow \quad V_A - V_B = W_{AB} = \vec{E}.d\vec{\ell}$

But $V_A = V_B \qquad \therefore \vec{E}.d\vec{\ell} = 0$

$\Rightarrow \quad Edl\cos\theta = 0 \Rightarrow \cos\theta = 0 \Rightarrow \theta = 90°$

$\therefore \quad \vec{E} \perp d\vec{\ell}$

$\therefore$ Electric field $(\vec{E})$ is directed perpendicular to the equipotential surface.

22. Charge on gold nucleus $= q = Ze = 79 \times 1.6 \times 10^{-19}$

$V = \dfrac{kq}{r} = \dfrac{9 \times 10^9 \times 79 \times 1.6 \times 10^{-19}}{6.6 \times 10^{-15}}$

$= 1.724 \times 10^7 \, V.$

Practice Exercise-2

1. (a) Force on a charge q in a uniform electric field E is, $F = qE$, work done = force × distance = qEy.

2. (d) In an external electric field, the positive and negative charges of a non-polar molecule are displaced in opposite directions. The displacement stops when the external force on the constituent charges of the molecule is balanced by the restoring force (due to internal fields in the molecule). The non-polar molecule thus develops an induced dipole moment. The dielectric is said to be polarised by the external field.

3. (d) $W = PE(\cos 90° - \cos 270°) = 0$

4. (b) $A \to (2); B \to (3); C \to (4); D \to (1)$

Electrice field is zero inside a conductor placed in an external field.

Electrice potential is zero at the centre of a dipole.

Torque is zero when a dipole in stable equilibrium.

Potential energy is zero if a electric dipole perpendicular to uniform electice field.

5. (c) Since $V = \dfrac{W}{Q}$, more work will be done for a positive charge of two units as compared to positive charge of one unit, but the ratio $\dfrac{W}{Q}$ is same. Therefore potential difference is same.

6. (a) As $(V_B - V_A) = \dfrac{W_{AB}}{q} = -\int_A^B \vec{E}.d\vec{\ell}$

$= kq\left[\dfrac{1}{r_A} - \dfrac{1}{r_B}\right]$

Which depends on the initial and final position.

7. (c) 8. (c) 9. (a)

10. (c) The potential energy is negative whenever there is attraction. Since a positive and negative charge attract each other therefore their energy is negative. When both the charges are separated by infinite distance, they do not attract each other and their energy is zero.

11. (b) When the charge is released to move freely, the work done by electric field is equal to change in kinetic energy

$\therefore \quad W_{EF} = \Delta KE$

$- q\,\Delta V = \Delta KE$

$KE = -3 \times 10^{-6}(1-5) = 12 \times 10^{-6} \, J$

12. (a) Here, $V_A = V_B = \dfrac{1}{4\pi\varepsilon_0} \cdot \dfrac{Q}{a/\sqrt{2}}$

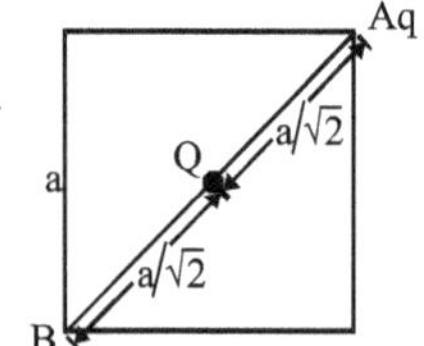

Hence, $V_A - V_B = 0$

Work done, $W = q(V_A - V_B) = 0$

13. (a) 14. (d)

15. The dotted circle is an equipotential surface, so work done will be zero.

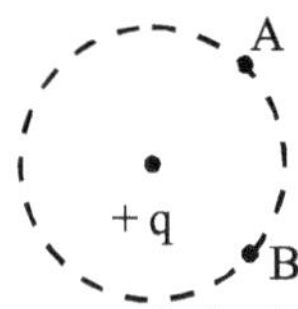

16. Work done will be same in both the paths as electrostatic force is conservative in nature, so work done doesn't depend on the path followed.

17. (a) $q_A = +2 \, \mu C, q_B = +4 \, \mu C, r = 0.5 \, m.$

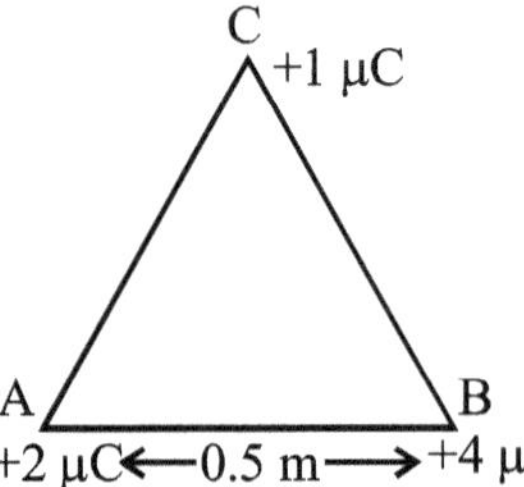

Electrostatic Potential energy $= \dfrac{kq_A q_B}{r}$

$= \dfrac{9 \times 10^9 \times 2 \times 10^{-6} \times 4 \times 10^{-6}}{0.5} = 0.144 \, J$

(b) Potential energy of the system,

$U = k\left[\dfrac{q_A q_B}{0.5} + \dfrac{q_A q_C}{1} + \dfrac{q_B q_C}{1}\right]$

$= 9 \times 10^9 [2 \times 4 \times 2 + 2 \times 1 + 4 \times 1] \times 10^{-12}$

$= 9 \times 10^9 [16 + 2 + 4] \times 10^{-12} = 198 \times 10^{-3} \, J.$

18. Potential difference between the plates

$\Delta V = 10 - 0 = 10$ V (B is grounded so its potential is zero)

(i) $E = \dfrac{\Delta V}{d} = \dfrac{10}{10^{-2}} = 10^3$ V/m

(ii) Plate A is an equipotential surface.
Hence work done in moving a charge of 10 μC from X to Y is zero.

Practice Exercise-3

1. **(d)** Since capacitance $C = \dfrac{\varepsilon_0 A}{d}$, as d decreases capacitance increases.

2. **(d)** (A) → (3); (B) → (1); (C) → (4); (D) → (2)

W.d. by battery A, $= 2\left(\dfrac{1}{2}C_1 V_1^2\right) = 2 \times 2^2 = 8$J

W.d. by battery B, $= 2\left[\dfrac{1}{2}CV_2^2\right]$

$= 2\left[\dfrac{1}{2} \times \dfrac{4 \times 2}{4+2} \times 4^2\right] = \dfrac{64}{3}$ J

$q_2 = CV_2 = \left(\dfrac{4 \times 2}{4+2}\right) \times 4 = \dfrac{16}{3}$

$q_1 = C_1 V_1 = 2 \times 2 = 4$

3. **(a)** PE, $U_0 = Q^2/2C$

When a slab of dielectric constant k is inserted, then $C' = Ck$

$U' = \dfrac{Q^2}{2C'} = \dfrac{Q^2}{2Ck} = \dfrac{U_0}{k}$

4. **(c)** $\dfrac{1}{C'} = \dfrac{1}{C} + \dfrac{1}{C} + \dfrac{1}{C} = \dfrac{3}{C} \Rightarrow C' = \dfrac{C}{3}$

$V' = V_1 + V_2 + V_3 = V + V + V = 3V$

5. **(c)** Battery is disconnected so Q will be constant as $C \propto k$. So with introduction of dielectric slab capacitance will increase using Q = CV, V will decrease and using $U = \dfrac{Q^2}{2C}$, energy will decrease.

6. **(a)** A, B, C and D are equipotential points (see fig.)

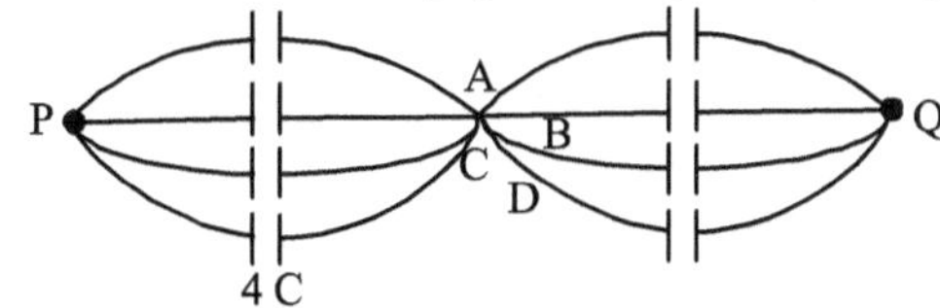

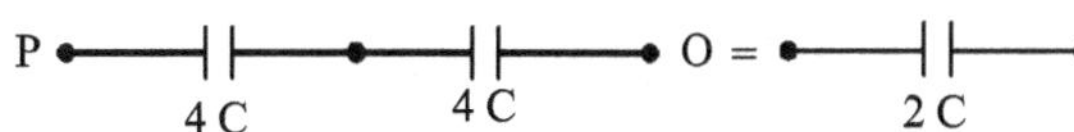

7. **(c)** $C' = kC$, and so, $U' = \dfrac{1}{2}(kC)V^2 = kU$. Also $q' = C'V$ $= kCV = kq$, and so charge density increases.

8. **(a)**

9. **(a)** In the battery connected capacitor V remains constant while C increases with the introduction of dielectric.

10. **(d)**

11. **(c)** Plate 2 and plate 3 jointly.

$\dfrac{(150-x)}{3} + \dfrac{(600-x)}{6} - 200 = 0$

12. **(b)** Hence, find charge on 6 μF capacitor is $q_1 = 700$ μC

13. **(d)** Charge on 3 μF is $q_2 = 250$ μC

$q_1 = (600 - x)$ $\quad$ $q_2 = (150 - x)$

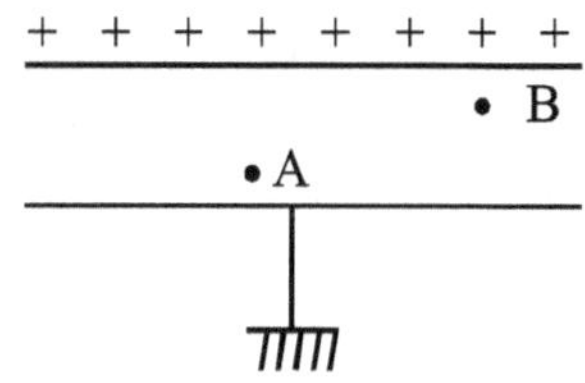

200 V

14. **(d)** Plates 2 and 3 and plates 1 and 4 form isolated system.

Hence $q_1 = q_2 = q_3 = x = -100$ μC

15. **(b)** Energy stored in capacitor will convert into heat.

$= \dfrac{1}{2}CV^2 = \dfrac{1}{2} \times 2 \times 10^{-6} \times (100)^2 = 0.01$ J

16. Electric field between the plates of a capacitor is uniform that is constant at every point $\left(E = \dfrac{\sigma}{\varepsilon_0}\right)$

$\therefore$ Electric field is same at A and B.

17. Energy $= \dfrac{1}{2}CV^2 = \dfrac{1}{2} \times 470 \times 10^{-6} \times (20)^2$
$= 94 \times 10^{-3}$ J.

18. The quantity is capacitance $\left(C = \dfrac{Q}{V}\right)$. It is a scalar quantity.

19. Two 10 μF capacitors are in parallel,

$\therefore$ $C_p = 10 + 10 = 20$ μF

20 μF and C are in series, $C_{eq} = \dfrac{20 \times C}{20 + C}$

$\Rightarrow 15 = \dfrac{20 + C}{20 + C} \Rightarrow C = 60$ μF

20. C and 20 μF are in series. $C_{eq} = 15$ μF

$\therefore$ $\dfrac{1}{15} = \dfrac{1}{20} + \dfrac{1}{C} \Rightarrow \dfrac{1}{C} = \dfrac{1}{15} - \dfrac{1}{20}$

$\Rightarrow \dfrac{1}{C} = \dfrac{4-3}{60} = \dfrac{1}{60} \Rightarrow C = 60$ μF.

21. As volume of bigger drop = Volume of n small drop.

i.e., $\dfrac{4}{3}\pi R^3 = n \times \dfrac{4}{3}\pi r^3$ $\quad$ i.e., $R = n^{1/3}$ r.

As capacity varies directly to radius, capacity of bigger radius becomes $n^{1/3}$ times the capacity of each small drop.

22. Combining the capacitances in series in the each branch between the points A and B and then, combining them in parallel, we get

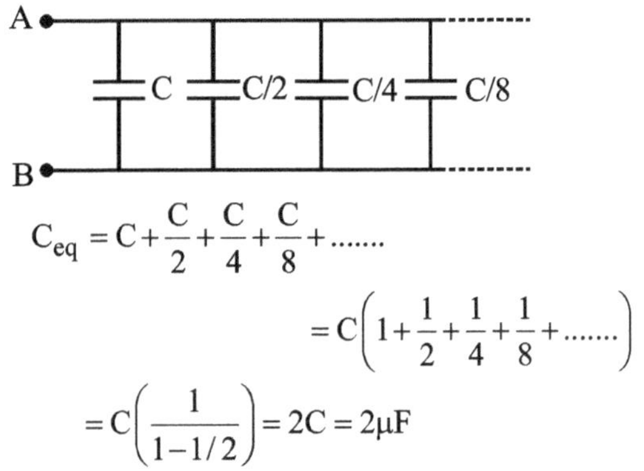

$$C_{eq} = C + \frac{C}{2} + \frac{C}{4} + \frac{C}{8} + \dots$$

$$= C\left(1 + \frac{1}{2} + \frac{1}{4} + \frac{1}{8} + \dots\right)$$

$$= C\left(\frac{1}{1 - 1/2}\right) = 2C = 2\mu F$$

23. We have $Q = CV$ or $V = \dfrac{Q}{C}$

$$\Rightarrow \quad \frac{Q}{4\pi\varepsilon_0 r} = \frac{9\times 10^9 \times 1}{10^{-2}} = 9 \times 10^{11} \text{ Volt.}$$

So it is not possible for a metallic sphere to hol d a charge of 1C because the potential is so high that electric breakdown of air will occur and the entire charge will leak out.

24. Here $C_1 = \dfrac{\varepsilon_0 A}{d} = 10 \text{ pF}$, $C_2 = \dfrac{k\varepsilon_0 A}{d/2}$

$$= 10 \times 10 \times 2 \text{ pF} = 200 \text{ pF.}$$

25. 5 μF, 10 μF and 15 μF are in parallel

$5 + 10 + 15 = 30 \text{ μF}$

2, 30 μF capacitors are in series.

$$\frac{1}{30} + \frac{1}{30} = \frac{1}{C_s} \Rightarrow \quad C_s = 15 \text{ μF.}$$

Past year Exercise

1. **(c)** Potential energy of a dipole in external field U is

$$U = -\vec{P} \cdot \vec{E}$$

for stable equilibrium $\theta = 0°$

$$U = -p E \cos 0° = -pE$$

$$\therefore \qquad U = -qLE$$

2. J/C is the SI unit of electric potential. It is a scalar quantity.

3. The electric potential at every point throughout the volume of the charged spherical shell is same.

Therefore, the electric potential at the center of sphere is 10 V.

4. Equipotential surfaces due to a single point charge are concentric sphere

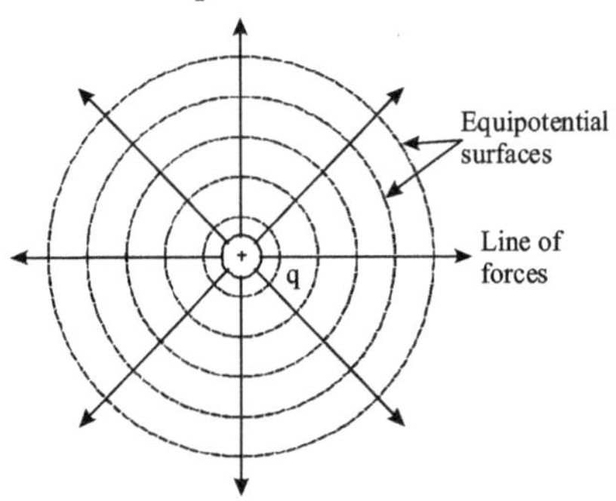

5. Electro field intensity inside the conductor is zero.

So, $\quad E = -\dfrac{\Delta V}{\Delta r}$

As, $E = 0 \Rightarrow \Delta V = 0$

or $\quad V_2 - V_1 = 0$ or, $V_2 = V_1$

The potential at every point inside the conductor remain same.

6. Work done, $W = 2pE$

7. The equipotential surface of the system is as shown :

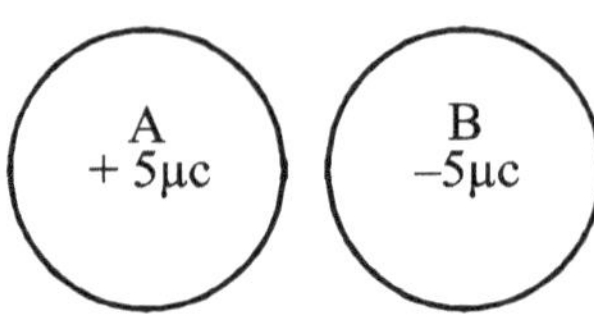

8. So, the work done (W) in moving a test charge along an equipotential surface is zero. Consider two points A and B on the equipotential surface.

By definition, potential difference between two points A and B = work done in carrying a unit positive charge from A to B.

$$\Rightarrow \quad V_A - V_B = W_{AB} = \vec{E}.d\vec{\ell}$$

But $\quad V_A = V_B \qquad \therefore \vec{E}.d\vec{\ell} = 0$

$$\Rightarrow Ed\ell \cos\theta = 0 \Rightarrow \cos\theta = 0 \Rightarrow \theta = 90°$$

$$\therefore \qquad \vec{E} \perp d\vec{\ell}$$

$\therefore$ Electric field $(\vec{E})$ is directed perpendicular to the equipotential surface.

9. Electric potential at a distance r from the point charge

$$V(r) = \frac{1}{4\pi\varepsilon_0} \frac{Q}{r}$$

Potential at point A will be

$$V(r_A) = \frac{1}{4\pi\varepsilon_0} \frac{Q}{r_A}$$

Similarly, potential at point B will be

$$V(r_B) = \frac{1}{4\pi\varepsilon_0} \frac{Q}{r_A} \qquad \because r_A < r_B$$

$$\Rightarrow V_A > V_B \qquad \therefore V_A - V_B > 0$$

10. Spherical.

11. (i) The figure is shown below.

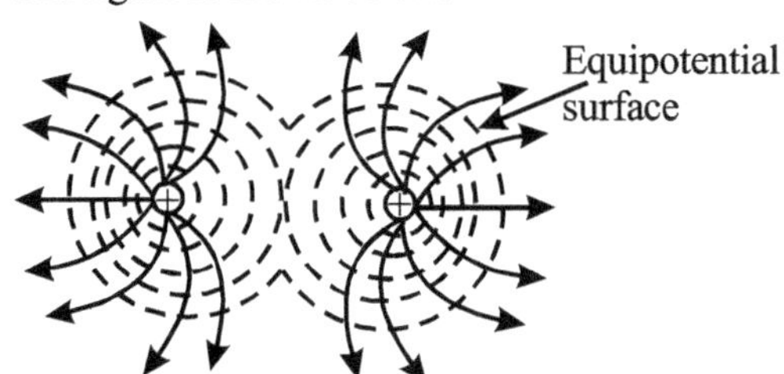

Equipotential surfaces of two identical positive charges

(ii) By definition, electric potential energy of any charge q placed in the region of electric field is equal to the work done in bringing charge q from infinity to that point and given by

$$U = qV$$

Now, considering the electric potentials at positions r_1 and r_2 as V_1 and V_2 respectively. Therefore, total potential energy of the system of two charges q_1 and q_2 placed at points with position vectors r_1 and r_2 in the region of E is given by

U = Work done in bringing charge q, from infinite to that position in E is equal to work done for charge q_2 from infinite to that position in E + work done to that of charge q_2 at these positions in presence of q_1.

i.e., $U = q_1 V_1 + q_2 V_2 = \dfrac{1}{4\pi\varepsilon_0} \cdot \dfrac{q_1 q_2}{|r_2 - r_1|}$

12. In series combination,

$$C_s = \dfrac{C}{n}$$

In parallel combination,

$\Rightarrow \quad C_p = nC$

According to problem,

$C = nC_s = 3 \times 1\mu F = 3\mu F$

In parallel combination,

$$C_p = nC = 3 \times 3 = 9\mu F$$

$$C_p = 9\mu F$$

For same voltage,

Energy stored, $U \propto C$

$$\therefore \quad \dfrac{U_s}{U_p} = \dfrac{C_s}{C_p} \Rightarrow \dfrac{U_s}{U_p} = \dfrac{1}{9}$$

or, $\quad U_s : U_P = 1 : 9$

13. Two identical capacitors C_1 and C_2 gets fully charged with 5V battery initially.

So, the charge and potential difference on both capacitors becomes

$q = CV$

$= 2 \times 10^{-6} \times 5V = 10\,\mu C$

and $V = 5V$

On introduction of dielectric medium of $K = 5$.

For C_1 (Continue to be connected with battery) potential difference of C_1, $(V') = 5V$

Capacitance of $C_1' = KC = 5 \times 2\mu F = 10\,\mu F$

Charge $q' = C'V; = (10\,\mu F)(5\,V) = 50\,\mu C$

For C_2 (Disconnected with battery)

Charge $q' = q = 10\,\mu C$

Potential difference

$$V' = \dfrac{V}{K} = \dfrac{5}{5} = 1\,V$$

14. (i) Equipotential surfaces due to an Electric dipole is as shown:-

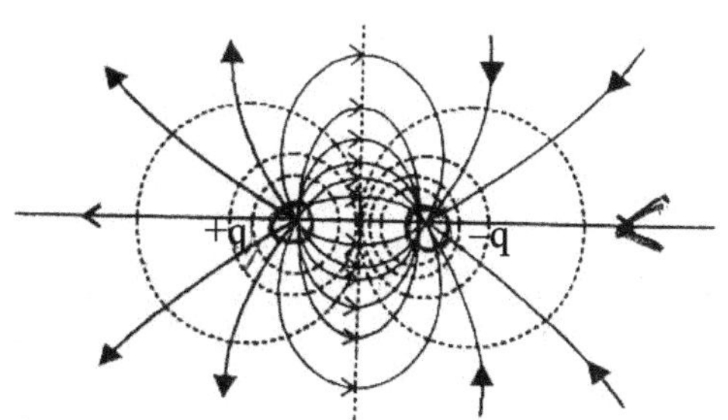

(ii) Equipotential surfaces get closer to each other near the point charges as strong electric field is produced there.

15. (i) $\because$ Electric field intensity and potential difference are related as

$$E = -\dfrac{\Delta V}{\Delta r}$$

$\Rightarrow \Delta V = -E\Delta r \Rightarrow V_A - V_C = -(2+2)E$

$V_A - V_C = -4E$

$V_C - V_A = 4E$

(ii) As $V_C - V_A = 4E$, is positive

$\therefore \quad V_C > V_A$

Potential is greater at point C than point A, as potential decreases along the direction of electric field.

16. Let C farad be the capacity of the unknown capacitor. Charge stored in the capacitor

$Q = C \times V = 300 \times 10^{-6}$ ...(i)

When the potential is reduced by 100 volts, the new potential will be $(V - 100)$ volts and charge

$= C \times (V - 100) = 100 \times 10^{-6}$ ...(ii)

Dividing eq. (i) by (ii), we have

$$\dfrac{V}{V - 100} = \dfrac{300}{100} = 3$$

or $\qquad V = 3V - 300$

$\therefore \qquad V = 150$ volt

Putting this value in eq. (i), we have

$C \times 150 = 300 \times 10^{-6}$

$\therefore \qquad C = 2 \times 10^{-6}$ farad

When the voltage is increased by 100 volts, the new voltage will be

$150\,V + 100\,V = 250\,V$

$\therefore$ New charge $\qquad Q' = CV$

$= 2 \times 10^{-6} \times 250\,C$

$= 500\,\mu C$

17. Let the potential difference across the plates of a parallel plate capacitor be V and d is the distance between them

A = area of the plates

Then electric field E_0 between them is given by

$$E_0 = \dfrac{V}{d} = \dfrac{Q}{A\,\varepsilon_0}$$

When a slab of thickness $t = \dfrac{2}{3}d$ and dielectric constant K is introduced between the plates

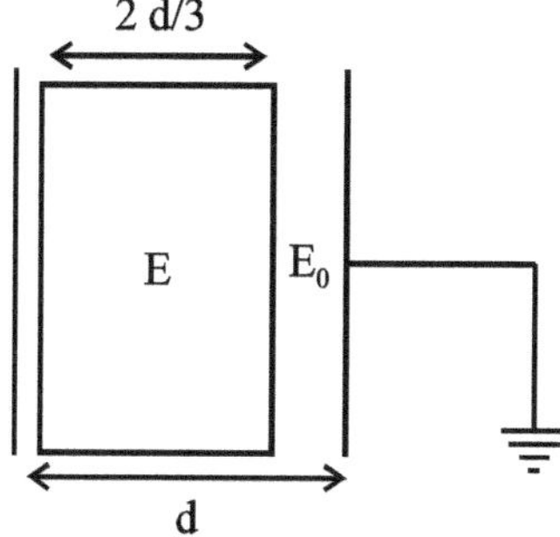

Then $\quad V = E_0\left(d - \dfrac{2d}{3}\right) + E \times \dfrac{2d}{3}$

$$= E_0\,\dfrac{d}{3} + \dfrac{E_0}{K}\dfrac{2d}{3} = E_0\,\dfrac{d}{3}\left[1 + \dfrac{2}{K}\right]$$

or $\quad V = \dfrac{Q}{A\,\varepsilon_0}\dfrac{d}{3}\left[1 + \dfrac{2}{K}\right] \quad \left(\because E_0 = \dfrac{Q}{A\,\varepsilon_0}\right)$

Therefore capacitance

$$C = \frac{Q}{V} = \frac{3A\,\epsilon_0}{d\left(1+\dfrac{2}{K}\right)}$$

This is the required expression.

18. Energy stored in a charged capacitor

$$U = q^2/2C$$

where 'q' is the charge on the charged capacitor.

When another similar uncharged capacitor is connected, the net capacitance of the system is $C' = 2C$

The charge on the system is constant. So, the energy stored in the system now is

$$U' = q^2/2(C') \Leftrightarrow U' = q^2/2(2C) \Rightarrow U' = q^2/4C$$

Thus, the required ratio is

$$\frac{U'}{U} = \frac{q^2/4c}{q^2/2c} = \frac{1}{2}$$

19. (i) When the dielectric slab is introduced between the plates of the capacitor, its capacitance will increase. Hence, the potential drop across the capacitor will decrease (since both are connected in series) ($V = Q/c$), as a result, the potential drop across the bulb will increase. So, its brightness will increase.

(ii) As the resistance (R) is increased, the potential drop across the resistor will increase (since both are connected in series) as a result, the potential drop across the bulb will decrease. So, its brightness will decrease.

20. (a) Let Q = Total charge on each plate of the capacitor, A = Area of each plate,

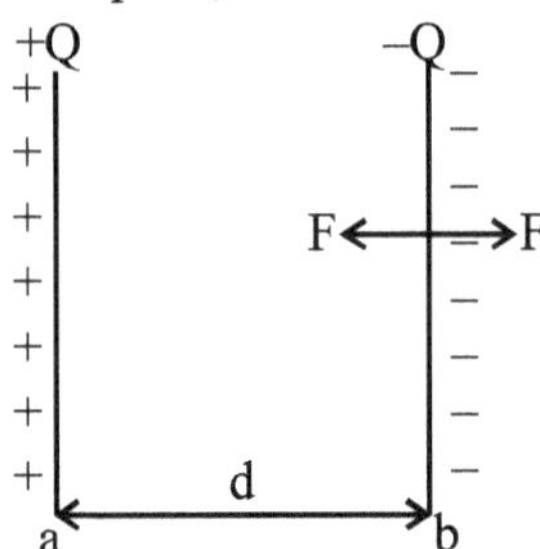

Suppose the plates of the capacitor are almost touching each other and a charge Q is given to the capacitor. One of the plates, say a, is kept fixed and other say b, is slowly pulled away from plate a to increase the separation from zero to d. The attractive force on the plate b at any instant

due to first plate is given by, $F = \dfrac{Q^2}{2A\varepsilon_0}$

The person pulling the plate b must apply an equal and opposite force (F) in the opposite direction if the plate is moved slowly.

Work done by the person during the displacement of the

second plate; $W = F.d = \dfrac{Q^2 d}{2A\varepsilon_0} = \dfrac{Q^2}{2C}$

Here, $C = \dfrac{A\varepsilon_0}{d}$ which is the capacitance of the capacitor in the final position.

The work done by the person must be equal to the increase in the energy of the system.

Thus, the capacitor has a stored energy, $U = \dfrac{Q^2}{2C}$

Now, if we pull the plates of the capacitor apart, we have to do work against the electrostatic attraction between the plates. When we increase the separation between the

plates from d_1 to d_2, an amount $\dfrac{Q^2}{2A\varepsilon_0}(d_2 - d_1)$ of work is performed by us and this much energy goes into the capacitor. On the other hand, new electric field is created in a volume $A(d_2 - d_1)$.

The energy stored per unit volume is thus given by,

$$u = \frac{Q^2(d_2 - d_1)}{2A\varepsilon_0}$$

$$A(d_2 - d_1) = \frac{Q^2}{2A^2\varepsilon_0} = \frac{1}{2}\varepsilon_0\left(\frac{Q}{A\varepsilon_0}\right)^2 = \frac{1}{2}\varepsilon_0 E^2$$

Here, E is the intensity of the electric field.

(b) Work done is given as $W = F.d$

Here, F is the force exerted on the charge (q) due to electric field (E) and is given by, $F = qE$

Net displacement, $d = 0$

$\therefore W = 0$

OR

(a) A parallel plate capacitor consists of two large plane parallel conducting plates separated by a small distance.

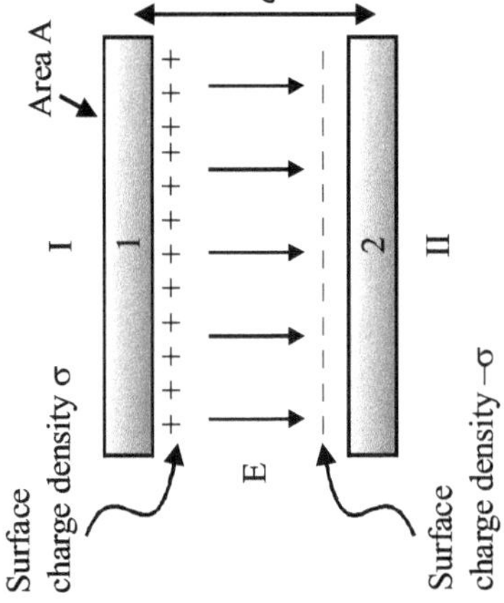

Let A be the area of each plate and d be the separation between them. The two plates have charges Q and −Q. Plate 1 has surface charge density, $\sigma = Q/A$, And plate 2 has a surface charge density −σ.

Electric field in, Outer region I,

$$E = \frac{\sigma}{2\varepsilon_0} - \frac{\sigma}{2\varepsilon_0} = 0$$

In outer region II,

$$E = \frac{\sigma}{2\varepsilon_0} - \frac{\sigma}{2\varepsilon_0} = 0$$

In the inner region between plates 1 and 2, the electric fields due to the two charged plates add up.

$$E = \frac{\sigma}{2\varepsilon_0} + \frac{\sigma}{2\varepsilon_0} = \frac{\sigma}{\varepsilon_0} = \frac{Q}{\varepsilon_0} = \frac{Q}{\varepsilon_0 A}$$

The direction of electric field is from positive to the negative plate. For uniform electric field, potential difference is simply the electric field times the distance between the plates.

$$V = E\,d = \frac{1}{\varepsilon_0}\frac{Qd}{A}$$

Capacitance (C) of the parallel plate capacitor,

$$C = \frac{Q}{V} = \frac{\varepsilon_0 A}{d}$$

(b) The surface charge density for a spherical conductor is given by, $\sigma = \dfrac{Q}{4\pi r^2}$

For spherical conductor R_1, the surface charge density is given by, $\sigma_1 = \dfrac{q_1}{4\pi R_1^2}$

Similarly, for spherical conductor R_2, the surface charge density is given by, $\sigma_2 = \dfrac{q_2}{4\pi R_2^2}$

$$\therefore \quad \frac{\sigma_1}{\sigma_2} = \left(\frac{q_1}{q_2}\right)\left(\frac{R_2^2}{R_1^2}\right)$$

Since the two conductors are connected, we have, $q_1 = q_2$

$$\therefore \quad \frac{\sigma_1}{\sigma_2} = \frac{R_2^2}{R_1^2} = \left(\frac{R_2}{R_1}\right)^2$$

21. An equipotential surface is that surface at every point of which, the electric potential is the same.

(i)

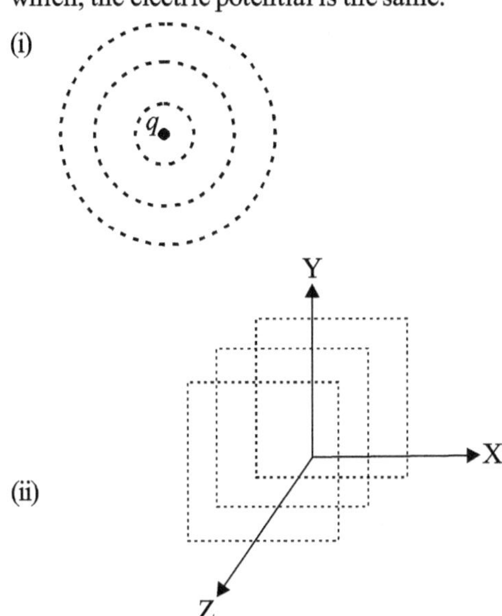

(ii)

The equipotential surfaces about a single charge are not equidistant because electric field due to a single charge is not constant.

(iii) If the electric field exist along tangential to an equipotential surface, a charged particle will experience a force along the tangential line and can move along it. As a charged particle can move only due to the potential difference (along the direction of change of potential), this contradicts the concept of an equipotential surface.

22. Capacitance of capacitor in case *I*

$$C_1 = \frac{K\varepsilon_0 A}{d.}$$

For, case 2, the capacitor are connected in series. Therefore equivalent capacitance would be

$$\frac{1}{C_2} = \frac{\dfrac{1}{K_1\varepsilon_0 A}}{d/2} + \frac{\dfrac{1}{K_2\varepsilon_0 A}}{d/2}$$

$$\frac{1}{C_2} = \frac{d}{2\varepsilon_0 A}\left[\frac{1}{K_1} + \frac{1}{K_2}\right]$$

$$C_2 = \frac{2\varepsilon_0 A}{d}\left[\frac{K_1 K_2}{K_1 + K_2}\right]$$

Given that $C_1 = C_2$

$$\therefore \quad \frac{k\varepsilon_0 A}{d} = \frac{2\varepsilon_0 A}{d}\left[\frac{K_1 K_2}{K_1 + K_2}\right]$$

$$K = \left[\frac{2K_1 K_2}{K_1 + K_2}\right]$$

23. Current charging the capacitor, $I = \dfrac{dQ}{dt}$

Displacement current, due to time varying electric field,

$$I_D = \varepsilon_0 \frac{d\phi_E}{dt} = \varepsilon_0 \frac{d(EA)}{dt}\;(\because \phi_E = EA)$$

$$\therefore\; I_D = \varepsilon_0 A\frac{dE}{dt} = \varepsilon_0 A\frac{d}{dt}\left(\frac{Q}{\varepsilon_0 A}\right) = \frac{dQ}{dt}\left(\because E = \frac{Q}{\varepsilon_0 A}\right)$$

Clearly, $I = I_D$

24. (a) Force on charge, Q due to other charges is shown in the figure

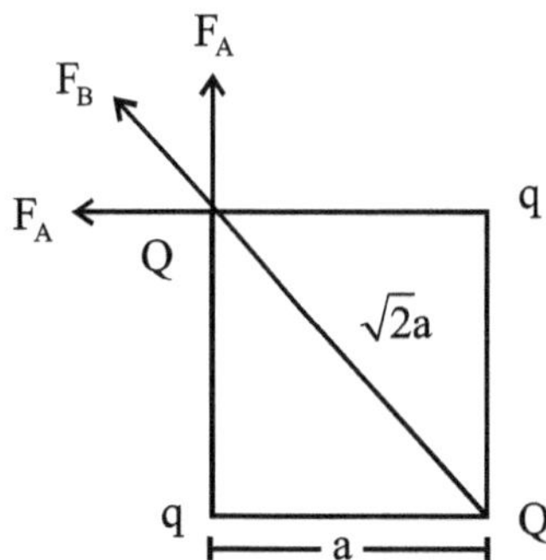

Here, F_A is force acting on Q due to q
F_B is force acting on Q due to Q
Using Coulomb's law

$$F_A = K\frac{Qq}{a^2}\ \text{and}\ F_B = K\frac{Q^2}{a^2}\left[\text{here, } K = \frac{1}{4\pi\,\epsilon_\circ}\right]$$

Net force is equal to resultant of two perpendicular forces F_A (acting in different direction) + force F_B

$$F_{net} = \sqrt{2}\,F_A + F_B \Rightarrow F_{net} = k\left[\sqrt{2}\frac{Qq}{a^2} + \frac{Q^2}{2a^2}\right]$$

(b) Potential energy of a system of two charges (q_1 and q_2) separated by a distance 'a' is given by

$$V = k\frac{q_1 q_2}{a}$$

There are 6 pairs, as shown in the figures.

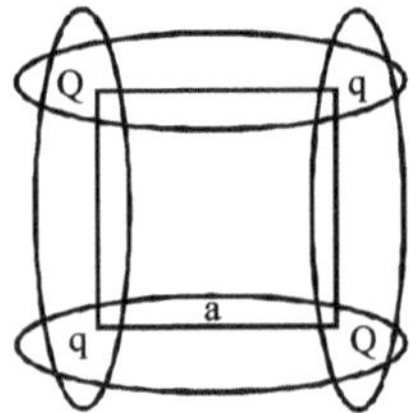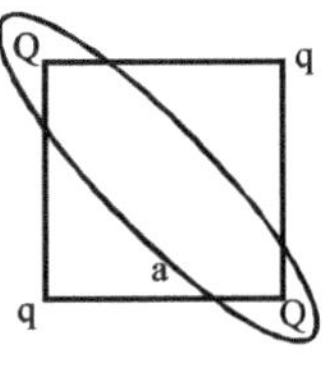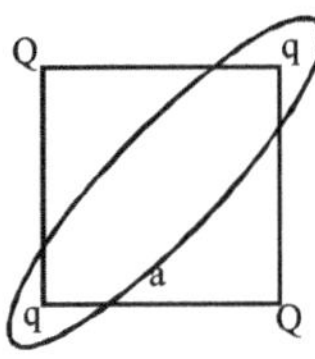

$\therefore$ Potential energy of the system

$$= \frac{4kQq}{a} + \frac{kQ^2}{\sqrt{2}a} + \frac{kq^2}{\sqrt{2}a}$$

OR

(a) The forces on the charge q due to other charges are shown in the figure

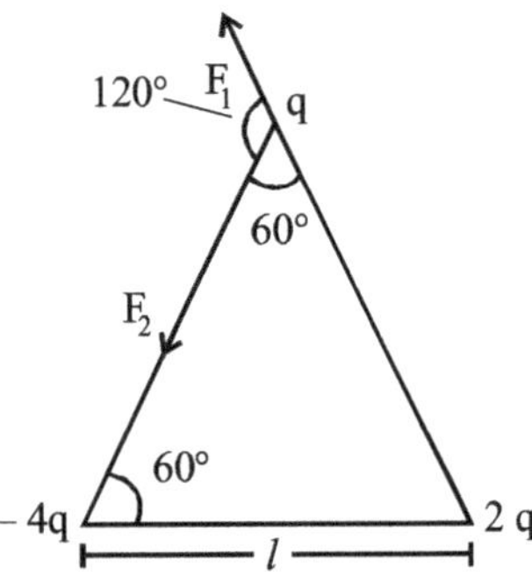

The resultant electric force acting on the charge q is the resultant of forces F_1 and F_2

Using Coulomb's law,

$$\left|F_1\right| = k\frac{2qq}{l^2} = k\frac{2q^2}{l^2} \text{ and } \left|F_2\right| = k\frac{4qq}{l^2} = k\frac{4q^2}{l^2}$$

Now, resulant force $F = \sqrt{F_1^2 + F_2^2 + 2F_1F_2\cos\theta}$

$$= \sqrt{F_1^2 + F_2^2 + 2F_1F_2\cos120°}$$

Resultant force

$$F = \sqrt{F_1^2 + F_2^2 - 2F_1F_2} \qquad \left[\because \cos120° = -\frac{1}{2}\right]$$

(b) The amount of the work done to separate the charges at infinite distance is difference in initial and final potential energy i.e.,

Work done = (final potential energy) – (initial potential energy)

Final potential energy (when charges are at infinite distance) = 0

Initial potential energy $= -k\dfrac{4q^2}{\ell} - k\dfrac{8q^2}{\ell} + k\dfrac{2q^2}{\ell}$

$$= -k\frac{10q^2}{\ell}$$

$\therefore$ Work done = (final potential energy) – (initial potential

energy) $= 0 - \left(-k\dfrac{10q^2}{\ell}\right)$

$\therefore$ Work done $= k\dfrac{10q^2}{\ell}$

25. As two capacitors are connected in parallel
So, the potential on each of them remains the same.
Charge on each, $Q_A = CV = Q_B$

Hence, the energy stored in the system

$$U_{initial} = \frac{1}{2}CV^2 + \frac{1}{2}CV^2 = CV^2 \qquad ...(i)$$

When a dielectric slab of dielectric constant (k) is introduced, the capacitance changes to KC.

As the switch is open, only voltage across capacitor, A remains the same.

The voltage across capacitor, B changes to $V' = Q/C'$
$= Q/KC = V/K$

Hence, new energy stored in the system

$$U_{final} = \frac{1}{2}KCV^2 + \frac{1}{2}KC\frac{V^2}{K^2}$$

$\therefore$ $U_{final} = \dfrac{1}{2}KCV^2 + \dfrac{1}{2}\dfrac{CV^2}{K} = \dfrac{1}{2}CV^2\left(k + \dfrac{1}{K}\right)$

$\therefore$ $\dfrac{U_{initial}}{U_{final}} = \dfrac{1}{K + \dfrac{1}{K}} = \dfrac{K}{K^2 + 1}$

26. Torque on a dipole which is placed in an uniform electric field (E) is given by,

$$\tau = PE\sin\theta = (ql)\,E\sin\theta \qquad ...(1)$$

Here, l is the length of the dipole, Q is the charge and E is the electric field.

Potential energy,

$$U = -PE\cos\theta = -(ql)\,E\cos\theta \qquad ...(2)$$

Dividing (2) by (1), $\dfrac{\tau}{U} = \dfrac{q l E \sin\theta}{-q l E \cos\theta} = -\tan\theta$

$$\Rightarrow U = \frac{-\tau}{\tan\theta}$$

$$\Rightarrow U = \frac{-\tau}{\tan60°} \Rightarrow U = \frac{-4\sqrt{3}}{\sqrt{3}} \Rightarrow U = -4J$$

NCERT Exemplar 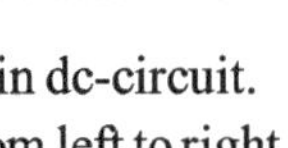

1. **(d)** As capacitor offers infinite resistance in dc-circuit. So, current flows through $2\,\Omega$ resistance from left to right, given by

$$I = \frac{V}{R + r} = \frac{2.5V}{2 + 0.5} = \frac{2.5}{2.5} = 1\,A$$

So, the potential difference across $2\,\Omega$ resistance
$V = IR = 1 \times 2 = 2$ volt.

Since, capacitor is in parallel with $2\,\Omega$ resistance, so it also has 2V potential difference across it.

As current does not flow through capacitor branch so no potential drop will be accross $10\,\Omega$ resistance. The charge on capacitor

$$q = CV = (4\,\mu F) \times 2V = 8\,\mu C$$

2. **(c)** The direction of electric field is always perpendicular to the direction of electric field and equipotential surface maintained at high electrostatic potential to other equipotential surface maintained at low electrostatic potential.

The positively charged particle experiences the electrostatic force in the direction of electric field i.e., from high electrostatic potential to low electrostatic potential. Thus, the work done by the electric field on the positive charge, so electrostatic potential energy of the positive charge decreases because speed of charged particle moves in the direction of field due to force $q\vec{E}$.

3. **(c)** The work done (in displacing a charge particle) by a electric force is given by $W_{12} = q(V_2 - V_1)$. Here initial and final potentials are same in all three cases are equal (20V) and same charge is moving from A to B, so work done is (ΔVq) same in all three cases.

4. **(c)** As we know that the relation between electric field intensity E and electric potential V is

$$E = -\frac{dV}{dr}$$

Electric field intensity $E = 0$ then $\frac{dV}{dr} = 0$

This imply that $V = $ constant

Thus, $E = 0$ inside the charged conducting sphere then the constant electrostatic potential 100V at every where inside the sphere and it verifies the shielding effect also.

5. **(a)** Here we have to findout the shape of equipotential surface, these surface are perpendicular to the field lines, so there must be electric field which can not be without charge. So, the collection of charges, whose total sum is not zero, with regard to great distance can be considered as a point charge. The equipotentials due to point charge are spherical in shape as electric potential due to point charge q is given by

$$V = K_e \frac{q}{r}$$

This suggest that electric potentials due to point charge is same for all equidistant points. The locus of these equidistant points which are at same potential, form spherical surface.

The lines of field from point charge are radial. So the equipotential surface perpendicular to field lines from a sphere.

6. **(c)** The capacitance of parallel plate capacitor filled with dielectric of thickness d_1 and dielectric constant K_1 is

$$C_1 = \frac{K_1 \varepsilon_o A}{d_1}$$

Similarly, capacitance of parallel plate capacitor filled with dielectric of thickness d_2 and dielectric constant K_2 is

$$C_2 = \frac{K_2 \varepsilon_o A}{d_2}$$

Since both capacitors are in series combination, then the equivalent capacitance is

$$\frac{1}{C} = \frac{1}{C_1} + \frac{1}{C_2}$$

$$\text{or} \quad C = \frac{C_1 C_2}{C_1 + C_2} = \frac{\dfrac{K_1 \varepsilon_0 A}{d_1} \dfrac{K_2 \varepsilon_0 A}{d_2}}{\dfrac{K_1 \varepsilon_0 A}{d_1} + \dfrac{K_2 \varepsilon_0 A}{d_2}}$$

$$C = \frac{K_1 K_2 \varepsilon_0 A}{K_1 d_2 + K_2 d_1} \qquad \ldots (i)$$

So multiply the numerator and denominator of equation (i) with $(d_1 + d_2)$

$$C = \frac{K_1 K_2 \varepsilon_0 A}{(K_1 d_2 + K_2 d_1)} \times \frac{(d_1 + d_2)}{(d_1 + d_2)}$$

$$= \frac{K_1 K_2 (d_1 + d_2)}{(K_1 d_2 + K_2 d_1)} \times \frac{\varepsilon_0 A}{(d_1 + d_2)} \qquad \ldots (ii)$$

So, the equivalent capacitances is

$$C = \frac{K \varepsilon_0 A}{(d_1 + d_2)} \qquad \ldots (iii)$$

Comparing, (ii) and (iii), the dielectric constant of new capacitor

$$K = \frac{K_1 K_2 (d_1 + d_2)}{K_1 d_2 + K_2 d_1}$$

7. More

8. As electric field is conservative, work done will be zero in both the cases.

9. Suppose this were not true. The potential just inside the surface would be different from that at the surface resulting in a potential gradient. This would mean that there are field lines pointing inwards or outwards from the surface. These lines cannot at the other end be again on the surface, since the surface is equipotential. Thus, this is possible only if the other end of the lines are at charges inside, contradicting the premise. Hence, the entire volume inside must be at the same potential.

10. $U_1 > U_2$ because particles move in a direction where potential energy of the system is decreased.

11. When the body of the car is given a sudden electric charge, an equal but opposite charge is polarized on the surface of the paint around it. Therefore, the mist of paint is attracted to the body of the car and it is uniformly painted.

12. $$U = \frac{-qQ}{4\pi\varepsilon_0 R\sqrt{1 + z^2/R^2}}$$

The variation of potential energy u with z is shown in the figure.

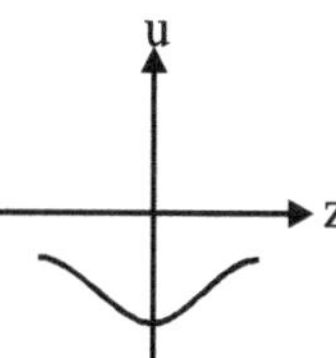

The charge $-q$ displaced would perform oscillations. We cannot conclude anything just by looking at the graph.

13. The potential inside the shell will be the same everywhere as on its surface. As we add $-3Q$ charge on the surface, the potential on the surface changes by the same amount as that inside. Therfore the potential difference remains the same.

14. Charge on smaller sphere

$$q = C\left(\frac{V}{2}\right) = \frac{4\pi\varepsilon_0 R V}{2}$$

Potential difference $= \dfrac{q}{4\pi\varepsilon_0}\left(\dfrac{1}{R} - \dfrac{1}{2R}\right)$

$$= \left(\frac{VR}{2}\right)\left(\frac{1}{2R}\right) = \frac{V}{4}$$

Objective Practice Exercise 

1. **(c)** Electric potential inside a conductor is constant and it is equal to that on the surface of the conductor.

2. **(b)**   3. **(a)**

4. **(a)** Since $V = \dfrac{1}{4\pi\varepsilon_0}\dfrac{q}{r}$, for a given point charge, q is constant, therefore V depends only on r. Hence V is a function of distance.

5. **(d)** Surface of metallic cube is an equipotential surface. Therefore, electric field is normal to the surface of the cube.

6. **(c)** Because in case of metallic spheres either solid or hollow, the charge will reside on the surface of the sphere. Since both spheres have same surface area, so they can hold equal maximum charge.

7. **(a)**   8. **(c)**

9. **(b)** Electric field is always zero inside a conductor. If there is any excess of charge on a hollow conductor it always resides on the outer surface of conductor. Therefore inside a hollow conductor there is no charge and hence charge density is zero.

10. **(d)** When negative terminal is grounded, positive terminal of battery is at +12 V. When positive terminal is grounded, the negative terminal will be at –12 V.

11. **(c)** The component of electric field in any direction is negative of the rate of change of electric potential with distance in that direction.

$$\therefore \ E_x = -\frac{dV}{dx}$$

12. **(b)**

13. **(b)** As, $E = -\dfrac{dV}{dr}$ or, $0 = -\dfrac{dV}{dr}$ because electric field inside a charged hollow sphere is zero.
or, v = constant

14. **(a)**

15. **(a)** Potential at B, V_B is maximum
$V_B > V_C > V_A$
As in the direction of electric field potential decreases.

16. **(b)**

17. **(b)** Potential at the centre of the triangle,
$$V = \frac{\Sigma q}{4\pi\varepsilon_0 r} = \frac{2q - q - q}{4\pi\varepsilon_0 r} = 0$$
Obviously, $E \neq 0$

18. **(c)** The potential energy is negative whenever there is attraction. Since a positive and negative charge attract each other therefore their energy is negative. When both the charges are separated by infinite distance, they do not attract each other and their energy is zero.

19. **(d)** When $\dfrac{Q_1}{R_1} - \dfrac{Q_2}{R_2}$; current will flow in connecting wire so that energy decreases in the form of heat through the connecting wire.

20. **(c)** As work is done by the field, K.E. of the body increases by

$$\text{K.E.} = W = q(V_A - V_B)$$
$$= 10^{-8}(600 - 0) = 6 \times 10^{-6} \text{ J}$$

21. **(a)** We know that $\dfrac{W_{AB}}{q} = V_B - V_A$
$$\therefore \ V_B - V_A = \frac{2\,\text{J}}{20\,\text{C}} = 0.1\,\text{J/C} = 0.1\,\text{V}$$

22. **(c)** $\dfrac{W_{PQ}}{q} = (V_Q - V_P)$
$$\Rightarrow \ W_{PQ} = q(V_Q - V_P)$$
$$= (-100 \times 1.6 \times 10^{-19})(-4 - 10)$$
$$= +2.24 \times 10^{-16}\text{J}$$

23. **(c)** Since $W_{A \to B} = q(V_B - V_A)$
$$\Rightarrow \ V_B - V_A = \frac{16}{4} = 4\text{V}$$

24. **(c)** Potential energy decreases whenever there is attraction. A negative charge placed at centroid causes attraction.

25. **(c)** In a round trip, displacement is zero. Hence, work done is zero.

26. **(d)** Since capacitance $C = \dfrac{\varepsilon_0 A}{d}$, as d decreases capacitance increases.

27. **(b)**   28. **(b)**

29. **(b)** $C_{medium} = K \times C_{air}$

30. **(b)**

31. **(c)** As the capacitor remains connected to the battery, the potential difference provided by the battery remains constant.

32. **(b)** In oil, C becomes twice, V becomes half. Therefore, E = V/d becomes half.

33. **(a)** Capacitance of spherical conductor $= 4\pi\varepsilon_0 a$ where a is radius of conductor.
Therefore, $C = \dfrac{1}{9 \times 10^9} \times 1 = \dfrac{1}{9} \times 10^{-9}$
$$= 0.11 \times 10^{-9} \text{ F} = 1.1 \times 10^{-10} \text{ F}$$

34. **(d)**

35. **(a)** Due to insertion of a dielectric slab capacitance increase by K times. The potential difference, the electric field and the stored energy decreases by $\dfrac{1}{K}$ times.

36. **(a)** In parallel grouping of capacitors
$$C_{eq} = C_1 + C_2 + \ldots\ldots\ldots\ldots C_n$$

37. **(b)** Energy will be lost during transfer of charge (heating effect).

38. **(c)**

39. **(c)** $C = \dfrac{2 \times 2}{2 + 2} + 2 = 3\ \mu F$

40. **(b)** In series combination of capacitors
$$V_{eff} = V + V + V = 3V$$
$$\frac{1}{C_{eff}} = \frac{1}{C} + \frac{1}{C} + \frac{1}{C} \ \Rightarrow \ C_{eff} = \frac{C}{3}$$

Thus, the capacitance and breakdown voltage of the combination will be $\dfrac{C}{3}$ and 3V.

41. (c) Energy of given to conductor, $U = \dfrac{1}{2}CV^2$

or $\quad U = \dfrac{1}{2} \times 5 \times 10^{-6} \times (800)^2 = 1.6\,\text{joule}$

42. (a) C = equivalent capacitance

$\therefore \quad \dfrac{1}{C} = \dfrac{1}{2} + \dfrac{1}{3} + \dfrac{1}{6} \Rightarrow \therefore \ C = 1\mu F$

Charge in series circuit will be same.

$\therefore \ q = CV = (1 \times 10^{-6}) \times 10 = 10\mu C$

$\therefore \quad$ Charge across '3µF' capacitor will be 10µC.

43. (c) Potential energy of a dipole in external field U is

$U = \quad -\vec{P} \cdot \vec{E}$

for stable equilibrium $\theta = 0°$

$U = \quad -p\,E\cos 0° = -pE$

$\therefore \quad U = \quad -qLE$

44. (d) As capacitor offers infinite resistance in dc-circuit. So, current flows through 2Ω resistance from left to right, given by

$I = \dfrac{V}{R+r} = \dfrac{2.5V}{2+0.5} = \dfrac{2.5}{2.5} = 1\,A$

So, the potential difference across 2Ω resistance
$V = IR = 1 \times 2 = 2\,\text{volt.}$

Since, capacitor is in parallel with 2Ω resistance, so it also has 2V potential difference across it.

As current does not flow through capacitor branch so no potential drop will be accross 10Ω resistance. The charge on capacitor
$q = CV = (4\,\mu F) \times 2V = 8\,\mu C$

45. (c) The direction of electric field is always perpendicular to the direction of electric field and equipotential surface maintained at high electrostatic potential to other equipotential surface maintained at low electrostatic potential.

The positively charged particle experiences the electrostatic force in the direction of electric field i.e., from high electrostatic potential to low electrostatic potential. Thus, the work done by the electric field on the positive charge, so electrostatic potential energy of the positive charge decreases because speed of charged particle moves in the direction of field due to force $q\vec{E}$.

46. (c) The work done (in displacing a charge particle) by a electric force is given by $W_{12} = q(V_2 - V_1)$. Here initial and final potentials are same in all three cases are equal (20V) and same charge is moving from A to B, so work done is (ΔVq) same in all three cases.

47. (c) As we know that the relation between electric field intensity E and electric potential V is

$E = -\dfrac{dV}{dr}$

Electric field intensity $E = 0$ then $\dfrac{dV}{dr} = 0$

This imply that V = constant

Thus, E = 0 inside the charged conducting sphere then the constant electrostatic potential 100V at every where inside the sphere and it verifies the shielding effect also.

48. (c) The capacitance of parallel plate capacitor filled with dielectric of thickness d_1 and dielectric constant K_1 is

$C_1 = \dfrac{K_1 \varepsilon_o A}{d_1}$

Similarly, capacitance of parallel plate capacitor filled with dielectric of thickness d_2 and dielectric constant K_2 is

$C_2 = \dfrac{K_2 \varepsilon_o A}{d_2}$

Since both capacitors are in series combination, then the equivalent capacitance is

$\dfrac{1}{C} = \dfrac{1}{C_1} + \dfrac{1}{C_2}$

or $\quad C = \dfrac{C_1 C_2}{C_1 + C_2} = \dfrac{\dfrac{K_1 \varepsilon_0 A}{d_1} \dfrac{K_2 \varepsilon_0 A}{d_2}}{\dfrac{K_1 \varepsilon_0 A}{d_1} + \dfrac{K_2 \varepsilon_0 A}{d_2}}$

$C = \dfrac{K_1 K_2 \varepsilon_0 A}{K_1 d_2 + K_2 d_1} \quad \ldots (i)$

So multiply the numerator and denominator of equation (i) with $(d_1 + d_2)$

$C = \dfrac{K_1 K_2 \varepsilon_0 A}{(K_1 d_2 + K_2 d_1)} \times \dfrac{(d_1 + d_2)}{(d_1 + d_2)}$

$= \dfrac{K_1 K_2 (d_1 + d_2)}{(K_1 d_2 + K_2 d_1)} \times \dfrac{\varepsilon_0 A}{(d_1 + d_2)} \quad \ldots (ii)$

So, the equivalent capacitances is

$C = \dfrac{K \varepsilon_0 A}{(d_1 + d_2)} \quad \ldots (iii)$

Comparing, (ii) and (iii), the dielectric constant of new capacitor

$K = \dfrac{K_1 K_2 (d_1 + d_2)}{K_1 d_2 + K_2 d_1}$

49. (a) As shown in the figure, the resultant electric fields before and after interchanging the charges will have the same magnitude, but opposite directions.

Also, the potential will be same in both cases as it is a scalar quantity.

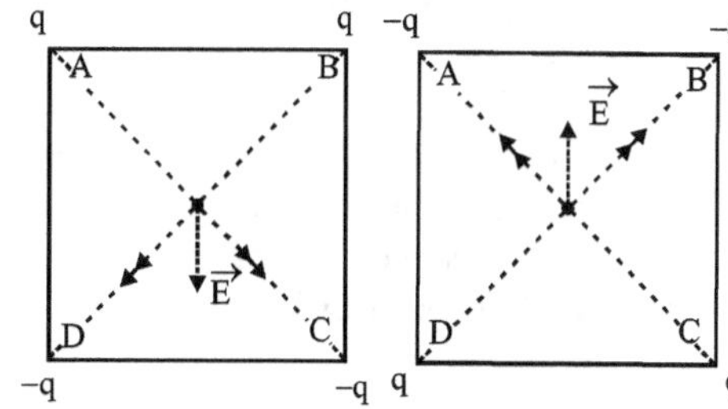

50. **(d)** When $\dfrac{Q_1}{R_1} - \dfrac{Q_2}{R_2}$; current will flow in connecting wire so that energy decreases in the form of heat through the connecting wire.

Chapter Test

1. **(a)** As shown in the figure, the resultant electric fields before and after interchanging the charges will have the same magnitude, but opposite directions.

Also, the potential will be same in both cases as it is a scalar quantity.

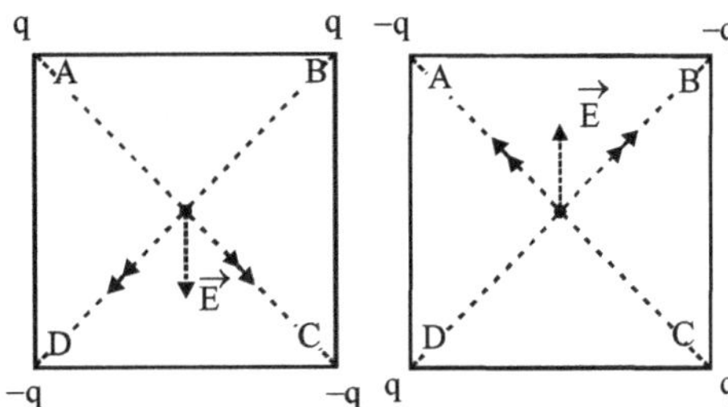

2. **(d)** When $\dfrac{Q_1}{R_1} - \dfrac{Q_2}{R_2}$; current will flow in connecting wire so that energy decreases in the form of heat through the connecting wire.

3. **(a)** The equivalent circuit diagram as shown in the figure.

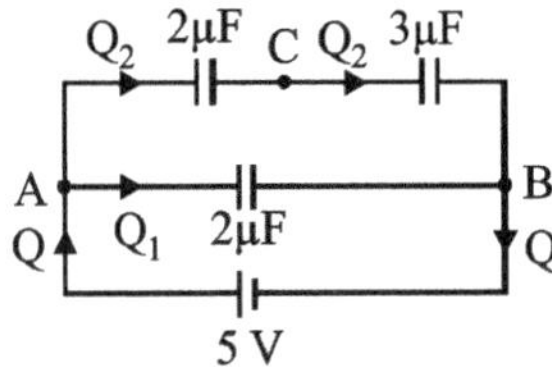

The equivalent capacitance between A and B is

$$C_{eq} = \frac{2\mu F \times 3\mu F}{2\mu F + 3\mu F} + 2\mu F = \frac{16}{5}\mu F$$

Total charge of the given circuit is

$$Q = \frac{16}{5}\mu F \times 5V = 16\mu C$$

$$Q_1 = (2\mu F) \times 5V = 10\mu C$$

$\therefore$ $Q_2 = Q - Q_1 = 16\,\mu C - 10\,\mu C = 6\,\mu C$

$\therefore$ Voltage between B and C is

$$V_{BC} = \frac{Q_2}{3\mu F} = \frac{6\mu C}{3\mu F} = 2\,V$$

4. **(d)** $V = 5x^2 + 10x - 4$

$$E = \frac{-dV}{dx} = -(10x + 10).$$

At $x = 1\,m$, $E = -20\,V/m$.

5. **(b)** Since force on both the charges of a dipole is equal but opposite in direction, so net force $= 0$

6. **(a)** In the battery connected capacitor V remains constant while C increases with the introduction of dielectric

7. **(a)** In series $\dfrac{1}{C} = \dfrac{1}{C_1} + \dfrac{1}{C_2} + \dfrac{1}{C_3}$ and charge on each capacitor is same.

8. **(c)** Capacitance are in series

$$\frac{1}{c} = \frac{1}{2} + \frac{1}{2} + \frac{1}{2} \Rightarrow c = \frac{2}{3}F$$

9. **(c)** $C = \dfrac{2 \times 2}{2 + 2} + 2 = 3\,\mu F$

10. **(c)** Before introducing a slab capacitance of plates

$$C_1 = \frac{\varepsilon_0 A}{3}$$

If a slab of dielectric constant K is introduced between plates then

$$C = \frac{K\varepsilon_0 A}{d} \text{ then } C_1' = \frac{\varepsilon_0 A}{2.4}$$

C_1 and C_1' are in series hence,

$$\frac{\varepsilon_0 A}{3} = \frac{k\dfrac{\varepsilon_0 A}{3} \cdot \dfrac{\varepsilon_0 A}{2.4}}{k\dfrac{\varepsilon_0 A}{3} + \dfrac{\varepsilon_0 A}{2.4}}$$

$3\,k = 2.4\,k + 3 \qquad 0.6\,k = 3$

Hence, the dielectric constant of slap is given by,

$$k = \frac{30}{6} = 5$$

11. **(b)**

12. As $r_A > r_B \Rightarrow V_A < V_B \left[\because \quad V = \dfrac{kq}{r} \right]$

$\therefore$ Charge will flow from B to A.

13. $\because$ $V = \dfrac{q}{C}$

$\therefore$ $3\,\mu F$ will have more electric potential.

14. $\because$ $C_1 = C_2 = C_3 = C$ (say)

C_2 and C_3 are in parallel.

$\therefore$ $C_{23} = 2C$

C_{23} and C_1 are in series.

$\therefore$ $C_{eq} = 2C \times C/(2C + C)$

$\qquad = \dfrac{2}{3}C$ Charge $= \dfrac{2}{3}C \times e$

$\therefore$ $V_1 = \dfrac{\text{charge}}{C_1} = \dfrac{2/3C \times e}{C} = \dfrac{2}{3}e$

$\qquad V_2 = V_3 = V_{23} = \dfrac{2Ce/3}{2C} = \dfrac{e}{3}$

15. The capacitance of the capacitor remains unchanged when a sheet of Al foil is introduced between them.

3 Current Electricity

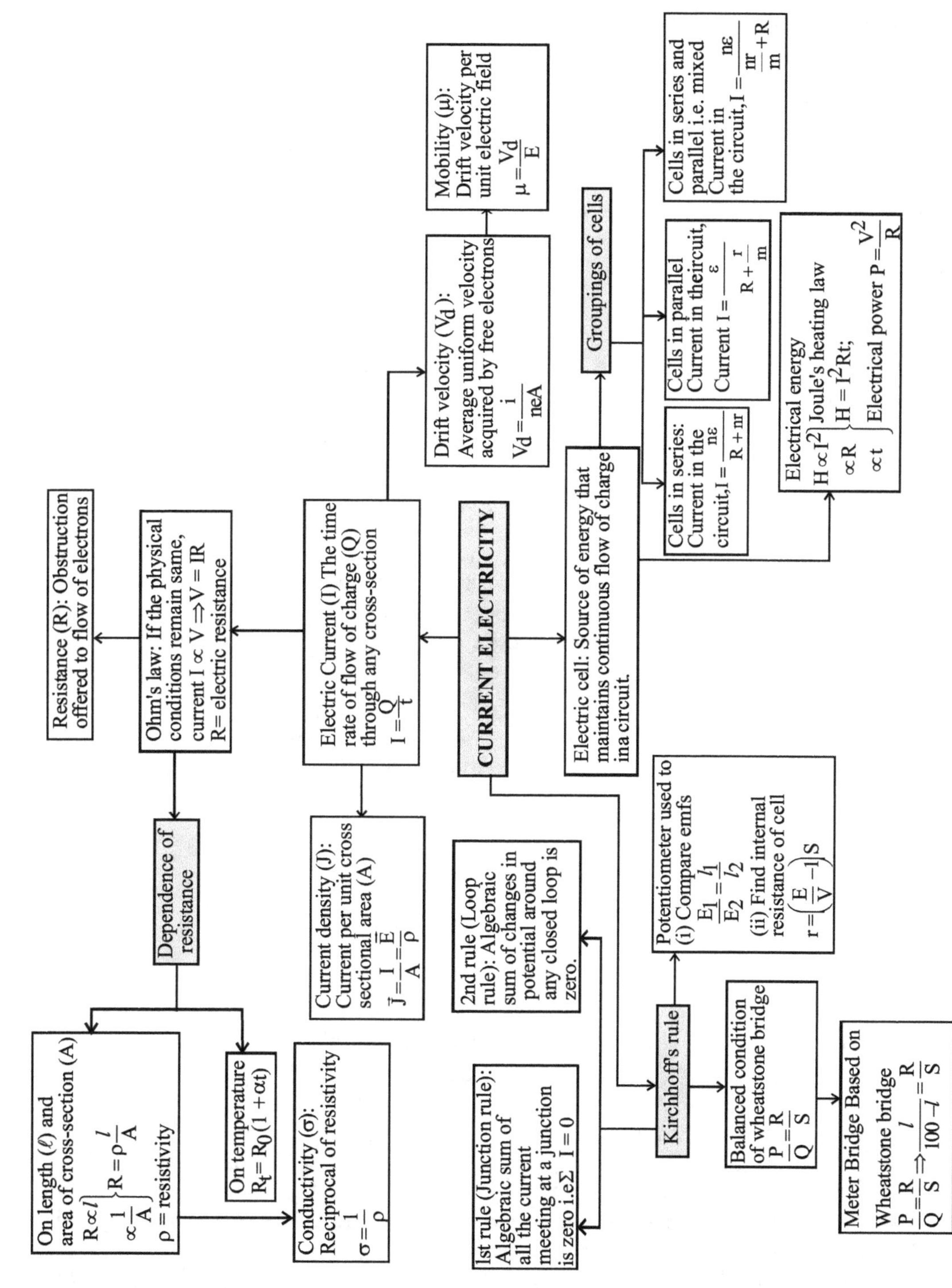

Topic 1 — Electric Current, Current Density, Drift Velocity, Mobility Ohm's Law, Resistance & Conductance & Resistivity

ELECTRIC CURRENT

The time rate of flow of charge through any cross-section is called electric current.

If Δq charge passes through a cross-section in time Δt then, *average current* $I_{av} = \dfrac{\Delta q}{\Delta t}$

Instantaneous current $I = \lim\limits_{\Delta t \to 0} \dfrac{\Delta q}{\Delta t} = \dfrac{dq}{dt}$

Electric current is measured in **ampere (A).** It is a scalar fundamental physical quantity.

One ampere : *The current through a conductor is said to be one ampere, if one coulomb of charge is flowing per second through a cross-section of wire.*

The conventional direction of current is the direction of flow of positive charge or applied field. It is opposite to direction of flow of negatively charged electrons.

CURRENT DENSITY

It is the current flowing per unit area.

Current density $J = \dfrac{I}{A} = \dfrac{ne}{At}$ where A is the cross-sectional area of the conductor.

It is a vector quantity. its S.I. unit is A/m^2

Carriers of current : Free electrons are the current carriers in solid conductors. Positive and negative ions are the current carriers in liquid conductors.

DRIFT VELOCITY

The motion of free electrons in a conductor are continuous and random. They collide with positive metal ions and change direction during each collision. So thermal velocities are randomly distributed and average velocity is zero.

When a potential difference is applied across the ends of a conductor, electrons are drifted towards the positive terminal of the field, this velocity is called drift velocity (v_d).

$$v_d = -\frac{e\vec{E}\tau}{m} = \frac{i}{neA}$$

Relaxation time (τ) is the time interval between two successive collisions of electrons with the positive ions.

Relation between current (I) and drift velocity(v_d) : Drift velocity is directly proportional to current, $I = nAev_d$

MOBILITY

It is the drift velocity per unit electric field.

i.e., $\mu = \dfrac{v_d}{E}$

Its S.I. unit is $Volt^{-1}\, sec^{-1}\, m^2$

OHM'S LAW

It states that if the physical state i.e. temperature, nature of material and dimensions of a conductor remain unchanged then the ratio of potential difference applied across its ends to current flowing through it remains constant.

i.e., $V \propto I$ or $V = IR$, where $R = \dfrac{V}{I}$ is the resistance of conductor.

$$I = neAv_d = neA\,\frac{eE}{m}\tau = \left(\frac{ne^2\tau}{m}\right)AE = \left(\frac{ne^2\tau}{m}\right)A\frac{V}{L} \qquad \text{so } R = \frac{V}{I} = \left(\frac{m}{ne^2\tau}\right)\frac{L}{A}, \text{ R is resistance of conductor.}$$

*The substances which obey ohm's law are called **ohmic** or **linear** conductors* e.g., silver, copper, mercury, carbon, mica etc. The resistance of such conductors is independent of magnitude and polarity of applied potential difference. Here the graph between I and V. **V-I characteristics** is a straight line passing through the origin. The reciprocal of slope of straight line gives resistance,

$$R_{sta} = \frac{V}{I} \text{ and, } R_{dyna} = \frac{\Delta V}{\Delta I} = \frac{1}{\tan\theta} = \text{constant.}$$

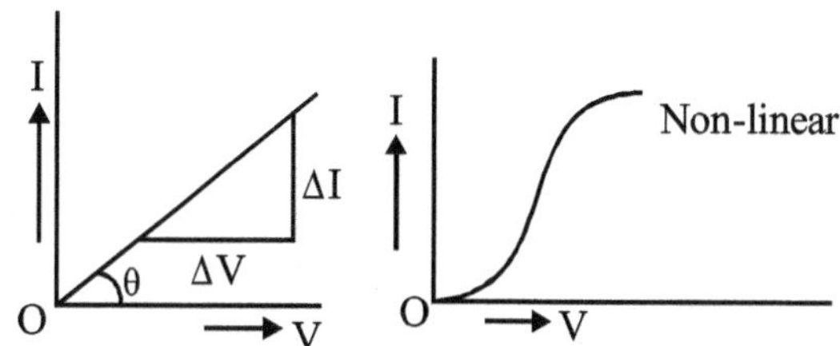

*The substances which do not obey ohm's law are called **non-ohmic** or **non-linear** conductors.* The I–V curve is not a straight line. e.g., p-n junction diode, transistors, thermionic valves, rectifiers etc. This is the **limitation of Ohm's law**.

RESISTANCE

It is the property of a substance due to which it opposes the flow of current through it. It is a scalar quantity with **SI unit** volt/ampere called **ohm (Ω)**.

Factors Affecting the Resistance of a Conductor

The resistance of a conductor depends on the following factors :

1. **Temperature :** The **temperature dependence of resistance** is given by $R = R_0(1 + \alpha\,\Delta\theta)$, where α is temperature coefficient of resistance and $\Delta\theta$ is change in temperature.

    The temperature coefficient of resistance $\alpha = \dfrac{R - R_0}{R_0\Delta\theta}$ is defined as change in resistance per unit resistance at 0°C per degree rise of temperature.

    For maximum metals, $\alpha = \dfrac{1}{273}$ per °C   so, $R = R_0\left(1 + \dfrac{\Delta\theta}{273}\right) = R_0\left(\dfrac{273 + \Delta\theta}{273}\right) = R_0\dfrac{T}{273}$

    so, $R \propto T$ i.e., the resistance of pure metallic conductor is proportional to its absolute temperature.

2. **Length of the conductor :** The resistance of a conductor is directly proportional to its length. i.e., $R \propto L$

3. **Cross-sectional area of the conductor :** The resistance of the conductor is inversely proportional to the cross-sectional area.

    i.e. $R \propto \dfrac{1}{A}$

    $R \propto L$ and $R \propto \dfrac{1}{A}$ so, $R \propto \dfrac{L}{A}$ or $R = \rho\dfrac{L}{A}$

    where L = length, A = area of cross-section of wire and ρ is called **resistivity** or **specific resistance**.
    The **fractional change in resistance without change in volume or mass are :**

    (a) When change in length is small ($\leq 5\%$) fractional change in R is, $\dfrac{\Delta R}{R} = \dfrac{2\Delta L}{L}$

    (b) When change in radius is small ($\leq 5\%$) fractional change in R is, $\dfrac{\Delta R}{R} = \dfrac{-4\Delta r}{r}$

    (c) When change in area is small ($\leq 5\%$) fractional change in R is, $\dfrac{\Delta R}{R} = \dfrac{-2\Delta A}{A}$

4. **Nature of the material of the wire :** The resistance is less for conductors and more for semiconductors and insulators.

CONDUCTANCE (G) & RESISTIVITY (ρ)

It is the reciprocal of resistance i.e., $G = 1/R$.
Its **SI unit** is ohm^{-1} or mho or siemen (s)

Resistivity or specific resistance (ρ)

In terms of microscopic quantities, $E = \rho J$
Resistivity is numerically equal to ratio of magnitude of electric field to current density.

Specific resistance, $\rho = \dfrac{RA}{L}$ so, if $L = 1$ m, $A = 1$ m^2 then $\rho = R$.

Resistivity is numerically equal to resistance of substance having unit area of cross-section and unit length.
It is a scalar with **SI unit** ohm-meter (Ω-m).
*The reciprocal of resistivity is called **conductivity or specific conductance**.*

Conductivity $\sigma = \dfrac{1}{\rho} = \dfrac{ne^2\tau}{m} = ne\mu$

Its **SI unit** mho/m

The resistivity is independent of shape and size of conductor and it depends on nature of material of body. The resistivity is the property of material while resistance is property of object.

Temperature Dependence of Resistivity

Resistivity depends on temperature and is given by relation $\rho = \rho_0(1 + \alpha\,\Delta\theta)$ where α is temperature coefficient of resistivity and $\Delta\theta$ is change in temperature.

For metals, α is positive so resistivity increases with temperature while for non-metals α is negative so resistivity decreases with temperature.

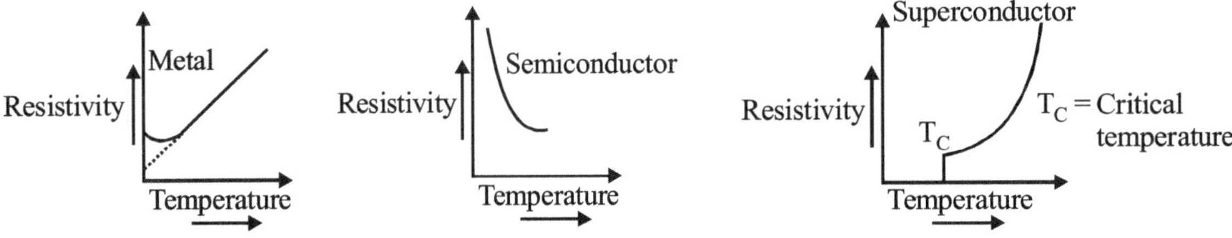

Superconductors : Conductors possess some resistance at room temperature which increases with the rise in temperature and decreases with the decrease in temperature. If the temperature is decreased drastically, the resistance of the conductor becomes very low and its conductivity rises very much. At a very low temperature, the resistance of the conductor may vanish completely. When it happens, the conductor is called a **superconductor**. For example, helium is a super conductor at 4.2 K $(-268.8°C)$.

Illustration 1 :

The resistance of a wire of length 100 cm and of uniform area of cross-section 0.020 cm^2, is found to be 2.0 ohm. Calculate specific resistance of wire.

Sol.

Here, $\quad \ell = 100$ cm, $A = 0.020$ cm^2, $R = 2.0\,\Omega$

Specific resistance $\rho = \dfrac{RA}{\ell} = \dfrac{2.0 \times 0.020}{100} = 0.0004\,\Omega$ cm

Practice Exercise-1

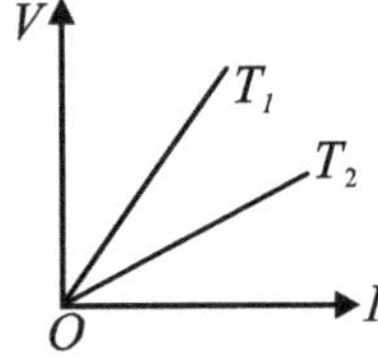

Multiple Choice Questions

1. In the equation AB = C, A is the current density, C is the electric field, Then B is
   (a) resistivity
   (b) conductivity
   (c) potential difference
   (d) resistance

2. A wire X has half the diameter and half the length of a wire Y of similar material. The ratio of resistance of X to that of Y is
   (a) $8:1$
   (b) $4:1$
   (c) $2:1$
   (d) $1:1$

3. The voltage V and current I graphs for a conductor at two different temperatures T_1 and T_2 are shown in the figure. The relation between T_1 and T_2 is

   (a) $T_1 > T_2$
   (b) $T_1 < T_2$
   (c) $T_1 = T_2$
   (d) $T_1 = \dfrac{1}{T_2}$

4. The I-V characteristics shown in figure represents
   (a) ohmic conductors
   (b) non-ohmic conductors
   (c) insulators
   (d) superconductors

5. If the resistance of a conductor is $5\,\Omega$ at $50°$ C & $7\,\Omega$ at $100°$ C, then mean temperature coefficient of resistance (of material) is
   (a) $0.013/°C$
   (b) $0.004/°C$
   (c) $0.006/°C$
   (d) $0.008/°C$

6. At what temperature will the resistance of a copper wire becomes three times its value at 0°C? (Temperature coefficient of resistance of copper is $4 \times 10^{-3}/°C$)
   (a) $550°C$
   (b) $500°C$
   (c) $450°C$
   (d) $400°C$

DIRECTIONS (Qs. 7-12) : *Each of these questions contains an assertion followed by reason. Read them carefully and answer the question on the basis of following options. You have to select the one that best describes the two statements.*

(a) If both Assertion and Reason are correct and the Reason is a correct explanation of the Assertion.

(b) If both Assertion and Reason are correct but Reason is not a correct explanation of the Assertion.

(c) If the Assertion is correct but Reason is incorrect.

(d) If the Assertion is incorrect but the Reason is correct.

7. **Assertion :** Bending a wire does not effect electrical resistance.

  Reason : Resistance of wire is proportional to resistivity of material.

8. **Assertion :** The electric bulbs glows immediately when switch is on.

  Reason : The drift velocity of electrons in a metallic wire is very high.

9. **Assertion:** For a conductor resistivity increases with increase in temperature.

  Reason: Since $\rho = \dfrac{m}{ne^2\tau}$, when temperature increases the random motion of free electrons increases and vibration of ions increases which decreases τ.

10. **Assertion :** The current density $\bar{j}$ at any point in ohmic resistor is in direction of electric field $\bar{E}$ at that point.

  Reason : A point charge when released from rest in a region having only electrostatic field always moves along electric lines of force.

11. **Assertion :** Free electrons always keep on moving in a conductor even then no magnetic force act on them in magnetic field unless a current is passed through it.

  Reason : The average velocity of free electron is zero.

12. **Assertion :** Drift speed v_d is the average speed between two successive collisions.

  Reason : If $\Delta\ell$ is the average distance moved between two collisions and Δt is the corresponding time, then $v_d = \lim\limits_{\Delta t \to 0} \dfrac{\Delta\ell}{\Delta t}$.

Case / Passage Based Questions

The motion of free electrons in a conductor are continuous and random. They collide with positive metal ions and change direction during each collision. So thermal velocities are randomly distributed and average velocity is zero.

When a potential difference is applied across the ends of a conductor, electrons are drifted towards the positive terminal of the field, this velocity is called drift velocity (v_d).

$$v_d = -\dfrac{e\bar{E}\tau}{m} = \dfrac{i}{neA}$$

13. If N, e, τ and m are representing electron density, charge, relaxation time and mass of an electron respectively, then the resistance of wire of length ℓ and cross-sectional area A is given by

  (a) $\dfrac{m\ell}{Ne^2A^2\tau}$

  (b) $\dfrac{2m\tau A}{Ne^2\ell}$

  (c) $\dfrac{Ne^2\tau A}{2m\ell}$

  (d) $\dfrac{Ne^2A}{2m\tau\ell}$

14. When a current I is set up in a wire of radius r, the drift velocity is v_d. If the same current is set up through a wire of radius 2 r, the drift velocity will be

  (a) $4\,v_d$

  (b) $2\,v_d$

  (c) $v_d/2$

  (d) $v_d/4$

15. A straight conductor of uniform cross-section carries a current I. If s is the specific charge of an electron, the momentum of all the free electrons per unit length of the conductor, due to their drift velocity only is

  (a) $I\,s$

  (b) $\sqrt{I/s}$

  (c) I/s

  (d) $(I/s)^2$

16. The resistance of a wire at room temperature 30°C is found to be 10 Ω. Now to increase the resistance by 10%, the temperature of the wire must be [The temperature coefficient of resistance of the material of the wire is 0.002 per °C]

  (a) 36°C

  (b) 83°C

  (c) 63°C

  (d) 33°C

17. The number of free electrons per 100 mm of ordinary copper wire is 2×10^{21}. Average drift speed of electrons is 0.25 mm/s. The current flowing is

  (a) 5 A

  (b) 80 A

  (c) 8 A

  (d) 0.8 A

18. How does the drift velocity of electrons in a metallic conductor vary with increase in temperature?

19. A wire of resistivity ρ is stretched to double its length. What will be its new resistivity?

20. Manganin is used for making standard resistors. Why?

21. If the length of a wire conductor is doubled by stretching it, keeping the potential difference across it constant, by what factor does the drift speed of electrons change?

22. If the temperature of a good conductor increases, how does the relaxation time of electron in the conductor change?

23. Two wires, one of manganin and the other copper have equal lengths and equal resistances. Which one of these wires will be thicker?

24. Which physical quantity does the voltage vs current graph for a metallic conductor depict? Give its SI unit.

25. The metallic conductor is at a temperature Q_1. The temperature of the metallic conductor is increased to Q_2. How will the product of its resistivity and conductivity change?

26. Specific resistance of copper, silver and constantan are $1.18 \times 10^{-6}\ \Omega$ cm, $1 \times 10^{-6}\ \Omega$ cm and $48 \times 10^{-6}\ \Omega$ cm respectively. Which is the best electrical conductor and why?

27. Two wires A and B of the same metal, have the same area of cross-section and have their lengths in the ratio 2 : 1. What will be the ratio of currents flowing through them respectively when the same potential difference is applied across length of eachs of them?

28. If p.d. V applied acorss a conductor is increased to 2V, how will the drift velocity of the electrons change?

Short Answer Questions

29. Deduce Ohm's law using the concept of drift velocity.

30. Derive a relation between the current flowing through a conductor and drift velocity.

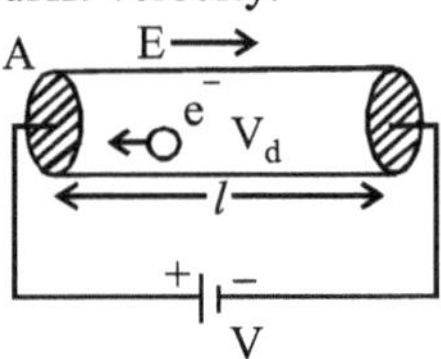

31. Define the term resistivity of a conductor. Give its S.I. unit. Show that the resistivity of a conductor is given by $\dfrac{m}{ne^2\tau}$ where symbols have their usual meanings.

32. Calculate the electrical resistivity of the material of a conductor of length 3m, area of cross section 0.02 mm^2 having a resistance of 20 ohm.

Topic 2   Electrical Energy and Power 

ELECTRICAL ENERGY AND POWER

Electrical energy developed by a voltage V supplying a current I in time t is given by $E = VIt = I^2Rt$ (Joule's Heating law).

The power is, thus, given by $P = \dfrac{E}{t} = VI = \dfrac{V^2}{R}$

The S.I. unit of electric energy is joule.

The commercial unit of electric energy, (B. O. T. U) board of trade unit is kilo-watt hour (kwh)

$1\ \text{kwh} = 3.6 \times 10^6\ \text{joule}$

Practice Exercise-2 

Multiple Choice Questions

1. Three identical resistances A, B and C are connected as shown in fig.

The heat produced will be maximum

(a) In B
(b) In B and C
(c) In A
(d) Same for A, B and C

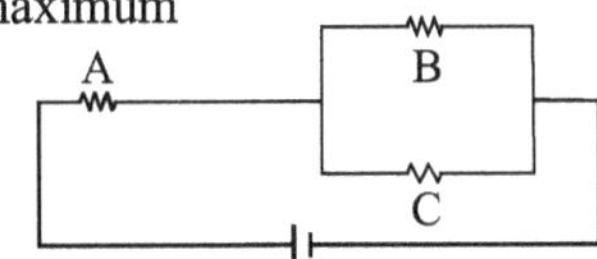

2. Match the Column I and Column II.

Column I	Column II
(A) Smaller the resistance greater the current	(1) If the same voltage is applied and resistance are in series
(B) Greater or smaller the resistance the current is same	(2) If the same current is passed
(C) Greater the resistance smaller the power	(3) When resistances are connected in series
(D) Greater the resistance greater the power	(4) When resistances are connected in parallel

(a) $(A) \to (3)$; $(B) \to (1)$; $(C) \to (2)$; $(D) \to (4)$
(b) $(A) \to (1)$; $(B) \to (3)$; $(C) \to (2)$; $(D) \to (4)$
(c) $(A) \to (2)$; $(B) \to (1)$; $(C) \to (4)$; $(D) \to (3)$
(d) $(A) \to (4)$; $(B) \to (3)$; $(C) \to (1)$; $(D) \to (2)$

3. A wire of radius r and another wire of radius 2r, both of same material and length are connected in series to each other. The combination is connected across a battery. The ratio of the heats produced in the two wires will be

(a) 4.00   (b) 2.00   (c) 0.50   (d) 0.25

Assertion & Reason Questions

DIRECTIONS (Qs. 4-7) : *Each of these questions contains an assertion followed by reason. Read them carefully and answer the question on the basis of following options. You have to select the one that best describes the two statements.*

(a) If both Assertion and Reason are correct and the Reason is a correct explanation of the Assertion.
(b) If both Assertion and Reason are correct but Reason is not a correct explanation of the Assertion.
(c) If the Assertion is correct but Reason is incorrect.
(d) If the Assertion is incorrect but the Reason is correct.

4. **Assertion :** Fuse wire must have high resistance and low melting point.
Reason : Fuse is used for voltage stablisation only.

5. **Assertion :** The (100w, 220 v) bulb glow with more brightness than, (50w, 220v) bulb.
Reason : 100w bulb has more resistance than 50w bulb.

6. **Assertion :** When current through a bulb decreases by 0.5%, the glow of bulb decreases by 1%.
   Reason : Glow (Power) which is directly proportional to square of current.

7. **Assertion :** Long distance power transmission is done at high voltage.
   Reason : At high voltage supply power losses are less.

Case / Passage Based Questions

Heating Effect of Current: The electric energy consumed in a circuit is defined as *the total work done in maintaining the current in an electric circuit for a given time.*

Electric energy $= VIt = Pt = I^2 Rt = V^2 t / R$

The **S.I. unit** of electric energy is joule (denoted by J)

where 1 joule $= 1$ watt $\times 1$ second $= 1$ volt $\times 1$ ampere $\times 1$ sec.

In **household circuits** the electrical appliances are connected in parallel and the electrical energy consumed is measured in kWh

8. An electric fan and a heater are marked as 100 W, 220 V and 1000 W, 220 V respectively. The resistance of heater is
   (a) equal to that of fan
   (b) lesser than that of fan
   (c) greater than that of fan
   (d) zero

9. Which of the following statement is false?
   (a) Some of the energy produced by the light bulb takes the form of heat.
   (b) The battery is the source of all the electrons flowing around the circuit.
   (c) The current entering the light bulb equals the current leaving the light bulb.
   (d) The potential in the wire to the left of the light bulb differs from the potential in the wire to the right of that bulb.

10. Resistance of conductor is doubled keeping the potential difference across it constant. The rate of generation of heat will
    (a) become one fourth
    (b) be halved
    (c) be doubled
    (d) become four times

11. The heating element of an electric heater should be made with a material, which should have
    (a) high specific resistance and high melting point
    (b) high specific resistance and low melting point
    (c) low specific resistance and low melting point
    (d) low specific resistance and high melting point

12. If R_1 and R_2 are respectively the filament resistances of a 200 watt bulb and a 100 watt bulb designed to operate on the same voltage
    (a) R_1 is two times R_2
    (b) R_2 is two times R_1
    (c) R_2 is four times R_1
    (d) R_1 is four times R_2

Very Short Answer Questions

13. Two 120 V light bulbs, one of 25 W and other of 200 W were connected in series across a 240 V line. One bulb burnt out almost instantaneously. Which one has burnt and why?

14. What happens to the power dissipation if the value of electric current passing through a conductor of constant resistance is doubled?

15. What is the largest voltage that you can safely put across a resistor marked 196 Ω-1 W?

Topic 3 — Internal Resistance, Terminal Potential Difference Electromotive Force of a Cell, Grouping of Cells

INTERNAL RESISTANCE, TERMINAL POTENTIAL DIFFERENCE, AND ELECTROMOTIVE FORCE OF A CELL

Internal Resistance of a Cell (r)

It is the resistance offered by the electrolyte and electrodes of a cell when current flows through it. It depends on the following factors:
(i) Distance between the plates.
(ii) The nature of the electrolyte and electrodes.
(iii) Area of the plates immersed in the electrolyte. If area increases, internal resistance decreases.

Terminal Potential Difference (V) and Electromotive Force (E) of a Cell

Terminal potential difference of a cell is defining the potential difference between the two electrodes of a cell when the cell is in closed circuit i.e. current is withdrawn from it.

Electromotive force or e.m.f of a cell is the maximum potential difference between the two electrodes of a cell when the cell is in open circuit i.e. no current is taken from the cell.

$V = E - Ir \leftarrow$ when current is withdrawn from the cell

$V = E + Ir \leftarrow$ when the cell is charged.

The S.I. unit of emf and potential difference is same i.e., volt.

GROUPING OF CELLS

Series Grouping of Cells : *The cells are said to be connected in series, if negative terminal of first cell is connected to positive of second whose negative terminal is connected to positive of third cell and so on.* **The external resistance is connected between free terminals of first and last cells.**

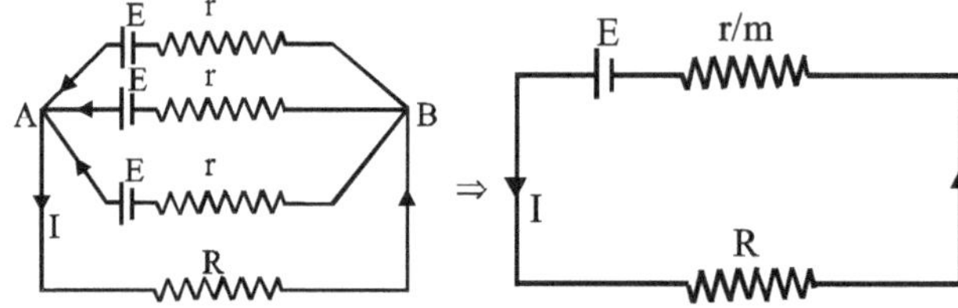

Let n identical cells each of emf E and internal resistance r be connected in series.
The combination can be replaced by a single cell of emf nE and internal resistance nr.

The current flowing through load, $I = \dfrac{nE}{R+nr}$

(1) If nr << R then $I = \dfrac{nE}{R}$. If equivalent internal resistance nr is less than external resistance R then current in circuit is equal to n times circuit current due to single cell.

(2) If nr >> R then I = E/r. If equivalent internal resistance nr is greater than external resistance R then current in circuit is equal to short circuited current obtained from one cell.

(3) Maximum current can be drawn from series combination of cells if external resistance is very large as compared to equivalent internal resistance.

(4) If in series combination of n cells p cells are reversed than equivalent emf

$$E_{eq} = (n-p)\,E - pE = (n-2p)E \text{ and } r_{eq} = nr \text{ so current } \quad I = \frac{(n-2p)E}{nr+R}$$

(5) If unidentical cells are connected in series then

$$E_{eq} = E_1 + E_2 + ... = \Sigma\,E_i \text{ and } r_{eq} = r_1 + r_2 + ... = \Sigma r_i. \text{ so current } I = \frac{\Sigma E_i}{R + \Sigma r_i}.$$

Parallel Grouping of Cells : *The cells are said to be connected in parallel if positive terminals of all the cells are connected together at one point and their negative terminals at another point.* The external resistor is connected between these two points A and B.

Let m identical cells each of emf E and internal resistance r be connected in parallel.
The combination can be replaced by a single cell of emf E and internal resistance r/m.

The current $I = \dfrac{E}{R + r/m}$

(1) If r/m << R then $I = \dfrac{E}{R}$. If equivalent internal resistance r/m is less than external resistance R then current in circuit is equal to current produced by a single cell.

(2) If r/m >> R then $I = \dfrac{mE}{r}$. If equivalent internal resistance r/m is greater than external resistance then current in circuit is equal to m times the current produced by a short circuited cell.

Thus maximum current can be drawn from parallel combination of cells if external resistance is small as compared to net internal resistance of cells.

Mixed Grouping of Cells : Let there be n identical cells each of emf E and internal resistance r, in one row and m rows of cells in parallel.

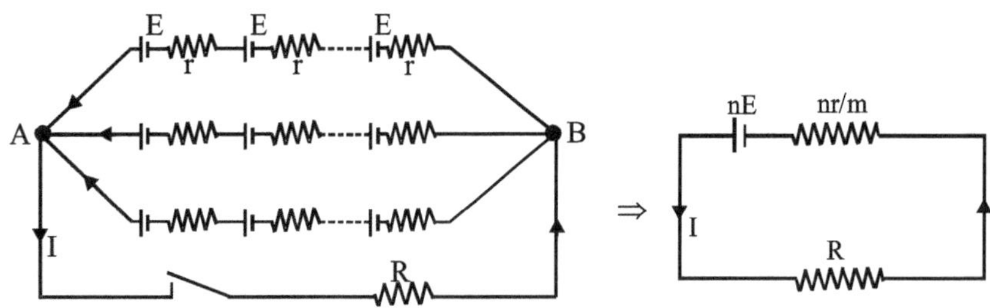

The combination of cells can be replaced by a single cell of emf nE and internal resistance $\dfrac{nr}{m}$.

The current $I = \dfrac{nE}{R + \dfrac{nr}{m}} = \dfrac{E}{\dfrac{R}{n} + \dfrac{r}{m}}$ where, n × m = p = total number of cells.

(1) The current in the circuit is maximum when $\dfrac{R}{n} + \dfrac{r}{m}$ is minimum

so, $\dfrac{d}{dm}\left(\dfrac{R}{n} + \dfrac{r}{m}\right) = 0$ or $\dfrac{d}{dm}\left(\dfrac{mR}{p} + \dfrac{r}{m}\right) = 0$ or $\dfrac{R}{p} - \dfrac{r}{m^2} = 0$ or $\dfrac{R}{p} = \dfrac{R}{mn} = \dfrac{r}{m^2}$ or $\dfrac{R}{n} = \dfrac{r}{m}$

In mixed grouping of cells current in circuit is maximum if $\dfrac{R}{n} = \dfrac{r}{m}$ and $I_{max} = \dfrac{nE}{2R} = \dfrac{mE}{2r}$

(2) In mixed grouping of cells power transferred to the load is maximum when external resistance R is equal to total internal resistance.

i.e., $R = \dfrac{nr}{m}$ or $\dfrac{R}{n} = \dfrac{r}{m}$.

This shows power transfer is maximum when current is maximum.

$$P = \dfrac{E^2 R}{\left(\dfrac{R}{n} + \dfrac{r}{m}\right)^2} \quad \text{and} \quad P_{max} = \dfrac{n^2 E^2}{4R} = \dfrac{m^2 E^2 R}{4r^2}$$

(3) In mixed grouping of cells current in circuit and power transferred to load become maximum under same condition. This is why it is preferred over series and parallel combination of cells.

Practice Exercise-3

Multiple Choice Questions

1. Emf of a cell is
   (a) the maximum potential difference between the terminals of a cell when no current is drawn from the cell.
   (b) the force required to push the electrons in the circuit.
   (c) the potential difference between the positive and negative terminal of a cell in a closed circuit.
   (d) less than terminal potential difference of the cell.

2. An energy source will supply a constant current into the load if its internal resistance is
   (a) very large as compared to the load resistance
   (b) equal to the resistance of the load
   (c) non-zero but less than the resistance of the load
   (d) zero

3. To draw a maximum current from a combination of cells, how should the cells be grouped?
   (a) Parallel
   (b) Series
   (c) Mixed grouping
   (d) Depends upon the relative values of internal and external resistances

4. A cell of internal resistance r is connected across an external resistance nr. Then the ratio of the terminal voltage to the emf of the cell is
   (a) $\dfrac{1}{n}$
   (b) $\dfrac{1}{n+1}$
   (c) $\dfrac{n}{n+1}$
   (d) $\dfrac{n-1}{n}$

5. If n cells each of emf ε and internal resistance r are connected in parallel, then the total emf and internal resistances will be
   (a) $\varepsilon, \dfrac{r}{n}$
   (b) ε, nr
   (c) $n\varepsilon, \dfrac{r}{n}$
   (d) $n\varepsilon, nr$

6. Under what condition will the strength of current in a wire of resistance R be the same for connection is series and in parallel of n identical cells each of the internal resistance r? When
   (a) $R = nr$
   (b) $R = r/n$
   (c) $R = r$
   (d) $R \to \infty, r \to 0$

7. The internal resistance of a 2.1 V cell which gives a current of 0.2 A through a resistance of 10 Ω is
   (a) $0.5\,\Omega$
   (b) $0.8\,\Omega$
   (c) $1.0\,\Omega$
   (d) $0.2\,\Omega$

Assertion & Reason Questions

DIRECTIONS (Qs. 8-9) : *Each of these questions contains an assertion followed by reason. Read them carefully and answer the question on the basis of following options. You have to select the one that best describes the two statements.*
(a) If both Assertion and Reason are correct and the Reason is a correct explanation of the Assertion.
(b) If both Assertion and Reason are correct but Reason is not a correct explanation of the Assertion.
(c) If the Assertion is correct but Reason is incorrect.
(d) If the Assertion is incorrect but the Reason is correct.

8. Assertion : A larger dry cell has higher emf.

Reason : The emf of a dry cell is proportional to its size.

9. Assertion : In a simple battery circuit, the point of the lowest potential is negative terminal of the battery.

Reason : The current flows towards the point of the higher potential, as it does in such a circuit from the negative to the positive terminal.

Case / Passage Based Questions

Terminal potential difference of a cell is defining the potential difference between the two electrodes of a cell when the cell is in closed circuit i.e. current is withdrawn from it.

Electromotive force or e.m.f of a cell is the maximum potential difference between the two electrodes of a cell when the cell is in open circuit i.e. no current is taken from the cell.

$V = E - Ir \leftarrow$ when current is withdrawn from the cell

$V = E + Ir \leftarrow$ when the cell is charged.

The S.I. unit of emf and potential difference is same i.e., volt.

10. A cell of internal resistance r is connected to an external resistance R. The current will be maximum in R, if

(a) R = r   (b) R < r   (c) R > r   (d) R = r/2

11. A capacitor is connected to a cell of emf E having some internal resistance r. The potential difference across the

(a) cell is < E   (b) cell is E

(c) capacitor is > E   (d) capacitor is < E

12. A primary cell has an e.m.f. of 1.5 volt. When short-circuited it gives a current of 3 ampere. The internal resistance of the cell is

(a) 4.5 ohm   (b) 2 ohm

(c) 0.5 ohm   (d) (1/4.5) ohm

13. A dc source of emf E_1 = 100 V and internal resistance $r = 0.5\,\Omega$, a storage battery of emf $E_2 = 90$ V and an external resistance R are connected as shown in figure. For what value of R no current will pass through the battery ?

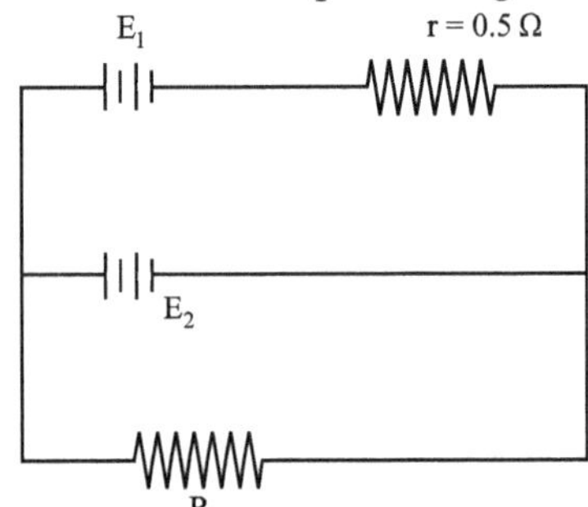

(a) $5.5\,\Omega$ (b) $3.5\,\Omega$ (c) $4.5\,\Omega$ (d) $2.5\,\Omega$

14. Three batteries of emf 1 V and internal resistance 1Ω each are connected as shown. Effective emf of combination between the points PQ is

(a) zero

(b) 1V

(c) 2V

(d) (2/3) V

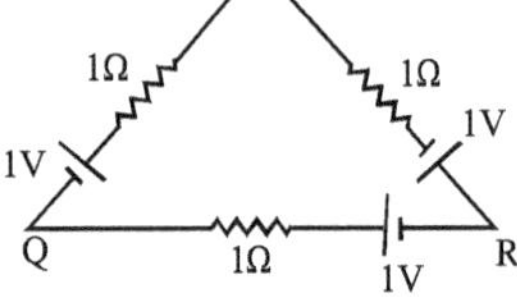

Very Short Answer Questions

15. State the condition in which terminal voltage across a secondary cell is equal to its e.m.f

16. A cell of e.m.f 2V and internal resistance $0.1\,\Omega$ is connected to a $3.9\,\Omega$ external resistance. What will be the p.d across the terminals of the cell?

17. Why is the terminal voltage less than the emf of the cell?

18. A cell of emf 'E' and internal resistance 'r' draws a current 'I'. Write the relation between terminal voltage 'V' in terms of E, I and r.

Short Answer Questions

19. Derive an expression for the internal resistance of a cell in terms of e.m.f and terminal potential difference of a cell.

20. Consider n cells connected in series in a row and m such rows connected in parallel. Obtain an expression for the maximum current from such a combination.

21. A battery of e.m.f 3V and internal resistance r is connected in series with a resistor of 55 Ω through an ammeter of resistance 1 Ω. The ammeter reads 50 mA. Draw the circuit diagram and calculate the value of r.

22. Two identical cells of e.m.f 1.5V each joined in parallel provide supply to an external circuit consisting of two resistance of 17 Ω each joined in parallel. A very high resistance voltmeter reads the terminal voltage of cells to be 1.4 V. Calculate the internal resistance of each cell.

23. Three identical cells each of e.m.f 2V and unknown internal resistance are connected in parallel. The combination is connected to a 5 Ω resister. If the terminal voltage across the cells is 1.5 V, what is the internal resistance of each cell?

24. A storage battery of e.m.f +8V, internal resistance 1 Ω is being charged by a 120 V d.c. source, using a 15 Ω resistor in series in the circuit.

Calculate (i) current in the circuit, (ii) terminal voltage across the battery during charging, (iii) chemical energy stored in the battery in 5 minutes.

25. Calculate the terminal voltage across the cells X and Y in the circuit given below. The cell X has an e.m.f 4V, internal resistance 0.5 Ω and cell Y has an e.m.f 8V and internal resistance 1 Ω.

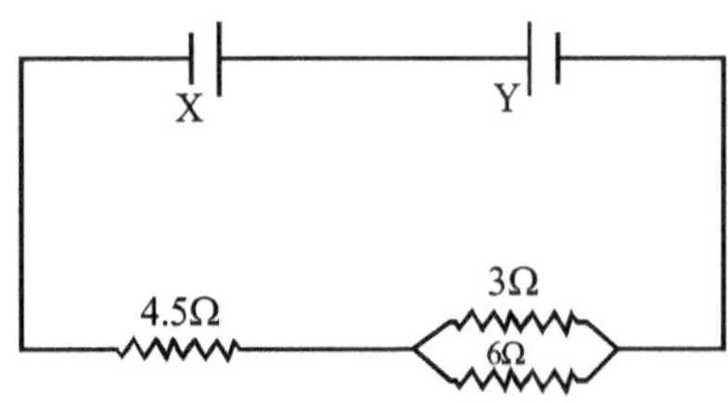

Topic 4	**Kirchhoff's Rules, Wheatstone Bridge, Meter Bridge and Potentiometer**

KIRCHHOFF'S RULES

Ist rule (Junction rule) : The algebraic sum of the currents meeting at a junction on electric circuit is always zero. i.e. $\sum I = 0$

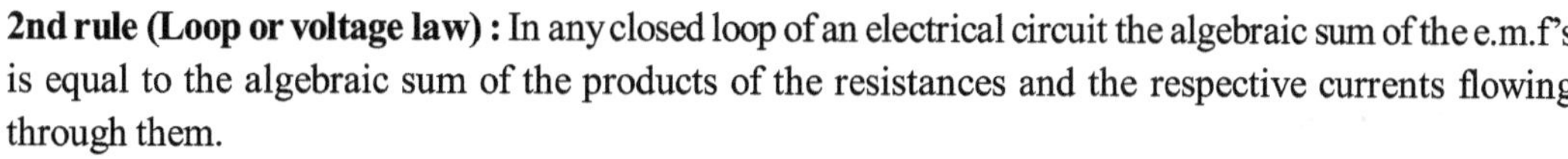

Here, $I_1 + I_2 + I_3 - I_4 + I_5 = 0$ or $I_1 + I_2 + I_3 + I_5 = I_4$

i.e, The Sum of currents entering the junction is equal to the sum of currents leaving the junction.

The current flowing in a conductor towards the junction is taken as positive and the current flowing away from the junction is taken as negative.

2nd rule (Loop or voltage law) : In any closed loop of an electrical circuit the algebraic sum of the e.m.f's is equal to the algebraic sum of the products of the resistances and the respective currents flowing through them.

i.e., $\sum E = \sum IR$

Sign Convention:

(i)   The e.m.f. of a cell is taken negative if in travelling the loop, the negative terminal comes first otherwise it is positive.

(ii)   The product of current and resistance in an arm of the loop is positive if the direction of current is same as the direction of the loop otherwise it is negative.

WHEATSTONE BRIDGE

It is a combination of four resistances used to measure one resistance in terms of other three.

Principle : The bridge is said to be balanced when no current flows through the galvanometer G. Then the potentials at points B and D are same.

Then, $\dfrac{P}{Q} = \dfrac{R}{S}$

Proof : When no current flows through the galvanometer then for the closed loop ABDA from kirchhoff's 2nd law

$$PI_1 - R(I - I_1) = 0$$

or $PI_1 = R(I - I_1)$ ...(i)

And for the closed loop BCDB

$$Q(I_1 - I_g) = S(I - I_1 + I_g)$$

Here $I_g = 0$

$\therefore$ $QI_1 = S(I - I_1)$ ...(ii)

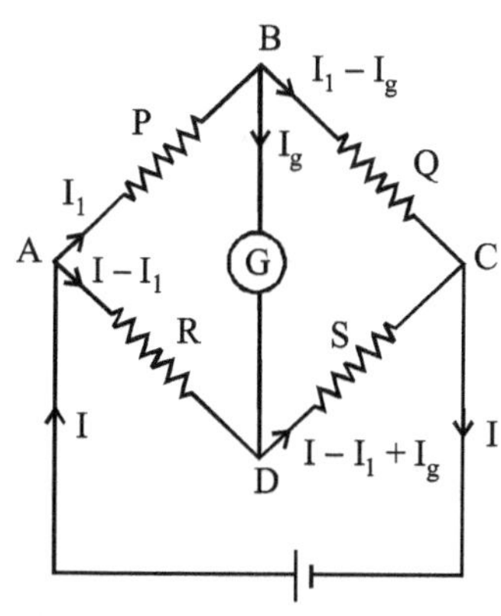

Dividing equation (i) by (ii) $\dfrac{P}{Q} = \dfrac{R}{S}$

METRE BRIDGE

It is an application of Wheatstone Bridge. It is also known as slide wire bridge. At balancing condition of bridges

$$\frac{R}{S} = \frac{P}{Q} = \frac{\sigma l_1}{\sigma(100 - l_1)} \quad \Rightarrow \quad \frac{R}{S} = \frac{l_1}{100 - l_1} \quad \Rightarrow \quad R = S\frac{l_1}{100 - l_1}$$

where σ is the resistance per unit length of the wire and l_1 is the length of the wire from one end where null point is obtained. The bridge is most sensitive when null point is somewhere near the middle point of the wire. This is due to end resistances.

Applications :

(i)   To measure an unknown resistance

(ii) To compare the two unknown resistances.

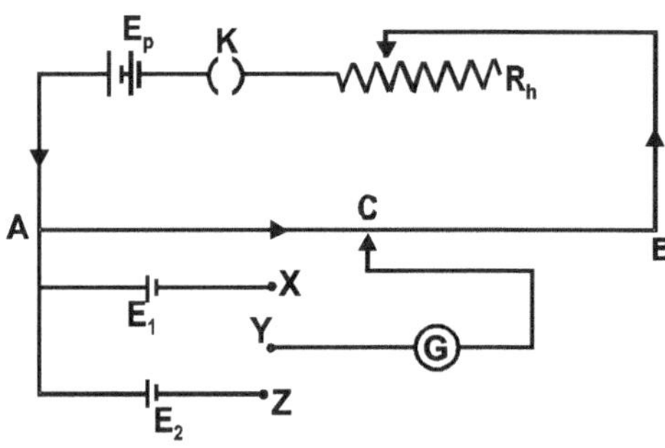

A meter bridge. Wire AC is 1 m long.

POTENTIOMETER

It it an instrument based on wheatstone bridge.

Principle:– The fall of potential across any portion of the wire is directly proportional to the length of that portion provided the wire of uniform cross-section and a constant current is flowing through it.

Theory : If A be the area of cross-section of the wire, ρ be the specific resistance of the material of the wire.

V be the potential difference across the portion of the wire whose length is ℓ and resistance R.

I be the current flowing through the wire then by Ohm's law,

$$V = IR = I\frac{\ell\rho}{A} = \left(\frac{I\rho}{A}\right)\ell = k\ell \quad \left[\text{where } k = \frac{\rho\ell}{A}\right]$$

$\therefore$ $V \propto \ell$ if A and I are constants

or, $\dfrac{V}{\ell} = k$ = Potential gradient or fall of potential/length of the wire.

Applications:

(i)   Potentiometer is used to compare the e.m.f's of two cells

Formula used : $\dfrac{E_1}{E_2} = \dfrac{\ell_1}{\ell_2}$

(ii) It is also used to find the internal resistance of a cell

Formula used : $r = \left(\dfrac{E}{V} - 1\right)R = \left(\dfrac{\ell_1}{\ell_2} - 1\right)R$

Practice Exercise-4

Multiple Choice Questions

1. The figure below shows currents in a part of electric circuit. The current i is
   (a) 1.7 amp
   (b) 3.7 amp
   (c) 1.3 amp
   (d) 1 amp

2. Match the entries of Column I with their correct mathematical expressions in Column II

Column I		Column II
(A) Balanced condition of wheatstone bridge	(1)	$\dfrac{R_1}{R_2} = \dfrac{R_3}{R_4}$
(B) Comparison of emf of two cells.	(2)	$\dfrac{R}{S} = \dfrac{l_1}{100 - l_1}$
(C) Determination of internal resistance of a cell	(3)	$\dfrac{E_1}{E_2} = \dfrac{l_1}{l_2}$
(D) Determination of unknown resistance by meter bridge	(4)	$r = R\left(\dfrac{l_1}{l_2} - 1\right)$

   (a) (A) → (4); (B) → (2); C → (3); (D) → (1)
   (b) (A) → (1); (B) → (3); C → (4); (D) → (2)
   (c) (A) → (3); (B) → (4); C → (2); (D) → (1)
   (d) (A) → (4); (B) → (3); C → (2); (D) → (1)

3. The resistances in the two arms of the meter bridge are 5Ω and $R\Omega$, respectively. When the resistance R is shunted with an equal resistance, the new balance point is at $1.6\,l_1$. The resistance 'R' is :
   (a) 10Ω
   (b) 15Ω
   (c) 20Ω
   (d) 25Ω

4. Sensitivity of potentiometer can be increased by
   (a) increasing the e.m.f of the cell
   (b) increasing the length of the potentiometer
   (c) decreasing the length of the potentiometer wire
   (d) None of these

5. AB is a wire of potentiometer with the increase in value of resistance R, the shift in the balance point J will be
   (a) towards B
   (b) towards A
   (c) remains constant
   (d) first towards B then back towards A

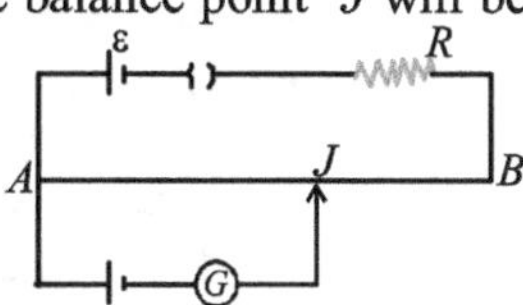

6. In the figure in balanced condition of wheatstone bridge
   (a) B is at higher potential.
   (b) D is at higher potential.
   (c) Any of the two B or D can be at higher potential than other arbitrarily.
   (d) B and D are at same potential.

7. The resistance of an ammeter is 13 Ω and its scale is graduated for a current upto 100 amps. After an additional shunt has been connected to this ammeter it becomes possible to measure currents upto 750 amperes by this meter. The value of shunt-resistance is
   (a) $2\,\Omega$　　(b) $0.2\,\Omega$　　(c) $2\,k\Omega$　　(d) $20\,\Omega$

Assertion & Reason Questions

DIRECTIONS (Qs. 8-11) : *Each of these questions contains an assertion followed by reason. Read them carefully and answer the question on the basis of following options. You have to select the one that best describes the two statements.*
(a) If both Assertion and Reason are correct and the Reason is a correct explanation of the Assertion.
(b) If both Assertion and Reason are correct but Reason is not a correct explanation of the Assertion.
(c) If the Assertion is correct but Reason is incorrect.
(d) If the Assertion is incorrect but the Reason is correct.

8. **Assertion** : Kirchoff's junction rule can be applied to a junction of several lines or a point in a line.
   Reason : When steady current is flowing, there is no accumulation of charges at any junction or at any point in a line.

9. **Assertion** : A potentiometer of longer length is used for accurate measurement.
   Reason : The potential gradient for a potentiometer of longer length with a given source of e.m.f becomes small.

10. **Assertion** : Kirchoff's junction rule follows from conservation of charge.
    Reason : Kirchoff's loop rule follows from conservation of momentum.

11. **Assertion** : A potentiometer of longer length is used for accurate measurment.
    Reason : The potential gradient for a potentiometer of longer length with a given source of e.m.f becomes small.

Case / Passage Based Questions

Potentiometer: A potentiometer is an ideal voltmeter since a voltmeter draws some current through the circuit while potentiometer needs no current to work. A potentiometer works on the principle of emf comparison. In working condition, a constant current flows throughout the wire of a potentiometer using standard cell of emf e_1. The wire of potentiometer is made of uniform material and cross-sectional area, and it has uniform resistance per unit length. The potential gradient depends upon the current in the wire.
A potentiometer with a cell of emf 2 V and internal resistance 0.4 Ω is used across the wire AB. A standard cadmium cell of

emf 1.02 V gives a balance point at 66 cm length of wire. The standard cell is then replaced by a cell of unknown emf e (internal resistance r), and the balance point found similarly turns out to be 88 cm length of the wire. The length of potentiometer wire AB is 1 m.

12. The value of e is
  (a) 1.36 V   (b) 2.63 V
  (c) 1.83 V   (d) None of these

13. The reading of the potentiometer, if a 4 V battery is used instead of e, is
  (a) 88.3 cm   (b) 47.3 cm
  (c) 95 cm   (d) cannot be calculated

14. If the resistance is connected across the cell e, the balancing length will
  (a) increase   (b) decrease
  (c) remain same   (d) None of these

15. The length of a wire of a potentiometer is 100 cm, and the emf of its standard cell is E volt. It is employed to measure the emf of a battery whose internal resistance is 0.5 Ω. If the balance point is obtained at $l = 30$ cm from the positive end, the emf of the battery is
  (a) $\dfrac{30E}{100}$ (b) $\dfrac{30E}{100.5}$
  (c) $\dfrac{30E}{(100-0.5)}$ (d) $\dfrac{30(E-0.5i)}{100}$
  where i is the current in the potentiometer wire.

16 In a potentiometer experiment, the balancing with a cell is at length 240 cm. On shunting the cell with a resistance of 2 Ω, the balancing length becomes 120 cm. The internal resistance of the cell is
  (a) 2 Ω   (b) 4 Ω   (c) 0.5   (d) 1 Ω

Very Short Answer Questions

17. At which point on a meter bridge wire, it is most sensitive?
18. Write any one use of potentiometer.

Short Answer Questions

19. Derive the balanced condition of wheatstone's bridge principle.
20. Explain the principle and working of a potentiometer. How will you find the value of e.m.f of a cell using a potentiometer?
21. Explain with a circuit diagram how the e.m.f of two cells can be compared with the help of a potentiometer.

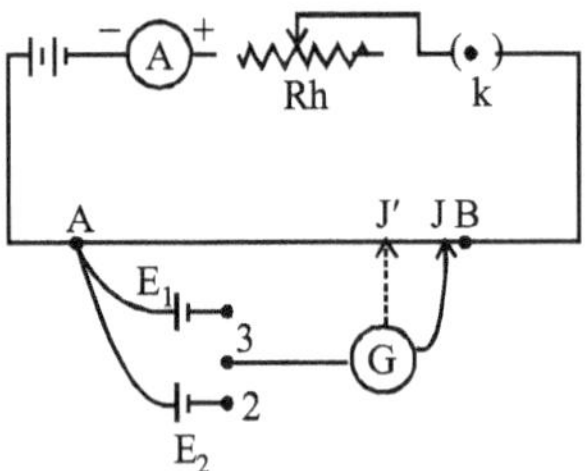

22. A voltmeter of a resistance 400 Ω is used to measure the potential difference across a 100 Ω ressitor in the circuit shown below.
  (a) What will be the reading on the voltmeter?
  (b) Calculate the potential difference across a 100 Ω resistor before the voltmeter is connected.

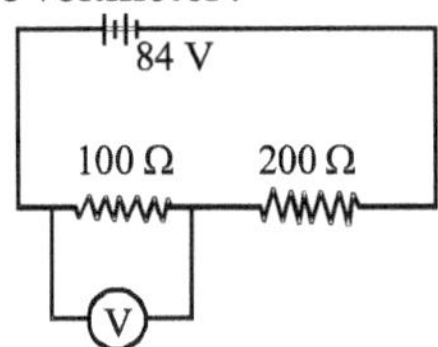

23. The length of a potential wire is 600 cm and it carries a current of 40 mA. For a cell of e.m.f. 2V and internal resistance 10 Ω, the null point is found to be at 500 cm. If a voltmeter is connected across the cell, the balancing length is decreased by 10 cm. Find
  (i) the resistance of whole wire
  (ii) reading of voltmeter and
  (iii) resistance of voltmeter.

24. Find the value of unknown resistance X and the current drawn by the circuit from the battery, if no current flows through the galvanometer. Assume the resistance per unit length of the wire AB to be 0.01 Ω/cm.

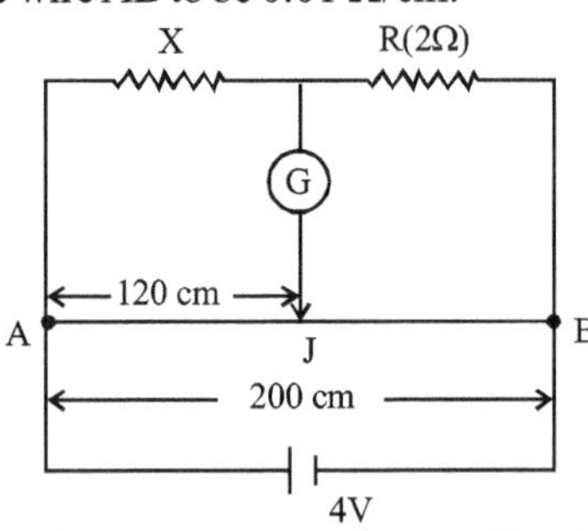

25. Find the value of the unknown resistance X in the following circuit, if no current flows through the section AO. Also calculate the current drawn by the circuit from the battery of e.m.f 6V and negligible internal resistance.

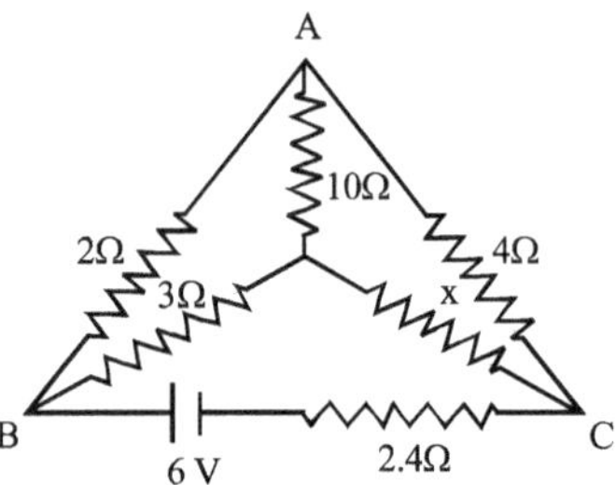

26. The variation of potential difference V with length in case of two potentiometers X and Y is as should in the given diagram. Which one of these two will you prefer for comparing e.m.f's of two cells and why?

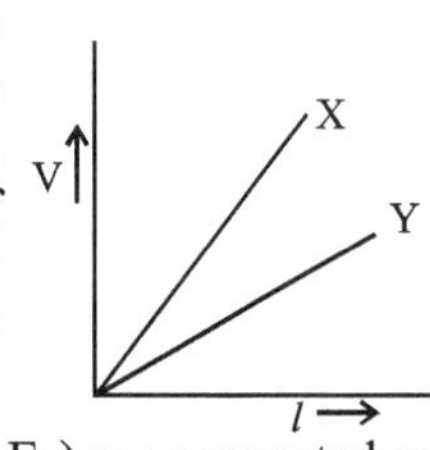

27. Two cells of e.m.f E_1 and E_2 ($E_1 > E_2$) are connected as shown in the figure. When a potentiometer is connected between A and B, the balancing length of the potentionmeter wire is 300 cm. On connecting the same potentiometer between A and C, the balancing length is 100 cm. Calculate the ratio of E_1 and E_2.

28. Explain with a circuit diagram how the internal resistance of a cell can be measured by a potentiometer.

29. Draw a circuit diagram to explain how an unknown resistance and the specific resistance of its material is calculated by a metre bridge.

30. Two cells of e.m.f 6V and 12 V and internal resistances 1 Ω and 2 Ω respectively are connected in parallel so as to send current in the same direction through an external resistance of 15 Ω.
  (i) Draw the circuit diagram.
  (ii) Using Kirchhoff's laws calculate
  (a) Current through each branch of the circuit
  (b) Potential difference across the 15 Ω resistance.

Important Tips & Formulae

- The drift velocity of electrons is small due to frequent collisions suffered by electrons.

- Electric field is zero inside a charged conductor, but it is non zero inside a current carrying conductor and is given by $E = \dfrac{V}{l}$ where V = potential difference across the conductor.

- The electric field established throughout the circuit, almost instantly. So the current established is almost instant. Due to this reason the electric bulb glows immediately when switch is on.

- The resistance of conductor increases with decrease density of material.

- Emf of cell does not depend on the resistance of the circuit. It depends upon the nature of electrolyte of the cell while potential difference depends upon the resistance between the two points of the circuit and current flowing through the circuit.

- Wheatstone bridge is most sensitive if all the four arms have equal resistances *i.e.*, $P = Q = R = S$

- A potentiometer can act as an ideal voltmeter.

- Resistance for an ideal voltmeter $= \infty$

- Resistance for an ideal ammeter $= 0$

- The maximum value of current which can be passed through the fuse wire without melting it is called safe current. The safe current is independent of the length of the wire.

- If length of wire is increased by n times then resistance will increase by n^2 times *i.e.*, $|R_2 = n^2 R_1|$. Similarly if radius of wire is reduced to $\dfrac{1}{n}$ times then area of cross-section will decrease $\dfrac{1}{n^2}$ times so the resistance becomes n^4 times *i.e.*, $R_2 = n^4 R_1$.

- The relation between current density $\vec{J}$, conductivity σ and electric field $\vec{E}$ applied across conductor is given by
$$\vec{J} = \sigma \vec{E}$$
Here $\sigma = \dfrac{ne^2}{m} \tau$

- If length of a conductor increases by x% then resistance will increase by 2x % (valid only if 2x < 10%) but its resistivity remains unchanged.

- If we have n conductor, each of equal resistance, the number of possible combinations is 2^{n-1}.

- If we have n conductors, each of different resistance then the number of possible combinations will be 2^n.

- If a wire of resistance R, is cut into n equal parts and then these parts are collected to form a bundle then resistance of combination formed will be $\dfrac{R}{n^2}$.

- If two resistance of R_1 and R_2 are connected first in series and then in parallel. If R_s and R_p are their equivalent resistance in series and parallel combination respectively then $R_1 = \dfrac{1}{2}\left[R_s + \sqrt{R_s^2 - 4R_s R_p} \right]$ and
$$R_2 = \dfrac{1}{2}\left[R_s + \sqrt{R_s^2 - 4R_s R_p} \right]$$

- If in the series combination of n identical cells (each having emf E and internal resistance r) if x cells are wrongly connected then equivalent emf will be $E_{eq} = (n - 2x)E$ and equivalent internal resistance will be $r_{eq} = nr$.

- Consider the parallel combination of two cells having emf E_1 and E_2 respectively, if they are connected with reversed polarity then equivalent emf is given by
$$E_{eq} = \dfrac{E_1 r_2 - E_2 r_1}{r_1 + r_2}$$

- Thus, power consumed by a n equal resistors in parallel combination is n^2 times that of power consumed in series combination if V remains same.

- Short circuited current, $I = \dfrac{n\varepsilon}{nr} = \dfrac{\varepsilon}{r}$ *i.e.*, I is independent of n in parallel combination of n cells in of internal resistance r.

NCERT Questions

3.1. The storage battery of a car has an emf of 12 V. If the internal resistance of the battery is 0.4 Ω what is the maximum current that can be drawn from the battery?

Sol. Given, $E = 12V$, $r = 0.4\,\Omega$, $I_{max.} = ?$

By formula, $I = \dfrac{E}{R+r}$

For maximum current, $R = 0$.

So, $I_{max.} = E/r = 12/0.4 = 30A$.

3.2. A battery of emf 10 V and internal resistance 3 Ω is connected to a resistor. If the current in the circuit is 0.5 A, what is the resistance of the resistor? What is the terminal voltage of the battery when the circuit is closed?

Sol. Given, $E = 10\ V$, $r = 3\,\Omega$, $I = 0.5\ A$, $R = ?$, $V = ?$

By formula, $I = \dfrac{E}{R+r}$ and

$R = (E/I) - r = (10/0.5) - 3 = 20 - 3 = 17\ \Omega$

By relation, $V = IR = 0.5 \times 17 = 8.5\ V$

3.3. (a) Three resistors of resistances $1\,\Omega$, $2\,\Omega$ and $3\,\Omega$ are combined in series. What is the total resistance of the combination?

(b) If the combination is connected to a battery of emf 12 V and negligible internal resistance, obtain the potential drop across each resistor.

Sol. (a) Given, $R_1 = 1\,\Omega$, $R_2 = 2\,\Omega$, $R_3 = 3\,\Omega$, $R_s = ?$

(b) $\varepsilon = 12\ V$, $V_1 = ?$, $V_3 = ?$

(a) By formula, $R_s = R_1 + R_2 + R_3$
$= 1 + 2 + 3 = 6\ \Omega$

(b) By relation, $I = E/R = 12/6 = 2A$
& $V = RI$
$V_1 = R_1 I = 1 \times 2 = 2V$
$V_2 = R_2 I = 2 \times 2 = 4V$
$V_3 = R_3 I = 3 \times 2 = 6V$.

3.4. (a) Three resistors of $2\,\Omega$, $4\,\Omega$ and $5\,\Omega$ are combined in parallel. What is the total resistance of the combination?

(b) If the combination is connected to a battery of emf 20 V and negligible internal resistance then determine the current through each resistor, and the total current drawn from the battery.

Sol. (a) Given, $R_1 = 2\,\Omega$, $R_2 = 4\,\Omega$, $R_3 = 5\,\Omega$, $R_p = ?$

(b) $V = 20\ V$, $I_1 = ?$, $I_2 = ?$, $I_3 = ?$, $I = ?$

(a) By formula, $\dfrac{1}{R_p} = \dfrac{1}{R_1} + \dfrac{1}{R_2} + \dfrac{1}{R_3}$

$= \dfrac{1}{2} + \dfrac{1}{4} + \dfrac{1}{5} = \dfrac{10+5+4}{20} = \dfrac{19}{20}$

$R_p = \dfrac{20}{19}$ ohm.

(b) By formula, $I = \dfrac{V}{R}$;

$I_1 = \dfrac{V}{R_1} = \dfrac{20}{2} = 10A$;

$I_2 = \dfrac{V}{R_2} = \dfrac{20}{40} = 5A$;

$I_3 = \dfrac{V}{R_3} = \dfrac{20}{5} = 4A$

By relation, $I = I_1 + I_2 + I_3 = 10 + 5 + 4 = 19A$.

3.5. At room temperature (27°C) the resistance of a heating element is 100 Ω. What is the temperature of the element if the resistance is found to be 117 Ω given that the temperature coefficient of the material of the resistor is $1.70 \times 10^{-4}\ °C^{-1}$.

Sol. Given, $R_1 = 100\ \Omega$, $R_2 = 117\ \Omega$,
$\alpha = 1.7 \times 10^{-4}\ °C^{-1}$, $t_1 = 27°C$, $t_2 = ?$
By formula, $R_2 = R_1\,[1 + \alpha(t_2 - t_1)]$
$R_2 - R_1 = R_1\alpha(t_2 - t_1)$

$t_2 = \dfrac{R_2 - R_1}{R_1\alpha} + t_1$

$= \dfrac{117 - 100}{100 \times 1.7 \times 10^{-4}} + 27$

$= \dfrac{17 \times 10^4}{100 \times 1.7} + 27 = 1000 + 27 = 1027°\ C$.

3.6. A negligibly small current is passed through a wire of length 15 m and uniform cross-section 6.0×10^{-7} m², and its resistance is measured to be 5.0 Ω. What is the resistivity of the material?

Sol. Given, $l = 15\ m$, $A = 6.0 \times 10^{-7}\ m^2$, $R = 5\ \Omega$, $\rho = ?$

By relation, $R = \rho\dfrac{\ell}{A}$

or, $\rho = \dfrac{RA}{\ell} = \dfrac{5 \times 6.0 \times 10^{-7}}{15} = 2 \times 10^{-7}$ ohm-m.

3.7. A silver wire has a resistance of 2.1 Ω at 27.5°C, and a resistance of 2.7 Ω at 100°C. Determine the temperature coefficient of resistivity of silver.

Sol. Given, $R_1 = 2.1\ \Omega$, $t_1 = 27.5°\ C$, $R_2 = 2.7\ \Omega$,
$t_2 = 100°\ C$, $\alpha = ?$
By formula, $R_2 = R_1\,[1 + \alpha(t_2 - t_1)]$

$\alpha = \dfrac{R_2 - R_1}{R_1(t_2 - t_1)} = \dfrac{2.7 - 2.1}{2.1(100 - 27.5)}$

$= \dfrac{0.6}{2.1 \times 72.5} = 3.941 \times 10^{-3}\ °C^{-1}$.

3.8. A heating element using nichrome connected to a 230 V supply draws an initial current of 3.2 A which settles after a few seconds to a steady value of 2.8 A. What is the steady temperature of the heating element if the room temperature is 27.0°C? Temperature coefficient of resistance of nichrome averaged over the temperature range involved is 1.70×10^{-4} °C^{-1}.

Sol. Given, $R_1 = \dfrac{230}{3.2}\Omega$, $R_2 = \dfrac{230}{2.8}\Omega$, $\alpha = 1.7 \times 10^{-4}$ °C^{-1},

$t_1 = 27$°C, $t_2 = ?$

By formula, $R_2 = R_1 [(1 + \alpha(t_2 - t_1)]$

$$t_2 = \frac{R_2 - R_1}{R_1 \alpha} + t_1 = \frac{\dfrac{230}{2.8} - \dfrac{230}{3.2}}{\dfrac{230}{3.2} \times 1.7 \times 10^{-4}} + 27$$

$$= \frac{3.2 - 2.8}{3.2 \times 2.8 \times \dfrac{1}{3.2} \times 1.7 \times 10^{-4}} + 27$$

$$= \frac{0.4}{2.8 \times 1.7 \times 10^{-4}} + 27 = 840.34 + 27 = 867.34°C.$$

3.9. Determine the current in each branch of the network shown in Figure.

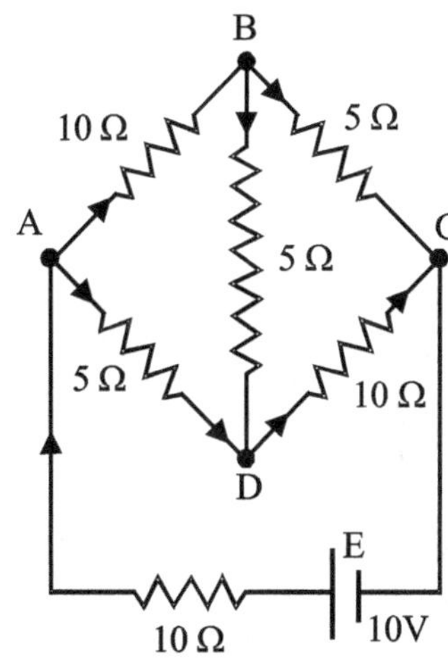

Sol. From Kirchhoff's loop rule,

For loop ADCEA,

$- 5(I - I_1) - 10(I - I_2) - 10I + 10 = 0$

i.e., $25I - 5I_1 - 10I_2 = 10$

or $5I - I_1 - 2I_2 = 2$ ...(1)

For loop ABDA,

$- 10I_1 - 5(I_1 - I_2) + 5 (I - I_1) = 0$

i.e., $- 20I_1 + 5I_2 + 5I = 0$

or $I - 4I_1 + I_2 = 0$ ...(2)

For loop BCDB,

$- 5I_2 + 10(I - I_2) + 5 (I_1 - I_2) = 0$

i.e., $-20I_2 + 10I + 5I_1 = 0$

or $2I + I_1 - 4I_2 = 0$ ...(3)

Adding (2) and (3), $3I - 3I_1 - 3I_2 = 0$

i.e., $I - I_1 - I_2 = 0$

or $I = I_1 + I_2$ ...(4)

Applying value of I in eq. (1),

$5I_1 + 5I_2 - I_1 - 2I_2 = 2$

i.e., $4I_1 + 3I_2 = 2$ ...(5)

Applying value of I in eq. (2),

$I_1 + I_2 - 4I_1 + I_2 = 0$

or $- 3I_1 + 2I_2 = 0 \Rightarrow I_2 = \dfrac{3}{2}I_1$

Putting values in eq. (5), $4I_1 + \dfrac{9}{2}I_1 = 2$

$\Rightarrow I_1 = \dfrac{4}{17}$A ; $I_2 = \dfrac{3}{2}I_1 = \dfrac{6}{17}$A

$\Rightarrow I = I_1 + I_2 = \dfrac{4}{17} + \dfrac{6}{17} = \dfrac{10}{17}$A

Currents in different branches can be calculated from these values.

3.10. **(a)** In a metre bridge, the balance point is found to be at 39.5 cm from the end A. When the resistor Y is of $12.5\,\Omega$ determine the resistance of X. Why are the connections between resistors in a Wheatstone or meter bridge made of thick copper strips?

(b) Determine the balance point of the bridge above if X and Y are interchanged.

(c) What happens if the galvanometer and cell are interchanged at the balance point of the bridge? Would the galvanometer show any current?

Sol. **(a)**

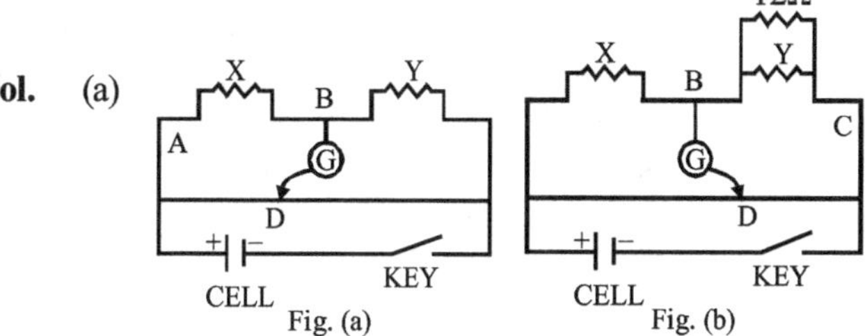

Given that Y = $12.5\Omega, l_1 = 39.5$cm,

$\ell_2 = 100 - 39.5 = 60.5$ cm, X = ?

By formula, $\dfrac{X}{Y} = \dfrac{\ell_1}{\ell_2}$ and

$X = Y\dfrac{\ell_1}{\ell_2} = \dfrac{12.5 \times 39.5}{60.5} = 8.1612\Omega.$

Thick copper strips are used for connections to minimise resistance of connection which are not accounted for in bridge formula.

(b) When X and Y are interchanged, values of ℓ_1 and ℓ_2 also become interchanged. Then $\ell_1 = 60.5$ cm. Hence balance point will be at 60.5 cm.

(c) When galvanometer and cell are interchanged, condition for balance of bridge remains satisfied. Hence galvanometer will not show any current.

3.11. A storage battery of emf 8.0 V and internal resistance $0.5\,\Omega$ is being charged by a 120 V D.C. supply using a series resistor of $15.5\,\Omega$. What is the terminal voltage of the battery during charging? What is the purpose of having a series resistor in the charging circuit?

Sol. The total circuit resistance becomes
$$15.5 + 0.5 = 16\Omega.$$

The total e.m.f. of circuit will be $120 - 8 = 112$ V (Battery emf opposing supply emf)

Charging current becomes $\dfrac{112}{16} = 7.0$A.

For battery being charged, terminal voltage,
$$V = E + Ir = 8.0 + 7 \times 0.5 = 11.5V.$$

A series resistor is used to reduce charging current to a proper value.

3.12. In a potentiometer arrangement, a cell of emf 1.25 V gives a balance point at 35.0 cm length of the wire. If the cell is replaced by another cell and the balance point shifts to 63.0 cm. what is the emf of the second cell?

Sol. Given, $\ell_1 = 35$ cm, $\ell_2 = 63$ cm,

$E_1 = 1.25$ V, $E_2 = ?$

By relation, $\dfrac{E_2}{E_1} = \dfrac{\ell_2}{\ell_1}$

or $E_2 = E_1 \dfrac{\ell_2}{\ell_1} = 1.25 \times \dfrac{63}{35} = 2.25$ V.

3.13. The number density of free electrons in a copper conductor estimated in Example 3.1 is 8.5×10^{28} m^{-3}. How long does an electron take to drift from one end of a wire 3.0 m long to its other end? The area of cross-section of the wire is 2.0×10^{-6} m^2 and it is carrying a current of 3.0 A.

Sol. Given, $n = 8.5 \times 10^{28}$ m^{-3}, $A = 2.0 \times 10^{-6}$ m^2, $e = 1.6 \times 10^{-19}$ C, $I = 3.0$ A, $v_d = ?$

By formula, $I = nAv_d e$ or $v_d = \dfrac{I}{nAe}$

$$= \dfrac{3}{8.5 \times 10^{28} \times 2.0 \times 10^{-6} \times 1.6 \times 10^{-19}}$$

$$= \dfrac{3}{85 \times 2 \times 16 \times 10}\,\text{m/sec}$$

Time taken to travel 3m,
$$t = \dfrac{\ell}{v_d} = \dfrac{3 \times 85 \times 2 \times 16 \times 10}{3} = 27200\,\text{sec}.$$

ADDITIONAL EXERCISES

3.14. The earth's surface has a negative surface charge density of 10^{-6} m^{-2}. The potential difference of 400 kV between the top of the atmosphere and the surface results (due to the low conductivity to the lower atmosphere) in a current of only 1800 A over the entire globe. If there were no mechanism of sustaining atmospheric electric field, how much time (roughly) would be required to neutralise the earth's surface? (This never happens in practice because there is a mechanism to replenish electric charges, namely the continual thunderstorms and lightning in different parts of the globe). (Radius of earth $= 6.37 \times 10^6$ m.)

Sol. Given, charge per unit area of surface of earth
$$= 10^{-9}\,\text{Cm}^{-2},$$

Current $= 1800$ A, radius of earth $= 6400$ km
$$= 6.4 \times 10^6\,\text{m}$$

Charge on entire surface of the earth
$$= 4\pi\,(6.4 \times 10^6)^2 \times 10^{-9}\text{C}.$$

As rate of flow of charge is 1800 C per sec, time taken for flow of entire charge,
$$t = \dfrac{4 \times 3.14 \times (6.4 \times 10^6) \times 10^{-9}}{1800}$$

$$= \dfrac{4 \times 314 \times 64 \times 64}{18} \times 10^{-3} = 285.8\,\text{sec}.$$

3.15. (a) Six lead-acid type of secondary cells each of emf 2.0 V and internal resistance 0.015 Ω are joined in series to provide a supply to a resistance of 8.5 Ω. What are the current drawn from the supply and its terminal voltage?

(b) A secondary cell after long use has an emf of 1.9 V and a large internal resistance 380 Ω. What maximum current can be drawn from the cell? Could the cell drive the starting motor of a car?

Sol. (a) Given, number of secondary cells, $N = 6$,

E.m.f. of each cell, $E = 2.0$ V

Internal resistance of each cell, $r = 0.015\ \Omega$,

External resistance, $R = 8.5\ \Omega$

By formula, current,
$$I = \dfrac{NE}{R + Nr} = \dfrac{6 \times 2}{8.5 + 6 \times 0.015} = \dfrac{12}{8.5 + 0.09} = 1.397\,\text{A}.$$

Terminal voltage $V = IR = \dfrac{12 \times 8.5}{8.59} = 11.874$ V.

(b) Given, $E = 1.9$ V, $r = 380\ \Omega$, $I_{max} = ?$

Maximum current can be drawn by short circuit,

$$I_{max} = \frac{E}{r} = \frac{1.9}{380} = 0.005 \text{ A}.$$

Which cannot start a car, because a starter motor requires a large current (≈ 700 A) for few seconds.

3.16. **Two wires of equal length, one of aluminium and the other of copper have the same resistance. Which of the two wires is lighter? Hence explain why aluminium wires are preferred for overhead power cables.**

(ρ_{Al} = 2.63 × 10⁻⁸ Ω m, ρ_{Cu} = 1.72 × 10⁻⁸ Ω m, Relative density of Al = 2.7 of Cu = 8.9)

Sol. By formula, $R = \rho\dfrac{\ell}{a} = \rho\dfrac{\ell^2}{a\ell} = \rho\dfrac{\ell^2}{V} = \dfrac{\rho\ell^2 d}{m}$

where $V = a\ell$ = volume of wire,
ma = mass of wire, d = density of wire material.

For aluminium wire, $R_{Al} = \dfrac{\rho_{Al}\ell^2_{Al}d_{Al}}{m_{Al}}$

For copper wire, $R_{cu} = \dfrac{\rho_{Cu}\ell^2_{Cu}d_{Cu}}{m_{Cu}}$

For equal length and resistance,

$$\frac{\rho_{Al}d_{Al}}{m_{Al}} = \frac{\rho_{Cu}d_{Cu}}{m_{Cu}} \Rightarrow \frac{m_{Cu}}{m_{Al}} = \frac{\rho_{Cu}d_{Cu}}{\rho_{Al}d_{Al}}$$

$$\Rightarrow \frac{m_{Cu}}{m_{Al}} = \frac{1.72\times10^{-8}\times8.9}{2.63\times10^{-8}\times2.7} = \frac{172\times89}{263\times27} = 2.1558.$$

Aluminium wires are preferred for overhead cables because the ratio shows that aluminium wire is lighter than copper wire.

3.17. **What conclusion can you draw from the following observations on a resistor made of alloy manganin?**

Current	Voltage	Current	Voltage
A	V	A	V
0.2	3.94	3	59.2
0.4	7.87	4	78.8
0.6	11.8	5	98.6
0.8	15.7	6	118.5
1	19.7	7	138.2
2	39.4	8	158

Sol. Ohm's law is valid to a high accuracy; the resistivity of the alloy manganin is nearly independent of temperature.

3.18. **Answer the following questions:**

(a) **A steady current flows in a metallic conductor of nonuniform cross-section. Which of these quantities is constant along the conductor: current, current density, electric field, drift speed?**

(b) **Is Ohm's law universally applicable for all conducting elements? If not, give examples of elements which do not obey Ohm's law.**

(c) **A low voltage supply from which one needs high currents must have very low internal resistance. Why?**

(d) **A high tension (HT) supply of say, 6 kV must have a very large internal resistance. Why?**

Sol. (a) Only current (because it is given to be steady!). The rest depends on the area of cross section inversely.

(b) No, examples of non-ohmic elements vacuum diode, semiconductor diode etc.

(c) Because the maximum current drown from source is equal to ε/r.

(d) Because, if the circuit is shorted (accidentally), the current drown will exceed safety limits, if internal resistance is not large.

3.19. **Choose the correct alternative:**

(a) **Alloys of metals usually have (greater/less) resistivity than that of their constituent metals.**

(b) **Alloys usually have much (lower/higher) temperature coefficients of resistance than pure metals.**

(c) **The resistivity of the alloy manganin is nearly independent of/increases rapidly with increase of temperature.**

(d) **The resistivity of a typical insulator (e.g., amber) is greater than that of a metal by a factor of the order of ($10^{22}/10^3$).**

Sol. (a) greater

(b) lower

(c) nearly independent of

(d) 10^{22}

3.20. (a) **Given n resistors each of resistance R, how will you combine them to get the (i) maximum (ii) minimum effective resistance? What is the ratio of the maximum to minimum resistance?**

(b) **Given the resistances of $1\,\Omega$, $2\,\Omega$, $3\,\Omega$, how will be combine them to get an equivalent resistance of (i) $(11/3)\,\Omega$ (ii) $(11/5)\,\Omega$, (iii) $6\,\Omega$ (iv) $(6/11)\,\Omega$?**

(c) **Determine the equivalent resistance of networks shown in Fig (i) and (ii).**

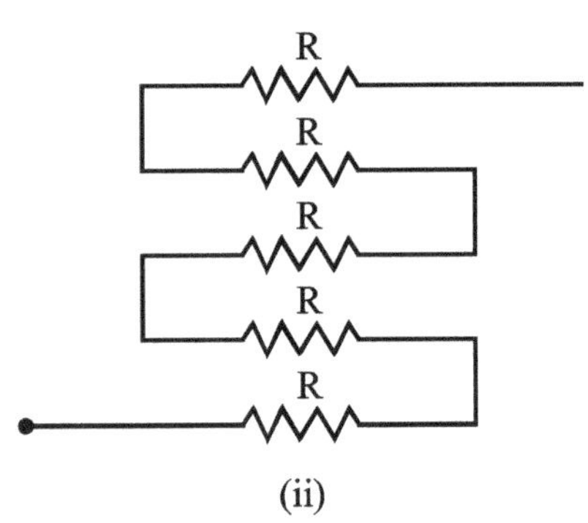

(ii)

Sol. (a) For maximum effective resistance, resistors must be combined in series.

Maximum effective resistance = nR

For minimum effective resistance, resistors must be combined in parallel.

Minimum effective resistance = $\dfrac{R}{n}$

Ratio, $\dfrac{\text{maximum}}{\text{minimum}}$ of effective resistance = $\dfrac{nR}{\dfrac{R}{n}} = n^2$.

(b) (i) 1Ω and 2Ω in parallel with 3Ω in their series.

Equivalents resistance = $\dfrac{1\times 2}{1+2}+3 = \dfrac{2}{3}+3 = \dfrac{11}{3}\Omega$.

(ii) 2Ω and 3Ω in parallel with 1Ω in their series.

Equivalents resistance = $\dfrac{2\times 3}{2+3}+1 = \dfrac{6}{5}+1 = \dfrac{11}{5}\Omega$.

(iii) All in series, equivalent resistance
= 1 + 2 + 3 = 6 Ω.

(iv) All resistance in parallel,

$$\dfrac{1}{\text{Eq.resistance}} = \dfrac{1}{1}+\dfrac{1}{2}+\dfrac{1}{3}+ = \dfrac{11}{6}$$

or equivalent resistance = $\dfrac{6}{11}\Omega$.

(c) (i) It is equivalent to four $2\,\Omega - 4\,\Omega$ parallel combination in series.

Each combination = $\dfrac{2\times 4}{2+4} = \dfrac{8}{6} = \dfrac{4}{3}\Omega$

Since such four combination are in series.

$\therefore$ Total resistance = $4\times\dfrac{4}{3} = \dfrac{16}{3}\Omega$.

(ii) It is equivalent to 5 resistors, each of resistance R in series. Total resistance = 5R.

3.21. Determine the current drawn from a 12 V supply with internal resistance $0.5\,\Omega$ by the infinite network shown in fig. Each resistor has $1\,\Omega$ resistance.

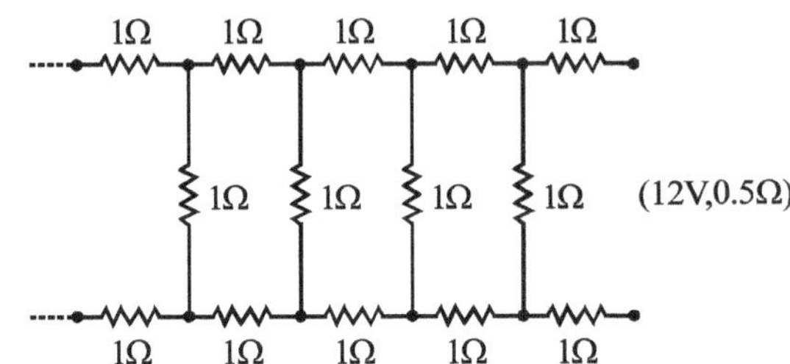

Sol. Let the network have resistance R. Adding one more set to it on battery end the network now becomes as shown in figure.

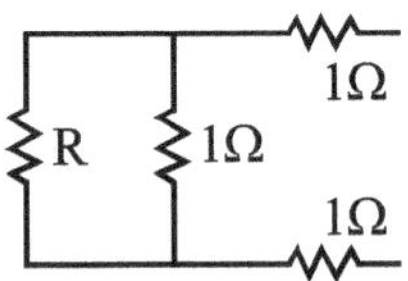

This has resistance = $1+\dfrac{R\times 1}{R+1}+1 = 2+\dfrac{R}{R+1}$

The network has infinite such sets. So, this resistance must still be R.

Hence, $2+\dfrac{R}{R+1} = R$

or, $2R + 2 + R = R^2 + R$

$R^2 - 2R - 2 = 0$

$\Rightarrow \quad R = \dfrac{2\pm\sqrt{4+8}}{2} = \dfrac{2\pm 2\sqrt{3}}{2} = 1\pm\sqrt{3}$

Taking only positive value,

$R = 1+\sqrt{3} = 2.732\Omega$.

Now total circuit resistance = 2.732 + 0.5 = 3.232 Ω

$\therefore$ Current = $\dfrac{12}{3.232} = 3.71292$ A.

3.22. Figure shows a potentiometer with a cell of 2.0 V and internal resistance $0.40\,\Omega$ maintaining a potential drop across the resistor wire AB. A standard cell which maintains a constant emf of 1.02 V (for very moderate currents upto a few mA) gives a balance point at 67.3 cm length of the wire. To ensure very low currents drawn from the standard cell, a very high resistance of $600\,k\,\Omega$ is put in series with it, which is shorted close to the balance point. The standard cell is then replaced by a cell of unknown emf E and the balance point found similarly, turns out to be at 82.3 cm length of the wire.

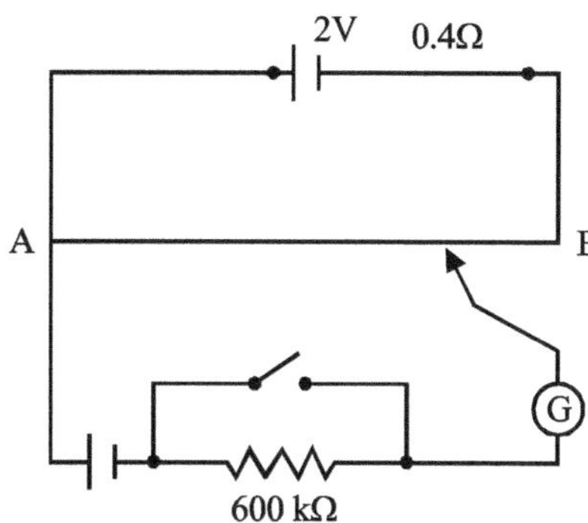

(a) What is the value of E?

(b) What purpose does the high resistance of 600 kΩ have?

(c) Is the balance point affected by this high resistance?

(d) Is the balance point affected by the internal resistance of the driver cell?

(e) Would the method work in the above situation if the driver cell of the potentiometer had an emf of 1.0 V instead of 2.0 V?

(f) Would the circuit work well for determining an extremely small emf, say of the order of a few mV (such as the typical emf of the thermo-couple)? If not, how will you modify the circuit?

Sol. **(a)** By formula, $\dfrac{E}{E_{standard}} = \dfrac{l}{l_{standard}}$

$\Rightarrow$ $E = \dfrac{l \times E_{standard}}{l_{standard}} = \dfrac{82.3 \times 1.02}{67.3} = 1.2474$ V.

(b) To reduce current through the galvanometer when the movable contact is far from the balance point.

(c) No.

(d) No.

(e) No. If E is greater than the emf of the drive cell of the potentiometer, there will be no balance point on the wire AB.

(f) The circuit, as it is, would be unsuitable because the balance point (for ε of the order a few mV) will be very close to the end A and the percentage error in measurement will be very large. The circuit is modified by putting a suitable resistor R in series with the wire AB so that potential drop across AB is only slightly greater than the emf to be measured. Then the balance point will be at larger length of the wire and the percentage error will be much smaller.

3.23. Figure shows a potentiometer circuit for comparison of two resistances. The balance point with a standard resistor R = 10.0 Ω is found to be 58.3 cm, while that with the unknown resistance X is 68.5 cm. Determine the value of X. What might you do if you failed to find a balance point with the given cell of emf E?

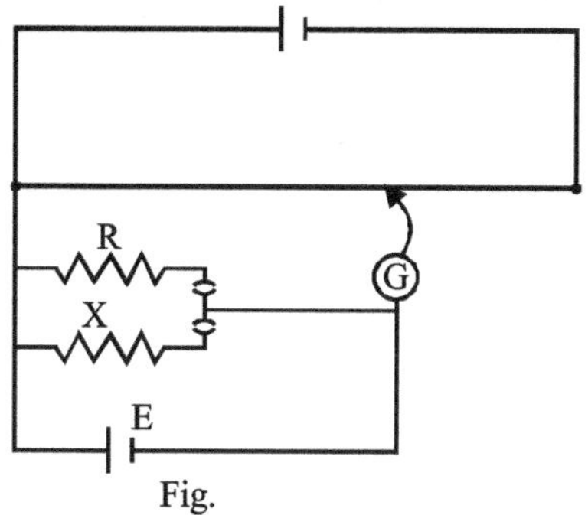

Fig.

Sol. In this case, $\dfrac{R}{X} = \dfrac{l_1}{l_2}$

or $X = R\dfrac{l_2}{l_1} = \dfrac{10 \times 68.5}{58.3} = 11.75\Omega$

In case of failure, a high resistance is put in series with the cell E. This will reduce current through R and X and potential difference across them will be reduced to values lower than the potential difference across wire AB.

3.24. Figure shows a 2.0 V potentiometer used for the determination of internal resistance of a 1.5 V cell. The balance point of cell in open circuit is 76.3 cm. When a resistor of 9.5 Ω is used in the external circuit of the cell, the balance point shifts to 64.8 cm length of the potentiometer wire. Determine the internal resistance of the cell.

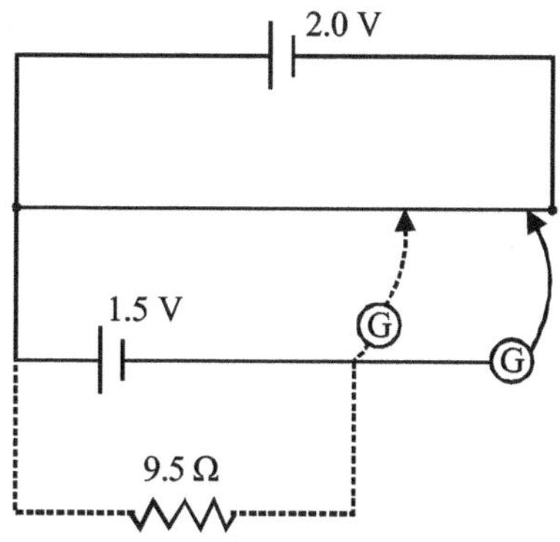

Sol. In open circuit, balance point at 76.3 cm balances e.m.f. of the cell. In close circuit balance point at 64.8 cm balances terminal voltage V of the cell.

Hence E = 76.3 kV and V = 64.8 kV

By formula internal resistance,

$r = R\dfrac{E-V}{V} = \dfrac{9.5(76.3 - 64.8)}{64.8} = \dfrac{9.5 \times 11.5}{64.8} = 1.686\Omega.$

Past year Exercise

Very Short Answer Questions

1. A potentiometer can measure emf of a cell because
   (a) the sensitivity of potentiometer is large.
   (b) no current is drawn from the cell at balance.
   (c) no current flows in the wire of potentiometer at balance.
   (d) internal resistance of cell is neglected.

2. Two resistors R_1 and R_2 of $4\,\Omega$ and $6\,\Omega$ are connected in parallel across a battery. The ratio of power dissipated in them, $P_1 : P_2$ will be
   (a) $4 : 9$ (b) $3 : 2$
   (c) $9 : 4$ (d) $2 : 3$

3. A resistance R is connected across a cell of emf E and internal resistance r. Now, a potentiometer measures the potential difference between the terminals of the cells as V. Write the expression for r in terms of E, V and R.

4. Two identical slabs, of a given metal, are joined together, in two different ways, as shown in figures (a) and (b). What is the ratio of the resistances of these two combinations?

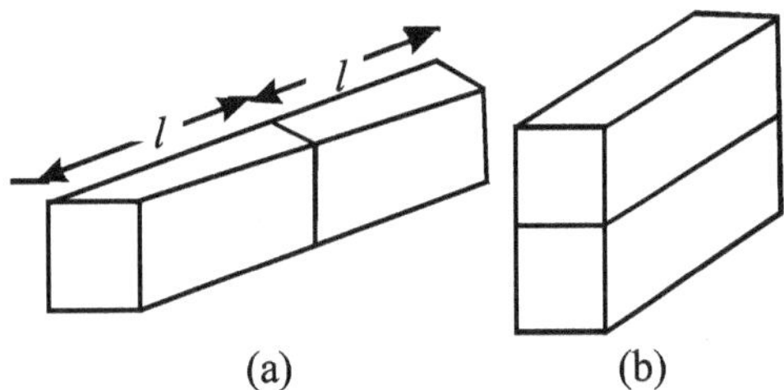

       (a)   (b)

5. Define resistivity of a conductor. Write its *SI* unit.

6. In an experiment on meter bridge, if the balancing length AC is X, what would be its value, when the radius of the meter bridge wire AB is doubled? Justify your answer.

7. When electrons drift in a metal from lower to higher potential, does it mean that all the free electrons of the metal are moving in the same direction?

8. Two wires of equal length, one of copper and the other of manganin have the same resistance. Which wire is thicker?

9. Two students A and B were asked to pick a resistor of $15\,k\Omega$ from a collection of carbon resistors. A picked a resistor with bands of colours brown, green, orange while B choose a resistor with bands of black green, red. Who picked the correct resistor?

10. What does the voltmeter connected to the two terminals of a cell read-emf or terminal potential difference?

11. A heating element is marked 210 V, 630 W. Find the resistance of the element when connected to a 210V dc source.

12. A 5V battery of negligible internal resistance is connected across a 200 V battery and a resistance of $39\,\Omega$ as shown in the figure. Find the value of the current.

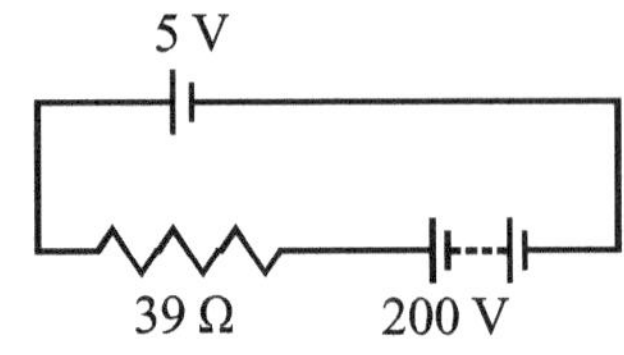

13. The emf of a cell is always greater than its terminal voltage. Why? Give reason.

14. Two identical cells, each of emf E, having negligible internal resistance, are connected in parallel with each other across an external resistance R. What is the current through this resistance?

15. Define the term 'Mobility' of charge carriers in a conductor. Write its S.I. unit

16. Show variation of resistivity of copper as a function of temperature in a graph.

17. Define the term 'electrical conductivity' of a metallic wire. Write its S.I. unit.

18. Define the term 'drift velocity' of charge carriers in a conductor and write its relationship with the current flowing through it.

19. Distinguish between emf and terminal voltage of a cell.

20. Graph showing the variation of current versus voltage for a material GaAs is shown in the figure. Identify the region of
    (i) negative resistance
    (ii) where Ohm's law is obeyed.

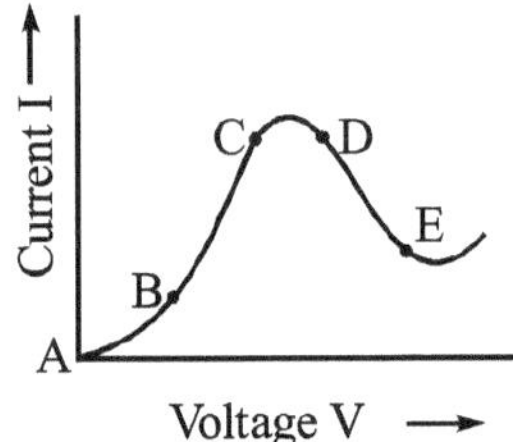

21. The plot of the variation of potential difference across a combination of three identical cells in series, versus current is shown below. What is the emf and internal resistance of each cell ?

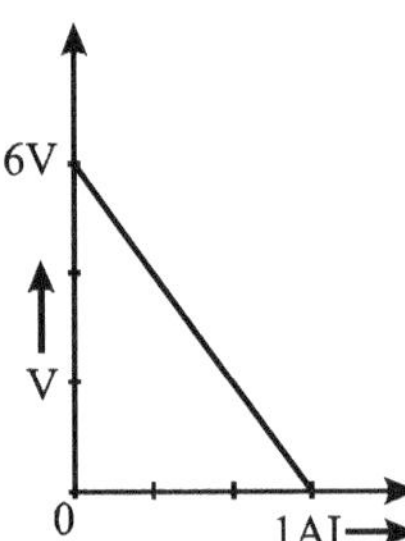

22. Name the charge carriers for the flow of current in a
    (i) conductor and (ii) electrolyte

23. Nichrome and copper wires of same length and same radius are connected in series. Current I is passed through them. Which wire gets heated up more? Justify your answer.

Short Answer Questions

24. (i) State Kirchhoff's rules.

(ii) A battery of 10V and negligible internal resistance is connected across the diagonally opposite corners of a cubical network consisting of 12 resistors each of 1 Ω resistance. Use Kirchhoff's rules to determine.

    (a) the equivalent resistance of the network and

    (b) the total current in the network.

25. In the meter bridge experiment, balance point was observed at J with $AJ = l$.

(i) The values of R and X were doubled and then interchanged. What would be the new position of balance point?

(ii) If the galvanometer and battery are interchanged at the balanced position, how will the balance point get affected?

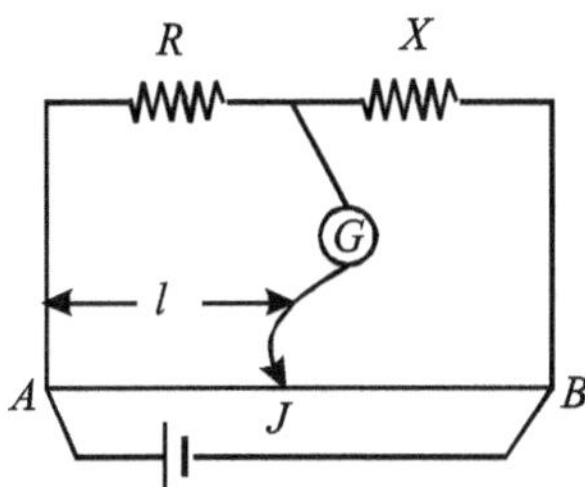

26. Two cells of emf E_1 and E_2 having internal resistances r_1 and r_2 respectively are connected in parallel as shown. Deduce the expressions for the equivalent emf and equivalent internal resistance of a cell which can replace the combination between the points B_1 and B_2.

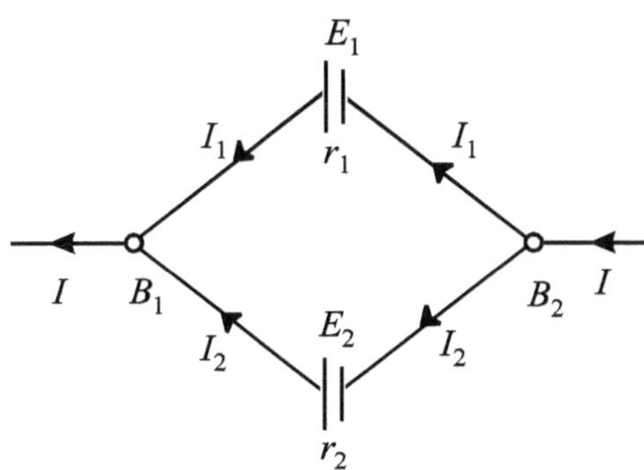

27. Two heating elements of resistances R_1 and R_2 when operated at a constant supply of voltage V, consume powers P_1 and P_2, respectively. Deduce the expressions for the power of their combination when they are, in turn, connected in

(i) series and

(ii) parallel across their same voltage supply.

28. Define relaxation time of the free electrons drifting in a conductor. How is it related to the drift velocity of free electrons? Use this relation to deduce the expression for the electrical resistivity of the material.

29. State the underlying principle of a potentiometer. Write two factors on which the sensitivity of a potentiometer depends.

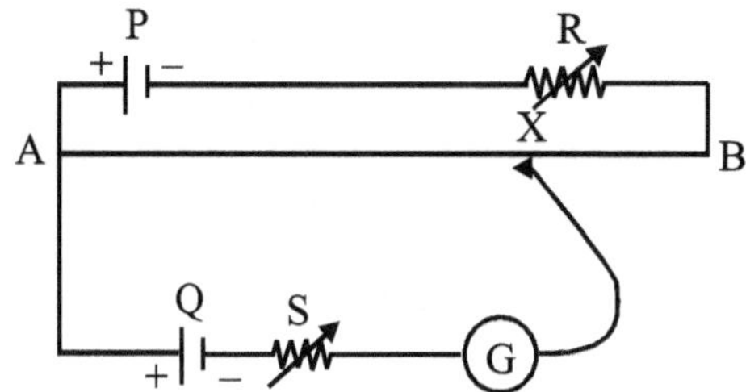

In the potentiometer circuit shown in the figure, the balance point is at X. State, giving reason, how the balance point is shifted when:

(i) resistance R is increased?

(ii) resistance S is increased, keeping R constant?

30. Write a relation between current and drift velocity of electrons in a conductor. Use this relation to explain how the resistance of a conductor changes with the rise in temperature.

31. Use Kirchhoff's rules to determine the value of the current I_1 flowing in the circuit shown in the figure.

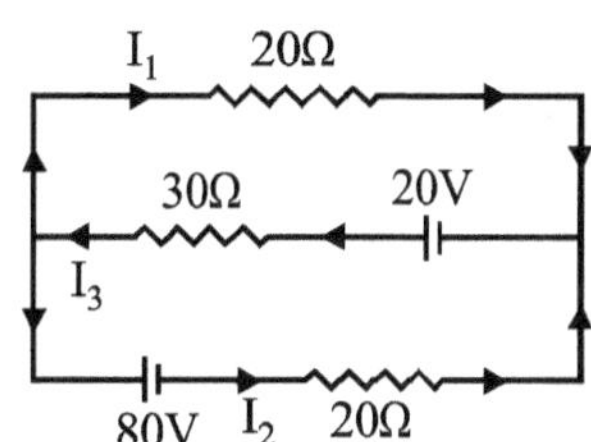

32. A uniform wire of resistance 12 Ω is cut into three pieces so that the ratio of the resistances $R_1 : R_2 : R_3$ = 1 : 2 : 3 and the three pieces are connected to form a triangle across which a cell of emf 8 V and internal resistance1 Ω is connected as shown. Calculate the current through each part of the circuit.

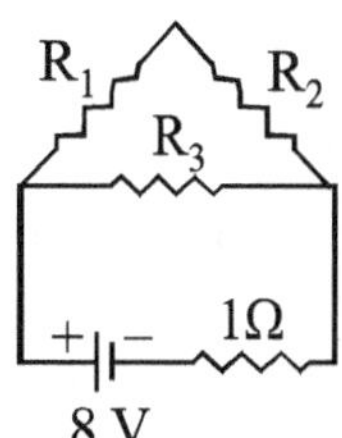

33. Draw a graph showing the variation of resistivity with temperature for nichrome. Which property of nichrome is used to make standard resistance coils ?

34. A battery of emf E and internal resistance r when connected across an external resistance of 12 ohm produces a current of 0.5 A. When connected across a resistance of 25 ohm it produces a current of 0.25 A. Determine the (i) emf and (ii) internal resistance of the cell.

35. An ammeter of resistance $0.6\,\Omega$ can measure current upto $1.0\,A$. Calculate (i) the shunt resistance required to enable the ammeter to measure current upto $5.0A$ (ii) The combined resistance of the ammeter and the shunt.

36. A cell of emf 'E' and internal resistance 'r' is connected across a variable resistor 'R'. Plot a graph showing variation of terminal voltage 'V' of the cell versus the current 'I'. Using the plot, show how the emf of the cell and its internal resistance can be determined.

37. Estimate the average drift speed of conduction electrons in a copper wire of cross-sectional area $1.0 \times 10^{-7}\,m^2$ carrying a current of $1.5\,A$. Assume the density of conduction electrons to be $9 \times 10^{28}\,m^{-3}$.

38. Answer the following:
- (a) Why are the connections between the resistors in a meter bridge made of thick copper strips?
- (b) Why is it generally preferred to obtain the balance point in the middle of the meter bridge wire?
- (c) Which material is used for the meter bridge wire and why?

OR

A resistance of $R\,\Omega$ draws current from a potentiometer, as shown in the figure. The potentiometer has a total resistance $R_0\,\Omega$. A voltage V is supplied to the potentiometer. Derive an expression for the voltage across R when the sliding contact is in the middle of the potentiometer.

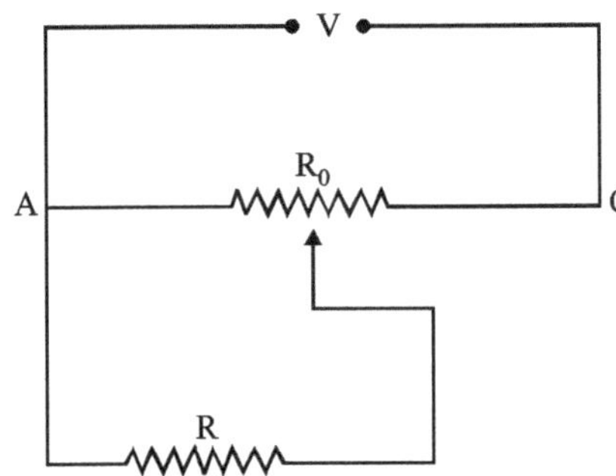

39. A potentiometer wire of length 1 m has a resistance of 10 Ω. It is connected to a 6 V battery in series with a resistance of $5\,\Omega$. Determine the emf of the primary cell which gives a balance point at 40 cm.

40. During a thunderstorm the 'live' wire of the transmission line fell down on the ground from the poles in the street. A group of boys, who passed through, noticed it and some of them wanted to place the wire by the side. As they were approaching the wire and trying to lift the cable, Anuj noticed it and immediately pushed them away, thus preventing them from touching the live wire. During pushing some of them got hurt. Anuj took them to a doctor to get them medical aid.

Based on the above paragraph, answer the following questions :

- (a) Write the two values which Anuj displayed during the incident.
- (b) Why is it that a bird can sit on a suspended live wire without any harm whereas touching it on the ground can give a fatal shock ?
- (c) The electric power from a power plant is set up to a very high voltage before transmitting it to distant consumers. Explain, why.

41. In a meter bridge shown in the figure, the balance point is found to be 40 cm from end A. If a resistance of 10 Ω is connected in series with R, balance point is obtained 60 cm from A. Calculate the values of R and S.

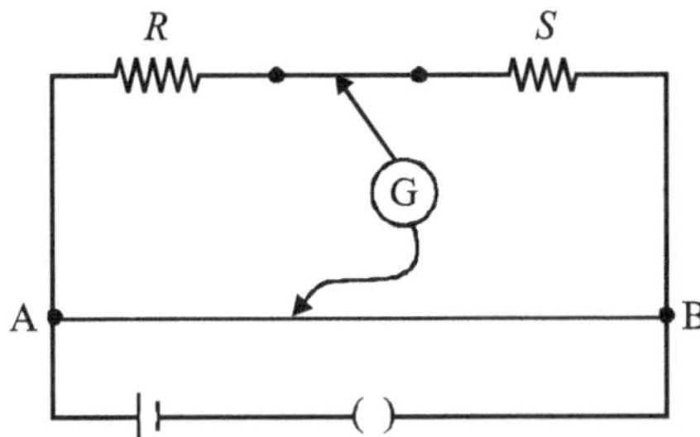

42. State the underlying principle of a potentiometer. Write two factors by which current sensitivity of a potentiometer can be increased. Why is a potentiometer preferred over a voltmeter for measurirg the emf of a cell?

43. Use Kirchhoff's rules to obtain conditions for the balance condition in a Wheatstone bridge.

44. A cell of emf 'E' and internal resistance 'r' is connected across a variable load resistor R. Draw the plots of the terminal voltage V versus (i) R and (ii) the current I.

45. (i) Derive an expression for drift velocity of free electrons.
- (ii) How does drift velocity of electrons in a metallic conductor vary with increase in temperature ?

46. Explain the principle of working of a meter bridge. Draw the circuit diagram for determination of an unknown resistance using it.

47. (a) Two cells of emf E_1 and E_2 have their internal resistances r_1 and r_2 respectively. Deduce an expression for the equivalent emf and internal resistance of their parallel combination when connected across an external resistance R. Assume that the two cells are supporting each other.
- (b) In case the two cells are identical, each of emf $E = 5$ V and internal resistance $r = 2\Omega$, calculate the voltage across the external resistance $R = 10\,\Omega$.

48. Two electric bulbs P and Q have their resistances in the ratio of 1 : 2. They are are connected in series across a battery. Find the ratio of the power dissipation in these bulbs.

49. A 10 V cell of negligible internal resistance is connected in parallel across a battery of emf 200 V and internal resistance 38W as shown in the figure. Find the value of current in the circuit.

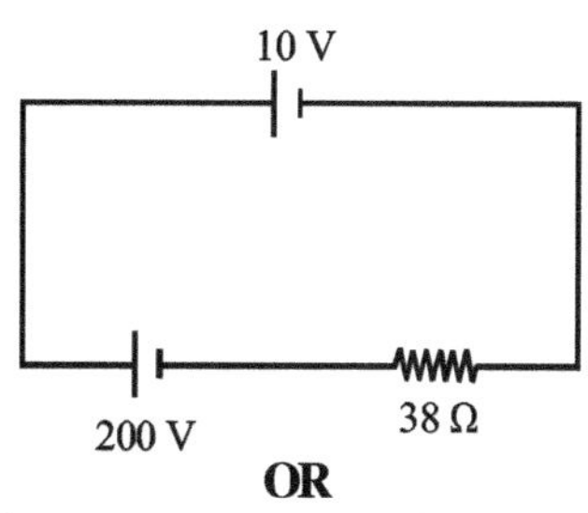

OR

In a potentiometer arrangement for determining the emf of a cell, the balance point of the cell in open circuit is 350 cm. When a resistance of 9 Ω is used in the external circuit of the cell, the balance point shifts to 300 cm. Determine the internal resistance of the cell.

50. (a) Define the term 'conductivity' of a metallic wire. Write its SI unit.

(b) Using the concept of free electrons in a conductor, derive the expression for the conductivity of a wire in terms of number density and relaxation time. Hence obtain the relation between current density and the applied electric field E.

51. (a) The potential difference applied across a given resistor is altered so that the heat produced per second increases by a factor of 9. By what factor does the applied potential difference change?

(b) In the figure shown, an ammeter A and a resistor of 4 Ω are connected to the terminals of the source. The emf of the source is 12V having an internal resistance of 2Ω. Calculate the voltmeter and ammeter readings.

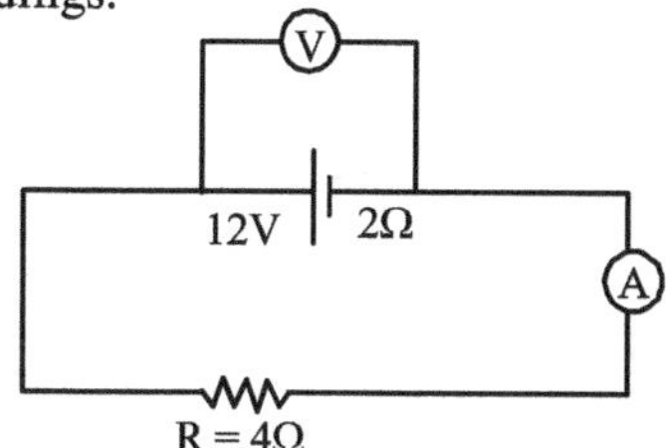

52. (a) Write the principle of working of a metre bridge.

(b) In a metre bridge, the balance point is found at a distance l_1 with resistances R and S as shown in the figure.

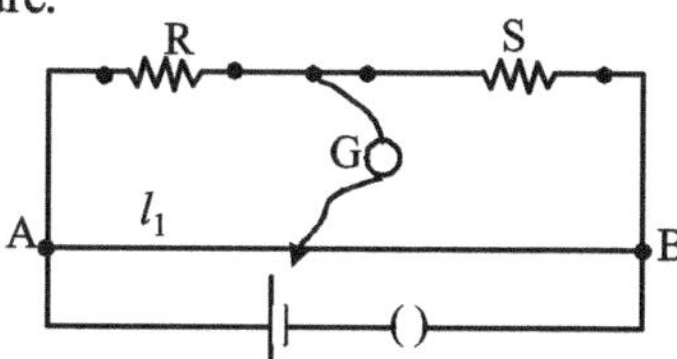

An unknown resistance X is now connected in parallel to the resistance S and the balance point is found at a distance l_2. Obtain a formula for X in terms of l_1, l_2 and S.

NCERT Exemplar

Multiple Choice Questions

1. Consider a current carrying wire (current I) in the shape of a circle.

(a) source of emf

(b) electric field produced by charges accumulated on the surface of wire

(c) the charges just behind a given segment of wire which push them just the right way by repulsion

(d) the charges ahead

2. Two batteries of emf ε_1 and $\varepsilon_2 (\varepsilon_2 > \varepsilon_1)$ and internal resistances r_1 and r_2 respectively are connected in parallel as shown in figure.

(a) The equivalent emf ε_{eq} of the two cells is between ε_1 and ε_2, i.e., $\varepsilon_1 < \varepsilon_{eq} < \varepsilon_2$

(b) The equivalent emf ε_{eq} is smaller than ε_1

(c) The ε_{eq} is given by $\varepsilon_{eq} = \varepsilon_1 + \varepsilon_2$ always

(d) ε_{eq} is independent of internal resistances r_1 and r_2

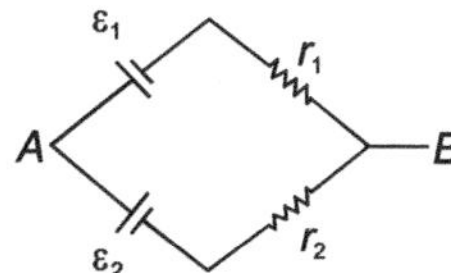

3. A resistance R is to be measured using a meter bridge, student chooses the standard resistance S to be 100Ω. He finds the null point at $l_1 = 2.9$ cm. He is told to attempt to improve the accuracy.

Which of the following is a useful way?

(a) He should measure I_1 more accurately

(b) He should change 5 to 1000Ω and repeat the experiment

(c) He should change S to 3Ω and repeat the experiment

(d) He should given up hope of a more accurate measurement with a meter bridge

4. Two cells of emfs approximately 5 V and 10 V are to be accurately compared using a potentiometer of length 400 cm.

(a) The battery that runs the potentiometer should have voltage of 8V

(b) The battery of potentiometer can have a voltage of 15 V and R adjusted so that the potential drop across the wire slightly exceeds 10 V

(c) The first portion of 50 cm of wire itself should have a potential drop of 10 V

(d) Potentiometer is usually used for comparing resistances and not voltages

5. A metal rod of length 10 cm and a rectangular cross-section of $1 \text{cm} \times \dfrac{1}{2}$ cm is connected to a battery across opposite faces. The resistance will be

(a) maximum when the battery is connected across $1 \text{ cm} \times \dfrac{1}{2}$ cm faces

(b) maximum when the battery is connected across 10 cm × 1 cm faces

(c) maximum when the battery is connected across 10 cm $\times \dfrac{1}{2}$ cm faces

(d) same irrespective of the three faces

6. Which of the following characteristics of electrons determines the current in a conductor?

(a) Drift velocity alone

(b) Thermal velocity alone

(c) Both drift velocity and thermal velocity

(d) Neither drift nor thermal velocity

Very Short Answer Questions

7. Is the motion of a charge across junction momentum conserving? Why or why not?

8. Power P is to be delivered to a device via transmission cables having resistance R_C. If V is the voltage across R and I the current throuh it, find the power wasted and how can it be reduced?

9. While doing an experiment with potentiomete r (Fig.) it was found that the deflection is one sided and (i) the deflection decreased while moving from one end A of the wire to the end B; (ii) the deflection increased, while the jockey was moved towards the end B.

(i) Which terminal + or −ve of the cell E_1, is connected at

X in case (i) and how is E_1 related to E?

(ii) Which terminal of the cell E_1 is connected at X in case (ii) ?

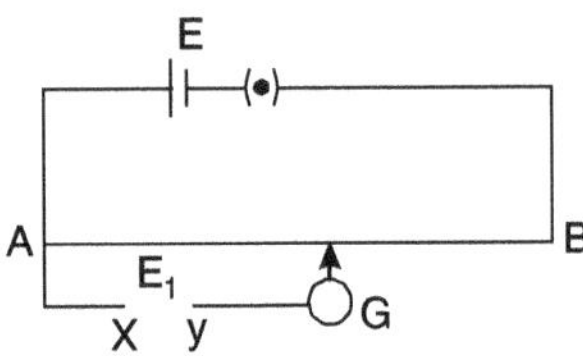

10. The potential difference across the terminals of a battery is 10 V when there is a current of 3A in the battery from the negative to the positive terminal. When the current is 2A in the reverse direction, the potential difference become 15 V. What is the internal resistance of the battery ?

11. A battery has internal resistance, so , if the current it supplies goes up, the voltage it supplies goes down. If too many bulbs are connected in parallel across a battery, will their brightness diminish? Explain.

Short Answer Questions

12. Two cells of same emf E but internal resistance r_1 and r_2 are connected in series to an external resistor R (Fig.).

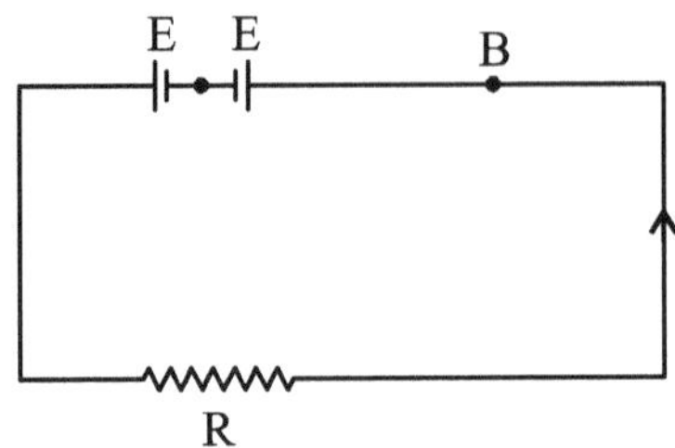

What should be the value of R so that the potential difference across the terminals of the first cell becomes zero.

13. Two conductors are made of the same material and have the same length. Conductor A is a solid wire of diameter 1mm. Conductor B is a hollow tube of outer diameter 2mm and inner diameter 1mm. Find the ratio of resistance R_A to R_B.

14. You are given two resistors X and Y whose resistances are to be determined using an ammeter of resistance $0.5\,\Omega$ and a voltmeter of resistance $20 \times 10^3\,\Omega$. It is known that X is in the range of a few ohms, while Y is in the range of several thousand ohms.

In each case which of the following two connections would you choose for the measurement of resistance. Justify your answer quantitatively.

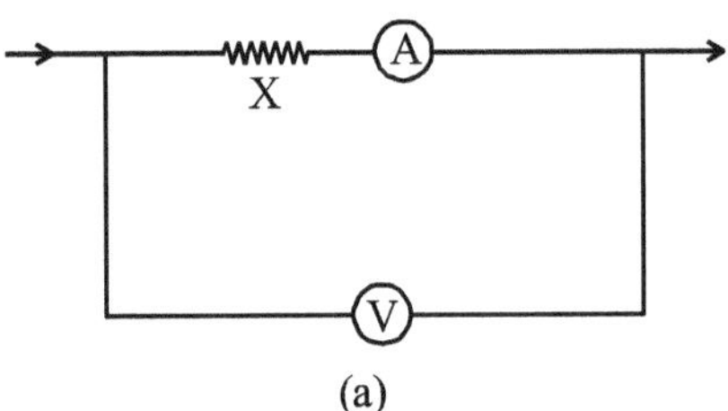

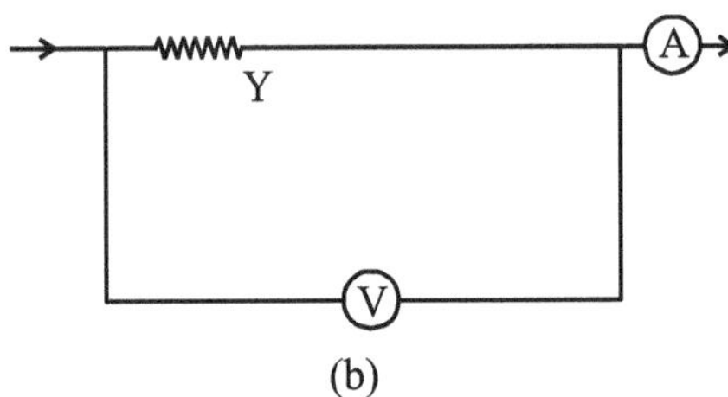

15. Four cells of identical emf E, internal resistance r are connected in series to a variable resistor. The following graph shows the variation of voltage of the combination with the current output.

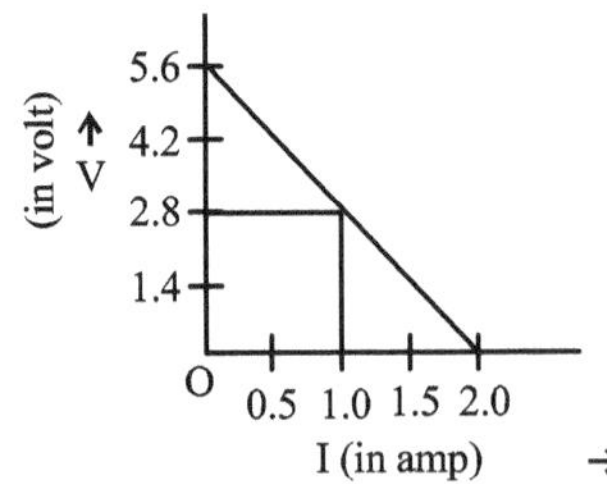

(a) What is the emf of each cell used?

(b) For what current from the cells does maximum power dissipation occurs in the circuit.

(c) Calculate the internal resistance of each cell.

Objective Practice Exercise

Multiple Choice Questions

DIRECTIONS : *This section contains multiple choice questions. Each question has four choices (a), (b), (c) and (d) out of which only one is correct.*

1. Drift velocity of electrons is due to
  (a) motion of conduction electrons due to random collisions.
  (b) motion of conduction electrons due to electric field $\vec{E}$.
  (c) repulsion to the conduction electrons due to inner electrons of ions.
  (d) collision of conduction electrons with each other.

2. For which of the following dependence of drift velocity v_d on electric field E, is Ohm's law obeyed?
  (a) $v_d \propto E^2$ (b) $v_d = E^{1/2}$
  (c) $v_d =$ constant   (d) $v_d = E$

3. When a potential difference V is applied across a conductor at a temperature T, the drift velocity of electrons is proportional to
  (a) $\sqrt{V}$ (b) V   (c) $\sqrt{T}$ (d) T

4. In the absence of an electric field, the mean velocity of free electrons in a conductor at absolute temperature (T) is
  (a) zero   (b) independent of T
  (c) proportional to T   (d) proportional to T^2

5. A current passes through a wire of nonuniform cross-section. Which of the following quantities are independent of the cross-section?
  (a) The charge crossing   (b) Drift velocity
  (c) Current density   (d) Free-electron density

6. If N, e, τ and m are representing electron density, charge, relaxation time and mass of an electron respectively, then the resistance of wire of length ℓ and cross-sectional area A is given by
  (a) $\dfrac{m\ell}{Ne^2 A^2 \tau}$ (b) $\dfrac{2m\tau A}{Ne^2 \ell}$ (c) $\dfrac{Ne^2 \tau A}{2m\ell}$ (d) $\dfrac{Ne^2 A}{2m\tau\ell}$

7. The example of non-ohmic resistance is
  (a) diode   (b) copper wire
  (c) filament lamp   (d) carbon resistor

8. The electric field intensity E, current density J and specific resistance k are related to each other through the relation
  (a) $E = J/k$ (b) $E = Jk$ (c) $E = k/J$ (d) $k = JE$

9. Nichrome or Manganin is widely used in wire bound standard resistors because of their
  (a) temperature independent resistivity
  (b) very weak temperature dependent resistivity.
  (c) strong dependence of resistivity with temperature.
  (d) mechanical strength.

10. Two resistors A and B have resistances R_A and R_B respectively with $R_A < R_B$. The resistivities of their materials are ρ_A and ρ_B. Then
  (a) $\rho_A > \rho_B$
  (b) $\rho_A = \rho_B$
  (c) $\rho_A < \rho_B$
  (d) insufficient information to predict relation

11. The figure shows the circuit diagram of five resistors, a battery and a switch. If the switch S is closed then current drawn from the battery
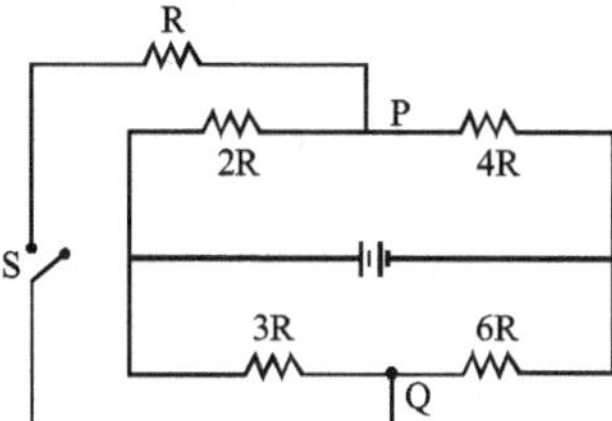
  (a) increases
  (b) decreases
  (c) remains same
  (d) initially increases and when the resistance R gets heated then decreases.

12. The relaxation time in conductors
  (a) increases with the increases of temperature
  (b) decreases with the increases of temperature
  (c) it does not depends on temperature
  (d) all of sudden changes at $400\ K$

13. In the circuit shown in Fig, the current in 4 Ω resistance is 1.2 A. What is the potential difference between B and C?
  (a) 3.6 volt
  (b) 6.3 volt
  (c) 1.8 volt
  (d) 2.4 volt
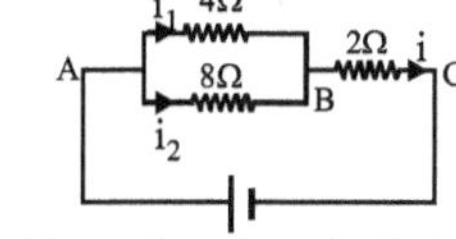

14. Kirchhoff's first and second laws for electrical circuits are consequences of
  (a) conservation of electric charge and energy respectively
  (b) conservation of electric charge
  (c) conservation of energy and electric charge respectively
  (d) conservation of energy

15. Emf of a cell is
  (a) the maximum potential difference between the terminals of a cell when no current is drawn from the cell.
  (b) the force required to push the electrons in the circuit.
  (c) the potential difference between the positive and negative terminal of a cell in a closed circuit.
  (d) less than terminal potential difference of the cell.

16. When potential difference is applied across an electrolyte, then Ohm's law is obeyed at
  (a) zero potential   (b) very low potential
  (c) negative potential   (d) high potential

17. To draw a maximum current from a combination of cells, how should the cells be grouped?
  (a) Parallel
  (b) Series
  (c) Mixed grouping
  (d) Depends upon the relative values of internal and external resistances.

18. A cell of internal resistance r is connected to an external resistance R. The current will be maximum in R, if
  (a) R = r   (b) R < r   (c) R > r   (d) R = r/2

19. The amount of charge Q passed in time t through a cross-section of a wire is $Q = 5t^2 + 3t + 1$. The value of current at time $t = 5$ s is
    (a) 9 A   (b) 49 A
    (c) 53 A   (d) None of these

20. A capacitor is connected to a cell of emf E having some internal resistance r. The potential difference across the
    (a) cell is $< E$ (b) cell is E
    (c) capacitor is $> E$ (d) capacitor is $< E$

21. Two cells of the same emf E have different internal resistances r_1 and r_2. They are connected in series with an external resistance R and the potential difference across the first cell is found to be zero. Therefore, the external resistance R must be
    (a) $r_1 - r_2$ (b) $r + r_2$ (c) $2r_1 - r_2$ (d) $r_1 - 2r_2$

22. If n cells each of emf ε and internal resistance r are connected in parallel, then the total emf and internal resistances will be
    (a) $\varepsilon, \dfrac{r}{n}$ (b) ε, nr (c) $n\varepsilon, \dfrac{r}{n}$ (d) $n\varepsilon, nr$

23. An electric fan and a heater are marked as 100 W, 220 V and 1000 W, 220 V respectively. The resistance of heater is
    (a) equal to that of fan   (b) lesser than that of fan
    (c) greater than that of fan   (d) zero

24. Three resistances R, 2R and 3R are connected in parallel to a battery. Then
    (a) the potential drop across 3R is maximum
    (b) the current through each resistance is same
    (c) the heat developed in 3R is maximum
    (d) the heat developed in R is maximum.

25. A current of 30A is registered when the terminals of a dry cell of emf 1.5V are connected through an ammeter. (Neglect the ammeter resistance). The amount of heat produced in the battery in 20s is
    (a) 450 J   (b) 900 J   (c) 1000 J   (d) 50 J

26. The powers of two electric bulbs are 100 watt and 200 watt. Both of them are joined with 220 volt. The ratio of resistance of their filament will be
    (a) $4:1$ (b) $1:4$ (c) $1:2$ (d) $2:1$

27. Forty electric bulbs are connected in series across a 220 V supply. After one bulb is fused the remaining 39 are connected again in series across the same supply. The illumination will be
    (a) more with 40 bulbs than with 39
    (b) more with 39 bulbs than with 40
    (c) equal in both the cases
    (d) in the ratio $40^2 : 39^2$

28. A heater boils a certain quantity of water in time t_1 Another heater boils the same quantity of water in time t_2. If both heaters are connected in parallel, the combination will boil the same quantity of water in time
    (a) $\dfrac{1}{2}(t_1 + t_2)$ (b) $(t_1 + t_2)$ (c) $\dfrac{t_1 t_2}{t_1 + t_2}$ (d) $\sqrt{t_1 t_2}$

29. How much heat is developed in 210 watt electric bulb in 5 minutes? (Chemical equivalent of heat = 4.2 J/C)
    (a) 30000 cal (b) 22500 cal (c) 15000 cal (d) 7500 cal

30. Why is the Wheatstone bridge better than the other methods of measuring resistances?
    (a) It does not involve Ohm's law
    (b) It is based on Kirchoff's law
    (c) It has four resistor arms
    (d) It is a null method

31. If in the experiment of Wheatstone's bridge, the positions of cells and galvanometer are interchanged, then balance point will
    (a) change
    (b) remain unchanged
    (c) depend on the internal resistance of cell and resistance of galvanometer
    (d) None of these

32. In meter bridge or Wheatstone bridge for measurement of resistance, the known and the unknown resistance are interchanged. The error so removed is
    (a) end correction
    (b) index error
    (c) due to temperature effect
    (d) random error

33. Potentiometer is based on
    (a) deflection method   (b) zero deflection method
    (c) both (a) and (b)   (d) None of these

34. In potentiometer a balance point is obtained, when
    (a) the e.m.f. of the battery becomes equal to the e.m.f of the experimental cell
    (b) the p.d. of the wire between the +ve end of battery to jockey becomes equal to the e.m.f. of the experimental cell
    (c) the p.d. of the wire between +ve point of cell and jockey becomes equal to the e.m.f. of the battery
    (d) the p.d. across the potentiometer wire becomes equal to the e.m.f. of the battery

35. In the experiment of potentiometer, at balance point, there is no current in the
    (a) main circuit
    (b) galvanometer circuit
    (c) potentiometer circuit
    (d) both main and galvanometer circuits

36. Sensitivity of potentiometer can be increased by
    (a) increasing the e.m.f of the cell
    (b) increasing the length of the potentiometer
    (c) decreasing the length of the potentiometer wire
    (d) None of these

37. Potentiometer measures potential more accurately because
    (a) it measures potential in open circuit
    (b) it uses sensitive galvanometer for null deflection
    (c) it uses high resistance potentiometer wire
    (d) it measures potential in closed circuit

38. For measuring voltage of any circuit, potentiometer is preferred to voltmeter because
    (a) the potentiometer is cheap and easy to handle.
    (b) calibration in the voltmeter is sometimes wrong.
    (c) the potentiometer almost draws no current during measurement.
    (d) range of the voltmeter is not as wide as that of the potentiometer.

39. The emf developed by a thermocouple is measured with the help of a potentiometer and not by a moving coil millivoltmeter because
    (a) the potentiometer is more accurate than the voltmeter
    (b) the potentiometer is more sensitive than voltmeter
    (c) the potentiometer makes measurement without drawing any current from the thermocouple
    (d) measurement using a potentiometer is simpler than with a voltmeter

Chapter Test

Time : 30 minutes   **Max. Marks : 15**

Direction :

Each question number **1-15** carry **1 mark** each.

1. A wire of a certain material is stretched slowly by ten per cent. Its new resistance and specific resistance become respectively:
   (a) 1.2 times, 1.3 times   (b) 1.21 times, same
   (c) both remain the same   (d) 1.1 times, 1.1 times

2. In the circuit shown in figure, with steady current, the potential drop across the capacitor must be
   (a) V   (b) $\dfrac{V}{2}$

   (c) $\dfrac{V}{3}$ (d) $\dfrac{2V}{3}$

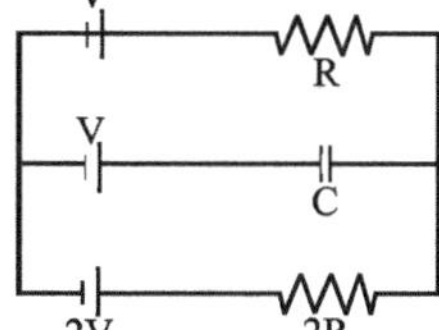

3. The current in the primary circuit of a potentiometer wire is 0.5 A, ρ for the wire is 4×10^{-7} Ω–m and area of cross-section of wire is 8×10^{-6} m^2. The potential gradient in the wire would be
   (a) 25 mV/meter   (b) 2.5 mV/meter
   (c) 25 V/meter   (d) 10 V/meter

4. Kirchhoff's first law, i.e., $\Sigma i = 0$ at a junction, deals with the conservation of
   (a) charge   (b) energy
   (c) momentum   (d) angular momentum

DIRECTIONS (Qs. 5-6) : *Each of these questions contains an assertion followed by reason. Read them carefully and answer the question on the basis of following options. You have to select the one that best describes the two statements.*
(a) If both Assertion and Reason are correct and the Reason is a correct explanation of the Assertion.
(b) If both Assertion and Reason are correct but Reason is not a correct explanation of the Assertion.
(c) If the Assertion is correct but Reason is incorrect.
(d) If the Assertion is incorrect but the Reason is correct.

5. **Assertion :** Voltmeter is connected in parallel with the circuit.
   Reason : Resistance of a voltmeter is very small.

6. **Assertion :** The drift velocity of electrons in a metallic wire will decrease, if the temperature of the wire is increased.
   Reason : On increasing temperature, conductivity of metallic wire inecreases.

DIRECTIONS : (Qs. 7-11) *are case based questions.*

It an instrument based on wheatstone bridge.
Principle:– The fall of potential across any portion of the wire is directly proportional to the length of that portion provided the wire of uniform cross-section and a constant current is flowing through it.
Theory : If A be the area of cross-section of the wire,
ρ be the specific resistance of the material of the wire.
V be the potential difference across the portion of the wire whose length is ℓ and resistance R.
I be the current flowing through the wire then by Ohm's law,
$$V = IR = I\frac{\ell\rho}{A} = \left(\frac{I\rho}{A}\right)\ell = k\ell \quad \left[\text{where } k = \frac{\rho\ell}{A}\right]$$

$\therefore$ $V \propto \ell$ if A and I are constants

or, $\dfrac{V}{\ell} = k =$ Potential gradient or fall of potential / length of the wire.

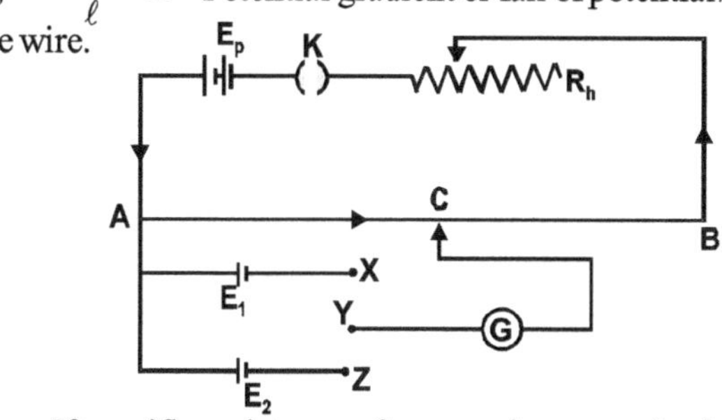

7. If specific resistance of a potentiometer wire is $10^{-7}\Omega$m current flowing through it, is 0.1 amp and cross sectional area of wire is 10^{-6} m^2, then potential gradient will be
   (a) 10^{-2} volt/m   (b) 10^{-4} volt/m
   (c) 10^{-6} volt/m   (d) 10^{-8} volt/m

8. A cell when balanced with potentiometer gave a balance length of 50 cm. 4.5 Ω external resistance is introduced in the circuit, now it is balanced on 45 cm. The internal resistance of cell is
   (a) 0.25 Ω (b) 0.5 Ω (c) 1.0 Ω (d) 1.5 Ω

9. A potentiometer consists of a wire of length 4m and resistance 10Ω. It is connected to a cell of e.m.f. 3V. The potential gradient of wire is
   (a) 5V/m   (b) 2V/m   (c) 5V/m   (d) 10V/m

10. In an experiment to measure the internal resistance of a cell, by a potentiometer, it is found that the balance point is at a length of 2 m, when the cell is shunted by a 5 Ω resistance and is at a length of 3 m when the cell is shunted by a 10 Ω resistance. The internal resistance of the cell is
    (a) 1.5 Ω (b) 10 Ω (c) 15 Ω (d) 1 Ω

11. 125 cm of potentiometer wire balances the emf. of a cell and 100 cm of the wire is required for balance, if the poles of the cell are joined by a 2Ω resitor. Then the internal resistance of the cell is
    (a) 0.25Ω (b) 0.5Ω (c) 0.75Ω (d) 1.25Ω

Very Short Answer Type Questions

12. What is the effect of heating of a conductor on a drift velocity of free electrons?

13. State Kirchhoff's rules.

14. Three identical resistors R_1, R_2 and R_3 are connected to a battery as shown in the following figure.

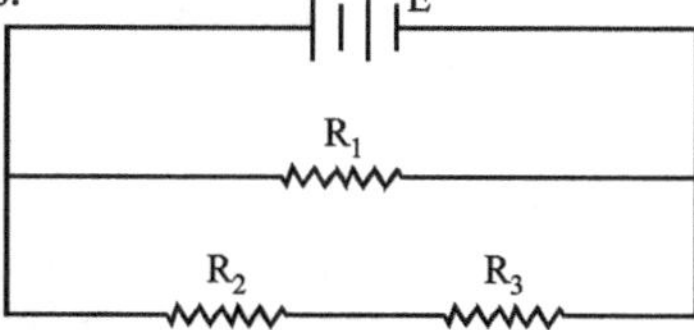

What will be the ratio of voltages across R_1 and R_2 ?

15. What is the potential difference between A and B?

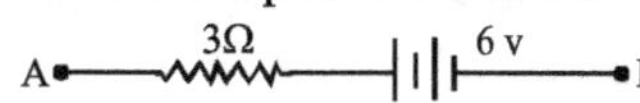

Solutions

1. (a) $J = \sigma E \Rightarrow J\rho = E$

J is current density, E is electric field

so $B = \rho =$ resistivity.

2. (c) $R = \dfrac{\rho\ell}{A} \Rightarrow R = \dfrac{\rho\ell}{\pi r^2}$

Given, $\ell_x = \dfrac{\ell_y}{2}$

$r_x = \dfrac{r_y}{2}$

So, ratio of resistance of x to that of Y is,

$\Rightarrow \dfrac{R_x}{R_y} = \dfrac{\ell_x}{\ell_y} \times \dfrac{r_y^2}{r_x^2} \Rightarrow \dfrac{(\ell_y/2)}{\ell_y} \times \dfrac{r_y^2}{\left(\dfrac{r_y^2}{2}\right)^2}$

$\Rightarrow \dfrac{\ell_y}{2\ell_y} \times \dfrac{\ell_y^2}{\ell_y^2} \times 4 \Rightarrow \dfrac{2}{1}$

3. (a) The slope of V–I graph gives the resistance of a conductor at a given temperature. From the graph, it follows that resistance of a conductor at temperature T_1 is greater than at temperature T_2 As the resistance of a conductor is more at higher temperature and less at lower temperature, hence $T_1 > T_2$.

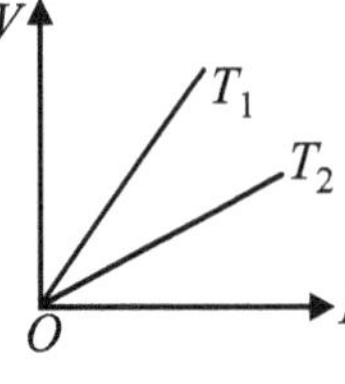

4. (b) The figure is showing $I - V$ characteristics of non ohmic or non linear conductors.

5. (a) [Hint $\Rightarrow R_t = R_0(1 + \alpha\, t)$]

$5\Omega = R_0(1 + \alpha \times 50)$ and $7\Omega = R_0(1 + \alpha \times 100)$

or $\dfrac{5}{7} = \dfrac{1 + 50\alpha}{1 + 100\alpha}$ or $\alpha = \dfrac{2}{150} = 0.0133/{}^\circ C$

6. (b) $R_t = R_0(1 + \alpha t)$ at $t^\circ C$ $R_t = 3R_0$

$\alpha = 4 \times 10^{-3}/{}^\circ C$

$3R_0 = R_0(1 + 4 \times 10^{-3} \times t)$

$\therefore \quad 3 - 1 = 4 \times 10^{-3}t$

$\therefore \quad t = \dfrac{2}{4 \times 10^{-3}} = 500^\circ C$

7. (a) Resistance wire $R = \rho\dfrac{\ell}{A}$, where ρ is resistivity of material which does not depend on the geometry of wire. Since when wire is bent resistivity, length and area of cross-section do not change, therefore resistance of wire also remain same.

8. (c)

9. (a) When temperature increases the random motion of electrons and vibration of ions increases which results in more frequent collisions of electrons with the ions. Due to this the average time between the successive collisions, denoted by τ, decreases which increases ρ.

10. (c) From relation $\vec{J} = \sigma\vec{E}$, the current density $\vec{J}$ at any point in ohmic resistor is in direction of electric field $\vec{E}$ at that point. In space having non-uniform electric field, charges released from rest may not move along ELOF. Hence Assertion is correct while Reason is incorrect.

11. (a) In the absence of the electric current, the free electrons in a conductor are in a state of random motion, like molecule in a gas. Their average velocity is zero. i.e. they do not have any net velocity in a direction. As a result, there is no net magnetic force on the free electrons in the magnetic field. On passing the current, the free electrons acquire drift velocity in a definite direction, hence magnetic force acts on them, unless the field has no perpendicular component.

12. (c) Drift speed is the average speed between two successive collisions.

13. (a)

14. (d) $I = nAev_d$ or $v_d \propto 1/\pi r^2$

15. (c)

16. (b) $R_t = R_0(1 + \alpha t)$

Initially, $R_0(1 + 30\alpha) = 10\,\Omega$

Finally, $R_0(1 + \alpha t) = 11\,\Omega$

$\therefore \dfrac{11}{10} = \dfrac{1 + \alpha t}{1 + 30\alpha}$

or, $10 + (10 \times 0.002 \times t) = 11 + 330 \times 0.002$

or, $0.02t = 1 + 0.66 = 1.066$ or $t = \dfrac{1.66}{0.02} = 83^\circ C$.

17. (d) $I = neAv_d = 2 \times 10^{21} \times 1.6 \times 10^{-19} \times 10 \times 0.25 \times 10^{-3}$

$= 2 \times 1.6 \times 0.25 = \dfrac{8}{10} = 0.8\,A$

18. Drift velocity $v_d = \dfrac{\rho E\tau}{m}$

With increase in temperature, relaxation time (τ) decreases.

$\therefore$ Drift velocity also decreases.

19. Resistivity will not change as it depends on the material not on the length.

20. Manganin is an alloy whose temperature coefficient of resistance is almost negligible. So its resistance does not change with change in temperature, that is why it is used in making standard resistors.

21. $|v_d| = \dfrac{eE\tau}{m} = \dfrac{e\tau}{m}\cdot\dfrac{V}{\ell}$ when l is doubled, the drift speed becomes half.

22. If the temperature of a good conductor increases, the K.E of electrons increases, so more no. of collisions will take place.

$\therefore$ Time between successive collision will decrease and the relaxation time of electrons will also decrease.

23. $R = \dfrac{\rho\ell}{A}$ $\therefore$ $\dfrac{R_{Cu}}{R_{man}} = \dfrac{\rho_{Cu}}{\rho_{man}}\cdot\dfrac{A_{man}}{A_{Cu}}$

$\because \quad R_{Cu} = R_{Man} \Rightarrow \dfrac{\rho_{Cu}}{\rho_{man}} \cdot \dfrac{A_{man}}{A_{Cu}} = 1$

$\Rightarrow \rho_{Cu} \cdot A_{man} = \rho_{man} \cdot A_{Cu}$

$\because \quad \rho_{man} > \rho_{Cu} \qquad \therefore \quad A_{man} > A_{Cu}$

24. Slope of voltage vs. current graph gives resistance of a metallic conductor. S.I. unit is ohm.

25. When the temperature increases, the resistivity increases and the conductivity decreases. So their product remains same.

26. The specific resistance of silver is least. So it is the best conductor as the conductivity is the reciprocal of specific resistance.

27. $R_A = \dfrac{\rho \ell_A}{A}$ and $R_B = \dfrac{\rho \ell_B}{A} \qquad \because V = IR$ and V is constant

$\therefore \quad I_A R_A = I_B R_B \Rightarrow \dfrac{I_A}{I_B} = \dfrac{R_B}{R_A} = \dfrac{\ell_B}{\ell_A}$

But $\ell_A : \ell_B = 2:1 \Rightarrow \dfrac{I_A}{I_B} = 1:2$

28. $v_d = \dfrac{eE\tau}{m} = \dfrac{e\tau}{m}\left(\dfrac{V}{\ell}\right) \qquad \therefore \quad v_d \propto V$

$\therefore$ Drift velocity will be double if the voltage becomes 2V.

29. As we know, $I \propto v_d$ and $v_d \propto E$ and $E \propto V$

$\therefore I \propto V =$ which is ohm's law.

$v_d = -\dfrac{eE\tau}{m}$ and $E = -\dfrac{V}{\ell} \qquad \therefore \quad v_d = \dfrac{eV\tau}{m\ell}$ and $I = nAev_d$

$\therefore \quad I = neA\left(\dfrac{eV}{m\ell}\right)\tau = \left(\dfrac{ne^2 A\tau}{m\ell}\right)V = \dfrac{1}{R}V$

or $\quad V = IR$ where $R = \dfrac{m\ell}{nAe^2\tau}$ is a constant for a particular conductor at a particular temperature and is called the resistance of the conductor.

30. Let n be the number of free electrons per unit volume of the conductor.

Volume of the conductor $= A\ell$

Number of free electrons of the conductor $= n$

Total free charge of the conductor $= nA\ell e$, where e is the charge of an electron.

If t be the time taken to cover a distance ℓ by this change,

then $t = \dfrac{\ell}{v_d}$

$\therefore \quad I = \dfrac{q}{t} = \dfrac{nAe\ell}{\ell/v_d} = nAev_d \Rightarrow v_d = \dfrac{I}{enA} \quad \therefore \quad v_d \propto I$

31. Specific resistance of a material is defined as the resistance of unit length and unit cross-sectional area of the conductor. S.I. unit is ohm - m.

$R = \dfrac{m\ell}{ne^2 A\tau} = \left(\dfrac{m}{ne^2\tau}\right)\dfrac{\ell}{A} \qquad$ Also $\quad R = \dfrac{\rho\ell}{A}$

32. $R = \dfrac{\rho\ell}{A} \Rightarrow \rho = \dfrac{RA}{\ell} = \dfrac{R \times \pi d^2}{4\ell}$

$\Rightarrow \rho = \dfrac{2 \times 3.14 \times (0.02 \times 10^{-3})^2}{4 \times 3} = 7.5 \times 10^{-7}\,\Omega m$

Practice Exercise-2

1. **(c)** $\because$ Current in A is maximum

$\therefore$ Heat produced in it will be maximum.

2. **(c)** $A \to (2); B \to (1); C \to (4); D \to (3)$

3. **(a)** $H = I^2 Rt$. Here $R_1 = \rho \dfrac{\ell}{\pi r^2}$ and

$R_2 = \rho \dfrac{\ell}{\pi(2r)^2}$.

That is, $R_1 = 4R_2$. Hence, $\dfrac{H_1}{H_2} = 4$.

4. **(c)** **5.** **(c)**

6. **(a)** Glow $=$ Power $(P) = I^2 R$

$\therefore \quad \dfrac{dP}{P} = 2\left(\dfrac{dI}{I}\right) = 2 \times 0.5 = 1\%$

7. **(a)** Power loss $= i^2 R = \left(\dfrac{P}{V}\right)^2 R$

[P = Transmitted power]

8. **(b)** As $R \propto V^2/P$ or $R \propto 1/P$, so resistance of heater is less than that of fan.

9. **(b)** Most of the charges flowing around the circuit are valence electrons stripped off the metal atoms in the wires and light bulbs. A battery doesn't "supply" all of the charges. It merely pushes around charges already present in the circuit.

Statements (c) and (d) are both true. All charges flowing into the light bulb also flow back out; no current gets " used up" But inside the bulb, those charges lose energy. This lost electrical energy converts into light and heat. So, the current has lower "potential" after flowing through the bulb.

10. **(b)** The rate of generation of heat, for a given potential difference is, $P = V^2/R$

11. **(a)** A heating wire should be such that it produces more heat when current is passed through it and also does not melt. It will be so if it has high specific resistance and high melting point.

12. **(b)** $R_1 = \dfrac{V^2}{P_1}$ and $R_2 = \dfrac{V^2}{P_2}$

$\therefore \quad \dfrac{R_2}{R_1} = \dfrac{P_1}{P_2} = \dfrac{200}{100} = 2 \ (\because V = \text{constant})$

$R_2 = 2R_1$

13. As $P = \dfrac{V^2}{R}$.

$\therefore$ 25 W bulb has more resistance. Same current flows through both of them. So the 25 W bulb will develop more heat and burns out instantaneously.

14. $\because P = I^2 R$, If I is developed, it becomes 4 times.

15. $V^2 = PR \Rightarrow V = \sqrt{196 \times 1} = 14$ volt.

Practice Exercise-3 

1. (a)

2. (d) $I = \dfrac{E}{R+r}$, Internal resistance (r) is zero,

$I = \dfrac{E}{R} = $ constant.

3. (d)

4. (c) Internal resistance = r, External resistance = nr.
Let terminal voltage = V

then $V = E - Ir \Rightarrow V = E - \dfrac{Er}{(n+1)r}$

$V = \dfrac{nE}{n+1} \Rightarrow \dfrac{V}{E} = \dfrac{n}{n+1}$

5. (a) In the parallel combination,

$$\dfrac{\varepsilon_{eq}}{r_{eq}} = \dfrac{\varepsilon_1}{r_1} + \dfrac{\varepsilon_2}{r_2} + ... + \dfrac{\varepsilon_n}{r_n}$$

$$\dfrac{1}{r_{eq}} = \dfrac{1}{r_1} + \dfrac{1}{r_2} + ... + \dfrac{1}{r_n}$$

$(\because \varepsilon_1 = \varepsilon_2 = \varepsilon_3 = ... = \varepsilon_n = \varepsilon$ and $r_1 = r_2 = r_3 = ... \, r)$

$\therefore \quad \dfrac{\varepsilon_{eq}}{r_{eq}} = \dfrac{\varepsilon}{r} + \dfrac{\varepsilon}{r} + ... + \dfrac{\varepsilon}{r} = n\dfrac{\varepsilon}{r}$ .... (i)

$\dfrac{\varepsilon}{r_{eq}} = \dfrac{1}{r} + \dfrac{1}{r} + ... + \dfrac{1}{r} = \dfrac{n}{r}$ $r_{eq} = r/n$ ....(ii)

From (i) and (ii)

$$\varepsilon_{eq} = n\dfrac{\varepsilon}{r_{eq}} \times r_{eq} = n \times \dfrac{\varepsilon}{r} \times \dfrac{\varepsilon}{r} = \varepsilon$$

6. (c)

7. (a) Given : emf $\varepsilon = 2.1$ V
$I = 0.2$ A, $R = 10\,\Omega$
Internal resistance r = ?
From formula.
$\varepsilon - Ir = V = IR$
$2.1 - 0.2r = 0.2 \times 10$
$2.1 - 0.2\,r = 2$ or $0.2\,r = 0.1 \Rightarrow r = \dfrac{0.1}{0.2} = 0.5\,\Omega$

8. (d) The e.m.f. of a dry cell is dependent upon the electrode potential of cathode and anode which in turn is dependent upon the reaction involved as well as concentration of the electrolyte. It has nothing to do with size of the cell.

9. (c) Positive terminal of a battery is point of highest potential and current flows from highest to lowest potential i.e. from +ve to –ve potential.

10. (a)

11. (b) In the given case cell is in open circuit (i = 0) so voltage across the cell is equal to its e.m.f.

12. (c) $r = E / I = 1.5 / 3 = 0.5$ ohm.

13. (c) $\dfrac{100}{R+r} = \dfrac{90}{R} \Rightarrow \dfrac{R+r}{R} = \dfrac{10}{9}$

$\Rightarrow 1 + \dfrac{0.5}{R} = \dfrac{10}{9} \Rightarrow \dfrac{0.5}{R} = \dfrac{1}{9} \Rightarrow R = 4.5\,\Omega$

14. (a)

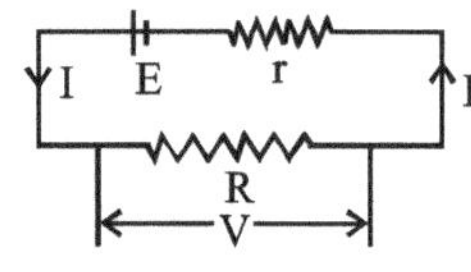

$E_{net} = \dfrac{E_1 r_2 - E_2 r_1}{r_1 + r_2}$ or $E_{net} = \dfrac{2-2}{2+1} = 0$

15. Since, $V = E - Ir$, therefore, if $r = 0$ i.e the internal resistance of the cell is zero then the terminal voltage across a secondary cell is equal to its e.m.f.

16. $V = E - Ir = 2 - I \times 0.1$

Also $I = \dfrac{E}{R+r} = \dfrac{2}{3.9+0.1} = \dfrac{2}{4} = \dfrac{1}{2} = 0.5$ A.

$\therefore \quad V = 2 - 0.5 \times 0.1 = 2 - 0.05 = 1.95$ V

17. When cell is in use there is potential drop across the cell i.e., $V = E - ir$

18. The required relation of terminal voltage in terms of E, I and r is $V = E - ir$

19. Let R be the external resistance and r be the internal resistance of the cell of e.m.f E.
$\therefore$ In closed circuit, total resistance of the circuit = R + r

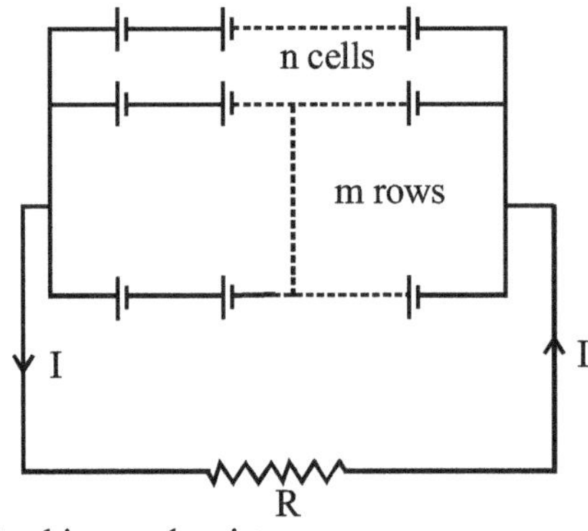

$\therefore$ Current = $I = \dfrac{E}{R+r}$

Potential difference = $V = E - Ir$
(Ir = Potential drop across internal resistance)

$Ir = E - V \Rightarrow r = \dfrac{E-V}{I}$

By ohm's law, $V = IR$ $\therefore$ $I = \dfrac{V}{R}$

$\therefore \quad r = \left(\dfrac{E-V}{V}\right)R = \left(\dfrac{E}{V} - 1\right)R.$

20. Total e.m.f = nE, Total resistance = $R + \dfrac{nr}{m}$

[$\because$ Total internal resistance

$\dfrac{1}{r_p} = \dfrac{1}{nr} + \dfrac{1}{nr} + ... \, m$ times $= \dfrac{m}{nr}$ $\therefore r_p = \dfrac{nr}{m}$]

$\therefore$ Current = $I = \dfrac{nE}{R + \dfrac{nr}{m}} \Rightarrow I = \dfrac{mnE}{mR + nr}$

I will be maximum if mR + nr is minimum.

That is possible if mR = nr   i.e. R = $\dfrac{nr}{m}$

i.e. External resistance of the circuit = Total internal resistance of all the cells.

21. Here, E = 3V, I = 50 mA = 50 × 10⁻³ A.

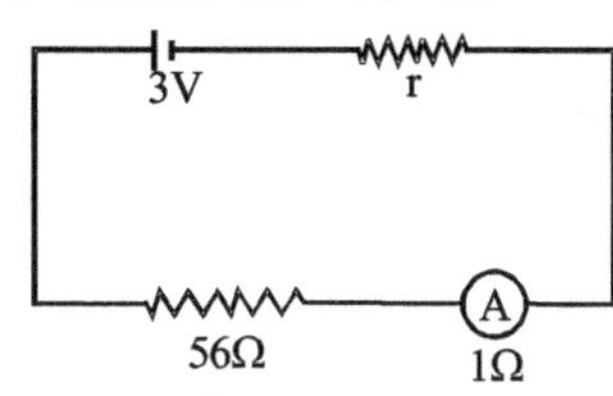

$$I = \frac{E}{R+r} \Rightarrow \frac{3}{56+r} = 50 \times 10^{-3}$$

∴   r = 4 Ω.

22.

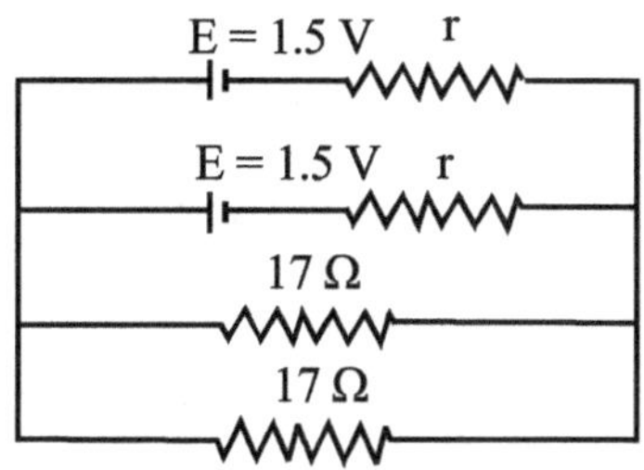

Let the internal resistance of each cell is r.

E = 1.5 volt, V = 1.4 volt.

The equivalent resistance of two 17 Ω in parallel is

$$R = \frac{17 \times 17}{17+17} = \frac{17}{2} = 8.5\,\Omega$$

∴ $I = \dfrac{E}{R+\dfrac{r}{2}}$ and V = IR

∴ $R + \dfrac{r}{2} = \dfrac{E}{I} = \dfrac{ER}{V}$

∴ $\dfrac{r}{2} = \dfrac{E}{V}R - R = \left(\dfrac{E}{V} - 1\right)R$

$\Rightarrow$ $r = 2\left(\dfrac{E}{V} - 1\right)R = 2\left(\dfrac{1.5}{1.4} - 1\right)8.5 = 1.21\,\Omega.$ (approx.)

23.

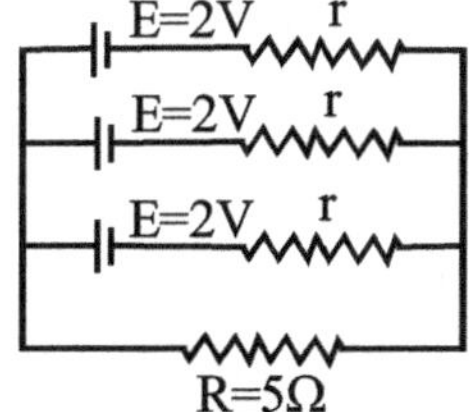

Here equivalent internal resistance is r/3 since the 3 cells are connected in parallel

∴ $I = \dfrac{E}{R + \dfrac{r}{3}}$

Potential difference across R

= terminal voltage of each cell = 1.5V

∵ $V = IR \Rightarrow 1.5 = \dfrac{2 \times 5}{R + \dfrac{r}{3}}$

$\Rightarrow$ $5 + \dfrac{r}{3} = \dfrac{10}{1.5} \Rightarrow \dfrac{r}{3} = \dfrac{20}{3} = -5 \Rightarrow r = 5\,\Omega.$

24. E = 8V, r = 1 Ω, charging voltage = V = 120 volt, R = 15 Ω

(i)   Current $= I = \dfrac{V-E}{R+r} = \dfrac{120-8}{15+1} = \dfrac{112}{16} = 7A.$

(ii)   Terminal voltage during charging = V = E + Ir
= 8 + 7 × 1 = 15 volt.

(iii)   Energy stored = VIt = 8 × 7 × 6 × 60
= 16800 J in 5 minutes

25. 3 Ω and 6 Ω are in parallel, $\dfrac{1}{R} = \dfrac{1}{3} + \dfrac{1}{6} = \dfrac{3}{6} = \dfrac{1}{2}$

$\Rightarrow$ R' = 2 Ω

∴   4.5 Ω and 2 Ω are in series, 4.5 + 2 = 6.5 Ω
Net resistance in the circuit = R = 1 + 0.5 + 6.5 = 8 Ω

Net e.m.f = 8 − 4 = 4V. ;   ∴ $I = \dfrac{E}{R} = \dfrac{4}{8} = 0.5A.$

Terminal voltage across
X = V$_X$ = E + Ir = 4 + 0.5 × 0.5
V$_X$ = 4.25 V.
Terminal voltage across
Y = V$_Y$ = E − Ir = 8 − 0.5 × 1 = 7.5 V.

Practice Exercise-4

1. **(a)**   According to Kirchhoff's first law
At junction A, $i_{AB} = 2 + 2 = 4$ A
At junction B, $i_{AB} = i_{BC} + 1 \Rightarrow i_{BC} = 4 - 1 \Rightarrow 3$A

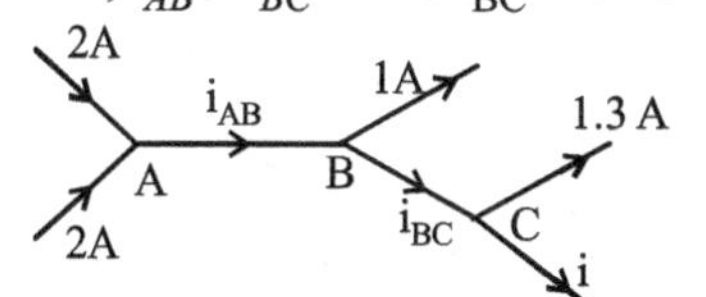

At junction C, $i = i_{BC} - 1.3 = 3 - 1.3 = 1.7$ A

2. **(b)**   A → (1); B → (3); C → (4); D → (2)

3. **(b)**   This is a balanced wheatstone bridge condition,

$$\frac{5}{R} = \frac{\ell_1}{100 - \ell_1} \text{ and } \frac{5}{R/2} = \frac{1.6\ell_1}{100 - 1.6\ell_1} \Rightarrow R = 15\,\Omega$$

4. **(b)**

5. **(a)**   Due to increases in resistance R the current through the wire will decrease and hence the potential gradient also decreases, which results in increase in balancing length. So. J will shift towards B.

6. **(d)**   In balance condition, since no current flows through the galvanometer therefore B and D are at the same potential.

7. **(a)**   We know

$$\frac{I}{I_S} = 1 + \frac{G}{S}$$

$$\frac{750}{100} = 1 + \frac{13}{S}$$

$$S \Rightarrow 2\,\Omega$$

8. **(a)**

9. **(a)** Sensitivity $\propto \dfrac{1}{\text{Potential gradient}} \propto$ (Length of wire)

10. **(c)** Kirchoff's loop rule follows from conservation of energy.

11. **(a)** Sensitivity $\propto \dfrac{1}{\text{Potential gradient}} \propto$ Length of wire.

12 **(a)** $\dfrac{e}{1.02} = \dfrac{88}{66}$

or $e = 1.36$ V

13. **(d)** 4 V is greater than applied emf 2 V, hence no balance point is obtained. On connecting the resistance across e, current will flow in e due to which terminal potential difference will be less than emf and the balancing length will decrease.

14. **(b)**

15. **(a)** $\because\ V \propto l$ $\therefore\ \dfrac{V}{E} = \dfrac{l}{L}$ or $V = \dfrac{l}{L}E = \dfrac{30}{100}E$

16. **(a)** $r = \dfrac{l_1 - l_2}{l_2}R = \dfrac{240 - 120}{120} \times 2 = 2\,\Omega$

17. Somewhere near the middle point of the wire.

18. Potentiometer is used to find internal resistance of a cell.

19. Refer to theory

20. **Principle:** The fall of potential across any portion of the potentiometer wire is directly proportional to the length of that portion provided the wire is of uniform cross - sectional area and a constant current is flowing through it.

Working:

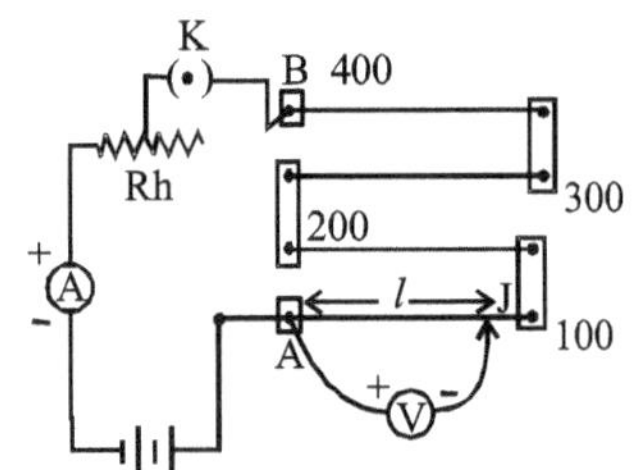

Let A be the area of cross-section of the wire. ρ be the specific resistance of the material of the wire V is the potential drop across the portion of the wire whose length is ℓ and resistance R and I be the current flowing through the wire.

$V = IR = \dfrac{I\rho\ell}{A} = k\ell\ \therefore\ V \propto \ell$ where I and A are constants

$\dfrac{V}{\ell} = k = $ potential gradient or falls of potential per unit length of the wire.

To find the e.m.f of a cell the following circuit is used.

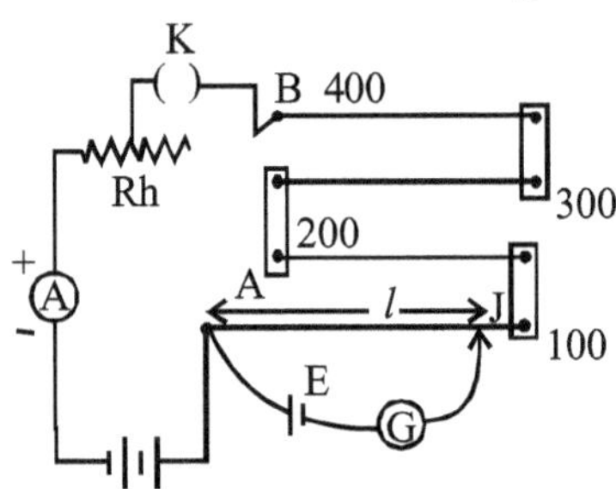

The cell of e.m.f E to be measured is connected in parallel along with a galvanometer to the potentiometer wire. Let the null point is found at J and AJ = ℓ

$\therefore$ The potential drop across the potentiometer wire AJ is equal to the unknown e.m.f E.

$\therefore$ E = kℓ where k is the potential gradient of the potentiometer wire. Knowing k and measuring ℓ from the attached scale E can be calculated.

21. AB is the potentiometer wire. The two cells of e.m.f E_1 and E_2 to be compared are connected in parallel with the end A of the potentiometer wire with a three way key and a galvanometer. When the key is put between 1 and 3 terminals the balancing length for cell E_1 is found to be AJ = ℓ_1

$\therefore$ $E_1 = k\,\ell_1$ [where k = Potential gradient of the potentiometer wire]

When the key is put between 2 and 3 terminals, cell of e.m.f E_2 is connected in the circuit and the corresponding balancing length is found to be ℓ_2

$\therefore$ $E_2 = k\,\ell_2$ $\therefore$ $\dfrac{E_1}{E_2} = \dfrac{\ell_1}{\ell_2}$

Measuring ℓ_1 and ℓ_2 from the attached scale the ratio of E_1 and E_2 can be calculated.

22. $100\,\Omega$ resister and $400\,\Omega$ voltmeter are in parallel.

$\therefore$ Their equivalent resistance $= \dfrac{100 \times 400}{100 + 400} = 80\,\Omega$

$\therefore$ Total resistance of the circuit $= 80 + 200 = 280\,\Omega$

$\therefore$ Current $= \dfrac{84}{280} = \dfrac{3}{10}$ A

$\therefore$ Voltage the voltmeter is connected, the total resistance of the loop $= 100 + 200 = 300\,\Omega$

$\therefore$ Current $= \dfrac{84}{300}$ A. Potential difference across $100\,\Omega$

$= \dfrac{84}{300} \times 100 = 28$ volt.

23. **(i)** When voltmeter is not connected
Length of wire $= 600$ cm,
I $= 40$ mA, null point $= 500$ cm,
e.m.f. applied $= 2$V

$\therefore$ Potential difference across wire $= \dfrac{6}{5} \times 2 = 2.4$V

$\therefore$ Resistance of wire $= \dfrac{2.4}{40 \times 10^{-3}} = 60\,\Omega$

(ii) Reading of voltmeter = Potential gradient $\times$ balancing length $= \dfrac{2}{500} \times 490 = 1.96$ V.

(iii) Current drawn by voltmeter $= \dfrac{2 - 1.96}{10} = 4 \times 10^{-3}$ A

$\therefore$ Resistance of voltmeter $= \dfrac{1.96}{4 \times 10^{-3}} = 0.49 \times 10^3$

$= 490\,\Omega$

24. Since the bridge is balanced,

$\therefore$ $\dfrac{P}{Q} = \dfrac{R}{S}$ $\Rightarrow$ $\dfrac{X}{2} = \dfrac{\ell}{200 - \ell}$

$\Rightarrow$ $\dfrac{X}{2} = \dfrac{120}{200 - 120}$ $\Rightarrow$ $\dfrac{X}{2} = \dfrac{120}{8}$ $\Rightarrow$ X $= 3\,\Omega$

25. The given circuit can be simplified as follows:

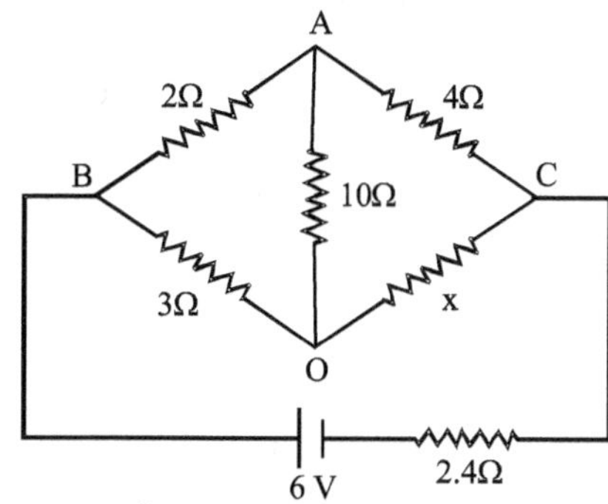

∵ No current flows through the arm AO.

∴ This is a balanced Wheatstone bridge. i.e.

$$\frac{2}{4} = \frac{3}{X} \Rightarrow X = 6\,\Omega,$$

$2\,\Omega$ and $4\,\Omega$ are in series $2 + 4 = 6\,\Omega$

$3\,\Omega$ and $6\,\Omega$ are in series. $3 + 6 = 9\,\Omega$

Equivalent resistance of the $9\,\Omega$ and $6\,\Omega$, connected in

parallel, $R = \dfrac{9 \times 6}{9 + 6} = 3.6\,\Omega$.

∴ Equivalent resistance of the network is $3.6 + 2.4 = 6\,\Omega$

∴ $I = \dfrac{6}{6} = 1A.$

26. Here slope of V-ℓ graph $= \dfrac{V}{\ell} = k = $ Potential gradient

Slope of X $>$ Slope of γ.

∴ γ has a smaller potential gradient than X. A potentiometer with smaller potential gradient is preferred because a larger length of the wire will be required to balance the e.m.f so that measurement will be accurate.

27. For the points AB, $E_1 = k\ell_1 = k \times 300$ .... (1)

For the points AC, $E_1 - E_2 = k\ell_2 = k \times 100$ .... (2)

$$\frac{E_1 - E_2}{E_1} = \frac{1}{3} \Rightarrow 3E_1 - 3E_2 = E_1$$

$$\Rightarrow 3E_1 - E_1 = 3E_2 \qquad \Rightarrow 2E_1 - 3E_2$$

$$\Rightarrow \frac{E_1}{E_2} = \frac{3}{2} \qquad \Rightarrow E_1 : E_2 = 3 : 2$$

28.

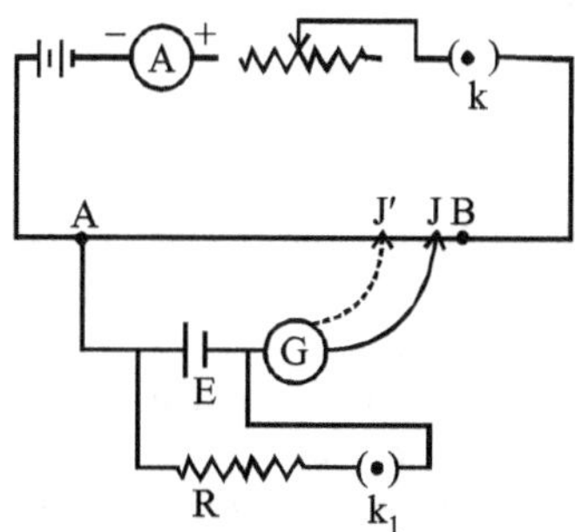

When the key k_1 is off, the cell of e.m.f E is in open circuit.

Let the null point in that case be J and $AJ = \ell_1$

∴ $E = k\ell_1$

When the key is closed, the new null point is at J' and let

$AJ' = \ell_2$

Then the potential difference between two poles of the cell $= V = k\ell_2$

∴ $\dfrac{E}{V} = \dfrac{\ell_1}{\ell_2}$

∴ Internal resistance of the cell

$$= r = \left(\frac{E}{V} - 1\right)R \Rightarrow r = \left(\frac{\ell_1}{\ell_2} - 1\right)R$$

knowing R and measuring ℓ_1 and ℓ_2, r can be calculated.

29.

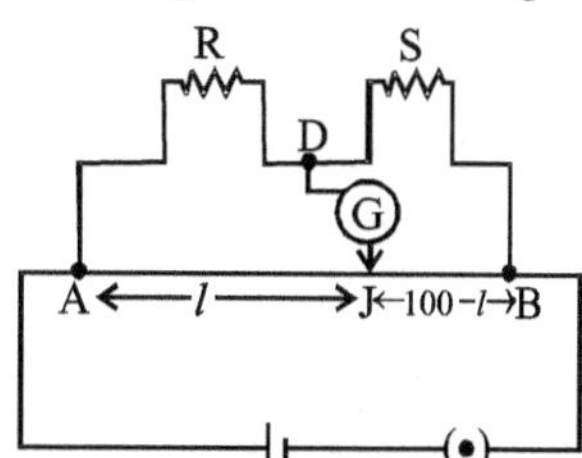

Here, AB is a one metre long, metre bridge wire.

R is the unknown resistance.

S is a known resistance from the resistance box.

J is the position of the null point when no current flows through the galvanometer.

Let $AJ = \ell$

∴ $JB = 100 - \ell$

P = Resistance of the length ℓ of the wire $= \ell r$

Q = Resistance of the length $100 - \ell$ of the wire $= (100 - \ell)r$

where $\ell = $ resistance/unit length of the wire.

∴ $\dfrac{\ell r}{(100 - \ell)r} = \dfrac{R}{S} \Rightarrow R = \left(\dfrac{\ell}{100 - \ell}\right)S$

Measuring ℓ from the scale attached to AB and knowing S, R can be calculated.

30. (i)

(ii) Applying Kirchhoff's 1st law at point F,

$$I_1 + I_2 = I_3 \qquad ..... (1)$$

For the loop ABCFA, applying Kirchhoff's

2nd law, $12 - 6 = -1I_1 + 2I_2$

$$\Rightarrow 6 = 2I_2 - I_1 \qquad .... (2)$$

For the loop FCDEF applying Kirchhoff's 2nd law,

$$-12 = -2I_2 - 15I_3$$

$$12 = 2I_2 + 15(I_1 + I_2)$$

$$12 = 2I_2 + 15I_1 + 15I_2$$

$$12 = 15I_1 + 17I_2 \qquad ..... (3)$$

Solving we get, $I_1 = -\dfrac{78}{47}$ A, $I_2 = \dfrac{102}{47}$ A and

$$I_3 = \frac{24}{47} A$$

Potential difference across the 15 Ω resistance

$$= 15 \times I_3 = 15 \times \frac{24}{47} = 7.66\,V.$$

Past year Exercise

1. **(b)**

2. **(b)** $P_1 = \dfrac{V^2}{R_1}$ and $P_2 = \dfrac{V^2}{R_2}$

   $\dfrac{P_1}{P_2} = \dfrac{R_2}{R_1} = \dfrac{6}{4} = \dfrac{3}{2}$

3. Internal resistance $r = R\left(\dfrac{E}{V} - 1\right)$

4. Let each conductor is of resistance R.

   Case I According to Fig. (a) the resistances are connected in series combination, so resistance

   $\qquad R_1 = R + R = 2R$

   Case II According to Fig. (b), the resistances are connected in parallel combination, so equivalent resistance.

   $\dfrac{1}{R_2} = \dfrac{1}{R} + \dfrac{1}{R} \Rightarrow R_2 = \dfrac{R}{2}$

   Ratio of the equivalent resistance in two combinations is

   $\therefore \quad \dfrac{R_1}{R_2} = \dfrac{2R}{(R/2)} = 4$

5. The resistivity of conductor is equal to the resistance offered by the conductor of unit length and unit cross-sectional area.

   SI unit of resistivity is ohm-metre (Ω-m)

6. The balancing length continue to be X even on doubling the radius of meter bridge wire

   As Resistance of wire $\propto l$ $\qquad \left(\dfrac{\delta}{A} = \text{constant}\right)$

7. Yes, all the free electrons drift in the same direction.

8. Given that resistance of both the wire is same.

   $i.e.,\ R_{Mn} = R_{Cu}\ \ \dfrac{\rho_{Mn}\, l_{Mn}}{A_{Mn}} = \rho_{Cu}\dfrac{l_{Cu}}{A_{Cu}}$

   As, $l_{Mn} = l_{Cu}\ \ \dfrac{\rho_{Mn}}{A_{Mn}} = \dfrac{\rho_{Cu}}{A_{Cu}}$

   We know that, $\rho_{Cu} < \rho_{Mn}$

   So, $A_{Mn} > A_{Cu}$

   i.e. Manganin wire is thicker.

9. $15\,k\Omega = 15 \times 10^3\,\Omega$ (1 for brown, 5 for green and multiplier 10^3 for orange. Hence A picked correct resistor.

10. Terminal potential difference.

11. Given : V = 210 V, P = 630 W, R = ?

    As we know $R = \dfrac{V^2}{P} = \dfrac{210 \times 210}{630} = 70\,\Omega$

12. It is clear that the cell and the battery send current in the opposite directions.

    $\therefore$ Net emf in the circuit $= 200 - 5 = 195V$

    Hence, current in the circuit

    $\qquad i = \dfrac{V}{R} = \dfrac{195}{39} = 5A$

13. Every cell has a characteristic emf E and some internal resistance. When the cell is in a closed circuit, a current flows through the cell. As a result some potential drop takes place inside the cell. The terminal voltage V = E – ir, clearly, V < E.

14. The net emf of cells, each of emf value E in parallel combination is E

    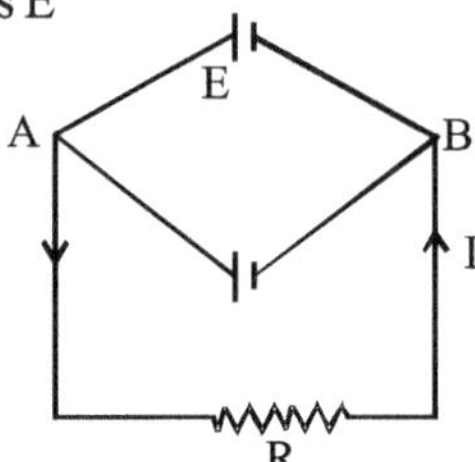

    Therefore, by Ohm's law, current in the resistor R is $I = \dfrac{E}{R}$

15. Drift velocity per unit electric field is called mobility. It is denoted by μ.

    $\mu = \dfrac{V_d}{E}$

    S.I. unit of mobility is $\dfrac{m^2}{volt\text{-}sec}$.

16. The value of temperature coefficient (α) is positive for metals, like copper, because resistance of metal increases with rise in temperature. Thus the variation of resistivity of copper with temperature is parabolic in nature. This is shown in the following graph:

    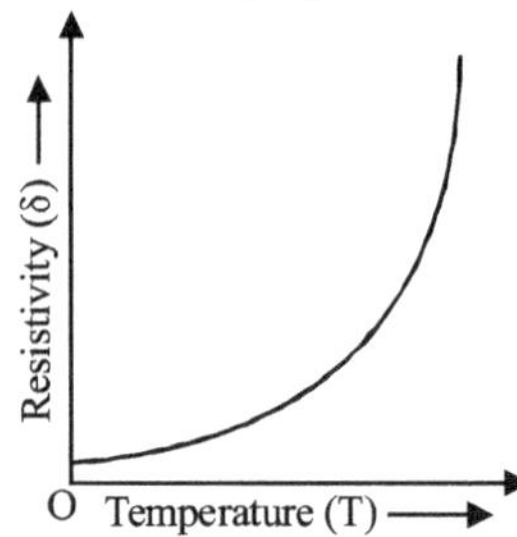

17. Conductivity of wire refers to its ability to carry an electrical charge with minimum resistance.

    The electrical conductivity of a metallic wire is defined as the ratio of the current density to the electric field it creates. It is represented by σ(sigma).

    Electrical conductivity, $\sigma = J/E$

    S.I. unit = (mho m^{-1}) or (ohm m)$^{-1}$

18. The motion of free electrons in a conductor are continuous and random. They collide with positive metal ions and change direction during each collision. So thermal velocities are randomly distributed and average velocity is zero.

    When a potential difference is applied across the ends of a conductor, electrons are drifted towards the positive terminal of the field, this velocity is called drift velocity (v_d)

    $\qquad v_d = -\dfrac{I}{neA}$

    Here, I is the current following through the conductor.
    n is the number density of an electron.
    A is the area of the conductor.
    e is the charge of the electron.

19.

Emf	Terminal voltage
It is the maximum potential differencethat can be delivered by a cell when no current flows through the circuit.	It is the potential difference across the terminals of the load when current flows through the circuit.
It is represented by E and remains constant for a cell.	It is represented by V and depends on the internal resistance of the cell.

20. (i) In region DE of the graph semiconductor has a negative resistance.

(ii) Ohm's law is obeyed when v $\propto$ I

21. According to the definition of the terminal potential difference,

$V = E - Ir$

E is the EMF and r is the total internal resistance of the circuit.

$I = 0 \Rightarrow V = E$

From the graph we can see $E = 6\,V$

As there are three cells we can write, $E = 3 \times e \Rightarrow e = 2\,V$

And, when, $V = 0 \Rightarrow E = Ir$

$r = \dfrac{E}{I} = \dfrac{6}{1} = 6\Omega$

As per the question the cells are connected in series, so

$r' = \dfrac{r}{3} = 2\Omega$

22. The charge carriers for the flow of current in a

(i) Conductor are electrons and

(ii) electrolyte are ions.

23. Nichrome wire is heated more.

Heat dissipated in a wire is given by Joule's heating law

$H = I^2 Rt = I^2 \dfrac{\rho \ell}{A} t$

$H \propto \rho$ ($\because$ I, ℓ and A remains same)

As $\rho_{nichrome} > \rho_{copper} \therefore H_{nichrome} > H_{copper}$

24. (i) Refer to Theory

(ii) Let $6I$ current be drawn from the cell. Since the paths AA', AD and AB are symmetrical, current through them is same.

As per Kirchhoff's junction rule, the current distribution is shown in the figure.

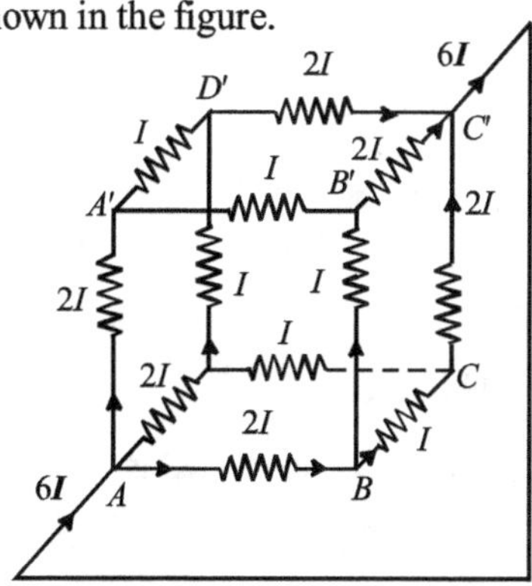

Let the equivalent resistance across the combination be R.

$E = V_A - V_B = (6I) R$

$\Rightarrow \quad 6IR = 10 \qquad [\because E = 10V] \,...(i)$

Applying Kirchhoff's second rule in loop $AA'B'C'A$

$-2I \times 1 - I \times 1 - 2I \times 1 + 10 = 0$

$\Rightarrow \quad 5I = 10$

$\quad I = 2A$

Total current in the network $= 6I = 6 \times 2 = 12\,A$

From Eq. (i), $6IR = 10$

$6 \times 2 \times R = 10$

$R = \dfrac{10}{12} = \dfrac{5}{6}\Omega = \dfrac{5}{6}\Omega$

25. (i) The balancing condition state that

$\dfrac{R}{X} = \dfrac{l}{(100-l)} \Rightarrow \dfrac{X}{R} = \dfrac{100-l}{l}$

when X and R both are doubled then $\dfrac{2X}{2R} = \dfrac{X}{R} = \dfrac{100-l}{l}$

balancing length would be at $(100 - l)$ cm

(ii) On changing the position of galvanometer and battery, the meter bridge continue to be balanced and hence no change across in the balance point.

26. By Kirchhoff's current rule

$I = I_1 + I_2$

Across cell E_1, potential difference (V)

$V = V_{B_2} - V_{B_1} = E_1 - I_1 r_1$

Across cell E_2, potential difference (V)

$V = V_{B_2} - V_{B_1} = E_2 - I_2 r_2$

On solving above equations we get,

$I_1 = \dfrac{E_1 - v}{r_1}$ and $I_2 = \dfrac{E_2 - v}{r_2}$

$\therefore \quad I = \left(\dfrac{E_1 - V}{r_1}\right) + \left(\dfrac{E_2 - V}{r_2}\right)$

$I = \left(\dfrac{E_1}{r_1} + \dfrac{E_2}{r_2}\right) - V\left(\dfrac{1}{r_1} + \dfrac{1}{r_2}\right)$

$V\left(\dfrac{r_1 + r_2}{r_1 r_2}\right) = \left(\dfrac{E_1 r_2 + E_2 r_1}{r_1 r_2}\right) - I$

$V = \left(\dfrac{E_1 r_2 + E_2 r_1}{r_1 + r_2}\right) - I\left(\dfrac{r_1 r_2}{r_1 + r_2}\right)$

Let equivalent emf and equivalent internal resistance of combination are E_{eq} and r_{eq}, then potential difference across combination is given

$V = E_{eq} - Ir_{eq}$

On comparing we get, $E_{eq} = \dfrac{E_1 r_2 + E_2 r_1}{r_1 + r_2}$ and $r_{eq} = \dfrac{r_1 r_2}{r_1 + r_2}$

27. Resistance of two heating elements are:

$$P_1 = \frac{V^2}{R_1} \Rightarrow R_1 = \frac{V^2}{P_1}$$

$$P_2 = \frac{V^2}{R_2}, \; R_2 = \frac{V^2}{P_2}$$

(i) In series combination

$$R_S = R_1 + R_2 = \frac{V^2}{P_1} + \frac{V^2}{P_2} = V^2\left(\frac{P_1 + P_2}{P_1 P_2}\right)$$

$$\therefore \quad P_S = \frac{V^2}{R_s} = \frac{V^2}{V^2\left(\dfrac{P_1 + P_2}{P_1 P_2}\right)} = \frac{P_1 P_2}{P_1 + P_2}$$

(ii) In parallel combination

$$\frac{1}{R_p} = \frac{1}{R_1} + \frac{1}{R_2} = \frac{1}{\dfrac{V^2}{P_1}} + \frac{1}{\dfrac{V^2}{P_2}} = \frac{P_1}{V^2} + \frac{P_2}{V^2}$$

$$\frac{1}{R_p} = \frac{1}{V^2}(P_1 + P_2)$$

power consumption in parallel combination

$$P_p = \frac{V^2}{R_p}$$

$$P_p = V^2\left[\frac{1}{V^2}(P_1 + P_2)\right]$$

$$P_p = P_1 + P_2$$

28. The average time difference between two successive collisions of drifting electrons inside the conductor under the influence of electric field is known as relaxation time. Drift speed and relaxation time are related as:

$$V_d = -\frac{eE\tau}{m}$$

As current $I = - ne \, Av_d$

$$I = -neA\left(-\frac{eE\tau}{m}\right)$$

$$I = \frac{ne^2 A\tau}{m}\left(\frac{V}{l}\right) \qquad \left(\because E = \frac{V}{l}\right)$$

$$\Rightarrow \frac{V}{I} = \frac{ml}{ne^2 A\tau} = \rho\frac{l}{A} = R \Rightarrow \rho = \frac{m}{ne^2\tau}$$

29. Principle of a potentiometer : If a constant current is passed through a wire of uniform area of cross section the potential drop across a section of the wire is directly proportional to the length of that section of the wire.

The factors on which sensitivity of a potentiometer depends.

(i) Length of the potentiometer wire and (ii) Current through the wire.

(i) The balance point will shift towards B. Increase in resistance R decreases the current through the potentiometer wire. This decreases the least count of the potentiometer (k = V/L). Now, to balance the same potential greater length of wire will be required.

(ii) No change in the balance point as R is constant. Resistance S is only to ensure that the deflection in the galvanometer remain within scale.

30. Relation between current (I) and drift velocity (v_d) :

$$I = V_d \, enA$$

$$I = \frac{e^2 VnA}{mL}\tau \qquad \left(\because V_d = \frac{eV}{mL}T\right)$$

It is clear from this expression that with the rise in temperatue τ decreases, this decreases the current in the circuit, which in turn increases the resistance of the conductor.

31. 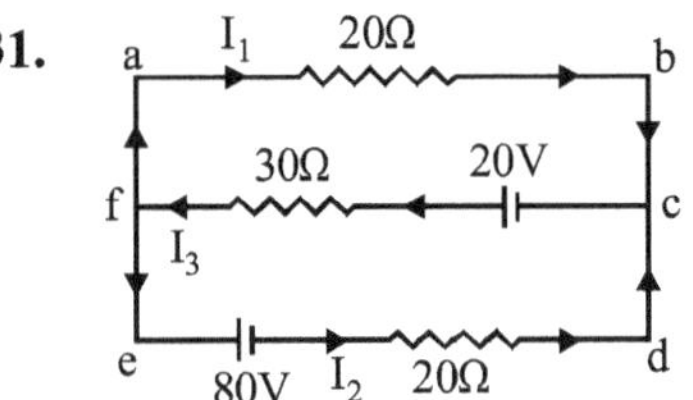

From Kirchoff's Ist rule or junction rule

For junction f, I

$$_1 + I_2 = I_3$$

or, $\quad I_1 = I_3 - I_2 \qquad$ ... (i)

From kirchoff's 2nd rule or loop rule

In loop 'abcfa'

$$-20I_1 + 20 - 30I_3 = 0$$

or, $\qquad 2I_1 + 3I_3 = 2 \qquad$ ... (ii)

In loop 'fcdef,'

$$30I_3 - 20 + 20I_2 - 80 = 0$$

or, $\quad 3I_3 + 2I_2 = 10 \qquad$ ... (iii)

Substituting equation (i) in (ii)

$$2(I_3 - I_2) + 3I_3 = 2$$

or, $\qquad 5I_3 - 2I_2 = 2 \qquad$ ...(iv)

Adding equations (iii) and (iv)

$$8I_3 = 12$$

or, $\quad I_3 = 3/2$ A

Substituting in equation (iii) and solving

$$I_2 = 11/4 A$$

Substituting for I_3 and I_2 in equation (i)

$$I_1 = 3/2 - 11/4 = -5/4 \text{ A}$$

32. Given : $\quad R_1 : R_2 : R_3 = 1 : 2 : 3$

and $\qquad R_1 + R_2 + R_3 = 12 \, \Omega$

The three resistance are

$$R_1 = \frac{1}{6} \times 12 = 2\Omega, \; R_2 = \frac{2}{6} \times 12 = 4\Omega \text{ and}$$

$$R_3 = \frac{3}{6} \times 12 = 6\Omega$$

Resistance R_1 and R_2 are connected in series

$$\therefore \quad R = R_1 + R_2 = 2 + 4 = 6\Omega$$

This resistance R and R_3 are connected in parallel,

∴ net resistance $R_P = \dfrac{RR_3}{R+R_3} = \dfrac{6 \times 6}{6+6} = 3\Omega$

Again R_P and the internal resistance of the cell (r) are connected in series, therfore, net resistance of the circuit

$$R_N = R_P + r = 3 + 1 = 4\,\Omega$$

Hence, current in the circuit

$$I = V/R_N = 8/4 = 2\,A$$

From the circuit, it is clear that I/2 (= 1A) through resistors R_1, R_2 and I/2 (=1A) through resistor R_3

33. Graph of variation of resistivity with temperature for nichrome

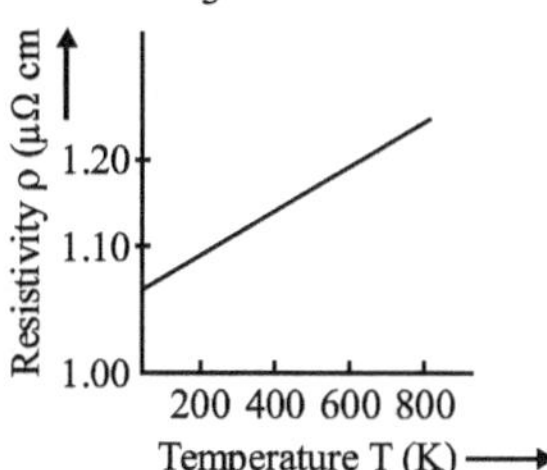

Property of nichrome used to make standard resistance coils : Its low temperature coefficient of resistance.

34. Given : $I_1 = 0.5\,A$, $R_1 = 12\,ohm$, $I_2 = 0.25\,A$, $R_2 = 25\,ohm$

From formula, $I = \dfrac{E}{(R+r)}$ or $E = I(R+r)$

$0.5 \times (12+r) = 0.25 \times (25+r)$

Solving we get, r = 1 ohm and emf, E = 0.5 (12 + 1) = 6.5 V

35. (i) Given : $G = 0.6\,\Omega$, $I_g = 1.0\,A$, $I = 5A$, $S = ?$

We know that $S = \dfrac{GI_g}{I - I_g} = \dfrac{0.6 \times 1}{5-1} = \dfrac{0.6}{4} = 0.15\,\Omega$

∴ Required shunt resistance $= 0.15\,\Omega$

(ii) Since the ammeter and shunt are in parallel, their combined resistance

$$R_C = \dfrac{G \times S}{G+S} = \dfrac{0.6 \times 0.15}{0.6 + 0.15} = \dfrac{0.6 \times 0.15}{0.75} = 0.12\,\Omega$$

36. If E is the emf of the cell, r is the internal resistance of the cell and I is the current through the circuit. Then Terminal voltage 'V' of the cell is $V = E - Ir$

So, $V = -Ir + E$

Comparing with the equation of a straight line

$y = mx+c$, we get: $y = V$; $x = I$; $m = -r$; $c = E$

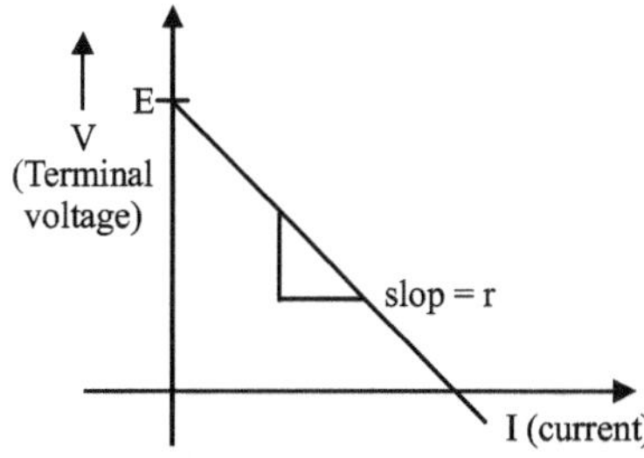

Graph showing variation of terminal voltage 'V' of the cell versus the current 'I'

Where, Emf of the cell = Intercept on V axis

Internal resistance = slope of line.

37. Drift velocity, $V_d = \dfrac{I}{neA}$

where, I is the current, n is charge density, e is charge of electron and A is cross-section area.

$$V_d = \dfrac{1.5}{9 \times 10^{28} \times 1.6 \times 10^{-19} \times 1.0 \times 10^{-7}}$$

$$V_d = \dfrac{1.5}{14.4 \times 10^2}$$

$$V_d = 10.4 \times 10^{-4}\,m/s$$

38. (a) The resistivity of a copper wire is very low, and when the connections are thick, so that the area is quite large and hence the resistance of the wires is almost negligible. So, the connections between the resistors in a meter bridge made of thick copper strips

(b) To improves the sensitivity of the meter bridge, it is preferred to obtain the balance point in the middle of the meter bridge.

(c) Constantan is used for meter bridge wire because the temperature coefficient of constantan is almost negligible due to which the resistance of the wire does not change with increase in temperature of the wire due to flow of current.

OR

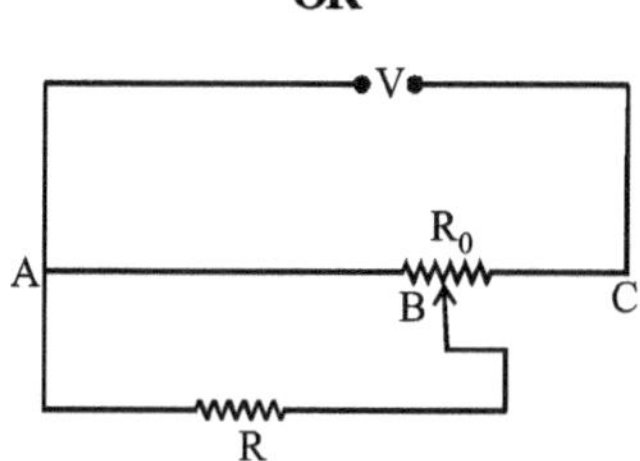

Total resistance between A and B

$$R_{AB} = \dfrac{\dfrac{R_0}{2} \times R}{R + \dfrac{R_0}{2}} = \dfrac{RR_0}{2R + R_0}$$

Total resistance between A and C

$$R_{AC} = R_{AB} + \dfrac{R_0}{2} = \left[\dfrac{RR_0}{2R + R_0} + \dfrac{R_0}{2}\right]$$

The current through the potentiometer wire

$$I = \dfrac{V}{R_{AC}}$$

The potential difference between A and B

$$V_{AB} = I\,R_{AB} = \dfrac{V}{R_{AC}} \times R_{AB}$$

$$= \dfrac{V}{\dfrac{RR_0}{R+R_0} + \dfrac{R_0}{2}} \times \dfrac{RR_0}{(2R+R_0)}$$

$$= \dfrac{V}{\dfrac{2RR_0 + R_0(2R+R_0)}{2(2R+R_0)}} \times \dfrac{RR_0}{(2R+R_0)}$$

$$= \dfrac{2V\,RR_0}{R_0[2R + 2R + R_0]}$$

$$V_{AB} = \dfrac{2VR}{R_0 + 4R}$$

39. Total resistance of the circuit,

$R = (R_{PQ} + 5)\,\Omega = 15\,\Omega$

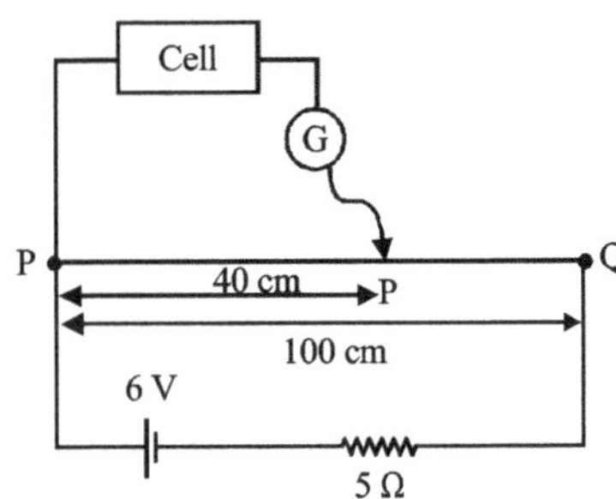

Current in the circuit, $i = \dfrac{V}{R} = \dfrac{6}{15}$ A

$\therefore$ Voltage across PQ, $V_{PQ} = i.R_{OQ} = 4$ V

emf of the cell, $e = \dfrac{l}{L} V_0$

Here: balance point is at, $l = 40$ cm

Total length of wire $PQ = L = 1$ m $= 100$ cm

$\therefore\quad e = \dfrac{40}{100}(4) = 1.6$ V

40. (a) During this incident, Anuj reflected the following values:

(i) He was concerned about the lives of the individuals.

(ii) He was well aware about what would be the after effect of touching a live wire with naked hands and he immediately acted upon this situation and saved lives of the boys.

(b) When the bird perches on a live wire, its body becomes charged for the moment and has same voltage as the live wire; however, no current flows into its body. Body is a poor conductor of electricity as compared to the copper wire, so there is no reason for electrons to take a detour through the bird's body. Therefore, no current flows from the body of the bird.

On the other hand, if the bird touches the ground while being in contact with the high voltage live wire, then the electric circuit gets complete and high current flows through the body of the bird, giving it a fatal shock.

(c) The electric power from a power plant is set up at a very high voltage before transmitting it to distant consumers to reduce the loss of power during transmission.

The power loss during the transmission = $\mathbf{I}^2\,\mathbf{R}$. So the power loss can be minimised by reducing the value of the current. Thus, to reduce the value of current, value of the voltage of the electric power should be kept high before transmitting.

Power = Voltage × Current

From the above equation, we can see that the current can be reduced by increasing the voltage of the electric power.

41. When balance point is at 40 cm, we have

$\dfrac{R}{S} = \dfrac{40}{100 - 40} = \dfrac{40}{60} \Rightarrow \dfrac{R}{S} = \dfrac{2}{3}$

$\Rightarrow\quad 3\,R = 2\,S$ .... (i)

When a resistance of 10 Ω is added in series with R, Then, equivalent reistance of $R' = R + 10$

Now, balance point is obtained at 60 cm.

$\therefore\quad \dfrac{R+10}{S} = \dfrac{60}{100-60} = \dfrac{60}{40}$

$\Rightarrow\quad \dfrac{R+10}{S} = \dfrac{3}{2}$

$\Rightarrow\quad 2\,R + 20 = 3S$ ...(ii)

Solving eqs (i) and (ii), we get

$S = 12\,\Omega$ and $R = 8\,\Omega$

42. (a) **Principle of potentiometer:** When a steady current flows through the potentiometer wire then, the potential difference across the uniform wire is directly proportional to the length of the part across which the potential is measured.

(b) Current sensitivity can be increased by

(i) increasing the length of the wire

(ii) decreasing the current in the wire using a rheostat

(c) Potentiometer is preferred over voltmeter because it measures accurate emf of the cell. It uses null method, so no current is drawn by the galvanometer from the cell in balanced condition of potentiometer and a voltmeter measures the voltage across the terminals of a cell when the cell is in closed circuit. This voltage is called terminal voltage of a cell not emf.

43. Refer to Theory

44. (i) Graph between terminal voltage V and resistance (R)

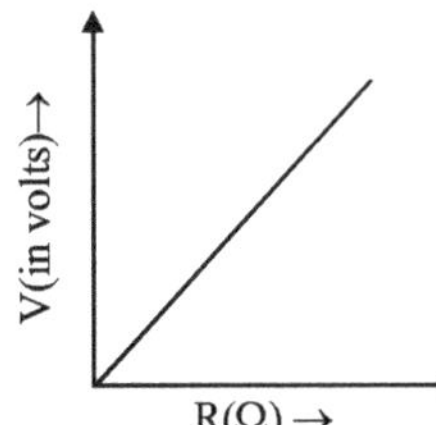

(ii) Graph between terminal voltage (V) and current (I)

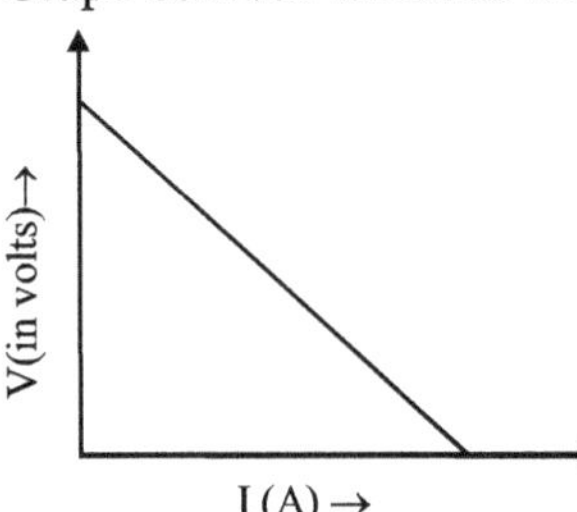

45. (i) Refer to theory

(ii) Drift velocity of electrons in a metallic conductor decreases with increase in temperature.

As, we increase the temperature of the metallic conductor the collision between the electrons and ions increases, which results in the decrease in the relaxation time.

So, $v_d \propto \tau$

Hence, the drift velocity decreased.

46. Working principle of meter bridge:
The working principle of meter bridge is based on wheatstone bridge. It is an arrangement of four resistances used to determine one of these resistances quickly in terms of the remaining three resistances.
When the bridge is balanced,
$$\frac{R}{S} = \frac{l}{100 - l} \; ; l = \text{balanced length}$$

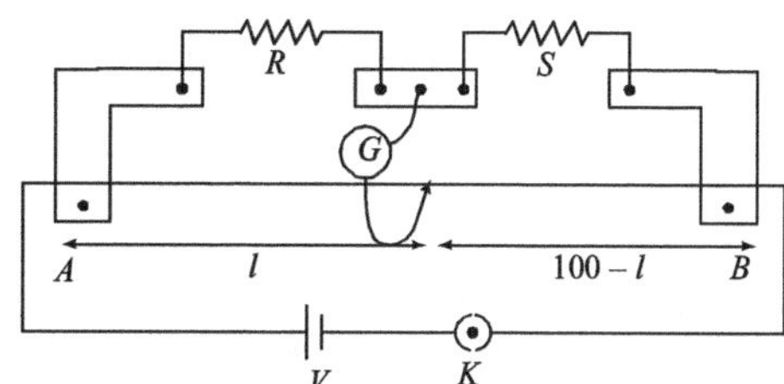

47. (a) From the circuit, we can write
$$V_1 = E_1 - I_1 r_1 \qquad \qquad \dots(1)$$
$$V_2 = E_2 - I_2 r_2 \qquad \qquad \dots(2)$$
Since E_1 and E_2 are parallel
$$V_1 = V_2 = V \text{ and } I = I_1 + I_2$$

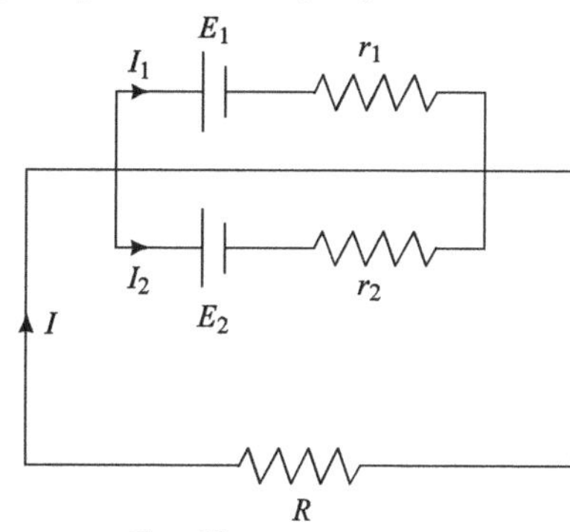

From (1), $I_1 = \dfrac{E_1 - V}{r_1}$

From (2), $I_2 = \dfrac{E_2 - V}{r_2}$

Similarly, for equivalent cell
$$I = \frac{E_{eq} - V}{r_{eq}}$$

48. For series combination, power dissipated (P) by a bulb is directly proportional to its resistance (R).
i.e., $P \propto R$
$P_1/P_2 = R_1/R_2 = 1:2.$

49. Let i be the current in the circuit and its direction is in anticlockwise direction.

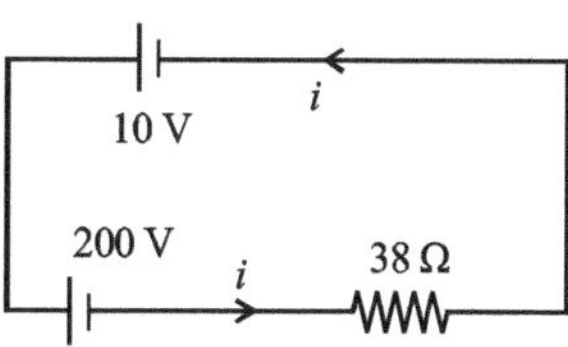

Applying kirchhoff's voltage law, $E - V + iR = 0$
$10 - 200 + 38\,i = 0 \Rightarrow 38\,i = 190 \Rightarrow i = 5A$

OR

Given : $R = 9\Omega$, $l_1 = 350$, $l_2 = 300$
Internal resistance of a cell is given by, $r = R\left(\dfrac{l_2}{l_1} - 1\right)$
Substituting values of l_2, l_1 and R, we get
$$r = R\left(\frac{350}{300} - 1\right) = 9\left(\frac{7}{6} - 1\right) = 1.5\Omega.$$

50. (a) The reciprocal of the resistivity (ρ) of a material is called its conductivity and is denoted by σ.
$$\text{i.e., } \sigma = \frac{1}{\rho}$$
The SI unit of conductivity: siemen per meter (sm^{-1})
(b) The average time difference between two successive collisions of drifting electrons inside the conductor under the influence of electric field is known as relaxation time. Drift speed and relaxation time are related as:
$$V_d = -\frac{eE\tau}{m}$$
As current $I = -ne\,Av_d$
$$I = -neA\left(-\frac{eE\tau}{m}\right)$$
$$I = \frac{ne^2 A\tau}{m}\left(\frac{V}{l}\right) \qquad \left(\because E = \frac{V}{l}\right)$$
$$\Rightarrow \frac{V}{I} = \frac{ml}{ne^2 A\tau} = \rho\frac{l}{A} = R$$
$$\rho = \frac{m}{ne^2\tau}$$
Now, we know that conductivity of a conductor (σ) is mathematically defined as the reciprocal of resistivity of the conductor. Thus, $\rho = \dfrac{1}{\sigma}$

$\therefore$ Conductivity, $\sigma = \dfrac{ne^2\tau}{m}$

Now, from above equations
$\dfrac{I}{A} = \sigma E$ Current density is given as $J = \dfrac{I}{A}$
Thus, $J = \sigma E$

51. (a) According to question, heat produced per second (H/t) increases 9 times by changing potential difference (V) i.e., $H' = 9H$
$$\therefore \quad \frac{V'^2 t}{R} = 9 \times \frac{V^2 t}{R}$$
[from joule's heating law, $H = I^2 Rt = \dfrac{V^2 t}{R}$]
$\therefore \quad V'^2 = 9 \times V^2 \quad \text{ or, } V' = 3V$
Hence applied potential difference increases by a factor of 3.
(b) Given : emf of cell /source E 12 V
Internal resistance $r = 2\Omega$
External resistance $R = 4\Omega$
$$\text{Current } I = \frac{E}{R+r} = \frac{12}{4+2} = \frac{12}{6} = 2\,A$$
Using $V = E - Ir$
$V = 12 - (2 \times 2) = 8\,V$
Thus, reading of the ammeter will be 2 A and of the voltmeter will be 8 V.

52. (a) **Principle of working of a meter bridge:** Meter bridge works on the principle of Wheatstone bridge. According to the principle, the balancing condition for balancing length l_1,

$$\frac{R}{S} = \frac{P}{Q} = \frac{\sigma l_1}{\sigma(100 - l_1)}$$

$$\Rightarrow \frac{R}{S} = \frac{l_1}{100 - l_1} \Rightarrow R = S\frac{l_1}{100 - l_1}$$

where σ is the resistance per unit length of the wire and l_1 is the length of the wire from one end where null point is obtained. The bridge is most sensitive when null point is somewhere near the middle point of the wire. This is due to end resistances.

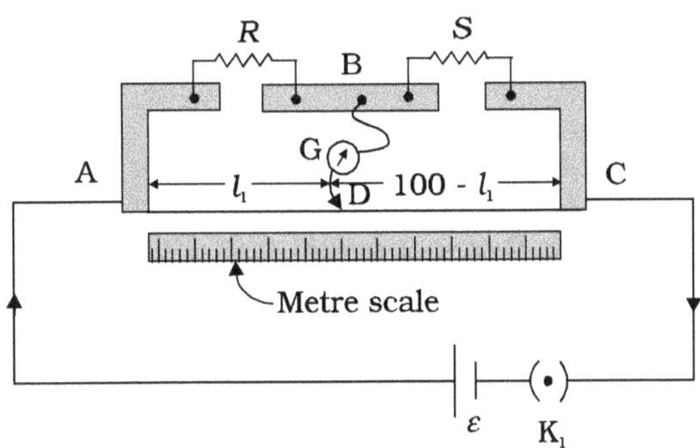

A meter bridge. Wire AC is 1 m long.

(b)   For balancing length l_1, the condition is

$$\frac{R}{S} = \frac{l}{100 - l_1} \qquad \text{...(i)}$$

When a resistance x is connected in parallel with S, the net resistance becomes

$$S_{new} = \frac{XS}{X + S}$$

For balancing length l_2, the condition is $\dfrac{R}{S_{new}} = \dfrac{l_2}{100 - l_2}$

$$\therefore \frac{R(X+S)}{XS} = \frac{l_2}{100 - l_2} \qquad \text{...(ii)}$$

From eqn. (i) and (ii), $\dfrac{l_1}{100 - l_1} \times \dfrac{X \times S}{X} = \dfrac{l_2}{100 - l_2}$

$$\therefore \frac{X + S}{X} = \frac{l_2}{100 - l_2} \times \frac{100 - l_1}{l_1}$$

$$\therefore \frac{X + S}{X} = \frac{l_2(100 - l_1)}{l_1(100 - l_2)} \Rightarrow \frac{S}{X} + 1 = \frac{l_2(100 - l_1)}{l_1(100 - l_2)}$$

NCERT Exemplar

1.   **(b)** As we know, electric current per unit area I/A, is called current density j i.e., $j = \dfrac{I}{A}$

The SI units of the current density are A/m^2.
The current density is also directed along E and is also a vector and the relationship is

$$j = \sigma E$$

Current density changes due to electric field produced by charges accumulated on the surface of wire.

2.   **(a)** As we know the equivalent emf (ε_{eq}) in the parallel combination

$$\varepsilon_{eq} = \frac{\varepsilon_2 r_1 + \varepsilon_1 r_2}{r_1 + r_2}$$

So according to formula the equivalent emf ε_{eq} of the two cells in parallel combination is between ε_1 and ε_2. Thus $(\varepsilon_1 < \varepsilon_{eq} < \varepsilon_2)$.

3.   **(c)** Adjusting the blance point near the middle of the bridge, i.e.. when l_1 is close to 50 cm. requires a suitable choice of S, R is unknown resistance :

Since, $\dfrac{R}{S} = \dfrac{R l_1}{R(100 - l_1)}$

$$\frac{R}{S} = \frac{l_1}{100 - l_1} \quad \text{or} \quad R = S\left[\frac{l_1}{100 - l_1}\right]$$

$$R = S\left[\frac{2.9}{97.1}\right]$$

So, here, R : S = 2.9 : 97.1 implies that the S is nearly 33 times to that of R. In orded to make this ratio 1 : 1 it is necessary to reduce the value of S nearly $\dfrac{1}{33}$ times i.e., nearly 3 Ω,

4.   **(b)** The potential drop across wires of potentiometer should be more than emfs of primary cells. Here, values of emfs of two cells are given as 5V and 10V, so the potential drop along the potentiometer wire must be more than 10V. So battery should be of 15V and about 4V potential is droped by using variable resistance.

5.   **(a)** As we known that the resistance of wire is $R = \rho\dfrac{l}{A}$

For maximum value of R, l must be higher and A should be lower and it is possible only when the battery is connected

across area of cross section $= 1cm \times \left(\dfrac{1}{2}\right)cm$.

6.   **(a)** We know that the relationship between current and drift speed is

$$I = ne\, Av_d$$

Where, I is the current and V_d is the drift velocity.
So, $I \propto V_d$
Hence, only drift velocity determines the current in a conductor.

7.   When an electron approaches a junction, in addition to the uniform **E** that it normally faces (which keep the drift velocity v_d fixed), there are accumulation of charges on the surface of wires at the junction. These produce electric field. These fields alter direction of momentum.

8.   Power wasted $P_C = I^2 R_C$
where R_C is the resistance of the connecting wires.

$$P_C = \frac{P^2}{V^2} R_C$$

In order to reduce P_C. Power should be transmitted at high voltage.

9.   (i)   Positive terminal of E_1 is connected at X and $E_1 > E$.
      (ii) Negative terminal of E_1 is connected at X.

10. $E - 3r = 10$ ....(i)
      $E + 2r = 15$ ....(ii)
      solving these two equations, we get, $r = 1\ \Omega$

11. In parallel connection, same voltage exists across each bulb. As the overall voltage of the circuit will decrease, the voltage across each bulb will also decrease. Hence, the brightness of the bulbs will diminish.

12. $I = \dfrac{E + E}{R + r_1 + r_1}$

$V_1 = E - Ir_1 = E - \dfrac{2E}{r_1 + r_2 + R} r_1 = 0$

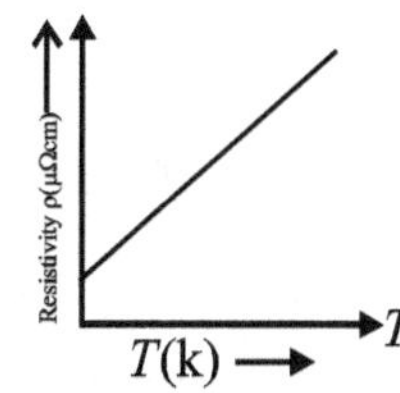

or $\quad E = \dfrac{2Er_1}{r_1 + r_2 + R} \qquad I = \dfrac{2r_1}{r_1 + r_2 + R}$

$r_1 + r_2 + R = 2r_1$
$R = r_1 - r_2$

13. $R_A = \dfrac{\rho l}{\pi (10^{-3} \times 0.5)^2}$

$R_B = \dfrac{\rho l}{\pi [(10^{-3})^2 - (0.5 \times 10^{-3})^2]}$

$\dfrac{R_A}{R_B} = \dfrac{(10^{-3})^2 - (0.5 \times 10^{-3})^2}{(.5 \times 10^{-3})^2} = 3 : 1$

14. Resistance, $\quad X = \dfrac{\text{Reading of V}}{\text{Reading of A}}$

For X use (b)
For Y use (a).

15. (a) When $I = 0$

Total emf = terminal Voltage $4E = 5.6$

$E = 1.4\,V$

(b) For maximum current external resistance $= 4r$

$I = \dfrac{4E}{R + 4r} = \dfrac{4E}{8r} = \dfrac{5.6}{8 \times 0.7} = 1A$

(c) Internal resistance of 4 cells $= 4r$.

For $I = 1.0\,A$, $V = 2.8\,V$ [from graph]

External resistance, $R = \dfrac{V}{I} = 2.8\,\Omega \Rightarrow r = 0.7\Omega$.

Objective Practice Exercise

1. **(b)** Motion of conduction electrons due to random collisions has no preffered direction and average to zero. Drift velocity is caused due to motion of conduction electrons due to applied electric field $\vec{E}$.

2. **(d)** **3.** **(b)** **4.** **(a)** **5.** **(d)** **6.** **(a)**

7. **(a)** **8.** **(b)**

9. **(b)** These materials exhibit a very weak dependence of resistivity on temperature. Their resistance values would be changed very little with temperature as shown in figure. Hence these materials are widely used as heating element.

10. **(d)** Resistivity depends on various other factors like temp.

11. **(c)** No current flows through the resistor R as P and Q are at same potential. Hence current drawn from battery will remain same on closing the switch.

12. **(b)**

13. **(a)** The potential difference across 4Ω resistance is given by $V = 4 \times i_1 = 4 \times 1.2 = 4.8$ volt

So, the potential across 8Ω resistance is also 4.8 volt.

Current $i_2 = \dfrac{V}{8} = \dfrac{4.8}{8} = 0.6\,\text{amp}$

Current in 2Ω resistance $i = i_1 + i_2$

$\therefore i = 1.2 + 0.6 = 1.8\,\text{amp}$

Potential difference across 2Ω resistance

$V_{BC} = 1.8 \times 2 = 3.6$ volts

14. **(a)** Kirchhoff 's first law deals with conservation of electrical charge & the second law deals with conservation of electrical energy.

15. **(a)** Because of internal resistance of cell.

16. **(d)** **17. (d)** **18. (a)** **19. (c)**

20. **(b)** In the given case cell is in open circuit ($i = 0$) so voltage across the cell is equal to its e.m.f.

21. **(a)**

22. **(a)** In the parallel combination,

$\dfrac{\varepsilon_{eq}}{r_{eq}} = \dfrac{\varepsilon_1}{r_1} + \dfrac{\varepsilon_2}{r_2} + ... + \dfrac{\varepsilon_n}{r_n}$

$\dfrac{1}{r_{eq}} = \dfrac{1}{r_1} + \dfrac{1}{r_2} + ... + \dfrac{1}{r_n}$

$(\because \varepsilon_1 = \varepsilon_2 = \varepsilon_3 = ... = \varepsilon_n = \varepsilon$ and $r_1 = r_2 = r_3 = ... \, r)$

$\therefore \quad \dfrac{\varepsilon_{eq}}{r_{eq}} = \dfrac{\varepsilon}{r} + \dfrac{\varepsilon}{r} + ... + \dfrac{\varepsilon}{r} = n\dfrac{\varepsilon}{r} \qquad .... (i)$

$\dfrac{\varepsilon}{r_{eq}} = \dfrac{1}{r} + \dfrac{1}{r} + ... + \dfrac{1}{r} = \dfrac{n}{r} \quad r_{eq} = r/n \qquad ...(ii)$

From (i) and (ii)

$\varepsilon_{eq} = n\dfrac{\varepsilon}{r_{eq}} \times r_{eq} = n \times \dfrac{\varepsilon}{r} \times \dfrac{\varepsilon}{r} = \varepsilon$

23. **(b)** As $R \propto V^2/P$ or $R \propto 1/P$, so resistance of heater is less than that of fan.

24. **(d)** $H \propto \dfrac{1}{R}$ [as $V = $ constant in parallel connection]

25. **(b)** $i = \dfrac{E}{r} \Rightarrow 30 = \dfrac{1.5}{r}$

$r = 0.05\,\Omega \Rightarrow H = i^2 rt = (30)^2 \times 0.05 \times 20 = 900\,J$

26. **(d)** As $R \times \dfrac{1}{\text{Power}} \quad \therefore R_1 : R_2 = 2 : 1$

27. **(b)** Since, the voltage is same for the two combinations, therefore $H \propto \dfrac{1}{R}$. Hence, the combination of 39 bulbs will glow more.

28. **(c)** If a heater boils m kg water in time t_1 and another heater boils the same water in t_2, then both connected in series will boil the same water in time $t_s = t_1 + t_2$ and if in parallel $t_p = \dfrac{t_1 t_2}{t_1 + t_2}$ [Use time taken $\propto$ Resistance]

29. **(c)** $H = P \times t = \dfrac{210 \times 5 \times 60}{4.2} = 15000\,\text{cal.}$

30. **(d)**

31. **(b)** The deflection in galvanometer will not be changed due to interchange of cells and the galvanometer.

32. **(a)** In meter bridge experiment, it is assumed that the resistance of the L shaped plate is negligible, but actually it is not so. The error created due to this is called end error. To remove this the resistance box and the unknown resistance must be interchanged and then the mean reading must be taken.

33. **(b)** Potentiometer is based on zero deflection method.

34. **(b)**   **35.** **(b)**   **36.** **(b)**   **37.** **(a)**   **38.** **(c)**

39. **(c)**

Chapter Test

1. **(b)** Resistance of a wire is given by $R = \rho \dfrac{l}{a}$

If the length is increased by 10% then new

length $l' = l + \dfrac{1}{10} = \dfrac{11}{10} l$

In that case, area of cross-section of wire would decrease by 10%

∴ New area of cross-section

$A' = A - \dfrac{A}{10} = \dfrac{9}{10} A$

$\therefore R' = \rho \dfrac{l'}{A'} = \rho \dfrac{\frac{11}{10} l}{\frac{9}{10} A}$

$R' = \dfrac{11}{9} \rho \dfrac{l}{R}$ $R' = 1.21 R$

Thus the new resistance increases by 1.21 times. The specific resistance (resistivity) remains unchanged as it depends on the nature of the material of the wire.

2. **(c)** Applying Kirchhoff's law in BCDEFAB we get,

$I = \dfrac{V}{3R}$

Let A be at 0 V. Then potential at G is V.
Applying Krichhoff's law for AFED, we get

$0 + V + IR = V_D$

$\Rightarrow 0 + V + \dfrac{V}{3R} \times R = V_D \Rightarrow V_D = \dfrac{4V}{3}$

∴ potential different across capacitor $= \dfrac{4V}{3} - V = \dfrac{V}{3}$

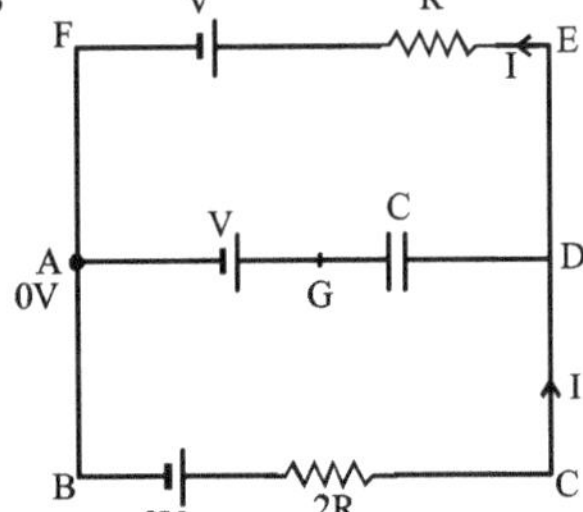

3. **(a)** Potential gradient of wire $= \dfrac{V}{\ell} = \left(\dfrac{\rho}{A}\right) \times I$

where ℓ & A are the length and cross-section of wire

so $\dfrac{V}{\ell} = \dfrac{4 \times 10^{-7}}{8 \times 10^{-6}} \times 0.5 = 25\,\text{mV/meter}$

4. **(a)**

5. **(c)** Voltmeter is a galvanometer with high resistance. It measures potential drop across any part of an electrical circuit. It is connected in parallel so that it does not draw any current itself (due to high resistance) and does not affect net resistance of the circuit.

6. **(c)** On increasing temperature of wire the kinetic energy of free electrons increase and so they collide more rapidly with each other and hence their drift velocity decreases. Also when temperature increases, resistivity increases and resistivity is inversely proportional to conductivity of material.

7. **(a)** Potential gradient $= \dfrac{V_A - V_B}{\ell} = \dfrac{i \times \rho}{A} = \dfrac{0.1 \times 10^{-7}}{10^{-6}}$

$= 10^{-2}\,\text{V/m}$

8. **(a)**

9. **(a)** Potential gradient $= \dfrac{\text{Pot. Difference}}{\text{length of wire}} = \dfrac{V_A - V_B}{\ell}$

10. **(b)** In case of internal resistance measurement by potentiometer,

$\dfrac{V_1}{V_2} = \dfrac{\ell_1}{\ell_2} = \dfrac{\{E\,R_1/(R_1+r)\}}{\{E\,R_2/(R_2+r)\}} = \dfrac{R_1(R_2+r)}{R_2(R_1+r)}$

Here $\ell_1 = 2\,\text{m}$, $\ell_2 = 3\,\text{m}$, $R_1 = 5\,\Omega$ and $R_2 = 10\,\Omega$

$\therefore \dfrac{2}{3} = \dfrac{5(10+r)}{10(5+r)}$ or $20 + 4r = 30 + 3r$ or $r = 10\,\Omega$

11. **(b)** $r = \dfrac{\ell_1 - \ell_2}{\ell_2} \times R\,\Omega$

Here, $\ell_1 = 125\,\text{cm}$, $\ell_2 = 100\,\text{cm}$, $R = 2\,\Omega$.   ∴ $r = 0.5\,\Omega$

12. Drift velocity of electrons will decrease as the temperature increases.2.

13. Refer to Theory.

14. Voltage across $R_1 = E$

Voltage across R_2 and $R_3 = E$

               (∵ they are connected in series)

Current

$I = \dfrac{E}{\dfrac{R_1(R_2+R_3)}{R_1+R_2+R_3}} = \dfrac{E(R_1+R_2+R_3)}{R_1(R_2+R_3)}$,

Current across $R_1 = \dfrac{E}{R_1}$

$\therefore$ Current across $R_2 = \dfrac{E(R_1+R_2+R_3)}{R_1(R_2+R_3)} - \dfrac{E}{R_1}$

$= \dfrac{E}{R_1}\left[\dfrac{R_1+R_2+R_3}{R_2+R_3} - 1\right]$

$= \dfrac{E}{R_1}\left[\dfrac{R_1+R_2+R_3-R_2-R_3}{R_2+R_3}\right]$

$= \dfrac{E}{R_1} \times \dfrac{R_1}{R_2+R_3} = \dfrac{E}{R_2+R_3}$

$\therefore$ Voltage across $R_2 = \dfrac{ER_2}{R_2+R_3}$

But $R_1 = R_2 = R_3 = R = \dfrac{ER}{2R} = \dfrac{E}{2}$

$\therefore$ Ratio of voltage across R_1 and $R_2 = E : E/2 = 2 : 1$

15. Potential difference between A and B $= V = E - Ir = 6$

[∵ no current is taken from the cell]

4 · Moving Charges and Magnetism

MOVING CHARGES AND MAGNETISM

Magnetic field: Space in the surrounding of a magnet or any current carrying conductor in which its magnetic influence can be experienced

Direction of magnetic field-Depends upon the direction of current. Right hand thumb rule-Thumb points in the direction of current, curling of fingers represents direction of magnetic field.

Magnetic field due to a solenoid. Inside a long solenoid $B = \mu_0 nI$. At a point on one end $B = \dfrac{\mu_0 nI}{2}$

Ampere's circuital law $\oint B dl = \mu_0 I$

Magnetic field due to a toroid $B = \mu_0 nI$

Force acting on a charged particle moving in a uniform magnetic field $F = qVB \sin\theta = q(V \times B)$

Lorentz force $F = q(E + V \times B)$

Motion of a charged particle in a uniform magnetic field follows a circular path, radius $r = \dfrac{MV}{Bq \sin\theta}$

Force on a conductor carrying current in a uniform magnetic field, $F = I\,Bl \sin\theta$ $F = I(B \times l)$

Magnetic field due to a straight current carrying conductor of infinite length $B = \dfrac{\mu_0 I}{2\pi R}$

Biot-Savart's law: Magnetic field due to current carrying element, $dB = \dfrac{\mu_0}{4\pi} \cdot \dfrac{Idl \sin\theta}{r^2}$

Magnetic field due to a current carrying circular loop

At the centre of circular loop $B = \dfrac{\mu_0 NI}{2R}$

Force between two parallel current carrying conductors $F = \dfrac{\mu_0}{4\pi} \cdot \dfrac{2I_1 I_2}{r} \times \ell$

Galvanometer to ammeter conversion : Low resistance or shunt connected in parallel $S = \left(\dfrac{I_g}{I - I_g}\right) G$

Galvanometer to voltmeter conversion : High resistance in series $R = \dfrac{V}{I_g} - G$

Galvanometer : It is a device used to detect current in a circuit.

On the axis of circular loop $B = \dfrac{\mu_0 NIa^2}{2(r^2 + a^2)^{3/2}}$

Torque experienced by a current carrying loop in a uniform magnetic field $\tau = MB \sin\theta\ \hat{n} = M \times B$

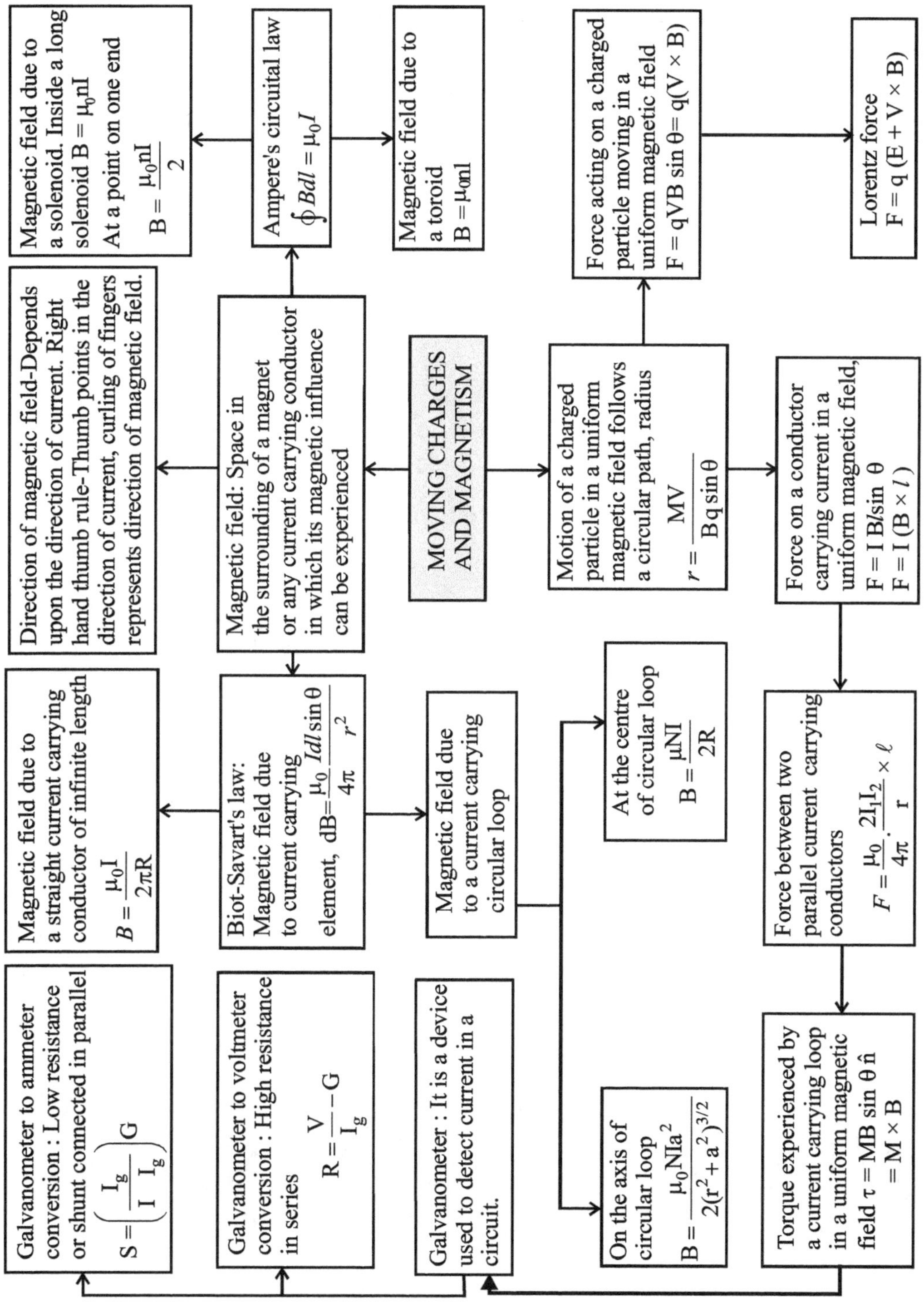

Topic 1 — Oersted Experiment, Magnetic Field, Magnetic Field due to a Current Element-Biot-Savart's Law & its Applications, Ampere's Circuital Law 

OERSTED EXPERIMENT

Magnetic effect of electric current means-an electric current flowing in a conductor produces a magnetic field in the space around it. In 1820, **Hans Christian Oersted** Showed that electricity and magnetism are related phenomena.

Oersted discovered a magnetic field around a conductor carrying electric current.

(a) A magnet at rest produces a magnetic field around it while an electric charge at rest produces an electric field around it.

(b) A current carrying conductor has a magnetic field and not an electric field around it. On the other hand, a charge moving with a uniform velocity has an electric as well as a magnetic field around it.

(c) An electric field cannot be produced without a charge whereas a magnetic field can be produced without a magnet.

(d) No poles are produced in a coil carrying current but such a coil shows north and south polarities.

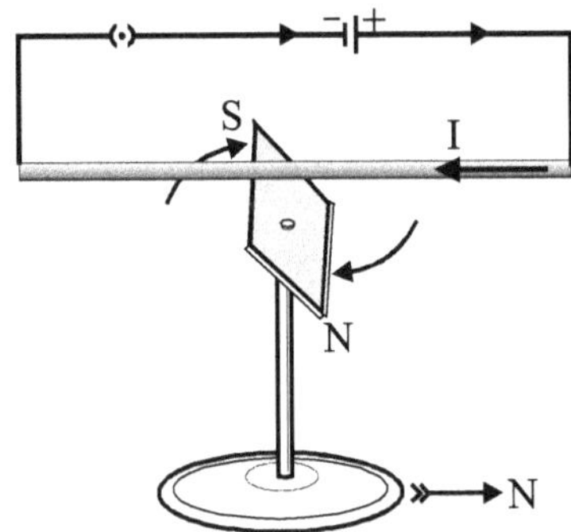

(e) All oscillating or an accelerated charge produces E.M. waves also in addition to electric and magnetic fields.

MAGNETIC FIELD

It is the space around a magnet/current carrying conductor where magnetic influence can be experienced. Its S.I. unit is tesla or weber/m^2. 1 tesla = 10^4 gauss. The C.G.S. unit of magnetic field is gauss.

Rules to Find the Direction of Magnetic Field

Right hand thumb rule: *If we grasp the conductor in the palm of the right hand so that the thumb points in the direction of the flow of current, then the direction in which the fingers curl, gives the direction of magnetic field lines.*

Right hand grip rule: *If we hold the thumb of right hand mutually perpendicular to the grip of the fingers such that the curvature of the finger represents the direction of current in the wire loop, then the thumb of the right hand will point in the direction of magnetic field near the centre of the current loop.*

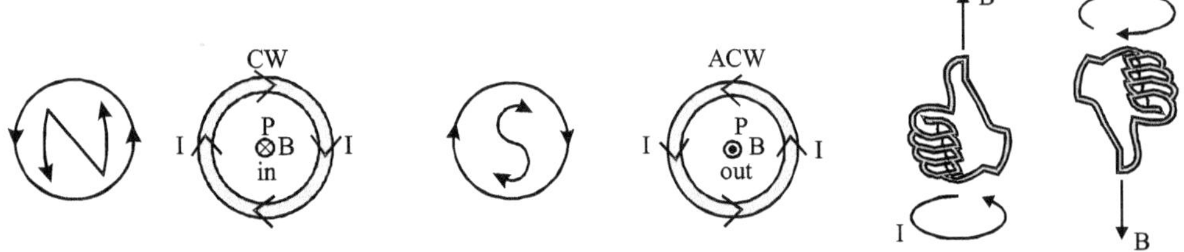

MAGNETIC FIELD DUE TO A CURRENT ELEMENT – BIOT-SAVART'S LAW

The strength of magnetic field or magnetic flux density (dB) at a point P due to current element dl depends on,

(i) $dB \propto I$

(ii) $dB \propto dl$

(iii) $dB \propto \sin\theta$

(iv) $dB \propto \dfrac{1}{r^2}$,

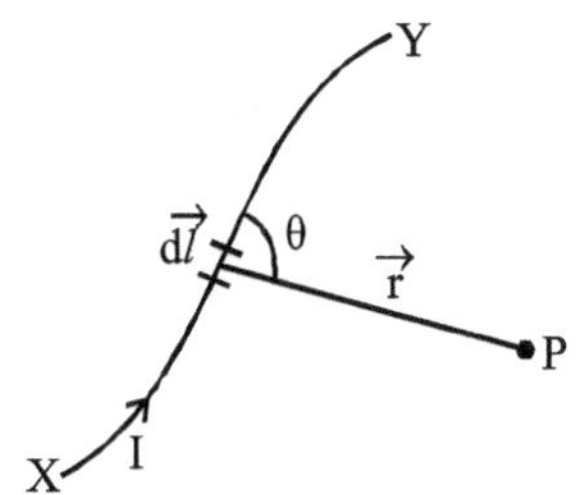

Combining these we get,

$$dB \propto \frac{Idl\sin\theta}{r^2} \Rightarrow dB = k\frac{Idl\sin\theta}{r^2} \qquad \text{here, k is a Proportionality constant}$$

In S.I. units, $k = \dfrac{\mu_0}{4\pi}$ where μ_0 is called **permeability of free space**.

$$\mu_0 = 4\pi\times10^{-7}\ TA^{-1}m$$

$$\therefore \qquad dB = \frac{\mu_0}{4\pi}\frac{Idl\sin\theta}{r^2} \text{ and } d\vec{B} = \frac{\mu_0}{4\pi}I\frac{(\vec{dl}\times\vec{r})}{r^3} \text{ (in vector form)}$$

$d\vec{B}$ is perpendicular to the plane containing $\vec{dl}$ and $\vec{r}$ and is directed inwards.

Relation between μ_0, ε_0 and C :

$$C = \frac{1}{\sqrt{\mu_0\varepsilon_0}} \text{ here, } \varepsilon_0 \text{ is the electric permittivity in free space and C is the speed of light in vacuum.}$$

$$C_{vacuum} = 3\times10^8\ m/s$$

APPLICATIONS OF BIOT-SAVART'S LAW

Magnetic Field due to a Infinitely Long Straight Conductor

Consider a long straight conductor XY through which current I is flowing from X to Y. Let P be the observation point at a distance 'r' from the conductor XY. Let us consider an infinitesimally small current element CD of length $d\ell$. Let s be the distance of P from the mid-point O of the current element. Let θ be the angle which OP makes with the direction of current.

The magnetic field at P due to the current element CD is

$$dB = \frac{\mu_0}{4\pi}\frac{I\,d\ell\sin\theta}{s^2} \quad \text{[Biot-Savart's law]}$$

The magnetic field at P due to the whole of the conductor XY

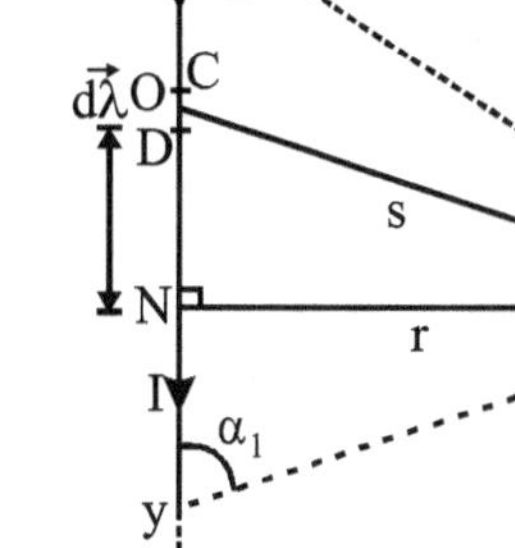

$$B = \int dB = \int_{-\theta_1}^{\theta_2}\frac{\mu_0 I}{4\pi r}\cos\theta\,d\theta = \frac{\mu_0 I}{4\pi r}\int_{-\theta_1}^{\theta_2}\cos\theta\,d\theta$$

$$= \frac{\mu_0 I}{4\pi r}[\sin\theta]_{-\theta_1}^{\theta_2}$$

$$B = \frac{\mu_0 I}{4\pi r}[\sin\theta_2 - \sin(-\theta_1)] \text{ or } B = \frac{\mu_0 I}{4\pi r}(\sin\theta_1 + \sin\theta_2)$$

Special Cases :

(i) For the conductor of infinite length :

Here, $\theta_1 = \theta_2 = \dfrac{\pi}{2}$ $\therefore$ $B = \dfrac{\mu_0 I}{4\pi r}(\sin\theta_1 + \sin\theta_2) = \dfrac{\mu_0 I}{2\pi R}$

(ii) Magnetic field at a point on the line of current carrying wire :

If a point lies on the line of current carrying wire then magnetic field at this point is always zero.

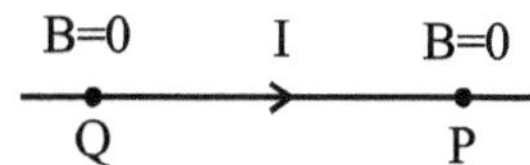

(iii) At a point exactly in front of one end of semi-infinite wire :

Here, $\theta_1 = 0$ and $\theta_2 = \dfrac{\pi}{2}$

$\therefore \quad B = \dfrac{\mu_0 I}{4\pi R}$

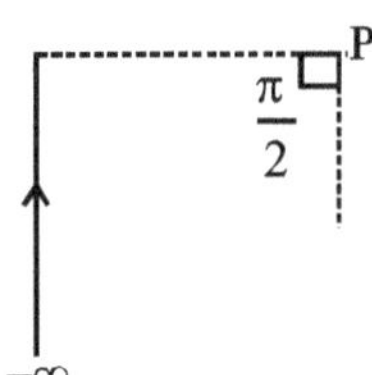

(iv) On perpendicular bisector of finite length of wire :

Here, $\sin\theta_1 = \sin\theta_2 = \dfrac{a}{\sqrt{a^2 + 4d^2}}$

$\therefore \quad$ Magnetic field $B = \dfrac{\mu_0 I}{4\pi R} \dfrac{2a}{\sqrt{a^2 + 4d^2}}$

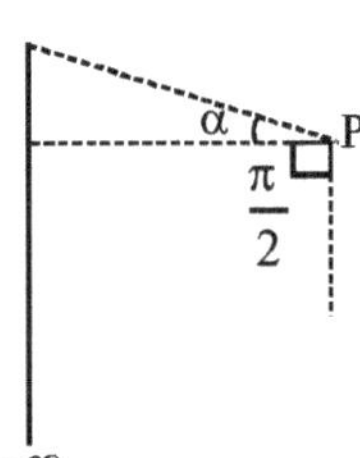

$a \rightarrow$ length of the wire

$d \rightarrow$ perpendicular distance of the field point then

(v) At a point not exactly in front of the end of a semi infinite wire :

Here $\theta_1 = \alpha$ and $\theta_2 = \pi/2$

$\therefore \quad B = \dfrac{\mu_0 I}{4\pi R}(1 + \sin\alpha)$

Magnetic Field Due to a Circular arc at the Centre (Subtending an angle θ at the centre)

Consider a current element that subtends an angle θ as shown in figure.

Magnetic field due to this element is

$B = \dfrac{\mu_0 I \theta}{4\pi R}$

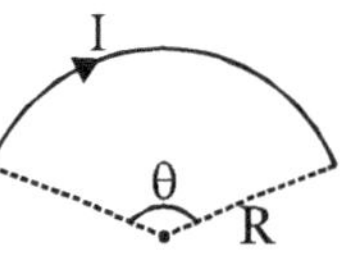

Special Case :

(i) Magnetic field at the centre of a loop

Here the loop makes an angle $\theta = 2\pi$ at the centre

$\therefore \quad B = \dfrac{\mu_0 I}{2R}$

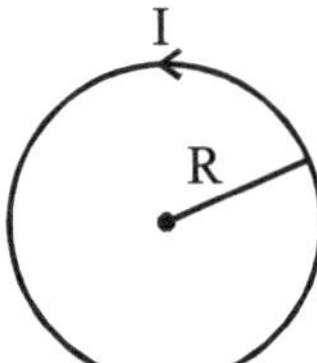

(ii) Magnetic field at a point on the axis of a circular coil carrying current when point P lies far away from the centre of the coil

$B = \dfrac{\mu_0}{4\pi} \cdot \dfrac{2M}{x^3}$ where $M = nIA$ = magnetic dipole moment of the coil.

x is the distance of the point where the field is to be measured, n is the number of turns, I is the current and A is the area of the coil.

AMPERE'S CIRCUITAL LAW

Ampere's circuital law states that *the line integral of magnetic field induction $\vec{B}$ around any closed path in vacuum is equal to μ_0 times the total current crossing the area bounded by the closed path provided the electric field inside the loop remains constant.*

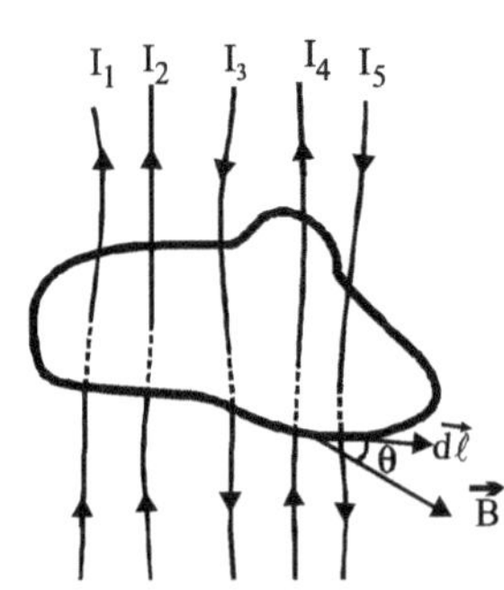

i.e., $\oint \vec{B} \cdot \vec{d\ell} = \mu_0 \sum I$ here $\sum I = I_1 + I_2 - I_3 + I_4 - I_5$

Application of Ampere's Circuital Law

(i) **Magnetic Field due to a Long Current Carrying Wire :** Consider a long straight conductor Z-Z' along z-axis. Let I be the current flowing in the direction as shown in Fig. The magnetic field is produced around the conductor. The magnetic lines of force are concentric circles in the XY plane as shown by dotted lines. Let the magnitude of the magnetic field induction produced at a point P at distance r

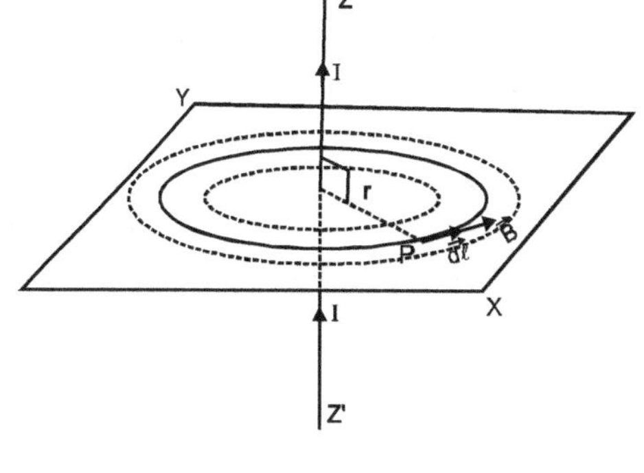

from the conductor is $\vec{B}$

Consider a close circular loop as shown in figure.

According to Ampere's law $\oint \vec{B}.\vec{d\ell} = \mu_0 \Sigma I$

The direction of $\vec{B}$ at every point is along the tangent to the circle.

Consider a small element $\vec{d\ell}$ of the circle of radius r at P. The direction of $\vec{B}$ and $\vec{d\ell}$ is the same. Therefore, angle between them is zero.

Line integral of $\vec{B}$ around the complete circular path of radius r is given by

$$\oint \vec{B}.\vec{d\ell} = \oint B\, d\ell \cos 0^\circ = B \oint d\ell = B \times 2\pi r$$

$(\oint d\ell = 2\pi r = $ circumference of the circle) and $\Sigma I = I$

So we get, $B \times 2\pi r = \mu_0 I$ or $B = \dfrac{\mu_0 I}{2\pi r} = \dfrac{\mu_0}{4\pi} \times \dfrac{2I}{r}$ $B \propto I$ and $B \propto \dfrac{1}{r}$

The Solenoid and The Toroid

(ii) **The Solenoid :** It consists of a long wire wound in the form of a helix where the neighbouring turns are closely spaced. So each turn can be regarded as a circular loop. The net magnetic field is the vector sum of the fields due to all the turns.
$B = \mu_0 nI$

At the edge of a short solenoid, $B = \dfrac{1}{2}\mu_0 nI$

where n = number of turns per unit length of a solenoid.
The direction of the field is given by the right-hand rule. The solenoid is commonly used to obtain a uniform magnetic field.

(iii) **The Toroid :** The toroid is a hollow circular ring on which a large number of turns of a wire are closely wound. It can be viewed as a solenoid which has been bent into a circular shape to close on itself.

Magnetic field due to a toroid, $B = \dfrac{\mu_0 NI}{2\pi r}$

Let r be the average radius of the toroid and n be the number of turns per unit length then
$N = 2\pi r \times n = $ (average) perimeter of the toroid × number of turns per unit length
and thus, $B = \mu_0 nI$,

Illustration 1 :

A semicircular arc of radius 20 cm carries a current of 10 A. Calculate the magnitude of the magnetic field at the centre of the sphere.

Sol. Here, r = 20 cm = 0.2m, I = 10A, $\mu_0 = 4\pi \times 10^{-7}$ TmA^{-1};

For a semicircular arc the magnetic field at the centre is $B = \dfrac{\mu_0 I}{4r}$

$B = \dfrac{4\pi \times 10^{-7} \times 10}{4 \times 0.2} = 1.57 \times 10^{-5}$ T.

It is perpendicular to the plane of the paper directed inwards.

Illustration 2 :

A pair of stationary and infinitely long bent wires are placed in the XY plane as shown in fig. The wires carry currents of $i = 10A$. The segments L and M are along the X-axis. The segments P and Q are parallel to the Y-axis such that $OS = OR = 0.02$ m. Find the magnitude and direction of the magnetic induction at the origin O.

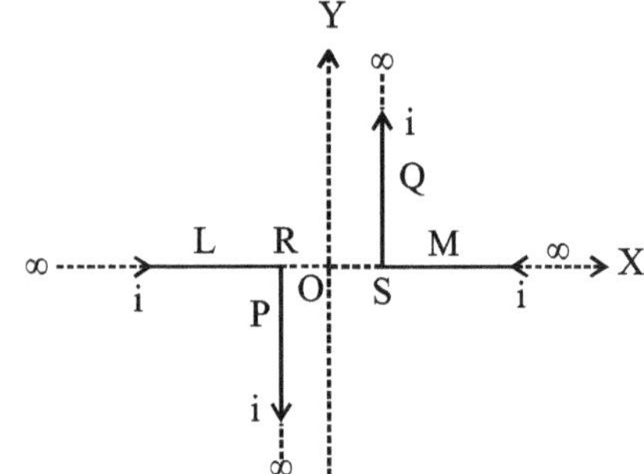

Sol. The magnetic field due to an infinitely long current carrying conductor at one end of the conductor at a distance r is given by

$$B = \frac{\mu_0}{4\pi} \frac{i}{r}$$

∴ Magnetic field due to current carrying conductor P at point O is

$$B_1 = \frac{\mu_0}{4\pi} \frac{i}{(OR)}$$ directed towards the reader perpendicular to the plane of paper.

Magnetic field due to current carrying conductor Q at point O is directed towards the reader perpendicular to the plane of paper.

$$B_2 = \frac{\mu_0}{4\pi} \frac{i}{(OS)}$$

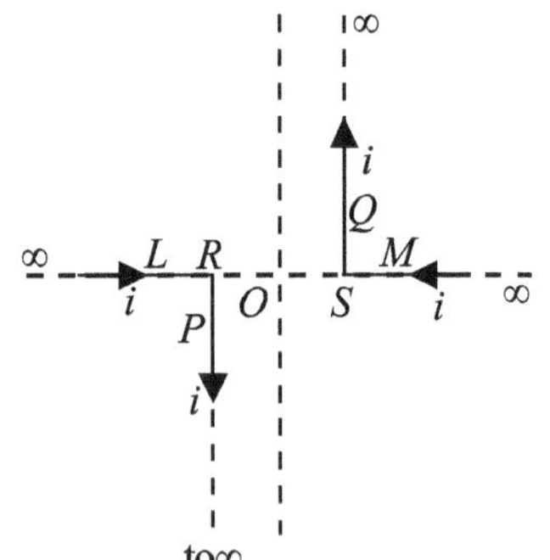

Magnetic field due to current carrying conductors L and M at O is zero.

∴ Resultant magnetic field at O
$$B = B_1 + B_2$$
(directed towards the reader perpendicular to the plane of paper)

$$B = \frac{\mu_0}{4\pi} \frac{i}{OR} + \frac{\mu_0}{4\pi} \frac{i}{OS} = \frac{\mu_0}{4\pi} i \left[\frac{1}{OR} + \frac{1}{OS} \right] = 10^{-7} \times 10 \times \left[\frac{1}{0.02} + \frac{1}{0.02} \right] = 10^{-4} \text{ tesla.}$$

Practice Exercise-1

Multiple Choice Questions

1   Magnetic field at the centre of a circular coil of radius r, through which a current I flows is
(a) directly proportional to r
(b) inversely proportional to I
(c) directly proportional to I
(d) directly proprotional to I^2

2. A current of I ampere flows in a wire forming a circular arc of radius r metres subtending an angle θ at the centre as shown. The magnetic field at the centre O in tesla is

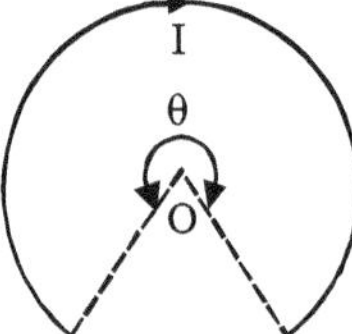

(a) $\dfrac{\mu_0 I\theta}{4\pi r}$ (b) $\dfrac{\mu_0 I\theta}{2\pi r}$

(c) $\dfrac{\mu_0 I\theta}{2r}$ (d) $\dfrac{\mu_0 I\theta}{4r}$

3. A long solenoid carrying a current produces a magnetic field B along its axis. If the current is double and the number of turns per cm is halved, the new value of the magnetic field is
(a) 4 B   (b) B/2   (c) B   (d) 2 B

4. Biot-Savart law indicates that the moving electron velocity (V) produce a magnetic field B such that
(a) $B \| V$
(b) $B \perp V$
(c) it obeys inverse cube law
(d) it is along the line joining electron and point of observation

5. The magnetic field around a long straight current carrying wire is
(a) spherical symmetry   (b) cylindrical symmetry
(c) cubical symmetry   (d) unsymmetrical

6. Magnetic field at the centre of a circular coil of radius r, through which a current I flows is
(a) directly proportional to r
(b) inverseley proportional to I
(c) directly proportional to I
(d) directly proprotional to I^2

7. Which of the following statements is/are correct?
I. The magnetic field in the open space inside the toroid is constant.
II. The magnetic field in the open space exterior to the toroid is constant.
III. The magnetic field inside the core of toroid is constant.
(a) I and II   (b) II and III
(c) III only   (d) I only

Assertion & Reason Questions

DIRECTIONS (Qs. 8-11) : *Each of these questions contains an assertion followed by reason. Read them carefully and answer the question on the basis of following options. You have to select the one that best describes the two statements.*
(a) If both Assertion and Reason are correct and the Reason is a correct explanation of the Assertion.
(b) If both Assertion and Reason are correct but Reason is not a correct explanation of the Assertion.
(c) If the Assertion is correct but Reason is incorrect.
(d) If the Assertion is incorrect but the Reason is correct.

8. **Assertion:** Ampere's circuital law is analogous of Biot-Savart's law.
Reason: Ampere's circuital law cannot be derived from the Biot-savart's law.

9. **Assertion :** Figure shows a current carrying circular loop. The magnetic field at the centre of loop is zero.

Reason : Magnitude of magnetic field at the centre of circular loop carrying current i is given by $B = \dfrac{\mu_0 ni}{R}$.

10. **Assertion :** A current I flows along the length of an infinitely long straight and thin walled pipe. Then the magnetic field at any point inside the pipe is zero.
Reason : $\oint \vec{B}.\vec{d\ell} = \mu_0 I$ and $\sum I_{in} = 0$

11. **Assertion :** The magnetic field at the end of a very long current carrying solenoid is half of that at the center.
Reason : If the solenoid is sufficiently long, the field within it is uniform.

Case / Passage Based Questions

Ampere's circuital law states that *the line integral of magnetic field induction $\vec{B}$ around any closed path in vacuum is equal to μ_0 times the total current crossing the area bounded by the closed path provided the electric field inside the loop remains constant.*

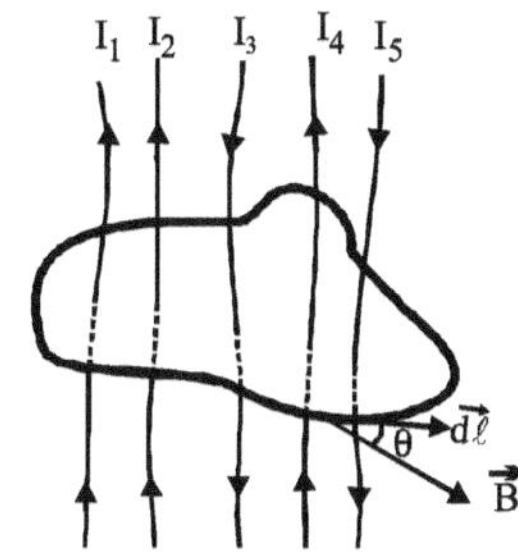

i.e., $\oint \vec{B}.\vec{d\ell} = \mu_0 \sum I$ here $\sum I = I_1 + I_2 - I_3 + I_4 - I_5$

12. The magnetic field B at a point on one end of a solenoid having n turns per metre length and carrying a current of i ampere is given by
(a) $\dfrac{\mu_0 ni}{e}$ (b) $\dfrac{1}{2}\mu_0 ni$ (c) $4\pi\mu_0 ni$ (d) ni

13. If a long hollow copper pipe carries a direct current, the magnetic field associated with the current will be
(a) only inside the pipe
(b) only outside the pipe
(c) neither inside nor outside the pipe
(d) both inside and outside the pipe

14. The correct plot of the magnitude of magnetic field $\vec{B}$ vs distance r from centre of the wire is, if the radius of wire is R

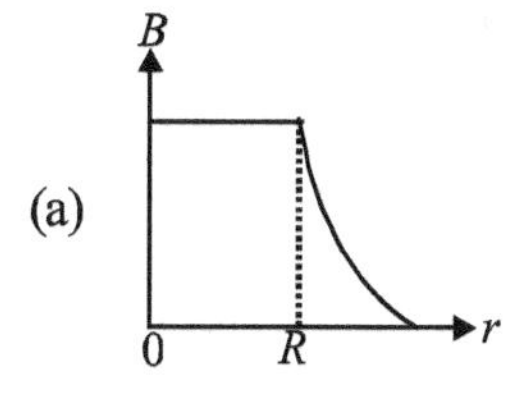
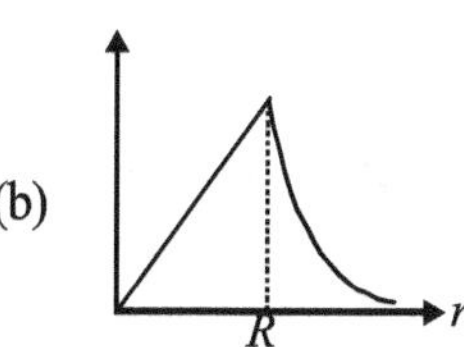
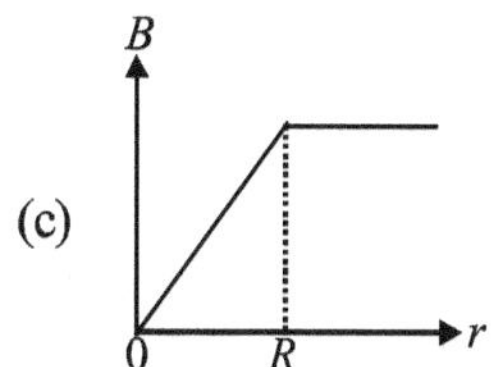
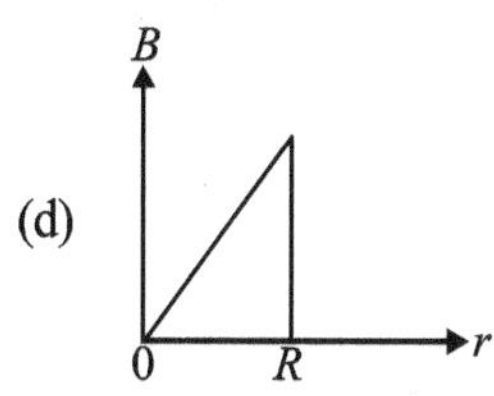

15. A current of I ampere flows in a wire forming a circular arc of radius r metres subtending an angle θ at the centre as shown. The magnetic field at the centre O in tesla is
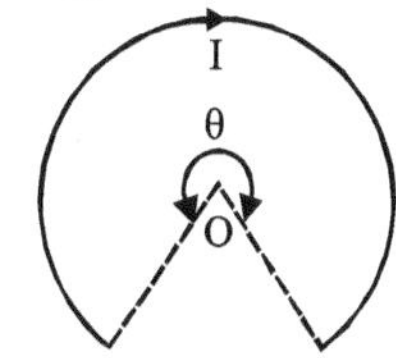
(a) $\dfrac{\mu_0 I\theta}{4\pi r}$ (b) $\dfrac{\mu_0 I\theta}{2\pi r}$ (c) $\dfrac{\mu_0 I\theta}{2r}$ (d) $\dfrac{\mu_0 I\theta}{4r}$

16. The figure shows n (n being an even number) wires placed along the surface of a cylinder of radius r. Each wire carries current i in the same direction. The net magnetic field on the axis of the cylinder is

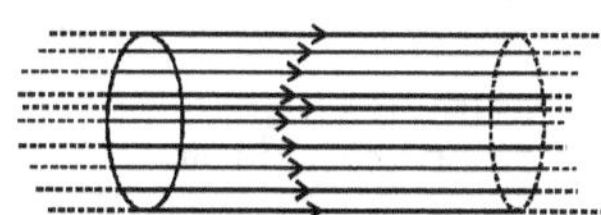

(a) $\mu_0\, ni$ (b) $\dfrac{\mu_0 ni}{2\pi r}$ (c) zero (d) $\dfrac{\mu_0 ni}{4\pi r}$

Very Short Answer Questions

17. Consider the circuit shown here where APB and AQB are semi circles. What will be the magnetic field at the centre C of the circular loop?
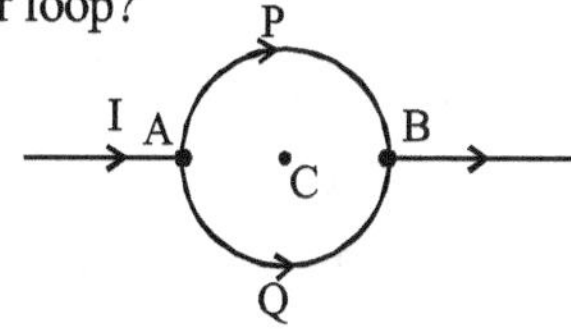

18. A current is set up in a long copper pipe. Is there a magnetic field (i) inside (ii) outside the pipe?

19. How will the magnetic field intensity at the centre of a circular coil carrying current change, if the current through the coil is doubled and the radius of the coil is halved?

Short Answer Questions

20. Derive an expression for the magnetic field at the centre of a circular current carrying coil using Biot – Savart's law.

21. Derive from Biot - Savart's law the magnetic field due to a straight current carrying conductor of infinite length.

Topic 2 — Force on a Moving Charge in Uniform Magnetic & Electric Fields 

FORCE ON A MOVING CHARGE IN A UNIFORM MAGNETIC FIELD

If a charge q is moving with velocity $\vec{v}$ enters in a region of uniform magnetic field $\vec{B}$, it experiences force. The force experienced by the charged particle is given by the expression $\vec{F} = q(\vec{v} \times \vec{B})$

The direction of magnetic force is same as $\vec{v} \times \vec{B}$ if charge is positive and opposite to $\vec{v} \times \vec{B}$ if charge is negative (determined by right hand thumb rule)

As the magnetic force is always perpendicular to the direction of motion of particle it can never do work on it. Thus kinetic energy of charged particle in magnetic field can never change.

If a charge q is moving with velocity $\vec{v}$ enters in a region in which electric field $\vec{E}$ and magnetic field $\vec{B}$ both exist, it experiences force due to both fields simultaneously then force is given by

$\vec{F} = q(\vec{v} \times \vec{B}) + q\vec{E}$. This force is called **Lorentz force**.

Magnetic Field Strength $\left(\vec{B}\right)$: In the equation $F = qBv \sin\theta$, if $q = 1$, $v = 1$,

$\sin\theta = 1$ i.e. $\theta = 90°$ then $F = B$.

$\therefore$ Magnetic field strength is defined as the force experienced by a unit charge moving with unit velocity perpendicular to the direction of magnetic field.

Special Cases: (i)   If $\theta = 0°$ or $180°$, $\sin\theta = 0$ $\therefore$ $F = 0$

A charged particle moving parallel to the magnetic field, will not experience any force.

(ii)   If $v = 0$, $F = 0$

A charged particle at rest in a magnetic field will not experience any force.

(iii)   If $\theta = 90°$, $\sin\theta = 1$ then the force is maximum $F_{max.} = qvB$

A charged particle moving perpendicular to magnetic field will experience maximum force.

Motion of a Charged Particle in a Uniform Magnetic Field

Case 1 : (Straight line motion)

If a charge particle q is projected into a uniform magnetic field B with a velocity which is parallel to the field lines, the force experienced by the charge is zero and hence it travels in a straight line with uniform velocity.

$$\vec{F} = q(\vec{v} \times \vec{B}) = \vec{0} \text{ for } \vec{v} \parallel \vec{B}$$

Case II : (Uniform circular motion)

If a charged particle q is projected into a uniform magnetic field B with a initial velocity perpendicular to the lines of force, it gets trapped in a circular path.

The force exerted by the field provides the necessary centripetal force

Mathematically, we have $qvB = \dfrac{mv^2}{r} \Rightarrow r = \dfrac{mv}{qB}$

The time period of revolution is $T = \dfrac{2\pi r}{v} \Rightarrow T = \dfrac{2\pi m}{qB}$

Note that the plane of the circular path is perpendicular to the lines of force.

Motion of Charged Particle in Combined Electric and Magnetic Fields

Let a moving charged particle is subjected simultaneously to both electric field $\vec{E}$ and magnetic field $\vec{B}$.

The moving charged particle will experience **electric force $\vec{F}_e = q\vec{E}$** and **magnetic force $\vec{F}_m = q\,(\vec{v} \times \vec{B})$**

Net force on the charged particle $\vec{F} = q\,(\vec{E} + \vec{v} \times \vec{B})$ "Lorentz-force"

Depending on the direction of $\vec{v}$, $\vec{E}$ and $\vec{B}$ various situations are possible and the motion in general is quite complex.

Case I : ($\vec{v}$, $\vec{E}$ and $\vec{B}$ are collinear) :

As the particle is moving parallel or antiparallel to the field the magnetic force on it will be zero and only electric force will act.

So, acceleration of the particle $\vec{a} = \dfrac{\vec{F}}{m} = \dfrac{q\vec{E}}{m}$

Hence, the particle will pass through the field following a straight line path (parallel to the field) with change in its speed. In this situation speed, velocity, momentum and kinetic energy all will change without change in direction of motion.

Case II : $\vec{v}$, $\vec{E}$ and $\vec{B}$ are mutually perpendicular :

If in this situation direction and magnitude of $\vec{E}$ and $\vec{B}$ are such that

resultant force $\quad \vec{F} = \vec{F_e} + \vec{F_m} = 0 \qquad$ i.e., $\qquad \vec{a} = \dfrac{\vec{F}}{m} = 0$

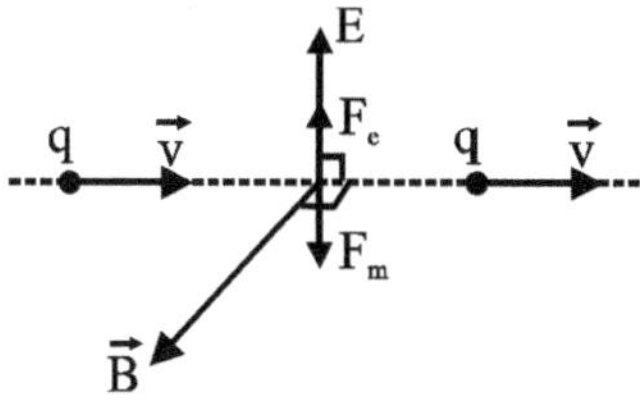

Then as shown in fig., the particle will pass through the field with same velocity

$\because \quad F_e = F_m \quad$ i.e., $\quad qE = qvB$

or $v = \dfrac{E}{B}$ This principle is used in 'Velocity-selector' to get a charged beam having a specific velocity.

Illustration 3 :

An electron moves through a uniform magnetic field given by $\vec{B} = B_x \tilde{i} + \left(3B_x\right)\hat{j}$. At a particular instant, the electron has the velocity $\vec{v} = \left(2.0\hat{i} + 4.0\hat{j}\right)$ m/s and the magnetic force acting on it is $\left(6.4 \times 10^{-19}\hat{k}\right)N.$ Find B_x.

Sol. Magnetic force, $\qquad \vec{F} \quad = \quad q(\vec{v} \times \vec{B})$

$\qquad$ or $\qquad 6.4 \times 10^{-19}\hat{k} \quad = \quad -e\left[(2.0\hat{i} + 4.0\hat{j}) \times (B_x\hat{j} + 3B_x\hat{j})\right]$

$\qquad \therefore \qquad\qquad\quad B_x \quad = \quad -2.0\,\text{T}$

Practice Exercise-2

Multiple Choice Questions

1. A particle of mass m and charge q enters a magnetic field B perpendicularly with a velocity v. The radius of the circular path described by it will be
   (a) Bq/mv (b) mq/Bv (c) mB/qv (d) mv/Bq

2. Which of the following statement(s) is/are true/false?
   I. A charged particle moves perpendicular to the magnetic field. Its kinetic energy remains constant, but momentum changes.
   II. Force acts perpendicular to the velocity of particle.
   (a) F, F (b) F, T (c) T, T (d) T, F

3. In a region, steady and uniform electric and magnetic fields are present. These two fields are parallel to each other. A charged particle is released from rest in this region. The path of the particle will be a
   (a) helix (b) straight line
   (c) ellipse (d) circle

4. Direction of force due to magnetic field on a moving charged particle is
   I. perpendicular to direction of velocity of charged particle.
   II. perpendicular to direction of magnetic field.
   III. parallel to direction of velocity of charged particle.
   IV. parallel to the direction of magnetic field.
   True/false statements are
   (a) T, F, F, T (b) T, T, F, F
   (c) T, F, T, F (d) F, F, T, T

5. Lorentz force is _________ charged particle.
   (a) electrostatic force acting on a
   (b) magnetic force acting on a moving

   (c) the vector sum of electrostatic and magnetic force acting on a moving
   (d) the vector sum of gravitational and magnetic force acting on a moving

6. In cyclotron the gyro-radius is
   (a) proportional to momentum
   (b) proportional to energy
   (c) inversely proportional to momentum
   (d) inversely proportional to energy

7. Consider the following statements and select the true/false.
   I. Force on the charged particle will be zero if it is at rest.
   II. Direction of force on moving charge particle is given by Fleming's Left Hand Rule.
   III. A charged particle enters a region of uniform magnetic field at an angle of 45° to the magnetic lines of force, the path of the particle is a circle.
   IV. There is no change in the kinetic energy of a charged particle moving in a magnetic field although a magnetic force is acting on it.
   (a) F, F, F, T (b) F, T, F, F
   (c) T, T, F, T (d) F, F, T, T

8. A beam of electrons is moving with constant velocity in a region having simultaneous perpendicular electric and magnetic fields of strength 20 Vm^{-1} and 0.5 T respectively at right angles to the direction of motion of the electrons. Then the velocity of electrons must be
   (a) 8 m/s (b) 20 m/s (c) 40 m/s (d) $\dfrac{1}{40}$ m/s

9. An electric charge $+q$ moves with velocity $\vec{v} = 3\hat{i} + 4\hat{j} + \hat{k}$ in an electromagnetic field given by $\vec{E} = 3\hat{i} + \hat{j} + 2\hat{k}$ and $\vec{B} = \hat{i} + \hat{j} - 3\hat{k}$. The y-component of the force experienced by $+q$ is :
   (a) $11q$ (b) $5q$ (c) $3q$ (d) $2q$

Assertion & Reason Questions

DIRECTIONS (Qs. 10-15) : *Each of these questions contains an assertion followed by reason. Read them carefully and answer the question on the basis of following options. You have to select the one that best describes the two statements.*

(a) If both Assertion and Reason are correct and the Reason is a correct explanation of the Assertion.

(b) If both Assertion and Reason are correct but Reason is not a correct explanation of the Assertion.

(c) If the Assertion is correct but Reason is incorrect.

(d) If the Assertion is incorrect but the Reason is correct.

10. Assertion : Magnetic field interacts with a moving charge and not with a stationary charge.
Reason : A moving charge produces a magnetic field.

11. Assertion : If a charged particle is released from rest in a region of uniform electric and magnetic fields parallel to each other, it will move in a straight line.
Reason : The electric field exerts no force on the particle but the magnetic field does.

12. Assertion : A charged particle moves in a uniform magnetic field. The velocity of the particle at some instant makes an acute angle with the magnetic field. The path of the particle is a helix with constant pitch.
Reason : The force on the particle is given by $\vec{F} = q\left(\vec{v}.\vec{B}\right)$.

13. Assertion: The work done by magnetic force on a moving charged particle is zero.
Reason: The work done by magnetic force on a charged particle is zero as the force is always parallel to velocity of particle.

14. Assertion : A direct current flows through a thin conductor produces magnetic field only outside the conductor.
Reason : There is no flow of charge carriers inside the conductor.

15. Assertion : The net charge in a current carrying wire is zero and so magnetic force on the wire in magnetic field is zero.
Reason : The force on a current carrying wire is given by $F = qVB \sin\theta$ [where q = charge, V = potential difference, B = field, θ = angle]

Case / Passage Based Questions

The moving charged particle will experience **electric force** $\vec{F}_e = q\vec{E}$ and **magnetic force** $\vec{F}_m = q\,(\vec{v} \times \vec{B})$

Net force on the charged particle $\vec{F} = q\,(\vec{E} + \vec{v} \times \vec{B})$ "Lorentz-force"

Depending on the direction of $\vec{v}$, $\vec{E}$ and $\vec{B}$ various situations are possible and the motion in general is quite complex.

16. An electron having a charge e moves with a velocity v in X-direction. An electric field acts on it in Y-direction? The force on the electron acts in
(a) positive direction of Y-axis
(b) negative direction of Y-axis
(c) positive direction of Z-axis
(d) negative direction of Z-axis

17. Lorentz force is
(a) electrostatic force acting on a charged particle.
(b) magnetic force acting on a moving charged particle.
(c) the vector sum of electrostatic and magnetic force acting on a moving charged particle.
(d) the vector sum of gravitational and magnetic force acting on a moving charged particle.

18. A certain region has an electric field $\vec{E} = (2\hat{i} - 3\hat{j})$ N/C and a uniform magnetic field $\vec{B} = (5\hat{i} + 3\hat{j} + 4\hat{k})$ T. The force experienced by a charge 1C moving with velocity $(\hat{i} + 2\hat{j})$ ms^{-1} is

(a) $(10\hat{i} - 7\hat{j} - 7\hat{k})$ (b) $(10\hat{i} + 7\hat{j} + 7\hat{k})$

(c) $(-10\hat{i} + 7\hat{j} + 7\hat{k})$ (d) $(10\hat{i} + 7\hat{j} - 7\hat{k})$

19. A proton moving with a constant velocity passes through a region of space without any change in its velocity. If E and B represent the electric and magnetic fields respectively, this region of space may not have
(a) E = 0, B = 0   (b) E = 0, B ≠ 0
(c) E ≠ 0, B = 0   (d) E ≠ 0, B ≠ 0

20. A charged particle with velocity 2×10^3 m/s passes undeflected through electric and magnetic field. Magnetic field is 1.5 tesla. The electric field intensity would be
(a) 2×10^3 N/C   (b) 1.5×10^3 N/C
(c) 3×10^3 N/C   (d) $4/3 \times 10^{-3}$ N/C

Very Short Answer Questions

21. The force $\vec{F}$ experienced by a particle of charge q moving with velocity $\vec{v}$ in a magnetic field $\vec{B}$ is given by $\vec{F} = q(\vec{v} \times \vec{B})$. Which pair of vectors is always at right angles to each other?

22. Under what condition, an electron moving through a magnetic field experiences maximum force?

23. An electron beam is moving vertically upwards. If it passes through a magnetic field which is directed from south to north in a horrizontal plane, then in which direction will the beam be deflected?

24. An electron and a proton moving with the same speed enter the same magnetic field region at right angles to the direction of the field. For which of the two particles will the radius of circular path be smaller?

25. Which one of the following will experience maximum force, when projected with the same velocity 'v' perpendicular to the magnetic field 'B' (i) α-particle and (ii) β-particle?

26. No force is experienced by a stationary charge in a magnetic field. Why?

27. An electron moving with a velocity 10^7 ms^{-1} enters a uniform magnetic field of IT, along a direction parallel to the field. What would be its trajectory?

Short Answer Questions

28. Define the S.I. unit of magnetic field. "A charge moving at right angles to a uniform magnetic field does not undergo change in kinetic energy." – Why?

29. A stream of electrons travelling with speed 'v m/s' at right angles to a uniform magnetic field 'B', is deflected in a circular path of radius 'r'. Prove that $\dfrac{e}{m} = \dfrac{v}{rB}$

30. A charged particle moving in a perpendicular uniform magnetic field penetrates a layer of lead and there by loses one half of it's kinetic energy. How will the radius of curvature of its path change?

31. An electron of kinetic energy 25 keV moves perpendicular to the direction of a uniform magnetic field of 0.2 millitesla. Calculate the time period of rotation of the electron in the magnetic field.

32. A proton and an alpha particle of the same velocity enter in a region of uniform magnetic field acting in a plane perpendicular to the magnetic field. Deduce the ratio of the radii of the circular path so described by the particles. Explain why the kinetic energy of the particle after emerging from the magnetic field remains unaltered.

33. An electron being accelerated through 100 V enters a uniform magnetic field of 0.004 T perpendicular to direction of motion. Calculate the radius of path described by electron.

Topic 3

Force on a Current Carrying Conductor Placed in a Uniform Magnetic Field, Force Between Two Parallel Current Carrying Conductors-Definition of Ampere and Torque on a Current Carrying Loop in Uniform Magnetic Field

FORCE ON A CURRENT CARRYING CONDUCTOR PLACED IN A UNIFORM MAGNETIC FIELD

In a uniform magnetic field, force on a current carrying conductor.

$$\vec{F} = I\left|\vec{\ell}\times\vec{B}\right| \quad \text{or} \quad F = I\ell B \sin\theta$$

where I is the current through the conductor B is the magnetic field intensity, ℓ is the length of the conductor and θ is the angle between the direction of current and magnetic field.

(i) When $\theta = 0°$ or $180°$, $\sin\theta = 0 \Rightarrow F = 0$

∴ When a conductor is placed along the magnetic field, no force will act on the conductor.

(ii) When $\theta = 90°$, $\sin\theta = 1$, F is maximum.

$$F_{max} = I\ell B$$

when the conductor is placed perpendicular to the magnetic field, it will experience maximum force.

FORCE BETWEEN TWO PARALLEL CURRENT CARRYING CONDUCTORS AND DEFINITION OF ONE AMPERE

- When the current is in same direction the two conductors will attract each other with a force

$$F = \frac{\mu_0}{4\pi}\cdot\frac{2I_1 I_2}{r} \quad \text{per unit length of the conductor. Force per unit length} = 2\times 10^{-7}\,\text{N/m if } I_1 = I_2 = 1 \text{ and } r = 1\text{ m}.$$

- When the current is in opposite direction the two conductors will repel each other with the same force.

  The S.I. unit of current is 1 ampere. (A).

  One ampere *is the current which on flowing through each of the two parallel uniform linear conductor placed in free space at a distance of 1 m from each other produces a force of 2×10^{-7} N/m along their lengths.*

TORQUE ON A CURRENT CARRYING LOOP IN UNIFORM MAGNETIC FIELD

We take uniform magnetic field in each case.

Case I : When plane of the loop is perpendicular to the magnetic field

Length of AB = DC = ℓ and that of BC = AD = b

Force experienced by all the sides are shown in the figure.

∴ Force on AB and DC are equal and opposite to each other and that on BC and AD too therefore, $\sum \vec{F} = 0$

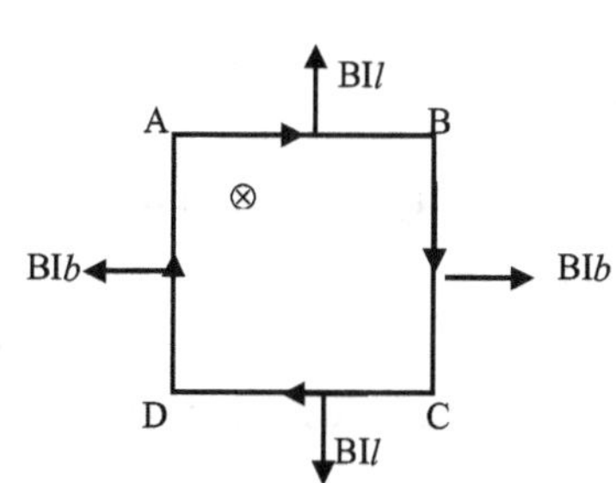

Since the line of action of the forces on AB and DC is same and also the line of action of the forces BC and AD is same, therefore torque is zero. i.e., $\sum \vec{\tau}_{av} = 0$

Case II : When the plane of the loop is inclined to the magnetic field

In this case again $\Sigma F = 0$

$\therefore$ Lines of action of the forces on AB and DC are different, therefore this forms a couple and produces a torque.

Side view of the loop is shown in the figure.

Torque, $\tau = BI\ell(b\sin\theta) = BI(\ell b)\sin\theta = BIA\sin\theta$

If loop has N turns then $\tau = BNIA\sin\theta$

In vector form, $\vec{\tau} = \vec{M} \times \vec{B}$, where $\vec{M} = NI\vec{A} = $ **Magnetic moment of the loop**

where $\vec{A}$ is the area vector of the loop whose magnitude is area of the loop and direction is out of the plane for anti-clockwise sense of the current and into the loop for clockwise sense of current.

Torque $\vec{\tau} = \vec{M} \times \vec{B}$ is analogous to the torque on electric dipole in an electric field $(\vec{\tau} = \vec{P} \times \vec{E})$. Hence we can consider current carrying coil as a magnetic dipole, (North pole $\rightarrow$ Anticlockwise current sense and South pole $\rightarrow$ Clockwise current sense)

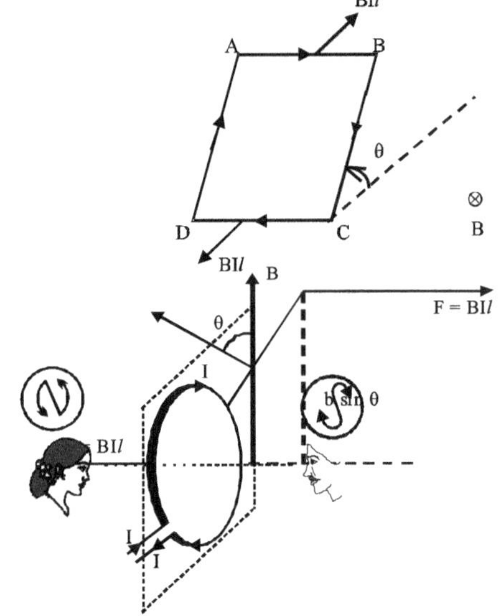

Illustration 4 :

Find the force on a wire (of negligible mass) of length 4 cm placed inside a solenoid near its centre, making an angle of 60° with its axis. The wire carries a current of 12A and magnetic field due to solenoid has a magnitude of 0.25 T.

Sol.   As we know, $\vec{F} = I(\vec{\ell} \times \vec{B}) \Rightarrow F = I\ell B\sin\theta = 12 \times 4 \times 10^{-2} \times 0.25 \times \sin 60° = 0.104\,\text{N}.$

Practice Exercise-3

Multiple Choice Questions

1. Two thin, long, parallel wires, separated by a distance 'd' carry a current of 'i' A in the same direction. They will

   (a) repel each other with a force of $\mu_0 i^2/(2\pi d)$

   (b) attract each other with a force of $\mu_0 i^2/(2\pi d)$

   (c) repel each other with a force of $\mu_0 i^2/(2\pi d^2)$

   (d) attract each other with a force of $\mu_0 i^2/(2\pi d^2)$

2. Three wires A, B and C are situated at the same distance. A current of 1A, 2A, 3A flows through these wires in the same direction. Then the resultant force on B is directed

   (a) Towards A

   (b) Towards C

   (c) Perpendicular to the plane of paper and outward

   (d) Perpendicular to the plane of paper and inward

3. The magnetic dipole moment of a current loop is independent of

   (a) magnetic field in which it is lying

   (b) number of turns

   (c) area of the loop

   (d) current in the loop

4. Match Column I and Column II.

Column I		Column II
(A) Biot-Savart's law	(1)	$\dfrac{\mu_0 I_1 I_2}{2\pi d}$
(B) Ampere's circuital law	(2)	$q[\vec{E}+(\vec{V}\times\vec{B})]$
(C) Force between two parallel current carrying conductors	(3)	$\oint \vec{B}.\vec{dl} = \mu_0 \Sigma i$
(D) Lorentz force	(4)	$\vec{B} = \dfrac{\mu_0 i}{4\pi}\int \dfrac{dl\sin\theta}{r^2}\hat{n}$

   (a) $(A)\rightarrow(4)$; $(B)\rightarrow(3)$; $(C)\rightarrow(1)$; $(D)\rightarrow(2)$

   (b) $(A)\rightarrow(2)$; $(B)\rightarrow(2)$; $(C)\rightarrow(4)$; $(D)\rightarrow(3)$

   (c) $(A)\rightarrow(4)$; $(B)\rightarrow(3)$; $(C)\rightarrow(2)$; $(D)\rightarrow(1)$

   (d) $(A)\rightarrow(2)$; $(B)\rightarrow(1)$; $(C)\rightarrow(4)$; $(D)\rightarrow(3)$

5. If m is magnetic moment and B is the magnetic field, then the torque is given by

   (a) $\vec{m}.\vec{B}$

   (b) $\dfrac{|\vec{m}|}{|\vec{B}|}$

   (c) $\vec{m}\times\vec{B}$

   (d) $|\vec{m}|\cdot|\vec{B}|$

6. A current carrying loop is placed in a uniform magnetic field. The torque acting on it does not depend upon
(a) shape of the loop   (b) area ot the loop
(c) value of the current   (d) magnetic field

7. A square current carrying loop is suspended in a uniform magnetic field acting in the plane of the loop. If the force on one arm of the loop is $\vec{F}$, the net force on the remaining three arms of the loop is

(a) $3\,\vec{F}$ (b) $-\vec{F}$

(c) $-3\,\vec{F}$ (d) $\vec{F}$

8. A current carrying conductor placed in a magnetic field experiences maximum force when angle between current and magnetic field is
(a) $3\pi/4$ (b) $\pi/2$
(c) $\pi/4$ (d) zero

9. An 8 cm long wire carrying a current of 10 A is placed inside a solenoid perpendicular to its axis. If the magnetic field inside the solenoid is 0.3 T, then magnetic force on the wire is
(a) 0.14 N   (b) 0.24 N
(c) 0.34 N   (d) 0.44 N

Case / Passage Based Questions

A rigid circular loop has a radius of 0.20 m and is in the x-y plane. A clockwise current I is carried by the loop, as shown. The magnitude of the magnetic moment of the loop is 0.75 A-m². A uniform external magnetic field, B = 0.20 T in the positive x-direction, is present

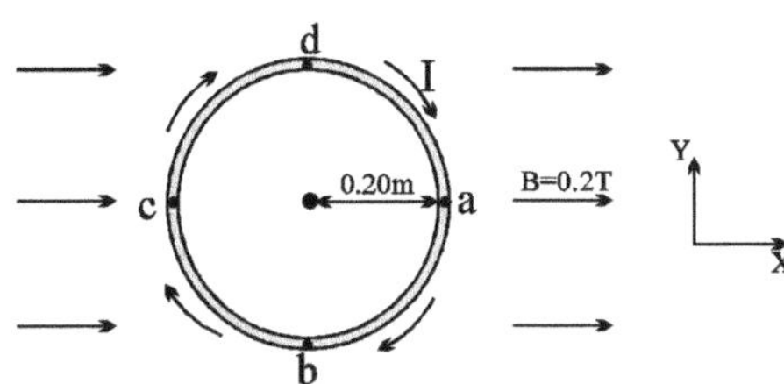

10. In figure, the magnitude of the magnetic torque exerted on the loop is closest to
(a) 0.55 N-m   (b) 0.15 N-m   (c) 0.45 N-m   (d) 0.35 N-m

11. In figure the loop is released from rest. The initial motion of the loop is described by
(a) point a moves out of the plane, point c moves into the plane
(b) points a, b, c and d move counterclockwise
(c) point a, b, c and d move clockwise
(d) point c moves out of the plane, point a moves into the plane

12. In figure, an external torque changes the orientation of loop from one of lowest potential energy to one of highest potential energy. The work done by the external torque is closest to
(a) 0.5 J   (b) 0.2 J   (c) 0.3 J   (d) 0.4 J

13. A wire is placed parallel to the lines of force in a magnetic field and a current flows in the wire. Then
(a) the wire will experience a force in the direction of the magnetic field
(b) the wire will not experience any force at all
(c) the wire will experience a force in a direction opposite to the field
(d) it experiences a force in a direction perpendicular to lines of force

14. A current carrying coil is subjected to a uniform magnetic field. The coil will orient so that its plane becomes
(a) inclined at 45° to the magnetic field
(b) inclined at any arbitrary angle to the magnetic field
(c) parallel to the magnetic field
(d) perpendicular to the magnetic field

Very Short Answer Questions

15. Equal currents (I) are flowing through two infinitely long parallel wires. What will be the magnetic field at a point mid-way when the currents are flowing in the same direction?

Short Answer Questions

16. Derive an expression for the force on a current carrying conductor placed in a magnetic field

17. Explain why two straight parallel current carrying conductors carrying current in same direction attract and carrying current in opposite direction repel each other. Hence define 1A current.

18. What is the torque acting on a coil placed in a magnetic field of strength B?

19. What is the magnetic moment associated with a coil of 1 turn, area of cross-section $10^{-4}\,\text{m}^2$, carrying a current of 2A?

20. A long straight wire AB carries a current of 4A. A proton P travels at 4×10^6 m/s parallel to the wire 0.2 m from it and in a direction opposite to the current. Calculate the force which the magnetic field of current exerts on the proton. Also specify the direction of the force.

21. A short conductor of length 5 cm is placed parallel to a long conductor of length 1.5 m near its cetre. The conductors carry currents 4 A and 3A respectively in the same direction. What is the total force experienced by the long conductor when they are 3 cm apart?

Topic 4 — Moving Coil Galvanometer its Current Sensitivity and Conversion of Galvanometer into Voltmeter and Ammeter

MOVING COIL GALVANOMETER

The moving coil galvanometer was first designed by Kelvin and later on modified by D'Arsonaval. This is used for detection and measurement of small electric current.

The **principle of a moving coil galvanometer** is based on the fact that when a current carrying coil is placed in a magnetic field, it experiences a torque.

Construction: A moving coil ballistic galvanometer is shown in figure. It essentially consists of a rectangular coil PQRS or a cylindrical coil of large number of turns of fine insulated wire wound over a non-conducting frame of ivory or bamboo. This coil is suspended by means of phosphor bronze wire between the pole pieces of a powerful horse shoe magnet NS. The poles of the magnet are curved to make the field radial. The lower end of the coil, is attached to a spring of phosphor-bronze wire. The spring and the free ends of phosphor bronze wire are joined to two terminals T_2 and T_1 respectively on the top of the case of the instrument. L is a soft iron core. A small mirror M is attached on the suspension wire. Using lamp and scale arrangement, the deflection of the coil can be recorded. The whole arrangement is enclosed in a non-metallic case.

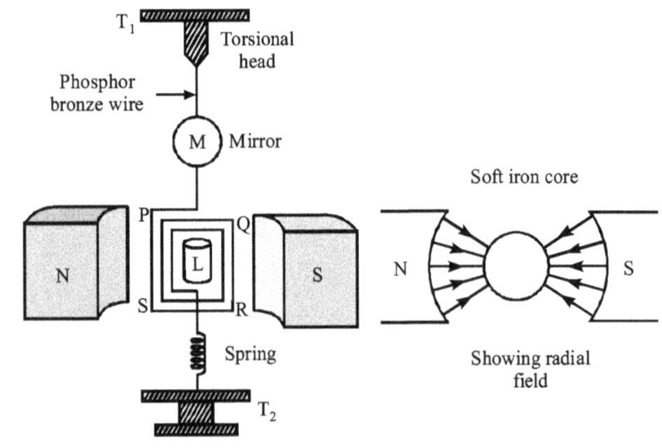

Theory and working : Let the coil be suspended freely in the magnetic field.

Suppose, n = number of turns in the coil

A = area of the coil

B = magnetic field induction of radial magnetic field in which the coil is suspended.

Here, the magnetic field is radial, i.e., the plane of the coil always remains parallel to the direction of magnetic field, and hence the torque acting on the coil

$$\tau = niAB \qquad \qquad \dots(i)$$

Due to this torque, the coil rotates. As a result, the suspension wire gets twisted. Now a restoring torque is developed in the suspension wire. The coil will rotate till the deflecting torque acting on the coil due to flow of current through it is balanced by the restoring torque developed in the suspension wire due to twisting. Let C be the restoring couple for unit twist in the suspension wire and θ be the angle through which the coil has turned. The couple for this twist θ is $C\theta$.

In equilibrium, deflecting couple = restoring couple

$$\therefore \quad ni\,AB = C\theta \ \text{ or } \ i = C\theta/(nAB)$$

$$\text{or} \quad i = K\theta \, (\text{where } C/nAB = K) \qquad \qquad \dots(ii)$$

K is a constant for galvanometer and is known as galvanometer constant.

$$\text{Hence } i \propto \theta$$

Therefore, the deflection produced in the galvanometer is directly proportional to the current flowing through it.

Current sensitivity (I_s) of the galvanometer is *the deflection produced when unit current is passed through the galvanometer.*

$$\text{i.e.,} \quad I_s = \frac{\theta}{I} = \frac{nBA}{k}$$

Voltage sensitivity is defined as *the deflection produced when unit potential difference is applied across the galvanometer.*

$$\text{i.e.,} \quad V_s = \frac{\theta}{V} = \frac{\theta}{IR} = \frac{nBA}{kR} \quad [R = \text{Resistance of the galvanometer}]$$

Condition for the maximum sensitivity of the galvanometer

The galvanometer is said to be sensitive if a small current produces a large deflection.

$$\because \quad \theta = \frac{nBA}{k} I$$

$$\therefore \quad \theta \text{ will be large if (i) n is large, (ii) B is large (iii) A is large and (iv) k is small.}$$

CONVERSION OF GALVANOMETER INTO VOLTMETER AND AMMETER

(a) A galvanometer is converted to voltmeter by putting a high resistance in series with it.

Total resistance of voltmeter = G + R where G is the galvonometer resistance.

R is the resistance added in series.

Current through the galvanometer, $I_g = \dfrac{V}{G+R}$

where V is the potential difference across the voltmeter.

And resistance, $R = \dfrac{V}{I_g} - G$

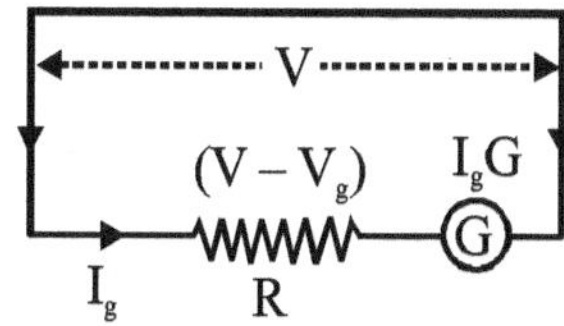

(b) A galvanometer is converted into an ammeter by connecting a low resistance (shunt) in parallel with it .

Shunt $S = \left(\dfrac{I_g}{I - I_g}\right) G$ where G is the galvanometere resistance.

I is the total current through the ammeter.

I_g is the current through the ammeter.

Effective resistance of the ammeter $R = \dfrac{GS}{G+S}$

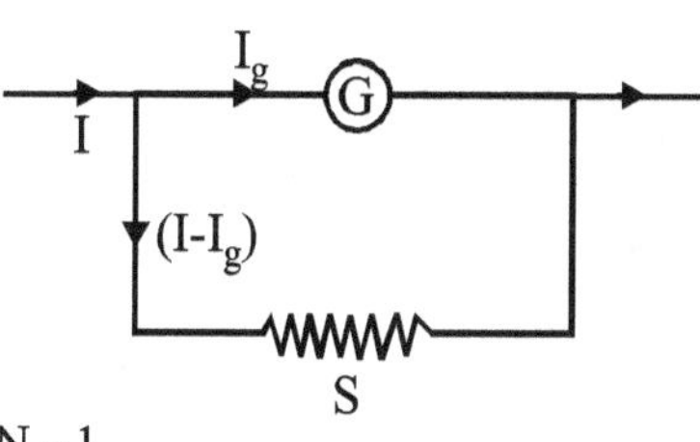

The range of an ammeter can be increased N times by reducing shunt S = G/N – 1

An ideal ammeter has zero resistance.

Illustration 5 :

A voltmeter reads 5V at full scale deflection and is graded according to its resistance per volt at full scale deflection as 2000 Ω / V. How will you convert it into a voltmeter that reads 15 V at full scale deflection?

Sol. Resistance/volt at full scale deflection = 2000 Ω / V

$\therefore$ Current at full scale deflection $= \dfrac{1}{\text{Resistance/volt}} = \dfrac{1}{2000} = 5 \times 10^{-4}$ A

Reading of voltmeter at full scale deflection = 5 V

$\therefore$ Resistance of the voltmeter $= \dfrac{5}{5 \times 10^{-4}} = 10^4 \Omega$

Range of voltmeter = 15 V

$\therefore$ Resistance to be added with the voltmeter in series, $R = \dfrac{V}{I_g} - G$

$= \dfrac{15}{5 \times 10^{-4}} - 10^4 = (3-1) \times 10^4 = 2 \times 10^4 \, \Omega.$

Illustration 6 :

In a galvanometer there is a deflection of 10 divisions per mA. The internal resistance of the galvanometer is 78 Ω. If a shunt of 2 Ω is connected to the galvanometer and there are 75 division in all on the scale of the galvanometer, calculate the maximum current which the galvanometer can read.

Sol. Given, G = 78 Ω, S = 2 Ω;

Figure of merit of the galvanometer = current per division

$\Rightarrow k = \dfrac{10^{-3}}{10} = 10^{-4} A \Rightarrow I_g = nk = 75 \times 10^{-4} A$

$S = \left(\dfrac{I_g}{I - I_g}\right) G$ $\therefore I = \left(\dfrac{G}{S} + 1\right) I_g = 3000 \times 10^{-4} = 0.3$ A.

Practice Exercise-4

Multiple Choice Questions

1. The current sensitivity of a galvanometer is defined as
(a) the current flowing through the galvanometer when a unit voltage is applied across its terminals.
(b) current per unit deflection.
(c) deflection per unit current.
(d) dflection per unit current when a unit voltage is applied across its terminals.

2. The deflection in a moving coil galvanometer is
(a) directly proportional to the torsional constant
(b) directly proportional to the number of turns in the coil
(c) inversely proportional to the area of the coil
(d) inversely proportional to the current flowin g

3. The galvanometer cannot as such be used as an ammeter to measure the value of current in a given circuit. The following reasons are
I. galvanometer gives full scale deflection for a small current.
II. galvanometer has a large resistance.
III. a galvanometer can give inaccurate values.
The correct reasons are:
(a) I and II   (b) II and III
(c) I and III   (d) I, II and III

4. A galvanometer having a resistance of 80 ohms is shunted by a wire of resistance 2 ohms. If the total current is 1 amp., the part of it passing through the shunt will be
(a) 0.25 amp (b) 0.8 amp (c) 0.02 amp (d) 0.5 amp

5. The resistance of an ammeter is 13 Ω and its scale is graduated for a current upto 100 amps. After an additional shunt has been connected to this ammeter it becomes possible to measure currents upto 750 amperes by this meter. The value of shunt-resistance is
(a) 2 Ω (b) 0.2 Ω (c) 2 kΩ (d) 20 Ω

Case / Passage Based Questions

(a) A galvanometer is converted to voltmeter by putting a high resistance in series with it.
Total resistance of voltmeter $= G + R$ where G is the galvonometer resistance.
R is the resistance added in series.

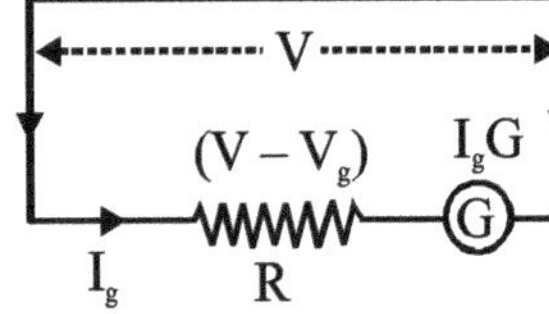

Current through the galvanometer, $I_g = \dfrac{V}{G + R}$
where V is the potential difference across the voltmeter.
And resistance, $R = \dfrac{V}{I_g} - G$

(b) A galvanometer is converted into an ammeter by connecting a low resistance (shunt) in parallel with it.
Shunt $S = \left(\dfrac{I_g}{I - I_g}\right) G$ where G is the galvanometere resistance.

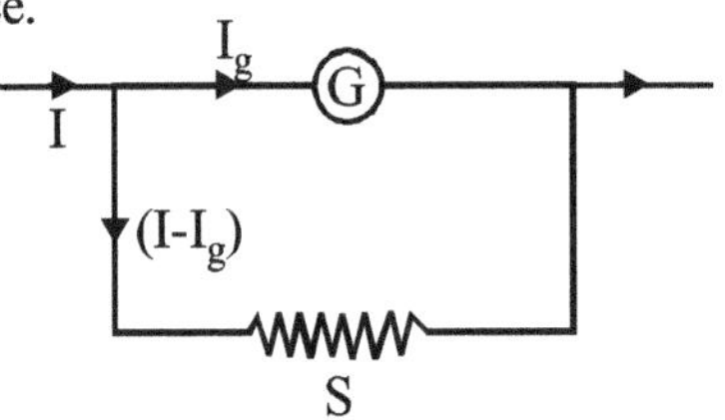

I is the total current through the ammeter.
I_g is the current through the ammeter.
Effective resistance of the ammeter $R = \dfrac{GS}{G + S}$
The range of an ammeter can be increased N times by reducing shunt $S = G/N - 1$
An ideal ammeter has zero resistance.

6. A galvanometer of resistance, G is shunted by a resistance S ohm. To keep the main current in the circuit unchanged, the resistance to be put in series with the galvanometer is
(a) $\dfrac{S^2}{(S+G)}$ (b) $\dfrac{SG}{(S+G)}$ (c) $\dfrac{G^2}{(S+G)}$ (d) $\dfrac{G}{(S+G)}$

7. A galvanometer having a coil resistance of 60 Ω shows full scale deflection when a current of 1.0 amp passes through it. It can be converted into an ammeter to read currents upto 5.0 amp by
(a) putting in series a resistance of 15Ω
(b) putting in series a resistance of 240Ω
(c) putting in parallel a resistance of 15Ω
(d) putting in parallel a resistance of 240Ω

8. A milli voltmeter of 25 milli volt range is to be converted into an ammeter of 25 ampere range. The value (in ohm) of necessary shunt will be
(a) 0.001   (b) 0.01   (c) 1   (d) 0.05

9. A moving coil galvanometer of resistance 100Ω is used as an ammeter using a resistance 0.1Ω. The maximum deflection current in the galvanometer is 100μA. Find the minimum current in the circuit so that the ammeter shows maximum deflection
(a) 100.1 mA   (b) 1000.1 mA
(c) 10.01 mA   (d) 1.01 mA

10. A galvanometer of resistance 5 ohms gives a full scale deflection for a potential difference of 10 mV. To convert the galvanometer into a voltmeter giving a full scale deflection for a potential difference of 1V, the size of the resistance that must be attached to the voltmeter is
(a) 0.495 ohm   (b) 49.5 ohm
(c) 495 ohm   (d) 4950 ohm

Very Short Answer Questions

11. What is the nature of the magnetic field in a moving coil galvanometer?

12. Name the physical quantity whose S.I. unit is Wb - m^{-2}. Is it a scalar or a vector quantity?

13. State two properties of the material of the wire used for suspension of the coil in a moving coil galvanometer.

14. What is the advantage of using radial magnetic field in a moving coil galvanometer?

15. An ammeter and a milliammeter are converted from the same galvanometer. Out of the two, which current measuring instrument has higher resistance?

Short Answer Questions

16. How will you convert a galvanometer into an ammeter?

17. How will you convert a galvanometer into a voltmeter?

18. The coil of a galvanometer has resistance of 100 ohm. It shows full scale deflection for a current of 5×10^{-4}A. How will you convert into a voltmeter to read a maximum potential difference of 5V?

19. A galvanometer having a coil resistance of 100Ω gives full scale deflection when a current of 1 mA is passed through it. Calculate the value of resistance required to convert it into an ammeter of the range of 1A.

Important Tips & Formulae

- When charged particle is moving perpendicular to the direction of magnetic field, the path of particle will be circular. In this motion, the magnitude of momentum of the particle remain constant but its direction keeps changing. Also, KE of particle in magnetic field is constant.

- Magnetic force depends on velocity, while electric force is independent of the state of rest or motion of the charged particle.

- If current carrying straight wire is placed along the axis of a current carrying coil then it will not experience magnetic force as magnetic field produced by the coil is parallel to the wire.

- Magnetic force does no work when the charged particle is displaced while electric force does work in displacing the charged particle.

- If two linear parallel conductors are carrying equal currents in the same direction then magnetic field induction at the centre of seperation of two wire is zero.

- The force acting on a curved wire joining any two point in a plane is the same as that on a straight wire joining these points.

- A radial magnetic field used in moving coil galvanometer to make the scale of galvanometer linear.

- Magnetic field inside a current carrying conductor $B = kd$ $i.e.$, straight line passing through origin.

  At surface $(d = R)$ $B = \dfrac{\mu_0 I}{2\pi d}$

  Same $B = \dfrac{\mu_0 I}{2\pi d}$ outside the conductor $i.e.$, hyperbolic.

- We can decide the polarity of the magnetic dipole due to current loop. If the direction of current flowing through the coil is anticlockwise then that face of coil will be north pole. If the direction of current is clockwise, then that face has south polarity.

- A charge will move in combined electric and magnetic field if

  $$qE = qVB \text{ or } V = \dfrac{E}{B}$$

- If a current carrying circular loop (n = 1) is bent sharply so as to convert into a coil having n identical turns then magnetic field at the centre of the coil becomes n^2 times the previous field $i.e.$, $B_{(n\,turn)} = n^2 B_{(single\,turn)}$.

- If an electron moves in a circular path of radius r with speed v then magnetic field produced at the centre of circular path will be

  $$B = \dfrac{\mu_0}{4\pi} \cdot \dfrac{ev}{r^2} \Rightarrow r \propto \sqrt{\dfrac{v}{B}}$$

- If two coils of radius r_1 and r_2 are connected in series to the source of direct current, then the ratio of magnetic field inductions at their centres is given by

  $$\dfrac{B_1}{B_2} = \dfrac{r_2}{r_1}$$

  If the same coil is connected in parallel combination, then

  $$\dfrac{B_1}{B_2} = \dfrac{r_2^2}{r_1^2}$$

- Magnetic field induction at one end of solenoid is given by

  $$B = \dfrac{\mu_0 NI}{2\ell}$$

- To increase the range of voltmeter having resistance G from V to $\dfrac{V}{n}$, a shunt of resistance nG should be connect in parallel to it.

- If velocity of charge particle v and magnetic field $\vec{B}$ are not perpendicular to each other then the charge will move in helical motion with pitch of helix is given by

  $$P = 2\pi m V_{\parallel}/qB$$

  here $V_{\parallel}$ is the component of velocity parallel to the magnetic field.

NCERT Questions

4.1. A circular coil of wire consisting of 100 turns, each of radius 8.0 cm carries a current of 0.40 A. What is the magnitude of the magnetic field B at the centre of the coil?

Sol. Given, $N = 100, r = 8$ cm $= 0.08$ m
$I = 0.4$ A, B $= ?$

As we know, $B = \dfrac{\mu_0 NI}{2r}$

$$= \dfrac{4\pi \times 10^{-7} \times 100 \times 0.4}{2 \times 0.08} = \pi \times 10^{-4}\,\text{T}.$$

4.2. A long straight wire carries a current of 35 A. What is the magnitude of the field B at a point 20 cm from the wire?

Sol. Given, $I = 35$ A, $a = 20$ cm $= 0.2$ m, B $= ?$

$$B = \dfrac{\mu_0 I}{2\pi a} = \dfrac{4\pi \times 10^{-7} \times 35}{2\pi \times 0.2} = 3.5 \times 10^{-5}\,\text{T}.$$

4.3. A long straight wire in the horizontal plane carries a current of 50 A in north to south direction. Give the magnitude and direction of B at a point 2.5 m east of the wire.

Sol. Given, $I = 50$ A, $a = 2.5$ m, B $= ?$

$$B = \dfrac{\mu_0 I}{2\pi a} = \dfrac{4\pi \times 10^{-7} \times 50}{2\pi \times 2.5} = 4 \times 10^{-6}\,\text{T}.$$

It will be in vertically upward direction (right hand thumb rule)

4.4. A horizontal overhead power line carries a current of 90 A in east to west direction. What is the magnitude and direction of the magnetic field due to the current 1.5 m below the line?

Sol. Given, $I = 90$ A, $a = 1.5$ m, $\mu_0 = 4\pi \times 10^{-7}$, B $= ?$

$$B = \dfrac{\mu_0 I}{2\pi a} = \dfrac{4\pi \times 10^{-7} \times 90}{2\pi \times 1.5} = 1.2 \times 10^{-5}\,\text{T}.$$

From right hand thumb rule, its direction is towards South.

4.5. What is the magnitude of magnetic force per unit length on a wire carrying a current of 8 A and making an angle of 30° with the direction of a uniform magnetic field of 0.15 T?

Sol. Given, $I = 8$ A, $d\ell = 1$m, B $= 0.15$ T, $\theta = 30°$
$\Rightarrow \sin\theta = 0.5$, force per unit length F $= ?$

$F = I\,d\ell\,B\sin\theta = 8 \times 1 \times 0.15 \times 0.5 = 0.6$ N/m.

4.6. A 3.0 cm wire carrying a current of 10 A is placed inside a solenoid perpendicular to its axis. The magnetic field inside the solenoid is given to be 0.27 T. What is the magnetic force on the wire?

Sol. Given, $d\ell = 3$ cm $= 0.03$ m, $I = 10$ A, B $= 0.27$ T, $\theta = 90° \Rightarrow \sin\theta = 1$, F $= ?$

$F = I\,d\ell\,B\sin\theta = 10 \times 0.03 \times 0.27 \times 1$
$\quad = 8.1 \times 10^{-2}\,\text{N}$

The direction can be obtained by Fleming's left hand rule.

4.7. Two long and parallel straight wires A and B carrying currents of 8.0 A and 5.0 A in the same direction are separated by a distance of 4.0 cm. Estimate the force on a 10 cm section of wire A.

Sol. Given, $I_1 = 8$A, $I_2 = 5$A, $r = 4$cm $= 0.04$ m
$\ell = 10$ cm $= 0.1$ m, F $= ?$

Force per unit length $= \dfrac{\mu_0}{2\pi}\dfrac{I_1 I_2}{r}$

Force on length ℓ

$$F = \dfrac{\mu_0}{2\pi}\dfrac{I_1 I_2 \ell}{r} = \dfrac{4\pi \times 10^{-7} \times 8 \times 5 \times 0.1}{2\pi \times 0.04}$$

$\quad = 2 \times 10^{-5}$ N. Force is attractive.

4.8. A closely wound solenoid 80 cm long has 5 layers of windings of 400 turns each. The diameter of the solenoid is 1.8 cm. If the current carried is 8.0 A, estimate the magnitude of B inside the solenoid near its centre.

Sol. Given, $\ell = 80$ cm $= 0.8$ m
$N = 5 \times 400 = 2000, I = 8$ A, B $= ?$

$$B = \mu_0 nI = 4\pi \times 10^{-7} \times \dfrac{2000}{0.8} \times 8$$

$$= 8\pi \times 10^{-3} = 2.51 \times 10^{-2}\,\text{T}$$

4.9. A square coil of side 10 cm consists of 20 turns and carries a current of 12 A. The coil is suspended vertically and the normal to the plane of the coil makes an angle of 30° with the direction of a uniform horizontal magnetic field of magnitude 0.80 T. What is the magnitude of torque experienced by the coil?

Sol. Given, $A = 10 \times 10 = 100$ cm$^2 = 10^{-2}$ m^2
$N = 20, I = 12$ A, B $= 0.8$ T, $\theta = 30° \Rightarrow \sin\theta = 0.5$
As we know, $\tau = NIAB\sin\theta$
$\quad\quad\quad = 20 \times 12 \times 10^{-2} \times 0.8 \times 0.5$
$\quad\quad\quad = 96 \times 10^{-2}$ Nm

4.10. Two moving coil galvanometers, M_1 and M_2 have the following particulars:
$R_1 = 10\ \Omega,\ N_1 = 30,$
$A_1 = 3.6 \times 10^{-3}$ m^2, $B_1 = 0.25$ T
$R_2 = 14\ \Omega,\ N_2 = 42,$
$A_2 = 1.8 \times 10^{-3}$ m^2, $B_2 = 0.50$ T
(The spring constants are identical for the two meters). Determine the ratio of (a) current sensitivity and (b) voltage sensitivity of M_2 and M_1.

Sol. Given, for meter M_1
$R_1 = 10\,\Omega, N_1 = 30, A_1 = 3.6 \times 10^{-3}$ m^2,
$B_1 = 0.25$ T, $k_1 = k$
For meter M_2
$R_2 = 14\,\Omega, N_2 = 42, A_2 = 1.8 \times 10^{-3}$ m^2,
$B_2 = 0.5$ T, $k_2 = k$

$\because$ Current sensitivity $I_s = \dfrac{NAB}{k}$

$$\therefore \quad \frac{I_{S2}}{I_{S1}} = \frac{N_2 A_2 B_2}{k_2} \times \frac{k_1}{N_1 A_1 B_1}$$

$$= \frac{42 \times 1.8 \times 10^{-3} \times 0.50 \times k}{k \times 30 \times 3.6 \times 10^{-3} \times 0.25}$$

$$= \frac{42 \times 18 \times 50}{30 \times 36 \times 25} = 7 : 5$$

(b) Voltage sensitivity $v_s = \dfrac{NAB}{Rk}$

$$\therefore \quad \frac{V_{S2}}{V_{S1}} = \frac{N_2 A_2 B_2}{R_2 k_2} \times \frac{R_1 k_1}{N_1 A_1 B_1}$$

$$= \frac{42 \times 18 \times 10^{-3} \times 0.50 \times 10 \times k}{14 \times k \times 30 \times 36 \times 10^{-3} \times 0.25}$$

$$= \frac{42 \times 18 \times 50 \times 10}{14 \times 30 \times 36 \times 25} = 1$$

4.11. In a chamber, a uniform magnetic field of 6.5 G $(1\ \text{G} = 10^{-4}\ \text{T})$ is maintained. An electron is shot into the field with a speed of $4.8 \times 10^6\ \text{m s}^{-1}$ normal to the field. Explain why the path of the electron is a circle. Determine the radius of the circular orbit. $(e = 1.6 \times 10^{-19}\ \text{C},\ m_e = 9.1 \times 10^{-31}\ \text{kg})$

Sol. Given, $B = 6.5\ \text{G} = 6.5 \times 10^{-4}\ \text{T}$
$v = 4.8 \times 10^6\ \text{m/s}, q = e = 1.6 \times 10^{-19}\text{C}$
$m = 9.1 \times 10^{-31}\ \text{kg}.$

$$\because \frac{mv^2}{r} = qvB \Rightarrow r = \frac{mv}{Bq} = \frac{9.1 \times 10^{-31} \times 4.8 \times 10^6}{1.6 \times 10^{-19} \times 6.5 \times 10^{-4}}$$

$$= \frac{91 \times 48 \times 10^{-27}}{16 \times 65 \times 10^{-25}} = 4.2 \times 10^{-2}\ \text{m} = 4.2\ \text{cm}.$$

4.12. In question 4.11 obtain the frequency of revolution of the electron in its circular orbit. Does the answer depend on the speed of the electron?

Sol. We know, $\omega_c = \dfrac{qB}{m} \Rightarrow 2\pi v = \dfrac{qB}{m} \Rightarrow v = \dfrac{qB}{2\pi m}$

$$= \frac{1.6 \times 10^{-19} \times 6.5 \times 10^{-4}}{2 \times 3.14 \times 9.1 \times 10^{-31}} = 0.182 \times 10^8 = 18.2 \times 10^6$$

$$= 18.2\ \text{MHz}.$$

Answer does not depend on the speed of the electron.

4.13 (a) A circular coil of 30 turns and radius 8.0 cm carrying a current of 6.0 A is suspended vertically in a uniform horizontal magnetic field of magnitude 1.0 T. The field lines make an angle of 60° with the normal of the coil. Calculate the magnitude of the counter torque that must be applied to prevent the coil from turning.

(b) Would your answer change, if the circular coil in (a) were replaced by a planar coil of some irregular shape that encloses the same area? (All other particulars are also unaltered.)

Sol. (a) Given, $N = 30, r = 8\ \text{cm} = 0.08\ \text{m}$
$A = \pi(0.08)^2\ \text{m}^2, I = 6\ \text{A}, B = 1\text{T}, \theta = 60°$
$\Rightarrow \sin\theta = 0.866$
Restoring torque = deflecting torque
$$= NIAB \sin\theta$$
$$\tau = 30 \times 6 \times \pi \times 0.0064 \times 1 \times 0.866$$
$$= 3.1341\ \text{Nm}.$$

(b) The torque depends upon area of coil and not shape. Answer will be same. No change.

ADDITIONAL EXERCISES

4.14. Two concentric circular coils X and Y of radii 16 cm and 10 cm, respectively, lie in the same vertical plane containing the north to south direction. Coil X has 20 turns and carries a current of 16 A; coil Y has 25 turns and carries a current of 18 A. The sense of the current in X is anticlockwise, and clockwise in Y, for an observer looking at the coils facing west. Give the magnitude and direction of the net magnetic field due to the coils at their centre.

Sol. Given, for coil X, $r_1 = 16\ \text{cm} = 0.16\ \text{m}, N_1 = 20$
$I_1 = 16\ \text{A}$ (anti-clockwise)
For coil Y, $r_2 = 10\ \text{cm} = 0.1\text{m}, N_2 = 25$
$I_2 = 18\ \text{A}$(clockwise)

$\because$ Magnetic field, $B = \dfrac{\mu_0 NI}{2r}$

$$\therefore B_1 = \frac{\mu_0 \times 20 \times 16}{2 \times 0.16} = 1000\mu_0\ \text{T towards east.}$$

$$B_2 = \frac{\mu_0 \times 25 \times 18}{2 \times 0.10} = 2250\mu_0\ \text{T towards west.}$$

Resultant $B = (2250 - 1000)\ \mu_0$ T towards west
$$= 1250 \times 4\pi \times 10^{-7}\ \text{T towards west}$$
$$= 1.5715 \times 10^{-3}\ \text{T towards west.}$$

4.15. A magnetic field of 100 G $(1\ \text{G} = 10^{-4}\ \text{T})$ is required which is uniform in a region of linear dimension about 10 cm and area of cross - section about $10^{-3}\ \text{m}^2$. The maximum current carrying capacity of a given coil of wire is 15 A and the number of turns per unit length that can be wound round a core is at most 1000 turns m^{-1}. Suggest some appropriate design particulars of a solenoid for the required purpose. Assume the core is not ferromagnetic.

Sol. Given, $B = 100\ \text{G} = 10^{-2}\ \text{T}, I = 15\ \text{A}, n = 1000/\text{m}$

$$B = \mu_0 nI \Rightarrow nI = \frac{B}{\mu_0} = \frac{10^{-2}}{4\pi \times 10^{-7}} = \frac{10^5}{4\pi} \approx 8000$$

we may have $I = 10\ \text{A}, n = 800$
The core length may be 50 cm having 400 turns and cross-section $5 \times 10^{-3}\ \text{m}^2$

4.16. For a circular coil of radius R and N turns carrying current I, the magnitude of the magnetic field at a point on its axis at a distance x from its centre is given by,

$$B = \frac{\mu_0 IR^2 N}{2(x^2 + R^2)^{3/2}}$$

(a) Show that this reduces to the familiar result for field at the centre of the coil.

(b) Consider two parallel co–axial circular coils of equal radius R, and number of turns N, carrying equal currents in the same direction, and separated by a distance R. Show that the field on the axis around the mid–point between the coils is uniform over a distance that is small as compared to R, and

is given by, $B = 0.72\dfrac{\mu_0 NI}{R}$, approximately.

(Such an arrangement to produce a nearly uniform magnetic field over a small region is known as Helmholtz coils.)

Sol. **(a)** $B = \dfrac{\mu_0 I R^2 N}{2(x^2 + R^2)^{3/2}}$

At the centre of the coil $x = 0$

$B = \dfrac{\mu_0 I R^2 N}{2R^3} = \dfrac{\mu_0 IN}{2R}$ —which is same standard result.

(b) In a small region of length 2d about the mid-point between the coils,

$$B = \dfrac{\mu_0 I R^2 N}{2} \times \left[\left\{ \left(\dfrac{R}{2} + d \right)^2 + R^2 \right\}^{-3/2} + \left\{ \left(\dfrac{R}{2} - d \right)^2 + R^2 \right\}^{-3/2} \right]$$

$$= \dfrac{\mu_0 I R^2 N}{2} \times \left(\dfrac{5R^2}{4} \right)^{3/2} \left[\left(1 + \dfrac{4d}{5R} \right)^{-3/2} + \left(1 - \dfrac{3d}{5R} \right)^{-3/2} \right]$$

$$\approx \dfrac{\mu_0 I R^2 N}{2R^3} \times \left(\dfrac{4}{5} \right)^{-3/2} \times \left[1 - \dfrac{6d}{5R} + 1 + \dfrac{6d}{5R} \right]$$

(Neglecting term with d^2/R^2 and higher powers of d/R since d/R<<1).

$\therefore \quad B = \left(\dfrac{4}{5} \right)^{3/2} \dfrac{\mu_0 IN}{R} \approx 0.72 \dfrac{\mu_0 IN}{R}$

4.17. **A toroid has a core (non–ferromagnetic) of inner radius 25 cm and outer radius 26 cm, around which 3500 turns of a wire are wound. If the current in the wire is 11 A, what is the magnetic field (a) outside the toroid, (b) inside the core of the toroid, and (c) in the empty space surrounded by the toroid.**

Sol. Average radius, $a = \dfrac{25 + 26}{2} = 25.5 \text{ cm} = 0.255 \text{ m}$;

$N = 3500$

$n = \dfrac{N}{2\pi a} = \dfrac{3500}{2\pi \times 0.255} = \dfrac{3500}{0.51\pi} \text{ m}^{-1}$;

$I = 11 \text{A}, \mu_0 = 4\pi \times 10^{-7}, B = ?$

(a) Field outside the toroid is zero.

(b) Field inside the core,

$B = \mu_0 nI = 4\pi \times 10^{-7} \times \dfrac{3500}{0.51\pi} \times 11$

$= 3 \times 10^{-2}$ tesla

(c) Field in space surrounded by toroid is zero.

4.18. **Answer the following questions:**

(a) A magnetic field that varies in magnitude from point to point but has a constant direction (east to west) is set up in a chamber. A charged particle enters the chamber and travels undeflected along a straight path with constant speed. What can you say about the initial velocity of the particle?

(b) A charged particle enters an environment of a strong and non–uniform magnetic field varying from point to point both in magnitude and direction, and comes out of it following a complicated trajectory. Would its final speed equal the initial speed if it suffered no collisions with the environment?

(c) An electron travelling west to east enters a chamber having a uniform electrostatic field in north to south direction. Specify the direction in which a uniform magnetic field should be set up to prevent the electron from deflecting from its straight line path.

Sol. **(a)** Initial velocity v is either parallel or antiparallel to B.

(b) Yes, because magnetic force can change the direction of v, not its magnitude.

(c) B should be in a vertically downward direction.

4.19. **An electron emitted by a heated cathode and accelerated through a potential difference of 2.0 k V, enters a region with uniform magnetic field of 0.15 T. Determine the trajectory of the electron if the field (a) is transverse to its initial velocity, (b) makes an angle of 30° with the initial velocity.**

Sol. A electron which is accelerated by a potential difference of 2.0 kV will have a kinetic energy gained 2000 eV.

$E = 1/2\, m_e\, v^2 = 2000 \times 1.6 \times 10^{-19}$

$v = \sqrt{\dfrac{4 \times 1.6 \times 10^{-16}}{9 \times 10^{-37}}} = 2.66 \times 10^7 \text{ ms}^{-1}$

(a) When the electron enters in the uniform magnetic field which is normal to the velocity of electron follows a circular path of radius.

$r = \dfrac{mv}{Bq} = \dfrac{9 \times 10^{-31} \times 2.66 \times 10^7}{0.15 \times 1.6 \times 10^{-19}}$

$= 99.75 \times 10^{-1} \text{ m} \approx 1 \text{mm}$

(b) When the magnetic field makes an angle 30° with the initial velocity, the trajectory of the electron becomes helical.

radius of the helical path is

$r = \dfrac{mv \sin \theta}{Bq}$

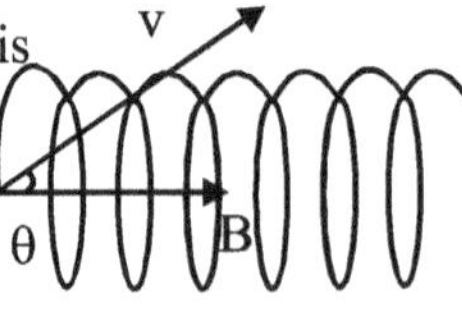

$r = 99.75 \times 10^{-7} \times \dfrac{1}{2}$

$r = 49.875 \times 10^{-7} \text{ m} \approx 0.5 \text{ mm}$

Pitch of the helical path is

$$\text{Pitch} = T \times v \cos\theta = \frac{2\pi\, m}{Bq} \times v \cos\theta$$

$$= \frac{2\pi \times 9 \times 10^{-31} \times 2.66 \times 10^{7}}{0.15 \times 1.6 \times 10^{-19}} = \frac{\sqrt{3}}{2}$$

$$= 542.5 \times 10^{-5}\,\text{m}$$

So, pitch $= 5.42$ mm.

4.20. **A magnetic field set up using Helmholtz coils (described in question 4.16) is uniform in a small region and has magnitude of 0.75 T. In the same region, a uniform electrostatic field is maintained in a direction normal to the common axis of the coils. A narrow beam of (single species) charged particles all accelerated through 15 kV enters this region in a direction perpendicular to both the axis of the coils and the electrostatic field. If the beam remains undeflected when the electrostatic field is 9.0×10^{-5} V m^{-1}, make a simple guess as to what the beam contains. Why is the answer not unique?**

Sol. Narrow beam of charged particles remains undeflected and is perpendicular to both electric field and magnetic fields which are mutually perpendicular. So, the electric force is balanced by magnetic force.

$$qE = qv\text{B}$$

speed of charged particles

$$v = E/B = \frac{9 \times 10^{-5}}{0.75} = 12 \times 10^{-5}\,\text{ms}^{-1}$$

Because the beam is accelerated through 15 kV, if charge is q, then kinetic energy gained by charged particles

$$\frac{1}{2}mv^2 = qV \;\Rightarrow\; \frac{m}{q} = \frac{2V}{v^2}$$

$$= \frac{2 \times 15 \times 10^3}{\left(12 \times 10^{-5}\right)^2} = 20.8 \times 10^{11}$$

Here, we can only obtain charge to mass ratio and same ratio can be in Deuterium ions, He^{++}, Li^{++}, so the beam can contain any of these charged particles.

4.21. **A straight horizontal conduction rod of length 0.45 m and mass 60 g is suspended by two vertical wires at its ends. A current of 5.0 A is set up in the rod through the wires.**
(a) What magnetic field should be set up normal to the conductor in order that the tension in the wires is zero?
(b) What will be the total tension in the wires if the direction of current is reversed keeping the magnetic field same as before?
[Ignore the mass of the wires.] $g = 9.8$ m s^{-2}

Sol.

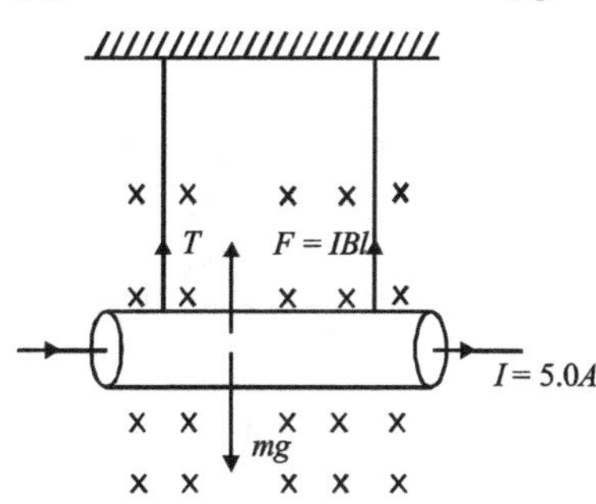

At balance tension in the strings and magnetic force IBl balance the weight of wire.

$$2T + IBl = mg$$

(a) For tension in the wire to be zero.

$$IBl = mg \;\Rightarrow\; B = \frac{mg}{Il}$$

$$= \frac{60 \times 10^{-3} \times 9.8}{5 \times 0.45} = 0.26\ \text{T}$$

(b) If the direction of current is now reversed, keeping the current and magnetic field same, then

$$2T = IBl + mg$$
$$2T = 2\,mg = 2 \times 60 \times 10^{-3} \times 9.8$$

Total tension $= 1.176$ N.

4.22. **The wires which connect the battery of an automobile to its starting motor carry a current of 300 A (for a short time). What is the force per unit length between the wires if they are 70 cm long and 1.5 cm apart? Is the force attractive or repulsive?**

Sol. Two wires connecting battery of an automobile to the starting motor carry 300 current in opposite direction. So, the force is repulsive between them. Force per unit length

$$F/l = \frac{\mu_0}{4\pi}\frac{2I_1 I_2}{r}\,10^{-7} \times \frac{2 \times 300 \times 300}{1.5 \times 10^{-2}} = 1.2\ \text{N/m}$$

4.23. **A uniform magnetic field of 1.5 T exists in a cylindrical region of radius 10.0 cm, its direction parallel to the axis along east to west. A wire carrying current of 7.0 A in the north to south direction passes through this region. What is the magnitude and direction of the force on the wire if,**
(a) the wire intersects the axis,
(b) the wire is turned from N-S to northeast-northwest direction.
(c) the wire in the N-S direction is lowered from the axis by a distance of 6.0 cm?

Sol. The magnetic field is in the direction east to west and in the cylindrical region of radius 10 cm.

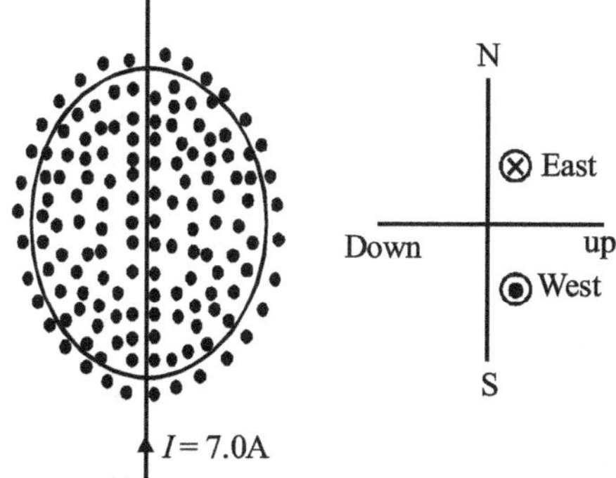

(a) A current carrying wire, intersects the axis.
Force on wire
$$F = IBl = IB(2r) = 7 \times 1.5 \times 2 \times 1 \times 10^{-2}$$
$$= 2.1\ \text{N upwards}$$

(b) By turning the wire by an angle 45° in NE and SW direction the force remain the same $f = 2.1$ N.

(c) Now the wire is lowered from the axis by a distance of 6.0 cm.

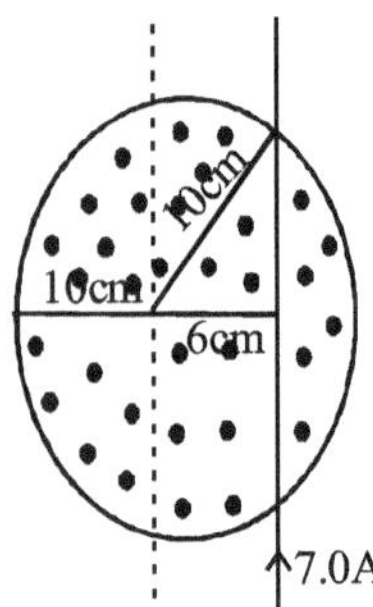

↑7.0A

Length of wire inside cylindrical region is 16cm now.

So, the force is $F = IBl = 7 \times 1.5 \times 16 \times 10^{-2}$

$$= 1.68 \text{ N}$$

4.24. A uniform magnetic field of 3000 G is established along the positive Z-direction. A rectangular loop of sides 10 cm and 5 cm carries a current of 12 A. What is the torque on the loop in the different cases shown in figure? What is the force on each case? Which case corresponds to stable equilibrium?

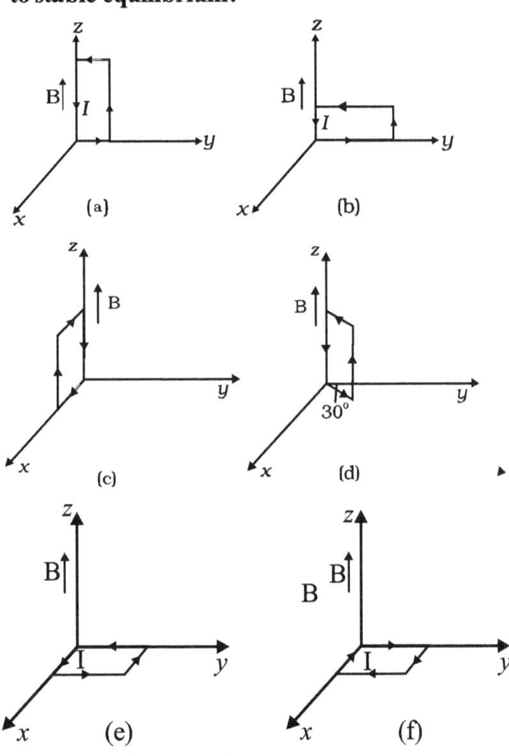

Sol. (a) Let us detail each case separately,

Dipole moment $(\vec{M})$ is along +x direction

$$\vec{M} = 10 \times 5 \times 10^{-4} \times 12 \,\hat{i}$$
$$= 0.06\hat{i}$$

$$\vec{B} = 3000 \times 10^{-4} \,\hat{k}$$

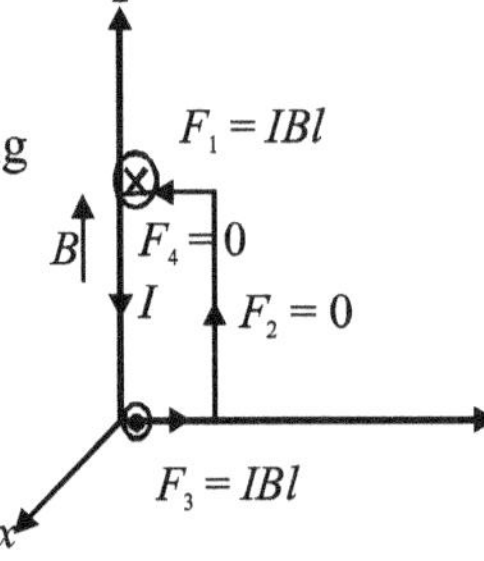

Torque $\vec{C} = \vec{M} \times \vec{B} = -1.8 \times 10^{-2} \,\hat{J}$ N.m

Torque is 1.8×10^{-2} N-m along $-y$ direction, Net force on the coil is zero, coil is not in equilibrium.

(b) Dipole moment is along $+ x$ direction

$$\vec{M} = 0.06\,\hat{i}, \ \vec{B} = 0.3\,\hat{k}$$

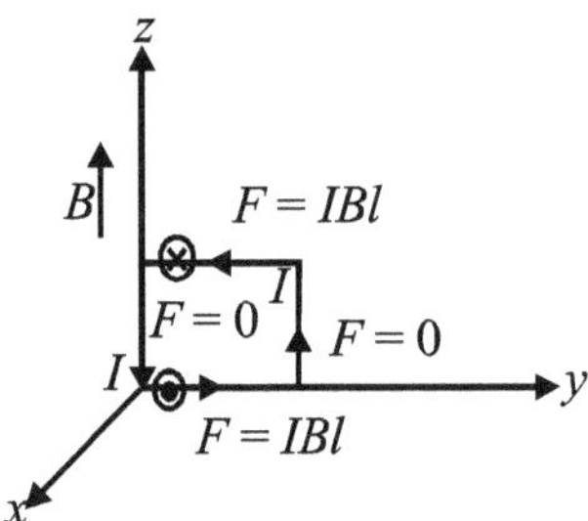

Torque $\vec{\tau} = \vec{M} \times \vec{B}$

So, torque is 1.8×10^{-2} N-m along $-y$ direction.

Net force on the coil is zero, coil is not in equilibrium.

(c) Dipole moment is along $-y$ direction

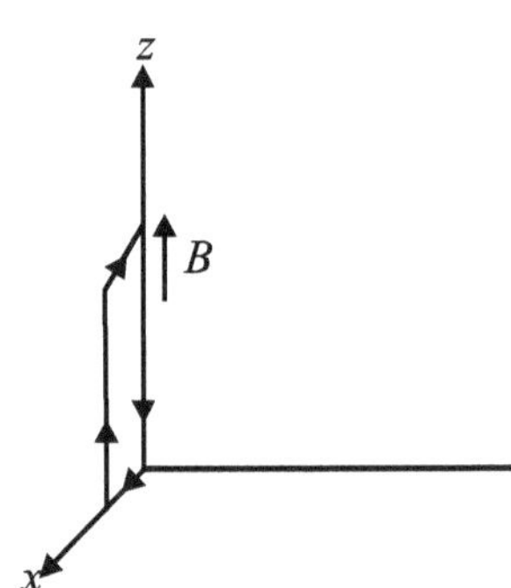

$$\vec{M} = -0.06\,\hat{j}, \ \hat{B} = 0.3\,\hat{k}$$

Torque $\vec{\tau} = \vec{M} \times \vec{B} = -1.8 \times 10^{-2} \,\hat{i}$ N–m.

So, the torque is 1.8×10^{-2} Nm along $-x$ direction.

Net force on the coil is zero, coil is not in equilibrium.

(d) Dipole moment is at an angle 150° with the $+x$ direction.

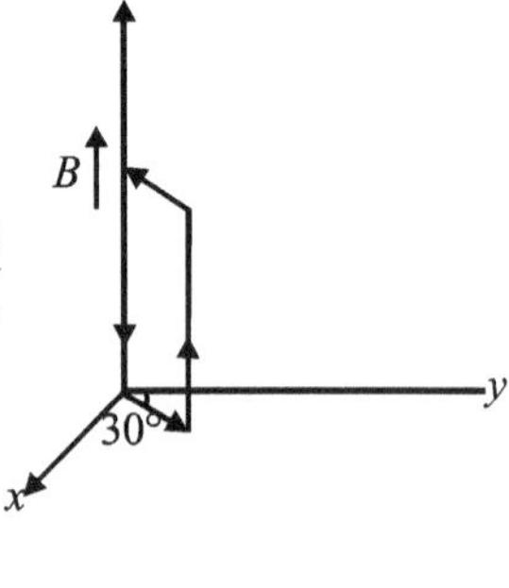

Torque $\tau = MB \sin\theta$

$$= 1.8 \times 10^{-2} \sin\frac{\pi}{2}$$

$$= 1.8 \times 10^{-2} \text{ N.m}$$

At an angle 240° with the $+x$ direction, net force on the coil is zero, coil is not in equilibrium.

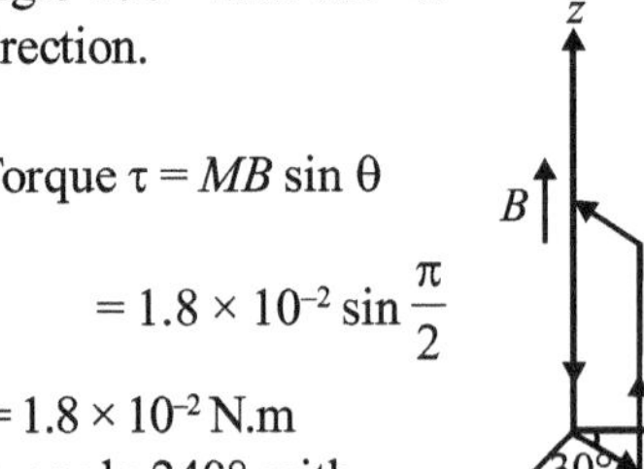

(e) Dipole moment is along +z direction.

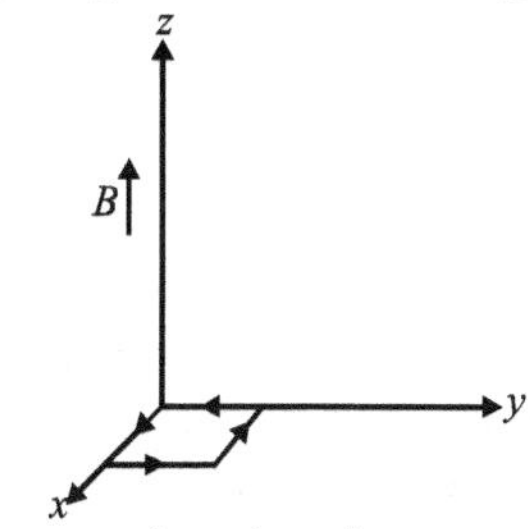

Torque $\vec{\tau} = \vec{M} \times \vec{B} = 1.8 \times 10^{-2} \, \hat{k} \times \hat{k} = 0$

Potential energy $U = \vec{M} . \vec{B}$

$U = -1.8 \times 10^{-2} \left(\hat{k}.\hat{k} \right) = -1.8 \times 10^{-2} \, \text{J}$

negative sign shows equilibrium is stable.

(f) Dipole moment is along $-z$ direction

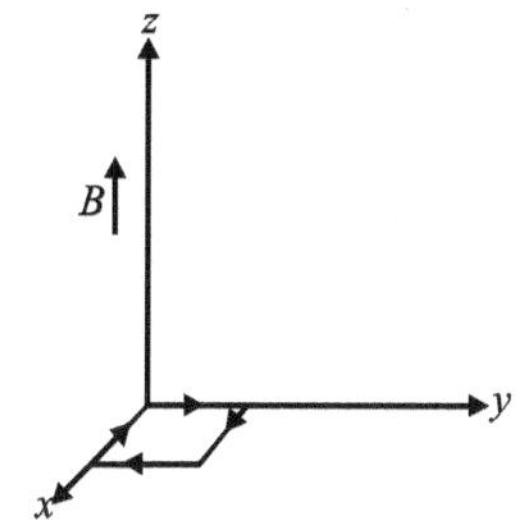

Torque $\vec{\tau} = \vec{M} \times \vec{B} = 1.8 \times 10^{-2} \left(-\hat{k}.\hat{k} \right) = 0$

Potential energy, $U = -\vec{M} . \vec{B} = +1.8 \times 10^{-2} \, \text{J}$

Positive energy so, equilibrium is unstable.

4.25. **A circular coil of 20 turns and radius 10 cm is placed in a uniform magnetic field of 0.10 T normal to the plane of the coil. If the current in the coil is 5.0 A, what is the**

(a) **total torque on the coil,**

(b) **total force on the coil,**

(c) **average force on each electron in the coil due to the magnetic field?**

(The coil is made of copper wire of cross-sectional area 10^{-5} m^2 and the free electron density in copper is given to about 10^{29} m^{-3}.)

Sol. The magnetic field is normal to the plane of the coil, so condition of minimum torque.

(a) Torque on the coil

$\tau = NI_{AB} \sin \theta$

Here, $\theta = 0° \therefore \tau = 0$

(b) Force on every element of the coil cancelled force on corresponding element. Therefore, net force on the coil is zero.

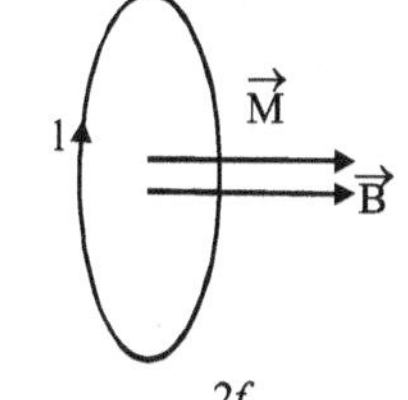

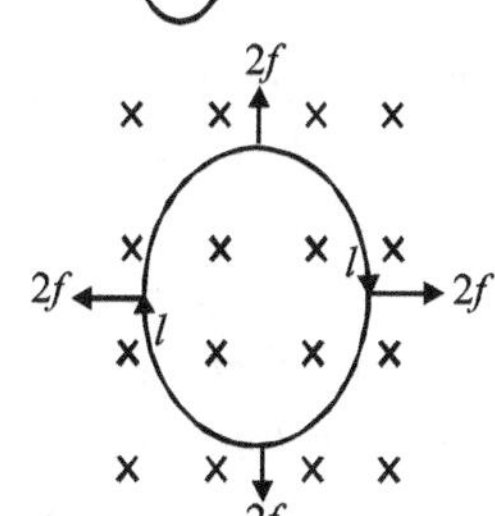

(c) To calculate force on each electron, let us find drift velocity.

$I = Anev$

$5 = 10^{-5} \times 10^{29} \times 1.6 \times 10^{-19} v_d$

or $v_d = 3.125 \times 10^{-5} \, \text{ms}^{-1}$

Now force, $F = ev_d B$

$F = 1.6 \times 10^{-19} \times 3.125 \times 10^{-5} \times 0.1 = 5 \times 10^{-25} \, \text{N}$

4.26. **A solenoid 60 cm long and of radius 4.0 cm has 3 layers of windings of 300 turns each. A 2.0 cm long wire of mass 2.5 g lies inside the solenoid (near its centre) normal to its axis; both the wire and the axis of the solenoid are in the horizontal plane. The wire is connected through two leads parallel to the axis of the solenoid to an extenal battery which supplies a current of 6.0 A in the wire. What value of current [with appropriate sense of circulation] in the windings the solenoid can support the weight of the wire? g = 9.8 ms^{-2}.**

Sol. Magnetic field in the solenoid

$B = \mu_0 nl$

where $n = \dfrac{300 \times 3}{60 \times 10^{-2}} = 1500 \, \dfrac{\text{turns}}{\text{m}}$

$B = 4\pi \times 10^{-7} \times 1500 \times I = 18.84 \, I \times 10^{-4} \, \text{T}$

A current carrying wire is suspended inside solenoid and a current $I = 6.0$ A is flowing in it.

To balance the weight of the wire by the magnetic force

$IBl = mg$

or, $6 \times [18.84 \, I \times 10^{-4}] \times 2 \times 10^{-2} = 2.5 \times 10^{-3} \times 9.8$

$\therefore \quad I = 108.4 \, \text{A}.$

4.27. **A galvanometer coil has a resistance of 12Ω and the metre show full scale deflection for a current of 3 mA. How will you convert the metre into a voltmeter of range 0 to 18 V?**

Sol. By using the formula

$R_V = \dfrac{V}{I_g} - G$

We can calculate required resistance to be connected in series.

$R_V = \dfrac{18}{3 \times 10^{-3}} - 12 = 5,988 \, \Omega$

4.28. **A galvanometer coil has a resistance of 15 Ω and the metre shows full scale deflection for a current of 4 mA. How will you convert the metre into an ammeter of range 0 to 6 A?**

Sol. For converting galvanometer into ammeter of required range, required shunt can be calculated by using formula

$S = \dfrac{I_g \, G}{I - I_g} = \dfrac{4 \times 10^{-3} \times 15}{6 - 0.004} = 0.01\Omega = 10 \, \text{m}\Omega.$

Past year Exercise

Multiple Choice Question

1. The magnetic dipole moment of a current carrying coil does *not* depend upon
   (a) number of turns of the coil.
   (b) cross-sectional area of the coil.
   (c) current flowing in the coil.
   (d) material of the turns of the coil.

Very Short Answer Questions

2. A beam of α-particles projected along + X-axis, experiences a force due to a magnetic field along the + Y-axis. What is the direction of the magnetic field?

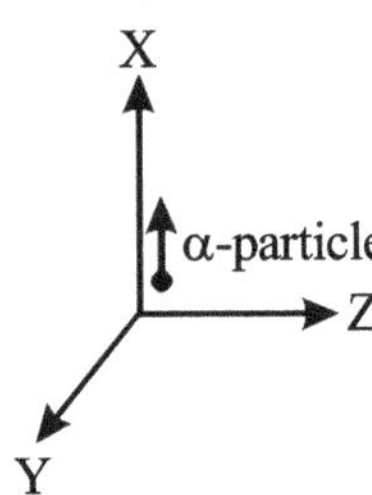

3. Use the expression $\mathbf{F} = q\,(\mathbf{v} \times \mathbf{B})$, to define the SI unit of magnetic field.

4. A narrow beam of protons and deuterons, each having the same momentum, enters a region of uniform magnetic field directed perpendicular to their direction of momentum. What would be the ratio of the radii of circular path described by them?

5. Two particles A and B of masses m and 2m have charges q and 2q respectively. They are moving with velocities v_1 and v_2 respectively, in the same direction, enters the same magnetic field, B acting normally to their direction of motion. If the two forces F_A and F_B acting on them are in the ratio of 1 : 2, find the ratio of their velocities.

6. Is the steady electric current the only source of magnetic field? Justify your answer.

7. Using the concept of force between two infinitely long parallel current carrying conductors, define one ampere of current.

8. Write the expression, in a vector form, for the Lorentz magnetic force due to a charge moving with velocity in a magnetic field . What is the direction of the magnetic force?

9. The field lines of a negative point charge are as shown in the figure. Does the kinetic energy of a small negative charge increase or decrease in going from B to A?

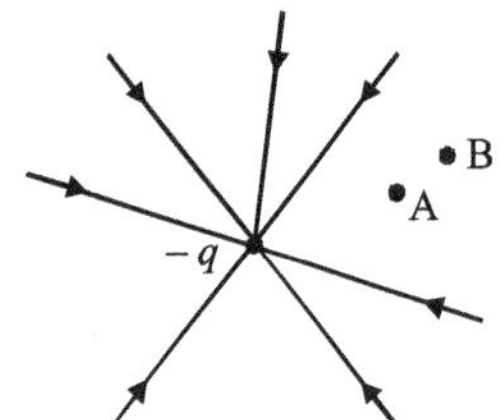

10. Write the underlying principle of a moving coil galvanometer.

Short Answer Questions

11. A square coil of side 10 cm has 20 turns and carries a current of 12 A. The coil is suspended vertically and normal to the plane of the coil makes an angle θ with the direction of a uniform horizontal magnetic field of 0.80 T. If the torque, experienced by the coil equals 0.96 N-m, find the value of θ.

12. An electron and a proton moving with a same speed enter the same magnetic field region at right angles to the direction of the field. Show the trajectory followed by the two particles in the magnetic field. Find the ratio of the radii of the circular paths which the particles may describe.

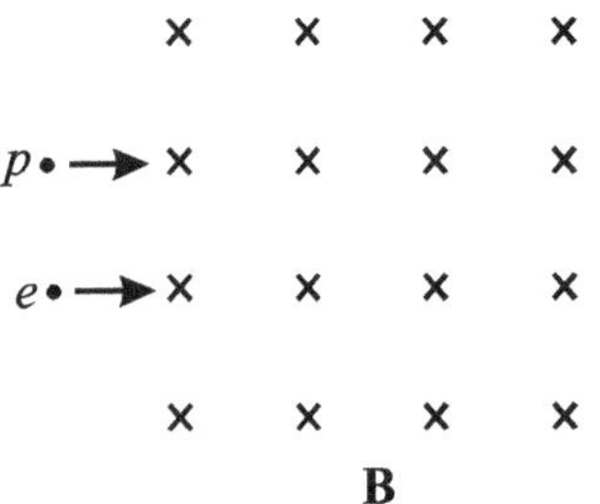

13. Obtain, with the help of necessary diagram, the expression for the magnetic field in the interior of a toroid carrying current.

14. State Biot-Savart law and give the mathematical expression for it.
    How does a circular loop carrying current behave as a magnet?

15. Write the expression for Lorentz magnetic field on a particle of charge q moving with velocity $\mathbf{v}$ in a magnetic field $\mathbf{B}$. Show that no work is done by this force on the charged particle.

16. A circular coil of closely wound N turns and radius, r carries a current, I. Write the expression for the following
    (i) the magnetic field at its centre.
    (ii) the magnetic moment of this coil.

17. Starting from the expression for the energy $W = \frac{1}{2} LI^2$, stored in a solenoid of self-inductance L to build up the current I, obtain the expression for the magnetic energy in terms of the magnetic field B, area A and length l of the solenoid having n number of turns per unit length.

    Hence, show that the energy density is given by $\frac{B^2}{2m_0}$.

18. A wire AB is carrying a steady current of 6 A and is lying on the table. Another wire CD carrying 4A is held directly above AB at a height of 1 mm. Find the mass per unit length of the wire CD so that it remains suspended at its position when left free. Give the direction of the current flowing in CD with respect to that in AB.
    [Take the value of $g = 10\,\text{ms}^{-2}$]

19. (a) Define the current sensitivity of a galvanometer.
    (b) The coil area of a galvanometer is 25×10^{-4} m^2. It consists of 150 turns of a wire and is in a magnetic field of 0.15 T. The restoring torque constant of the suspension fibre is 10^{-6} N m per degree. Assuming the magnetic field to be radial, calculate the maximum current that can be measured by the galvanometer, if the scale can accommodate $30°$ deflection.

20. Use Biot-Savart law to derive the expression for the magnetic field on the axis of a current carrying circular loop of radius R.
    Draw the magnetic field lines due to a circular wire carrying current I.

21. (a) Write an expression of magnetic moment associated with a current (I) carrying circular coil of radius r having N turns.
    (b) Consider the above mentioned coil placed in YZ plane with its centre at the origin. Derive expression for the value of magnetic field due to it at point $(x, 0, 0)$.

OR

(a) Define current sensitivity of a galvanometer. Write its expression.
(b) A galvanometer has resistance G and shows full scale deflection for current I_g.
    (i) How can it be converted into an ammeter to measure current upto I_0 $(I_0 > I_g)$?
    (ii) What is the effective resistance of this ammeter?

22. (a) Depict the magnetic field lines due to a circular current carrying loop showing the direction of field lines.
    (b) A current I is flowing in a conductor placed along the x-axis as shown in the figure. Find the magnitude and direction of the magnetic field due to a small current element $d\vec{\ell}$ lying at the origin at points (i) (0, d, 0) and (ii) (0, 0, d).

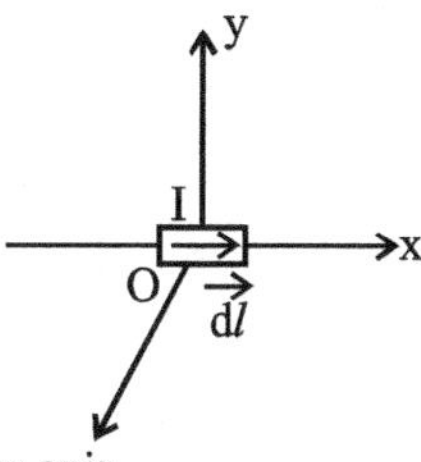

23. (a) Briefly explain how a galvanometer is converted into an ammeter.
    (b) A galvanometer coil has a resistance of 15 Ω and it shows full scale deflection for a current of 4 mA. Convert it into an ammeter of range 0 to 6 A.

24. Find the condition under which the charged particles moving with different speeds in the presence of electric and magnetic field vectors can be used to select charged particles of a particular speed.

25. (a) State Biot - Savart law and express this law in the vector form.
    (b) Two identical circular coils, P and Q each of radius R, carrying currents 1 A and $\sqrt{3}$A respectively, are placed concentrically and perpendicular to each other lying in the XY and YZ planes. Find the magnitude and direction of the net magnetic field at the centre of the coils.

26. Two long straight parallel wires A and B separated by a distance d, carry equal current I flowing in same direction as shown in the figure.

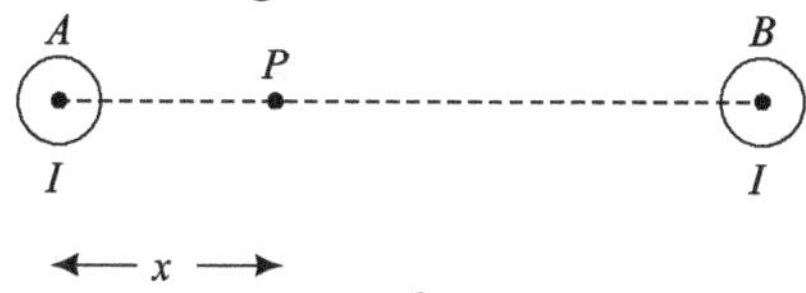

(a) Find the magnetic field at a point P situated between them at a distance x from one wire.
(b) Show graphically the variation of the magnetic field with distance x for $0 < x < d$.

NCERT Exemplar

Multiple Choice Questions

1. Two charged particles traverse identical helical paths in a completely opposite sense in a uniform magnetic field $\mathbf{B} = B_0\hat{\mathbf{k}}$.
   (a) They have equal z-components of momenta
   (b) They must have equal charges
   (c) They necessarily represent a particle, anti-particle pair
   (d) The charge to mass ratio satisfy
   $$\left(\frac{e}{m}\right)_1 + \left(\frac{e}{m}\right)_2 = 0$$

2. Biot-Savart law indicates that the moving electrons (velocity v) produce a magnetic field $\mathbf{B}$ such that
   (a) B is perpendicular of v
   (b) B is parallel to v
   (c) it obeys inverse cube law
   (d) it is along the line joining the electron and point of observationt.

3. A current carrying circular loop of radius R is placed in the x-y plane with centre at the origin. Half of the loop with x > 0 is now bent so that it now lies in the y-z plane.
   (a) The magnitude of magnetic moment now diminishes
   (b) The magnetic moment does not change
   (c) The magnitude of B at $(0, 0, z)$, $z > R$ increases
   (d) The magnitude of B at $(0, 0, z)$, $z \gg R$ is unchanged

4. An electron is projected with uniform velocity along the axis of a current carrying long solenoid. Which of the following is true?
    (a) The electron will be accelerated along the axis
    (b) The electron path will be circular about the axis
    (c) The electron will experience a force at 45° to the axis and hence execute a helical path
    (d) The electron will continue to move with uniform velocity along the axis of the solenoid

5. In a cyclotron, a charged particle
    (a) undergoes acceleration all the time
    (b) speeds up between the dees because of the magnetic field
    (c) speeds up in a dees
    (d) slows down within a dee and speeds up between dees

Very Short Answer Questions

6. Two long wires carrying current I_1 and I_2 are arranged as shown in Fig.. The one carrying current I_1 is along is the x-axis. The other carrying current I_2 is along a line parallel to the y-axis given by $x = 0$ and $z = d$. Find the force exerted at O_2 because of the wire along the x-axis.

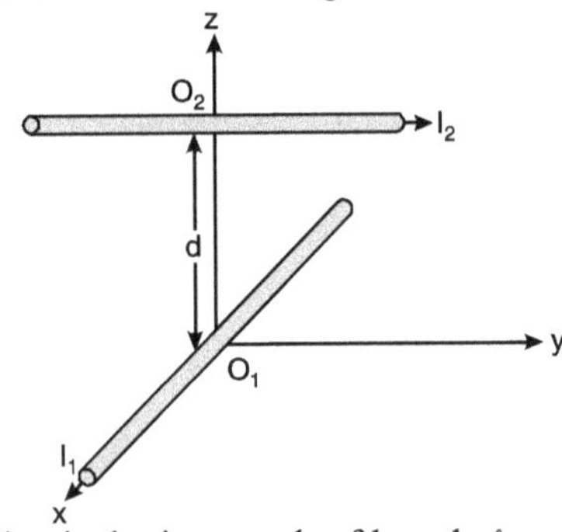

7. Four identical wires, each of length ℓ, are bent into the four loops P, Q, R and S, as shown, and placed in a uniform magnetic field $\vec{B}$. If they carry the same current I, which loop will experience the maximum torque ?

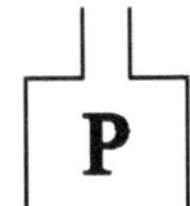 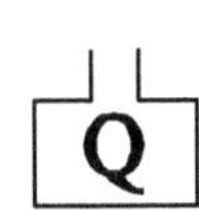  

8. Why is the magnetic field strength inside a current carrying loop of wire greater than the field strength about a straight section of wire ?

Short Answer Questions

9. A current carrying loop consists of 3 identical quarter circles of radius R, lying in the positive quadrants of the x-y, y-z and z-x planes with their centres at the origin, joined together. Find the direction and magnitude of **B** at the origin.

10. A long straight wire carrying current of 25A rests on a table as shown in Fig.. Another wire PQ of length 1m, mass 2.5 g carries the same current but in the opposite direction. The wire PQ is free to slide up and down. To what height will PQ rise?

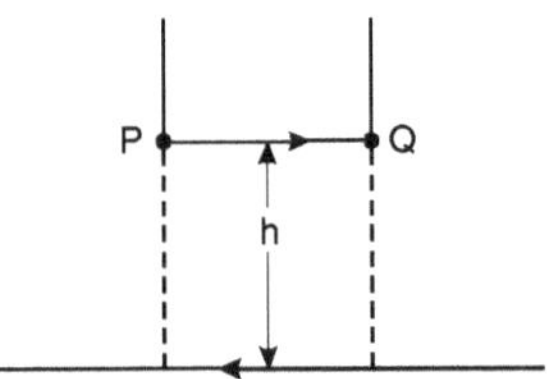

11. When a bar magnet is dropped through a vertical length of copper pipe, it falls noticeably more slowly than it does when it is dropped through a vertical length of plastic pipe. If the copper pipe is long enough, the dropped magnet will reach a terminal falling speed, Why ?

12. Two circular coils X and Y having radii R and R/2 respectively are placed in horizontal plane with their centres coinciding with each other. Coil X has a current I flowing through it in the clockwise sense. What must be the current in coil Y to make the total magnetic field at the common centre of the two coils, zero?

    With the same currents flowing in the two coils, if the coil Y is not lifted vertically upwards through a distance R, what would be the net magnetic field at the centre of coil Y?

Objective Practice Exercise

Multiple Choice Questions

DIRECTIONS : *This section contains multiple choice questions. Each question has four choices (a), (b), (c) and (d) out of which only one is correct.*

1. A charge q is moving with a velocity v parallel to a magnetic field B. Force on the charge due to magnetic field is
    (a) q v B   (b) q B/v
    (c) zero   (d) B v/q

2. Consider a moving charged particle in a region of magnetic field. Which of the following statements are correct?
    (a) If **v** is parallel to **B**, then path of particle is spiral.
    (b) If **v** is perpendicular to **B**, then path of particle is a circle.
    (c) If **v** has a component along **B**, then path of particle is zig-zag.
    (d) If **v** is along **B**, then path of particle is a circle.

3. Which of the above statements is/are incorrect?
   A velocity selector; (a region of perpendicular electric and magnetic field)
   (a) allows charged particles to pass straight when $v = E/B$.
   (b) deflects particles in the direction of electric field when $v < E/B$.
   (c) deflects particles in a direction perpendicular to both v and B, when $v < E/B$.
   (d) deflects all particles in a direction perpendicular to both E and B.

4. Select the incorrect statement about Lorentz Force.
   (a) In presence of electric field $\vec{E}(r)$ and magnetic field $\vec{B}(r)$ the force on a moving electric charge is
   $$\vec{F} = q[\vec{E}(r) + v \times \vec{B}(r)]$$
   (b) The force, due to magnetic field on a negative charge is opposite to that on a positive charge.
   (c) The force due to magnetic field become zero if velocity and magnetic field are parallel or antiparallel.
   (d) For a static charge the magnetic force is maximum.

5. Ampere's circuital law states that
   (a) the surface integral of magnetic field over the open surface is equal to μ_0 times the total current passing through the surface.
   (b) the surface integral of magnetic field over the open surface is equal to μ_0 times the total current passing near the surface.
   (c) the line integral of magnetic field along the boundary of the open surface is equal to μ_0 times the total current passing near the surface.
   (d) the line integral of magnetic field along the boundary of the open surface is equal to μ_0 times the total current passing through the surface.

6. A charged particle enters in a uniform magnetic field with a certain velocity. The power delivered to the particle by the magnetic field depends on
   (a) force exerted by magnetic field and velocity of the particle.
   (b) angular speed ω and radius r of the circular path.
   (c) angular speed ω and acceleration of the particle.
   (d) None of these

7. A proton moving with a constant velocity passes through a region of space without any change in its velocity. If E and B represent the electric and magnetic fields respectively, this region of space may not have
   (a) $E = 0, B = 0$　　　　(b) $E = 0, B \neq 0$
   (c) $E \neq 0, B = 0$　　　　(d) $E \neq 0, B \neq 0$

8. A charged particle with charge q enters a region of constant, uniform and mutually orthogonal fields $\vec{E}$ and $\vec{B}$ with a velocity $\vec{v}$ perpendicular to both $\vec{E}$ and $\vec{B}$, and comes out without any change in magnitude or direction of $\vec{v}$. Then
   (a) $\vec{v} = \vec{B} \times \vec{E}/E^2$　　　　(b) $\vec{v} = \vec{E} \times \vec{B}/B^2$
   (c) $\vec{v} = \vec{B} \times \vec{E}/B^2$　　　　(d) $\vec{v} = \vec{E} \times \vec{B}/E^2$

9. If an electron and a proton having same momenta enter perpendicular to a magnetic field, then
   (a) curved path of electron and proton will be same (ignoring the sense of revolution)
   (b) they will move undeflected
   (c) curved path of electron is more curved than that of the proton
   (d) path of proton is more curved

10. A beam of electrons is moving with constant velocity in a region having simultaneous perpendicular electric and magnetic fields of strength $20\,\text{Vm}^{-1}$ and 0.5 T respectively at right angles to the direction of motion of the electrons. Then the velocity of electrons must be
    (a) 8 m/s　　(b) 20 m/s　　(c) 40 m/s　　(d) $\dfrac{1}{40}$ m/s

11. A charge moving with velocity v in X-direction is subjected to a field of magnetic induction in negative X-direction. As a result, the charge will
    (a) remain unaffected
    (b) start moving in a circular path Y–Z plane
    (c) retard along X-axis
    (d) move along a helical path around X-axis

12. A proton (mass m and charge $+ e$) and an α-particle (mass 4m and charge $+ 2e$) are projected with the same kinetic energy at right angles to the uniform magnetic field. Which one of the following statements will be true ?
    (a) The α-particle will be bent in a circular path with a small radius that for the proton
    (b) The radius of the path of the α-particle will be greater than that of the proton
    (c) The α-particle and the proton will be bent in a circular path with the same radius
    (d) The α-particle and the proton will go through the field in a straight line

13. A positively charged particle moving into east enters a region of uniform magnetic field directed vertically upwards. The particle will
    (a) continue to move due east
    (b) move in a circular orbit with its speed unchanged
    (c) move in a circular orbit with its speed increased
    (d) gets deflected vertically upwards.

14. The negatively and uniformly charged nonconducting disc as shown is rotated clockwise.
    The direction of the magnetic field at point A in the plane of the disc is
    (a) into the page
    (b) out of the page
    (c) up the page
    (d) down the page

15. A proton (mass $= 1.67 \times 10^{-27}$ kg and charge $= 1.6 \times 10^{-19}$ C) enters perpendicular to a magnetic field of intensity 2 weber/m^2 with a velocity 3.4×10^7 m/sec. The acceleration of the proton should be
    (a) 6.5×10^{15} m/sec^2　　　　(b) 6.5×10^{13} m/sec^2
    (c) 6.5×10^{11} m/sec^2　　　　(d) 6.5×10^{9} m/sec^2

16. The magnetic field around a long straight current carrying wire is
  (a) spherical symmetry   (b) cylindrical symmetry
  (c) cubical symmetry   (d) unsymmetrical

17. A current is passed through a straight wire. The magnetic field established around it has its lines of force
  (a) circular and endless   (b) oval in shape and endless
  (c) straight   (d) All of the above

18. A current carrying coil is subjected to a uniform magnetic field. The coil will orient so that its plane becomes
  (a) inclined at $45°$ to the magnetic field
  (b) inclined at any arbitrary angle to the magnetic field
  (c) parallel to the magnetic field
  (d) perpendicular to the magnetic field

19. A small current element of length $d\ell$ and carrying current is placed at $(1, 1, 0)$ and is carrying current in '$+z$' direction. If magnetic field at origin be $\vec{B}_1$ and at point $(2, 2, 0)$ be $\vec{B}_2$ then
  (a) $\vec{B}_1 = \vec{B}_2$ (b) $|\vec{B}_1| = |2\vec{B}_2|$
  (c) $\vec{B}_1 = -\vec{B}_2$ (d) $\vec{B}_1 = -2\vec{B}_2$

20. A current I flows along the length of an infinitely long, straight, thin walled pipe. Then
  (a) the magnetic field at all points inside the pipe is the same, but not zero
  (b) the magnetic field is zero only on the axis of the pipe
  (c) the magnetic field is different at different points inside the pipe
  (d) the magnetic field at any point inside the pipe is zero

21. If a copper rod carries a direct current, the magnetic field associated with the current will be
  (a) only inside the rod
  (b) only outside the rod
  (c) both inside and outside the rod
  (d) neither inside nor outside the rod

22. Biot-Savart law indicates that the moving electrons velocity (V) produce a magnetic field B such that
  (a) B P V   (b) $B \perp V$
  (c) it obeys inverse cube law
  (d) it is along the line joining electron and point of observation

23. Ampere's circuital law is equivalent to
  (a) Biot-Savart law   (b) Coulomb's law
  (c) Faraday's law   (d) Kirchhoff's law

24. A solenoid of length 1.5 m and 4 cm diameter possesses 10 turns per cm. A current of 5A is flowing through it, the magnetic induction at axis inside the solenoid is
  ($\mu_0 = 4\pi \times 10^{-7}$ weber amp^{-1} m^{-1})
  (a) $4\pi \times 10^{-5}$ gauss   (b) $2\pi \times 10^{-5}$ gauss
  (c) $4\pi \times 10^{-5}$ tesla   (d) $2\pi \times 10^{-5}$ tesla

25. The magnetic field B at a point on one end of a solenoid having n turns per metre length and carrying a current of i ampere is given by
  (a) $\dfrac{\mu_0 ni}{e}$ (b) $\dfrac{1}{2}\mu_0 ni$ (c) $4\pi\mu_0 ni$ (d) ni

26. A long solenoid has 200 turns per cm and carries a current i. The magnetic field at its centre is 6.28×10^{-2} Weber/m^2. Another long solenoid has 100 turns per cm and it carries a current $\dfrac{i}{3}$. The value of the magnetic field at its centre is
  (a) 1.05×10^{-2} Weber/m^2 (b) 1.05×10^{-5} Weber/m^2
  (c) 1.05×10^{-3} Weber/m^2 (d) 1.05×10^{-4} Weber/m^2

27. Two concentric circular coils of ten turns each are situated in the same plane. Their radii are 20 and 40 cm and they carry respectively 0.2 and 0.4 ampere current in opposite direction. The magnetic field in weber/m^2 at the centre is
  (a) $\mu_0/80$ (b) $7\mu_0/80$ (c) $(5/4)\mu_0$ (d) zero

28. A coil of one turn is made of a wire of certain length and then from the same length a coil of two turns is made. If the same current is passed in both the cases, then the ratio of the magnetic inductions at their centres will be
  (a) $2 : 1$ (b) $1 : 4$ (c) $4 : 1$ (d) $1 : 2$

29. Magnetic field intensity at the centre of a coil of 50 turns, radius 0.5 m and carrying a current of 2 A is
  (a) 0.5×10^{-5} T   (b) 1.25×10^{-4} T
  (c) 3×10^{-5} T   (d) 4×10^{-5} T

30. A coil carrying electric current is placed in uniform magnetic field, then
  (a) torque is formed   (b) e.m.f is induced
  (c) both (a) and (b) are   (d) None of these

31. Two long wires are hanging freely. They are joined first in parallel and then in series and then are connected with a battery. In both cases which type of force acts between the two wires?
  (a) Attraction force when in parallel and repulsion force when in series
  (b) Repulsion force when in parallel and attraction force when in series
  (c) Repulsion force in both cases
  (d) Attraction force in both cases

32. A moving coil galvanometer has N number of turns in a coil of effective area A, it carries a current I. The magnetic field B is radial. The torque acting on the coil is
  (a) NA^2B^2I (b) $NABI^2$ (c) N^2ABI (d) $NABI$

33. A conducting circular loop of radius r carries a constant current i. It is placed in a uniform magnetic field $\vec{B}_0$ such that $\vec{B}_0$ is perpendicular to the plane of the loop. The magnetic force acting on the loop is
  (a) irB_0 (b) $2\pi irB_0$ (c) zero   (d) πirB_0

34. Two long conductors, separated by a distance d carry current I_1 and I_2 in the same direction. They exert a force F on each other. Now the current in one of them is increased to two times and its direction is reversed. The distance is also increased to $3d$. The new value of the force between them is
  (a) $-\dfrac{2F}{3}$ (b) $\dfrac{F}{3}$ (c) $-2F$ (d) $-\dfrac{F}{3}$

35. A current of 5 ampere is flowing in a wire of length 1.5 metres. A force of 7.5 N acts on it when it is placed in a uniform magnetic field of 2 tesla. The angle between the magnetic field and the direction of the current is

(a) 30° (b) 45°   (c) 60°   (d) 90°

36. A straight wire of length 0.5 metre and carrying a current of 1.2 ampere is placed in uniform magnetic field of induction 2 tesla. The magnetic field is perpendicular to the length of the wire. The force on the wire is

(a) 2.4 N (b) 1.2 N (c) 3.0 N (d) 2.0 N

37. An electric current of 30 ampere is flowing in each of two parallel conducting wires placed 5 cm apart. The force acting per unit length on either of the wires will be

(a) 3.6×10^{-3} N/m   (b) 3.6×10^{-3} dyne/cm

(c) 3.6×10^{-5} N/m   (d) 3.6×10^{-2} N/m

38. The distance between the wires of electric mains is 12 cm. These wires experience 4 mg wt. per unit length. The value of current flowing in each wire will be

(a) 4.85 A   (b) 0

(c) 4.85×10^{-2} A   (d) 4.85×10^{4} A

39. A current carrying conductor placed in a magnetic field experiences maximum force when angle between current and magnetic field is

(a) $3\pi/4$ (b) $\pi/2$ (c) $\pi/4$ (d) zero

40. A current of 3 A is flowing in a linear conductor having a length of 40 cm. The conductor is placed in a magnetic field of strength 500 gauss and makes an angle of 30° with the direction of the field. It experiences a force of magnitude

(a) 3×10^{-4} N   (b) 3×10^{-2} N

(c) 3×10^{2} N   (d) 3×10^{4} N

41. Two straight horizontal parallel wires are carrying the same current in the same direction, d is the distance between the wires. You are provided with a small freely suspended magnetic needle. At which of the following positions will the orientation of the needle be independent of the magnitude of the current in the wires ?

(a) At a distance $d/2$ from any of the wires

(b) At a distance $d/2$ from any of the wires in the horizontal plane

(c) Anywhere on the circumference of a vertical circle of radius d and centre halfway between the wires

(d) At points halfway between the wires in the horizontal plane

42. Two long parallel wires are at a distance of 1 metre. Both of them carry 5 ampere of current. The force of attraction per unit length between the two wires is

(a) 50×10^{-7} N/m   (b) 2×10^{-8} N/m

(c) 5×10^{-8} N/m   (d) 10^{-7} N/m

43. A and B are two conductors carrying a current i in the same direction. x and y are two electron beams moving in the same direction. Then

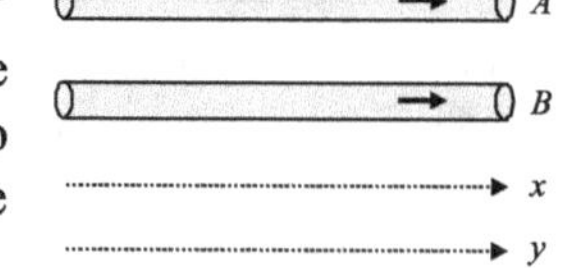

(a) there will be repulsion betwen A and B, attraction between x and y

(b) there will be attraction between A and B, repulsion between x and y

(c) there will be repulsion between A and B and also x and y

(d) there will be attraction between A and B and also x and y

Chapter Test

Time : 30 minutes   **Max. Marks : 15**

Direction :

Each question number **1-15** carry **1 mark** each.

1. The magnetic induction at a point P which is at a distance of 4 cm from a long current carrying wire is 10^{-3} T. The field of induction at a distance 12 cm from the current will be

(a) 3.33×10^{-4} T   (b) 1.11×10^{-4} T

(c) 3×10^{-3} T   (d) 9×10^{-3} T

2. A conducting circular loop of radius r carries a constant current i. It is placed in a uniform magnetic field **B** such that B is perpendicular to the plane of the loop. The magnetic force acting on the loop is

(a) i r B   (b) $2\pi r i B$

(c) zero   (d) $\pi r i B$

3. A galvanometer of resistance 100 Ω gives a full scale deflection for a current of 10^{-5} A. To convert it into a ammeter capable of measuring upto 1 A, we should connect a resistance of

(a) 1 Ω in parallel   (b) 10^{-3} Ω in parallel

(c) 10^{5} Ω in series   (d) 100 Ω in series

4. A charged particle of mass m and charge q travels on a circular path of radius r that is perpendicular to a magnetic field B. The time taken by the particle to complete one revolution is

(a) $\dfrac{2\pi q^2 B}{m}$ (b) $\dfrac{2\pi m q}{B}$

(c) $\dfrac{2\pi m}{qB}$ (d) $\dfrac{2\pi q B}{m}$

DIRECTIONS (Qs. 5-6) : *Each of these questions contains an assertion followed by reason. Read them carefully and answer the question on the basis of following options. You have to select the one that best describes the two statements.*

(a) If both Assertion and Reason are correct and the Reason is a correct explanation of the Assertion.

(b) If both Assertion and Reason are correct but Reason is not a correct explanation of the Assertion.

(c) If the Assertion is correct but Reason is incorrect.

(d) If the Assertion is incorrect but the Reason is correct.

5. **Assertion:** Electron moving perpendicular to $\vec{B}$ will perform circular motion ?

Reason: Force by magnetic field is perpendicular to velocity

6. **Assertion :** If the current in a solenoid is reversed in direction while keeping the same magnitude, the magnetic field energy stored in the solenoid remains unchanged.

Reason : Magnetic field energy density is proportional to the magnetic field.

DIRECTIONS : (Qs. 7-11) *are case based questions.*

A particle of mass m and charge q, moving with velocity V enters Region II normal to the boundary as shown in the figure. Region II has a uniform magnetic field B perpendicular to the plane of the paper. The length of the Region II is l.

Region
Region   II   Region
I   III
V
l

7. (a) The particle enters Region III only if its velocity $V > \dfrac{qB}{m}$

(b) The particle enters Region III only if its velocity $V < \dfrac{qlB}{m}$

(c) The particle enters Region III only if its velocity $V = \dfrac{qlB}{m}$

(d) All of the above

8. Path length of the particle in Region II is maximum when

(a) velocity $V = \dfrac{qlB}{2m}$

(b) velocity $V = \dfrac{2qlB}{m}$

(c) velocity

(d) velocity $V = \dfrac{4qlB}{m}$

9. Time spent in Region II as long as the particle returns to Region I is

(a) two times if velocity V is doubled

(b) halved if velocity is doubled

(c) halved if velocity is halved

(d) same for any value of V

10. If the direction of the initial velocity of the charged particle is neither along nor perpendicular to that of the magnetic field, then the orbit will be

(a) a straight line

(b) an ellipse

(c) a circle

(d) a helix

11. A charged particle moves with velocity $\vec{V}$ in a uniform magnetic field $\vec{B}$. The magnetic force experienced by the particle is

(a) always zero

(b) never zero

(c) zero, if $\vec{B}$ and $\vec{V}$ are perpendicular

(d) zero, if $\vec{B}$ and $\vec{V}$ are parallel

12. An electron and a proton, having equal momentum enter a uniform field at right angles to the field lines. What will be the ratio of the radii of curvature of their trajectories?

13. An electron is moving with velocity v along the axis of a long straight solenoid carrying current I. What will be the force acting on the electron due to the magnetic field of the solenoid?

14. Write the expression for the magnitude of force per unit length between two infinitely long parallel, straight current carrying conductors. Hence define the SI unit of current.

15. How can a moving coil galvanometer be converted to (i) an ammeter and (ii) a voltmeter?

Solutions 

1. **(c)** Field at the center of a circular coil of radius r is

$$B = \frac{\mu_0 I}{2r}$$

2. **(a)** $B = \frac{\mu_0 I}{2r} \times \frac{\theta}{2\pi} = \frac{\mu_0 I\theta}{4\pi r}$

3. **(c)** $B = \mu_0 N_0 i; \ B_1 = (\mu_0)\left(\frac{N_0}{2}\right)(2\,i) = \mu_0 N_0 i = B$

$\Rightarrow \ B_1 = B$

4. **(b)** $d\vec{B} = \frac{\mu_0}{4\pi} \frac{q(\vec{v} \times \vec{r})}{r^3}$ i.e. $\vec{B} \perp r \ \vec{v} \ \& \ \vec{r}$ both

5. **(b)** Magnetic field is given by $B = \frac{\mu_0 i}{2\pi r}$ i.e., $B \propto \frac{1}{r}$ which implies that field has cylindrical symmetry.

6. **(c)** Field at the center of a circular coil of radius r is

$$B = \frac{\mu_0 I}{2r}$$

7. **(c)**

8. **(d)** Ampere's circuital law can be derived from Biot-Savart law

9. **(c)** The magnetic field of two equal halfs of the loop is equal and opposite and so $\vec{B} = 0$.

10. **(a)**   **11.** **(b)**

12. **(b)** Magnetic field at a point on one end of a solenoid

$$B = \frac{1}{2}\mu_0 ni$$

13. **(b)**

14. **(b)** The magnetic field from the centre of wire of radius R is given by

$$B = \left(\frac{\mu_0 I}{2R^2}\right)r \quad (r < R) \Rightarrow B \propto r$$

and $B = \frac{\mu_0 I}{2\pi r} \quad (r > R) \Rightarrow B \propto \frac{1}{r}$

From the above descriptions, we can say that the graph (b) is a correct representation.

15. **(a)** $B = \frac{\mu_0 I}{2r} \times \frac{\theta}{2\pi} = \frac{\mu_0 I\theta}{4\pi r}$

16. **(c)** Since n is an even number, we can assume the wires in pairs such that the two wires forming a pair is placed diametrically opposite to each other on the surface of cylinder. The fields produced on the axis by them are equal and opposite and can get cancelled with each other.

17. Total magnetic field at the centre of the loop will be zero because direction of magnetic field due to semicircle APB and semicircle AQB are opposite and magnitude is equal.

18. The magnetic field inside the pipe is zero and outside it is maximum.

19. Magnetic field intensity at the centre of a circular coil

$$B = \frac{\mu_0 nI}{2r}$$

New field $B' = \frac{\mu_0 n(2I)}{2 \times r/2} = 2B$

$\therefore$ Magnetic field will increase two times.

20. From Biot – Savart's law, the magnetic field due to an element of length $2l$ of the current carrying conductor is

$$dB = \frac{\mu_0}{4\pi} \frac{Id\ell \sin\theta}{r^2}$$

Here $\theta = 90°$ ($\because \ d\ell$ is tangential, angle between the radius and the tangent is $90°$)

$$\therefore \quad dB = \frac{\mu_0}{4\pi} \cdot \frac{Id\ell}{r^2}$$

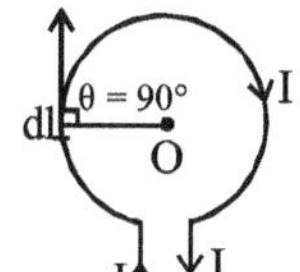

$\therefore$ Total magnetic field at the centre O due to the whole circular coil

$$= B = \int dB = \frac{\mu_0 I}{4\pi r^2}\int d\ell = \frac{\mu_0 I}{4\pi r^2}\cdot 2\pi r = \frac{\mu_0 I}{2r}$$

For a coil of n number of turns, $B = \frac{\mu_0 nI}{2r}$

It is perpendicular to the plane of the coil and directed inwards.

21. **Refer to Theory**

1. **(d)** Force, $F = qVB = \frac{mv^2}{R}$ $\therefore R = \frac{mv}{Bq}$

2. **(c)** A force which always perpendicular to velocity of the particle does no work on the particle, but changes the direction of momentum of the particle.

3. **(b)** The charged particle will move along the lines of electric field (and magnetic field). Magnetic field will exert no force. The force by electric field will be along the lines of uniform electric field. Hence the particle will move in a straight line.

4. **(b)** (i) Lorentz force depends on q, $\mathbf{v}$ and $\mathbf{B}$ (charge of the particle, the velocity and the magnetic field). Force on a negative charge is opposite to that on a positive charge.

(ii) The magnetic force $q \ [\mathbf{v} \times \mathbf{B}]$ includes a vector product of velocity and magnetic field. The vector product makes the force due to magnetic field vanish (become zero) if velocity and magnetic field are parallel or anti-parallel. The force acts in a (sideways) direction perpendicular to both the velocity and the magnetic field. Its direction is given by the screw rule.

5. **(c)** As Lorentz force is given by

$$\vec{F} = q\left(\vec{E} + \vec{V} \times \vec{B}\right) = q\vec{E} + q\left(\vec{V} \times \vec{B}\right)$$

$$\vec{F} = \vec{F}_E + \vec{F}_B$$

6. **(a)** $r = \dfrac{mv}{Bq}$ $r = \dfrac{mv}{Bq} = \dfrac{p}{Bq}$ $\left[\text{where } p = mv\right]$

$\Rightarrow r \propto$ momentum

7. **(c)** When charged particle enters perpendicularly in a magnetic field, it moves in a circular path with a constant speed. Hence its kinetic energy also remains constant.

8. **(c)** The electron moves with constant velocity without deflection. Hence, force due to magnetic field is equal and opposite to force due to electric field.

$qvB = qE \Rightarrow v = \dfrac{E}{B} = \dfrac{20}{0.5} = 40$ m/s

9. **(a)** Lorentz force acting on the particle

$$\vec{F} = q\left[\vec{E} + \vec{v} \times \vec{B}\right]$$

$$= q\left[\,3\hat{i} + \hat{j} + 2\hat{k} + \begin{vmatrix} \hat{i} & \hat{j} & \hat{k} \\ 3 & 4 & 1 \\ 1 & 1 & -3 \end{vmatrix}\right]$$

$$= q\left[3\hat{i} + \hat{j} + 2\hat{k} + \hat{i}(-12-1) - \hat{j}(-9-1) + k(3-4)\right]$$

$$F_y = 11q\hat{j}$$

10. **(a)** A moving charge experiences a force in magnetic fields. It is because of interaction of two magnetic fields, one which is produced due to the motion of charge and other in which charge is moving.

11. **(c)** Due to electric field, the force is $\vec{F} = q\vec{E}$ in the direction of $\vec{E}$. Since $\vec{E}$ is parallel to $\vec{B}$, the particle velocity $\vec{v}$ (acquired due to force $\vec{F}$) is parallel to $\vec{B}$. Hence $\vec{B}$ will not exert any force since $\vec{v} \times \vec{B} = 0$ and the motion of the particle is not affected by $\vec{B}$.

12. **(c)**

13. **(c)** Since the magnetic force is always perpendicular to the velocity of the charged particle so, work done is always zero.

14. **(d)**

15. **(d)** The magnetic force acts on moving electrons, and so net force on the conductor is non-zero.

16. **(b)**

17. **(c)** As Lorentz force is given by

$$\vec{F} = q\left(\vec{E} + \vec{V} \times \vec{B}\right) = q\vec{E} + q\left(\vec{V} \times \vec{B}\right)$$

$$\vec{F} = \vec{F}_E + \vec{F}_B$$

18. **(a)** Lorentz force, $\vec{F} = q\{\vec{E} + (\vec{v} \times \vec{B})\}$

$$\vec{v} \times \vec{B} = \begin{vmatrix} \hat{i} & \hat{j} & \hat{k} \\ 1 & 2 & 0 \\ 5 & 3 & 4 \end{vmatrix} = 8\hat{i} - 4\hat{j} - 7\hat{k}$$

$$\vec{F} = 1(2\hat{i} - 3\hat{j} + 8\hat{i} - 4\hat{j} - 7\hat{k}) = (10\hat{i} - 7\hat{j} - 7\hat{k})$$

19. **(c)**

20. **(c)** $E = vB = 2 \times 10^3 \times 1.5 = 3 \times 10^3$ V/m.

21. Pair of vectors always right angle are $\vec{F}$ and $\vec{v}$, $\vec{F}$ and $\vec{B}$.

22. $F = qvB \sin\theta$, if $\sin\theta = 1$ i.e. $\theta = 90°$ the force will be maximum.
When the charged particle will move perpendicular to the field, the force on it is maximum.

23. The electron beam will be deflected out of the plane of the paper or eastward.

24. Here, $\dfrac{mv^2}{r} = Bqv \Rightarrow r = \dfrac{mv}{Bq}$

$\dfrac{r_P}{r_e} = \dfrac{m_P}{m_e}$ $\qquad \because \; m_P > m_e$

$\therefore \quad r_P > r_e$

$\therefore \quad$ The radius of the path of electron will be smaller.

25. Since force $F = qBv$ and $q_\alpha > q_\beta$

$\therefore \quad \alpha$-particle will experience more force.

26. We have force $F = q\,(v \times B) = qvB \sin\theta$.
Since the charge is stationary, $v = 0$

$\therefore \quad F = 0$.

27. Electron move in a straight line.

28. The S.I. unit of magnetic field is tesla. (T)
The strength of magnetic field at a point is said to be 1T if a charge of 1C while moving at right angles to a magnetic field, with a velocity of 1 m/s experiences a force of 1 N at that point.

The force on a moving charged particle is $F = qBv\sin\theta$

If $\theta = 90°$, i.e. the particle moves at right angles to the magnetic field, $F = qBv$ which provides the necessary centripetal force for the circular motion of the particle. There is no linear acceleration. So no increase in linear velocity and hence in kinetic energy.

29. As, $\dfrac{mv^2}{r} = Bev \Rightarrow \dfrac{mv}{r} = Be \Rightarrow \dfrac{e}{m} = \dfrac{v}{rB}$

30. The radius (r) of circular path described by a charged particle in a magnetic field B is given by,

$$r = \dfrac{mv}{qB} \quad \left(\text{Since K.E.} = \dfrac{1}{2}mv^2 \text{ or } v = \sqrt{\dfrac{2K}{m}}\right)$$

$$= \dfrac{m}{qB}\sqrt{\dfrac{2K}{m}} = \sqrt{\dfrac{2mK}{qB}} \quad \text{i.e., } r \propto \sqrt{K}$$

i.e., when K.E. becomes one half, the radius is reduced to $\dfrac{1}{\sqrt{2}}$ times its initial value.

31. Given, $B = 0.2 \times 10^{-3}$ tesla.

$$T = ? \left(\dfrac{q}{m}\right)_{Proton} = 1.76 \times 10^{11} \text{ C/kg}$$

$$\text{K.E.} = \dfrac{1}{2}mv^2 = 25 \times 10^3 \text{ eV}$$

$$= 25 \times 10^3 \times 1.6 \times 10^{-19} \text{ J.}$$

$$T = \dfrac{2\pi m}{qB} = \dfrac{2 \times \dfrac{22}{7}}{1.76 \times 10^{11} \times 0.2 \times 10^{-3}} = 1.79 \times 10^{-7} \text{ s}$$

32. As we know, $\dfrac{mv^2}{r} = Bqv \Rightarrow r = \dfrac{mv}{Bq}$

$$\dfrac{r_1}{r_2} = \dfrac{m_1}{m_2} \cdot \dfrac{q_2}{q_1} \qquad \therefore \quad \dfrac{r_p}{r_\alpha} = \dfrac{m_p}{m_\alpha} \cdot \dfrac{q_\alpha}{q_p} = \dfrac{1}{4} \times \dfrac{2}{1}$$

$$[\because m_\alpha = 4m_p \text{ and } q_\alpha = 2q_p]$$

$$\therefore \quad \dfrac{r_p}{r_\alpha} = \dfrac{1}{2} \quad \therefore r_p = 2r_\alpha$$

$\because$ In circular motion, magnitude of velocity remains same so K.E. will not change after coming out from the magnetic field.

33. As we know, $\dfrac{1}{2}mv^2 = eV \Rightarrow m^2v^2 = 2meV$

$$\Rightarrow mv = \sqrt{2meV}$$

$$r = \dfrac{mv}{Be} = \dfrac{\sqrt{2meV}}{Be} = \sqrt{\dfrac{2mV}{B^2e}}$$

$$= \sqrt{\dfrac{2 \times 9.1 \times 10^{-31} \times 100}{0.004 \times 0.004 \times 1.6 \times 10^{-19}}} = 8.43 \times 10^{-3}\,\text{m}$$

Practice Exercise-3

1. (b) When the direction of currents are same, the force is attractive. Hence, both the wires will attract each other

Force per unit length.

$$\dfrac{F}{\ell} = \dfrac{\mu_0 i_1 i_2}{2\pi d} = \dfrac{\mu_0 i^2}{2\pi d}$$

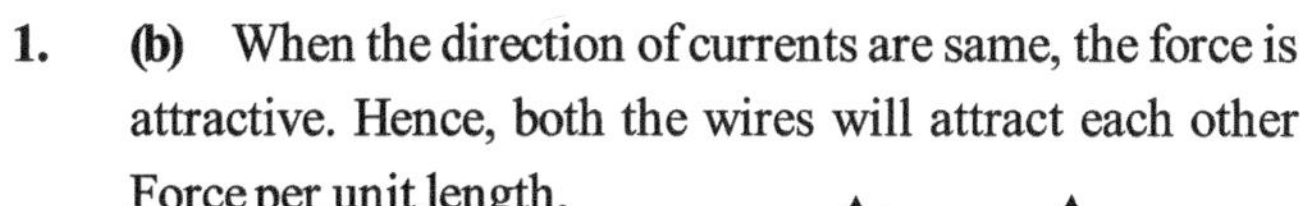

2. (b) $F \propto i_1 i_2$, so force on B due to C will be greater than that due to A. Hence net force on B acts towards C.

3. (a) Current loop acts as a magnetic dipole. Its magnetic moment is given by

$M = NIA$

where N = number of turns, I = current in a loop, A = area of the loop

From the above relation, we can conclude that magnetic dipole moment of a current loop is independent of magnetic field in which it is lying.

4. (a) $(A) \to (4)$; $(B) \to (3)$; $(C) \to (1)$; $(D) \to (2)$

5. (c)

6. (a) Because $\tau = NiAB\,\cos\theta$

7. (b) The force on the two arms parallel to the field is zero.

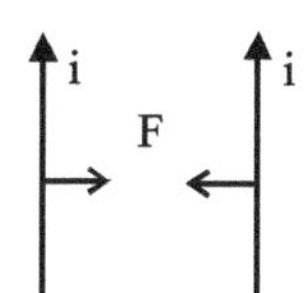

$\therefore$ Force on remaining arms $= -F$

8. (b) $F = iBl \sin\theta$. This is maximum when $\sin\theta = 1$ or $\theta = \pi/2$.

9. (b) $F = IlB$

Here, $\theta = 90°$, $I = 10\,A$

$l = 8\,\text{cm} = 8 \times 10^{-2}\,m$, $B = 0.3\,T$

$\therefore F = 10 \times 8 \times 10^{-2} \times 0.3 \times \sin 90° = 0.24\,N$

10. (b) $\tau = m\beta\sin\theta = 0.75 \times 0.20 = 0.15\,\text{Nm}$

11. (a)   **12. (c)**

13. (b) $F_m = I(\vec{\ell} \times \vec{B}) = 0$ because the directions of current $\vec{\ell}$ and magnetic field $\vec{B}$ are parallel.

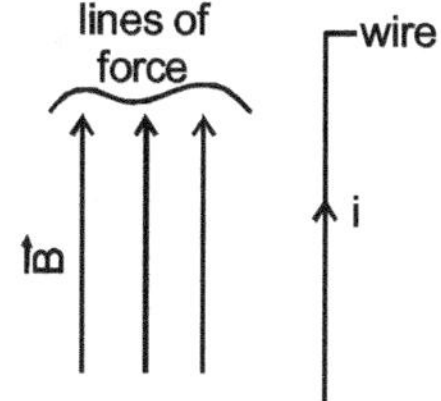

14. (d)

15. The net magnetic field at the centre will be zero as they are equal and opposite.

16. Let PQ be a conductor of length ℓ.
I be the current through the conductor.

$\vec{B}$ is the magnetic field intensity. $\vec{v_d}$ is the drift speed of electrons. θ is the angle between $\vec{B}$ and I.
n be the no. of electrons per unit volume of the conductor.
A is the cross-sectional area of the conductor.

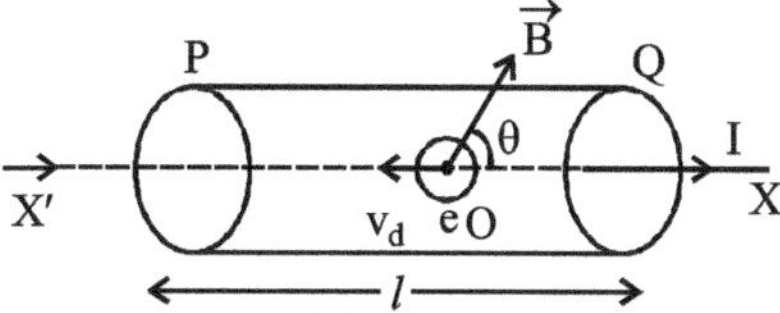

Total no. of free electrons in the conductor $N = nA\ell$

Magnetic Lorentz force on each electron $\vec{f} = -e\left(\vec{v_d} \times \vec{B}\right)$

$\therefore$ Total force of all free electrons

$$\vec{F} = N\vec{f} = -nA\,\ell\,e\left(\vec{v_d} \times \vec{B}\right)$$

But $I = nAev_d$

$\therefore \quad I\ell = nA\ell ev_d$

$I\vec{\ell}$ is called current element vector and is opposite to $\vec{v_d}$

$\therefore \quad I\vec{\ell} = -nA\ell e\vec{v_d}$

$\therefore \quad \vec{F} = I\vec{\ell} \times \vec{B}$

$\therefore \quad |\vec{F}| = I|\vec{\ell} \times \vec{B}| \Rightarrow F = I\ell B \sin\theta$

17. Magnetic field at P in C_2D_2 due to current I_1 through conductor $C_1D_1 = B_1 = \dfrac{\mu_0}{4\pi} \cdot \dfrac{2I_1}{r}$

$\therefore$ Force experienced by unit length of C_2D_2 due to magnetic field

$$\vec{B_1} = F_2 = B_1I_2 \times 1 = B_1I_2 = \dfrac{\mu_0}{4\pi} \cdot \dfrac{2I_1I_2}{r}$$

Similarly C_1D_1 will also experience a force F_1 due to magnetic field $\vec{B_2}$ of C_2D_2

$\overrightarrow{F_2}$ is directed towards C_1D_1 and F_1 is directed towards C_2D_2 and both act in the plane of the paper.

So C_1D_1 and C_2D_2 attract each other.

∴ Two linear conductors carrying current in same direction attract each other.

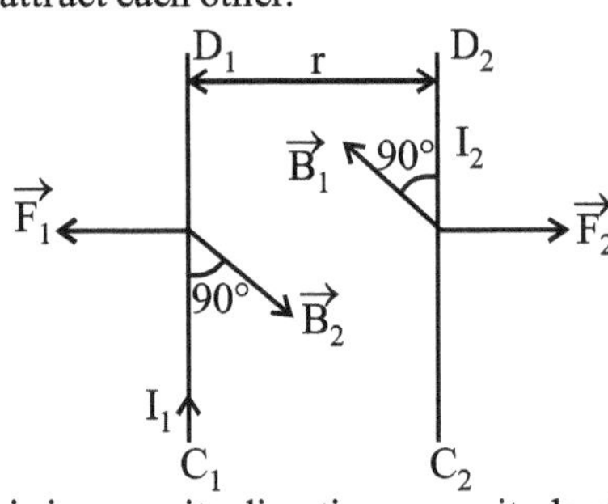

If current is in opposite direction, magnitude of F_1 and F_2 remains same but they are in opposite direction.

∴ They repel each other.

Definition of 1 A:

If $I_1 = I_2 = 1A$, $r = 1m$

$$F = \frac{\mu_0}{4\pi} \cdot \frac{2I_1I_2}{r} = \frac{10^{-7} \times 2 \times 1 \times 1}{1} = 2 \times 10^{-7} N$$

∴ 1 A is the current which on flowing through each of the two parallel uniform linear conductor placed in free space at a distance of 1m from each other produces a force of 2×10^{-7} N/m along their lengths.

18. Consider a coil of area A, n number of turns, carrying current I, when suspended in a magnetic field of strength B. The torque acting on it is given by,

$$\tau = nIBA \sin \alpha.$$

where α is the angle which a normal drawn on the plane of the coil makes with the direction of magnetic field. If the plane of the coil is perpendicular to the direction of magnetic field, $\theta = 90°$.

∴ $\tau_{max} = nIBA \sin 90° = nIBA.$

If the plane of the coil is in the direction of magnetic field, $\theta = 0°$.

∴ $\tau_{min} = nIBA \sin 0 = 0.$

19. Magnetic moment $M = nIA$

Here, $n = 1$, $I = 2A$, $A = 10^{-4} m^2$

$M = 1 \times 2 \times 10^{-4} = 2 \times 10^{-4} Am^2$

20. Here, $I = 4A$, $v = 4 \times 10^6$ m/s, $r = 0.2$ m,

$\mu_0 = 4\pi \times 10^{-7}$ Tm/A

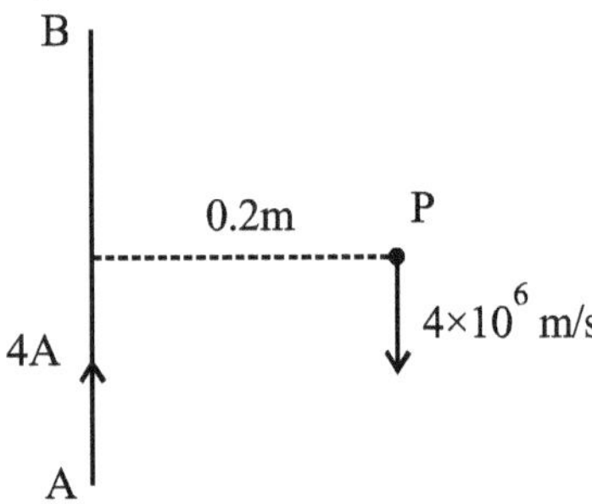

Magnetic field due to a straight wire carrying current

$$B = \frac{\mu_0 I}{2\pi r} = \frac{4\pi \times 10^{-7} \times 4}{2\pi \times 0.2} = 4 \times 10^{-6} T$$

The field acts at right angles to the direction of moving electron.

∴ Force exerted by the magnetic field on the moving proton $F = qvB \sin\theta$ [Here $\theta = 90°$]

$= 1.6 \times 10^{-19} \times 4 \times 10^6 \times 4 \times 10^{-6} \times 1$

$= 2.56 \times 10^{-20} N.$

21. Force on the short conductor due to magnetic field of the long conductor $F = \dfrac{\mu_0}{4\pi} \times \dfrac{2I_1I_2}{r} \times \ell$

∴ $F = \dfrac{10^{-7} \times 2 \times 4 \times 3}{0.03} \times 0.05 = 40 \times 10^{-7} N$

The force is attractive because the currents are in the same direction.

Practice Exercise-4 

1. **(c)** The current sensitivily of a galvanometer is defined as the deflection produced in the galvanometer per unit current flowing through it.

2. **(b)** $\theta = \dfrac{NiAB}{C} \Rightarrow \theta \propto N$ [Number of turns]

3. **(a)** The galvanometer cannot as such be used as an ammeter to measure the value of the current in a given circuit. This is for two reasons (i) Galvanometer is a very sensitive device, it gives a full-scale deflection for a current of the order of μA. (ii) For measuring currents, the galvanometer has to be connected in series and as it has a large resistance, this will change the value of the current in the circuit.

4. **(c)** [Hint $\Rightarrow S \times (I - I_g) = R_g \times I_g$]

5. **(a)** We know

$$\frac{I}{I_S} = 1 + \frac{G}{S} \quad \frac{750}{100} = 1 + \frac{13}{S} \quad\quad S \Rightarrow 2\Omega$$

6. **(c)** To keep the main current in the circuit unchanged, the resistance of the galvanometer should be equal to the net resistance.

$$\therefore G = \left(\frac{GS}{G+S}\right) + S' \Rightarrow G - \frac{GS}{G+S} = S' \quad \therefore S' = \frac{G^2}{G+S}.$$

7. **(c)** $G = 60\Omega$, $I_g = 1.0A$, $I = 5A$.

Let S be the shunt resistance connected in parallel to galvanometer

$I_g G = (I - I_g) S$,

$$S = \frac{I_g G}{I - I_g} = \frac{1}{5-1} \times 60 = 15\Omega$$

Thus by putting 15 Ω in parallel, the galvanometer can be converted into an ammeter.

8. **(a)** Galvanometer is converted into ammeter, by connected a shunt, in parallel with it.

$$\frac{GS}{G+S} = \frac{V_G}{I} = \frac{25\times10^{-3}}{25}$$

$$\frac{GS}{G+S} = 0.001\Omega$$

Here $S \ll G$ so $S = 0.001\ \Omega$

9. **(a)** $i_g = i\dfrac{SG}{S+G}$

or $\quad 100\times10^{-6} = i\left(\dfrac{0.1\times100}{100+0.1}\right)$ or $i = 100.1\times10^{-3}$ A.

10. **(c)** $I_g = 10\times10^{-3}/5 = 2\times10^{-3}$ A;

$$R = \frac{V}{I_g} - R_g = \frac{1}{2\times10^{-3}} - 5 = 495\Omega.$$

11. Radial magnetic field.

12. The quantity is magnetic field intensity $(\vec{B})$. It is a vector quantity.

13. It should have high tensile strength and be of non - magentic material.

14. It produces (i) maximum torque and (ii) the torque is uniform for all positions of the coil.

15. The value of shunt will be less as the range of the ammeter increases. Therefore, milliammeter will have higher resistance.

16. A galvanometer is converted into an ammeter by connecting a low resistance (shunt) in parallel with it.

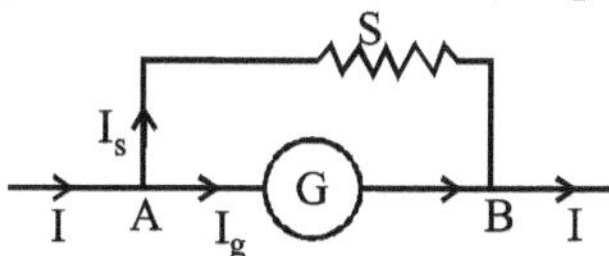

Let I be the total current through the combination. I_g and I_s be the currents through the galvanometer and the shunt respectively. G and S are the galvanometer resistance and shunt resistance respectively.

Here, $\quad I = I_g + I_s$

∵ Potential difference between A and B are same

∴ $\quad I_g G = I_s S \Rightarrow I_g G = (I - I_g)S$

$\Rightarrow I_g(G+S) = IS$

∴ $\quad I_g = I\left(\dfrac{S}{G+S}\right)$ and $S = \left(\dfrac{I_g}{I-I_g}\right)G$

The range of the ammeter is 0 to IA. The effective resistance of the ammeter

$$\frac{1}{R} = \frac{1}{S} + \frac{1}{G} \Rightarrow R = \frac{SG}{S+G}$$

17. A galvanometer can be converted into a voltmeter by adding a high resistance in series with it. If G be the galvanometer resitance and R is the high resistance added in series with it then total resistance of the voltmeter = G + R

∴ I_g= current through the combination $\dfrac{V}{G+R}$

Where V is the potential difference across the combination

∴ $\quad G + R = \dfrac{V}{I_g} \Rightarrow R = \dfrac{V}{I_g} - G$

Range of the voltmeter will be 0 to V volt.

18. Here $G = 100\Omega.\ I_G = 5\times10^{-4}$ A. $V = 5V$

$$R + G = \frac{V}{I_G} \Rightarrow R = \frac{V}{I_G} - G$$

$$= \frac{5}{5\times10^{-4}} - 100 = 9900\ \Omega$$

∴ A series resistance of 9900Ω is to be added to the galvanometer to convert it into a voltmeter.

19. Given, $G = 100\Omega$, $I_G = 1mA = 1\times10^{-3}$A, $I = 1A$, $S = ?$

$$S = \frac{I_G}{(I-I_G)}.G = \frac{1\times10^{-3}}{(1-1\times10^{-3})}.100 = \frac{10^{-1}}{1-0.001}$$

$$S = \frac{1}{10(0.999)} = \frac{1}{9.99} = 0.1\Omega$$

∴ Resistance to be added in parallel to the galvanometer to convert into ammeter is 0.1Ω.

Past year Exercise

1. **(d)**

2. Velocity of α-particles along x-axis, Magnetic force on α-particles is along y-axis

Therefore, The direction of magnetic field must be along (–Z) direction by Fleming's rule.

3. Given, $\quad F = q(v \times B)$

$\Rightarrow \quad F = qvB\sin\theta$

$\Rightarrow \quad B = \dfrac{F}{qv\sin\theta} = \dfrac{N}{(C)(m/s)} = N/A\text{-}m = T$

4. For given momentum of charge particle, radius of circular paths depends on charge and magnetic field as

$$r = \frac{mv}{qB} \Rightarrow r \propto \frac{1}{qB}$$

∴ For given momentum.

$r_{proton} : r_{deuteron} = 1:1$

As they have same momentum, charge and are moving in small magnetic field.

5. Ratio of forces acting on particles

$$\frac{F_A}{F_B} = \frac{qv_1 B\sin90°}{(2q)v_2 B\sin90°}$$

$$\Rightarrow \frac{F_A}{F_B} = \frac{v_1}{v_2}$$

As $\dfrac{F_A}{F_B} = \dfrac{1}{2}$ $\qquad$ ∴ $\dfrac{v_1}{v_2} = \dfrac{1}{2}$

6. No, it is also produced by alternating current.

7. The amount of current which when flowing (in same direction) through two infinitely long parallel wires separated by one metre produces an attractive force of 2×10^{-7} N/m is called one ampere. The wires must have negligible circular cross-section and they must be placed in vacuum.

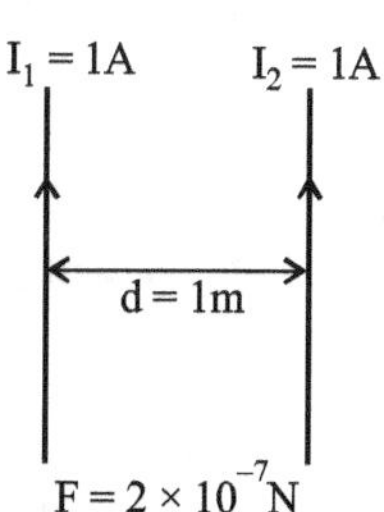

8. The force acting on a particle having a charge q and moving with velocity $\vec{v}$ in an uniform magnetic field $\vec{B}$ is given by, $\vec{F} = q(\vec{v}\times\vec{B})$

The direction of the magnetic force is perpendicular to the plane containing the velocity vector and the magnetic field vector .

9. Since we know that a negative charge always experiences a force in the direction opposite to that of the electric field present, the negative charge will experience the force away from the centre. This will cause its motion to retard while moving from B to A. Hence, its kinetic energy will decrease in going from B to A.

10. When a current-carrying coil is placed in a magnetic field, it experiences torque. This is the underlying principle of a moving coil galvanometer.

11. Here,

$$A = 10 \times 10 = 100 \text{ cm}^2 = 10^{-2} \text{ m}^2$$

$$N = 20 \text{ turns}$$

Current $I = 12$ A

Magnetic field $B = 0.8$ T

Torque $\tau = 0.96$ N-m

As we know, $\tau = NIAB \sin \theta$

$$0.96 = 20 \times 12 \times 10^{-2} \times 0.8 \times \sin \theta$$

$$\Rightarrow \quad \sin \theta = \frac{0.96}{1.92} = \frac{1}{2}$$

Therefore, $\theta = \dfrac{\pi}{6}$ rad

12. 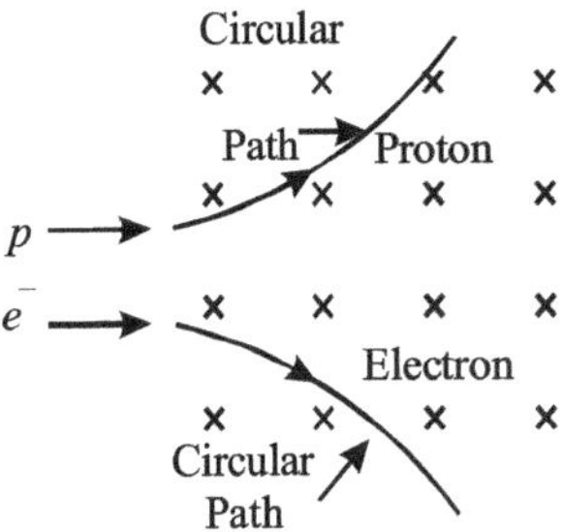

When a charged particle enters the magnetic field at right angle, then the particle experiences a magnetic force due to which it follows a circular path.

Radius of the circular path, $r = \dfrac{mv}{qB}$

For same speed v, and same charge
Magnetic field $r \propto m$

$\because$ As, $m_e < m_p$

$\Rightarrow$ therefore, $r_e < r_p$

The curvature of path of Proton is much more and in opposite direction of the curvature of path of electron.

13. Toroid is a hollow circular ring on which a large number of insulated turns of a metallic wire are closely wound. The direction of the magnetic field at a point P is given by tangent to the magnetic field line at that point.

Let B is the magnetic field in the open space interior to the toroid.

Considering a loop coplanar with toroid of radius x such that $x < R$ (radius of toroid) as shown in the figure.

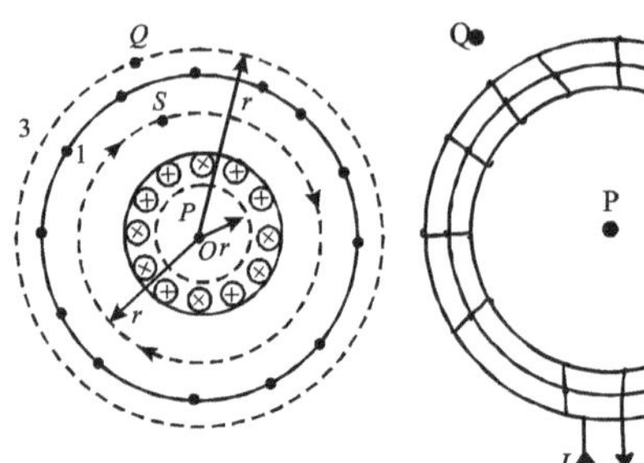

Applying Ampere's circuital law over loop, we have

$$\oint B.dl = \mu_0 \times \text{Current passes through the loop}$$

But no current passes through the loop.

$$\therefore \quad \oint B.dl = \mu_0 \times 0 = 0$$

$$\Rightarrow \quad B = 0$$

This is the magnetic field exist in the interior of toroid.

14. Biot-Savart law : For the magnetic field $\overrightarrow{dB}$ at a point P associated with a current element of length $\overrightarrow{d\ell}$ of a wire carrying a steady current I.

$dB \propto I$

$dB \propto d\ell$

$dB \propto \dfrac{1}{r^2}$

$dB \propto \sin \theta$

Combining all these

$$dB \propto \frac{Id\ell \sin \theta}{r^2}$$

or, $\quad dB = \dfrac{\mu_0}{4\pi} \times \dfrac{I\, d\ell \sin \theta}{r^2}$

μ_0 is called **permeability of free space**

As current carrying loop has the magnetic field lines around it, thus it behaves as a magnet with two mutually opposite poles.

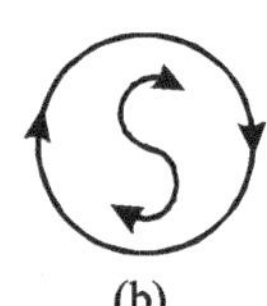

(a) (b)

The anticlockwise flow of current behaves like a north pole where clockwise flow as south pole. Hence, loop behaves as a magnet.

15. Magnetic Lorentz force

$$F_m = q(v \times B)$$

$\because \quad F \perp v$

$\therefore \quad W = Fd \cos 90° = 0$

No work is done by magnetic Lorentz force on charge particle.

16. (i) Magnetic field at centre due to circular current carrying coil $(B) = \dfrac{\mu_0 NI}{2r}$

(ii) Magnetic moment $M = NIA = NI\,(\pi r^2)$

$$M = \pi NIr^2$$

17. Given : $\quad W = \dfrac{1}{2} LI^2$

Now, $\quad L = \mu_0 n^2 Al$, and from $B = \mu_0 n I$

$$I = \frac{B}{\mu_0 n}$$

Therefore magnetic energy

$$U_B = W = \frac{1}{2}LI^2 = \frac{1}{2}(\mu_0 n^2 Al)\left(\frac{B}{\mu_0 n}\right)^2 = \frac{1}{2\mu_0}B^2 Al$$

Energy density $= \dfrac{U_B}{V} = \dfrac{U_B}{Al} = \dfrac{B^2}{2\mu_0}$

18. Given: $r = 1\,\text{mm} = 10^{-3}\,\text{m}$
    $i_1 = 6A,\ i_2 = 4A$
    mass per unit length of the wire CD, $m = ?$

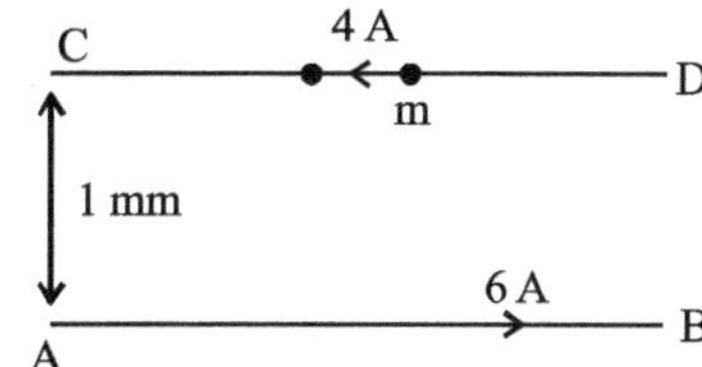

To support the wire CD the weight of its unit length must be equal to the force of repulsion on the wire per unit length.

i.e. $mg = \dfrac{dF}{dl} = \dfrac{\mu_0}{4\pi}\cdot\dfrac{2i_1 i_2}{r}$

or, $m = \dfrac{1}{g}\dfrac{dF}{dl} = \dfrac{1}{g}\times\dfrac{\mu_0}{4\pi}\cdot\dfrac{2i_1 i_2}{r} = \dfrac{1}{10}\times\dfrac{10^{-7}\times 2\times 6\times 4}{10^{-3}}$

$= 48\times 10^{-5} = 4.8\times 10^{-4}\,\text{kg m}^{-1}$

The direction of current in wire CD must be opposite to that in wire AB.

19. (a) The current sensitivity of a galvanometer is defined as the deflection per unit current.
    (b) Given:
    $A = 25\times 10^{-4}\,\text{m}^2,\ n = 150$
    $B = 0.15\,\text{T},\ C = 10^{-6}\,\text{Nm}$
    $\theta = 30°\quad I = ?$
    From the expression

    $I = \dfrac{c\theta}{nBA} = \dfrac{10^{-6}\times 30}{150\times 0.15\times 25\times 10^{-4}} = 5.3\text{mA}$

20. **Refer to theory.**
    Magnetic field lines due to a circular wire carrying current I.

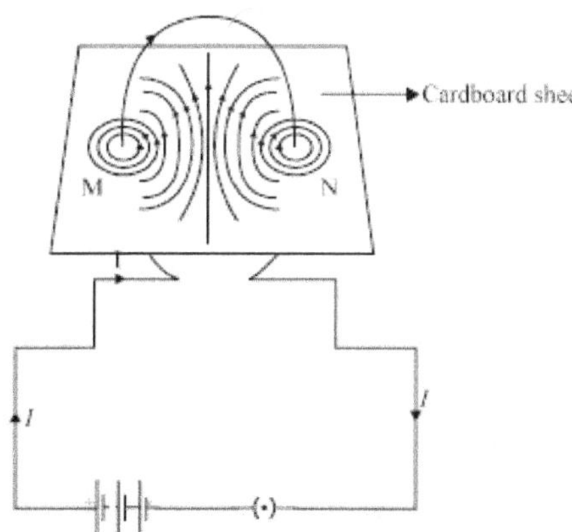

21. (a) Magnetic moment associated with a current carrying circular coil of radius r having N turns,

$$\vec{M} = NI(\pi r^2)\,\hat{n}$$

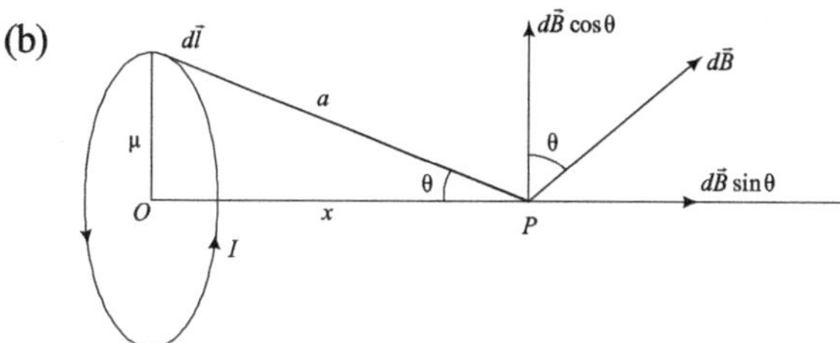

From Biot-savart law, the magnetic field at point $P(x, 0, 0)$ due to current element $\vec{dl}$,

$$\vec{dB} = \frac{\mu_0}{4\pi}\frac{I\,dl\sin 90°}{a^2}$$

Now, the vertical component $\cos\theta$ will cancel out for entire coil. So,

$$\vec{B}\ \text{at}\ P \Rightarrow B = \int dB\sin\theta$$

$$B = \frac{\mu_0 I}{4\pi a^2}\sin\theta\int dl$$

Now $\int dl = 2\pi r$

$\therefore\quad B = \dfrac{\mu_0 I}{4\pi a^2}\times\dfrac{r}{a}\times 2\pi r\quad \left[\because \sin\theta = \dfrac{r}{a}\right]$

$$B = \frac{\mu_0 I r^2}{2a^3} = \frac{\mu_0 I r^2}{2(r^2 + x^2)^{3/2}}\,\hat{i}.$$

For coil having N turns,

$$= \frac{\mu_0 I N r^2}{2(r^2 + x^2)^{3/2}}\,\hat{i}.$$

OR

(a) Current sensitivity

It is defined as the deflection produced in the galvanometer when a unit current flows through it.

Current sensitivity $I_c = \dfrac{NBA}{K}$

Where $N =$ no. of turns in the coil
$B =$ Magnetic field
$A =$ area of coil of galvanometer.

(b) (i)

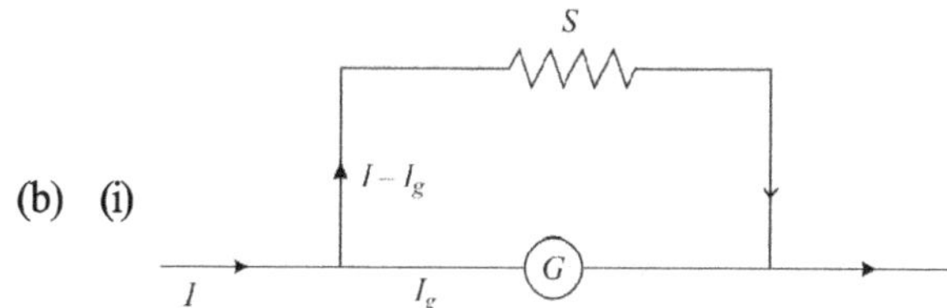

Galvanometer can be converted into ammeter by connecting a shunt (small resistance) S with parallel to galvanometer.

As galvanometer and shunt are connected in parallel, so,

Potential across $G =$ Potential across the S

$$I_g G = (I - I_g)S$$

$\therefore\quad S = \dfrac{I_g}{I - I_g}G.$

(ii) Effective resistance of this ammeter will be

$$\frac{1}{R_A} = \frac{1}{G} + \frac{1}{S}$$

$$R_A = \frac{GS}{G+S}.$$

22. (a) Magnetic field lines due to a circular current carrying loop showing the direction of field lines.

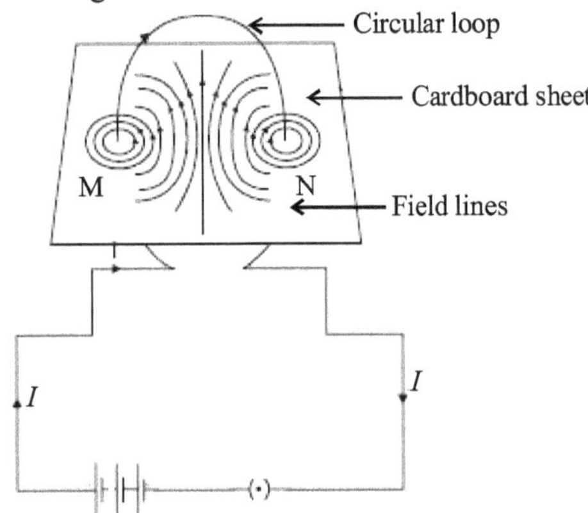

(b) (i) When current carrying element at point $(0, d, 0)$

$$d_B = \frac{\mu_0}{4\pi} \frac{id\ell \sin\theta}{r^2}$$

$$= \frac{2\times10^{-7}\, Idl}{d^2}(-\hat{k})$$

(ii) When current carrying element at point $(0, 0, d)$

$$d_B = \frac{\mu_0}{4\pi} \frac{id\ell \sin\theta}{r^2}$$

$$= \frac{2\times10^{-7}\, Idl}{d^2}(-\hat{J})$$

23. (a) A galvanometer is converted into an ammeter by connecting a low resistance (shunt) in parallel with it.

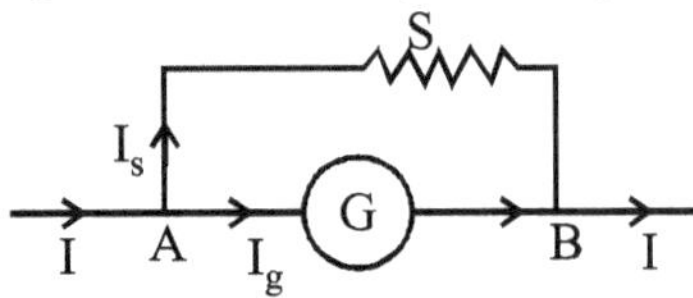

Let I be the total current through the combination. I_g and I_s be the currents through the galvanometer and the shunt respectively. G and S are the galvanometer resistance and shunt resistance respectively.

Here, $I = I_g + I_s$

∵ Potential difference between A and B are same

∴ $I_g G = I_s S \Rightarrow I_g G = (I - I_g)S$

$\Rightarrow I_g(G+S) = IS$ ∴ $I_g = I\left(\dfrac{S}{G+S}\right)$

and $S = \left(\dfrac{I_g}{I - I_g}\right)G$

The range of the ammeter is 0 to IA. The effective resistance of the ammeter

$$\frac{1}{R} = \frac{1}{S} + \frac{1}{G} \quad \Rightarrow \quad R = \frac{SG}{S+G}$$

(b) For converting galvanometer into ammeter of required range, required shunt can be calculated by using formula

$$S = \frac{I_g\, G}{I - I_g} = \frac{4\times10^{-3}\times15}{6 - 0.004} = 0.01\Omega = 10\text{ m}\Omega.$$

24. Let a charge q moving with velocity v in the presence of electric field E and magnetic field B.

The force on an electric charge q due to both E and B

$$F = q\,[E(r) + v \times B\,(r)]$$

$$F = F_{electric} + F_{magnetic} \qquad \dots(i)$$

Let us consider a simple case in which electric field, E and magnetic field, B are perpendicular to each other and also perpendicular to the velocity of the particle.

$$F_E = qE = qEj \,.\, F_B = q\,v \times B$$

or, $F_E = q(v\hat{i} \times B\hat{k}) = -qB\hat{j}$

∴ $F = q(E - vB)\hat{j}$

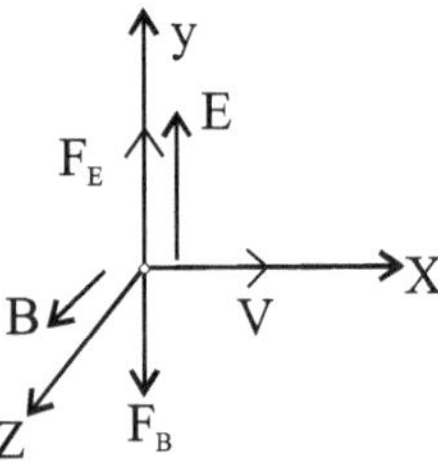

i.e., Electric and magnetic forces are in opposite directions. Suppose we adjust the values of E and B such that magnitudes of the two forces are equal, then the total force on the charge is zero and the charge will move in the fields undeflected. This happens when

$$qE = qvB \qquad \text{or,} \qquad v = \frac{E}{B}$$

This condition can be used to select charged particles of a particular velocity out of a beam containing charges moving with different speeds. The crossed E and B fields serve as a velocity selector.

25. (a) Biot–Savart law states that the magnetic field (dB) due to the current element dl at any point P is

(i) directly proportional to the current, I i.e., $dB \propto I$

(ii) directly proportional to the length dl of the element i.e., $dB \propto dl$

(iii) directly proportional to $\sin\theta$, where θ is the angle between dl and r, i.e., $dB \propto \sin\theta$

(iv) inversely proportional to the square of the distance r from the current element AB i.e., $dB \propto \dfrac{1}{r^2}$

Therefore, we have

$$dB \propto \frac{Idl \sin\theta}{r^2}$$

∴ $$dB = \frac{\mu_0}{4\pi}\frac{Idl \sin\theta}{r^2}$$

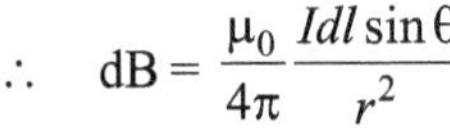

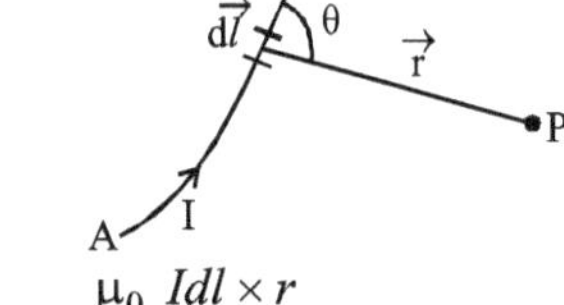

In vector notation, $dB = \dfrac{\mu_0}{4\pi}\dfrac{Idl \times r}{r^3}$

(b) Two coils P and Q are placed as shown in the figure:

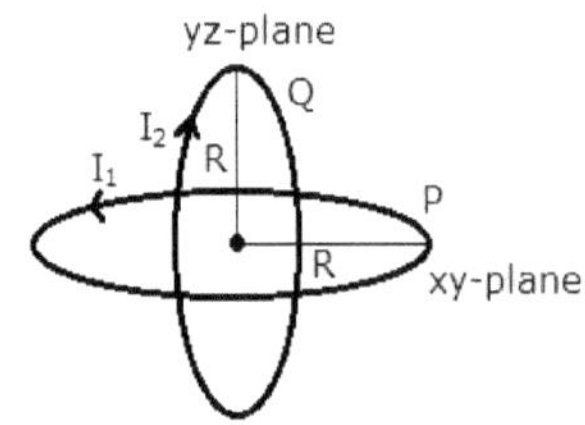

Given: Current through coil P, $I_1 = 1\,A$
Current through coil Q, $I_2 = \sqrt{3}\,A$
The magnetic field due to coil P at its centre

$$B_P = \frac{\mu_0 I_1}{2R} \text{ along z-axis}$$

The magnetic field due to coil Q at its centre

$$B_Q = \frac{\mu_0 I_2}{2R} \text{ along X-axis}$$

Hence, the field structure is as shown in figure
Therefore, the resultant field at the centre of the coils,

$$\therefore \quad B = \sqrt{B_P^2 + B_Q^2}$$

$$\therefore \quad B = \sqrt{\left(\frac{\mu_0 I_1}{2R}\right)^2 + \left(\frac{\mu_0 I_2}{2R}\right)^2}$$

$$= \sqrt{\left(\frac{\mu_0}{2R}\right)^2 + 3\left(\frac{\mu_0^2}{2R}\right)^2}$$

$$\therefore \quad B = 2\left(\frac{\mu_0}{2R}\right) = \frac{\mu_0}{R}$$

Direction of this field is in the x–z plane.

26.

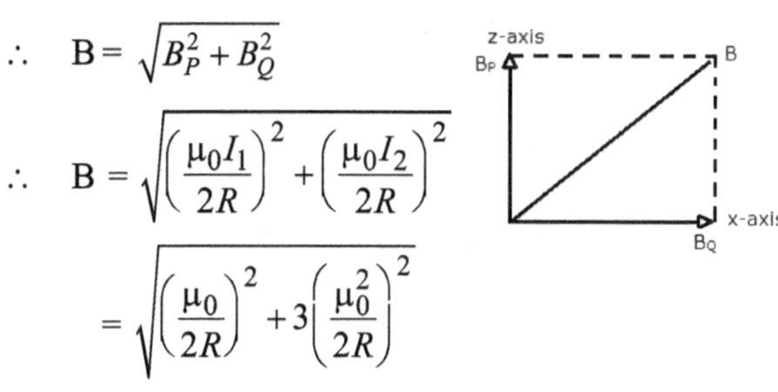

Field at P due to wire at A

$$\vec{B}_A = \frac{\mu_0 I}{2\pi x} \text{ (upward)}$$

Field at P due to wire at B

$$\vec{B}_B = \frac{\mu_0 I}{2\pi(d-x)} \text{ (downward)}$$

Therefore, total field at P

$$\vec{B} = \vec{B}_A + \vec{B}_B$$

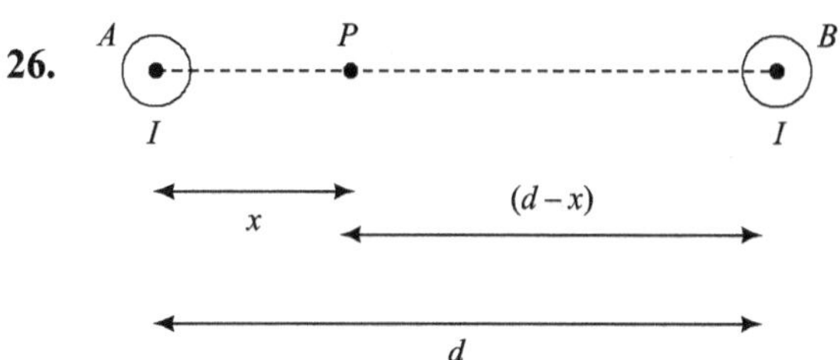

$$\vec{B} = \frac{\mu_0 I}{2\pi x} - \frac{\mu_0 I}{2\pi(d-x)}$$

$$\vec{B} = \frac{\mu_0 I}{2\pi}\left[\frac{1}{x} - \frac{1}{d-x}\right]$$

$$\vec{B} = \frac{\mu_0 I}{2\pi}\left[\frac{d-x-x}{x(d-x)}\right]$$

$$= \frac{\mu_0 I(d-2x)}{2\pi x(d-x)} \text{ upward.}$$

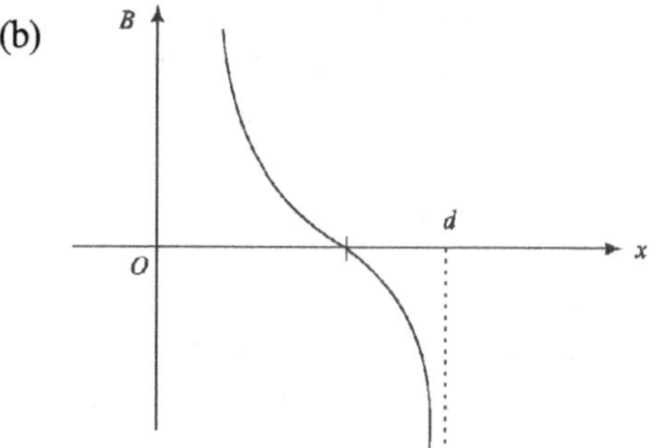

> **NCERT Exemplar**

1. **(d)** As we know that the uniqueness of helical path is determined by its pitch

$$P(\text{Pitch}) = \frac{2\pi\, mv \cos\theta}{Bq}$$

Where θ is angle of velocity of charge particle with x-axis
For the given pitch d correspond to charge particle, we have

$$\frac{q}{m} = \frac{2\pi v \cos\theta}{BP} = \text{constant}$$

If motion is not helical, $(\theta = 0)$
As charged particles traverse identical helical paths in a completely opposite direction in a same magnetic field **B**, LHS for two particles should be same and of opposite sign.

$$\therefore \quad \left(\frac{e}{m}\right)_1 + \left(\frac{e}{m}\right)_2 = 0$$

2. **(a)** By Biot-Savart law

$$dB = \frac{I dl \sin\theta}{r^2} = \left(\frac{I \times dl}{r}\right)$$

In Biot-Savat's law, magnetic field $\mathbf{B} \| idl \times \mathbf{r}$ and idl due to flow of electron is in opposite direction of v and by direction of cross product of two vectors

$$B \perp V$$

So, the magnetic field is $\perp$ to the direction of flow of charge.

3. **(a)** As the direction of magnetic moment of circular loop of radius R placed in the x-y plane is along z-direction and given by $M = I\,(\pi r^2)$, when half of the loop with $x > 0$ is now bent so that it now lies in the y-z plane, the magnitudes of magnetic field moment of each semicircular loop of radius R lie in the x-y plane and the y-z plane is $M' = I(\pi r^2)/4$ and the direction of magnetic field moments are along z-direction and x-direction respectively.
Then resultant is :

$$M_{net} = \sqrt{M'^2 + M'^2} = \sqrt{2}\,M' = \sqrt{2}\,I(\pi r^2)/4$$

So, $M_{net} < M$ or M diminishes.
Hence, the magnitude of magnetic moment is now diminishes.

4. **(d)** Magnetic Lorentz force :
$$F = qVB \sin\theta$$

Magnetic Lorentz force electron is projected with uniform velocity along the axis of a current carrying long solenoid $F = -qvB \sin 180° = 0 (\theta = 0°)$ as magnetic field and velocity are parallel and electric field is zero ($E = 0$) due to this magnetic field (B) perpendicular to the direction of motion (V). So it will not affect the velocity of moving charge particle. So the electron will continue to move with uniform velocity along the axis of the solenoid

5. **(a)** There is crossed electric and magnetic field between dees so the charged particle accelerates by electric field between dees towards other dees.

So, the charged particle undergoes acceleration as

(i) speeds up between the dees because of the oscillating electric field.

(ii) speed remain the same inside the dees because of the magnetic field but direction undergoes change continuously.

Hence, the charge particle accelerates inside and between Dees always.

6. At O_2, the magnetic field due to I_1 is along the y-axis. The second wire is along the y-axis and hence the force is zero.

7. The torque acting on each of the four loops is $\tau = MB \sin \theta$, where M is the magnetic moment. $M = IA$ where I is the current and A is the area of loop. For the same perimeter ℓ of four loops the circular loop has maxium area A and hence the torque will be maximum.

8. When a current carrying wire is bent into a loop, the magnetic field lines become bunched up inside the loop. Hence magnetic field intensity increases.

9. $\mathbf{B} = \dfrac{1}{4}(\hat{\mathbf{i}}+\hat{\mathbf{j}}+\hat{\mathbf{k}})\dfrac{\mu_0 I}{2R}$

10. $F = BIl \sin \theta = BIl$

$B = \dfrac{\mu_0 I}{2\pi h}$ $F = mg = \dfrac{\mu_0 I^2 l}{2\pi h}$

$h = \dfrac{\mu_0 I^2 l}{2\pi mg} = \dfrac{4\pi \times 10^{-7} \times 250 \times 25 \times 1}{2\pi \times 2.5 \times 10^{-3} \times 9.8}$

$= 51 \times 10^{-4} = 0.51$ cm

11. When a bar magnet is dropped through a vertical length of copper pipe, the pipe behaves as a magnet due to the alignment of the magnetic domains in it. The magnetic field of this magnet acts in a direction opposite to the magnetic field of the moving magnet. Therefore, the motion of the magnet slows down. But it doesn't happen so with the plastic pipe as it has no magnetic domains.

As time passes, and if the copper pipe is long enough, the two oppositely acting magnetic fields equalize each other and then the magnet falls with a constant terminal speed.

12. Let n be the no. of turns in both coils. Magnetic field B_1 at the centre of circular coil X of radius R carrying current I is $B_1 = \dfrac{\mu_0}{4\pi} \cdot \dfrac{2\pi nI}{R}$

and magnetic field B_2 at the centre of circular coil Y of radius $\dfrac{R}{2}$ carrying current I_1 is

$B_2 = \dfrac{\mu_0}{4\pi} \cdot \dfrac{2\pi nI_1}{R/2} = \dfrac{\mu_0}{4\pi} \cdot \dfrac{2\pi nI_1}{R} \cdot 2$

Since the total magnetic field at the common centre of two coils is zero.

$$B_2 = B_1$$

$$\dfrac{\mu_0}{4\pi} \cdot \dfrac{2\pi nI_1}{R} \cdot 2 = \dfrac{\mu_0}{4\pi} \cdot \dfrac{2\pi nI}{R} \qquad (\because 2I_1 = I \text{ or } I_1 = \dfrac{I}{2} \cdot)$$

Objective Practice Exercise

1. **(c)**

2. **(b)** If $v \perp B$, then path is circular and if v has a component along B, then path will be helical.

3. **(c)** In a velocity selector, where F_e and F_B are electric and magetic field, we get

Case I $F_e = F_B \Rightarrow v = \dfrac{E}{B}$

Case II $F_e > F_B \Rightarrow v < \dfrac{E}{B}$

Case III $F_e < F_B \Rightarrow v > E/B$

4. **(d)** If charge is not moving then the magnetic force is zero.

Since $\vec{F}_m = q(\vec{v} \times \vec{B})$

As $\vec{v} = 0$, for stationary charge

$\therefore \quad \vec{F}_m = 0$

5. **(d)**

6. **(d)** Power $= \dfrac{\text{work done}}{\text{time}}$

As no work is done by magnetic force on the charged particle because magnetic force is perpendicular to velocity, hence power delivered is zero.

7. **(c)**

8. **(b)** Here, $\vec{E}$ and $\vec{B}$ are perpendicular to each other and the velocity $\vec{v}$ does not change; therefore

$qE = qvB \Rightarrow v = \dfrac{E}{B}$

If velocity $\vec{v}$ is $\perp^r$ to both $\vec{E}$ and $\vec{B}$,

Also, $\left|\dfrac{\vec{E}\times\vec{B}}{B^2}\right| = \dfrac{E\,B\sin\theta}{B^2} = \dfrac{E\,B\sin 90°}{B^2} = \dfrac{E}{B} = |\vec{v}| = v$

9. **(a)** $r = mv/Bq$ is same for both.

10. **(c)** As electron move with constant velocity without deflection. Hence, force due to magnetic field is equal and opposite to force due to electric field.

$qvB = qE \Rightarrow v = \dfrac{E}{B} = \dfrac{20}{0.5} = 40 \text{ m/s}$

11. **(a)** The force acting on a charged particle in magnetic field is given by $\vec{F} = q(\vec{v}\times\vec{B})$ or $F = qvB\sin\theta$, When angle between v and B is $180°$, $F = 0$

12. **(c)** $r = \dfrac{\sqrt{2mK}}{qB}$ i.e. $r \propto \dfrac{\sqrt{m}}{q}$

Here kinetic energy K and B are same.

$\therefore \quad \dfrac{r_p}{r_\alpha} = \dfrac{\sqrt{m_p}}{\sqrt{m_a}}\cdot\dfrac{q_\alpha}{q_p} = \dfrac{\sqrt{m_p}}{\sqrt{4m_p}}\cdot\dfrac{2q_p}{q_p} = 1$

13. **(b)** In a perpendicular magnetic field, the path of a charged particle is a circle, and the magnetic field does not cause any change in energy.

14. **(a)**

15. **(a)** $F = ma = qvB \Rightarrow a = \dfrac{qvB}{m}$

$= \dfrac{1.6\times10^{-19}\times2\times3.4\times10^{7}}{1.67\times10^{-27}} = 6.5\times10^{15} \text{ m/sec}^2$

16. **(b)** Magnetic field is given by $B = \dfrac{\mu_0 i}{2\pi r}$ i.e., $B \propto \dfrac{1}{r}$ which implies that field has cylindrical symmetry.

17. **(a)** **18.** **(d)** **19.** **(c)**

20. **(d)** There is no current inside the pipe. Therefore

$\oint \vec{B}.\overline{d\ell} = \mu_o I$

$I = 0 \quad \therefore B = 0$

21. **(c)** **22.** **(b)** **23.** **(a)**

24. **(d)** $B = \mu_0 nI = 4\pi\times10^{-7}\times10\times5 = 2\pi\times10^{-5}$ T.

25. **(b)** Magnetic field at a point on one end of a solenoid

$B = \dfrac{1}{2}\mu_0 ni$

26. **(a)** $\dfrac{B_2}{B_1} = \dfrac{\mu_0 n_2 i_2}{\mu_0 n_1 i_1} \Rightarrow \dfrac{B_2}{6.28\times10^{-2}} = \dfrac{100\times\dfrac{i}{3}}{200\times i}$

$\Rightarrow B_2 = \dfrac{6.28\times10^{-2}}{6} = 1.05\times10^{-2}$ Wb/m^2

27. **(d)** $B = \dfrac{\mu_0}{4\pi}\cdot\dfrac{2\pi ni_1}{r_1} - \dfrac{\mu_0}{4\pi}\cdot\dfrac{2\pi ni_2}{r_2} = \dfrac{\mu_0}{2}\left[\dfrac{ni_1}{r_1} - \dfrac{ni_2}{r_2}\right]$

28. **(b)** Let ℓ be length of wire.

Ist case : $\ell = 2\pi r \Rightarrow r = \dfrac{\ell}{2\pi}$

$B = \dfrac{\mu_0 In}{2r} = \dfrac{\mu_0 I\times2\pi}{2\ell} = \dfrac{\mu_0\pi I}{\ell}\;[\because n=1]...(1)$

2nd Case : $\ell = 2(2\pi r') \Rightarrow r' = \dfrac{\ell}{4\pi}$

$B' = \dfrac{\mu_0 In}{2\dfrac{\ell}{4\pi}} = \dfrac{2\mu_0 I\pi}{\dfrac{\ell}{2}} = 4\left(\dfrac{\mu_0\pi I}{\ell}\right) = 4B$

29. **(b)** We know that magnetic field at the centre of circular coil,

$B = \dfrac{\mu_0 In}{2r} = \dfrac{4\pi\times10^{-7}\times2\times50}{2\times0.5} = 1.25\times10^{-4}T$

30. **(a)** A current carrying coil has magnetic dipole moment.

Hence a torque $\vec{p}_m\times\vec{B}$ acts on it in magnetic field.

31. **(a)**

32. **(d)** $\tau = MB\sin\theta \Rightarrow \tau_{max} = NIAB$, $(\theta = 90°)$

33. **(c)** The magnetic field is perpendicular to the plane of the paper. Let us consider two diametrically opposite elements. By Fleming's left hand rule, on element AB the direction of force will be leftwards and the magnitude will be

$dF = I(d\ell)B\sin 90° = I(d\ell)B$

On element CD, the direction of force will be towards right on the plane of the paper and the magnitude will be dF

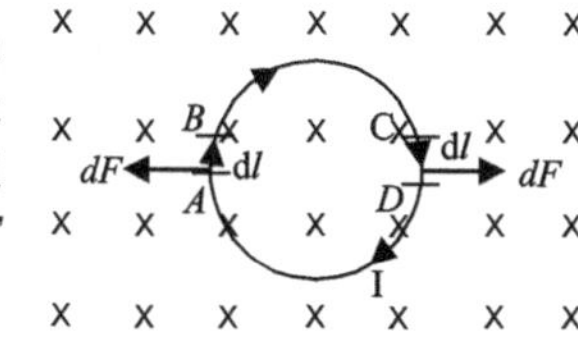

$= I(d\ell)B.$

These two forces will cancel out.

34. **(a)** Force between two long conductor carrying current,

$F = \dfrac{\mu_0}{4\pi}\dfrac{2I_1I_2}{d}\times\ell;\; F' = -\dfrac{\mu_0}{4\pi}\dfrac{2(2I_1)I_2}{3d}\ell$

$\therefore \dfrac{F'}{F} = \dfrac{-2}{3}$

35. **(a)** $F = Bil\sin\theta \Rightarrow 7.5 = 2\times5\times1.5\sin\theta \Rightarrow \theta = 30°$

36. **(b)** $F = Bi\ell = 2\times1.2\times0.5 = 1.2$ N

37. **(a)** $F = \dfrac{\mu_0 i_1 i_2}{2\pi r} = \dfrac{4\pi\times10^{-7}\times30\times30}{2\times\pi\times5\times10^{-2}} = 3.6\times10^{-3}$ N/m.

38. **(a)** $\dfrac{F}{\ell} = \dfrac{\mu_0 i^2}{2\pi d} = 9.8\times4\times10^{-6}$

$\Rightarrow i = \sqrt{\dfrac{4\times10^{-6}\times9.8\times0.12}{2\times10^{-7}}} = 4.85$ A

39.   **(b)** $F = iB\,l\,\sin\theta$. This is maximum when $\sin\theta = 1$ or $\theta = \pi/2$.

40.   **(b)** $F = I\ell\,B\,\sin\theta = 3 \times 0.40 \times (500 \times 10^{-4}) \times \sin 30^\circ$
$= 3 \times 10^{-2}\,\text{N}$.

41.   **(d)**   At these points, the resultant field $= 0$

42.   **(a)** $F = \dfrac{\mu_0}{4\pi} \times \dfrac{2i_1 i_2}{r}$

$= 50 \times 10^{-7}\,\text{N/m}$. Here F is force per unit length.

43.   **(b)**   Current carrying conductors will attract each other, while electron beams will repel each other.

Chapter Test

1.   **(a)** $B = \dfrac{\mu_0 I}{2\pi r} \Rightarrow B \propto \dfrac{1}{r}$

As the distance is increased to three times, the magnetic induction reduces to one third. Hence, $B = \dfrac{1}{3} \times 10^{-3}\,\text{tesla}$
$= 3.33 \times 10^{-4}\,\text{tesla}$

2.   **(c)**

3.   **(b)**   Here, $R_g = 100\,\Omega$; $I_g = 10^{-5}\,\text{A}$; $I = 1\text{A}$; $S = ?$

$$S = \dfrac{I_g R_g}{I - I_g} = \dfrac{10^{-5} \times 100}{1 - 10^{-5}} = 10^{-3}\,\Omega \text{ in parallel}$$

4.   **(c)**   Equating magnetic force to centripetal force,

$$\dfrac{mv^2}{r} = qvB\,\sin 90^\circ$$

Time to complete one revolution,

$$T = \dfrac{2\pi r}{v} = \dfrac{2\pi m}{qB}$$

5.   **(b)**   If $\vec{F} \perp \vec{V}$ at all instants then motion will be circular

6.   **(c)**

Sol. (7-11):

We know that $r = \dfrac{mV}{qB}$

$\therefore \quad V > \dfrac{qBl}{m}$

7.   **(a)**   If $r > l$ then particle enter the III region $\dfrac{mV}{qB} > l$

8.   **(c)**   If $V = \dfrac{qBl}{m}$ then particle will cover semi circular path in this condition the path length of the particle in region II is maximum.

9.   **(d)**   Time spent in region II, $T = \dfrac{\pi m}{qB}$

It does not depends upon the velocity.

10.   **(d)**

11.   **(d)** $F = q(\vec{V} \times \vec{B})$ if $V \parallel B$, then $\vec{F} = 0$

12.   As we know, $Bqv = \dfrac{mv^2}{r} \Rightarrow r = \dfrac{mv}{Bq}$

$$\therefore \quad \dfrac{r_e}{r_p} = \dfrac{m_e v_e}{eB} \times \dfrac{eB}{m_p v_p} \quad (\because m_e v_e = m_p v_p)$$

$$\therefore \quad r_e : r_p = 1 : 1$$

13.   Zero as $\vec{F} = q(\vec{v} \times \vec{B})$ [here $\theta = 0 \ \therefore \ \sin\theta = 0$]

14.   For two infinitely long parallel straight conductors kept at a distance r apart in vacuum and carrying currents I_1 and I_2,

Force/unit length of the conductor $\dfrac{F}{\ell} = \dfrac{\mu_0 I_1 I_2}{2\pi r}$

S.I. unit of current is 1 A.

If $I_1 = I_2 = 1\text{A}, r = 1\text{m}$ then

$$\dfrac{F}{\ell} = 2 \times 10^{-7}\,\text{N/m} \left[\because \dfrac{\mu_0}{4\pi} = 10^{-7} \right]$$

$\therefore$ 1 A is the amount of current flowing through two parallel wires separated by a distance of 1m, carrying a force of interaction of $2 \times 10^{-7}\,\text{N/m}$ between them.

15.   A moving coil galvanometer can be converted into an ammeter by putting a small resistance (shunt) in parallel with it.

A moving coil galavanometer can be converted into a voltmeter by adding a high resistance in series with it.

5 — Magnetism and Matter

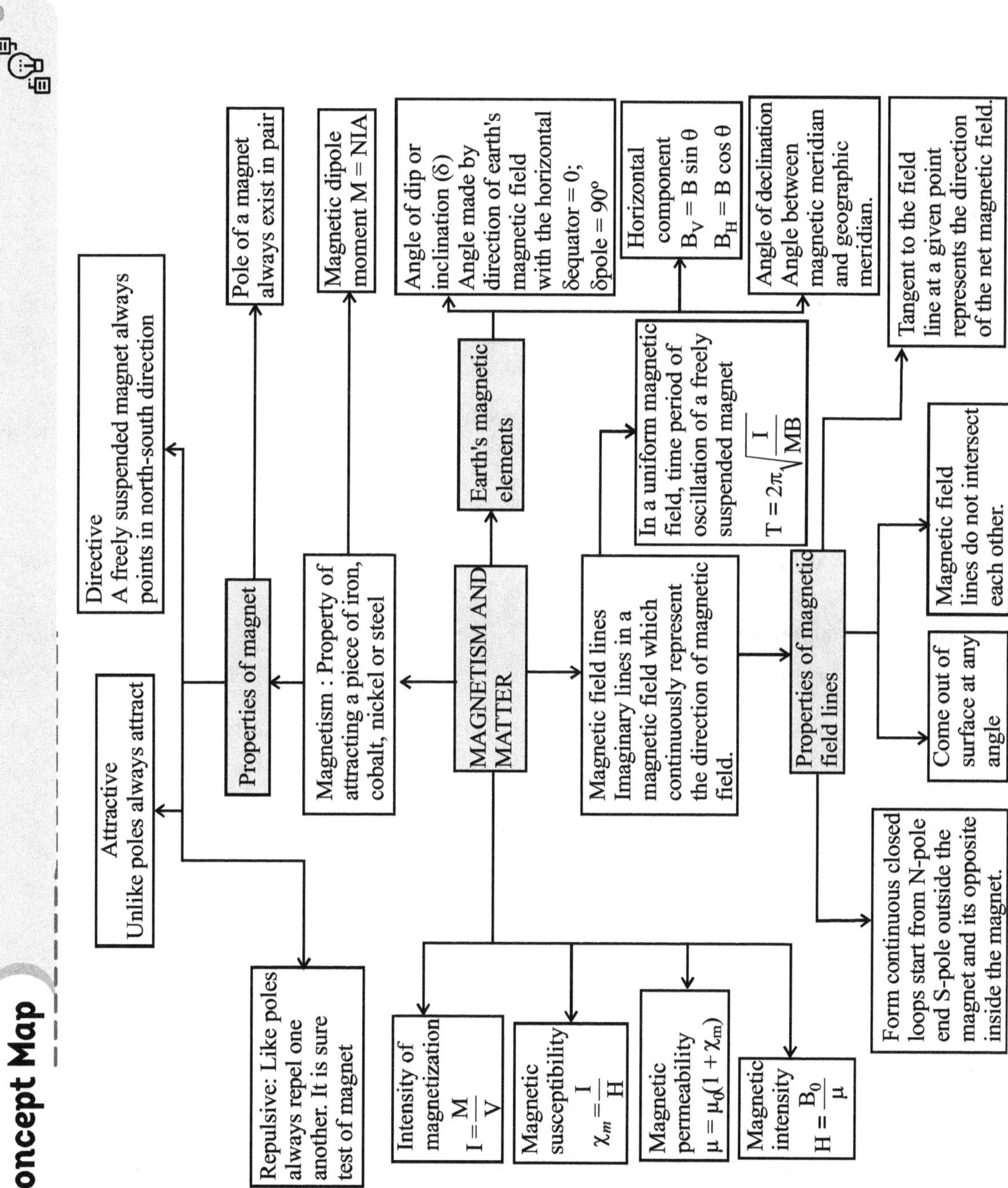

Topic 1 — **Magnetism, Bar Magnet, Magnetic field Lines, Bar Magnet as an Equivalent Solenoid, Current Loop as a Magnetic Dipole & Its Magnetic Dipole Moment, Magnetic Dipole Moment of a Revolving Electron, Magnetism and Gauss's Law**

MAGNETISM

The phenomenon of attraction of small bits of iron, cobalt, nickel (i.e., magnetic substance in which molecular magnets are randomly oriented, so net magnetic moment is zero) towards the ore of iron-magnetite (i.e., natural magnet in which molecular magnets are aligned in specific direction so, net magnetic moment is non-zero) is called magnetism.

Magnets are of two types : (i) Natural magnets like iron, cobalt, nickel. (ii) Artificial magnets like electromagnets.

Properties of Magnets

(i)   **Attractive property :** A magnet attracts a magnetic material, also two unlike poles attract each other.

(ii) **Directive property :** A freely suspended magnet always points towards geographical north-south direction.

(iii) **Poles of a magnet always exist in pair :** If a magnet is broken into number of pieces, each piece becomes a magnet with two equal and opposite poles. Monopole do not exists.

(iv) **Repulsive property :** A pole of a magnet attracts the opposite pole while repels similar pole. Repulsion is the sure test of polarity of a magnet.

BAR MAGNET

A bar magnet consists of two equal and opposite magnetic poles separated by a small distance. Poles are not exactly at the ends. The shortest distance between two poles is called effective length (L_e) and is less than its geometric length (L_g). For bar magnet $L_e = 2l$ and $L_e = (5/6) L_g$. For semicircular magnet, geometrical length $L_g = \pi R$ and $L_e = 2R$.

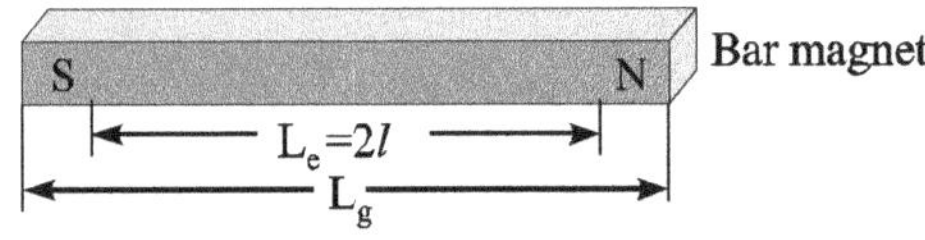

Equatorial line of a magnet: It is a line passing through the centre of the magnet and perpendicular to the length of the magnet.

Magnetic meridian is a vertical plane passing through the N-S poles of a freely suspended magnet.

Atomic/Molecular Theory of Magnetism

(i) Every molecule of a magnetic substance (magnetised or non-magnetised) is a complete magnet having a north and a south pole of equal strength.

(ii) In **unmagnetised** state, the molecular magnets are randomly oriented to form closed chains. Each north pole cancels the effect of south pole and the resultant magnetism of the specimen is zero.

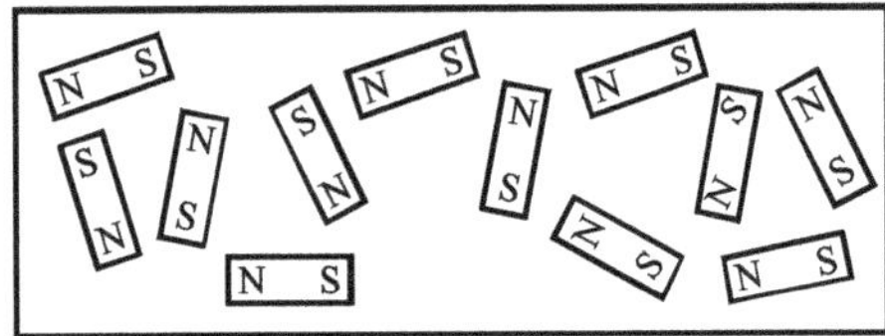

Unmagnetised

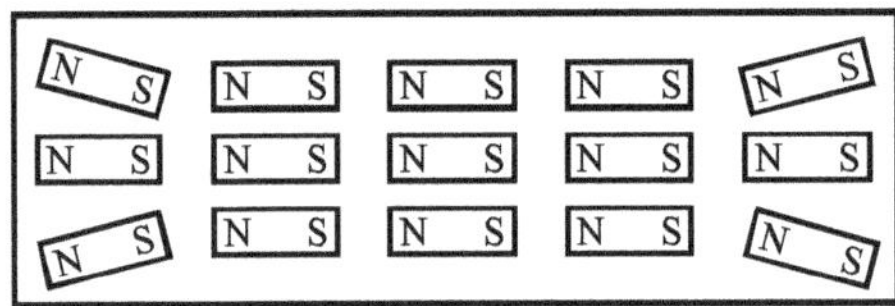

Magnetised

(iii) When **magnetised**, the molecular magnets are aligned themselves, all north poles in one direction and all south poles pointing in opposite direction.

MAGNETIC FIELD LINES

The path along which the N-pole of a magnetic compass needle is aligned itself in a magnetic field.

Properties of Magnetic Field Lines

(i)   They are closed curves, starting from N-pole and end to S-pole outside the magnet and from S-pole to N-pole inside the magnet.

(ii) The tangent to which at any point denotes the direction of magnetic field at that point.

(iii) No two lines of force intersect each other.

(iv) Crowding of more lines of force indicates stronger magnetic field.

Magnetic Dipole

Two unlike poles of equal strength separated by a small distance is called a magnetic dipole.

Where m is the magnetic pole strength, 2ℓ is the distance between the two poles. It is directed from S to N pole. Its **S.I. unit** is J/tesla.

Dipole moment, $\vec{M} = m(2\vec{\ell}\,)$

BAR MAGNETIC AS AN EQUIVALENT SOLENOID

A solenoid is a coil with a length greater than its diameter and is a type of electromagnet to produce controlled magnetic fields by passing an electric current through it.

By calculating the axial field of a finite solenoid carrying current, a bar magnet can be demonstrated as a solenoid. Consider a solenoid of radius a and length 2l with n number of turns per unit length that has current I passing through the solenoid. Considering a small element of thickness dx of the solenoid at distance x from O such that OP = r.

Magnetic field due to n turns at axis of solenoid $dB = \dfrac{\mu_0 n dx I a^2}{2(r-x)^2 + a^2]^{\frac{3}{2}}}$

Integrating x from -I to +I to magnitude of the total field

$$B = \dfrac{\mu_0 n I a^2}{2} \int_{-I}^{I} \dfrac{dx}{[r-x]^2 + a^2]^{\frac{3}{2}}} \quad [(r-x)^2]^{\frac{3}{2}} = r^3 \text{ and } B = \dfrac{\mu_0 n I a^2}{2r^3} \int_{-I}^{I} dx = \dfrac{\mu_0 n I}{2} \dfrac{2 I a^2}{r^3}$$

Therefore, $B = \dfrac{\mu_0}{4\pi} \dfrac{2m}{r^3}$

From the above expression, it is understood that the magnetic moment of a bar magnet is equal to the magnetic moment of a solenoid.

Difference between a Bar Magnet and a Solenoid

- The bar magnet is a permanent magnet whereas a solenoid is an electromagnet ie, it acts as a magnet only when an electric current is passed through.
- When a bar magnet is cut into two halves, both the pieces act as a magnet with the same magnetic properties whereas when a solenoid is cut into two halves, they will have weaker fields.
- The poles of the bar magnet are fixed whereas for a solenoid the poles can be altered.
- The strength of the magnetic field of a bar magnet is fixed ie, unaltered whereas the strength of the magnetic field of a solenoid depends on the electric current that is passed through it.

Illustration 1 :

How does a solenoid behave like a magnet?

Sol.

- A solenoid is a long coil of circular loops of insulated copper wire. Magnetic field lines are produced around the solenoid when a current is allowed to flow through it. The magnetic field produced by it is similar to the magnetic field of a bar magnet.
- The field lines produced in a current-carrying solenoid are shown in the following figure In the above figure when the north pole of a bar magnet is brought near the end connected to the negative terminal of the battery, the solenoid repels the bar magnet.
- Since like poles repel each other, the end connected to the negative terminal of the battery behaves as the North Pole of the solenoid and the other end behaves as the South Pole. Hence, one end of the solenoid behaves as the North Pole and the other end behaves as the South Pole.

CURRENT LOOP AS A MAGNETIC DIPOLE & ITS MAGNETIC DIPOLE MOMENT

A loop of wire carrying current behaves like a magnetic dipole, where the current is in clockwise direction that side of the loop is a south pole and at the opposite side current seems to be flowing in anticlockwise direction so it behaves like a north pole. They are seperated by a small distance. So the whole current loop behaves as a magnetic dipole.

Dipole moment (M) of the loop depends on,

$M \propto I$ (curent)

$M \propto A$ (area of the loop)

$\therefore$ $M \propto IA \Rightarrow M = kIA$ (k = 1 for SI units)

$\therefore$ $M = IA$ For n turns in the loop, $M = nIA$

MAGNETIC DIPOLE MOMENT OF A REVOLVING ELECTRON

In an atom electrons revolve around the nucleus. These moving electrons behave as small current loops. So atom possesses magnetic dipole moment and hence behaves as a magnetic dipole. The angular momentum of electron due to orbital motion,

$L = m_e vr.$ $[\because \vec{L} = \vec{r} \times m\vec{v}]$

The equivalent current due to orbital motion $I = -\dfrac{e}{T} = -\dfrac{ev}{2\pi r}$ As $T = \dfrac{2\pi r}{v}$

–ve sign shows direction of current is opposite to direction of motion of electron.

Magnetic dipole moment $M = IA = -\dfrac{ev}{2\pi r} \cdot \pi r^2 = -\dfrac{evr}{2}$

Using $L = m_e vr$, we have $M = -\dfrac{e}{2m_e} L$

In vector form: $\vec{M} = -\dfrac{e}{2m_e} \vec{L}$

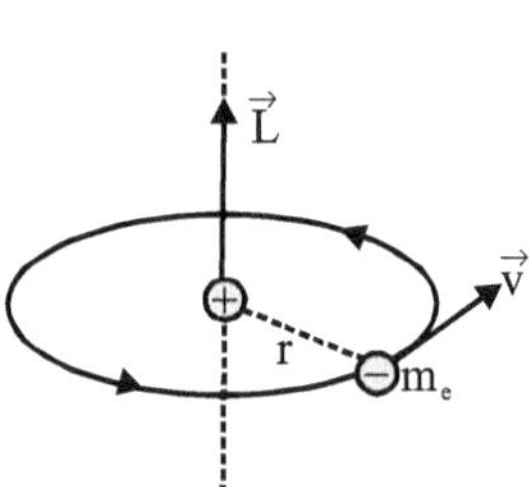

The direction of magnetic dipole moment vector is opposite to angular momentum vector.

Illustration 2 :

A current of 3 A flowing in a plane circular coil of radius 4 cm and number of turns 20. The coil is placed in a uniform magnetic filed of magnetic induction 0.5 T. Then what will be the dipole moment of the coil

Sol.   Dipole moment of coil $M = n\,i\,a = n\,i(\pi r^2) = 20 \times 3\left(\dfrac{22}{7}\right) \times (4 \times 10^{-2})^2 = 0.3 \text{ A m}^2$

MAGNETISM AND GAUSS'S LAW

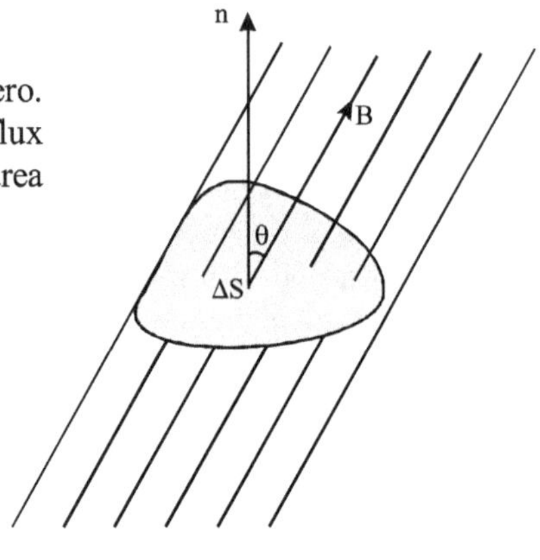

According to Gauss's law, the net magnetic flux (ϕ_B) through any closed surface is always zero. Consider a small vector area element $\Delta \mathbf{S}$ of a closed surface S as in Fig. The magnetic flux through $\Delta \mathbf{S}$ defined as $\Delta\phi_B = \mathbf{B} \cdot \Delta \mathbf{S}$, where $\mathbf{B}$ is the field at $\Delta \mathbf{S}$. We divide S into many small area elements and calculate the individual flux through each. Then, the net flux ϕ_B is,

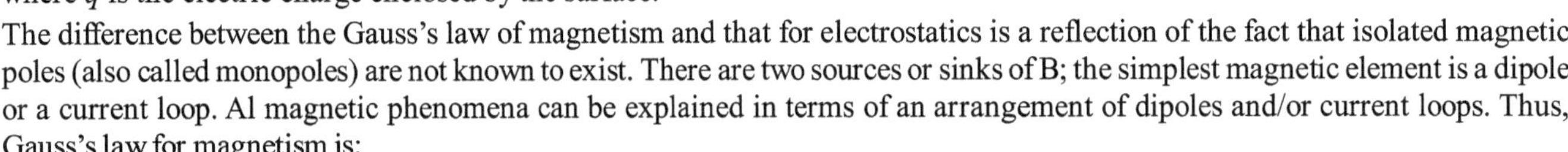

$$\phi_B = \sum_{'all'} \Delta\phi_B = \sum_{'all'} \mathbf{B} \cdot \Delta \mathbf{S} = 0$$

where 'all' stands for 'all' area elements $\Delta S'$.

Compare this with the Gauss's law of electrostatics.

The flux through a closed surface in that case is given by $\Sigma E \cdot \Delta S = \dfrac{q}{\epsilon_0}$

where q is the electric charge enclosed by the surface.

The difference between the Gauss's law of magnetism and that for electrostatics is a reflection of the fact that isolated magnetic poles (also called monopoles) are not known to exist. There are two sources or sinks of B; the simplest magnetic element is a dipole or a current loop. Al magnetic phenomena can be explained in terms of an arrangement of dipoles and/or current loops. Thus, Gauss's law for magnetism is:

The *net magnetic flux through any closed surface is zero.*

Oscillations of a Freely Suspended Magnet

In a uniform magnetic field the oscillations of a freely suspended magnet are simple harmonic and its time period is given by

$$T = 2\pi \sqrt{\dfrac{I}{MB}}$$

where   I = moment of inertia about the axis of the magnet

     M = magnetic moment   B = magnetic field intensity

Illustration 3 :

A thin rectangular magnet suspended freely has a period of oscillation of 4s. If it is broken into two equal halves, calculate the period of oscillation of each half.

Sol. For each half; mass is half and length is half; As $M.I. = \dfrac{m\ell^2}{12}$ $\quad \therefore$ M.I. becomes 1/8th. Also M becomes 1/2

As $t = 2\pi\sqrt{I/MB}$ $\quad \therefore$ t becomes $\sqrt{\dfrac{1/8}{1/2}}$ times $= \dfrac{1}{2}$ times $\qquad$ New time period $= \dfrac{1}{2} \times 4s = 2s$

Practice Exercise-1

Multiple Choice Questions

1. On cutting a solenoid in half, the field lines remain ...A..., emerging from one face of the solenoid and entering into the other face. Here, A refers to
    (a) irregular
    (b) discontinuous
    (c) continuous
    (d) alternate

2. An iron rod of length L and magnetic moment M is bent in the form of a semicircle. Now its magnetic moment will be
    (a) M
    (b) $2M/\pi$
    (c) M/π
    (d) M/π

Assertion & Reason Questions

DIRECTIONS (Qs. 3-5) : *Each of these questions contains an assertion followed by reason. Read them carefully and answer the question on the basis of following options. You have to select the one that best describes the two statements.*

(a) If both Assertion and Reason are correct and the Reason is a correct explanation of the Assertion.

(b) If both Assertion and Reason are correct but Reason is not a correct explanation of the Assertion.

(c) If the Assertion is correct but Reason is incorrect.

(d) If the Assertion is incorrect but the Reason is correct.

3. **Assertion :** Magnetic moment of an atom is due to both the orbital motion and spin motion of every electron.
    Reason : A charged particle produces magnetic field.

4. **Assertion :** Pole strength of bar magnet does not depends on area of a crossection.
    Reason : A bar magnet does exert a torque on itself due to its own field.

5. **Assertion :** The poles of magnet can not be separated by breaking into two pieces.

Reason : The magnetic moment will be reduced to half when a magnet is broken into two equal pieces.

Very Short Answer Questions

6. Define magnetic dipole moment.
7. No two magnetic lines of force intersect each other. Explain.
8. Magnetic lines of force are endless. Comment.
9. Draw magnetic field lines due to U-shaped magnet.
10. What happens if a bar magnet is cut in to two pieces along it's length?
11. Write the expression for Bohr magneton? What is it's value?
12. What is the significance of Gauss's Law in magnetism?

Short Answer Questions

13. Compare the magnetic field of a bar magnet and a solenoid.

14. A magnet of pole strength m and dipole moment M is cut as shown in the figure. Calculate new value of m and M.

    (a)
    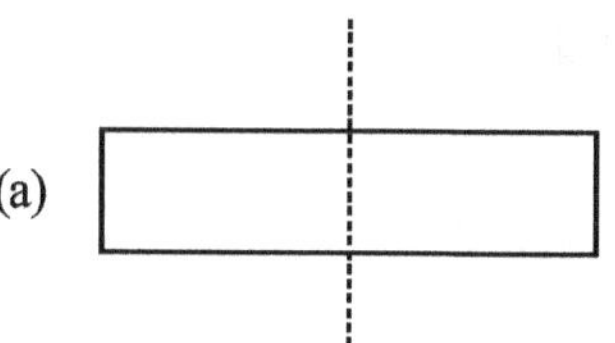

    (b)
    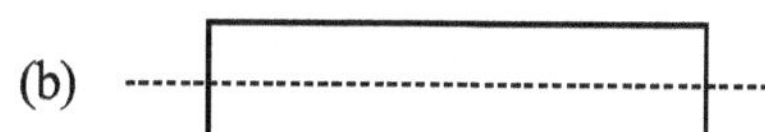

15. Write the expression for magnetic dipole moment of current loop.

16. State Gauss's law in magnetism.

Topic 2 — Earth's Magnetism – Earth's Magnetic Field & Magnetic Elements

EARTH'S MAGNETISM – EARTH'S MAGNETIC FIELD & MAGNETIC ELEMENTS

In the core of the earth various charged ions present in the molten state and constitute a current hence earth's magnetism.

Basic Terms of Earth's Magnetic Field

(i) Geographic Axis : It is straight line passing through the geographic poles of the earth. It is the axis of rotation of the earth. It is known as polar axis.

(ii) Geographic Meridian : It is a vertical plane passing through geographic north and south poles of the earth.

(iii) Geographic Equator : A great circle on the surface of the earth in a plane perpendicular to geographical axis is called geographic equator. All places on geographic equator are at equal distances from geographical poles.

(iv) Magnetic Axis : It is a straight line passing through the magnetic poles of the earth. It is inclined to geographic axis at nearly $17°$.

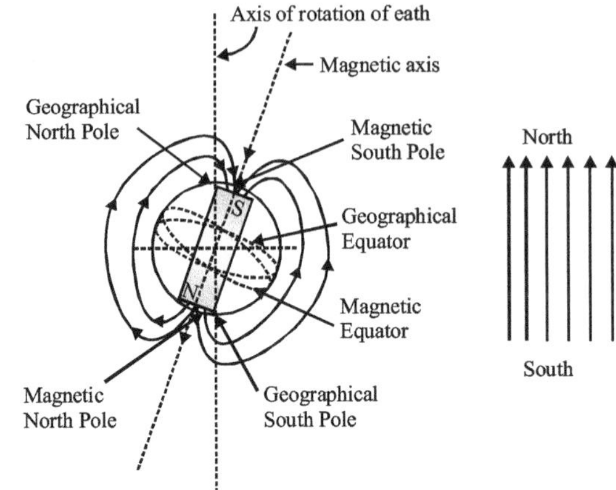

(v) Magnetic Meridian : It is a vertical plane passing through the magnetic north and south poles of the earth.

(vi) Magnetic Equator : A great circle on the surface of the earth in a plane perpendicular to magnetic axis is called magnetic equator. All places on magnetic equator are at equal distance from magnetic poles.

Elements of Earth's Magnetic Field

Magnetic elements of earth at a place are the quantities which can completely describe in magnitude and direction, the magnetic field of the earth. There are three elements of the magnetic field of the earth.

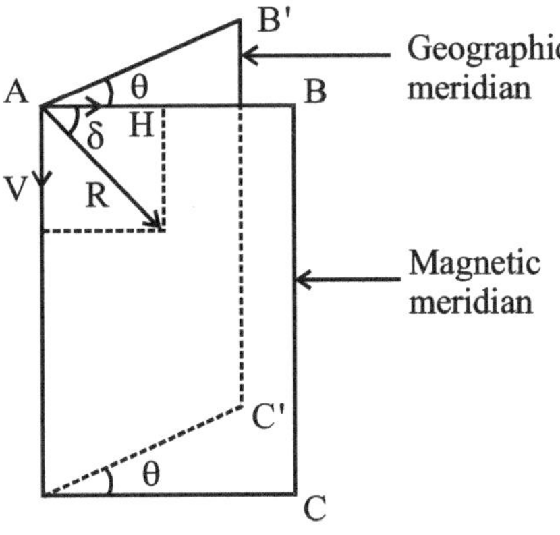

(i) Magnetic declination (θ): It is defined as the angle between the magnetic axis nd geographic axis. It can also be defined as the angle between magnetic and geographic meridian at a place.

(ii) Magnetic dip (δ) or inclination: It is defined as the angle between the direction of total intensity of earth's magnetic field and a horizontal line of magnetic meridian.

(iii) Horizontal component (H) : It is the component of total intensity of earth's magnetic field in the horrizontal direction in magnetic meridian.

Horizontal component of total intensity, $B_H = R \cos \delta$;

Vertical component of total intensity, $\quad B_V = R \sin \delta \Rightarrow B_H^2 + B_V^2 = R^2 \quad \therefore R = \sqrt{B_H^2 + B_V^2}$ and $\tan \delta = \dfrac{B_V}{B_H}$

Neutral Point

A neutral point in the magnetic field of a bar magnet is that point where the field due to the magnet is completely neutralized by the horizontal component of earth's magnetic field. At neutral point field due to bar magnet (B) is equal and opposite to horizontal component of earth's magnetic field (B_H) or $B = B_H$.

Neutral point when north pole of magnet is towards geographical north of earth.

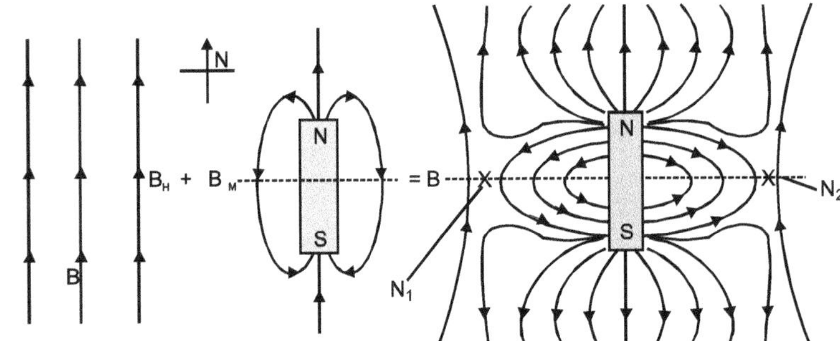

The neutral points N_1 and N_2 lie on the equatorial line. The magnetic field due to magnet at neutral point is $B = \dfrac{\mu_0}{4\pi} \dfrac{M}{(r^2 + \ell^2)^{\frac{3}{2}}}$, where M is magnetic dipole moment of magnet, 2ℓ is its length and r is distance of neutral point.

At neutral point, $B = B_H$ so $\dfrac{\mu_0}{4\pi} \dfrac{M}{(r^2 + \ell^2)^{\frac{3}{2}}} = B_H$ For a small bar magnet $(\ell^2 << r^2)$ then $\dfrac{\mu_0}{4\pi} \dfrac{M}{r^3} = B_H$

Neutral Point when South Pole of Magnet is Towards Geographical North of Earth.

The neutral points N_1 and N_2 lie on the axial line of magnet. The magnetic field due

to magnet at neutral point is $B = \dfrac{\mu_0}{4\pi} \dfrac{2Mr}{(r^2 - \ell^2)^2}$

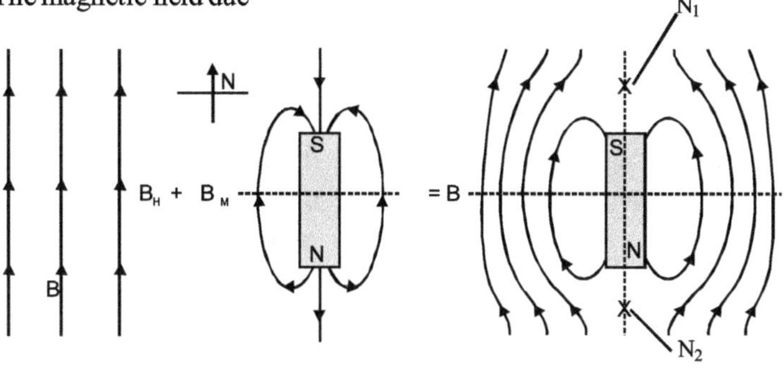

At neutral point, $B = B_H$ so $\dfrac{\mu_0}{4\pi} \dfrac{2Mr}{(r^2 - \ell^2)^2} = B_H$

For a small bar magnet $(\ell^2 \ll r^2)$ then $\dfrac{\mu_0}{4\pi} \dfrac{2M}{r^3} = B_H$

Illustration 4 :

If θ_1 and θ_2 are angles of dip in two vertical planes at right angle to each other and θ is true dip then prove $\cot^2\theta = \cot^2\theta_1 + \cot^2\theta_2$.

Sol.   If the vertical plane in which dip is θ_1 subtends an angle α with meridian than other vertical plane in which dip is θ_2 and is perpendicular to first will make an angle of $90 - \alpha$ with magnetic meridian. If θ_1 and θ_2 are apparent dips than

$$\tan\theta_1 = \frac{B_V}{B_H \cos\alpha} \;;\quad \tan\theta_2 = \frac{B_V}{B_H \cos(90-\alpha)} = \frac{B_V}{B_H \sin\alpha}$$

$$\cot^2\theta_1 + \cot^2\theta_2 = \frac{1}{(\tan\theta_1)^2} + \frac{1}{(\tan\theta_2)^2} = \frac{B_H^2 \cos^2\alpha + B_H^2 \sin^2\alpha}{B_V^2} = \frac{B_H^2}{B_V^2} = \left(\frac{B\cos\theta}{B\sin\theta}\right)^2 = \cot^2\theta$$

So, $\cot^2\theta_1 + \cot^2\theta_2 = \cot^2\theta$

Illustration 5 :

A magnetising field of $1600\,Am^{-1}$ produces a magnetic flux of 2.4×10^{-5} weber in a bar of iron of cross section $0.2\,cm^2$. Calculate permeability and susceptibility of the bar.

Sol.   Here, $H = 1600\,Am^{-1}$, $\phi = 2.4 \times 10^{-5}$ Wb.

$$a = 0.2\,cm^2 = 0.2 \times 10^{-4}\,m^2,\ \mu = ?\ \chi_m = ?$$

$$B = \frac{\phi}{a} = \frac{2.4\times10^{-5}}{0.2\times10^{-4}} = 1.2 \text{ weber}/m^2 \;;\ \mu = \frac{B}{H} = \frac{1.2}{1600} = 7.5\times10^{-4}\,TA^{-1}m \;;\ \text{As } \mu = \mu_0(1+\chi_m)$$

$$\therefore \chi_m = \frac{\mu}{\mu_0} - 1 = \frac{7.5\times10^{-4}}{4\pi\times10^{-7}} - 1 \;;\ \chi_m = \frac{7.5\times10^3}{4\pi} - 1 = 597.1 - 1 = 596.1$$

Practice Exercise-2

Multiple Choice Questions

1. Which of the following statement(s) is/are true/false about magnetism?

I.   The Earth behaves as a magnet with the magnetic field pointing approximately from the geographic South to the North.

II.   When a bar magnet is freely suspended, it points in the North–South direction. The tip which points to the geographic North is called the North –pole and the tip which points to georaphic South is called the South–pole of magnet.

III.   There is a repulsive force when North–poles (or South–poles) of two magnets are brought close together. Conversely, there is an attractive force between the North–pole of one magnet and the South–pole of other.

IV.   We can isolate the North or South–pole of a magnet.

(a)   T, T, F, F   (b)   T, T, F, T

(c)   F, F, T, T   (d)   T, T, T, F

2. At a certain place, the angle of dip is 30° and the horizontal component of earth's magnetic field is 0.50 oerested. The earth's total magnetic field (in oerested) is

(a) $\sqrt{3}$ (b)   1   (c) $\dfrac{1}{\sqrt{3}}$ (d) $\dfrac{1}{2}$

3. Match the column-I and column II.

Column I		Column II	
(A)	Horizontal component	(1)	$B_E \sin \phi$
(B)	Vertical component	(2)	$\dfrac{B_V}{B_H}$
(C)	$\tan \phi$	(3)	$B_E \cos \phi$
(D)	Tangent law	(4)	$B = B_H \tan \theta$

  (a) $A \rightarrow (3); B \rightarrow (2); C \rightarrow (1); D \rightarrow (4)$
  (b) $A \rightarrow (3); B \rightarrow (1); C \rightarrow (2); D \rightarrow (4)$
  (c) $A \rightarrow (2); B \rightarrow (3); C \rightarrow (1); D \rightarrow (4)$
  (d) $A \rightarrow (1); B \rightarrow (3); C \rightarrow (2); D \rightarrow (4)$

4. The horizontal component of the earth's magnetic field is 3.6×10^{-5} tesla where the dip angle is $60°$. The magnitude of the earth's magnetic field is
  (a) 2.8×10^{-4} tesla   (b) 2.1×10^{-4} tesla
  (c) 7.2×10^{-5} tesla   (d) 3.6×10^{-5} tesla

5. At a certain place, horizontal component is $\sqrt{3}$ times the vertical component. The angle of dip at this place is
  (a) 0 (b) $\pi/3$ (c) $\pi/6$ (d) $\pi/8$

6. Let V and H be the vertical and horizontal components of earth's magnetic field at any point on earth. Near the north pole
  (a) $V \gg H$ (b) $V \ll H$
  (c) $V = H$ (d) $V = H = 0$

7. The earth's magnetic field lines resemble that of a dipole at the centre of the earth. If the magnetic moment of this dipole is close to 8×10^{22} Am^2, the value of earth's magnetic field near the equator is close to (radius of the earth $= 6.4 \times 10^6$ m)
  (a) 0.6 Gauss   (b) 1.2 Gauss
  (c) 1.8 Gauss   (d) 0.32 Gauss

Case/Passage Based Questions

Magnetic elements of earth at a place are the quantities which can completely describe in magnitude and direction, the magnetic field of the earth. There are three elements of the magnetic field of the earth.

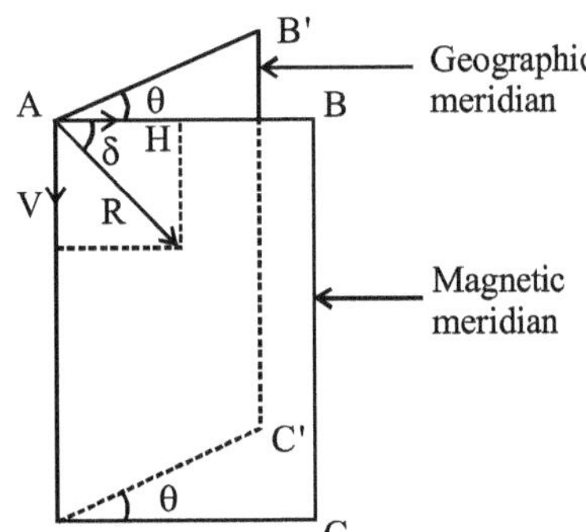

Horizontal component of total intensity, $B_H = R \cos \delta$;

Vertical component of total intensity,

$$B_V = R \sin \delta \Rightarrow B_H^2 + B_V^2 = R^2$$

$\therefore \quad R = \sqrt{B_H^2 + B_V^2}$ and $\tan \delta = \dfrac{B_V}{B_H}$

8. The strength of the earth's magnetic field is
  (a) constant everywhere
  (b) zero everywhere
  (c) having very high value
  (d) vary from place to place on the earth's surface

9. The lines of force due to earth's horizontal magnetic field are
  (a) parallel and straight   (b) concentric circles
  (c) elliptical   (d) curved lines

10. The earth's magnetic field always has a vertical component except at the
  (a) magnetic equator   (b) magnetic poles
  (c) geographic north pole   (d) latitude $45°$

11. At magnetic poles, the angle of dip is
  (a) $45°$ (b) $30°$ (c) zero   (d) $90°$

12. At the magnetic north pole of the earth, the value of the horizontal component of earth's magnetic field and angle of dip are respectively
  (a) zero, maximum   (b) maximum, minimum
  (c) maximum, maximum   (d) minimum, minimum

Very Short Answer Questions

13. Name the elements of earth's magnetic field.

14. What is the value of angle of dip at any place situated on the magnetic equator of the earth?

15. What is the angle of dip at a place where the horrizontal and vertical components of earth's magnetic field are equal?

16. The angle of dip at two places on the surface of the earth are respectively $0°$ and $90°$. Where are these places located?

17. Horizontal component of earth's magnetic field at a place is $\sqrt{3}$ times the vertical component. What is the value of angle of dip at this place?

18. If the ratio of horizontal component of earth's magnetic field to the resultant magnetic field at a place is $\dfrac{1}{\sqrt{2}}$, what is the angle of dip at that place?

19. Write mathematical form of tangent law in magnetism.

Short Answer Questions

20. Define the terms magnetic inclination and horizontal component of Earth's magnetic field at a place. Establish the relationship between the two with the help of a diagram.

21. What are the probable causes of the earth's magnetism?

22. A magnetic needle free to rotate in a vertical position orients itself with its axis horizontal at a certain place on the earth. What are the values of (i) angle of dip and (ii) horizontal component of earth's field at this place? Where will this place be on earth?

23. Horizontal and vertical component of magnetic field at a place are 0.22 gauss and 0.38 gauss. Calculate the angle of dip and resultant intensity of magnetic field.

24. The horizontal component of earth's magnetic field is 0.2 gauss and total magnetic field is 0.4 gauss. Find angle of dip.

25. A magnetic compass needle of magnetic moment 60 Am^2 is placed at a place. The needle points towards geographical north. Using the data given below, find the value of declination at that place. Horizontal component of earth's magnetic field $= 40 \times 10^{-6}$ Wb m^2 and torque experienced by the needle $= 1.2 \times 10^{-3}$ Nm.

26. How does the angle of dip vary as one moves from the equator towards the north pole? If the horizontal component of earth's magnetic field at a place where the angle of dip is 60° is 0.4×10^{-4} T, calculate the vertical component and the resultant magnetic field of earth at that point.

Important Tips & Formulae

- For a straight current carrying wire, magnetic moment is zero.
- Magnetic moment of toroid is zero.
- Atoms which have paired electrons have zero magnetic moment.
- The length of an iron bar changes when it is magnetised. When an iron bar is magnestised its length increases due to alignment of spins parallel to the field. This increase is in the direction of magnetisation.
- Horizontal component of earth's magnetic field is zero at poles. Vertical component of earth's magnetic field is zero at equator.
- Angle of dip at magnetic equator is 0° and at magnetic poles, it is 90°.
- Magnetic susceptibility is independent of temperature for diamagnetic substances.
- Material used for making soft iron should have high retentivity and low coercivity.
- The origin of diamagnetism is due to orbital motion of electrons. But, the origin of paramagnetism and ferromagnetism is due to magnetic moment of spinning of electrons.
- At curie temperature, substance undergo sharp change in their magnetic property.
- Time period of oscillation in difference position is always greater than that in sum position $T_d > T_s$.
- Intensity of magnetisation (I) is produced due to spin motion of electrons.
- To protect a magnetic material from the external magnetic field it should be placed inside a soft iron case. This phenomenon is called magnetic screening or shielding.
- Magnetic permeability of substance is given by
$\mu = \mu_0\mu_r = \mu_0(1+\chi)$
- Force between two bar magnets when their magnetic moments are parallel to each other is given by

$$f = \frac{\mu_0}{4\pi}\frac{6M_1M_2}{d^4}$$

If Magnetic moments are perpendicular to each other, then

$$f = \frac{\mu_0}{4\pi}\frac{3M_1M_2}{d^4}$$

- When a bar magnet is cut into two equal pieces along its length, then two magnets will have half pole strength and half the dipole moment.

- If a bar magnet is cut into two pieces perpendicular to its length, we get two magnet with same pole strength but half the dipole moment.
- A current carrying solenoid can be considered as the arrangement of small magnetic dipoles placed in line with each other. The number of such small magnetic dipoles is equal to the number of turns in the solenoid.
- Total intensity of earth's magnetic field is given by

$$I = I_0\sqrt{1+3\sin^2\delta}$$

Where $I_0 = \dfrac{M}{R^3}$

At equator, $\delta = 0°$ $\therefore$ $I = I_0$
At poles, $\delta = 90°$ $\therefore$ $I = 2I_0$

- Consider a vertical plane inclined at an angle β to the magnetic meridian. In such plane vertical component of earth's magnetic field will remain unchanged while in the new inclined plane, horizontal component of magnetic field is given by $B'_H = B_H \cos \beta$
$\phi' =$ apparent angle of dip

and $\tan\phi' = \dfrac{B_V}{B_H} = \dfrac{B_V}{B_H \cos\beta}$

$\Rightarrow \tan\phi' = \dfrac{\tan\phi}{\cos\beta}$

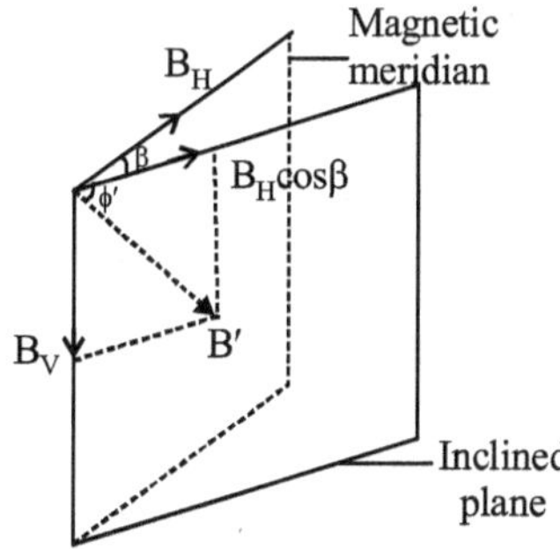

- If two bar magnets of magnetic moment M_1 and M_2 are lying at an angle to each other, then net magnetic moment,

$$M = \sqrt{M_1^2 + M_2^2 + 2M_1M_2\cos\theta}$$

- The area of hysteresis loop for soft iron is much smaller than for steel so energy loss per unit volume per cycle of soft iron is smaller than steel.
- If a bar magnet requires a magnetic intensity H to become demagnetised inside a long solenoid having n turns per unit length, then $H = nI$
Here, $I =$ current passing through the solenoid.

NCERT Questions

5.1. Answer the following questions regarding earth's magnetism:

    (a) A vector needs three quantities for its specification. Name the three independent quantities conventionally used to specify the earth's magnetic field.

    (b) The angle of dip at a location in southern India is about 18°. Would you expect a greater or smaller dip angle in Britain?

    (c) If you made a map of magnetic field lines at Melbourne in Australia, would the lines seem to go into the ground or come out of the ground?

    (d) In which direction would a compass free to move in the vertical plane point to, if located right on the geomagnetic north or south pole?

    (e) The earth's field, it is claimed, roughly approximates the field due to a dipole of magnetic moment 8×10^{22} J T^{-1} located at its centre. Check the order of magnitude of this number in some way.

    (f) Geologists claim that besides the main magnetic N-S poles, there are several local poles on the earth's surface oriented in different directions. How is such a thing possible at all?

Sol. (a) The three quantities are (1) magnetic declination (2) angle of dip and (3) horizontal component of earths magnetic field.

    (b) Since Britian is closer to the magnetic north pole hence angle of dip would be greater.

    (c) Since Australia is closer to magnetic south pole hence magnetic field lines would come out of the ground.

    (d) At the geomagnetic poles the direction of magnetic field would be in the vertical direction hence a magnetic needle moving in a horizontal plane would point in any direction.

    (e) Using formula for field at an equatorial point of a magnetic dipole

$$B = \frac{\mu_0 M}{4\pi r^3}, \text{ put } M \approx 8 \times 10^{22} \text{ J/T}$$

$$r = 6.4 \times 10^6 \text{m}, \frac{\mu_0}{4\pi} = 10^{-7}$$

$$\Rightarrow B = \frac{10^{-7} \times 8 \times 10^{22}}{(6.4 \times 10^6)^3} \approx \frac{8}{6.4 \times 6.4 \times 6.4} \times 10^{15-18}$$

$$\approx 0.031 \times 10^{-3} \simeq 0.3 \times 10^{-4} \text{ T} \simeq 0.3 \text{ G}$$

This is close to value of field due to earth (0.4 G) hence order of m is correct.

    (f) Local poles may happen due to deposites of magnetised mineral (iron etc.) Earths poles are the total sum of approximately all such magnetic fields inside the surface and in its core.

5.2 Answer the following questions:

    (a) The earth's magnetic field varies from point to point in space. Does it also change with time? If so, on what time scale does it change appreciably?

    (b) The earth's core is known to contain iron. Yet geologists do not regard this as a source of the earth's magnetism. Why?

    (c) The charged currents in the outer conducting regions of the earth's core are thought to be responsible for earth's magnetism. What might be the 'battery' (i.e., the source of energy) to sustain these currents?

    (d) The earth may have even reversed the direction of its field several times during its history of 4 to 5 billion years. How can geologists know about the earth's field in such distant past?

    (e) The earth's field departs from its dipole shape substantially at large distances (greater than about 30,000 km). What agencies may be responsible for this distortion?

    (f) Interstellar space has an extremely weak magnetic field of the order of 10^{-12} T. Can such a weak field be of any significant consequence? Explain.

[Note: Exercise 5.2 is meant mainly to arouse your curiosity. Answers to some questions above are tentative or unknown. Brief answers wherever possible are given at the end. For details, you should consult a good text on geomagnetism.]

Sol. (a) Yes, due to the motion of its plates and core the earth's magnetic field does shift. Noticeable changes occur over a large period of time (few hundred years) and variations are there even in small durations of time (few years) which cannot be ignored.

    (b) The core contains molten iron (magnetic domains are destroyed in molten form) which is not ferromagnetic hence it cannot contribute to magnetism of earth.

    (c) No, one really knows.

    (d) By study rock magnetism i.e., the solidification of rocks leads to trapping of materials in their magnetised states. Analysing these we can get clues to the history of geomagnetism.

    (e) At large distances external factors such as solar winds, ionospheric particles etc. influences the earths magnetic field, hence it gets distorted.

    (f) From cyclotron relation $r = \dfrac{mv}{e.B}$ we can say that small field can affect the path of moving charged particle whose radius is large eg. cosmic rays.

5.3 **A short bar magnet placed with its axis at 30° with a uniform external magnetic field of 0.25 T experiences a torque of magnitude equal to 4.5 × 10⁻² J. What is the magnitude of magnetic moment of the magnet?**

Sol. **Given:** magnetic field $B = 0.25$ T,
Torque $\tau = 4.5 \times 10^{-2}$ J,
Angle between axis of magnet and field $\theta = 30°$
To find: Magnetic moment = ?
Formula used: $\tau = MB \sin \theta$

$$M = \frac{\tau}{B \sin \theta} = \frac{4.5 \times 10^{-2}}{0.25 \times \sin 30°} = \frac{18 \times 10^{-2}}{1/2} = 0.36 \, A \, m^2$$

5.4 **A short bar magnet of magnetic moment m = 0.32 JT⁻¹ is placed in a uniform magnetic field of 0.15 T. If the bar is free to rotate in the plane of the field, which orientation would correspond to its (a) stable and (b) unstable equilibrium? What is the potential energy of the magnet in each case?**

Sol. **Given:** magnetic moment $M = 0.32$ J/T
Magnetic field $= 0.15$ T
To find: angle of orientation and potential energy in
(a) stable equilibrium
Formula used: $U = -MB \cos \theta$
Magnet is in stable equilibrium, M is parallel to B.
∴ $U = -MB \cos 0° = -MB = -0.32 \times 0.15 = -4.8 \times 10^{-2} \, J$
(b) Magnet is in unstable equilibrium,
M is antiparallel to B
∴ $U = -MB \cos 180° = MB = 0.32 \times 0.15 = 4.8 \times 10^{-2} \, J$

5.5 **A closely wound solenoid of 800 turns and area of cross section 2.5 × 10⁻⁴ m² carries a current of 3.0 A. Explain the sense in which the solenoid acts like a bar magnet. What is its associated magnetic moment?**

Sol. **Given:** No. of turns $N = 800$;
area $A = 2.5 \times 10^{-4}$ m²; current $I = 3.0$ A
To find: Magnetic moment
Formula used: $M = NIA$
Whenever current is passed through the solenoid, magnetic field is produced along its axis. The magnetic field lines comeout from one end and enter the other end of the solenoid. The ends acts as bar magnet poles. Magnetic moment $M = NIA = 800 \times 3 \times 2.5 \times 10^{-4} = 0.6 \, Am^2$

5.6. **If the solenoid in Exercise 5.5 is free to turn about the vertical direction and a uniform horizontal magnetic field of 0.25 T is applied, what is the magnitude of torque on the solenoid when its axis makes an angle of 30° with the direction of applied field?**

Sol. **Given:** Horizontal magnetic field $B = 0.25$ T,
magnetic moment (from Q. 5.5) $M = 0.6 \, Am^2$
angle $\theta = 30°$
To find: Torque τ
Formula used: $\tau = MB \sin \theta$

$$\tau = 0.6 \times 0.25 \times \sin 30° = 0.15 \times \frac{1}{2} = 0.075 \, Nm$$

5.7. **A bar magnet of magnetic moment 1.5 J T⁻¹ lies aligned with the direction of a uniform magnetic field of 0.22 T.**

What is the amount of work required by an external torque to turn the magnet so as to align its magnetic moment: (i) normal to the field direction, (ii) opposite to the field direction?
Also find the torque on the magnet in two cases (i) and (ii).

Sol. (i) Magnetic field $= 0.22$ T
magnetic moment of barmagnet
$M = 1.5$ J/T
To find: Work done in (i) normal direction (ii) opposite direction. Torque in (i) normal (ii) opposite direction
Formula used: $W = MB (\cos \theta_1 - \cos \theta_2)$ and $\tau = MB \sin \theta$
(i) To rotate the bar magnet from parallel alignment to normal direction, work done
$= W = MB (\cos 0° - \cos 90°)$
⇒ $W = 1.5 \times 0.22 \times (1 - 0) = 0.33$ J
Torque for $\theta = 90° \Rightarrow \tau = 1.5 \times 0.22 \times 1 = 0.33$ Nm
(ii) work done to rotate bar magnet from same direction to opposite is
$W = MB (\cos 0° - \cos 180°)$
$= 1.5 \times 0.22 (1 - (-1)) = 1.5 \times 0.22 \times 2 = 0.66$ J
Torque for $\theta = 180°$
$\tau = MB \sin 180° = 1.5 \times 0.22 \times 0 = 0$

5.8. **A closely wound solenoid of 2000 turns and area of cross-section 1.6 × 10⁻⁴ m², carrying a current of 4.0 A, is suspended through its centre allowing it to turn in a horizontal plane.**
(a) **What is the magnetic moment associated with the solenoid?**
(b) **What is the force and torque on the solenoid if a uniform horizontal magnetic field of 7.5 × 10⁻²T is set up at an angle of 30° with the axis of the solenoid?**

Sol. (a) **Given:** No. of turns $N = 2000$
area $= 1.6 \times 10^{-4}$ m²
current $I = 4.0$ A, magnetic field
$B = 7.5 \times 10^{-2}$ T
To find: Magnetic moment M
Torque for $\theta = 30°$, Force.
Formula: $M = NIA$
$\tau = MB \sin \theta$
The magnetic moment
$M = NIA = 40 \times 1.6 \times 10^{-4} \times 200 = 1.28 \, Am^2$
(b) Torque $\tau = MB \sin \theta = 1.28 \times 7.5 \times 10^{-2} \sin$

$$30° = 0.096 \times \frac{1}{2} = 0.048 \, Nm$$

Since force on both ends is equal and opposite hence net force is zero.

5.9. **A circular coil of 16 turns and radius 10 cm carrying a current of 0.75 A rests with its plane normal to an external field of magnitude 5.0 × 10⁻² T. The coil is free to turn about an axis in its plane perpendicular to the field direction. When the coil is turned slightly and released, it oscillates about its stable equilibrium with a frequency of 2.0 s⁻¹. What is the moment of inertia of the coil about its axis of rotation?**

Sol. **Given:** No. of turns $= 16$
radius $a = 10\,cm = 10 \times 10^{-2} = 0.1\,m$
current $I = 0.75\,A$
field $B = 5 \times 10^{-2}\,T$
frequency $v = 2.0\,s^{-1}$
To find: Moment of inertia $I = ?$

Formula used: $v = \dfrac{1}{2\pi}\sqrt{\dfrac{MB}{I}}$

The magnetic moment of the coil $M = NIA = NI\,\pi a^2$
$= 16 \times 0.75 \times \pi \times (0.1)^2 = 12 \times 3.14 \times 10^{-2} = 0.377\,Am^2$

Frequency $v = \dfrac{1}{2\pi}\sqrt{\dfrac{MB}{I}}$

$$\Rightarrow \quad I = \frac{MB}{4\pi^2 v^2} = \frac{0.377 \times 5 \times 10^{-2}}{4 \times (3.14)^2 \times 2^2} = \frac{0.377 \times 5 \times 10^{-2}}{16 \times 9.87}$$

$$= 1.2 \times 10^{-4}\,kg\,m^2$$

5.10. **A magnetic needle free to rotate in a vertical plane parallel to the magnetic meridian has its north tip pointing down at 22° with the horizontal. The horizontal component of the earth's magnetic field at the place is known to be 0.35 G. Determine the magnitude of the earth's magnetic field at the place.**

Sol. **Given:** Horizontal component of earth's magnetic field H $= 0.35\,G$
angle of dip $\delta = 22°$
To find: Earth's magnetic field B.
Formula: $H = B\cos\delta$

$$B = \frac{H}{\cos\delta} = \frac{0.35}{\cos 22°} \Rightarrow B = \frac{0.35}{0.9272} = 0.38\,G$$

5.11. **At a certain location in Africa, a compass points 12° west of the geographic north. The north tip of the magnetic needle of a dip circle placed in the plane of magnetic meridian points 60° above the horizontal. The horizontal component of the earth's field is measured to be 0.16 G. Specify the direction and magnitude of the earth's field at the location.**

Sol. **Given:** Angle of dip $\delta = 60°$; Horizontal component of earth's magnetic field $H = 0.16\,G$
To find: Earth's magnetic field $= B$
Formula used: $H = B\cos\delta$

$$H = B\cos\delta \Rightarrow B = \frac{H}{\cos\delta} = \frac{0.16}{\cos 60°} = \frac{0.16}{0.5} = 0.32\,G$$

The magnetic field of the earth lies 12° West of the geographic meridian (of Africa) at an angle of 60° (upwards) with respect to the horizontal.

5.12. **A short bar magnet has a magnetic moment of 0.48 J T⁻¹. Give the direction and magnitude of the magnetic field produced by the magnet at a distance of 10 cm from the centre of the magnet on (a) the axis, (b) the equatorial lines (normal bisector) of the magnet.**

Sol. **Given:** magnetic moment $m = 0.48\,J/T$
distance from magnets centre $= 10\,cm$.

To find: Magnetic field along (a) axis (b) normal bisector
Formula used: (a) Magnetic field due to bar magnet along

axis $B_{axis} = \dfrac{\mu_0}{4\pi}\dfrac{2M}{r^3}$

$$B_{axial} = \frac{\mu_0}{4\pi}\frac{2M}{r^3} = 10^{-7}\frac{2 \times 0.48}{(0.1)^3} = 9.6 \times 10^{-5}\,T \text{ (along } \vec{M})$$

(b)   Magnetic field along equatorial line,

$$B_{eq} = \frac{\mu_0}{4\pi}\frac{M}{r^3}$$

$$B_{eq} = \frac{\mu_0}{4\pi}\frac{M}{r^3} = 10^{-7} \times \frac{0.48}{(0.1)^3} = 4.8 \times 10^{-5}$$

$$T \text{ (opposite to } \vec{M})$$

5.13. **A short bar magnet placed in a horizontal plane has its axis aligned along the magnetic north-south direction. Null points are found on the axis of the magnet at 14 cm from the centre of the magnet. The earth's magnetic field at the place is 0.36 G and the angle of dip is zero. What is the total magnetic field on the normal bisector of the magnet at the same distance as the null-point (i.e., 14 cm) from the centre of the magnet? (At null points, field due to a magnet is equal and opposite to the horizontal component of earth's magnetic field).**

Sol. **Given:** Angle of dip $= 0°$; Distance of null point $= 14\,cm$
Earth's magnetic field $B = 0.36\,G$

To find: Total magnetic field on the normal bisector of the magnet B'
Formula used: $B = B_{axial} + B_{equatorial}$
In case of bar magnet placed in horizontal plane in N-S direction, null points wil lie along the axial line.
At the null point. H (Horizontal component of earth's field) is given by

$$H = B_{axial} \text{ and } B_{axial} = \frac{\mu_0}{4\pi}\frac{2M}{r^3} = H$$

Also $B_{eq} = \dfrac{\mu_0}{4\pi}\dfrac{M}{r^3}$

$$\Rightarrow \quad B_{eq} = \frac{H}{2} \text{ Hence, total magnetic field of magnet}$$

$$B = B_{axial} + B_{eq} = H + \frac{H}{2} = \frac{3}{2}H = \frac{3}{2} \times 0.36 \Rightarrow B = 0.54\,G$$

5.14. **If the bar magnet in exercise 5.13 is turned around by 180°, where will the new null points be located?**

Sol. **Given:** $\theta = 180° \Rightarrow$ position of null point changed from axial to equatorial location.

To find: Position of null point

Formula used: $B_{eq} = \dfrac{\mu_0}{4\pi}\dfrac{M}{r^3}$

In the given position of the magnet (S - N) the null points lie on the equatorial line

And $\quad B_{eq} = H$

Where $\quad B_{eq} = H = \dfrac{\mu_0}{4\pi} \dfrac{M}{r_{eq}^3}$

In previous question, null points were along axial line

and $B_{axial} = \dfrac{\mu_0}{4\pi} \dfrac{2M}{r_{axial}^3} \; (=H)$

Comparing the two, we get

$$r_{eq} = \dfrac{r_{axial}}{2^{1/3}} = \dfrac{14}{1.26} = 11.1 \text{ cm}$$

5.15. A short bar magnet of magnetic moment $5.25 \times 10^{-2} \text{ J T}^{-1}$ is placed with its axis perpendicular to the earth's field direction. At what distance from the centre of the magnet, the resultant field is inclined at $45°$ with earth's field on (a) its normal bisector and (b) its axis. Magnitude of the earth's field at the place is given to be 0.42 G. Ignore the length of the magnet in comparison to the distances involved.

Sol. **Given:** Magnetic moment $= 5.25 \times 10^{-2}$ J/T

$\quad \theta = 45°, H = 0.42 \text{ G} = 0.42 \times 10^{-4}$ T

To find: Distance at which angle between resultant field and H is $45°$ along

(i) equatorial line (ii) axial line

Formula used: (i) $B_{eq} = \dfrac{\mu_0}{4\pi} \dfrac{M}{r^3}$

(ii) $B_{axial} = \dfrac{\mu_0}{4\pi} \dfrac{2M}{r^3}$

(i) For the Bar magnet, the normal bisector field and horizontal component of earth's magnetic field will have a resultant at $45°$ only when both are equal and perpendicular.

i.e. $B_{eq} = H$

$\Rightarrow \quad B_{eq} = \dfrac{\mu_0}{4\pi} \dfrac{M}{r^3} = H$

$\Rightarrow \quad r = \left(\dfrac{\mu_0}{4\pi} \dfrac{M}{H} \right)^{1/3}$

$$= \left(\dfrac{10^{-7} \times 5.25 \times 10^{-2}}{0.42 \times 10^{-4}} \right)^{1/3}$$

$$= (125 \times 10^{-6})^{1/3} = 5 \times 10^{-2} \text{ m} = 5 \text{ cm}$$

(ii) Again resultant will be at $45°$

when $B_{axial} = H \Rightarrow B_{axial} = \dfrac{\mu_0}{4\pi} \dfrac{2M}{r^3} = H$

$\Rightarrow r = \left(\dfrac{\mu_0}{4\pi} \dfrac{2M}{H} \right)^{1/3} = \left(\dfrac{10^{-7} \times 5.25 \times 2 \times 10^{-2}}{0.42 \times 10^{-4}} \right)^{1/3}$

$$= (250 \times 10^{-6})^{1/3} = 6.3 \times 10^{-2} = 6.3 \text{ cm}$$

ADDITIONAL EXERCISES

5.16. Answer the following questions:

(a) Why does a paramagnetic sample display greater magnetisation (for the same magnetising field) when cooled?

(b) Why is diamagnetism, in contrast, almost independent of temperature?

(c) If a toroid used bismuth for its core, will the field in the core be (slightly) greater or (slightly) less than when the core is empty?

(d) Is the permeability of a ferromagnetic material independent of the magnetic field? If not, is it more for lower or higher fields?

(e) Magnetic field lines are always nearly normal to the surface of a ferromagnet at every point. (This fact is analogous to the static electric field lines being normal to the surface of a conductor at every point.) Why?

(f) Would the maximum possible magnetisation of a paramagnetic sample be of the same order of magnitude as the magnetisation of a ferromagnetic?

Sol. (a) In paramagnetics, the tendency to disrupt the alignment of molecular dipoles with the external magnetising field arising from random thermal motion is reduced at lower temperatures.

(b) In diamagnetics, the molecular dipole moments always align in direction opposite to that of external magnetising field, inspite of the internal motion of atoms.

(c) As bismuth is diamagnetic, so the field in the toroid with bismuth core will be slightly less than when the core is empty.

(d) No, the permeability of a ferromagnetic material is not independent of the magnetic field. It is more at higher fields.

(e) As the magnetic permeability μ of a ferromagnetic is much larger than unity i.e. $\mu \gg 1$, so magnetic field lines are always nearly normal to the surface of a ferromagnetic at every point.

(f) Yes, but for the maximum possible magnetisation of paramagnetic sample impractically very high magnetising fields are required.

5.17 Answer the following questions:

(a) **Explain qualitatively on the basis of domain picture the irreversibility in the magnetisation curve of a ferromagnet.**

(b) **The hysteresis loop of a soft iron piece has much smaller area than that of a carbon steel piece. If the material is to go through repeated cycles of magnetisation, which piece will dissipate greater heat energy?**

(c) **A system displaying a hysteresis loop such as a ferromagnet, is a device for storing memory?' Explain the meaning of this statement.**

(d) **What kind of ferromagnetic material is used for coating magnetic tapes in a cassette player, or for building 'memory stores' in modern computer?**

(e) **A certain region of space is to be shielded from magnetic fields. Suggest a method.**

Sol. (a) In a specimen of a ferromagnetic, the atomic dipoles are grouped together in domains. All the dipoles of a domain are aligned in the same direction and have net magnetic moment. In an unmagnetised substance these domains are randomly distributed so that the resultant magnetisation is zero. When the substance is placed in an external magnetic field, these domains align themselves in the direction of the field. Some energy is spent in the process of alignment when the external field is removed, these domains do nor come back into their random positions completely. The substance retains some magnetisation. The energy spent in the process of magnetisation is not fully recovered. The balance of energy is lost as heat. This is the basic cause for irreversibility of the magnetisation curve of a ferromagnetic substance.

(b) Carbon-Steel piece, because the heat produced in complete cycle of mangetisation is directly proportional to the area under the hysteresis loop.

(c) Magnetisation of a ferromagnet is not a single valued function of the magnetising field. Its value for a particular field depends both on the magnetising field and on the history of its magnetisation *i.e.* how many cycles of magnetisation it has gone through etc. So, the value of magnetisation is a record or memory of its cycles if magnetisation. If information bits can be made to correspond to these cycles, the system displaying such a hysteresis loop can act as a device for storing information.

(d) Ferrites or ceramics which is specially treated barium iron oxides.

(e) By surrounding the region with soft iron rings, as magnetic field lines will be drawn into the rings and the enclosed space becomes free of magnetic field.

5.18 A long straight horizontal cable carries a current of 2.5 A in the direction 10° south of west to 10° north of east. The magnetic meridian of the place happens to be 10° west of the geographic meridian. The earth's magnetic field at the location is 0.33 G, and the angle of dip is zero. Locate the line of neutral points (ignore the

thickness of the cable). (At *neutral points*, magnetic field due to a current-carrying cable is equal and opposite to the horizontal component of earth magnetic field.)

Sol.

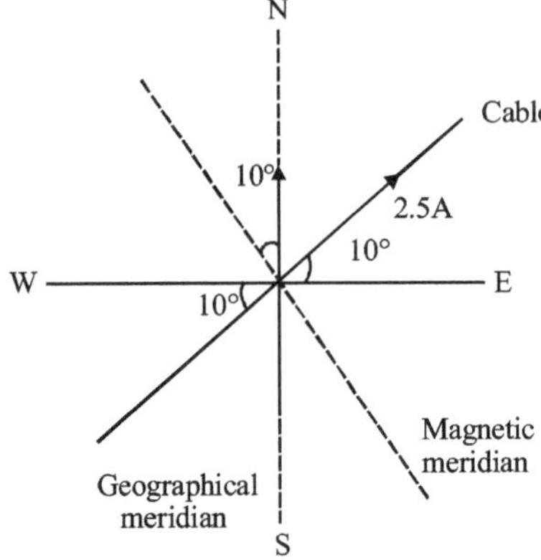

The neutural point can be achieved at a location above cable, where magnetic field of cable is balanced by earth magnetic field B_H.

$$B = \frac{\mu_0}{4\pi}\frac{2I}{r} = B_H$$

$$10^{-7} \times \frac{2 \times 2.5}{r} = 0.33 \times 10^{-4}$$

or $r = 15.15$ mm.

519. A telephone cable at a place has four long straight horizontal wire carrying a current of 1.0 A in the same direction east to west. The earth's magnetic field at the place is 0.39 G, and the angle of dip is 35°. The magnetic declination is nearly zero. What are the resultant magnetic fields at point 4.0 cm below the cable?

Sol. Let us first decide the directions which can best represent the situation.

here, $B_H = B\cos\delta$

$\qquad = 0.39 \times \cos 35°$ G

$B_H = 0.32$ G

and $B_V = B\sin\delta$

$\qquad = 0.39 \times \sin 35°$ G

$B_V = 0.22$ G

telephone cable carry a total current of 4.0 A in direction east to west. We want resultant magnetic field 4.0 cm below.

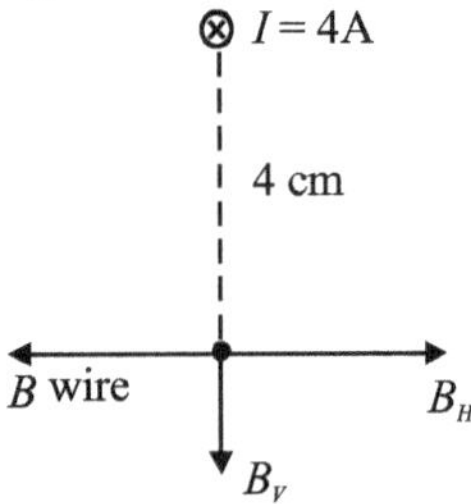

where $B_{wire} = \dfrac{\mu_0}{4\pi}\dfrac{2I}{r} = 10^{-7} \times \dfrac{2 \times 4}{4 \times 10^{-2}}$

$\qquad = 2 \times 10^{-5}$ T $= 0.2$ G

Net magnetic field

$$B_{net} = \sqrt{(B_H - B_W)^2 + B_V^2}$$

$$B_{net} = \sqrt{(0.12)^2 + (0.22)^2} = \sqrt{0.0144 + 0.0484}$$
$$= 0.25\,G$$

5.20 A compass needle free to turn in a horizontal plane is placed at the centre of circular coil of 30 turns and radius 12 cm. The coil is in a vertical plane making an angle of 45° with the magnetic meridian. When the current in the coil is 0.35 A, the needle points west to east.

(a) Determine the horizontal component of the earth's magnetic field at the location.

(b) The current in the coil is reversed, and the coil is rotated about its vertical axis by an angle of 90° in the anticlockwise sense looking from above. Predict the direction of the needle. Take the magnetic declination at the places to be zero.

Sol. (a) Given, for the coil,
$N = 30$, $r - 12\,cm = 0.12\,m$, $1 = 0.35\,A$

At center, $B = \dfrac{\mu_0 IN}{2r}$

Now B is inclined to B_H by 135° (being 90° to plane of coil) and resultant is at 90° with B_H (needle pointing from west to east)

From parallelogram law formula,

$$\tan 90° = \frac{B\sin 135°}{B_H + B\cos 135°}$$

or $\infty = \dfrac{B\sin 45°}{B_H - \cos 45°}$ i. e., $B_H - B\cos 45° = 0$

or, $B_H = B\cos 45° = \dfrac{\mu_0 IN}{2r}\cos 45°$

$$= \frac{4\pi\times 10^{-7}\times 0.35\times 30\times 0.707}{2\times 0.12} = \frac{4\times 22\times 35\times 3\times 707}{7\times 2\times 12}\times 10^{-9}$$
$$= 11\times 5\times 707\times 10^{-9} = 38885\times 10^{-9}T$$
$$= 0.38885\,G$$

(b) When current is reversed and coil rotated by 90°, resultant field is reversed. It points east to west, The needle will also stay east to west

5.21 A magnetic dipole is under the influence of two magnetic fields. The angle between the field directions is 60°, and one of the fields has a magnitude of 1.2×10^{-2} T. / If the dipole comes to stable equilibrium at an angle of 15° with this field, what is the magnitude of the other field?

Sol. The magnetic dipole experience torque due to both the fields and is in equilibrium

$$NB_1\sin 15° = MB_2\sin 45°$$

$$1.2\times 10^{-2}\times 0.26 = B_2(0.71)$$

or $B_2 = 0.44\times 10^{-2}\,T.$

5.22 A monoenergetic (18 keV) electron beam initially in the horizontal direction is subjected to a horizontal magnetic field of 0.04 G normal to the initial direction. Estimate the up or down deflection of the beam over a distance of 30 cm ($m_e = 9.11 \times 10^{-19}$ C). [Note: *Data* in this exercise are so chosen that the answer will give you an idea of the effect of earth's magnetic field on the

motion of the electron beam from the electron gun to the screen in a TV set.]

Sol. Kinetic energy of electron = 18 keV

$$\frac{1m_e v^2}{2} = 18\times 10^3 \times 1.6\times 10^{-19}\,joule$$

velocity $v = 8\times 10^7\,ms^{-1}$
velocity in x direction remain constant, hence time to cross 30 cm

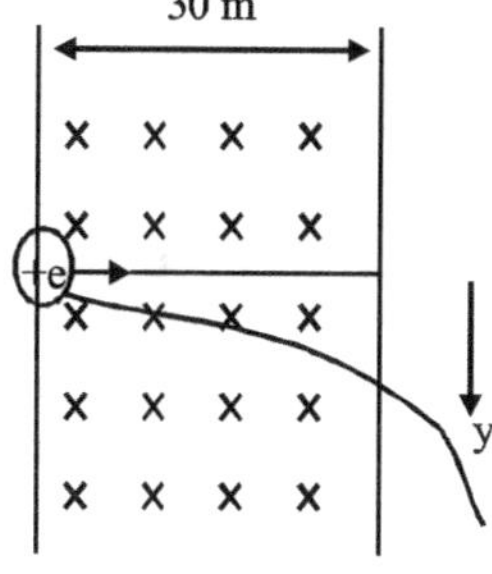

$$t = \frac{30\times 10^{-2}}{8\times 10^7}$$

$$t = \frac{3}{8}\times 10^{-9}\,sec$$

A magnetic force $F = evB$ is acting in vertical direction, which provides acceleration in vertical direction

$$a_y = \frac{evB}{m_e} = 5.63\times 10^{14}\,ms^{-2}$$

Vertical deflection $S_y = u_y t + \dfrac{1}{2}a_y t^2$

$$S_y = 0 + \frac{1}{2}\times 5.63\times 10^{14}\times \left[\frac{3}{8}\times 10^{-9}\right]^2$$

$$S_y = \frac{1}{2}\times \frac{9}{64}\times 5.63\times 10^{-4} = 395.85\times 10^{-7}\,meter.$$

5.23 A sample of paramagnetic salt contains 2.0×10^{24} atomic dipoles each of dipole moment 1.5×10^{-23} JT^{-1}. The sample is placed under a homogeneous magnetic field of 0.64 T, and cooled to a temperature of 4.2 K. The degree of magnetic saturation achieved is equal to 15%. What is the total dipole moment of the sample for a magnetic field of 0.98 T and a temperature of 2.8 K? (Assume Curie's law)

Sol. Dipole moment at complete saturation
$M = 2\times 10^{24}\times 1.5\times 10^{-23} = 30\,A\text{-}m^2$

at 0.84 T and 4.2 K, 15% of sample is magnetised.

$$M = C\frac{B_0}{T_0}$$

$$0.15\times 30 = C\frac{0.84}{4.2} \qquad\qquad ....(i)$$

at 0.98 T and 2.8 K

$$M = C\frac{0.98}{2.8} \qquad\qquad .... (ii)$$

Dividing (i) and (ii), $M = 7.875\,A\text{-}m^2$

5.24 A Rowland ring of mean radius 15 cm has 3500 turns of wire wound on a ferromagnetic core of relative permeability 800. What is the magnetic field B in the core for a magnetising current of 1.2 A?

Sol. Magnetic field B in the core

$$B = \mu_m nI = \frac{\mu_m NI}{2\pi r}$$

$$B = \frac{\mu_0\mu_r NI}{2\pi r} = \frac{4\pi\times 10^{-7}\times 800\times 3500\times 1.2}{2\pi\left(15\times 10^{-2}\right)} = 4.48\,T$$

5.25 The magnetic moment vectors $\vec{\mu}_s$ and $\vec{\mu}_l$ associated with the intrinsic spin angular momentum $\vec{S}$ and orbital angular momentum $\vec{l}$ respectively, of an electron are predicted by quantum theory (and rarified experimentally to a high accuracy) to be given by

$$\vec{\mu}_s = -\left(\frac{e}{m}\right)\vec{S} \quad \text{and} \quad \vec{\mu}_l = -\left(\frac{e}{2m}\right)\vec{l}$$

Which of these relations is in accordance with the result expected classically? Outline the derivation of the classical result.

Sol. Out of the two relations given, only one is in accordance with classical physics. This is

$$\vec{\mu}_1 = -\left(\frac{e}{2m}\right)\vec{l}$$

It follows from the definitions of μ_l and l.

$$\mu_l = iA = \left(\frac{-e}{T}\right)\pi r^2 \quad \dots\dots\dots (i)$$

$$l = mvr = m\left(\frac{2\pi r}{T}\right)r \quad \dots\dots\dots (ii)$$

where r is the radius of the circular orbit, which the electron of mass m and charge $(-e)$ completes in time T. Divide (i) by (ii),

$$\frac{\mu_l}{l} = \frac{-e}{T}\pi r^2 = \frac{T}{m 2\pi r^2} = \frac{-e}{2m} \qquad \therefore \ \vec{\mu}_l = \left(\frac{-e}{2m}\right)\vec{r}$$

clearly $\vec{\mu}_l$ and $\vec{l}$ will be antiparallel (both being normal to the plane of the orbit)

In contrast, $\dfrac{\mu_s}{S} = \dfrac{e}{m}$. It is obtained on the basis of quantum mechanics.

Past year Exercise

Fill in the Blank

1. The magnetic field and angle of dip at a place on the earth are 0.3 G and 30°, respectively. The value of vertical component of the earth's magnetic field at the place is _____________. **[CBSE 2020]**

Very Short Answer Questions

2. What is the characteristic property of a diamagnetic material?
3. How does a circular loop carrying current behave as a magnet?
4. The permeability of a magnetic material is 0.9983. Name the type of magnetic material it represents
5. Where on the surface of earth is vertical component of earth's magnetic field zero?
6. The susceptibility of a magnetic material is 1.9×10^{-5}. Name the type of magnetic material it represents.
7. The horizontal component of earth's magnetic field at a place is B and angle of dip is 60°. What is the value of vertical component of earth's magnetic field?
8. A magnetic needle, free to rotate in a vertical plane, orients itself verticaly at a certain plane on the earth. What are the values of
   (i) Horizontal component of earth's magnetic field and
   (ii) angle of dip at this place?
9. Where on the surface of Earth is the horizontal component of Earth's magnetic field zero?
10. Which of the following substances are paramagnetic?
    Bi, Al, Cu, Ca, Pb, Ni
11. Which of the following substances are diamagnetic?
    Bi, Al, No, Cu, Ca and Ni
12. What are permanent magnets? Give one example.
13. The motion of copper plates is damped when it is allowed to oscillate between the two poles of a magnet. If slots are cut in the plate, how will the damping be affected?
14. In what way is the behaviour of a diamagnetic material different from that of a paramagnetic, when kept in an external magnetic field

15. Write two properties of a material suitable for making (a) a permanent magnet, and (b) an electromagnet.

Short Answer Questions

16. The horizontal component of the earth's magnetic field at a place equals its vertical component there. Find the value of the angle of dip at that place. What is the ratio of the horizontal component to the total magnetic field of the earth at that place?
17. Three identical specimens of a magnetic materials, nickel, antimony, aluminium are kept in a non-uniform magnetic field. Draw the modification in the field lined in each case.
18. A circular coil of N turns and radius R carries a current I. It is unwound and rewound to make another coil of radius R/2, current I remaining the same. Calculate the ratio of the magnetic moments of the new coil and the original coil.
19. Show diagrammatically the behaviour of magnetic field lines in the presence of (i) paramagnetic and (ii) diamagnetic substances. How does one explain this distinguishing feature?
20. Out of the two magnetic materials, 'A' has relative permeability slightly greater than unity while 'B' has less than unity. Identify the nature of the materials 'A' and 'B'. Will their susceptibilities be positive or negative?
21. A bar magnet of magnetic moment 6 J/T is aligned at 60° with a uniform external magnetic field of 0.44 T. Calculate (a) the work done turning the magnet to align its magnetic moment (i) normal to the magnetic field, (ii) opposite to the magnetic field, and (b) the torque on the magnet in the final orientation in case (ii).
22. (a) An iron ring of relative permeability μ_r has windings of insulated copper wire of n turns per meter. When the current in the winding is I, find the expression for the magnetic field in the ring.
    (b) The susceptibility of a magnetic material is 0.9853. Identify the type of magnetic material. Draw the modification of the field pattern on keeping a piece of this material in a uniform magnetic field.

NCERT Exemplar

Multiple Choice Questions

1. A toroid of n turns, mean radius R and cross-sectional radius a carries current I. It is placed on a horizontal table taken as xy-plane. Its magnetic moment m

(a) is non-zero and points in the z-direction by symmetry

(b) points along the axis of the toroid ($m = m\phi$)

(c) is zero, otherwise there would be a field falling as $\dfrac{1}{r^3}$ at large distances outside the toroid

(d) is pointing radially outwards

2. The magnetic field of the earth can be modelled by that of a point dipole placed at the centre of the earth. The dipole axis makes an angle of 11.3° with the axis of the earth. At Mumbai, declination is nearly zero. Then,

(a) the declination varies between 11.3° W to 11.3° E

(b) the least declination is 0°

(c) the plane defined by dipole axis and the earth axis passes through Greenwich

(d) declination averaged over the earth must be always negative

3. In a permanent magnet at room temperature.

(a) magnetic moment of each molecule is zero

(b) the individual molecules have non-zero magnetic moment which are all perfectly aligned

(c) domains are partially aligned

(d) domains are all perfectly aligned

4. Consider the two idealised systems (i) a parallel plate capacitor with large plates and small separation and (ii) a long solenoid of length L >> R, radius of cross-section. In (i) E is ideally treated as a constant between plates and zero outside. In (ii) magnetic field is constant inside the solenoid and zero outside. These idealised assumptions, however, contradict fundamental laws as below

(a) case (i) contradicts Gauss' law for electrostatic fields

(b) case (ii) contradicts Gauss' law for magnetic fields

(c) case (i) agrees with $\oint E.dl = 0$.

(d) case (ii) contradicts $\oint H.dl = I_{en}$

5. A paramagnetic sample shows a net magnetisation of 8 Am^{-1} when placed in an external magnetic field of 0.6 T at a temperature of 4 K. When the same sample is placed in an external magnetic field of 0.2 T at a temperature of 16 K, the magnetisation will be

(a) $\dfrac{32}{3} Am^{-1}$ (b) $\dfrac{2}{3} Am^{-1}$

(c) $6 Am^{-1}$ (d) $2.4 Am^{-1}$

Very Short Answer Questions

6. A proton has spin and magnetic moment just like an electron. Why then its effect is neglected in magnetism of materials?

7. A ball of superconducting material is dipped in liquid nitrogen and placed near a bar magnet.

(i) In which direction will it move

(ii) What will be the direction of it's magnetic moment?

8. If a magnet is divided into n equal parts by cutting along the lines parallel to its length, then what will be the pole strength of each part ?

Short Answer Questions

9. Three identical bar magnets are rivetted together at centre in the same plane as shown in Fig.. This system is placed at rest in a slowly varying magnetic field. It is found that the system of magnets does not show any motion.

The north-south poles of one magnet is shown in the Fig.. Determine the poles of the remaining two.

10. A bar magnet of magnetic moment m and moment of inertia I (about centre, perpendicular to length) is cut into two equal pieces, perpendicular to length. Let T be the period of oscillations of the original magnet about an axis through the mix point, perpendicular to length, in a magnetic field B. What would be the similar period T' for each piece?

11. Why will a magnet placed in front of a television picture tube distort the picture?

12. A Rowland ring of mean radius 15 cm has 3500 turns of wire wound on a ferromagnetic core of relative permeability 800. What is the magnetic field B in the core for a magnetising current of 1.2A ?

Objective Practice Exercise

DIRECTIONS : *This section contains multiple choice questions. Each question has four choices (a), (b), (c) and (d) out of which only one is correct.*

1. The magnetism of magnet is due to
   (a) spin motion of electron
   (b) earth
   (c) pressure of big magnet inside the earth
   (d) cosmic rays

2. The primary origin (s) of magnetism lies in
   (a) atomic currents   (b) polar nature of molecules
   (c) extrinsic spin of electron (d) None of these

3. Which of these is correct in regard to a magnet?
   (a) Geometric length = 0.8 times the magnetic length
   (b) Magnetic length = 0.8 times the geometric length
   (c) Magnetic length = Geometric length
   (d) Geometric length = 10/9 of magnetic length

4. Magnetic dipole moment is a vector quantity directed from
   (a) south pole to north pole (b) north pole to south pole
   (c) east to west   (d) west to east

5. A bar magnet of magnetic moment M and length L is cut into two equal parts each of length L/2. The magnetic moment of each part will be
   (a) M   (b) M/4   (c) $\sqrt{2}$ M   (d) M/2

6. When a current in a circular loop is equivalently replaced by a magnetic dipole
   (a) the pole strength m of each pole is fixed
   (b) the distance d between the poles is fixed
   (c) the product md is fixed
   (d) None of these

7. The magnetic moment of atomic neon is equal to
   (a) zero   (b) $\dfrac{1}{2}\mu_B$ (c) μ_B (d) $\dfrac{3}{2}\mu_B$

8. Current i is flowing in a coil of area A and number of turns N, then magnetic moment of the coil, M is
   (a) NiA   (b) $\dfrac{Ni}{A}$ (c) $\dfrac{Ni}{\sqrt{A}}$ (d) N^2Ai

9. Magnetic field intensity is defined as
   (a) Magnetic moment per unit volume
   (b) Magnetic induction force acting on a unit magnetic pole
   (c) Number of lines of force crossing per unit area
   (d) Number of lines of force crossing per unit volume

10. The magnetic moment of a bar magnet is thus ...A... to the magnetic moment of an equivalent solenoid that produces the same magnetic field. Here, *A* refers to
    (a) unequal (b) different (c) equal   (d) same

11. The magnetic lines of force inside a bar magnet
    (a) are from north-pole to south-pole of the magnet
    (b) do not exist
    (c) depend upon the area of cross-section of the bar magnet
    (d) are from south-pole to north-pole of the Magnet

12. The strength of the earth's magnetic field is
    (a) constant everywhere
    (b) zero everywhere
    (c) having very high value
    (d) vary from place to place on the earths surface

13. The correct relation is
    (a) $B = \dfrac{B_V}{B_H}$ (b) $B = B_V \times B_H$
    (c) $|B| = \sqrt{B_H^2 + B_V^2}$ (d) $B = B_H + B_V$

14. The line on the earth surface joining the point where the field is horizontal, is called
    (a) magnetic equator   (b) magnetic line
    (c) magnetic axis   (d) magnetic inertia

15. Horizontal component of earth's field at a height of 1 m from the surface of earth is H. Its value at a height of 10 m from surface of earth is
    (a) H/10   (b) H/9   (c) H/100   (d) H

16. At the magnetic north pole of the earth, the value of the horizontal component of earth's magnetic field and angle of dip are respectively
    (a) zero, maximum   (b) maximum, minimum
    (c) maximum, maximum (d) minimum, minimum

17. Which of the following is responsible for the earth's magnetic field?
    (a) Convective currents in earth's core.
    (b) Diversive current in earth's core.
    (c) Rotational motion of earth.
    (d) Translational motion of earth.

18. Demagnetisation of magnets can be done by
    (a) rough handling
    (b) heating
    (c) magnetising in the opposite direction
    (d) All the above

19. A compass needle which is allowed to move in a horizontal plane is taken to a geomagnetic pole. It will
    (a) stay in north-south direction only
    (b) stay in east-west direction only
    (c) become rigid showing no movement
    (d) stay in any position

20. The time period of oscillation of a freely suspended bar magnet with usual notations is given by
    (a) $T = 2\pi\sqrt{\dfrac{I}{MB_H}}$ (b) $T = 2\pi\sqrt{\dfrac{MB_H}{I}}$
    (c) $T = \sqrt{\dfrac{I}{MB_H}}$ (d) $T = 2\pi\sqrt{\dfrac{B_H}{MI}}$

21. To measure the magnetic moment of a bar magnet, one may use
    (a) a deflection glavanometer if the earth's horizontal field is known
    (b) an oscillation magnetometer if the earth's horizontal field is known
    (c) both deflection and oscillation magnetometer if the earth's horizontal field is not known.
    (d) all of the above

22. For protecting a sensitive equipment from the external electric arc, it should be
    (a) wrapped with insulation around it when a current is passing through it
    (b) placed inside an iron core
    (c) surrounded with fine copper sheet
    (d) placed inside an aluminium can
23. The magnetic needle has magnetic moment $8.7 \times 10^{-2}\,Am^2$ and moment of inertia $11.5 \times 10^{-6}\,kgm^2$. It performs 10 complete oscillations in 6.70 s, what is the magnitude of the magnetic field?
    (a) 0.012 T (b) 0.120 T (c) 1.200 T (d) 2.10 T
24. The earth's magnetic field always has a vertical component except at the
    (a) magnetic equator   (b) magnetic poles
    (c) geographic north pole (d) latitude 45°
25. At magnetic poles, the angle of dip is
    (a) 45°   (b) 30°   (c) zero   (d) 90°

Chapter Test

Time : 30 minutes   **Max. Marks : 15**

Direction :

Each question number **1-15** carry **1 mark** each.

1. A bar magnet is cut into two equal halves by a plane parallel to the magnetic axis. Of the following physical quantities the one which remains unchanged is
   (a) pole strength
   (b) magnetic moment
   (c) intensity of magnetisation
   (d) None of these
2. One can define ...A... of a place as the vertical plane which passes through the imaginary line joining the magnetic North and the South–poles.
   Here, A refers to
   (a) geographic meridian   (b) magnetic meridian
   (c) magnetic declination   (d) magnetic inclination
3. The magnetic compass is not useful for navigation near the magnetic poles, since
   (a) R = 0   (b) V = 0   (c) H = 0   (d) $\theta = 0°$
4. The earth's magnetic field always has a vertical component except at the
   (a) magnetic equator   (b) magnetic poles
   (c) geographic north pole (d) latitude 45°
5. At magnetic poles, the angle of dip is
   (a) 45°   (b) 30°   (c) zero   (d) 90°
6. At the magnetic north pole of the earth, the value of the horizontal component of earth's magnetic field and angle of dip are respectively
   (a) zero, maximum   (b) maximum, minimum
   (c) maximum, maximum   (d) minimum, minimum
7. The ratio of intensity of magnetisation and magnetising field is called
   (a) permeability   (b) magnetic intensity
   (c) magnetic intensity   (d) magnetic susceptibility
8. At a certain place, horizontal component is $\sqrt{3}$ times the vertical component. The angle of dip at this place is
   (a) 0   (b) $\pi/3$ (c) $\pi/6$ (d) $\pi/8$
9. At a certain place, the angle of dip is 30° and the horizontal component of earth's magnetic field is 0.50 oerested. The earth's total magnetic field (in oerested) is
   (a) $\sqrt{3}$ (b) 1   (c) $\dfrac{1}{\sqrt{3}}$ (d) $\dfrac{1}{2}$

DIRECTIONS (Qs.10) : *Each of these questions contains an assertion followed by reason. Read them carefully and answer the question on the basis of following options. You have to select the one that best describes the two statements.*
(a) If both Assertion and Reason are correct and the Reason is a correct explanation of the Assertion.
(b) If both Assertion and Reason are correct but Reason is not a correct explanation of the Assertion.
(c) If the Assertion is correct but Reason is incorrect.
(d) If the Assertion is incorrect but the Reason is correct.

10. **Assertion :** If a compass needle be kept at magnetic north pole of the earth, the compass needle may stay in any direction
    Reason : Dip needle will stay vertical at the north pole of earth.

Very Short Answer Type Questions

11. What happens to the magnetic moment of a bar magnet if it is cut into two pieces (i) transverse to its length and (ii) along its length?
12. Which direction would a dip circle point to, if located right on the geomagnetic north or south pole?
13. Repulsion is a sure test of magnetism. Explain the statement.
14. How will you decide whether the magnetic field at a point is due to some current carrying conductor or due to earth?
15. You are given two identical looking bars A and B. One of them is a bar magnet and the other an ordinary piece of iron. Give an experiment to identify which one of the two is a bar magnet. You are not to use additional materials for the experiment.

Solutions

Practice Exercise-1

1. **(c)** The field lines remain continuous, emerging from one face of the solenoid and entering into the other face.

2. **(b)** On bending a rod it's pole strength remain unchanged where as its magnetic moment changes new magnetic moment $M' m(2R) = \left(\dfrac{2L}{\pi}\right) = \dfrac{2M}{\pi}$.

3. **(c)** In an atom, electrons revolve around the nuclear and such the circular orbits of electrons may be considered as the small current loops. In addition to orbital motion, an electron has got spin motion also. So the total magnetic moment of electron is the vector sum of its magnetic charge moments due to orbital and spin motion. Particles at rest do not produce magnetic field.

4. **(d)**

5. **(b)** When a magnet is cut into pieces, each piece becomes new magnet. $M' = \dfrac{m\ell}{2} = \dfrac{M}{2}$.

6. Magnetic dipole moment is defined as the product of the pole strength of either magnetic pole of the dipole and the distance between them. $\overrightarrow{M} = m \times \overrightarrow{2\ell}$. It is directed from S to N pole.

7. The tangent at any point at a magntic line of force gives the direction of magnetic field at that point. If two magnetic lines of force intersect then at the point of intersection there will be two different tangents and two directions of magnetic field which is not possible.

8. Magnetic lines of force are continuous closed loops.

9. 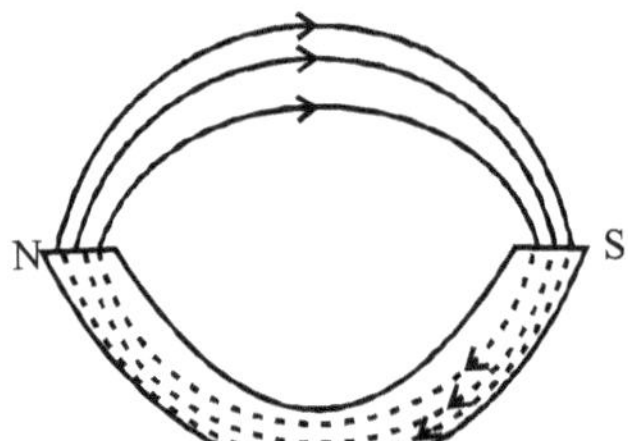

10. We get magnets each having north and south poles. Here the pole strength of each new magnet is half that of the original one; magnetic moment is halved.

11. Bohr Magneton $\mu_B = \dfrac{eh}{4\pi m} = 9.27 \times 10^{-24}\,\text{Am}^2$.

12. Magnetic monopole exist in equal and opposite pairs.

13. The North and South poles of a bar magnet are fixed, so the direction of magnetic field of a bar magnet is fixed. The poles of a solenoid can be reverse by reversing the direction of current through it. So the direction of magnetic field of a solenoid can be changed.

14. For figure (a), the new pole strength remains same as m but the dipole moment becomes M/2.
    For figure (b), the new pole strength will be m/2 and dipole moment also will be M/2.

15. Consider a plane loop of wire carrying current. A current carrying loop behaves as a magnetic dipole. The magnetic dipole moment is directly proportional to the strength of current (I) passing through the loop and area (A) enclosed by the loop.
    i.e., $\qquad M \propto IA$
    and $\qquad M = KIA$
    $M = IA$ (since $K = 1$)
    For n such turns magnetic moment $M = nIA$.

16. According to Gauss's law for magnetism, the net magnetic flux (ϕ_B) through any closed surface is always zero.
    Suppose a closed surface S is held in a uniform magnetic field $\overrightarrow{B}$. Consider a small element of area $\overrightarrow{ds}$ on this surface.

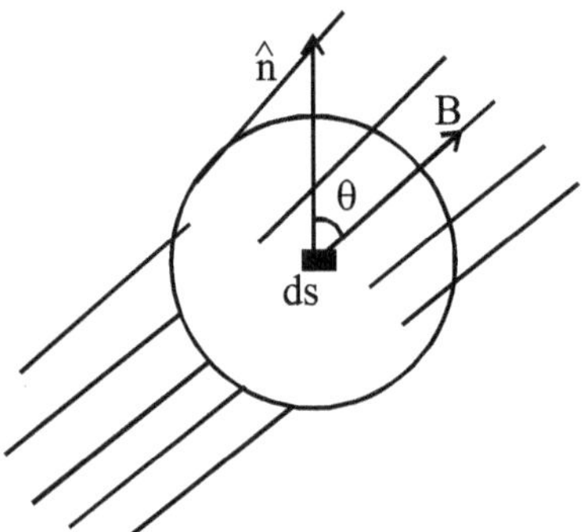

Magnetic flux through this element $d\phi_B = \overrightarrow{B}.\overrightarrow{ds}$.
If the area elements are really small, then the net magnetic flux through the surface is,
$$\phi_B = \int_S \overrightarrow{B}.\overrightarrow{ds} = 0.$$

Practice Exercise-2

1. **(d)** (i) The Earth behaves as a magnet with the magnetic field pointing appoximately from the geographic South to the North.
    (ii) When a bar magnet is freely suspended, it points in the North-South direction. The tip which points to the geographic North is called the North pole and the tip which points to the geographic South is called the South-pole of the magnet.
    (iii) There is a repulsive force when North poles (or South-poles) of two magnets are brought close together. Conversely there is an attractive force between the North-pole of one magnet and the South-pole of the other.
    (iv) We cannot isolate the North or South-pole of a magnet. If a bar magnet is broken into two halves, we get two similar bar magnets with somewhat weaker properties. Unlike electric charges, isolated magnetic North and South poles known as magnetic monopoles do not exist.

2. **(c)** $B = \dfrac{H}{\cos\theta} = \dfrac{0.50}{\cos 30^\circ} = \dfrac{0.50 \times 2}{\sqrt{3}} = 1/\sqrt{3}$

3. **(b)** $B_H = B_E \cos\phi$
    $B_V = B_E \sin\phi$

$\tan\phi = \dfrac{B_v}{B_H}$ and $B = B_H \tan\theta$

where, θ = magnetic declination

ϕ = Angle of inclination or dip angle

4. **(c)** Horizontal component of earth's field,
$H = B\cos\theta$, since, $\theta = 60°$

$$3.6\times10^{-5} = B\times\frac{1}{2}$$

$$\Rightarrow B = 7.2\times10^{-5} \text{ Tesla}$$

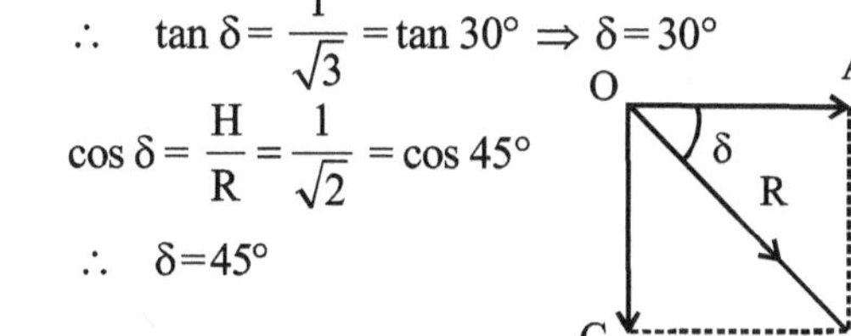

5. **(c)** $\tan\delta = \dfrac{V}{H} = \dfrac{V}{\sqrt{3}V} = \dfrac{1}{\sqrt{3}}$

$\therefore$ $\delta = 30° = \pi/6$ radian

6. **(a)**

7. **(a)** Given $M = 8\times10^{22}$ Am^2
$d = R_e = 6.4\times10^6$ m

Earth's magnetic field, $B = \dfrac{\mu_0}{4\pi}\cdot\dfrac{2M}{d^3}$

$$= \frac{4\pi\times10^{-7}}{4\pi}\times\frac{2\times8\times10^{22}}{(6.4\times10^6)^3} \cong 0.6 \text{ Gauss}$$

8. **(d)** The strength of the earths magnetic field is not constant. It varies from one place to other place on the surface of earth. Its value being of the order of 10^{-5} T.

9. **(b)** 10. **(a)** 11. **(d)** 12. **(a)**

13. (a) Angle of inclination, (b) angle of declination and (c) horizontal component of earth's magnetic field.

14. Angle of dip is 0° at magnetic equator.

15. $\tan\delta = \dfrac{V}{H}$. If $V = H$, $\tan\delta = 1$ i.e. $\delta = 45°$

16. The angle of dip is 0° at equator and that is 90° at poles.

17. $\tan\delta = \dfrac{H}{V}$, Here $H = \sqrt{3}V$ $\therefore \dfrac{V}{H} = \dfrac{1}{\sqrt{3}}$

$\therefore$ $\tan\delta = \dfrac{1}{\sqrt{3}} = \tan 30° \Rightarrow \delta = 30°$

18. $\cos\delta = \dfrac{H}{R} = \dfrac{1}{\sqrt{2}} = \cos 45°$

$\therefore$ $\delta = 45°$

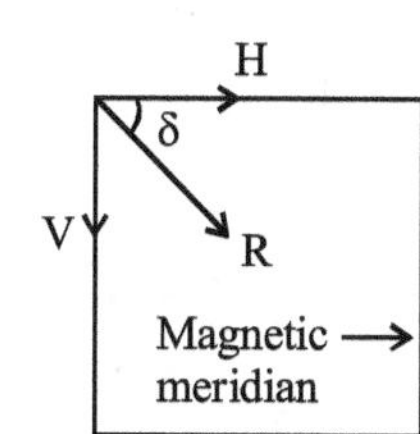

19. $F = H\tan\theta$

where F and H are the intensities of two uniform magnetic field acting perpendicular to each other and θ is the angle with which the freely suspended magnet makes with the direction of H.

20. Magnetic inclination (δ) at a place is the angle which the direction of earth's magnetic field makes with the horizontal plane at that place.

Horizontal component (H) of the earth's magnetic field is the component of the earth's magnetic field in the horizontal direction $H = R\cos\delta$

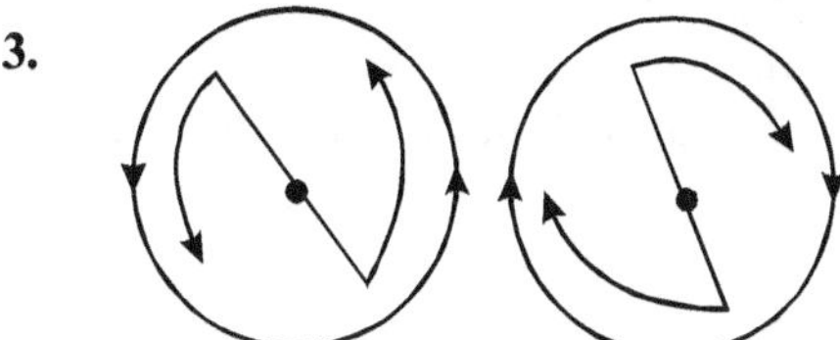

21. **(a)** Earth's magnetic field can be due to molten charged metallic fluid in the core of the earth. As the fluid rotates with the rotation of the earth, a current is developed which causes magnetism.

(b) Since every substance is made up of charged particles like protons and electrons, due to earth's rotation about its axis a circulating current is produced which can cause magnetism.

(c) In earth's atmosphere, gases are in ionised state due to cosmic rays. As earth rotates, an electric current is set up due to movement of charged ions which can be the cause of magnetism.

22. Angle of dip is $\pi/2$ and horizontal component will be zero. This places are North and South poles of the Earth.

23. Here, $H = 0.22$ gauss and $V = 0.38$ gauss.

$\tan\delta = \dfrac{V}{H} = \dfrac{0.38}{0.22} = 1.73$ $\therefore \delta = \tan^{-1}1.73 = 59.8 = 60°$

R = resultant intensity of magnetic field = $\sqrt{H^2 + V^2}$

$= \sqrt{(0.22)^2 + (0.38)^2} = \sqrt{0.048 + 0.1444} = 0.44$ gauss.

24. Here, $H = 0.2$ gauss, $R = 0.4$ gauss.

$\cos\delta = \dfrac{H}{R} = \dfrac{0.2}{0.4} = \dfrac{1}{2} = \cos 60°$

$\therefore$ $\delta = 60°$

25. Here, $M = 60$ Am^2, $H = 40\times10^{-6}$ Wb/m^2, $\tau = 1.2\times10^{-3}$ Nm

$\sin\theta = \dfrac{\tau}{MB} = \dfrac{1.2\times10^{-3}}{60\times40\times10^{-6}} = 0.5$ or $\theta = 30°$

26. Angle of dip increases from 0° to 90° one as moves from the equator towards the north pole.
Here, $H = 0.4\times10^{-4}$ T, $\delta = 60$

$\tan\delta = \dfrac{V}{H}$

$\therefore$ $V = H\tan\delta = 0.4\times10^{-4}\tan 60° = 0.4\times10^{-4}\times\sqrt{3}$

$\therefore$ $V = 0.69\times10^{-4}$ T

$B = \dfrac{H}{\cos\delta} = \dfrac{0.4\times10^{-4}}{\cos 60°} = \dfrac{0.4\times10^{-4}}{1/2} = 0.8\times10^{-4}$ T.

Past year Exercise

1. Vertical component of magnetic field B_v is
$B_v = B\sin\delta$
Given $B = 0.3$
$\delta = 30°$
$B_v = 0.3\sin 30°$
$B_v = 0.15$ G

2. When diamagnetic substances are placed in an external magnetic field they acquires feeble magnetisation in the direction opposite of the magnetic field.

3. 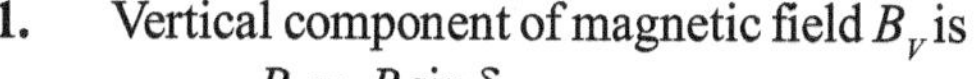

The current on one face is in anticlockwise direction, then this behaves as north pole where as when it viewed from other face then current is in clockwise direction forming south pole.

Hence, current loop has both magnetic poles and therefore behaves as a magnetic dipole.

4. The magnetic material is diamagnetic because for diamagnetic $\mu_r < 1$.

5. At equator there is only horizontal component of earth magnetic field.

6. The small and positive susceptibility represents paramagnetic substance.

7. Horizontal component

$$H = B_e \cos 60° = B \;\Rightarrow\; B_e \times \frac{1}{2} = B, B_e = 2B$$

Vertical component $V = B_e \sin 60° = 2B \times \dfrac{\sqrt{3}}{2} = \sqrt{3}B$

8. (i) Needle orients itself vertically therefore there is no component of earth's magnetic field in horizontal direction
(ii) The angle of dip is 90°.

9. At magnetic poles.

10. Al and Ca

11. Bi and Cu

12. The magnets which have high retentivity and high coercivity are called permanent magnets. Example - steel.

13. According to Lenz's law, induced emf opposes, the cause that produced it. Due to the oscillations of the copper plate, magnetic flux, changes and emf is induced. Hence, the motion of the copper plates is damped. When the slots are cut, oscillations will be less damped due to lesser eddy currents and copper plate will swing more freely.

14. When a bar of diamagnetic material is placed in an external magnetic field, the field lines are repelled or expelled and the field inside the material is reduced

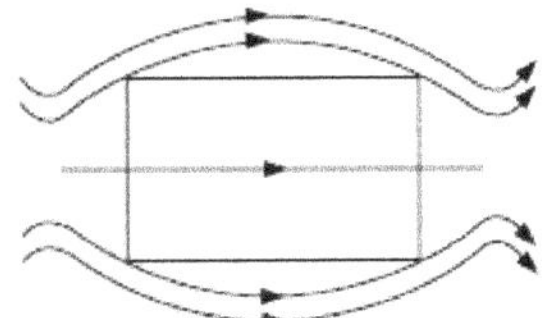

Whereas when a paramagnetic material is placed in an external magnetic field, the field lines are attracted towards it. Thus the field lines get concentrated inside the material and the field inside is enhanced.

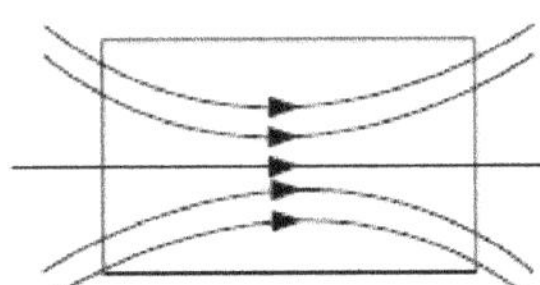

15. (a) Two properties of material suitable for making permanent magnets are
(i) high coercivity
(ii) high retentivity
(b) Two properties of material suitable for making electromagnets are
(i) low coercivity
(ii) low retentivity.

16. As given, H = V
If angle of dip at that place is δ, then

$$\tan \delta = \frac{V}{H} = \frac{V}{V} \quad \tan \delta = 1 \;\Rightarrow\; \delta = \frac{\pi}{4}\,rad$$

As, $H = B_e \cos \delta$

Therefore, $\dfrac{H}{B_e} = \cos \delta = \cos \dfrac{\pi}{4} = \dfrac{1}{\sqrt{2}}$ or $H : Be = 1 : \sqrt{2}$

17. Nickel is a ferromagnetic substance so field lines

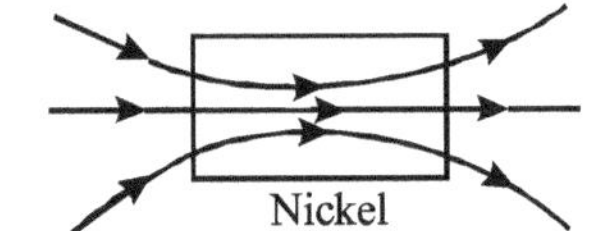

Nickel

Antimony is a diamagnetic substance so field lines

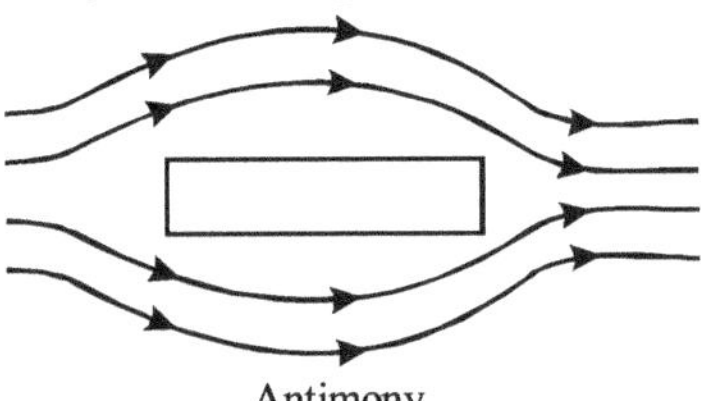

Antimony

Aluminium is a paramagnetic substance so field lines

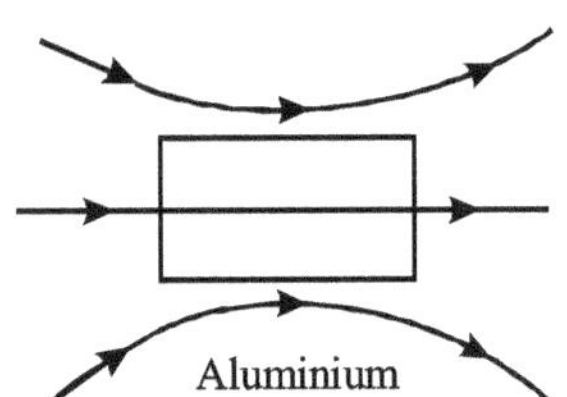

Aluminium

18. Length of the wire is same in both cases

$$\therefore \quad N_1 \times (2\pi R) = N_2 \times 2\pi \left(\frac{R}{2}\right)$$

So, $N_2 = 2N_1$

Now, the ratio of magnetic moments is given by

$$\frac{M_1}{M_2} = \frac{N_1 I A_1}{N_2 I A_2} = \frac{N_1 \times \pi R_1^2}{N_2 \times \pi R_2^2}$$

$$\frac{M_1}{M_2} = \left(\frac{N_1}{2N_1}\right) \times \left(\frac{R}{R/2}\right) = \frac{1}{2} \times 4 = 2$$

$$M_1 : M_2 = 2 : 1$$

19. (i) The behaviour of magnetic field lines in the presence of a diamagnetic substances (fig. a) and paramagnetic substances (fig. b) are shown below:

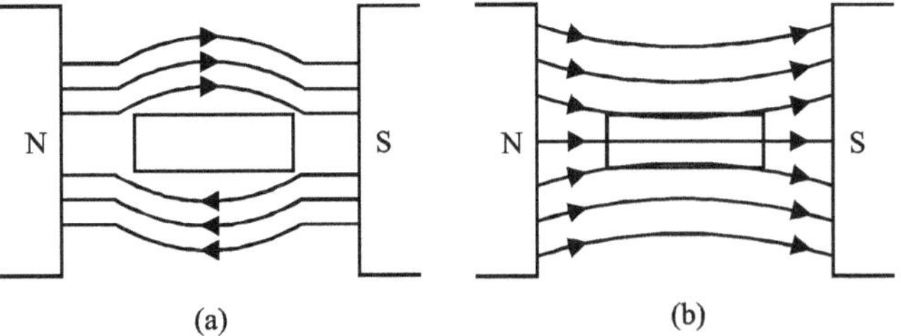

This distinguishing feature of magnetic substances is the difference in their relative permeabilities. The relative permeability of the diamagnetic substance is less than 1; so, the magnetic lines of force do not prefer passing through the substance. The relative permeability of a paramagnetic substance is greater than 1; so, the magnetic lines of force prefer passing through the substance.

20. Relation between relative permeability (μ_r) and susceptibility (x) of a magnetic material is, $\mu_r = 1 + \chi$

For a paramagnetic material, the relative permeability lies between $1 < \mu_r < 1 + E$ and its susceptibility lies between $0 < \chi < E$.

Hence, 'A' is a paramagnetic material and its susceptibility is positive.

For a diamagnetic material, the relative permeability lies between $0 \leq \mu_r < 1$ and its susceptibility lies between $-1 < \chi < 0$.

Hence, 'B' is a diamagnetic material and its susceptibility is negative.

21. (a) (i) Work done, $W = \vec{M}\vec{B}\,(\cos\theta_1 - \cos\theta_2)$

$= 6 \times 0.44 \times (\cos 60° - \cos 90°) = 6 \times 0.44 \times (0.5 - 0) = 1.32$

(ii) $W = \vec{M}\vec{B}\,(\cos\theta_2 - \cos\theta_1) = 6 \times 0.44 \times (\cos 60° - \cos 180°)$

$= 6 \times 0.44 \times [0.5 - (-1)] = 3.96\,J$

(b) Torque, $\tau = \vec{M} \times \vec{B} = 6 \times 0.44 \times \sin 180° = 0$.

22. (a) Here, an iron ring of relative permeability μr having windings of insulated copper wire of n turns per meter. It means it is acting as toroid.

A toroid consists of hollow circular ring on which a large number of turns of a wire are closely wound as shown in figure. Let N be the number of turns and I be the current passed through the toroid. r be the average radius. If the coils are closely spaced, the field inside the toroidal coil is tangent to the dotted circular path and is same at all points.

NCERT Exemplar

1. (c) Toroid is a hollow circular ring on which a large number of turns of a wire are closely wound. Thus, in this case magnetic field is only confined inside the body of toroid. So no magnetic field outside the toroid and magnetic field only inside the toroid.

In case of toroid, the magnetic field is in the form of concentric magnetic lines of force and there is no magnetic field outside the body of toroid. This is because the loop encloses no current. Thus, the magnetic moment of toroid is zero.

In other case, if we take r as a large distance outside the toroid, then $m \propto \dfrac{1}{r^3}$. Which is not possible.

2. (a) Magnetic declination is an angle between angle of magnetic meridian and the geographic meridian.

As the earth's magnetism, the magnetic field lines of the earth resemble that of a hypothetical magnetic dipole located at the centre of the earth.

The axis of the dipole does not coincide with the axis of rotation of the earth but is presently tilted by 11.3° (approx) with respect to geographical of axis earth. This results into two situations as given in the figure.

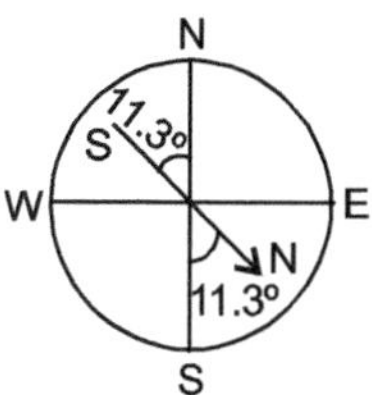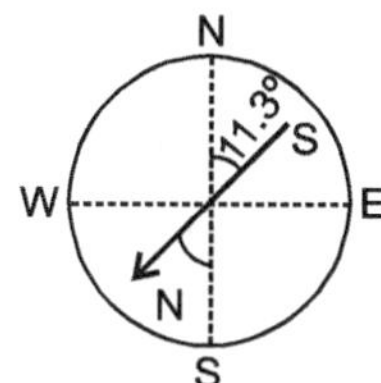

So, the declination varies between 11.3° W to 11.3° E.

3. (d) We know that a permanent magnet is a substance which at room temperature retain ferromagnetic property for a long period of time. The individual atoms in a ferromagnetic material possess a dipole moment as in a paramagnetic material. However, they interact with one another in such a way that they spontaneously align themselves in a common direction over a macroscopic volume i.e., domain.

Hence, in a permanent magnet at room temperature, domains are all perfectly aligned.

4. (b) The electric field lines, do not form a continuous path while the magnetic field lines form the closed paths.

Gauss's law states that, $\oint_s E.ds = \dfrac{q}{\varepsilon_0}$ for electrostatic field.

So, it does not contradict for electrostatic fields as the electric field lines do not form closed continuous path.

According to Gauss' law in magnetic field, $\oint_s E.ds = 0$

It contradicts for magnetic field, because there is a magnetic field inside the solenoid and no field outside the solenoid carrying current but the magnetic field lines form the closed path.

5. (b) According to the Curie law, the intensity of magnetisation (I) is directly proportional to the magnetic field induction and inversely proportional to the temperature (t) in kelvin.

So, I magnetisation $\propto \dfrac{B\,(\text{magnetic field induction})}{t\,(\text{temperature in kelvin})}$

$\Rightarrow \dfrac{I_2}{I_1} = \dfrac{B_2}{B_1} \times \dfrac{t_1}{t_2}$ ...(i)

As given that : $I_1 = 8\,Am^{-1}$, $I_2 = ?$

$B_1 = 0.6\,T$, $t_1 = 4K$

$B_2 = 0.2\,T$, $t_2 = 16K$

by putting the value of $B_1, B_2, t_1, t_2\, I_1$ in equation (i)

So, $\dfrac{0.2}{0.6} \times \dfrac{4}{16} = \dfrac{I_2}{8}$

We get, $I_2 = 8 \times \dfrac{1}{12}$

$I_2 = \dfrac{2}{3}\,A/m$

6. $\mu_p \approx \dfrac{eh}{2m_p}$ and $\mu_e \approx \dfrac{eh}{2m_e}$, $h = \dfrac{h}{2\pi}$

$\mu_e \gg \mu_p$ because $m_p \gg m_e$.

7. (i) Away from the magnet.

(ii) Magnetic moment is from left to right.

8. If a magnet of pole strength m is divided into n equal parts by cutting along the lines parallel to its length, then the pole strength of each part will be $m' = \dfrac{m}{n}$

9. Net $m = 0$. Only possibility is shown in Fig.

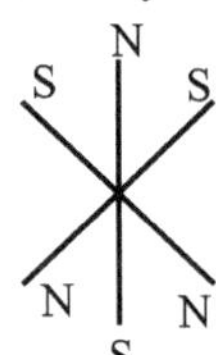

10. $T = 2\pi\sqrt{\dfrac{I}{mB}}$ $I' = \dfrac{1}{2} \times \dfrac{1}{4} I$ and $m' = \dfrac{m}{2}$. $T' = \dfrac{1}{2} T$

11. A magnet placed in front of a television picture tube produces a magnetic field which deflects the charged particles that constitute the picture in the television. This is why, a picture is distorted by a magnet placed in front of a television picture tube.

12. Here, $r = 15\,cm = 15 \times 10^{-2}\,m$, $N = 3500$, $\mu_r = 800$, $I = 1.2\,A$, $B = ?$

Number of turns/length, $n = \dfrac{N}{2\pi r} = \dfrac{3500}{2\pi \times 15 \times 10^{-2}}$

Also, $B = \mu_0 \mu_r n I = 4\pi \times 10^{-7} \times 800 \times \dfrac{3500 \times 1.2}{2\pi \times 15 \times 10^{-2}}$

$= 4.48$ T

1. **(a)** Spin motion of electron
2. **(a)**
3. **(b)** Magnetic length of a magnet is roughly 0.8 times the geometric length.
4. **(a)**
5. **(d)** As magnetic moment = pole strength x length and length is halved without affecting pole strength, therefore, magnetic moment becomes half.
6. **(c)**
7. **(a)** Magnetic moment is cancelled and $\mu_{net} = 0$.
8. **(a)**   **9.** **(b)**
10. **(c)** The magnetic moment of a bar magnet is thus equal to the magnetic moment of an equivalent solenoid that produces the same magnetic field.
11. **(d)** As shown in the figure, the magnetic lines of force are directed from south to north inside a bar magnet.

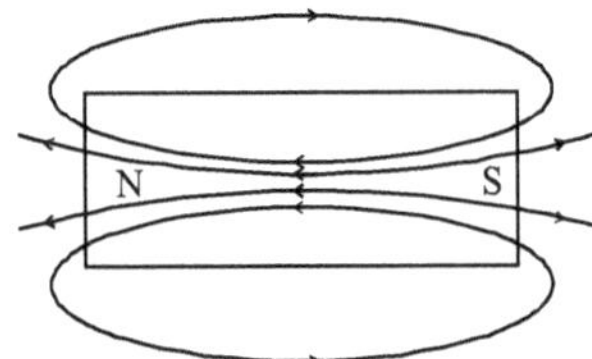

12. **(d)** The strength of the earth's magnetic field is not constant. It varies from one place to other place on the surface of earth. Its value being of the order of 10^{-5} T.
13. **(c)**   **14.** **(a)**
15. **(d)** The value of H is fairly uniform.
16. **(a)**
17. **(a)** The earth's core is hot and molten. Hence, convective current in earth's core is responsible for it's magnetic field.
18. **(d)**   **19.** **(d)**   **20.** **(a)**   **21.** **(d)**

22. **(b)** The iron core produces a magnetic screening for the equipment as lines of magnetic force can not enter iron enclosure.
23. **(a)** Magnetic moment, $M = 8.7 \times 10^{-2}\,Am^2$ moment of inertia, $I = 11.5 \times 10^{-6}\,kg\,m^2$ Time period of oscillation is

$T = \dfrac{6.70}{10} = 0.6755$

As, $T = 2\pi\sqrt{\dfrac{I}{MB}}$; $B = \dfrac{4\pi^2 I^2}{MT^2}$

$\therefore$ $B = \dfrac{4 \times (3.14)^2 \times 11.5 \times 10^{-6}}{8.7 \times 10^{-2} \times (0.67)^2} = 0.012$ T

24. **(a)**   **25.** **(d)**

1. **(c)**
2. **(b)** Magnetic meridian of a place is defined as the vertical plane which passes through the imaginary line joining the magnetic North and South-poles. This pane would intersect the surface of the Earth in a longitude like circle.
3. **(c)**   **4.** **(a)**   **5.** **(d)**   **6.** **(a)**   **7.** **(d)**
8. **(c)** $\tan\delta = \dfrac{V}{H} = \dfrac{V}{\sqrt{3}V} = \dfrac{1}{\sqrt{3}}$

$\therefore$ $\delta = 30° = \pi/6$ radian

9. **(c)** $B = \dfrac{H}{\cos\theta} = \dfrac{0.50}{\cos 30°} = \dfrac{0.50 \times 2}{\sqrt{3}} = 1/\sqrt{3}$

10. **(b)** We know that at magnetic poles the horizontal component of earth's field is zero, only vertical component exists. So compass needle may stay in any direction.
The dip needle rotates in a vertical plane and the angle of dip at poles is 90°. Hence, the dip needle will stand vertical at the north pole of earth.
11. When a magnet is cut into two pieces transverse to its length and along its length the dipole moment becomes half as when it is cut transverse to its length its distance becomes half and when it is cut along its length its pole strength becomes half.
12. Dip circle will become straight vertical showing the angle of dip 90° at the geomagnetic north or south pole.
13. Repulsion takes place only between two likes poles of a magnet whereas attraction takes place between two unlike poles of a magnet and between a magnet and a magnetic material. So by attraction it cannot be surely identified the substance is a magnet or not. So, repulsion is the surer test of magnetism.
14. The magnetic field due to a current carrying conductor changes its direction if the direction of current in the conductor is changed. Whereas the earth's magnetic field is always directed from geographical south to north direction.
15. The two rods A and B are touched at every point along their lengths. One rod will show attraction to the other at every point along its length, while the other will show attraction only at the two ends of the rod. The attractive power decreases from the ends towards the centre of the rod. At the centre there is no attractive power. The rod which shows uniform attractive power throughout its length is the ordinary piece of iron whereas the rod with maximum attractive power at the ends and no attractive power at the centre is the bar magnet.

6 Electromagnetic Induction

ELECTROMAGNETIC INDUCTION (EMI) Generation of current or emf by changing magnetic field

Faraday's laws of electromagnetic Induction

1st Law: When magnetic flux linked with the circuit changes an emf is induced in the circuit

2nd Law: Induced emf ∝ rate of change of magnetic flux
$$e = \frac{-d\phi}{dt}$$

Motional emf $e = -\frac{d\phi}{dt} = -Blv$

Across the end of rod, $e = \frac{1}{2}B\omega l^2$

Magnetic flux $\phi_B = \vec{B}.\vec{A} = BA\cos\theta$

Lenz's law: Direction of induced emf or current is always in such a way that it opposes cause due to which it is produced. It is in accordance with conservation of energy

Direction of induced current Fleming's Right Hand Rule: Thumb, forefinger, central finger of right hand stretched perpendicular to each other then if thumb → direction of motion; forefinger → direction of magnetic field then central finger → induced current

Induced current in a coil rotated in uniform magnetic field
$$I = \frac{NBA\,\omega\sin\omega t}{R}$$

AC Generator or Dynamo produces electrical energy from mechanical energy. It works on EMI principle

Inductance: It is analogous to inertia opposes any change of current in the circuit.

Mutual Inductance: Induced emf in a circuit due to change in magnetic flux in its neighbouring circuit. Coefficients of mutual inductance
$$M = \frac{\phi}{I}$$

Coefficient of mutual inductance between two long solenoids
$$M = \frac{\mu_0 N_1 N_2 A}{l}$$

Self inductance: Inertia of electricity. Coefficient of self inductance $L = \frac{\phi_B}{i}$

Self inductance of a long solenoid
$$L = \frac{\mu_0 N^2 A}{l}$$

Eddy current is induced, when magnetic flux linked with the conductor changes

Applications of eddy currents

→ Electromagnetic damping
→ Induction furnace
→ Magnetic braking
→ Electric power meter

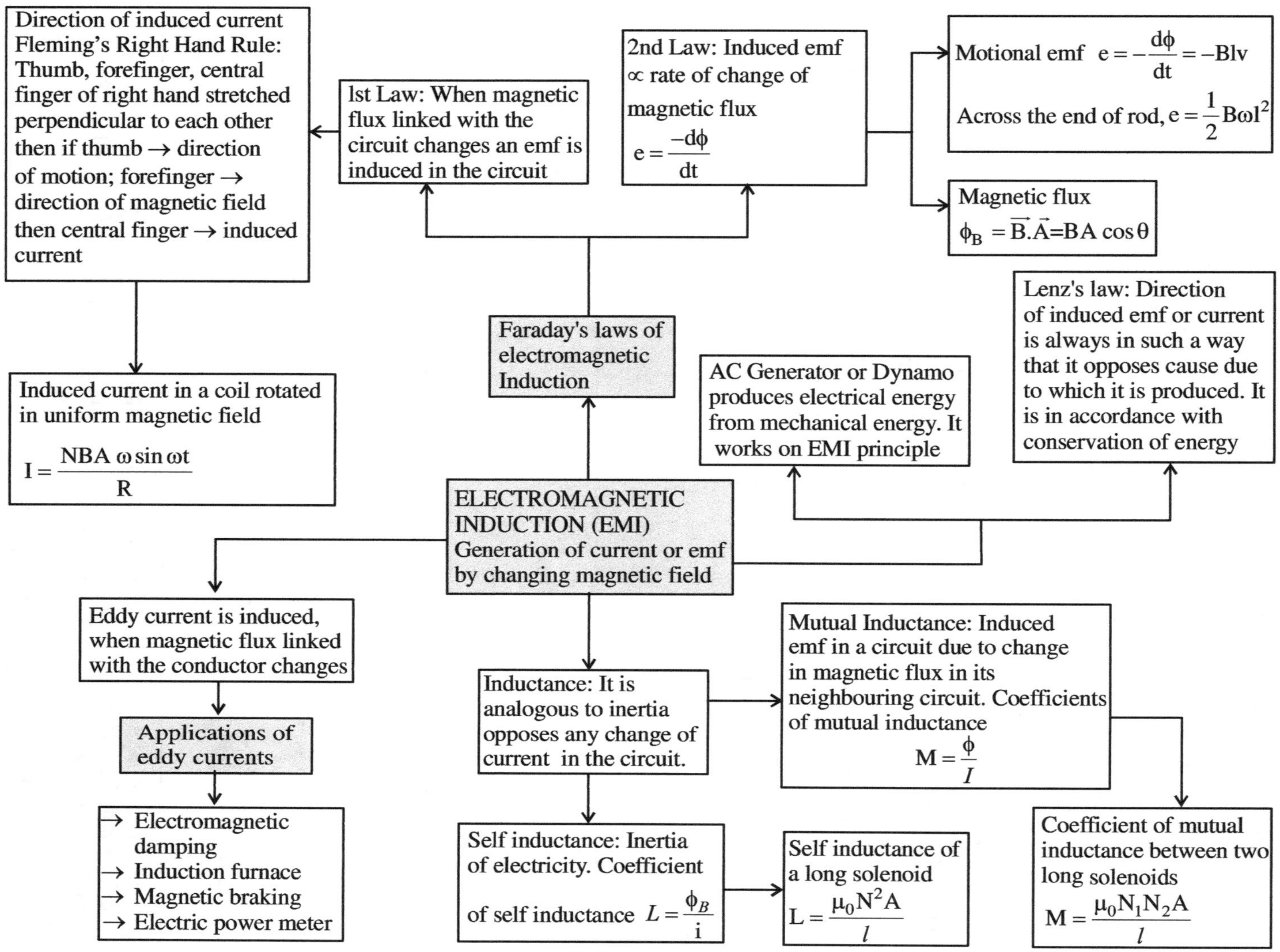

Topic 1   The Experiments of Faraday and Henry, Magnetic Flux, Faraday's Laws of Electromagnetic Induction and Lenz's Law

THE EXPERIMENTS OF FARADAY AND HENRY

Electromagnetic induction is the phenomenon of production of e.m.f. in a conductor due to change in magnetic flux linked with it. The discovery and understanding of electromagnetic induction are based on a long series of experiments carried out by Faraday and Henry. These experiments are illustrated by the following figures.

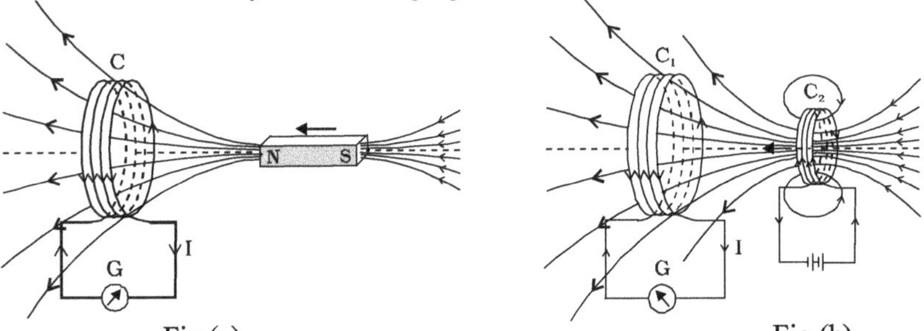

Fig (a)   Fig (b)

Current induced by a magnet : When the bar magnet is pushed towards the coil, the pointer in the galvanometer G deflects, fig (a).

Current induced by a current : Current is induced in coil C_1 due to motion of the current carrying coil C_2 fig (b).

A sensitive galvanometer (G) is connected to the free ends of a coil A, a strong magnet NS is brought near the coil and away from it and the following observations are made.

When the magnet with its N-pole facing the coil is moved towards the coil, the galvanometer shows some deflection while the magnet is in motion showing that an electric current is produced in the coil even though no conventional source of e.m.f. is in the circuit. The current is called the induced current and the e.m.f. responsible for it is called the **induced e.m.f.**

	Experiment	Observation	
1.	Place a magnet near a conducting loop with a galvanometer in the circuit	No current flows through the galvanometer	
2.	Move the magnet towards the loop	The galvanometer register a current	
3.	Reverse the direction of motion of the magnet	The galvanometer deflection reverses	
4.	Reverse the polarity of the magnet and move the magnet towards the loop	The galvanometer deflection reverses	
5.	Keep magnet fixed and move the coil towards the magnet	The galvanometer register a current	
6.	Increase the speed of the magnet	The deflection increases	
7.	Increase the strength of the magnet	The deflection increases	

8.	Increase the diameter of the coil	The deflection increases
9.	Fix the speed of the magnet but repeat the experiment with the magnet closer to the coil.	The deflection increases
10.	Move the magnet at an angle to the plane of the coil.	Deflection decreases it is maximum when the magnet moves perpendicular to the plane of the coil and it is zero when the magnet moves parallel to the plane of the coil.
11.	Increase the number of turns of the coil	Magnitude of current increases.

MAGNETIC FLUX (ϕ)

Magnetic flux through any surface held in a magnetic field $(\vec{B})$ is the total number of magnetic lines of force crossing the surface.

Magnetic flux through $\Delta S = \Delta\phi = (B) . (\Delta S \cos\theta) = \vec{B}.\overrightarrow{\Delta S}$

$\therefore$ Total flux through the surface $S = \phi = \int_S \vec{B}.d\vec{s}$

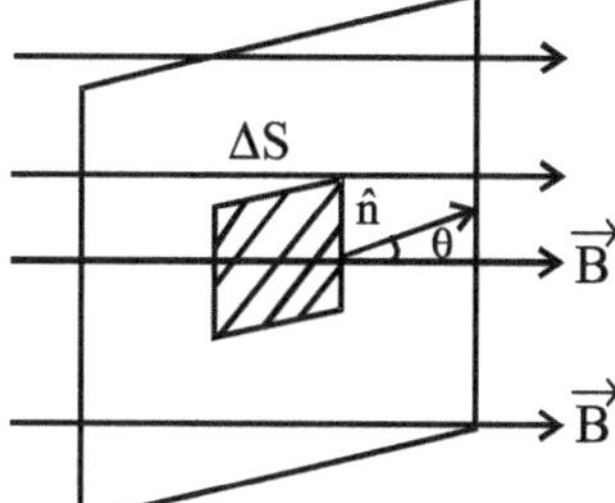

$\therefore$ For a plane surface of area A, total flux through it is $\phi = \vec{B}.\vec{A} = BA \cos\theta$

Unit of magnetic flux is weber. 1 weber = 1 tesla $\times 1$ m^2

FARADAY'S LAWS OF ELECTROMAGNETIC INDUCTION

Faraday gave two laws of electromagnetic induction.

1st law: Whenever the amount of magnetic flux linked with a coil changes, an e.m.f. is induced in the circuit. The e.m.f. lasts so long as the change in magnetic flux continues.

2nd law: The magnitude of e.m.f. induced in a circuit is directly proportional to the rate of change of magnetic flux linked with the circuit.

For a small change in magnetic flux $d\phi$ in a small time dt, induced e.m.f. $e = -\dfrac{d\phi}{dt} = \dfrac{-d}{dt}(BA \cos\theta)$

If the initial flux is ϕ_1, and final flux is ϕ_2 through a surface in time t, then rate of change of magnetic flux $= \dfrac{\phi_2 - \phi_1}{t}$

$\therefore$ Induced e.m.f. $= e \propto \dfrac{\phi_2 - \phi_1}{t}$ or, induced e.m.f. $e = -k\dfrac{\phi_2 - \phi_1}{t}$ [k = proportionality constant and k = 1 for all system of units]

The negative sign indicates induced e.m.f. opposes any change in magnetic flux associated with the circuit.

Induced e.m.f. and Different Methods of Production:

We know, induced e.m.f. $e = \dfrac{-d\phi}{dt}$ and flux $\phi = BA \cos\theta$ $\qquad \therefore \quad e = \dfrac{-d}{dt}(BA \cos\theta)$

Induced Current: $I = \dfrac{e}{R}$

This induced e.m.f. e can be produced either by changing B or by changing A or by changing θ alone.

(i) **By changing B alone:** If the magnetic field intensity B in a closed loop of conductor changes, then flux linked with the loop changes and an e.m.f. is produced.

$e = \dfrac{-d\phi}{dt} = \dfrac{-d}{dt}(BA \cos\theta) = -A \cos\theta \dfrac{dB}{dt}$ [A and θ are constants]

(ii) **By changing A alone:** If the area of the coil associated with magnetic flux B changes, keeping B and θ constant then,

$e = \dfrac{-d\phi}{dt} = \dfrac{-d}{dt}(BA \cos\theta) = -B \cos\theta \dfrac{dA}{dt}$

(iii) **By changing θ alone:** Consider a loop of N turns of area of cross-section A each placed in a magnetic field $\vec{B}$ in such a way that it is able to rotate about an axis perpendiular to $\vec{B}$. If ω is the constant angular velocity of the loop then induced e.m.f.

$e = \dfrac{-d\phi}{dt}$

$\phi = B(NA) \cos\theta$ and $\theta = \omega t$

Induced e.m.f. $e = \dfrac{-d}{dt}(BNA \cos\omega t) = BNA\omega \sin \omega t = e_0 \sin \omega t$ where $e_0 = BNA\omega = $ constant

Illustration 1 :

A coil having 100 turns and area of 0.001 metre^2 is free to rotate about an axis. The coil is placed perpendicular to a magnetic field of 1.0 weber/metre^2. If the coil is rotate rapidly through an angle of 180°, how much charge will flow through the coil? The resistance of the coil is 10 ohm.

Sol. The flux linked with the coil when the plane of the coil is perpendicular to the magnetic field is $\phi = nAB \cos\theta = nAB$.

The change in flux on rotating the coil by 180° is $d\phi = nAB - (-nAB) = 2nAB$

$$\therefore \quad \text{induced charge} = \frac{d\phi}{R} = \frac{2nAB}{R} = \frac{2 \times 100 \times 0.001 \times 1}{10} \qquad \therefore \text{ Induced charge} = 0.01 \text{ C.}$$

LENZ'S LAW

According to this law, *induced current will appear in such a direction that it opposes the change that produced it.*

Lenz's law complies with the law of conservation of energy because when N-pole of a magnet is moved towards the coil, the upper face of the coil acquires north polarity. So work has to be done against the force of repulsion in bringing the magnet closer to the coil.

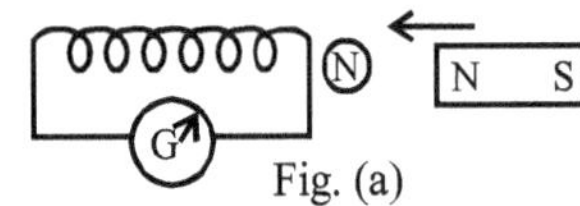
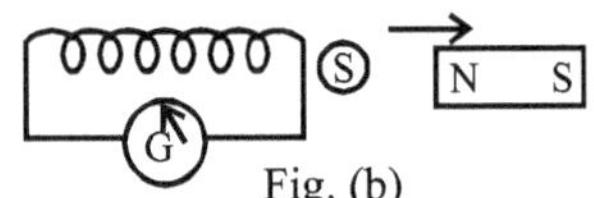

Fig. (a)   Fig. (b)

When the N-pole is moved away, south polarity is developed on the upper face of the coil. Therefore, work has to be done against the force of attraction in taking the magnet away from the coil.

And this mechanical work done is converted into electrical energy of the coil.

When the magnet does not move work done is zero, so no electrical energy is produced.

Practice Exercise 1

Multiple Choice Questions

1. In a coil of resistance $10\,\Omega$, the induced current developed by changing magnetic flux through it, is shown in figure as a function of time. The magnitude of change in flux through the coil in weber is
(a) 8   (b) 2   (c) 6   (d) 4

2. Whenever the magnetic flux linked with a coil changes, an induced e.m.f. is produced in the circuit. The e.m.f. lasts
I.   for a short time
II.   for a long time
III. so long as the change in flux takes place
The true/false statement(s) is/are
(a) T, T, F   (b) F, T, T
(c) T, F, T   (d) F, F, T

3. Consider coil and magnet

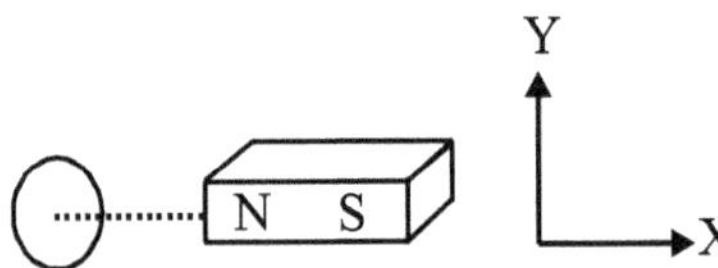

Current is induced in coil when
I.   coil and magnet both are at rest.
II.   coil is at rest and magnet moves along x.
III. magnet is at rest and coil moves along x.
Then true/false statements are
(a) T, F, F   (b) T, T, F
(c) F, F, T   (d) F, T, T

4. Two different wire loops are concentric and lie in the same plane. The current in the outer loop (I) is clockwise and increases with time. The induced current i in the inner loop______.
(a) is clockwise
(b) is zero
(c) is counter clockwise
(d) has a direction that depends on the ratio of the loop radii.

5. According to Faraday's law of electromagnetic induction
I.   The induced emf is not in the direction opposing the change in magnetic flux.
II.   The relative motion between the coil and magnet produces change in magnetic flux.
III. Only the magnet should be moved towards coil.
The true/false statement(s) are
(a) T,T,F   (b) F,T,F
(c) F,F,T   (d) F,T,T

6. A cylindrical bar magnet is kept along the axis a circular coil. If the magnet is rotated about its axis, then ________ in the coil.
(a) a current will be induced
(b) no current will be induced
(c) only an e.m.f. will induced
(d) an e.m.f and a current both will be induced

Assertion & Reason Questions

DIRECTIONS (Qs. 7-11) : *Each of these questions contains an assertion followed by reason. Read them carefully and answer the question on the basis of following options. You have to select the one that best describes the two statements.*

(a) If both Assertion and Reason are correct and the Reason is a correct explanation of the Assertion.

(b) If both Assertion and Reason are correct but Reason is not a correct explanation of the Assertion.

(c) If the Assertion is correct but Reason is incorrect.

(d) If the Assertion is incorrect but the Reason is correct.correct but the Reason is correct.

7. **Assertion :** Emf will always induce whenever there is change in magnetic flux associated with a circuit.

   Reason : Current will never induces whenever there is change in magnetic flux.

8. **Assertion :** Only a change in magnetic flux will maintain an induced current in the coil.

   Reason : The presence of constant magnetic field through a coil maintain an induced current in the coil of the circuit.

9. **Assertion :** Figure shows a horizontal solenoid connected to a battery and a switch. A copper ring is placed on a smooth surface, the axis of the ring being horizontal. As the switch is closed, the ring will move away from the solenoid.

   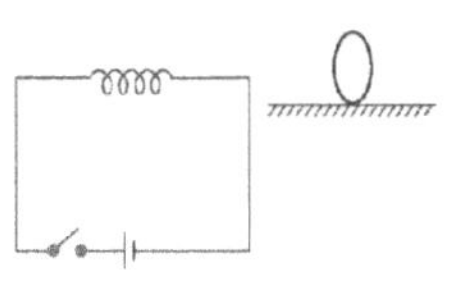

   Reason : Induced current in the ring, $i = -\dfrac{d\phi}{dt}$.

10. **Assertion :** An emf can be induced by moving a conductor in a magnetic field.

    Reason : An emf can be induced by changing the magnetic field.

11. **Assertion :** The induced charge that flows in the circuit does not depends on the time rate change of flux.

    Reason : $i = \dfrac{dq}{dt} = -\dfrac{1}{R}\left(\dfrac{d\phi}{dt}\right) \Rightarrow dq = -\dfrac{d\phi}{R}$

Case/Passage Based Questions

A magnet is moved with a fast speed towards a coil at rest. Due to this induced electromotive force, induced current and induced charge in the coil is E, I and Q respectively.

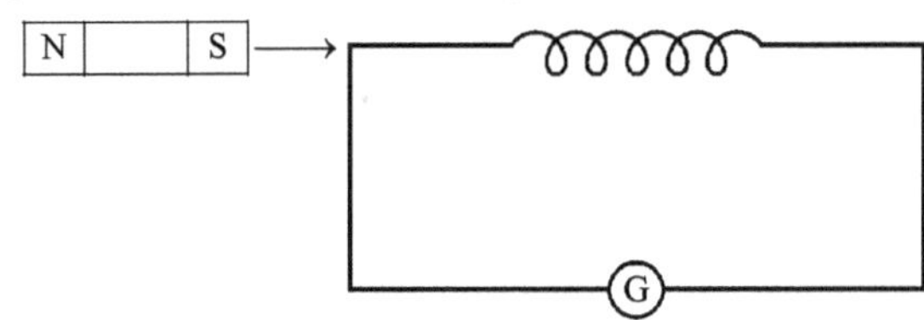

12. If the speed of the magnet is doubled, then
    (a) E decreases
    (b) E increases
    (c) E remains same
    (d) Either decreases or remains same

13. If the speed of the magnet is doubled, then
    (a) I increases
    (b) I decreases
    (c) I remains same
    (d) None of these

14. If the speed of the magnet is doubled, then
    (a) Q increases
    (b) Q decreases
    (c) Q remains same
    (d) Either increases or decreases

15. If the speed of the magnet is halved, then
    (a) E decreases
    (b) I decreases
    (c) Q decreases
    (d) both (a) and (b)

16. If the speed of the magnet is halved, then
    (a) E increases
    (b) I increases
    (c) Q remains same
    (d) None of these

Very Short Answer Questions

17. Define magnetic flux.

18. Give the direction in which induced current flows in the wire loop, when the magnet moves towards the loop as shown in the figure.

    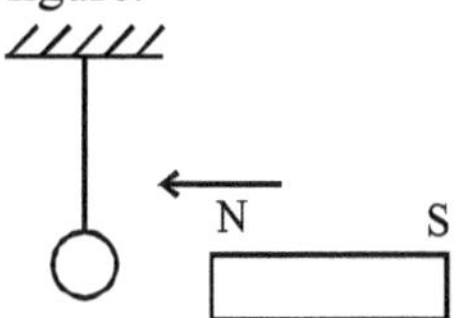

19. In which direction will the current be induced in the closed loop if the magnet is moved as shown in the figure.

    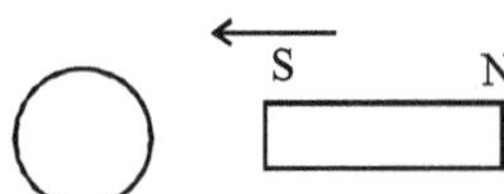

20. A magnet is moved in the direction indicated by an arrow between two coils AB and CD as shown in the figure. Find the direction of current in each coil.

    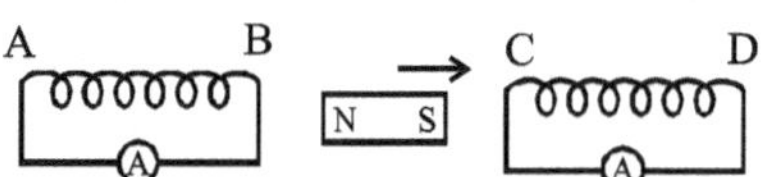

21. The following figure shows a horizontal solenoid 'PQ' connected to a battery 'B' and switch 'S'. A copper ring 'R' is placed on a frictionless track, the axis of the ring being along the axis of the solenoid. What would happen to the ring as the switch 'S' is closed?

    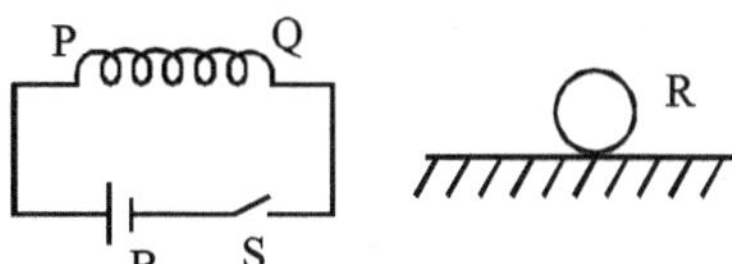

22. State Lenz's law.

Short Answer Questions

23. State Faraday's laws of electromagnetic induction. Express it mathematically.

24. The given figure shows an inductor L and resistor R connected in parallel to a battery B through a switch S. The resistance of R is same as that of the coil that makes L. Two identical bulbs, P and Q are put in each arm of the circuit as shown in the figure. When S is closed, which of the two bulbs will light up earlier? Justify your answer.

    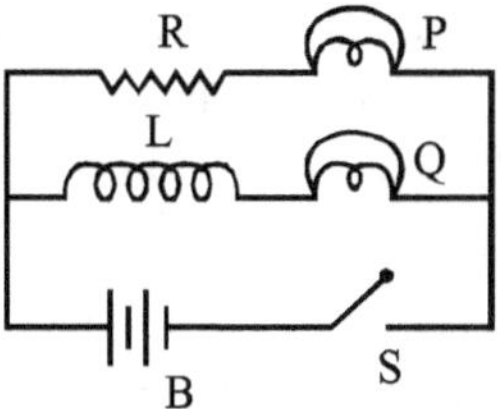

25. In the diagram given, a coil B is connected to low voltage bulb L and placed parallel to another coil 'A' as shown. Explain the following observations.
   (i) Bulb lights and
   (ii) Bulb gets dimmer if the coil 'B' is moved upwards.

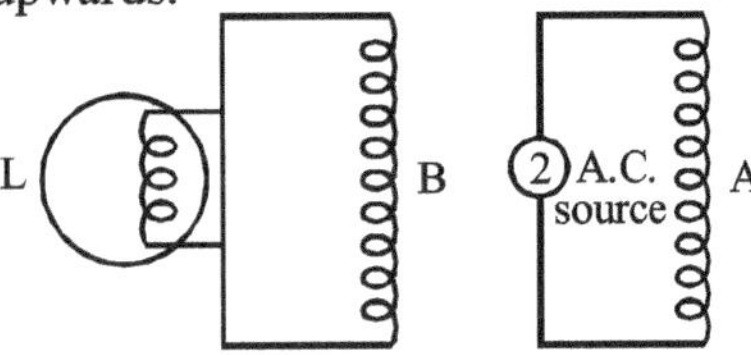

26. A small piece of metal wire is dragged across the gap between the pole piece of a magnet in 0.5 s. The magnetic flux between the pole pieces is known to be 8×10^{-4} Wb. Calculate the induced emf in the wire.
–ve sign gives the direction of e.m.f.

27. A bar magnet falls from a height 'h' through a metal ring. Will its acceleration be equal to g? Give reason for your answer.

28. A vertical metallic pole falls down through the plane of the magnetic meridian. Will any e.m.f. be produced between its ends? Give reason for your answer.

Topic 2   Motional Electromotive Force and Eddy Current

Fleming's Right Hand Rule

This law gives the direction of the induced e.m.f and current in a straight conductor moving perpendicular to the direction of magnetic field.

"If we stretch the right-hand thumb and two nearby fingers perpendicular to one another, and the first finger points in the direction of magnetic field and the thumb in the direction of motion of the conductor, then the middle finger will point in the direction of the induced current.

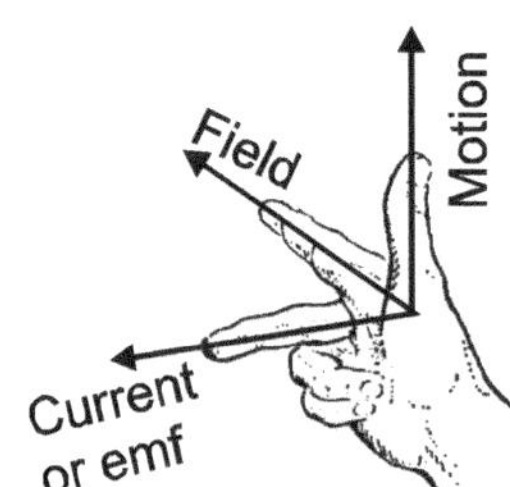

MOTIONAL ELECTROMOTIVE FORCE

Suppose the moving rod ab slides along a stationary U-shaped conductor, forming a complete circuit. Under the action of this field a counterclockwise current is established around this complete circuit. The moving rod becomes a source of electromotive force. Within it, charge moves from lower to higher potential and in the remainder of the circuit, charge moves from higher to lower potential. We call this a motional electromagnetic force denoted by e, we can write,

$$\text{Electromotive force. } e = Bv\ell$$

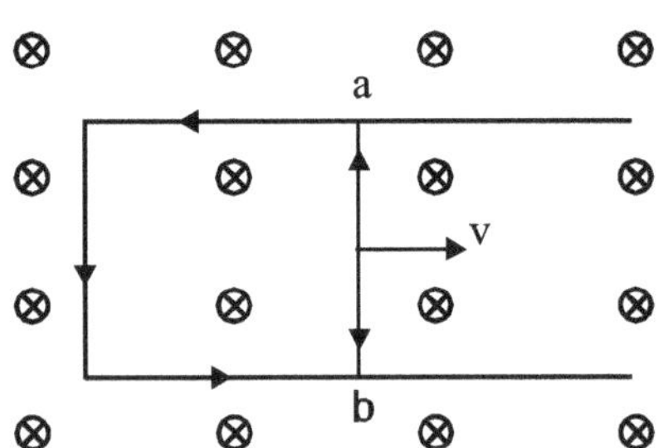

If R is the resistance of the circuit, then current in the circuit $\quad i = \dfrac{e}{R} = \dfrac{Bv\ell}{R}$

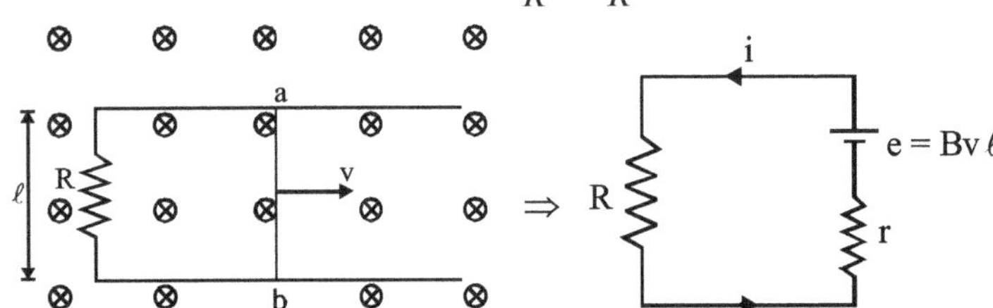

In the figure shown, we can replace the moving rod ab by a battery of emf Bvl with the positive terminal at a and the negative terminal at b. The resistance r of the rod ab may be treated as the internal resistance of the battery. Hence, the current in the circuit is,

$$i = \frac{e}{R+r} \quad \text{or} \quad i = \frac{Bv\ell}{R+r}$$

Illustration 2 :

A conductor of length 10 cm is moved parallel to itself with a speed of 10 m/s at right angles to a uniform magnetic induction 10^{-4} Wb/m². What is the induced e.m.f. in it?

Sol Given : $\quad \ell = 10\,\text{cm} = 0.1\,\text{m}, v = 10\,\text{m/s} \qquad B = 10^{-4}\,\text{Wb/m}^2$

e.m.f. induced in conductor $\quad e = B\ell V = 10^{-4} \times 0.1 \times 10 = 10^{-4}\,\text{V}$

Illustration 3 :

A copper rod of length l is rotated about one end perpendicular to the uniform magnetic field B with constant angular velocity ω. What is the induced e.m.f. between two ends.

Sol. Consider a small element of the rod of length dx at a distance x from the centre O.
Let v be the linear velocity of the element at right angles to the magnetic field B. The e.m.f.
developed across the element is $d\in = B\,v\,dx = B\,(\omega x)\,dx$ $(\because v = \omega x)$
The e.m.f. across the entire rod of length ℓ is given by

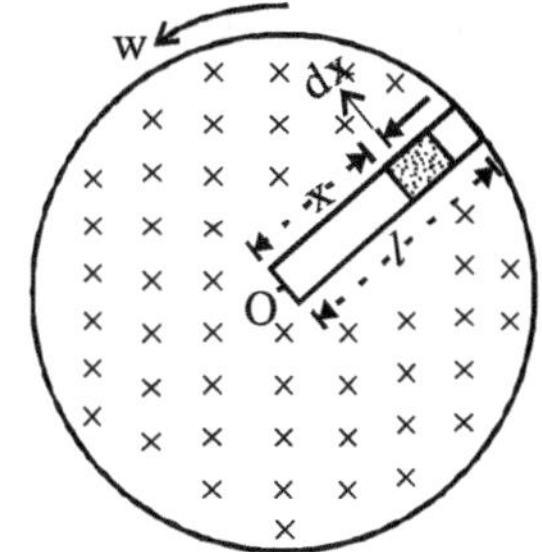

$$\in = \int d\in = B\omega \int_0^\ell x\,dx = B\omega \left[\frac{x^2}{2}\right]_0^\ell = B\omega(\ell^2/2) = \frac{1}{2}B\omega\ell^2$$

Energy Consideration : A Quantitative Study

In the figure shown, if you move the conductor ab with a constant velocity v,
the current in the circuit is,

$$i = \frac{B\,v\,\ell}{R}$$ (if, r = 0)

A magnetic force $F_m = i\,\ell\,B = \dfrac{B^2\ell^2 v}{R}$ acts on the conductor in opposite

direction of velocity. So, to move the conductor with a constant velocity
v an equal and opposite force F has to be applied in the conductor.

Thus, $F = F_m = \dfrac{B^2\ell^2 v}{R}$

The rate at which work is done by the applied force i.e. Power

$$P_{applied} = Fv = \frac{B^2\ell^2 v^2}{R}$$

And the rate at which energy is dissipated in the circuit

$$P_{dissipated} = i^2 R = \left(\frac{B\,v\,\ell}{R}\right)^2 \quad \therefore\ R = \frac{B^2\ell^2 v^2}{R}$$

This is just equal to the rate at which work is done by the applied force.

Illustration 4 :

**In a uniform magnetic field of induction B a wire in the form of a semicircle of radius r rotates about the diameter of the
circle with an angular frequency ω. The axis of rotation is perpendicular to the field. If the total resistance of the circuit
is R, what is the mean power generated per period of rotation?**

Sol. Magnetic flux $\phi = \vec{B}.\vec{A}$ $\phi = BA\cos\omega t$

$$\varepsilon = -\frac{d\phi}{dt} = \omega BA\sin\omega t\ ;\ i = \frac{\omega BA}{R}\sin\omega t \qquad\qquad P_{inst} = i^2 R = \left(\frac{\omega BA}{R}\right)^2 \times R\sin^2\omega t$$

$$P_{avg} = \frac{\displaystyle\int_0^T P_{inst}\times dt}{\displaystyle\int_0^T dt} = \frac{(\omega BA)^2}{R}\frac{\displaystyle\int_0^T \sin^2\omega t\,dt}{\displaystyle\int_0^T dt} = \frac{(\omega BA)^2}{R}\left(\frac{T}{2.T}\right) \qquad \therefore P_{avg} = \frac{(\omega B\pi r^2)^2}{2R}$$

EDDY CURRENT

Currents induced in the body of a conductor when the amount of magnetic flux linked with the conductor changes is called eddy
current.

Eddy currents often have large magnitudes and heat up the conductor. It is also known as Focault current as experimental concept
is given by Focault.

Magnitude of eddy current $i = \dfrac{\text{induced e.m.f.}}{\text{resistance}} = \dfrac{e}{R} = -\dfrac{d\phi/dt}{R}\ \left[\because e = -\dfrac{d\phi}{dt}\right]$

Applications of Eddy Current

(i) **Electromagnetic damping :** This is used in dead beat galvanometer. To avoid delay due to oscillations of galvanometer coil, it is wound over a metallic frame. As the coil is deflected, eddy current set up in the metallic frame which opposes the motion of the coil and the coil comes to rest quickly.

(ii) **Induction furnace :** Here heating effect of eddy current is used. The substance to be heated is kept in a high frequency magnetic field. Due to large eddy current, large amount of heat is produced which melts the substance.

(iii) Speedometer of an automobile

(iv) Dead-beat galvanometer

Disadvantages of Eddy Current

(i) It opposes the relative motion between the two objects.

(ii) It involves loss of energy in the form of heat.

(iii) Excessive heating may damage the insulation of electric appliances and may reduce their life.

Practice Exercise-2

Multiple Choice Questions

1. The figure shows a wire sliding on two parallel conducting rails placed at a separation I. A magnetic field B exists in a direction perpendicular to the plane of the rails. The force required to keep the wire moving at a constant velocity v will be

(a) evB

(b) $\dfrac{\mu_0 Bv}{4\pi I}$

(c) BIv

(d) zero

2. A sliding wire of length 0.25 m and having a resistance of 0.5 Ω moves along conducting guiding rails AB and CD with a uniform speed of 4 m/s. A magnetic field of 0.5 T exists normal to the plane of $ABCD$ directed into the page. The guides are short -circuited with resistances of 4 and 2 Ω as shown. The current through the sliding wire is :

(a) 0.27 A

(b) 0.37 A

(c) 1.0 A

(d) 0.72 A

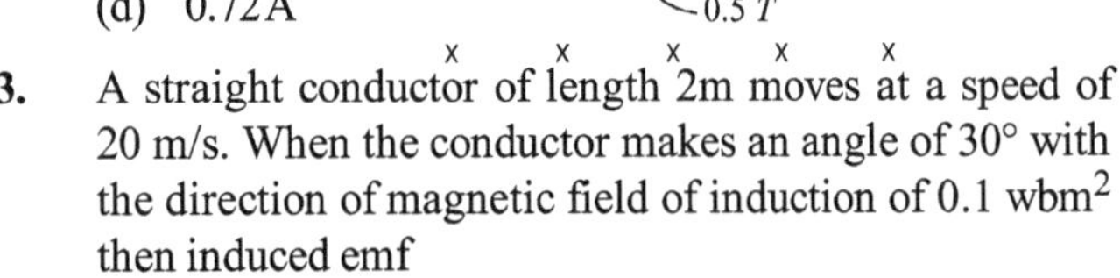

3. A straight conductor of length 2m moves at a speed of 20 m/s. When the conductor makes an angle of 30° with the direction of magnetic field of induction of 0.1 wbm^2 then induced emf

(a) 4V   (b) 3V   (c) IV   (d) 2V

4. A wire of length 1m is perpendicular to x-y plane. It is moved with velocity $\vec{v} = (3\hat{i} + 3\hat{j} + 2\hat{k})\,\text{m/s}$ through a region of uniform induction $\vec{B} = (\hat{i} + 2\hat{j})\,\text{T}$. The potential difference between the ends of the wire is

(a) IV   (b) 1.5V   (c) 2.5V   (d) 3V

5. A circular wire of radius r rotates about its own axis with angular speed ω in a magnetic field B perpendicular to its plane, then the induced e.m.f. is

(a) $\dfrac{1}{2}Br\omega^2$ (b) $Br\omega^2$ (c) $2Br\omega^2$ (d) zero

Assertion & Reason Questions

DIRECTIONS (Qs. 6-7) : *Each of these questions contains an assertion followed by reason. Read them carefully and answer the question on the basis of following options. You have to select the one that best describes the two statements.*

(a) If both Assertion and Reason are correct and the Reason is a correct explanation of the Assertion.

(b) If both Assertion and Reason are correct but Reason is not a correct explanation of the Assertion.

(c) If the Assertion is correct but Reason is incorrect.

(d) If the Assertion is incorrect but the Reason is correct.

6. **Assertion :** An emf can be induced by moving a conductor in a magnetic field.

Reason : An emf can be induced by changing the magnetic field.

7. **Assertion :** Figure shows a metallic conductor moving in magnetic field. The induced emf across its ends is zero.

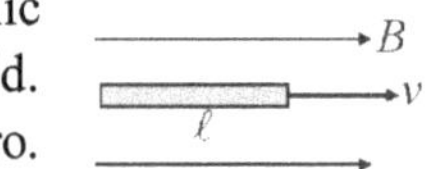

Reason : The induced emf across the ends of a conductor is given by $e = Bv\ell\sin\theta$.

Case/Passage Based Questions

Consider a region of cylindrical magnetic field, changing with time at the rate x. A triangular conducting loop PQR is placed in the field such that mid point of side PQ coincides with axis of the magnetic field region. $PQ = 2l$, PR = 2l.

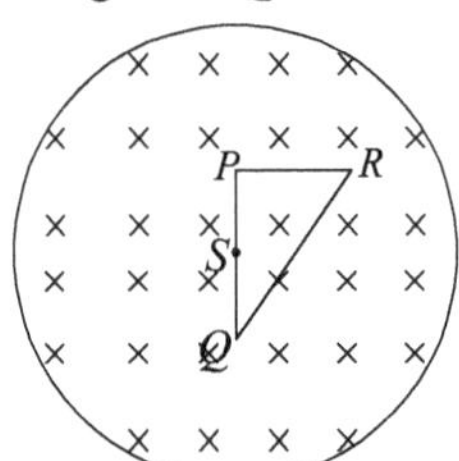

8. The emf induced in the side PQ of the loop is

(a) 0   (b) xl^2 (c) $\dfrac{xl^2}{2}$ (d) $2xl^2$

9. The emf induced in the side QR of the loop is

(a) 0   (b) xl^2 (c) $\dfrac{xl^2}{4}$ (d) $4xl^2$

10. The emf induced in the side PR of the loop is

   (a) xl^2 (b) $\dfrac{xl^2}{2}$ (c) $\dfrac{3}{2}xl^2$ (d) zero

11. Induced emf in the coil depends upon
  (a) conductivity of coil
  (b) amount of flux
  (c) rate of change of linked flux
  (d) resistance of coil

12. Whenever the magnetic flux linked with a coil changes, an induced e.m.f. is produced in the circuit. The e.m.f. lasts
  (a) for a short time
  (b) for a long time
  (c) for ever
  (d) so long as the change in flux takes place

Short Answer Questions

13. The closed loop PQRS is moving into a uniform magnetic field acting at right angles to the plane of the paper as shown in the following figure. State the direction in which the induced current flows in the loop.

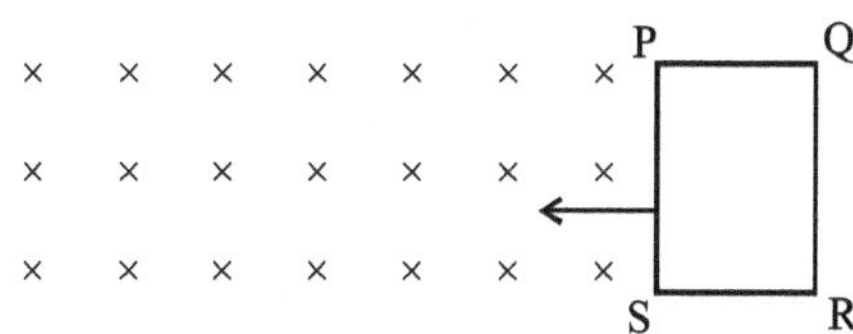

14. A rectangular loop KLMN is moved away with a uniform velocity 'v' at right angles to a uniform magnetic field B as shown in the figure.

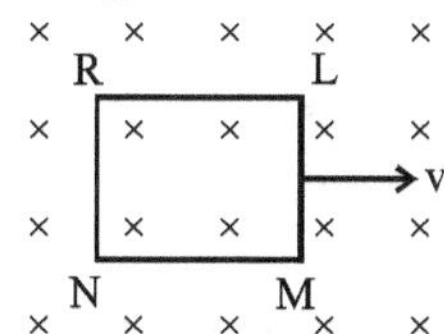

  (i) What is the magnitude of current induced in the loop?

  (ii) Will there be any work done by the loop? Give reason for your answer.

15. A uniform magnetic field exists normal to the plane of the paper over a small region of space. A rectangular loop of wire is slowly moved with a uniform velocity across the field as shown. Draw the graph showing the variation of (i) magnetic flux linked with the loop and (ii) the induced e.m.f with the loop with time.

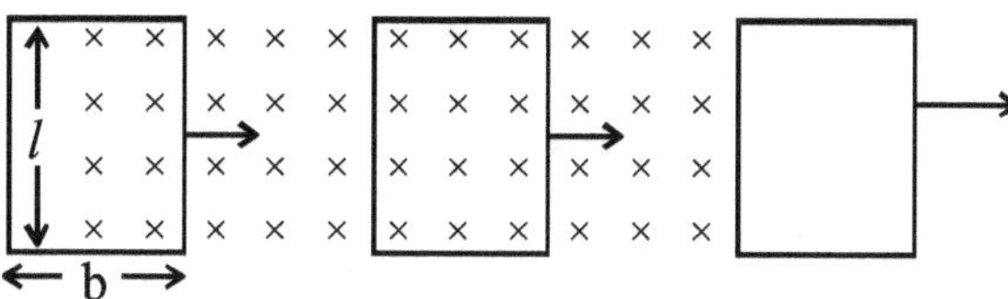

16. A circular copper wire 10 cm in radius rotates at 20π rad/s about an axis through its centre and perpendicular to the wire. A uniform magnetic field of 0.2 T acts perpendicular to the wire.
  (i) Calculate the potential difference developed between the axis of the wire and the rim.
  (ii) What is the induced current in the circuit whose terminals are connected between centre of disc and point of rim and the resistance of the circuit is 2Ω

17. A wheel with 10 metallic spokes, each 0.5 m long is rotated with a speed of 120 rev/min. in a plane normal to the earth's magnetic field at the place. If the magnitude of the field is 0.4 G, what is the induced e.m.f between the axle and rim of the wheel?

18. A wire of length 0.1 m moves with a speed of 10 m/s perpendicular to a magnetic field of induction 1T. Calculate the induced e.m.f.

19. A straight conductor 1m long moves at right angles to both its length and a uniform magnetic field. If the speed of conductor is 2 m/s and strength of magnetic field is 10^4 gauss, find the value of the induced e.m.f. in volt.

20. How are eddy currents produced? Give two applications of eddy current.

Topic 3   Self and Mutual Inductance and AC Generator 

SELF AND MUTUAL INDUCTANCE

Self Induction

It is a property of a coil due to which the coil opposes any change in the strength of current flowing through it by inducing an e.m.f. in itself.

Whenever the key in the circuit is closed or opened, the current in the circuit increases or decreases. The variation of current causes a variation in magnetic flux linked with the circuit $(\therefore \phi \propto B \propto i)$ hence, an induced emf is developed in the circuit.

The emf is called **self induced emf** and the phenomenon is called **self induction.** Induced emf follows Lenz's Law. i.e. induced current always opposes the change in the main current.

When the main current is increased (by the rheostat), the induced current flows opposite to the main current and opposes the increase in the main current (Fig.a) When the main current is decreased, then the induced current flows in the same direction as the main current and opposes the decrease in the main current (Fig.b).

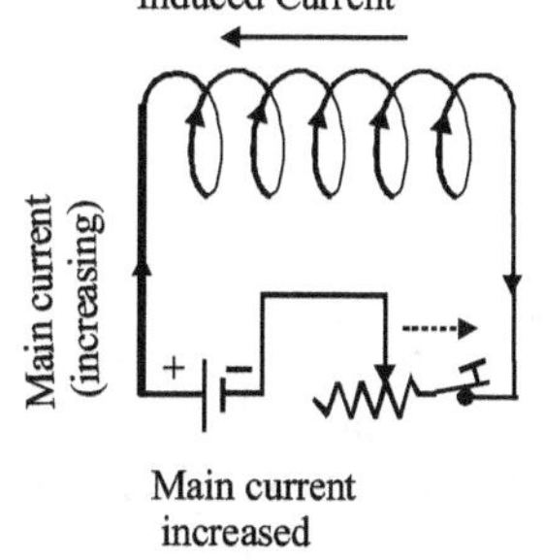

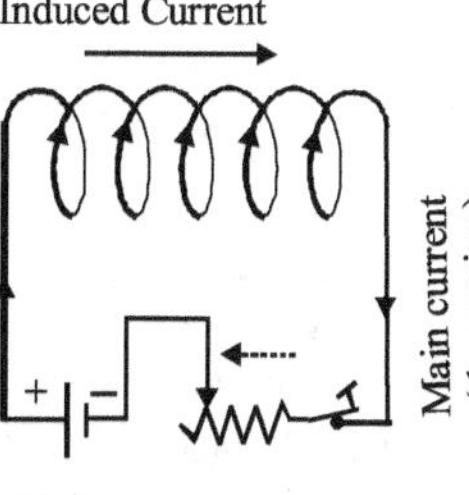

Coefficient of Self Inductance

Let us consider a coil having N turns. If the current flowing through the coil is i and the flux linked with each turn is ϕ, then the total flux linkage is $N\phi$. Now, $N\phi \propto i$ or $N\phi = Li$

where L is a constant called the **'coefficient of self-induction'** or **'self-inductance'** of the coil. By the above equation, we have

$$L = N\phi/i$$

In this equation, if $i = 1$, then $L = N\phi$. Hence the coefficient of self-induction of a coil is equal to the number of flux-linkages in the coil when unit current is flowing in the same coil.

According to Faraday's law of electromagnetic induction

$$e = -\frac{\Delta(N\phi)}{\Delta t}, \quad \text{But } N\phi = Li. \quad \text{Thus } e = \frac{-\Delta(Li)}{\Delta t} \quad \text{or} \quad e = -\frac{L\Delta i}{\Delta t}$$

If $\dfrac{\Delta i}{\Delta t} = 1$ ampere per second then $e = -L$

then, $e = L$ (numerically), hence the coefficient of self-induction of a coil is numerically equal to the emf induced in the coil due to unit rate of change of current in the same coil.

Units of self inductance of a coil

The **S.I.unit** of coefficient of self-induction is **henry.** If an emf of 1 volt is induced in a coil due to a change of current in it at the rate of 1 ampere/second, then the coefficient of self-induction of the coil is 1 henry. Thus

$$1 \text{ henry} = \frac{1 \text{ volt}}{1 \text{ ampere} / \text{ second}}$$

In practice, henry is a large unit for inductance. Smaller units for inductance are milli-henry and micro-henry. 1 milli-henry (mH) = 10^{-3} henry, 1 micro-henry (μH) = 10^{-6} henry.

Self inductance of a long solenoid: Self inductance of a long, air-cored solenoid of lenght l, having n turns per unit length of cross-sectional area A is given by $L = \mu_0 n^2 l A$

When a magnetic material of relative permeability μ_r is inserted into the solenoid as a core, then the self inductance becomes

$$L = \mu_0 \mu_r n^2 l A$$

Mutual Induction

It is the property of two coils due to which each opposes any change in the strength of current flowing through the other by developing an induced e.m.f.

Consider two coils A and B placed near to each other. When current in the coil A changed, there is a change in magnetic flux. As this flux is linked with the coil B, an e.m.f. induced is B. This phenomenon is called mutual induction.

The induced e.m.f. in secondary coil B is proportional to the rate of change of current in primary coil A.

Coefficient of Mutual Inductance

Consider two coils (Primary and secondary) placed very near to each other. Let N_1 and N_2 be the number of turns in the coils and i_1 be the current flowing in the first coil.

Let, due to this current, the magnetic flux linked with each turn of the secondary coil be ϕ_2. If N_2 be the number of turns in the secondary coil, then the number of flux-linkages in the coil will be $N_2\phi_2$. This number is proportional to the current i_1 flowing in the primary coil,

i.e. $N_2\phi_2 \propto i_1$ or $N_2\phi_2 = Mi_1$,

where M is a constant called the **'coefficient of mutual induction'** or **'mutual inductance'** between the two coils. From the above equation, we have $M = N_2\phi_2 / i_1$ In this equation, if $i_1 = 1$, then $M = N_2\phi_2$. Hence the coefficient of mutual induction between two coils is equal to the number of magnetic flux-linkage in one coil when a unit current flows in the other.

From Faraday's Law
$$e = -\frac{\Delta\phi}{\Delta t} = -\frac{\Delta(N_2\phi_2)}{\Delta t}$$

But $N_2\phi_2 = Mi_1$
$$\therefore \quad e = -\frac{\Delta(Mi_1)}{\Delta t} = -\frac{M\Delta i_1}{\Delta t}$$

If $\dfrac{\Delta i_1}{\Delta t} = 1$ ampere per second then $e = -M$

Hence, the coefficient of mutual induction between two coils is equal to the numerical value of the induced emf in one coil which is produced due to unit rate of change of current in the other.

The unit of the coefficient of mutual induction is 'henry'.

For a solenoid having a primary coil of N_1 turns and a secondary coil of N_2 turns, the coefficient of mutual inductance is given by

$$M = \frac{\mu_r \mu_0 N_1 N_2 A}{\ell} \qquad \text{where } \ell \text{ is the length of solenoid and A is the area of one turn of the secondary coil.}$$

Factors on which the Coeffecient of Mutual Induction of a Coil depends :

(i)   Size, shape, number of turns and nature of material of two coils.

(ii) Distance between two coils.

(iii) Orientation or relative placement of two coils.

Coefficient of Coupling

$$\text{Coefficient of coupling } K = \sqrt{\frac{M}{L_1 L_2}}$$

K is called the coefficient of coupling and is a measure of coupling between the two coils. Here, L_1 and L_2 are the self inductances of two coils and M is the mutual inductance between them.

Illustration 5 :

Find the self inductance of a coil in which an e.m.f. of 10 V is induced when the current in the circuit changes uniformly from 1 A to 0.5 A in 0.2 sec.

Sol. Given : $e = 10\,V$ and $\dfrac{dI}{dt} = \dfrac{1-0.5}{0.2} = \dfrac{0.5}{0.2} = 2.5\ A/s$

Self inductance of coil $\quad L = \dfrac{e}{dI/dt} = \dfrac{10}{2.5} = 4\ H \qquad \because\ e = L\dfrac{dI}{dt}$ (Considering magnitude only)

Illustration 6 :

Two coils are wound on the same iron rod so that the flux generated by one also passes through the other. The primary has 100 loops and secondary has 200 loops. When a current of 2 A flows through the primary the flux in it is 25×10^{-4} Wb. Determine value of M between the coils

Sol. $\left|e_s\right| = N_s\dfrac{d\phi_s}{dt}$ and $\left|e_s\right| = M\dfrac{di_p}{dt}$;

$\therefore\ N_s\dfrac{d\phi_s}{dt} = M\dfrac{di_p}{dt}$ or $M = N_s\dfrac{d\phi_s}{di_p} = \dfrac{200(2.5\times10^{-4} - 0)}{(2-0)} = 2.5\times10^{-2} = 25\ mH$

AC GENERATOR OR DYNAMO

It is used to convert mechanical energy into electrical energy.

Principle : It works on the principle of electromagnetic induction.

Construction : The main components of ac generator are :

(i)   Armature coil : It consist of large number of turns of insulated copper wire wound over iron core.

(ii) Magnet : Strong permanent magnet (for small generator) or an electromagnet (for large generator) with cylindrical poles in shape.

(iii) Slip rings : The two ends of the armature coil are connected to two brass rings R_1 and R_2. These rings rotate along with the armature coil.

(iv) Brushes : Two carbon brushes (B_1 and B_2), are pressed against the slip rings. These brushes are connected to the load through which the output is obtained.

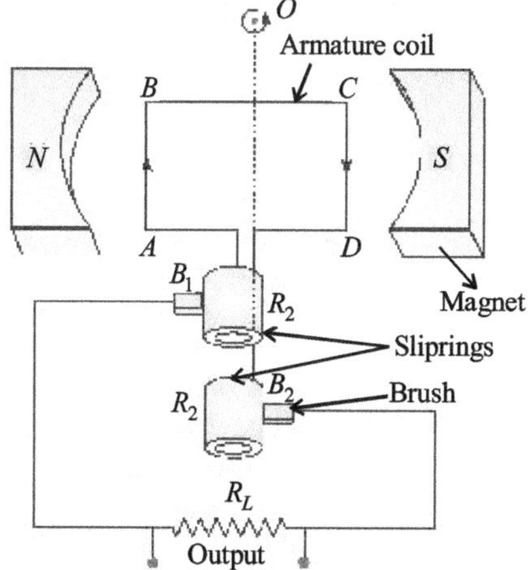

Theory and working: When a coil is rotated in magnetic field, an emf is induced in the coil. The coil may be rotated by water energy, steam energy or oil energy. Let at any instant magnetic flux through armature coil,

$$N\phi_B = NBA\cos\theta = NBA\cos\omega t$$

The induced emf $\qquad e = -\dfrac{d\phi_B}{dt} = NBA\omega\sin\omega t$

or $\qquad e = e_0\sin\omega t$, where $e_0 = NBA\omega$.

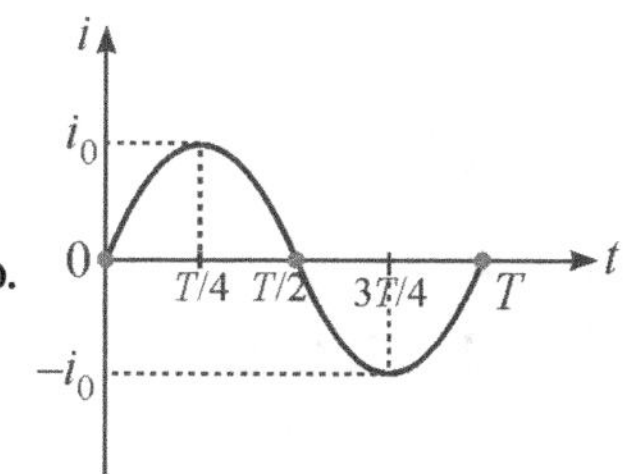

And induced current $\quad i = \dfrac{e}{R} = \dfrac{e_0}{R}\sin\omega t = i_0\sin\omega t$

The direction of current changes periodically and therefore the current is called alternating current.

Practice Exercise 3

Multiple Choice Questions

1. If the rate of change of current of 2A/s induces an emf of 10 mV in a solenoid, the self-inductance of the solenoid is
   (a) 5×10^{-3} Henry   (b) 8×10^{-3} Henry
   (c) 25×10^{-6} Henry   (d) 55×10^{-12} Henry

2. If N is the number of turns in a coil, the value of self inductance varies as
   (a) N^0 (b) N   (c) N^2 (d) N^{-2}

3. Two coils of self inductances 2 mH and 8 mH are placed so close together that the effective flux in one coil is completely linked with the other. The mutual inductance between these coils is
   (a) 6mH   (b) 4mH   (c) 16mH   (d) 10mH

4. Match the column-I and column-II

Column I	Column II
(A) AC generator	(1) Eddy current
(B) Dead beat galvanometer	(2) Slip rings
	(3) Split ring
(C) Solenoid	(4) Insulated copper wire wound in the form of a cylindrical coil

   (a) (A) → (2); (B) → (2); (C) → (1)
   (b) (A) → (4); (B) → (1); (C) → (3)
   (c) (A) → (2); (B) → (1); (C) → (4)
   (d) (A) → (2); (B) → (3); (C) → (4)

5. Two solenoids of same cross-sectional area have their lengths and number of turns in ratio of 1 : 2 both. The ratio of self-inductance of two solenoids is
   (a) 1:1   (b) 1:2   (c) 2:1   (d) 1:4

6. A small square loop of wire of side ℓ is placed inside a large square loop of side L (L >> ℓ). The loop are coplanar and their centres coincide. The mutual inductance of the system is proportional is
   (a) $\dfrac{\ell}{L}$ (b) $\dfrac{\ell^2}{L}$ (c) $\dfrac{L}{\ell}$ (d) $\dfrac{L^2}{\ell}$

Assertion & Reason Questions

DIRECTIONS (Qs. 7 & 8) : *Each of these questions contains an assertion followed by reason. Read them carefully and answer the question on the basis of following options. You have to select the one that best describes the two statements.*
(a) If both Assertion and Reason are correct and the Reason is a correct explanation of the Assertion.
(b) If both Assertion and Reason are correct but Reason is not a correct explanation of the Assertion.
(c) If the Assertion is correct but Reason is incorrect.
(d) If the Assertion is incorrect but the Reason is correct.

7. **Assertion :** When number of turns in a coil is doubled, coefficient of self-inductance of the coil becomes 2 times.
   Reason : This is because L ∝ 1/N.

8. **Assertion :** When number of turns in a coil is doubled, coefficient of self-inductance of the coil becomes double.
   Reason : This is because self inductance L ∝ N.

Case/Passage Based Questions

Self inductance of a long solenoid: Self-inductance of a long, air-cored solenoid of lenght *l*, having n turns per unit length of cross-sectional area A is given by $L = \mu_0 n^2 \ell A$

When a magnetic material of relative permeability μ_r is inserted into the solenoid as a core, then the self-inductance becomes

$$L = \mu_0 \mu_r n^2 \ell A$$

9. When current in a coil changes from 5 A to 2 A in 0.1 s, average voltage of 50 V is produced. The self-inductance of the coil is :
   (a) 6 H   (b) 0.67 H   (c) 3 H   (d) 1.67 H

10. The self inductance associated with a coil is independent of
    (a) current   (b) time
    (c) induced voltage   (d) resistance of coil

11. When the current in a coil changes from 2 amp. to 4 amp. in 0.05 sec., an e.m.f. of 8 volt is induced in the coil. The coefficient of self inductance of the coil is
    (a) 0.1 henry   (b) 0.2 henry
    (c) 0.4 henry   (d) 0.8 henry

12. The coefficient of self inductance of a solenoid is 0.18 mH. If a core of soft iron of relative permeability 900 is inserted, then the coefficient of self inductance will become nearly.
    (a) 5.4 mH   (b) 162 mH
    (c) 0.006 mH   (d) 0.0002 mH

13. The inductance of a closed-packed coil of 400 turns is 8 mH. A current of 5 mA is passed through it. The magnetic flux through each turn of the coil is
    (a) $\dfrac{1}{4\pi} \mu_0$ Wb   (b) $\dfrac{1}{2\pi} \mu_0$ Wb
    (c) $\dfrac{1}{3\pi} \mu_0$ Wb   (d) $0.4\,\mu_0$ Wb

Very Short Answer Questions

14. Define the term self inductance. Give its unit.

15. How does the self-inductance of an air core coil change, when (i) the number of turns in the coil is decreased and (ii) an iron rod is introduced in the coil.

16. If the number of turns in the solenoid is doubled, keeping other factors constant, how does the self-inductance of the coil change?

17. Write an expression for the energy stored in an inductor of inductance L, when a steady current is passed through it. Is the energy electric or the magnetic?

18. If the rate of change of current is 2 A/s and induces an e.m.f. of 40 mV in the solenoid, what is the self-inductance of the solenoid?

19. If the self inductance of an iron core inductor increases from 0.01 mH to 10 mH on introducing the iron core into it, what is the relative permeability of the core material used?

20. Write the expression for the efficiency of d.c. motor?

21. Name the main component which changes a.c generator in to d.c. generator.

Short Answer Questions

22. Define the term self-induction. Write two factors on which self-inductance of a coil depends.

23. Define the term mutual inductance. Write its S.I. unit. Give two factors on which the coefficient of mutual inductance between a pair of coil depends.

24. Derive the formula for the self-inductance of a long solenoid.

25. Derive the formula for the mutual inductance of two long solenoids of same length and cross-sectional area and having different number of turns.

26. How does the mutual inductance of a pair of coils change when:
   (i)   the distance between the coils is increased?
   (ii) the number of turns in each coil is dicreased? Justify your answer in each case.

Important Tips & Formulae

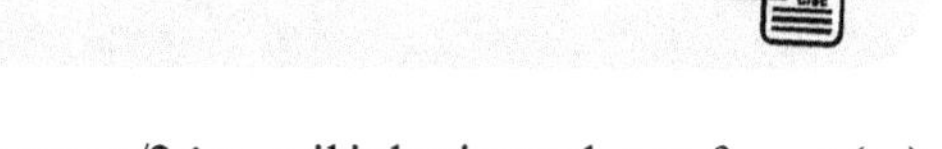

- When a conducting rod is allowed to fall freely in earth's magnetic field in such a way that its length lies along East-West direction then induced emf continuously increases w.r.t. time and induced current flows from West - East.

- If we drop a piece of metal and a piece of non-metal from the same height near the surface of the earth, the non-metallic piece will reach the ground first because there will be no induced current in it.

- If an aeroplane is landing down or taking off with its wings in the east-west direction, then emf will be induced across its wings. If an aeroplane is landing down or taking off with its wings in the north-south direction, then no emf will be induced.

- When a conducting rod is allowed to move on equator of earth, no emf will be induced due to absence of vertical component of earth's magnetic field. But at poles value of vertical component of magnetic field is maximum so maximum flux cutting will take place hence emf induces.

- Inductance of a solenoid at its end is half of its inductance at the centre.

$$\left(L_{end} = \frac{1}{2} L_{centre} \right)$$

- If current varies as a function of time then the induced e.m.f. produced in the inductor due to rate of current change through it is given by

$$e = -L \frac{dI}{dt}$$

- If instantaneous induced e.m.f. produced in a coil is $e = e_0 \sin \omega t = nBA\, \omega \sin \omega t$ (then for different cases)
   (i)   when $\omega t = 0, \pi$ *i.e.*, coil is vertical, e.m.f. $e = 0$

   (ii) when $\omega t = \pi/2$ *i.e.*, coil is horizontal, e.m.f. $e = +(ve)$ maximum.

   (iii) when $\omega t = \frac{3}{2}\pi$ *i.e.*, coil is horizontal, e.m.f. e $= -(ve)$ maximum.

- If two coils are connected in series having currents in the same direction, then we can calculate equivalent induction, $L = L_1 + L_2 + 2M$ Here, L_1 and L_2 are the self induction of two coils.
   If the direction of currents in the two coils is in opposite direction, then
   $$L = L_1 + L_2 - 2M$$

- If two solenoids have different area of cross-section, then $M = k\sqrt{L_1 L_2}$
   Here, k is coefficient of coupling between the two coils.

- If two coils are connected in parallel combination, then
$$\frac{1}{L} = \frac{1}{(L_1 + M)} + \frac{1}{(L_2 + M)}$$
$$\Rightarrow L = \frac{L_1 L_2 M^2 + M(L_1 + L_2)}{L_1 + L_2 + 2M}$$
   If $M = 0, L = \frac{L_1 L_2}{L_1 + L_2}$

- Mutual induction between two concentric coils having radii r_p and r_s and respective number of turns n_p and n_s is
$$M = \frac{\pi \mu_0 n_p n_s r_s^2}{2 r_p}$$

NCERT Questions

6.1. In the given experiment (a) What would you do to obtain a large deflection of the galvanometer ? (b) How would you demonstrate the presence of an induced current in the absence of a galvanometer ?

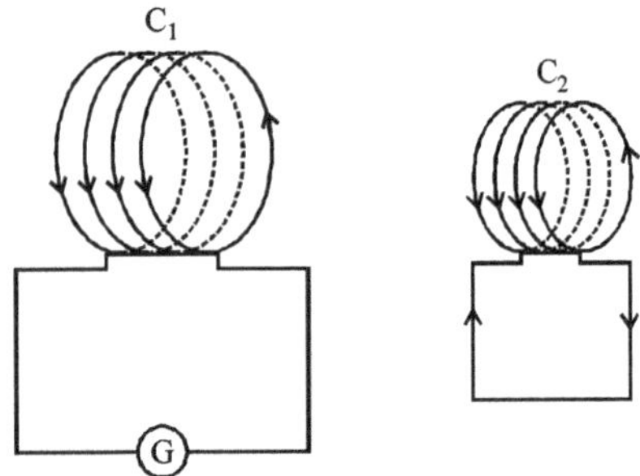

Sol. (a) To obtain large deflection in galvanometer we can take following steps
     (i) Connect the coal C_2 to a powerful battery for large current.
     (ii) Switch on and off the key at a rapid rate.
     (iii) Develop a relative shift/motion between the two coils.
     (iv) Use a Ferromagnetic material like Iron inside the coil C_2 to increase the magnetic flux.
   (b) Galvanometer is replaced by a torch bulb. Now a relative motion between two coils or switch on and off of the key glows the bulb and shows presence of induced current.

6.2. Predict the direction of induced current in the situations described by the following Figs. (a) to (f).

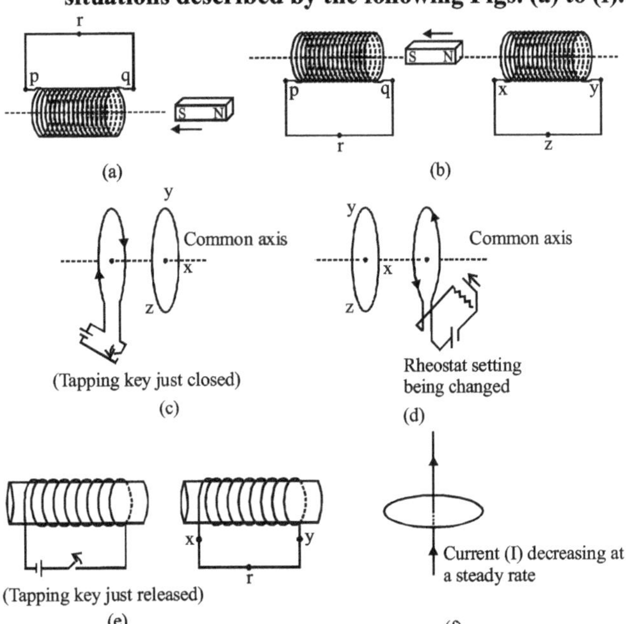

Sol. (a) Apply Lenz's law, induced current will flow to oppose the magnet. So South-pole is developed at end q and current flows in qrpq direction.
   (b) Same as above, South-pole developed at q and current is in prqp direction. For coil 2, North- is going away so attractive i.e., South pole is developed at end x and direction is yzxy.

(c) As key is closed, magnetic flux rises in the first coil, in other coil, induced current would be such as to oppose this increasing magnetic flux. This happenes when magnetic field produced in this coil is from right to left hence current is in yzx direction.

(d) As rheostat is changed to decrease resistance, current will increase and magnetic flux linked with it will rise. Applying Lenz's law, the induced current would oppose this increase, hence direction of magnetic field should be right to left and current is in direction zyx.

(e) When current is flowing before release of tapping key magnetic flux is from left to right (right end is N-pole). As key is released, current decreases magnetic flux decreases, hence induced flux would oppose this decrease and favour an increase in flux. Hence direction of induced current in adjoining coil is from left to right in direction xry.

(f) As current decreases in straight conductor, magnetic field in the plane of the coil remains to be in the same plane. The circular coil does not see the change in magnetic field (same plane) hence no current (or flux) is induced.

6.3. Use Lenz's law to determine the direction of induced current in the situations described by Fig.
(a) A wire of irregular shape turning into a circular shape;
(b) A circular loop being deformed into a narrow straight wire.

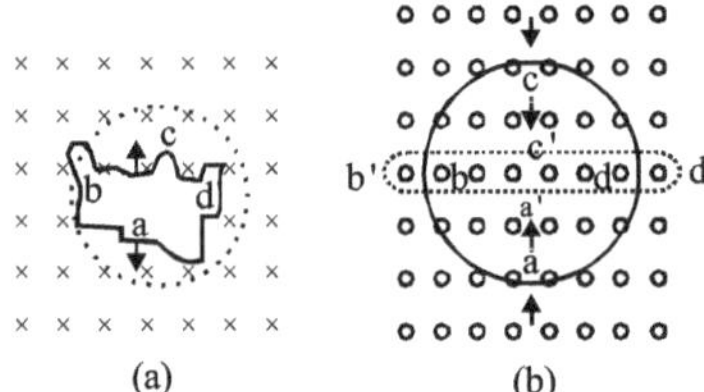

Sol. (a) As wire increases its area, the magnetic flux linked with the loop increases, the induced emf causes a current to oppose it. The force should be inward (to pull the wire back) hence direction of current is adcba
   (b) Here, the area decreases, hence current induced opposes this decrease in field and would try to increase the flux by pulling wire outward hence current is in direction A'D'C'B'A'.

6.4. A long solenoid with 15 turns per cm has a small loop of area 2.0 cm² placed inside the solenoid normal to its axis. If the current carried by the solenoid changes steadily from 2.0 A to 4.0 A in 0.1 s, what is the induced emf in the loop while the current is changing?

Sol. **Given:** no. of turns $= 15$/cm
     area $= 2$ cm²
   change in current $dI = 4 - 2 = 2$A
   change in time $dt = 0.1$ s
   To find: Induced emf $= e$

Formula used: $e = -\dfrac{d\phi}{dt} = \dfrac{-d}{dt}(\mu_0 n\, IA)$

Magnetic flux $\phi = BA = \mu_0 n\, IA$

induced emf $e = -\dfrac{d\phi}{dt} = -\mu_0 nA\dfrac{dI}{dt}$

$\mu_0 = 4\pi \times 10^{-7}, n = 15\ cm^{-1} = 1500\ m^{-1}$
$A = 2\ cm^2 = 2 \times 10^{-4}\ m^2$

$e = -4\pi \times 10^{-7} \times 1500 \times 2 \times 10^{-4} \times \dfrac{4-2}{0.1}$

$\quad = -4\pi \times 3 \times 10^{-7-4+3} \times 20$

$\quad = -4 \times 3.14 \times 6 \times 10^{-7} = -7.54 \times 10^{-6}\ V$

6.5. **A rectangular wire loop of sides 8 cm and 2 cm with a small cut is moving out of a region of uniform magnetic field of magnitude 0.3 T directed normal to the loop. (a) What is the emf developed across the cut if the velocity of the loop is 1 cm s⁻¹ in a direction normal to the (1) longer side, (2) shorter side of the loop? (b) For how long does the induced voltage last in each case?**

Sol. **Given:** Magnetic field $B = 0.3\ T$
velocity of loop $= 1\ cm/s = 10^{-2}\ m/s$
area of loop $= 8\ cm \times 2\ cm$

To find: (a) Voltage in the cut for (1) long side moving out (2) shorter side
(b) time of emf. for each case.

Formula: (a) $e = B\,\ell\,v$ (b) $t = \dfrac{length\ of\ wire}{v}$

(i) along longer side
length $= 8\ cm = 8 \times 10^{-2}\ m$
$\therefore\ e = B\ell v = 0.3 \times 8 \times 10^{-2} \times 10^{-2} = 0.24 \times 10^{-3}\ V = 0.24\ mV$

Time of emf $= \dfrac{length\ of\ shorter\ arm}{v}$

($\because$ emf develops as long as loop doesnot get out of the field ie, distance travelled by shorter arm)

$t = \dfrac{2 \times 10^{-2}}{10^{-2}} = 2 \times 10^{-2+2} = 2\ sec.$

(ii) along shorter side
$e = B\ell v = 0.3 \times 2 \times 10^{-2} \times 10^{-2} = 0.6 \times 10^{-4} = 0.06\ mV$

time of emf $= \dfrac{length\ of\ longer\ arm}{v} = \dfrac{8 \times 10^{-2}}{10^{-2}} = 8\ sec.$

6.6. **A 1.0 m long metallic rod is rotated with an angular frequency of 400 rad s⁻¹ about an axis normal to the rod passing through its one end. The other end of the rod is in contact with circular metallic ring. A constant and uniform magnetic field of 0.5 T parallel to the axis exists everywhere. Calculate the emf developed between the centre and the ring.**

Sol. **Given:** length of rod $= 1\ m$;
angular speed $\omega = 400\ rad/s$,
magnetic field $= 0.5T$

To find: emf developed $e = ?$

Formula used: $e = \dfrac{1}{2}B\ell^2\omega$

We know that the rod is rotating hence induced magnetic field passes parallel to the rod and normal to plane of the ring. An induced emf develops in the ring w.r.t centre of rod due to changing flux (as a result of rotation)

$e = B\ell v$

Here, $\ell = \dfrac{1}{2}\ell$ (distance from centre) and $v = \omega\ell$ ($v = \omega r$ where $r = \ell$)

$\Rightarrow\ e = \dfrac{1}{2}B\ell^2\omega = \dfrac{1}{2} \times 0.5 \times 1^2 \times 400 = 100V$

6.7. **A circular coil of radius 8.0 cm and 20 turns is rotated about its vertical diameter with an angular speed of 50 rad s⁻¹ in a uniform horizontal magnetic field of magnitude 3.0 × 10⁻² T. Obtain the maximum and average emf induced in the coil. If the coil forms a closed loop of resistance 10 W, calculate the maximum value of current in the coil. Calculate the average power loss due to Joule heating. Where does this power come from?**

Sol. **Given:** Radius of coil $r = 8\ cm = 8 \times 10^{-2}\ m$
no. of turns $= 20$
angular speed $\omega = 50\ rad/s$
magnetic field $= 3 \times 10^{-2}\ T$
resistance of coil $= 10\Omega$

To find: Power dissipated $P = ?$, max emf, average emf

Formula used: $P_{av} = \dfrac{I_0}{\sqrt{2}}\dfrac{E_0}{\sqrt{2}}$

emf $e = n\,BA\omega$
For varying current $e = nBA\,\omega\,\sin\omega t$
maximum emf $\Rightarrow \sin\omega t = 1$

$\Rightarrow e_0 = nBA\omega = 20 \times 3 \times 10^{-2} \times \pi r^2 \times 50$

$\quad = 3000 \times 10^{-2} \times 3.14 \times (8 \times 10^{-2})^2$

$\quad = 30 \times 3.14 \times 64 \times 10^{-4} = 0.603\ V$

The average value of emf is over one complete cycle
$\therefore\ e_{av} = 0$

The average power $P_{av} = \dfrac{e_0}{\sqrt{2}} \cdot \dfrac{I_0}{\sqrt{2}}$

$\Rightarrow P_{av} = \dfrac{e_0}{\sqrt{2}} \cdot \dfrac{e_0}{R.\sqrt{2}} = \dfrac{e_0^{\,2}}{2R} = \dfrac{(0.603)^2}{2 \times 10} \Rightarrow P_{av} = 0.018\ W.$

The source of this power is the external force (battery or motor) which is rotating this rod.

6.8. **A horizontal straight wire 10 m long extending from east to west is falling with a speed of 5.0 ms⁻¹, at right angles to the horizontal component of the earth's magnetic field, 0.30 ×10⁻⁴ Wb m⁻².**
(a) **What is the instantaneous value of the emf induced in the wire?**
(b) **What is the direction of the emf?**
(c) **Which end of the wire is at the higher electrical potential?**

Sol. **Given:** length of wire $\ell = 10\ m$;
velocity of wire $v = 5\ m/s$
horizontal component of earth's;
magnetic field $B = 0.3 \times 10^{-4}\ Wb/m^2$
To find: (a) instantaneous value of emf
(b) direction of emf
(c) end with higher potential

Formula used: $e = B\,\ell\,v$

(a) Here B = earth's field H

Hence, induced emf

$e = H\ell\,v = 0.3 \times 10^{-4} \times 10 \times 5 = 1.5 \times 10^{-3}$ V

(b) since wire falling down normal to earth field in E-W direction hence induced emf by Flemming rule is west to east

(c) This is induced emf, (increasing) hence eastern end has higher potential.

6.9. **Current in a circuit falls from 5.0 A to 0.0 A in 0.1 s. If an average emf of 200 V induced, give an estimate of the self-inductance of the circuit.**

Sol. **Given:** Change in current dI = (5 − 0) A

change in time dt = 0.1S   average emf e = 200 V

To find: self inductance L.

Formula: $e = \dfrac{-L\,dI}{dt}$ $|L| = \left|\dfrac{-e}{dI/dt}\right| = \dfrac{+200}{5/0.1} = 4$ H

6.10. **A pair of adjacent coils has a mutual inductance of 1.5 H. If the current in one coil changes from 0 to 20 A in 0.5 s, what is the change of flux linkage with the other coil?**

Sol. **Given:** Mutual inductance M = 1.5 H

change in current dI = 20 − 0 = 20 A

change in time dt = 0.5 s

To find: change in flux dφ = ?

Formula used: φ = MI

$\phi = MI \Rightarrow d\phi = MdI \Rightarrow d\phi = 1.5 \times 20 = 30$ Wb

6.11. **A jet plane is travelling towards west at a speed of 1800 km/h. What is the voltage difference developed between the ends of the wing having a span of 25 m, if the Earth's magnetic field at the location has a magnitude of 5×10^{-4} T and the dip angle is 30°.**

Sol. **Given:** velocity $v = 1800$ km/h. $= \dfrac{1800 \times 1000}{60 \times 60} = 500$ m/s

length $\ell = 25$ m

earth's field B = 5×10^{-4} T

angle of dip δ = 30°

To find: voltage developed or emf induced e = ?

Formula used: $e = B\ell v$

Since plane travels horizontally it is acted upon by vertical component of earth's field

$V = B\sin\delta = 5 \times 10^{-4} \times \sin 30° = 5 \times 10^{-4} \times \dfrac{1}{2} = 2.5 \times 10^{-4}$ T

Thus induced emf $e = B\ell v = 2.5 \times 10^{-4} \times 25 \times 500 = 3.125$ V

ADDITIONAL EXERCISES

6.12 **Suppose the loop shown in figure is stationary but the current feeding the electromagnet that produces the magnetic field is gradually reduced so that field decreases from its initial value of 0.3 T at the rate of 0.02 Ts⁻¹. If the cut is joined and the loop has a resistance of 1.6 ohm, how much power is dissipated by the loop as heat? What is the source of this power?**

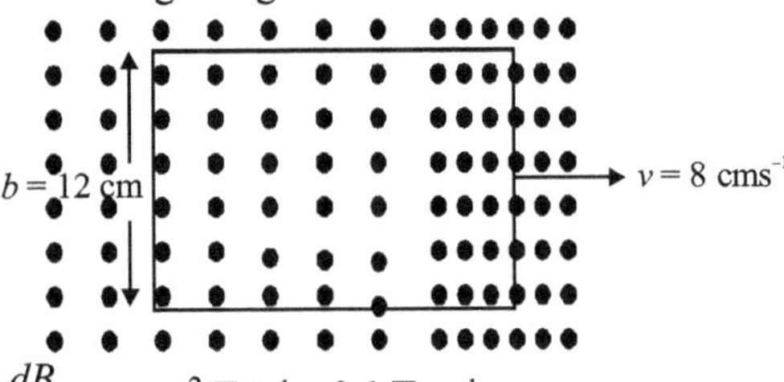

Sol. Here area is constant but the magnetic field is reducing at a constant rate.

$\dfrac{dB}{dt} = -(0.02)$ Ts⁻¹

Induced emf in the loop

$e = -\dfrac{d\phi}{dt} = -A\dfrac{dB}{dt}$

$e = -16 \times 10^{-4}[-0.02] = 32 \times 10^{-6}$ Volt

Induced current in the closed loop

$I = e/R = \dfrac{32 \times 10^{-6}}{1.6} = 20\ \mu$A

Power loop as heat $P = I^2 R$

$P = (20 \times 10^{-6})^2 \times 1.6 = 6.4 \times 10^{-10}$ W

Source of the power is work done in changing magnetic field.

6.13 **A square loop of side 12 cm with its sides parallel to X and Y axes is moved with a velocity of 8 cm s⁻¹ in the positive x-direction in an environment containing a magnetic field in the positive z-direction. The field is neither uniform in space nor constant in time. It has a gradient of 10^{-3} T cm⁻¹ along the negative x-direction (that is it increases by 10^{-3} T cm⁻¹ as one moves in the negative x-direction). and it is decreasing in time at the rate of 10^{-3} Ts⁻¹. Determine the direction and magnitude of the induced current in the loop if its resistance is 4.50 mΩ.**

Sol. Each side of square loop is 12 cm and magnetic field is decreasing along x direction.

$\dfrac{dB}{dx} = -10^{-3}$ Tᶜᵐ⁻¹ = 0.1 T m⁻¹

also the magnetic field is decreasing with time at constant rate

$\dfrac{dB}{dx} = -10^{-3}$ Ts⁻¹

Induced emf and rate of change of magnetic flux due to only time variation

$e_t = -\dfrac{d\phi}{dt} = -\dfrac{dBA}{dt} = -A\dfrac{dB}{dt}$

$e_t = -0.12 \times 0.12[-10^{-3}] = 144 \times 10^{-7}$ V

Induced emf and rate of change of magnetic flux due to changes in position

$$e_x = -\frac{dBA}{dt} = -A\frac{dB}{dx} \times \frac{dx}{dt}$$

$$e_x = -Av\frac{dB}{dx} = -0.12 \times 0.12 \times 0.08 \times (0.1) = 1152 \times 10^{-7}\text{ V}$$

Both the induced emf have same sign and thus adds to provide net Induced emf in the loop

$$e_{net} = e_t + e_x = 1296 \times 10^{-7}\text{ V}$$

Induced current $I = \dfrac{e_{net}}{R} = \dfrac{1296 \times 10^{-7}}{4.5 \times 10^{-3}} = 2.88 \times 10^{-2}$ A

6.14 It is desired to measure the magnitude of field between the poles of a powerful loud speaker magnet. A small flat search coil of area 2 cm² with 25 closely wound turns, is positioned normal to the field direction, and then quickly snatched out of the field region. Equivalently, one can give it quick 90° turns to bring its plane parallel to the field direction. The total charge flown in the coil (measured by a ballistic galvanometer connected to coil) is 7.5 mC. The combined resistance of coil and the galvanometer is 0.50 Ω. Estimate the field strength of magnet.

Sol. Let the magnetic field between poles of loud speaker magnet is B.

Initial flux through the coil

$$\phi_i = NBA = 25\,B\,(2 \times 10^{-4}) = 50 \times 10^{-4}\,B \quad ...(i)$$

Final flux through the coil is zero. Let coil is taken out in time 't'.

Magnitude of induced emf $e = \dfrac{\Delta\phi}{\Delta t}$

$$e = \frac{50 \times 10^{-4}\,B}{t}$$

Current in the coil

$$I = \frac{e}{R} = \frac{50 \times 10^{-4}\,B}{0.5t}$$

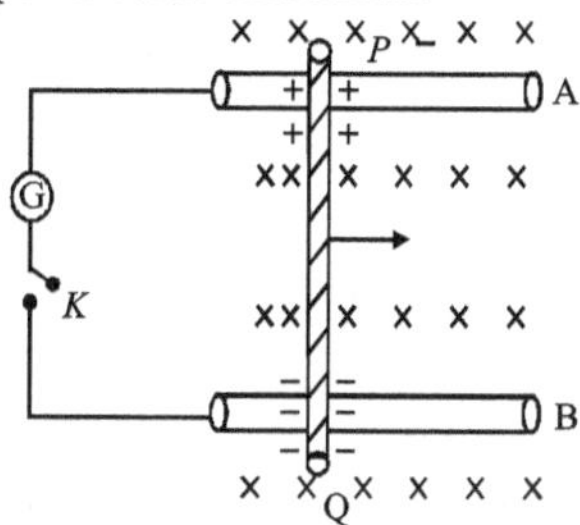

Total charge flowing in the coil

$q = It$

$$q = \frac{10^{-2}\,B}{t} \times t = 10^{-2}\,B \text{ or } 7.5\ 10^{-3} = 10^{-2}\,B$$

So, magnetic field between poles, $B = 0.75$ T

6.15 Figure shows a metal rod PQ resting on the smooth rails AB and positioned between the poles of a permanent magnet. The rails, the rod, and the magnetic field are in three mutual perpendicular directions. A galvanometer G connects the rails through a switch K. Length of the rod = 15 cm, B = 0.50 T, resistance of the closed loop containing the rod = 9.0 m Ω. Assume the field to be uniform.

(a) Suppose K is open and the rod is moved with a speed of 12 cm s⁻¹ in the direction shown. Give the polarity and magnitude of the induced emf.

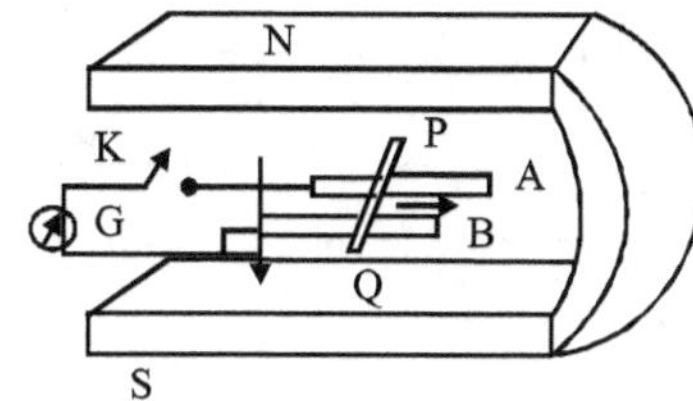

(b) Is there an excess charges built up at the ends of the rods when K is open? What if K is closed?

(c) With K open and the rod moving uniformly, there is *no net force* on the electrons in the rod PQ even though they do experience magnetic force due to the motion of the rod. Explain.

(d) What is the retarding force on the rod when K is closed?

(e) How much power is required (by an external agent) to keep the rod moving at the same speed (=12 cm s⁻¹) when K is closed?
How much power is required when K is open?

(f) How much power is dissipated as heat in the closed circuit? What is the source of this power?

(g) What is the induced emf in the moving rod if the magnetic field is parallel to the rails instead of being perpendicular?

Sol. Here rails, rod and magnetic field are in three mutually perpendicular directions.

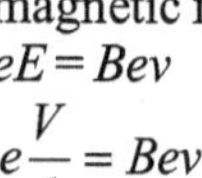

(a) Switch K is open and rod moves with speed of 12 cm s⁻¹.

Induced emf/motional emf

$e = Bvl = 0.5 \times 12 \times 10^{-2} \times 15 \times 10^{-2} = $ mV

(b) When the K is open upper end of the rod become positively charge, and lower end become negatively charged.

When the K is closed the charge flows in closed circuit but the excess charge is maintained by the flow of charge in the moving rod under magnetic force.

(c) In the state when K is open very soon a stage is reached when force due to electric field which is due to potential difference induced balance the magnetic force on electrons.

$eE = Bev$

$$e\frac{V}{l} = Bev$$

Motional emf $V = Bvl$.

(d) When the key is closed the current flows in a loop and the current carrying wire experience a retarding force in the magnetic field.

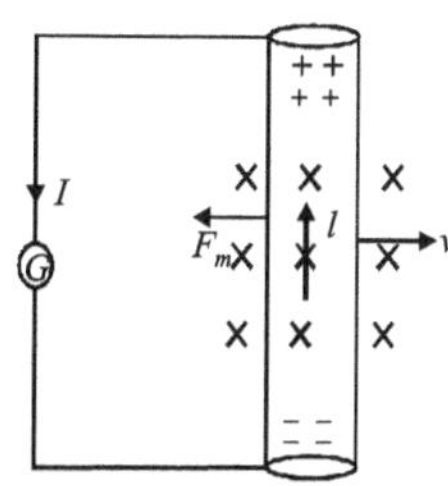

$F_m = IBl$

$$\text{where } I = \frac{Bvl}{R} = \frac{9 \times 10^{-3}}{9 \times 10^{-3}} = 1A$$

$F_m = 1 \times 0.5 \times 15 \times 10^{-2} = 0.075\text{ N}$

(e) To keep the rod moving in closed circuit at constant speed the force required is $f = 0.005$ N.

So, power required $P = \vec{F}\cdot\vec{v} = fv\cos 0° = fv$

$P = 0.075 \times 12 \times 10^{-2} = 9$ mW

when key K is open, no current flows and hence no retarding force, so no power is required to move at constant speed.

(f) Power lost in closed circuit due to flow to current
$P = I^2 R = (1)^2 \times 9 \times 10^{-3} = 9 \text{ mW}$
Power provided by external force to move the rod at constant speed is the source of this power lost.

(g) If $\vec{B}$ is parallel to rails, the induced/motional emf will be zero.

6.16 **An air cored solenoid with length 30 cm, area of cross-section 25 cm² and number of turns 500, carries a current of 2.5 A, The current is suddenly switched off in a brief time of 10^{-3} s. How much is the average back emf induced across the ends of the open switch in the circuit? Ignore the variation in magnetic field near the ends of the solenoid.**

Sol. Magnetic field inside solenoid

$B = \dfrac{\mu_0 NI}{l}$

Flux linked with solenoid

$\phi_i = BAN = \dfrac{\mu_0 N^2 \, AI}{l}$ ..(1)

Initial flux,

$\phi_i = \dfrac{4\pi \times 10^{-7} \times (500)^2 \times 25 \times 10^{-4} \times 2.5}{30 \times 10^{-2}}$ Wb

$\phi_i = 6.54 \times 10^{-3}$ Wb   Final flux, $\phi_f = 0 \, [I = 0]$

Average back emf

$e_{av} = \dfrac{\left(\phi_f - \phi_i\right)}{t} = -\left[\dfrac{0 - 6.45 \times 10^{-3}}{10^{-3}}\right] = 6.54 \text{ V}$

6.17 (a) **Obtain an expression for mutual inductance between a long straight wire and a square loop of side a as shown in figure.**

(b) **Now assume that the straight wire carries a current of 50 A and the loop is moved to the right with a constant velocity $v = 10$ ms⁻¹. Calculate the induced emf in the loop at the instant when $x = 0.2$ m. Take $a = 0.1$ m and assume that the loop has a large resistance.**

Sol. (a) As the magnetic field will be variable with distance from long straight wire, so the flux through square loop can be calculated by integration.

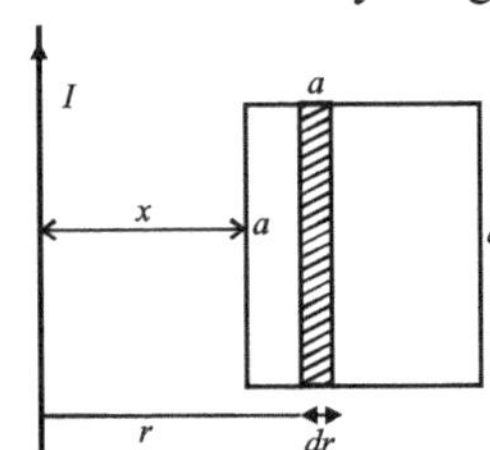

Let us assume a width dr of the square loop at a distance r from straight wire

$B = \dfrac{\mu_0 \, 2I}{4\pi \, r}$ $\phi = B a dr = \dfrac{\mu_0 \, 2I}{4\pi \, r} a dr$

Total flux associated with square loop

$\phi = \int d\phi = \dfrac{\mu_0}{4\pi} 2Ia \int\limits_{x}^{x+a} \dfrac{dr}{r}$

or $\phi = \dfrac{\mu_0}{4\pi} 2Ia \left[\log_e r\right]_x^{x+a}$ or $\phi = \dfrac{\mu_0}{4\pi} 2Ia \left[\log_e \dfrac{x+a}{x}\right]$

or $\quad \phi = \dfrac{\mu_0 Ia}{2\pi} \log_e(1 + a/x)$

(b) The square loop is moving right with a constant speed v, the instantaneous flux can be taken as

$\phi = \dfrac{\mu_0 Ia}{2\pi} \log_e(1 + a/x)$

Induced $Emf \; e = -\dfrac{d\phi}{dt} = -\dfrac{d\phi}{dx}\dfrac{dx}{dt} = -v\dfrac{d\phi}{dx}$

$e = -\dfrac{\mu_0 Iav}{2\pi} \dfrac{d \log_e(1 + a/x)}{dx}$

$e = -\dfrac{\mu_0 Iav}{2\pi} \dfrac{1}{\left(1 + \dfrac{a}{x}\right)}\left[-a/x^2\right]$ or $e = \dfrac{\mu_0}{2\pi} \dfrac{a^2 v}{x(x+a)} I$

or $\quad e = 2 \times 10^{-7} \dfrac{[0.1]^2 \; 10 \times 50}{0.2 \, [0.2 + 0.1]} = 1.67 \times 10^{-5}$ V

6.18 **A line charge λ per unit length is lodged uniformly onto the rim of a wheel of mass M and radius R. The wheel has light non-conducting spokes and is free to rotate without friction about its axis. A uniform magnetic field extends over a circular region within the rim. It is given by**
$$\vec{B} = -B_0 \, \hat{k} \; [r \le a, \, a < R] = 0 \; \text{(otherwise)}$$
What is the angular velocity of the wheel after the field is suddenly switched off?

Sol. According to Faraday's law of electromagnetic induction the

induced emf is $e = -\dfrac{d\phi}{dt}$

Thus a relation between electric field and rate of change of flux can be established.

$e = -\int \vec{E} \cdot \vec{dl} = -\dfrac{d\phi}{dt}$

$\vec{E}$ exist along circumference of radius 'a' due to change in magnetic flux.

$e \int dl = -\dfrac{d}{dt}\left(\pi a^2 B\right),\; E \times 2\pi a = -\pi a^2 \dfrac{dB}{dt}$

$E = -\dfrac{a}{2}\dfrac{dB}{dt}$ ....(i)

Linear charge density on rim is λ. so, total charge on rim
$Q = \lambda 2\pi a$ ... (ii)

Electric force on the charge

$F = QE = -\pi a^2 \lambda \dfrac{dB}{dt}, \quad m\dfrac{dv}{dt} = -\pi a^2 \lambda \dfrac{dB}{dt}$

In terms of angular velocity $v = R\omega$

$m\dfrac{dv}{dt}(R\omega) = -\pi a^2 \lambda \dfrac{dB}{dt}$

$m R \, d\omega = -\pi a^2 \lambda dB \quad d\omega = -\dfrac{\pi a^2 \lambda}{mR} dB$

Integrating both sides $\omega = -\dfrac{\pi a^2 \, \lambda B}{mR}$

As direction of angular velocity is along axis.

$\vec{\omega} = -\dfrac{\lambda a^2 \pi}{mR} B\hat{k}$

Past year Exercise

Fill in the Blank

1. The number of turns of a solenoid are doubled without changing its length and area of cross-section. The self-inductance of the solenoid will become __________ times.

Very Short Answer Questions

2. Define self-inductance of a coil. Write its SI unit.

3. A plot of magnetic flux (ϕ) versus current (I) is shown in the figure for two inductors, A and B. Which of the two has larger value of self-inductance?

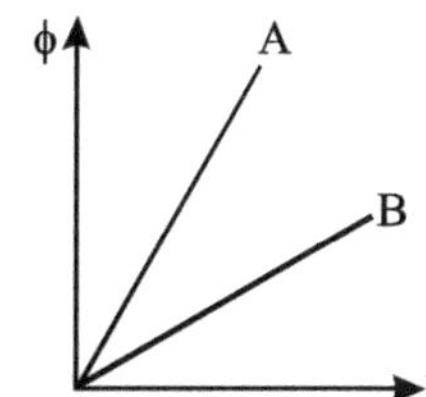

4. How can the self-inductance of a given coil having N number of turns, area of cross-section A and lengths l be increased?

5. The closed loop (PQRS) of wire is moved into a uniform magnetic field at right angles to the plane of the paper as shown in the figure. Predict the direction of the induced current in the loop.

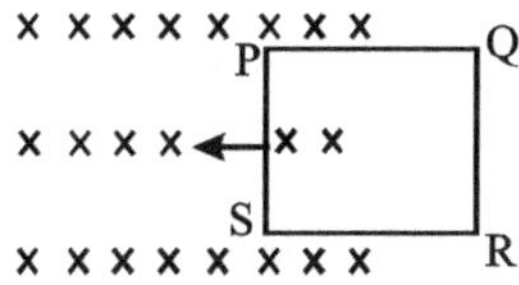

6. Predict the direction of induced current in metal rings 1 and 2 when current, I in the wire is steadily decreasing?

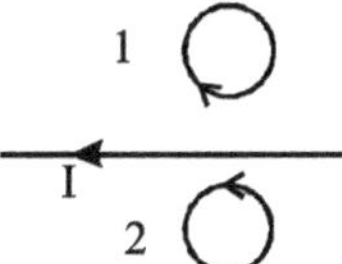

7. A bar magnet is moved in the direction indicated by the arrow between two coils PQ and CD. Predict the directions of induced current in each coil.

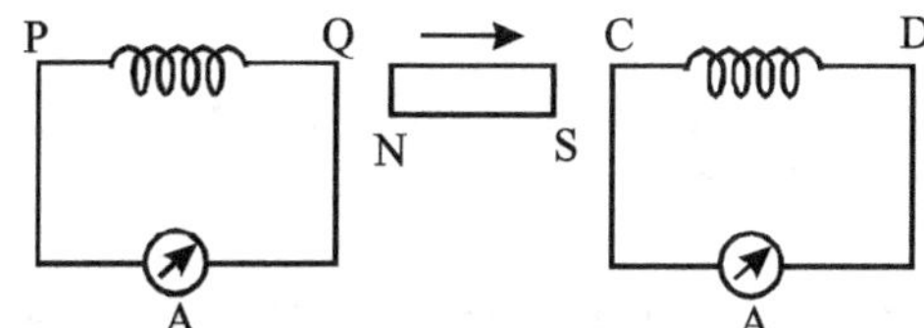

8. Predict the polarity of the capacitor in the situation described in the figure.

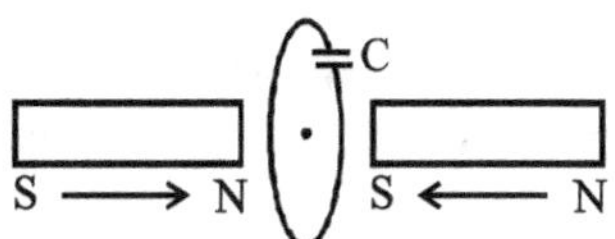

9. A light metal disc on the top of an electromagnet is thrown up as the current is switched on. Why? Give reason.

10. How does the mutual inductance of a pair of coils change when :
    (i) distance between the coils is increased and
    (ii) number of turns in the coils is increased?

11. The electric current flowing in a wire in the direction from B to A is decreasing. Find out the direction of the induced current in the metallic loop kept above the wire as shown.

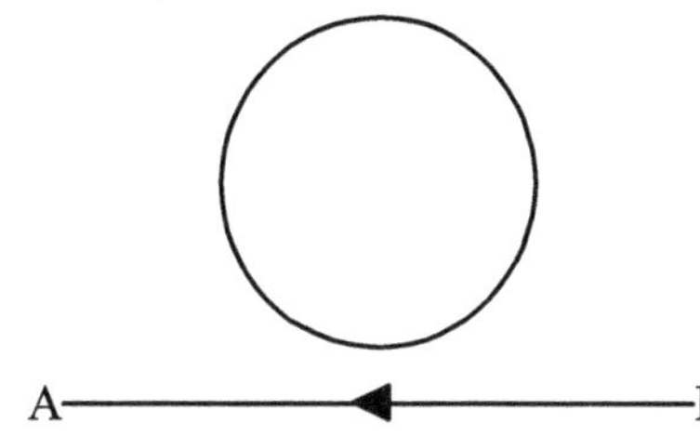

12. Two spherical bobs, one metallic and the other of glass, of the same size are allowed to fall freely from the same height above the ground. Which of the two would reach earlier and why?

13. Predict the polarity of the capacitor in the situation described below:

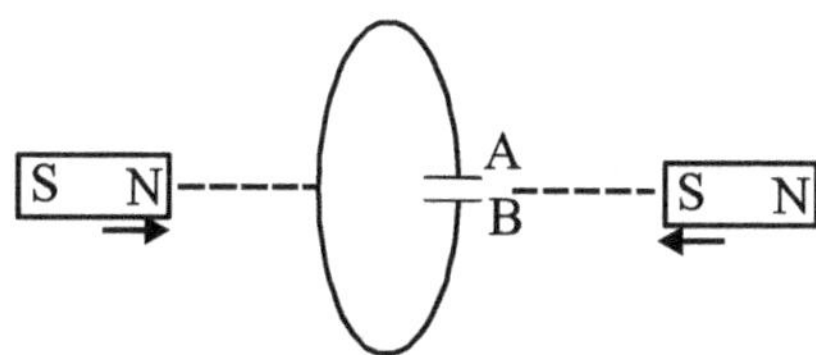

Short Answer Questions

14. A source, of emf ε is used to establish a current I through a coil of self-inductance L. Show that the work done by the source of build-up the current I is $\frac{1}{2}LI^2$.

15. Predict the polarity of the capacitor in the situation described by adjoining figure. Explain the reason too.

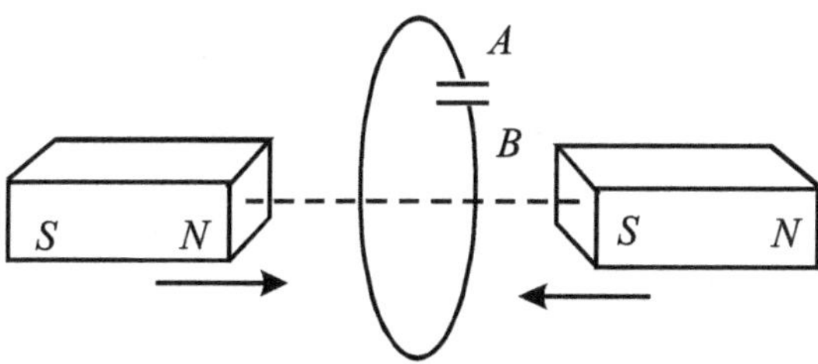

16. Current in a circuit falls steadily from 2.0 A to 0.0 A in 10 ms. If an average emf of 200 V is induced, calculate the self-inductance of the circuit.

17. Two concentric circular coils, one of small radius r and the other of large radius R, such that R >> r, are placed coaxially with centres coinciding. Obtain the mutual inductance of the arrangement.

18. A metallic rod of length, L is rotated with angular frequency of ω with one-end hinged at the centre and the other end at the circumference of a circular metallic ring of radius L, about an axis passing through the centre and perpendicular to the plane of the ring. A constant and uniform magnetic field, B parallel to the axis is present everywhere. Deduce the expression for the emf between the centre and the metallic ring.

19. State Lenz's law.

A metallic rod held horizontally along east-west direction, is allowed to fall under gravity. Will there be an emf induced at its ends? Justify your answer.

20. A rectangular conductor LMNO is placed in a uniform magentic field at 0.5 T. The field is directed perpendicular to the plane of the conductor. When the arm MN of length of 20 cm is moved towards left with a velocity of 10 ms⁻¹, calculate the emf inducted in the arm. Given the resistance of the arm to be 5Ω (assuming that other arms are of negligible resistance) find the value of the current in the arm.

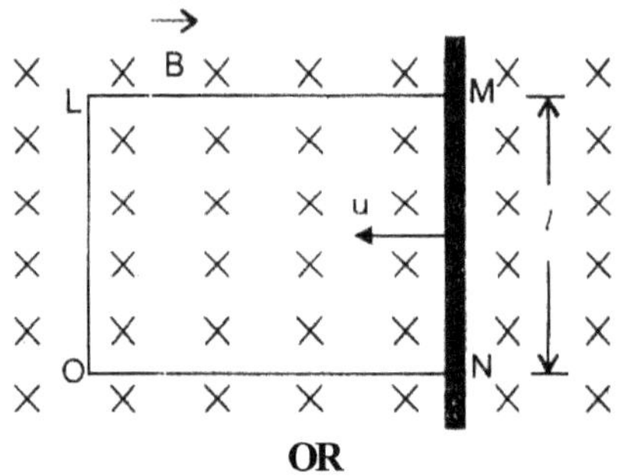

OR

A wheel with 8 metallic spokes each 50 cm long is rotated with a speed of 120 rev/min. in a plane normal to the horizontal component of the Earth's magnetic field. The earth's magnetic field at the place is 0.4 G and the angle of dip is 60°. Calculate the emf induced between the axle and the rim of the wheel. How will the value of emf be affected if the number of spokes were increased?

21. Define the term 'mutual inductance' between the two coils. Obtain the expression for mutual inductance of a pair of long coaxial solenoids each of length l and radii r_1 and r_2 $(r_2 \gg r_1)$. Total number of turns in the two solenoids are N_1 and N_2, respectively.

22. Define the term self-inductance of a solenoid. Obtain the expression for the magnetic energy stored in an inductor of self-inductance L to build up a current I through it.

23. (a) A rod of length l is moved horizontally with a uniform velocity 'v' in a direction perpendicular to its length through a region in which a uniform magnetic field is acting vertically downward. Derive the expression for the emf induced across the ends of the rod.

(b) How does one understand this motional emf by invoking the Lorentz force acting on the free charge carriers of the conductor? Explain.

24. (a) State Ampere's circuital law, expressing it in the integral form.

(b) Two long coaxial insulated solenoids, S_1 and S_2 of equal lengths are wound one over the other as shown in the figure. A steady current "I" flow thought the

inner solenoid S_1 to the other end B, which is connected to the outer solenoid S_2 through which the same current "I" flows in the opposite direction so as to come out at end A. If n_1 and n_2 are the number of turns per unit length, find the magnitude and direction of the net magnetic field at a point (i) inside on the axis and (ii) outside the combined system.

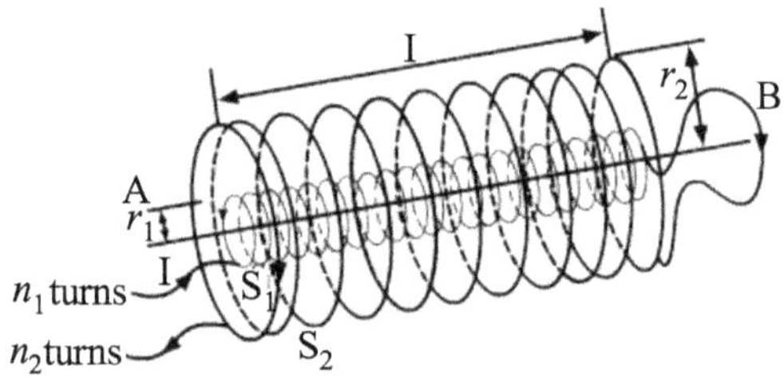

25. Ram is a student of class X in a village school. His uncle gifted him a bicycle with a dynamo fitted in it. He was very excited to get it. While cycling during night, he could light the bulb and see the objects on the road. He, however, did not know how this device works. He asked this question to his teacher. The teacher considered it an opportunity to explain the working to the whole class.

Answer the following question :

(a) State the principle and working of a dynamo.

(b) Write two values each displayed by Ram and his school teacher.

26. (i) Define mutual induction.

(ii) A pair of adjacent coils has a mutual inductance of 1.5 H. If the current in one coil changes from 0 to 20 A in 0.5 s. what is the change of flux linkage with the other coil?

27. The figure shows a rectangular conducting frame MNOP of resistance R placed partly in a perpendicular magnetic field $\vec{B}$ and moved with velocity $\vec{v}$ as shown in the figure

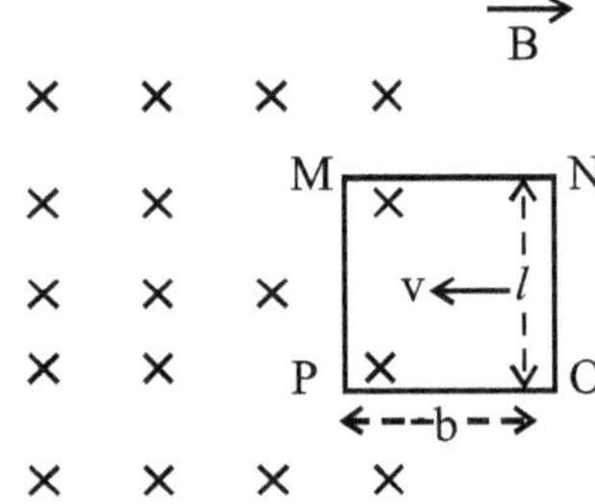

Obtain the expressions for the

(a) force acting on the arm 'ON' and its direction, and

(b) power required to move the frame to get a steady emf induced between the arms MN and PO.

28. Define mutual inductance between a pair of coils. Derive an expression for the mutual inductance of two long coaxial solenoids of same length wound one over the other.

OR

Define self-inductance of a coil. Obtain the expression for the energy stored in an indicator L connected across a source of emf.

NCERT Exemplar

Multiple Choice Questions

1. A square of side L metres lies in the xy-plane in a region, where the magnetic field is given by $B = B_0(2\hat{i} + 3\hat{j} + 4\hat{k})$ T, where B_0 is constant. The magnitude of flux passing through the square is

(a) $2B_0L^2$ Wb
(b) $3B_0L^2$ Wb
(c) $4B_0L^2$ Wb
(d) $\sqrt{29}B_0L^2$ Wb

2. A loop, made of straight edges has six corners at A (0, 0, 0), B (L, 0, 0), C (L, L, 0), D (0, L, 0), E (0, L, L) and F (0, 0, L). A magnetic field $B = B_0(\hat{i} + \hat{k})$ T is present in the region. The flux passing through the loop ABCDEFA (in that order) is

(a) B_0L^2 Wb
(b) $2B_0L^2$ Wb
(c) $\sqrt{2}B_0L^2$ Wb
(d) $4B_0L^2$ Wb

3. A cylindrical bar magnet is rotated about its axis. A wire is connected from the axis and is made to touch the cylindrical surface through a contact. Then,

(a) a direct current flows in the ammeter A
(b) no current flows through the ammeter A
(c) an alternating sinusoidal current flows through the ammeter A with a time period $T = \dfrac{2\pi}{\omega}$
(d) a time varying non-sinusoidal current flows through the ammeter A.

4. There are two coils A and B as shown in figure a current starts flowing in B as shown, when A is moved towards B and stops when A stops moving. The current in A is counter clockwise. B is kept stationary when A moves. We can infer that

(a) there is a constant current in the clockwise direction in A
(b) there is a varying current in A
(c) there is no current in A
(d) there is a constant current in the counter clockwise direction in A

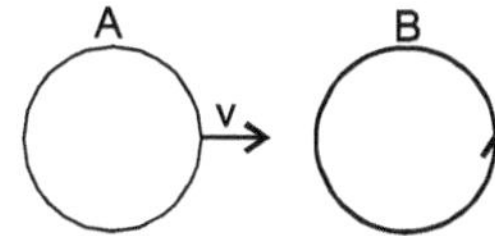

5. Same as problem 4 except the coil A is made to rotate about a vertical axis (figure). No current flows in B if A is at rest. The current in coil A, when the current in B (at t = 0) is counter-clockwise and the coil A is as shown at this instant, t = 0, is

(a) constant current clockwise
(b) varying current clockwise
(c) varying current counter clockwise
(d) constant current counter clockwise

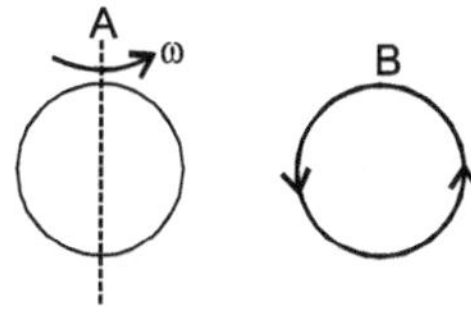

6. The self inductance L of a solenoid of length l and area of cross-section A, with a fixed number of turns N increases as

(a) l and A increase
(b) l decreases and A increases
(c) l increases and A decreases
(d) both l and A decrease

Very Short Answer Questions

7. Consider a magnet surrounded by a wire with an on/off switch S (Fig.). If the switch is thrown from the off position (open circuit) to the on position (closed circuit), will a current flow in the circuit? Explain.

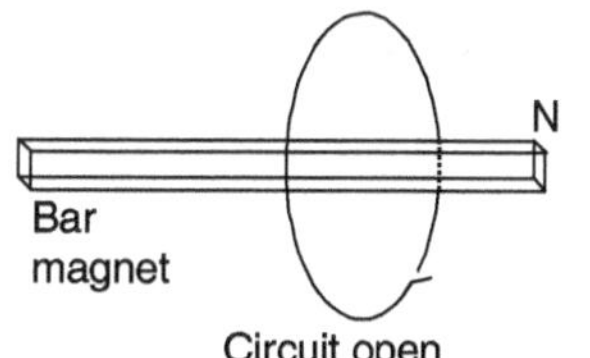

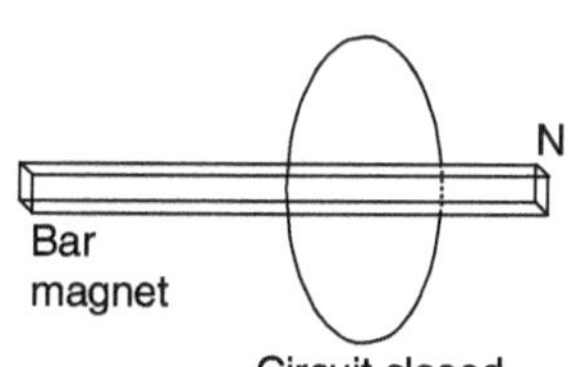

8. Consider a metal ring kept on top of a fixed solenoid (say on a carboard) (Fig.). The centre of the ring coincides with the axis of the solenoid. If the current is suddenly switched on, the metal ring jumps up. Explain

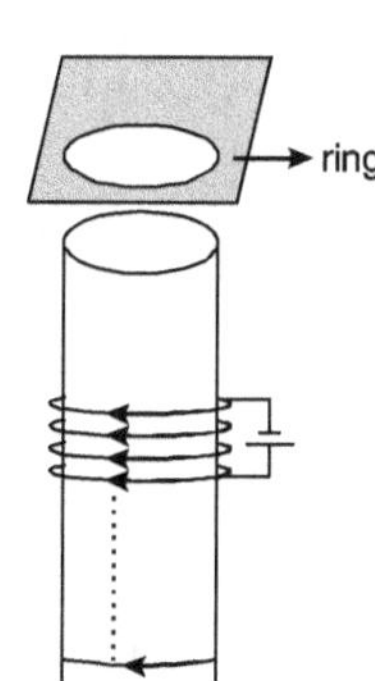

9. A rectangular wire frame, shown below, is placed in a uniform magnetic field directed upward and normal to the plane of the paper. The part AB is connected to a spring. The spring is stretched and released when the wire AB has come to the position A'B' (t = 0). How would the induced emf vary with time? Neglect damping.

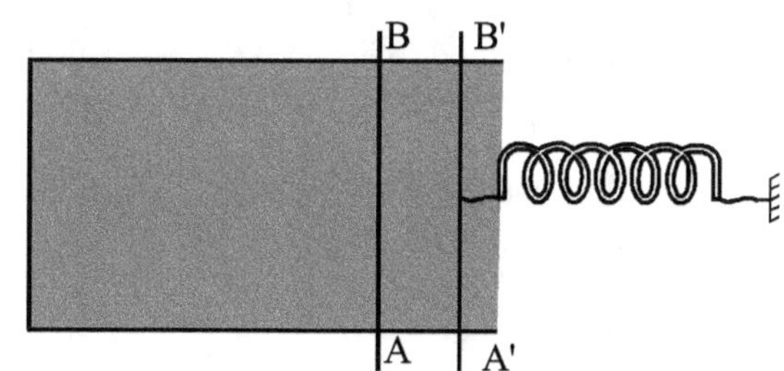

10. A rod PQ of length 0.5 m completes a circuit which is placed with its plane normal to a uniform magnetic field $\vec{B}$ of 0.15 T, as shown. If the resistance of rod is 3Ω, what will be the force required to move the rod with a constant velocity of 2 m/s ?

Short Answer Questions

11. A magnetic field in a certain region is given by $\mathbf{B} = B_0 \cos(\omega t)\,\hat{\mathbf{k}}$ and a coil of radius a with resistance R is placed in the x-y plane with its centre at the origin in the magnetic field (see Fig.). Find the magnitude and the direction of the current at $(a, 0, 0)$ at $t = \pi/2\omega$, $t = \pi/\omega$ and $t = 3\pi/2\omega$.

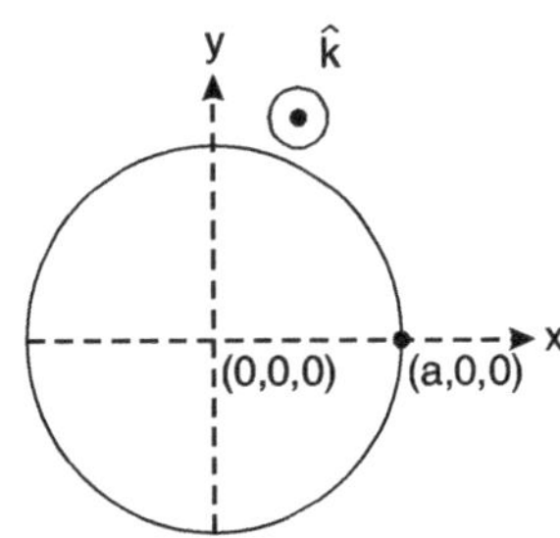

12. A (current vs time) graph of the current passing through a solenoid is shown in Fig. For which time is the back electromotive force (u) a maximum. If the back emf at $t = 3s$ is e, find the back emf at $t = 7s$. 15s and 40s. OA, AB and BC are straight line segments.

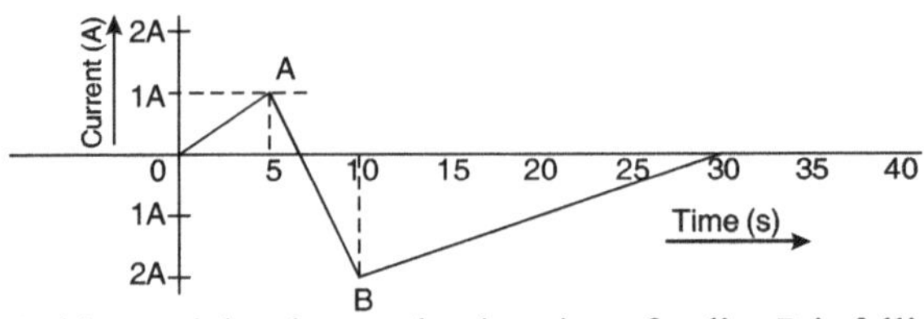

13. A thin semicircular conducting ring of radius R is falling with its plane vertical in a horizontal magnetic field $\vec{B}$. At the position MNQ of ring, the speed of ring is v. Then, what will be the potential difference developed across the ring ?

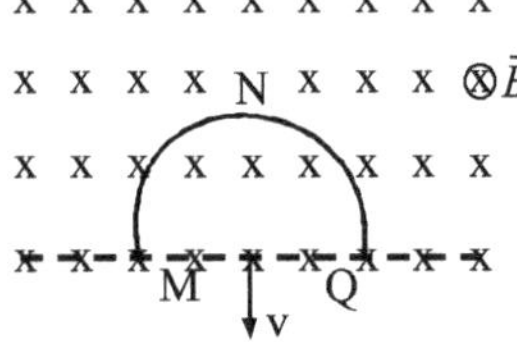

14. A horizontal square loop abcda is moved across the poles pieces of a magnet, as shown, with the speed **v**. When the side ab of loop enters the pole pieces at the time $\mathbf{t = 0}$, draw a graph which represents the emf **e** induced in the coil against the time **t**.

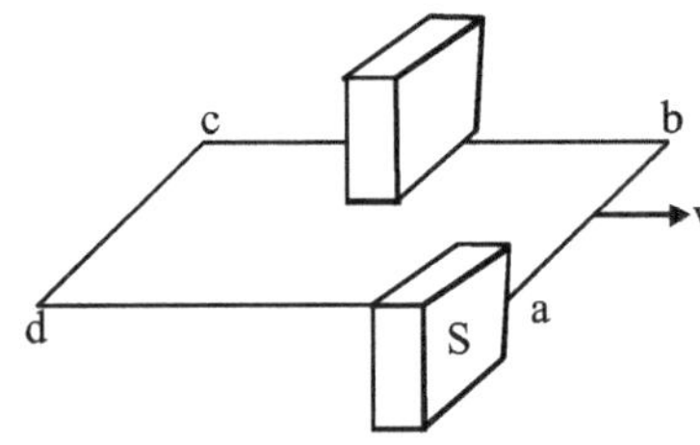

Objective Practice Exercise

Multiple Choice Questions

DIRECTIONS : *This section contains multiple choice questions. Each question has four choices (a), (b), (c) and (d) out of which only one is correct.*

1. The total charge induced in a conducting loop when it is moved in a magnetic field depends on
  (a) the rate of change of magnetic flux
  (b) initial magnetic flux only
  (c) the total change in magnetic flux
  (d) final magnetic flux only

2. According to Faraday's law of electromagnetic induction
  (a) the direction of induced force is such that it opposes the cause producing it
  (b) the magnitude of induced e.m.f. produced in a coil is directly proportional to the rate of change of magnetic flux
  (c) the direction of induced e.m.f. is such that it opposes the cause producing it
  (d) None of these

3. Lenz's law gives
  (a) the magnitude of the induced e.m.f.
  (b) the direction of the induced current
  (c) both the magnitude and direction of the induced current
  (d) the magnitude of the induced current

4. Induced emf in the coil depends upon
  (a) conductivity of coil
  (b) amount of flux
  (c) rate of change of linked flux
  (d) resistance of coil

5. An inductor may store energy in
  (a) its electric field
  (b) its coils
  (c) its magnetic field
  (d) both in electric and magnetic fields

6. A varying magnetic flux linking a coil is given by $\phi = xt^2$. If at a time $t = 3s$, the emf induced is 9V, then value of x is
  (a) $0.66\ \text{Wb/s}^2$ (b) $1.5\ \text{Wb/s}^2$
  (c) $-0.66\ \text{Wb/s}^2$ (d) $-1.5\ \text{Wb/s}^2$

7. The magnetic flux (in weber) linked with a coil of resistance $10\ \Omega$ is varying with respect to time t as $\phi = 4t^2 + 2t + 1$. Then the current in the coil at time $t = 1$ second is
  (a) 0.5 A   (b) 2 A   (c) 1.5 A   (d) 1 A

8. A rectangular coil of 100 turns and size 0.1 m × 0.05 m is placed perpendicular to a magnetic field of 0.1 T. The induced e.m.f. when the field drops to 0.05 T in 0.05 s is
   (a) 0.5 V (b) 1.0 V (c) 1.5 V (d) 2.0 V

9. A magnetic field of 2×10^{-2} T acts at right angles to a coil of area 100 cm^2, with 50 turns. The average e.m.f. induced in the coil is 0.1 V, when it is removed from the field in t sec. The value of t is
   (a) 10 s (b) 0.1 s (c) 0.01 s (d) 1 s

10. As a result of change in the magnetic flux linked to the closed loop shown in the fig, an e.m.f. V volt is induced in the loop. The work done (joule) in taking a charge Q coulomb once along the loop is 
    (a) QV (b) 2QV (c) QV/2 (d) Zero

11. A current $i = 2 \sin(\pi t/3)$ amp is flowing in an inductor of 2 henry. The amount of work done in increasing the current from 1.0 amp to 2.0 amp is
    (a) 1 J (b) 2 J (c) 3 J (d) 4 J

12. An electron moves along the line PQ which lies in the same plane as a circular loop of conducting wire as shown in figure. What will be the direction of the induced current in the loop?
    (a) Anticlockwise
    (b) Clockwise
    (c) Alternating
    (d) No current will be induced

13. A coil of circular cross-section having 1000 turns and 4 cm^2 face area is placed with its axis parallel to a magnetic field which decreases by 10^{-2} Wb m^{-2} in 0.01 s. The e.m.f. induced in the coil is:
    (a) 400 mV (b) 200 mV (c) 4 mV (d) 0.4 mV

14. A rectangular coil of 20 turns and area of cross-section 25 sq. cm has a resistance of 100 Ω. If a magnetic field which is perpendicular to the plane of coil changes at a rate of 1000 tesla per second, the current in the coil is
    (a) 1 A (b) 50 A (c) 0.5 A (d) 5 A

15. A coil of effective area 4 m^2 is placed at right angles to the magnetic induction B. The e.m.f. of 0.32 V is induced in the coil. When the field is reduced to 20% of its initial value in 0.5 sec. Find B.
    (a) 0.14 Wb/m^2 (b) 0.05 Wb/m^2
    (c) 0.4 Wb/m^2 (d) 0.14 Wb/m^2

16. Two identical circular loops of metal wire are lying on a table without touching each other. Loop–A carries a curent which increases with time. In response, the loop–B
    (a) Remains stationary
    (b) is attracted by the loop-A
    (c) is repelled by the loop-A
    (d) rotates about its CM, with CM fixed

17. The magnetic flux through a circuit of resistance R changes by an amount $\Delta\phi$ in a time Δt. Then the total quantity of electric charge Q that passes any point in the circuit during the time Δt is represented by
    (a) $R \cdot \dfrac{\Delta\phi}{\Delta t}$ (b) $\dfrac{1}{R} \cdot \dfrac{\Delta\phi}{\Delta t}$ (c) $\dfrac{\Delta\phi}{R}$ (d) $\dfrac{\Delta\phi}{\Delta t}$

18. A metal ring is held horizontally and bar magnet is dropped through the ring with its length along the axis of the ring. The acceleration of the falling magnet
    (a) is equal to g
    (b) is less than g
    (c) is more than g
    (d) depends on the diameter of ring and length of magnet

19. Two identical coaxial coils P and Q carrying equal amount of current in the same direction are brought nearer. The current in
    (a) P increases while in Q decreases
    (b) Q increases while in P decreases
    (c) both P and Q increases
    (d) both P and Q decreases

20. A solenoid has 2000 turns wound over a length of 0.3 m. Its cross-sectional area is 1.2×10^{-3} m^2. Around its central section a coil of 300 turns is wound. If an initial current of 2 A flowing in the solenoid is reversed in 0.25 s, the emf induced in the coil will be
    (a) 2.4×10^{-4} V (b) 2.4×10^{-2} V
    (c) 4.8×10^{-4} V (d) 4.8×10^{-2} V

21. Consider the situation shown in figure. If the switch is closed and after some time it is opened again, the closed loop will show
    (a) a clockwise current
    (b) an anticlockwise current
    (c) an anticlockwise current and then clockwise
    (d) a clockwise current and then an anticlock wise current.

22. A circular disc of radius 0.2 meter is placed in a uniform magnetic field of induction $\dfrac{1}{\pi}\left(\text{Wb}/\text{m}^2\right)$ in such a way that its axis makes an angle of 60° with $\vec{B}$. The magnetic flux linked with the disc is:
    (a) 0.02 Wb (b) 0.06 Wb
    (c) 0.08 Wb (d) 0.01 Wb

23. A 100 turns coil of area of cross section 200 cm^2 having 2 Ω resistance is held perpendicular to a magnetic field of 0.1 T. If it is removed from the magnetic field in one second, the induced charge produced in it is
    (a) 0.2 C (b) 2 C (c) 0.1 C (d) 1 C

24. If N is the number of turns in a coil, the value of self inductance varies as
    (a) N^0 (b) N (c) N^2 (d) N^{-2}

25. If the number of turns per unit length of a coil of solenoid is doubled, the self-inductance of the solenoid will
    (a) remain unchanged (b) be halved
    (c) be doubled (d) become four times

26. The self inductance of a long solenoid cannot be increased by
    (a) increasing its area of cross section
    (b) increasing its length
    (c) changing the medium with greater permeability
    (d) increasing the current through it

27. A 100 millihenry coil carries a current of 1 A. Energy stored in its magnetic field is
(a) 0.5 J   (b) 1 A   (c) 0.05 J   (d) 0.1 J

28. The self induced emf is 0.4 henry in the coil when current in it changes at the rate of 500 A/s, is
(a) 8×10^{-4} V   (b) 8×10^{-3} V
(c) 200 V   (d) 500 V

29. Find the self inductance of a coil in which an e.m.f. of 10 V is induced when the current in the circuit changes uniformly from 1 A to 0.5 A in 0.2 sec.
(a) 4 H   (b) 2 H   (c) 3 H   (d) 5 H

30. In an inductor of self-inductance $L = 2$ mH, current changes with time according to relation $i = t^2 e^{-t}$. At what time emf is zero?
(a) 4 s   (b) 3 s   (c) 2 s   (d) 1 s

31. The current in self inductance L = 40 mH is to be increased uniformly from 1 amp to 11 amp in 4 milliseconds. The e.m.f. induced in the inductor during the process is
(a) 100 volt   (b) 0.4 volt
(c) 4.0 volt   (d) 440 volt

32. In an induction coil the current increases from 0 to 6 amp in 0.3 sec by which induced emf of 30 volt is produced in it then the value of coefficient of self inductance of coil will be
(a) 3 henry   (b) 2 henry
(c) 1 henry   (d) 1.5 henry

33. When the current in a coil changes from 8 amp to 2 amp in 3×10^{-2} seconds, the emf induced in the coil is 2 volt. The self inductance of the coil is
(a) 10 mH   (b) 20 mH   (c) 5 mH   (d) 1 mH

34. When the current changes from +2 A to -2 A in 0.05 second, an e.m.f. of 8 V is induced in a coil. The coefficient of self-induction of the coil is
(a) 0.2 H   (b) 0.4 H   (c) 0.8 H   (d) 0.1 H

35. Two coils are placed close to each other. The mutual inductance of the pair of coils depends upon
(a) the rates at which currents are changing in the two coils
(b) relative position and orientation of the two coils
(c) the materials of the wires of the coils
(d) the currents in the two coils

36. Induction furnace is based on the heating effect of
(a) electric field   (b) eddy current
(c) magnetic field   (d) gravitational field

37. If rotational velocity of a dynamo armature is doubled, then induced e.m.f. will become
(a) half   (b) two times
(c) four times   (d) unchanged

38. The back e.m.f. in a d.c. motor is maximum, when
(a) the motor has picked up max speed
(b) the motor has just started moving
(c) the speed of motor is still on the increase
(d) the motor has just been switched off

39. Eddy currents are produced when
(a) a metal is kept in varying magnetic field
(b) a metal is kept in steady magnetic field
(c) a circular coil is placed in a magnetic field
(d) through a circular coil, current is passed

40. If a coil made of conducting wires is roated between poles pieces of the permanent magnet. The motion will generate a current and this device is called
(a) electric motor   (b) electric generator
(c) electromagnet   (d) All of the above.

Chapter Test

Time : *30 minutes*   **Max. Marks : *15***

Direction :

Each question number **1-15** carry **1 mark** each.

1. Fig shown below represents an area $A = 0.5$ m^2 situated in a uniform magnetic field $B = 2.0$ weber/m^2 and making an angle of 60° with respect to magnetic field.

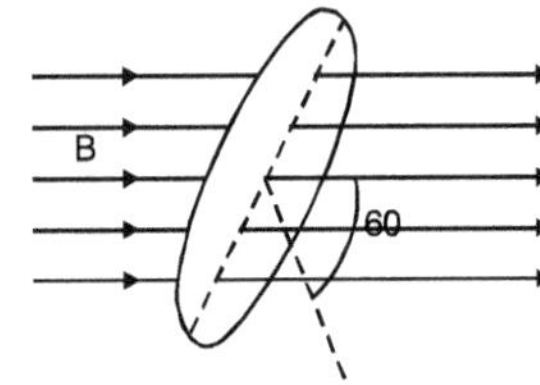

The value of the magnetic flux through the area would be equal to

(a) 2.0 weber   (b) $\sqrt{3}$ weber
(c) $\sqrt{3}/2$ weber   (d) 0.5 weber

2. A conductor of length 0.4 m is moving with a speed of 7 m/s perpendicular to a magnetic field of intensity 0.9 Wb/m^2. The induced e.m.f. across the conductor is
(a) 1.26 V   (b) 2.52 V   (c) 5.04 V   (d) 25.2 V

3. A coil is wound on a frame of rectangular cross-section. If all the linear dimensions of the frame are increased by a factor 2 and the number of turns per unit length of the coil remains the same, self-inductance of the coil increases by a factor of
(a) 4   (b) 8   (c) 12   (d) 16

4. In an AC generator, a coil with N turns, all of the same area A and total resistance R, rotates with frequency ω in a magnetic field B. The maximum value of emf generated in the coil is
   (a) N.A.B.R.ω (b) N.A.B.
   (c) N.A.B.R.   (d) N.A.B.ω

DIRECTIONS (Qs. 5-6) : *Each of these questions contains an assertion followed by reason. Read them carefully and answer the question on the basis of following options. You have to select the one that best describes the two statements.*

(a) If both Assertion and Reason are correct and the Reason is a correct explanation of the Assertion.

(b) If both Assertion and Reason are correct but Reason is not a correct explanation of the Assertion.

(c) If the Assertion is correct but Reason is incorrect.

(d) If the Assertion is incorrect but the Reason is correct.

5. **Assertion :** An induced emf appears in any coil in which the current is constant.
   Reason : Self induction phenomenon does not obey Faraday's law of induction.

6. **Assertion :** Faraday's laws are consequence of conservation of energy.
   Reason : In a purely resistive ac circuit, the current lags behind the emf in phase.

DIRECTIONS : (Qs. 7-11) *are case based questions.*
Suppose the moving rod ab slides along a stationary U-shaped conductor, forming a complete circuit. Under the action of this field a counterclockwise current is established around this complete circuit.

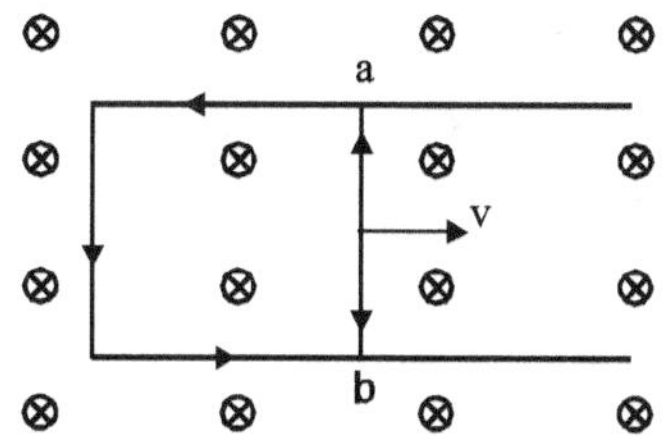

The moving rod becomes a source of electromotive force. Within it, charge moves from lower to higher potential and in the remainder of the circuit, charge moves from higher to lower potential. We call this a motional electromagnetic force denoted by e, we can write,

Electromotive force. $e = Bv\ell$

If R is the resistance of the circuit, then current in the circuit

$$i = \frac{e}{R} = \frac{Bv\ell}{R}$$

7. A 10-meter wire is kept in east-west direction. It is falling down with a speed of 5.0 meter/second, perpendicular to the horizontal component of earth's magnetic field of 0.30 $\times 10^{-4}$ weber/meter^2. The momentary potential difference induced between the ends of the wire will be
   (a) 0.0015 V   (b) 0.015 V
   (c) 0.15 V   (d) 1.5 V

8. A conductor AB of length l moves in x – y plane with velocity $\vec{v} = v_0 \left(\hat{i} - \hat{j} \right)$. A magnetic field $\vec{B} = B_0 \left(\hat{i} + \hat{j} \right)$ exists in the region. The iduced emf is
   (a) zero   (b) $B_0 l v_0$
   (c) $B_0 l v_0$ (d) $\sqrt{2} B_0 l v_0$

9. A rectangular loop is being pulled at a constant speed v, through a region of certain thickness d, in which a uniform magnetic field B is set up.
   The graph between position x of the right hand edge of the loop and the induced emf E will be

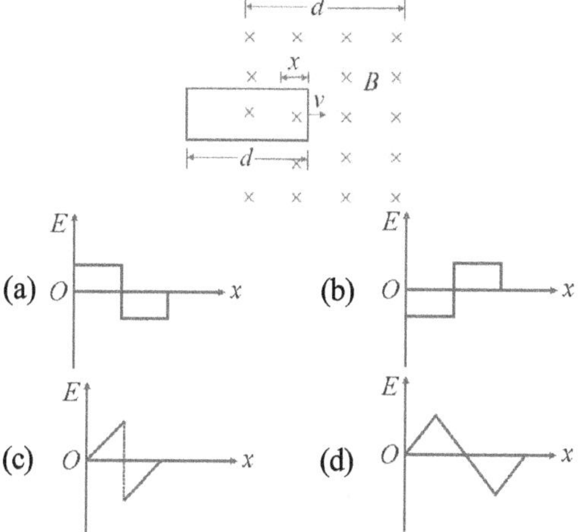

10. A six pole generator with fixed field excitation develops an e.m.f. of 100 V when operating at 1500 r.p.m. At what speed must it rotate to develop 120V?
    (a) 1200 r.p.m   (b) 1800 r.p.m
    (c) 1500 r.p.m   (d) 400 r.p.m

11. Consider the situation shown. The wire AB is sliding on fixed rails with a constant velocity. If the wire AB is replaced by semi-circular wire, the magnitude of induced e.m.f. will
    (a) increase
    (b) decrease
    (c) remain the same
    (d) increase or decrease depending on whether the semi-circle buldges towards the resistance or away from it.

Very Short Answer Type Questions

12. A cylindrical bar magnet is kept along the axis of a circular coil. Will there be a current induced in the coil if the magnet is rotated about its axis?

13. A wheel with a certain number of spokes is rotated in a plane normal to earth's magnetic field so that an e.m.f is induced between the axle and the rim of the wheel. Keeping all other things same, number of spokes is changed. How is the e.m.f affected?

14. State Faraday's laws of electromagnetic induction.

15. What are eddy current? Give one advantage and one disadvantage of it.

Solutions

1. **(b)** The charge through the coil = area of current-time $(i-t)$ graph

$$q = \frac{1}{2} \times 0.1 \times 4 = 0.2\,C$$

$$q = \frac{\Delta\phi}{R} \qquad [\because \text{Change in flux } (\Delta\phi) = q \times R]$$

$$q = 0.2 = \frac{\Delta\phi}{10}$$

$\Delta\phi = 2$ weber

2. **(d)** The induced e.m.f. is given by rate of change of magnetic flux linked with the circuit.

$$e = -\frac{d\phi}{dt}$$

For N turns $e = -N\dfrac{d\phi}{dt}$

Negative sign indicates that induced emf (e) opposes the change of flux.

3. **(d)** Relative motion between the magnet and the coil that is responsible for induction in the coil.

4. **(c)** As I increases, ϕ increases

$\therefore I_i$ is such that it opposes the increases in ϕ.

Hence, ϕ decreases (By Right Hand Rule). The induced current will be counter clockwise.

5. **(b)** The relative motion between the coil and the magnet produces change in the magnetic flux in the coil and the induced emf is always in such a direction that it opposes the change in the flux.

6. **(b)** Because there is no change in flux linked with coil.

7. **(c)** Emf will always induces whenever, there is change in magnetic flux.

8. **(c)**

9. **(c)** When switch is closed , the magnetic flux through the ring will increase and so ring will move away form the solenoid so as to compensate this flux. This is according to Lenz's law.

10. **(b)** In both the cases, the magnetic flux maybe change, and so there is an induced e.m.f.

11. **(a)** $\dfrac{dq}{dt} = -\dfrac{1}{R}\dfrac{d\phi}{dt} \Rightarrow dq = -\dfrac{d\phi}{R} \Rightarrow q = \dfrac{(\phi_1 - \phi_2)}{R}$

which is indipendent of time.

12. **(b)** E increases if the speed of the magnet increases.

13. **(a)** I increases if the speed of the magnet.

14. **(c)** Q remains same if the speed of the magnet is doubled.

15. **(d)** If the speed of the magnet is halved, then E and I decreases.

16. **(c)** Q does not depend upon the speed of the magnet.

17. The number of magnetic lines of force crossing a surface is called magnetic flux linked with the surface.

18. The induced current in the coil should be in such a direction that it opposes the motion of the magnet. So a N – pole will be created at the near end. Therefore from the side of the magnet the current in the coil will be anticlokwise direction.

19. Since the south pole of the magnet is approaching towards the loop, so by Lenz's law the induced current in the loop should be in such a direction that it should oppose the approach of the S-pole. So another S-pole should be produced at the near end of the coil. Therefore, the current should be in clockwise direction when viewed from the magnet side.

20. Induced current will be clockwise in both the coils, when viewed from the magnet side as the N-pole is moving away from coil AB so a S-pole should be created at the end B. The S-pole is approching towards CD, hence another S-pole should be produced at the end C to provent its approach.

21. As soon as the switch S is closed, an e.m.f. is induced in the ring R and it is repelled.

22. According to Lenz's law, the direction of induced e.m.f in a circuit is always such that it opposes the very case which produces it.

Thus $e = \dfrac{-d\phi}{dt}$

23. **Faraday's laws of electromagnetic induction:**
First law: Wherever there is a change in magnetic flux associted with a coil, an e.m.f. is induced in the coil. It last so long as the change continues.
Second law: The induced e.m.f. is directly proportional to the rate of change of magnetic flux of the coil and has a direction opposite to that of the change of magnetic flux.
Mathematically,

$$e \propto -\frac{d\phi}{dt} \quad \Rightarrow \quad e = -k\frac{d\phi}{dt}$$

$$[k = 1 \text{ for all system of units}]$$

$$\therefore \qquad e = -\frac{d\phi}{dt}$$

24. When the switch is closed the flux associated with L changes, an e.m.f. is induced in L which will oppose the growth of current in Q. But no such induced e.m.f. will be produced in R. So P will light up faster.

25. (i) When coil A is placed parallel to B and near to it, due to mutual induction an e.m.f is induced in B and the bulb lights up.

(ii) When the coil B is moved upwards, distance between A and B increases. Hence the magnetic flux linked with B decrease and mutual induction decreases and hence the bulb gets dimmer.

26. Induced emf $= e = -\dfrac{d\phi}{dt} = -\dfrac{8 \times 10^{-4}}{0.5}$

$$= -1.6 \times 10^{-3}\,V = -1.6\,mV$$

−ve sign gives the direction of e.m.f.

27. When the magnet falls, the magnetic flux linked through the metal ring changes, so current is induced in the ring will be in such a direction according to Lenz's law that it opposes the motion of the magnet, so its acceleration will be less than g.

28. No e.m.f. will be produced between the ends of a metallic pole falling vertically through the plane of magnetic meridian as the falling pole does not cut any magnetic lines of force.

Practice Exercise-2

1. **(d)** No change in flux, hence no force required.

2. **(a)** The induced emf across the sliding wire

$$e = Bv\ell = 0.5 \times 4 \times 0.25 = 0.5\,V$$

The effective circuit is shown in figure.

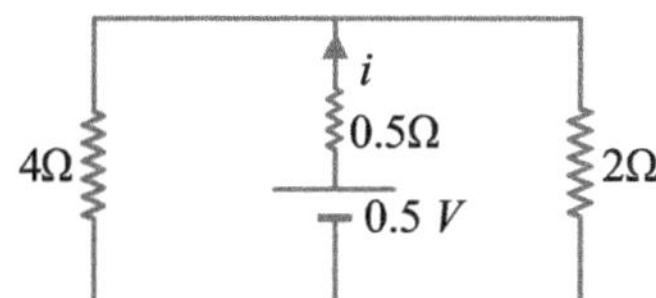

The equivalent resistance of the circuit

$$r = \frac{4 \times 2}{4 + 2} + 0.5 = 1.83\ \Omega$$

Now, $i = \dfrac{V}{R} = \dfrac{0.5}{1.83} = 0.27A$

3. **(d)** $|e| = BlV \sin\theta$

4. **(d)** $e = [Bv\ell]$

$$|e| = \begin{vmatrix} 3 & 3 & 2 \\ 1 & 2 & 0 \\ 0 & 0 & 1 \end{vmatrix}$$

(as length of conductor is $0\hat{i} + 0\hat{j} + 1\hat{k}$)

$\therefore |e| = 3V$

5. **(d)** The e.m.f. is induced when there is change of flux. As in this case there is no change of flux, hence no e.m.f. will be induced in the wire.

6. **(b)** In both the cases, the magnetic flux will change, and so there is an induced current.

7. **(a)** In the given case, there is no component of velocity in perpendicular to the magnetic field and so $e = Bv\ell \sin 0°$.

8. **(a)** $e = \dfrac{d}{2}\ell\left(\dfrac{dB}{dt}\right)$

For PQ, $\quad d = 0, e_{PQ} = 0$

For QR, $\quad d = \ell,\ ePR = \dfrac{\ell}{2} \times 2\ell \quad x = x\,\ell^2$

In close loop, $e_{QP} + e_{PR} + e_{RQ} = 0$

or $\quad 0 + e_{PR} + e_{RQ} = 0$

$\therefore \quad e_{RQ} = -e_{PR}$

$$= e_{RP}$$

$$= xl^2$$

9. **(b)** **10.** **(a)**

11. **(c)** Induced emf in the coil depends upon rate of change of linked flux.

12. **(d)** The emf lasts so long as the change in flux takes place.

13. The direction of induced current will be anti-clockwise i.e. along PSRQP. This is given by Fleming's right hand rule.

14. (i) Current induced in the loop is zero as there is no change in flux in the loop.

(ii) No work is done by the loop as there is no change in flux.

15. Magnetic flux, $\phi = BA = B\ell x = B\ell vt$

[Where x = distance covered by the loop in time t = vt]

$P_{max} = B\ell b$

$\therefore$ E.m.f induced $= e = \dfrac{d\phi}{dt} = B\ell v.$

(i)

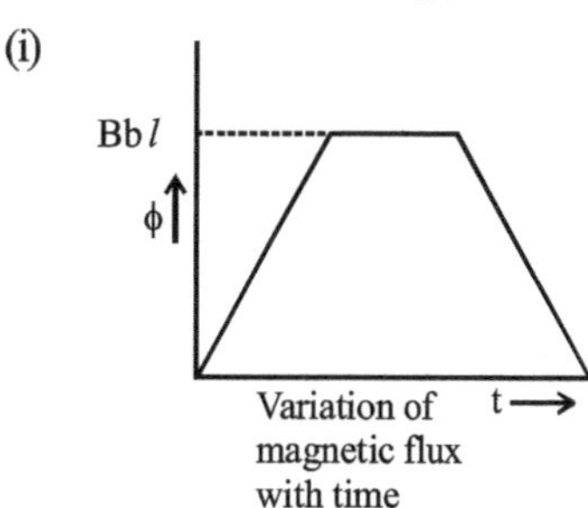

Variation of magnetic flux with time

(ii)

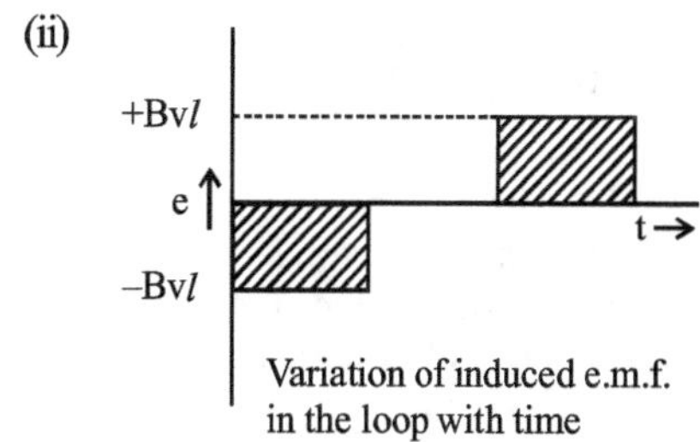

Variation of induced e.m.f. in the loop with time

16. The induced potential difference $= e = -\dfrac{d\phi}{dt}$

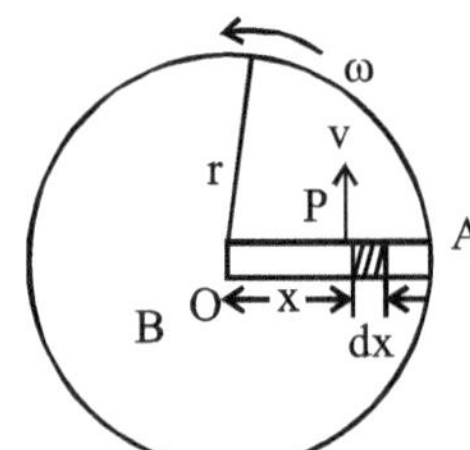

Consider a metallic disc of radius $OA = r$. Consider a small length element at P of length dx at a distance x from the centre O. The angular velocity (ω) of rotating disc is same for all elements, but linear velocity is different.

$\therefore$ The linear velocity of element of

$\qquad P = v = x\omega$

The potential difference across element at P,

$\qquad de = B\,vdx = Bx\omega\,dx$

$\therefore$ Total potential difference induced $= e = B\omega \int_0^r x\,dx$

$\qquad = B\omega\left[\dfrac{x^2}{2}\right]_0^r = \dfrac{B\omega r^2}{2}$

Here, $B = 0.2$T, $\omega = 20\pi$ rad/s, $r = 10$ cm $= 0.10$m

$e = \dfrac{0.2 \times 20\pi \times (0.10)^2}{2} = 2 \times 3.14 \times 10^{-2}$ V

$\quad = 6.28 \times 10^{-2}$ V

Induced current $= I = \dfrac{e}{R} = \dfrac{6.28 \times 10^{-2}}{2}$

$\qquad\qquad = 3.14 \times 10^{-2}$ A

17. Length of the spoke $= \ell = 0.5$m, number of spokes $= 10$, magnetic field $B = 0.4$ gauss $= 0.4 \times 10^{-4}$ T

Frequency of rotation $= f = 120$ rev/min

$\qquad = \dfrac{120}{60}$ rev/s $= 2$ rev/s

As the spokes are connected in parallel, the net emf induced will be the same as that for a single spoke.

$\therefore$ emf induced $= e = -\dfrac{d\phi}{dt} = -\dfrac{d}{dt}(BA)$

$\qquad\qquad = -B\dfrac{dA}{dt}$

$\Rightarrow \quad e = \dfrac{B\pi\ell^2}{\frac{1}{f}} = B\pi l^2 f \qquad$ (numerically)

$\qquad = 3.14 \times (0.5)^2 \times (0.4 \times 10^{-4}) \times 2 = 6.28 \times 10^{-5}$ V

18. Induced e.m.f. $= e = Blv = 1 \times 0.1 \times 10 = 1$ volt.

19. Here, $B = 10^4$ G $= 10^4 \times 10^{-4}$ T $= 1$T.

$l = 1$m, $v = 2$m/s

$e = Blv = 1 \times 1 \times 2 = 2$ volt.

20. When the magnetic flux linked with a conductor changes, a current is induced in the body of the conductor called eddy current. Eddy current is used for electromagnetic damping in dead beat galvanometer. It is used in Induction furnace to produce lot of heat sufficient to melt a metal.

Practice Exercise-3

1. **(a)** $L = \dfrac{\varepsilon}{dI/dt} = \dfrac{10 \times 10^{-3}}{2} = 5 \times 10^{-3}$ Henry

2. **(b)** $L = \dfrac{N\phi}{i}$

3. **(b)** Mutual Inductance of two coils

$\qquad M = \sqrt{L_1 L_2} = \sqrt{2\text{mH} \times 8\text{mH}} = 4\text{mH}$

4. **(c)** $(A) \to (2); (B) \to (1); (C) \to (4)$

Slip ring is a part of an AC generator.

In a dead beat galvanometer, eddy current helps in electromagnetic damping.

A solenoid is formed of long coil of circular loops of insulated copper wire

5. **(b)** Given $\dfrac{\ell_1}{\ell_2} = \dfrac{1}{2}$ and $\dfrac{N_1}{N_2} = \dfrac{1}{2}$ From

$\qquad L = \dfrac{\mu_0 N^2 A}{\ell}\alpha\dfrac{N^2}{\ell}$

we get, $\dfrac{L_1}{L_2} = \left(\dfrac{N_1}{N_2}\right)^2 \Big/ \left(\dfrac{\ell_1}{\ell_2}\right) = \dfrac{(1/2)^2}{1/2} = \dfrac{1}{2}$

6. **(b)**

7. **(c)** Number of flux linkages with the coil is proportional to the current i, $N f \mu i$

or $N\phi = Li \qquad$ [N is the number of turns in coils]

$\qquad\qquad$ [$N\phi$ is total flux linkage]

Hence, $L = \dfrac{N\phi}{i} = $ co-efficient of self-inductance.

8. **(d)** As $L = \mu_0\dfrac{N^2 A}{\ell}$

9. **(d)** According to Faraday's law of electromagnetic induction,

Induced emf, $e = \dfrac{Ldi}{dt}$

$50 = L\left(\dfrac{5-2}{0.1\text{sec}}\right)$

$\Rightarrow \quad L = \dfrac{50 \times 0.1}{3} = \dfrac{5}{3} = 1.67$ H

10. **(d)**

11. **(b)** $\varepsilon = M\dfrac{di}{dt}$ or $8 = M\left[\dfrac{(4-2)}{0.05}\right]$

$\therefore \quad M = \dfrac{8 \times 0.05}{2} = 0.2$ henry

12. **(b)** $L = \mu_0 nI$

$\therefore \quad \dfrac{L_2}{L_1} = \dfrac{\mu}{\mu_0} \qquad\qquad$ ----($\because$ n and I are same)

$\therefore \quad L_2 = \mu_r L_1 = 900 \times 0.18 = 162$ mH

13. **(a)** $N\phi = LI$

$$\therefore \quad \phi = \frac{LI}{N} = \frac{8\times 10^{-3}\times 5\times 10^{-3}}{400}$$

$$= 10^{-7} = \frac{\mu_0}{4\pi}\,Wb$$

14. The self-inductance of a coil is defined as the magnetic flux linked with the coil when unit current flows through it. S.I. unit is henry.

15. **(i)** $L = \mu_0 \dfrac{N^2}{\ell}A \quad \therefore L \propto N^2$

    If number of turns (N) of one coil is decreased, self inductance (L) also decreases.

    (ii) If an iron core is introduced in the coil, the permeability (μ) increases. So self inductance also increases.

16. Self-inductance $L \propto N^2$, so when the number of turns is doubled, self-inductance will become 4 times.

17. Energy stored in an inductor $= \dfrac{1}{2}LI^2$. It is magnetic energy.

18. Iuduced e.m.f. $= e = -L\dfrac{di}{dt}$

$$\therefore \quad L = \left|\frac{e}{di/dt}\right| = \frac{40\times 10^{-3}}{2}$$

$$= 20\times 10^{-3}\,H = 20\,mH.$$

19. Relative permeability $\mu_r = \dfrac{L_{medium}}{L_{air}} = \dfrac{10\,mH}{0.01\,mH} = 1000$.

20. Efficiency, $\eta = \dfrac{E}{V} = \dfrac{\text{back emf}}{\text{emf of battery}}$

21. Slipring arrangement in an a.c generator is replaced by split ring arrangement in the d.c generator.

22. Whenever there is a change in magnetic flux linked with a coil, an e.m.f. is induced in the coil. This is called self induction. Self-inductance of a coil depends on the number of turns and cross-sectional area of the coil.

23. Coefficient of mutual inductance between a pair of coils is numerically equal to the amount of magnetic flux linked with one coil when unit current flows through the other coil. Its S.I. unit is Henry.

    It depends on size, shape, number of turns and nature of material of two coils. It also depends on the relative placement of the two coils.

24. Magnetic field at a point inside the solenoid is $B = \dfrac{\mu_0 NI}{\ell}$

    Where N is the total number of turns of the solenoid and l is its length. B is constant throughout the length of the solenoid.

    Magnetic flux through each turn $= B \times$ area of each turn.

$$\therefore \quad \phi_1 = \mu_0 \frac{N}{\ell} I \times A$$

where A is the area of each turn.

$\therefore$ Total magnetic flux linked with the solenoid $= \phi = \mu_0 \dfrac{N}{\ell} IA \times N$

But from the definition of self inductance (L), $\phi = LI$.

$$\therefore \quad LI = \mu_0 \frac{N}{\ell} IA \times N \;\Rightarrow\; L = \frac{\mu_0 N^2 A}{\ell}$$

25. Let l be the length of each solenoid S_1 and S_2 and A be the cross-sectional area of each of them.

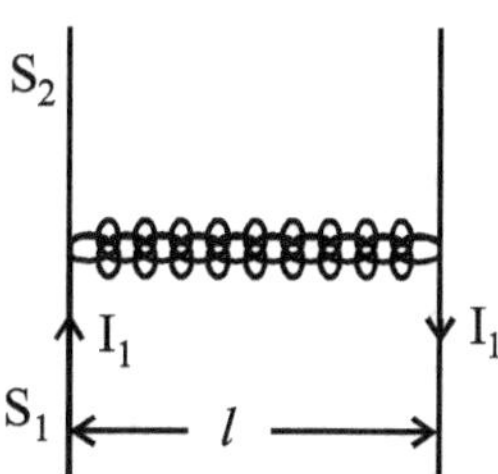

N_1 and N_2 be the total number of turns of S_1 and S_2.

Magnetic field in $S_1 = B_1 = \dfrac{\mu_0 N_1 I_1}{\ell}$

Magnetic flux linked with each turn of $S_2 = B_1 \times$ area of each turn $= B_1 A$

Total magnetic flux linked with $S_2 = B_1 A N_2$

$$\therefore \quad \phi_2 = \left(\frac{\mu_0 N_1 I_1}{\ell}\right)AN_2 = \frac{\mu_0 N_1 N_2 A I_1}{\ell}$$

But magnetic flux linked with S_2 is due to I_1

$$\therefore \quad \phi_2 \propto I_1 \qquad \text{or } \phi_2 = MI_1$$

Where M is the mutual inductance of S_2 and S_1

$$\therefore \quad MI_1 = \frac{\mu_0 N_1 N_2 A I_1}{\ell}$$

$$\therefore \quad M = \frac{\mu_0 N_1 N_2 A}{\ell}$$

26. **(i)** When the distance between the coils is increased the magnetic flux linked between them decreases as magnetic lines of force tend to diverge with distance. So mutual inductance also decreases.

    (ii) If the number of turns in each coil is decreased then also mutual inductance decreases as mutual inductance is directly proportional to the number of turns.

Past year Exercise

1. Self-inductance of a long solenoid

$$L = \frac{\mu_0 N^2 A}{l}$$

$$\therefore \quad L \propto N^2$$

So, the self-inductance of the solenoid will become 4 times.

2. Self-inductance of a coil is equal to the emf induced in coil when rate of change of current in coil is 1 A/s.

    SI unit of self-unductance is henry.

3. Inductor A have got greater slope than inductor B,

therefore self-inductance of A is greater than that of B.

4. The self-inductance can be increased by inserting a magnetic material having high permeability.

As, $L = \dfrac{\mu_0 N^2 A}{L}$ (for air)

5. By lenz's law induced current should oppose this increase in flux. Thus, flow of current will be from QPSRQ.

6. By lenz's law the direction of induced current in
 (i) ring 1 is clockwise
 (ii) ring 2 is anticlockwise

7. It is clear that north pole of the magnet is moving away from coil PQ, so to oppose this it will acquire south pole. The direction of curent will be anticlockwise. Again, the south pole is approaching towards coil CD, so end C of the coil will act as south pole. To oppose the approaching of south pole and the direction of current will be clockwise.

8. The polarity of upper plate will be positive with respect to the lower plate in the capacitor.

9. As the current is switched on the electromagnet is magnetised. It attracts the metal disc. Soon a change of flux takes place and an induced emf is produced which according to Lenz's law opposes the cause which produced it. Hence metal disc thrown up.

10. Mututal inductance $M = \dfrac{\mu_0 N_1 N_2 A}{1}$. Hence the mutual inductance will
 (i) decrease with the increase in distance and
 (ii) increase with increase of number of turns in the coils.

11. The current induced in the loop is in clockwise direction (using the right-hand thumb rule) because the decreasing magnetic field in the loop due to the decreasing current in wire AB is into the plane of the paper (perpendicular to the plane). So, the direction of the induced current in the loop will be such that it produces an inward magnetic field (perpendicular to the plane).

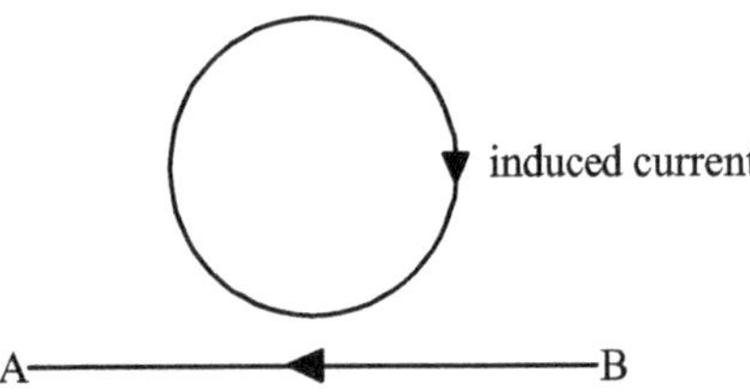

12. Glass bob is non-conducting in nature. Due to the non-conducting nature of the glass bob, it will only experience the Earth's gravitational pull. So, the glass bob will reach the ground earlier.

While a metallic bob is conducting in nature. So, Eddy current is induced in the metallic bob as it falls through the magnetic field of the Earth. By Lenz's law, the current induced is such that it opposes the motion of the metallic bob. So, the metallic bob will experience a force in the upward direction. This will slow down the metallic bob by some extent.

Hence, it will reach the Earth after the glass bob.

13. Polarity of capacitor Plate A will be positive with respect to Plate B. According to Lenz law, Plate A of the capacitor is at a higher potential than Plate B.

14. Let, I current flows through the coil of self-inductance L at any instant t when rate of change of current in coil is $\dfrac{dI}{dt}$.

∴ Induced emf, $E = -L\dfrac{dI}{dt}$

∴ Work done in establishing the current in small time interval dt is given by

$dW = Pdt = -\varepsilon I dt = -\left(-L\dfrac{dI}{dt}\right) I dt$

$dW = LI dI$

∴ Total work done in increasing the current from zero to I.

∴ $W = \displaystyle\int_0^1 LI dI = L\int_0^1 I dI = L\left[\dfrac{I^2}{2}\right]_0^I = \dfrac{1}{2}L\left(I^2 - 0^2\right)$

$W = \dfrac{1}{2}LI^2$

15. Induced current is in anticlockwise when seen from left hand side and its direction is in clockwise when seen from right hand side.

Therefore B is as negative plate while A is as (+) ve plate.

16. As $\Delta I = -2$ A
 $\Delta t = 10 \times 10^{-3}$ s
 $V = 200$ V

As we know, $e = -L\dfrac{\Delta I}{\Delta t}$

∴ $200 = -L\left(\dfrac{-2}{10 \times 10^{-3}}\right)$

$200 = L \times 2 \times 10^2$
$L = 1$H

17. Let a current I flows through the outer coil of radius R. The magnet field at the centre of the coil is

$B = \dfrac{\mu_0 I}{2R}$

As $r \ll R$, hence B may be considered to be constant over the centre cross-sectional area of inner coil of radius r. Hence, magnetic flux linked with the smaller coil will be

$\phi_1 = BA_1 = \dfrac{\mu_0 I}{2R} = r^2$

As we know, $\phi_1 = M_{12} I_2$

Now mutual inductance $M_{12} = \dfrac{\phi_1}{I_2} = \dfrac{\mu_0 r^2}{2R}$

But, $M_{12} = M_{21} =$ suppose, M

∴ $M = \dfrac{\mu_0 \pi r^2}{2R}$

18. Angular velocity of rod, $\omega = \dfrac{2\pi}{T}$

Changing flux associated with Ring $= BA = B\left(\pi L^2\right)$
According to Faraday's law of EMI, induced emf,

$e = \dfrac{\Delta\phi}{\Delta T} = \dfrac{B\pi L^2}{T}$ $e = \dfrac{B\pi L^2}{\left(\dfrac{2\pi}{\omega}\right)}$ $e = \dfrac{1}{2}B\omega L^2$

19. (i) **Lenz's law :** Whenever the magnetic flux linked with a circuit changes, an induced emf is produced and the direction of the induced current is such that it opposes the cause which produces it.

(ii) Yes, emf will be induced in the metallic rod because there will be a change of magnetic flux. The metallic rod will cut the magnetic lines of the earth's magnetic field.

20. Given, $B = 0.5\,T, l = 20\,cm = 0.2\,m$

Induced emf $e = BlV \Rightarrow 0.5 \times 0.2 \times 10$ Volt

or $e = 1.0\,V$

Current through this conductor

$$i = \frac{e}{R} = \frac{1V}{5\Omega} = 0.2\,A$$

OR

Given : Length of each spoke $= 50\,cm = 0.5\,m$

$$\omega = \frac{120}{60} = 2\ rps = 2 \times 2\pi = 4\pi\ \text{radian s}^{-1}$$

$B = 0.4\,G$

$\delta = 60°$

Horizontal component of Earth's magnetic field

$B_H = B\cos\delta = 0.4 \times \cos 60° = 0.2\,G$

Now, $e = \dfrac{1}{2}B_H\omega l^2 = \dfrac{1}{2} \times 0.2 \times 4\pi \times 0.5 \times 0.5\ V = 0.314\,V$

The emf will be unaffected by the increase in the number of spokes because they are in parallel.

21. Production of induced e.m.f. in a coil due to the change of current in a neighbouring coil, is called mutual induction.

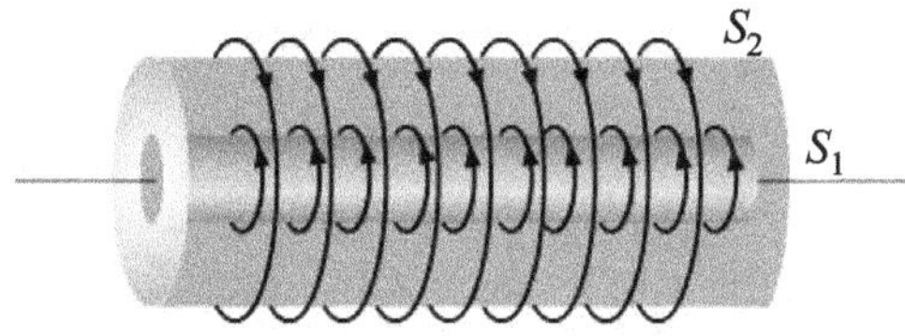

Suppose a current i is passed through the inner solenoid S_1. A magnetic field $B = \mu_0 n_1 i$ is produced inside S_1, whereas the field outside it is zero.

The flux through each turn S_2 is $B\pi r_1{}^2 = \mu_0 n_1 i\pi r_1{}^2$

The total flux through all the turns in a length l of S_2 is

$\phi = (\mu_0 n_1 i\pi r_1{}^2)n_2 l = (\mu_0 n_1 n_2 \pi r_1{}^2 l)i \Rightarrow M = \mu_0 n_1 n_2 \pi r_1{}^2 l$

22. The self-inductance of a solenoid is defined as the ratio of magnetic flux through the solenoid to the current passing through S.I. unit of self inductance is henry. It

is given by $= \dfrac{\phi}{i}$

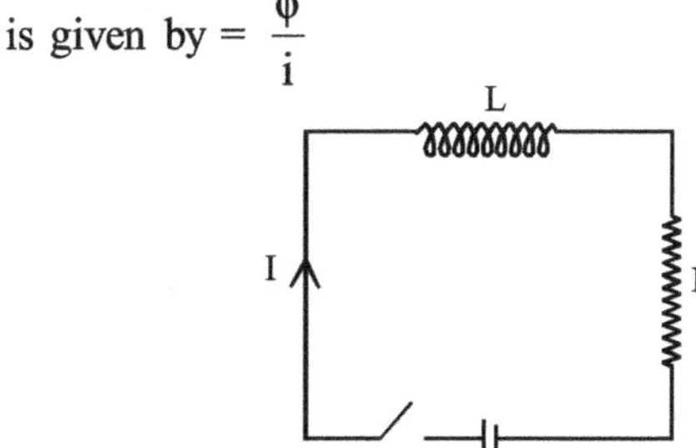

Consider the circuit shown above consisting of a inductor L and a resistor R, connected to a source of emf E. As the connections are made, the current grows in the circuit and the magnetic field increases in the inductor. Part of the work done by the battery during the process is stored in the inductor as magnetic field energy and

the rest appears as thermal energy in the resistor. After sufficient time, the current, and hence the magnetic field, becomes constant and further work done by the battery appears completely as thermal energy. If i be the current in the circuit at time t, we have

$$E - \frac{Ldi}{dt} = iR \Rightarrow Eidt = L^2Rdt + Lidi$$

$$\Rightarrow \int_0^t Eidt = \int_0^t i^2Rdt + \int_0^i Lidi \Rightarrow \int_0^t Eidt = \int_0^t i^2Rdt + \frac{1}{2}Li^2$$

Now (idt) is the charge flowing through the circuit during the time t to t+dt. Thus, (Eidt) is the work done by the battery in this period. The quantity on the left-hand side of the equation (i) is, therefore, the total work done by the battery in time 0 to t. Similarly, the first term on the right-hand side of equation (i) is the total thermal energy developed in the resistor at time t. Thus $\dfrac{1}{2}Li^2$ is the energy stored in the inductor as the current in it increases from 0 to i. As the energy is zero when the current is zero, when the current is zero, the energy in an inductor carrying a curretn i, is $U = \dfrac{1}{2}Li^2$

23. (a)

When a charge q moves with velocity $\vec{v}$ in a magnetic fields of strength $\vec{B}$, making an angle q, then magnetic Lorentz force,

$F = qvB\sin\theta$

If $\vec{v}$ and $\vec{B}$ are mutually perpendicular, then $\theta = 90°$

$\therefore F = qvB\sin 90° = qvB$

F is perpendicular to both $\vec{v}$ and $\vec{B}$.

Let a time conducting rod PQ is placed on two parallel metallic wires CD and MN in a magnetic field of strength $\vec{B}$. The direction of $\vec{B}$ is perpendicular to the plane of paper, downward represented by (X). Let the rod is moving with velocity $\vec{v}$, perpendicular to is own length, towards the right. Since a metallic conductor contain free electrons, they will move within the metal rod. Charge on each electron $= -e$. $\therefore$ Force experienced by each electron $= f_m = evB$ and will be directed from P to Q.

$\therefore$ The end P of the rod becomes positively charged and Q is negatively charged. So a potential difference is produced across the ends of the conductor. This is the induced e.m.f.

$\therefore$ Electric field produced in the rod $= E = \dfrac{V}{\ell}$

It is directed from P to Q.

The force on a free electron due to this electric field

$F_e = eE$

The direction of this force is from Q to P opposite to the electric field. $\therefore$ The emf produced opposes the force within electrons caused due to Lorentz force by Lenz's law. As the number of electrons at Q becomes more and more, the magnitude of electric force F_e goes on increasing and at a stage F_e become equal and opposite to F_m. Under this condition the potential difference produced across the ends of rod becomes constant.

In this case, $F_e = F_m \Rightarrow eE = evB \Rightarrow E = Bv$

$\therefore$ Potential difference produced, $V = El = Blv$ volt.

$\therefore$ Induced current $= I = \dfrac{V}{R} = \dfrac{Blv}{R}$ Ampere.

(b) The magnetic force $\left[q(\vec{v} \times \vec{B}) \right]$ component of the Lorentz force is responsible for motional electromotive force. When a conductor is moved through a magnetic field, the magnetic force tries to push the free electrons through the wire, and this creates the motional EMF.

24. (a) The line integral of magnetic field $\vec{B}$ around any closed path in vacuum is μ_0 times the total current through the closed path. Mathematically, $\oint \vec{B}.d\vec{\ell} = \mu_0 I$.

Proof:

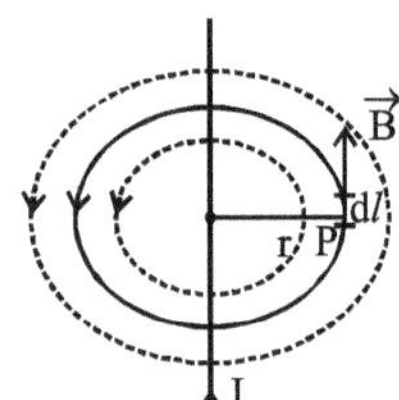

Magnetic field at a point P at a distance r from the conductor

$= B = \dfrac{\mu_0}{4\pi} . \dfrac{2I}{r}$

$\vec{B}$ is directed along the tangent to the circle at every point and is in same direction as $d\ell$ at the point.

$\therefore \quad \oint \vec{B}.d\vec{\ell} = \oint Bd\ell \cos 0° = \oint Bd\ell = \oint \dfrac{\mu_0 I}{2\pi r}.d\ell$

$\dfrac{\mu_0 I}{2\pi r} . \oint d\ell = \dfrac{\mu_0 I}{2\pi r} . 2\pi r = \mu_0 I$

(b) (i) The magnetic field due to a current carrying solenoid is given by, $B_0 = \mu_0 n_i$

where, n = number of turns per unit length

i = current through the solenoid

Now, the magnetic field due to solenoid S_1 will be in the upward direction and the magnetic field due to S_2 will be in the downward direction (by right-hand screw rule).

$B_{net} = B_{s_1} - B_{s_2} \Rightarrow B_{net} = \mu_0 n_1 I - \mu_0 n_2 I = \mu_0 n (n_1 - n_2)$

In the upward direction

(ii) The magnetic field is zero outside a solenoid.

25. (a) **Principle :** The underlying principle in the working of a dynamo is that changing magnetic flux in a conductor induces emf.

Working : A dynamo includes a coil attached to a small turbine fitted with a plastic cap. The coil is placed in a magnetic field. When the plastic cap comes in contact with moving tyres of the bicycle, the coil placed between the poles of a magnet rotates, thus the flux through the coil changes continuously. This induces a current in the coil which is connected to a bulb which lights up. As long as the bicycle is moving, the coil keeps on rotating, and hence, the flux keeps on changing. At a steady rate, we get a steady current and hence a light of steady intensity.

(b) The qualities shown by the teacher are: helpful and responsible as a teacher, and knowledgeable. The qualities shown by Ram are inquisitive and observing.

26. (i) Mutual induction: It is the phenomenon in which a change of current in one coil induces an emf in another coil placed near it. The coil in which the current changes is called the primary coil and the coil in which the emf is induced is called the secondary coil.

(ii) As we know, $e = -M \dfrac{dI}{dt}$

$e = -1.5 \times \dfrac{20-0}{0.5} = -60V$

So, the flux linked with the other coil is given by

$\Delta\phi = e \times \Delta t = -60 \times 0.5 = -30 \, Wb$

27. (a) current, $I = \dfrac{e}{R} = \dfrac{B\ell V}{R}$

Force acting on the arm 'ON'

$F = \ell IB = B\ell \left(\dfrac{B\ell V}{R} \right) = \dfrac{B^2 \ell^2 V}{R}$

And its direction towards left

(b) Power required to move the frame to get a steady emf induced between the arms MN and PO

$P = |F| |V| = \dfrac{B^2 \ell^2 V}{R} . V = \dfrac{B^2 \ell^2 V^2}{R}$

28. Mutual inductance is the property of two coils by the virtue of which each opposes any change in the strength of current flowing through the other by developing an induced emf.

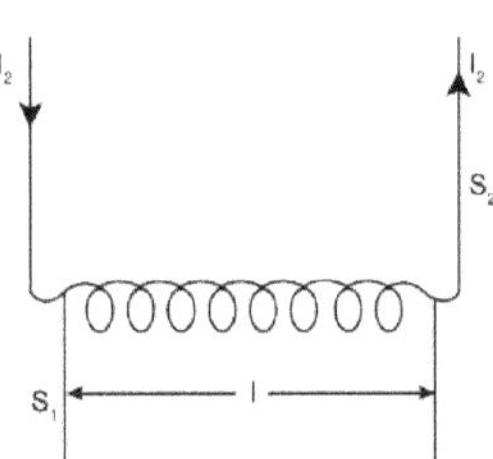

Consider two coils (Primary and secondary) placed very near to each other. Let N_1 and N_2 be the number of turns in the coils and i_1 be the current flowing in the first coil. Let, due to this current, the magnetic flux linked with each turn of the secondary coil be ϕ_2. If N_2 be the number of turns in the secondary coil, then the number of flux-linkages in the coil will be $N_2\phi_2$. This number is proportional to the current i_1 flowing in the primary coil,

i.e. $N_2\phi_2 \propto i_1$ or $N_2\phi_2 = Mi_1$,

where M is a constant called the **'coefficient of mutual induction'** or **'mutual inductance'** between the two coils.

From the above equation, we have $M = N_2\phi_2/i_1$ In this equation, if $i_1 = 1$, then $M = N_2\phi_2$. Hence the coefficient of mutual induction between two coils is equal to the number of magnetic flux-linkage in one coil when a unit current flows in the other.

From Faraday's Law $e = -\dfrac{\Delta\phi}{\Delta t} = -\dfrac{\Delta\left(N_2\phi_2\right)}{\Delta t}$

But $N_2\phi_2 = Mi_1$ $\therefore e = -\dfrac{\Delta\left(Mi_1\right)}{\Delta t} = -\dfrac{M\Delta i_1}{\Delta t}$

If $\dfrac{\Delta i_1}{\Delta t} = 1$ ampere/second then $e = -M$

Hence, the coefficient of mutual induction between two coils is equal to the numerical value of the induced emf in one coil which is produced due to unit rate of change of current in the other.

The unit of the coefficient of mutual induction is 'henry'.

For a solenoid having a primary coil of N_1 turns and a secondary coil of N_2 turns, the coefficient of mutual inductance is given by

$M = \dfrac{\mu_r\mu_0 N_1 N_2 A}{\ell}$ where ℓ is the length of solenoid

and A is the area of one turn of the secondary coil.

OR

Self-inductance of a coil is a property of a coil by virtue of which it opposes any change in self-flux linked with the coil. When a current is passed through a coil, it produces a magnetic field. A flux is linked with the magnetic field produced by the coil. This flux is called self-flux.

Self-flux is directly proportional to the current flowing through the coil. If I is current flowing through a coil and 'ϕ' is the magnetic flux linked with its own magnetic field, then

$\phi \propto I$ or, $\phi = LI$

where L is the proportionality constant and is known as self-inductance.

Expression for the energy stored in an inductor : Consider a simple circuit having a coil, a battery and a key. The coil has a self-inductance L. On pressing the key K, current flows through the circuit. However, self-inductance gives rise to induced current which opposes the growth of current in the circuit.

Thus, to increase the current from zero to its maximum value I_0, some work has to be done.

This work done is stored as the magnetic field of the inductor. Similarly, when the key is opened, the induced emf tends to maintain current in the circuit.

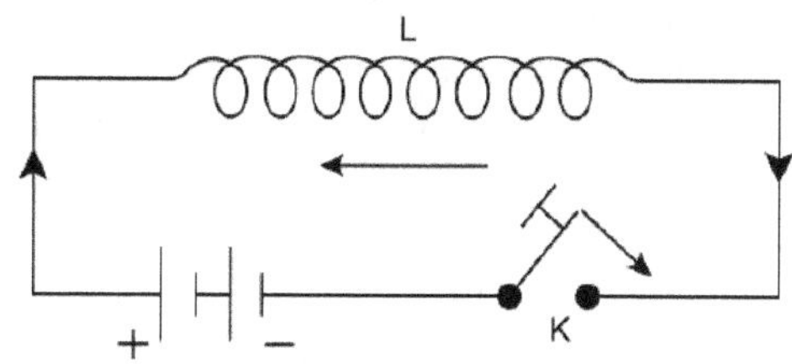

Let, I current flows through the coil of self-inductance L at any instant t when rate of change of current in coil is $\dfrac{dI}{dt}$.

$\therefore$ Induced emf, $E = -L\dfrac{dI}{dt}$

$\therefore$ Work done in establishing the current in small time interval dt is given by

$dW = Pdt = -\varepsilon Idt = -\left(-L\dfrac{dI}{dt}\right)Idt$

$dW = LIdI$

$\therefore$ Total work done in increasing the current from zero to I.

$\therefore$ $W = \int_0^I LIdI = L\int_0^I IdI = L\left[\dfrac{I^2}{2}\right]_0^I = \dfrac{1}{2}L\left(I^2 - 0^2\right)$

$W = \dfrac{1}{2}LI^2$

NCERT Exemplar

1.   **(c)** As we know that, the magnetic flux linked with uniform surface of area A in uniform magnetic field is $\phi = B.A$

The direction of A is perpendicular to the plane of square and square line in x-y plane in a region.

$A = L^2 k$

As given that, $B = B_0\left(2\hat{i} + 3\hat{j} + 4\hat{k}\right)$

So, $\phi = B.A = B_0\left(2\hat{i} + 3\hat{j} + 4\hat{k}\right).L^2\hat{k} = 4B_0 L^2$ Wb

2.   **(b)** The loop can be considered in two planes, Plane of ABCDA lies x-y plane whose area vector

$A_1 = |A|\hat{k}$, $A_1 = L^2\hat{k}$

whereas plane of ADEFA lies in y-z plane whose area vector

$A_2 = |A|\hat{i}$, $A_2 = L^2\hat{i}$.

Then the magnetic flux linked with uniform surface of area A in uniform magnetic field is

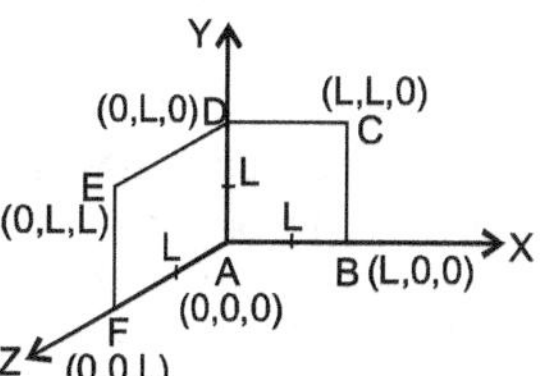

$\phi = B.A$

$A = A_1 + A_2 = \left(L^2\hat{k} + L^2\hat{i}\right)$ and $B = B_0\left(\hat{i} + \hat{k}\right)$

Now, $\phi = B.A = B_0\left(\hat{i} + \hat{k}\right)\cdot\left(L^2\hat{k} + L^2\hat{i}\right) = 2B_0 L^2$ Wb

3. **(b)** Induced current flow only when circuit is complete and there is a variation about circuit this problem is associated with the phenomenon of electromagnetic induction.

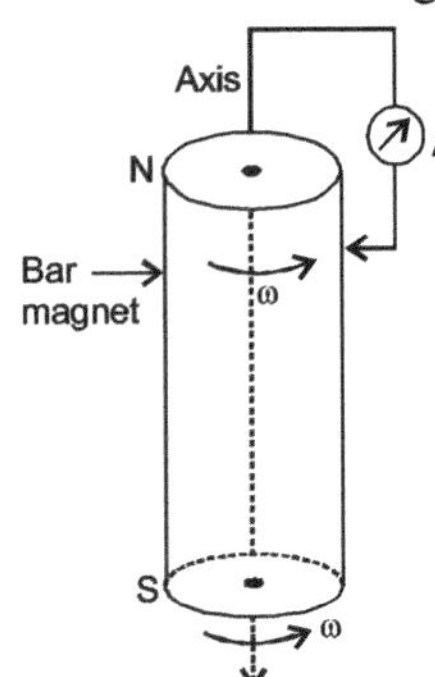

If there is a symmetry in magnetic field of cylindrical bar magnet is rotated about its axis, no change in flux linked with the circuit takes place, consequently no emf induces and hence, no current flows in the ammeter (A).

4. **(d)** When the coil A stops moving the current in B become zero, it possible only if the current in A is constant. If the current in A would be variable, there must be an induced emf (current) in B even if the A stops moving. So there is a constant current in same direction or counter clockwise direction in A as in B by lenz's law.

5. **(a)** By Lenz's law, at (t = 0) the current in B is counter-clockwise and the coil A is considered above to it. The counterclockwise flow of the current in B is equivalent to north pole of magnet and magnetic field lines are emanating upward to coil A.

   When coil A start rotating at t = 0, the current in A is constant along clockwise direction by Lenz's rule. As flux changes across coil A by rotating it near the N-pole formed by flowing current in B, in anticlockwise.

6. **(b)** The self-inductance of a long solenoid of cross-sectional area A and length l, having n turns per unit length, filled the inside of the solenoid with a material of relative permeability is given by

   $$L = \mu_r \mu_0 n^2 A l$$
   $$\therefore \quad n = N/l$$
   $$L = \mu_r \mu_0 \left[\frac{N^2 . A}{l.l} \right] l$$
   $$L = \mu_r \mu_0 [N^2 A/l] \quad \left(L \propto A, L \propto \frac{1}{l} \right)$$

   As μ_r and N are constant here so, to increase L for a coil, area A must be increased and l must be decreased.

7. No part of the wire is moving and so motional e.m.f is zero. The magnet is stationary and hence the magnetic field does not change with time. This means no electromotive force is produced and hence no current will flow in the circuit.

8. No flux was passing through the metal ring initially. When the current is switched on, flux passes through the ring. According to Lenz's law this increase will be resisted and this can happen if the ring moves away from the solenoid. One can analyse this in more detail (Fig.). If the current in the solenoid is as shown, the flux (downward) increases and this will cause a counterclockwise current (as seen form the top in the ring). As the flow of current is in the

opposite direction to that in the solenoid, they will repel each other and the ring will move upward.

9. As the magnetic flux changes continuously, so the emf changes with time as shown in the figure.

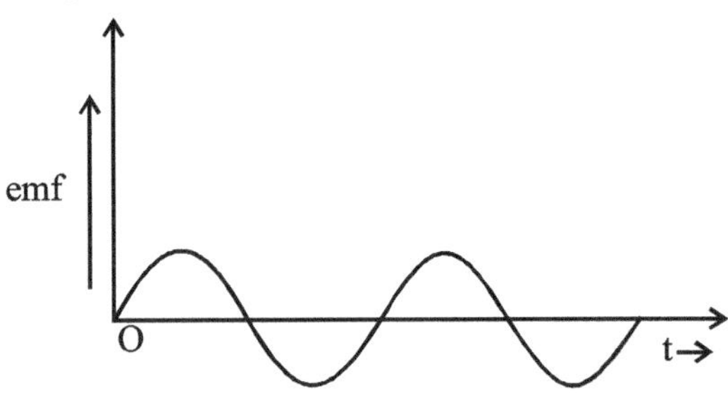

10. The force required to move the rod with a constant velocity is

$$F = \frac{B^2 l^2 v}{R} = \frac{(0.15)^2 \times (0.5)^2 \times 2}{3} \, N = 3.75 \times 10^{-3} \, N$$

11. Flux through the ring

$$\phi = B_o (\pi a^2) \cos \omega t$$
$$\varepsilon = B(\pi a^2) \omega \sin \omega t$$
$$I = B(\pi a^2) \omega \sin \omega t / R$$

Current at

$$t = \frac{\pi}{2\omega} ;$$

y
$\hat{k}$
x
(0,0,0)
(a,0,0)

$$I = \frac{B(\pi a^2) \omega}{R} \text{ along } \hat{j}$$

$$t = \frac{\pi}{\omega} ; I = 0$$

$$t = \frac{3}{2} \frac{\pi}{\omega} ; I = \frac{B(\pi a^2) \omega}{R} \text{ along } -\hat{j}$$

12. Maximum rate of change of current is in AB. So maximum back emf will be obtained between $5s < t < 10s$.

   If $u = L \, 1/5 \left(\text{for } t = 3s, \frac{dI}{dt} = 1/5 \right) (L \text{ is a constant})$

   For $5s < t < 10s$ $u_1 = -L \frac{3}{5} = -\frac{3}{5} L = -3e$

   Thus at $t = 7s$, $u_1 = -3e$

   For $10s < t < 30s$

   $$u_2 = L \frac{2}{20} = \frac{L}{10} = \frac{1}{2} e$$

   For $t > 30s$ $u_2 = 0$

13. At the position MNQ of ring, the ring moves out of the magnetic field $\vec{B}$ with the speed v, the magnetic flux through the ring decreases and hence, a potential difference e = (2R) v B is developed across the ring. The induced current will be clockwise, according to the Lenz's law, which means that Q will be at higher potential and M will be at lower potential.

14. Firstly, the square loop abcda enters more and more into the magnetic field between the pole pieces with the speed v, the magnetic flux through it increases and hence, the emf e induced in it will be constant and negative, i.e.,

   $$e = -B v l$$

Secondly, the entire loop remains well in the magnetic field for some time while moving across it, the magnetic flux remains constant and hence, the emf e induced in it will be zero. Thirdly, the loop comes out more and more from the magnetic field, the magnetic flux through it decreases and hence, the emf e induced in it will be constant and positive, i.e., $e = +Bvl$

Then, the graph for e will be, as shown below.

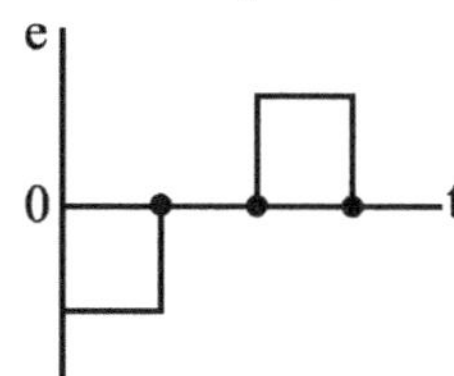

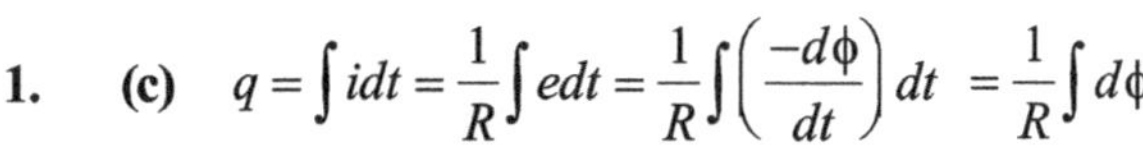

Objective Practice Exercise

1. **(c)** $q = \int i\,dt = \frac{1}{R}\int e\,dt = \frac{1}{R}\int\left(\frac{-d\phi}{dt}\right)dt = \frac{1}{R}\int d\phi$

   (taking only magnitude of e)

   Hence, total charge induced in the conducting loop depends upon the total change in magnetic flux.

2. **(b)** Induced of e.m.f., $e = -\dfrac{d\phi}{dt}$

3. **(b)**   4. **(c)**   5. **(c)**

6. **(d)** $e = -\dfrac{d\phi}{dt} = -2x\,t = 9$

   $\therefore\ -2x \times 3 = 9\quad \therefore\ x = -1.5\ \text{Wb/s}^2$ [At t = 3]

7. **(d)** Given : $\phi = 4t^2 + 2t + 1$ wb

   $\therefore\quad \dfrac{d\phi}{dt} = \dfrac{d}{dt}(4t^2 + 2t + 1) = 8t + 2 = |\varepsilon|$

   $I = \dfrac{|\varepsilon|}{R} = \dfrac{8t+2}{10\Omega} = \dfrac{8t+2}{10}A = 1A$ At t = 1 s

8. **(a)** $e = \dfrac{d\phi}{dt} = \dfrac{d}{dt}(NBA) = NA\dfrac{dB}{dt} = 0.5\,V$

9. **(b)** $e = \dfrac{-(\phi_2 - \phi_1)}{t} = \dfrac{-(0 - NBA)}{t} = \dfrac{NBA}{t}$

   $t = \dfrac{NBA}{e} = \dfrac{50 \times 2 \times 10^{-2} \times 10^{-2}}{0.1} = 0.1\,s$

10. **(a)** $\xi = \dfrac{W}{Q} \Rightarrow V = \dfrac{W}{Q} \Rightarrow W = QV$

11. **(c)**   12. **(a)**

13. **(a)** **Given:** No. of turns $N = 1000$

   Face area, $A = 4\,\text{cm}^2 = 4 \times 10^{-4}\,\text{m}^2$

   Change in magnetic field,
   $\Delta B = 10^{-2}\,\text{wbm}^{-2}$

   Time taken, $t = 0.01\,s = 10^{-2}$ sec

   Emf induced in the coil $e = ?$

   Applying formula,

   Induced emf, $e = \dfrac{-d\phi}{dt} = N\left(\dfrac{\Delta B}{\Delta t}\right)A\cos\theta = 400\,mV$

14. **(c)** $i = \dfrac{e}{R} = \dfrac{\dfrac{nAdB}{dt}}{R} = \dfrac{20 \times (25 \times 10^{-4}) \times 1000}{100} = 0.5A$

15. **(b)** Given : $A = 4\,\text{m}^2$, $e = 0.32$ V, $dt = 0.5$ sec.

   B_1 is the initial magnetic induction and when it is reduced to 20% $B_2 = 0.2\,B_1$

   $e = \dfrac{d\phi}{dt} = \dfrac{A(B_1 - B_2)}{\Delta t}$ or $0.32 = \dfrac{4(B_1 - 0.2\,B_1)}{0.5}$

   Magnetic induction $B_1 = \dfrac{0.16}{3.2} = 0.05\ \text{Wb/m}^2$

16. **(c)** If the current increases with time in loop A, then magnetic flux in B will increase. According to Lenz's law, loop -B is repelled by loop -A because current in loop B will be antiparallel to that in A.

17. **(c)** $\dfrac{\Delta\phi}{\Delta t} = \varepsilon = iR \Rightarrow \Delta\phi = (i\Delta t)R = QR \Rightarrow Q = \dfrac{\Delta\phi}{R}$

18. **(b)** Induced e.m.f. in the ring opposes the motion of the magnet.

19. **(d)** When the coils P and Q are brought nearer, the magnetic flux linked with each coil will increase and the induced current will induces in the direction opposite to original current according to Lenz, law and hence current in both P and Q decreases.

20. **(b)** $n = \dfrac{N}{\ell} = \dfrac{2000}{0.3} = \dfrac{20000}{3}$; $\xi = \dfrac{d}{dt}(NBA) = NA\dfrac{dB}{dt}$

   Since $B = \mu_0 nI \Rightarrow \xi = (\mu NAn)\dfrac{dt}{dt} \Rightarrow \xi = 0.024\,V$

21. **(d)** According to Lenz's law, when switch is closed, the flux in the loop increases out of plane of paper, so induced current will be clockwise.

22. **(a)** Here, $B = \dfrac{1}{\pi}$ (Wb/m^2)

   $\theta = 60°$

   Area normal to the plane of the disc

   $= \pi r^2 \cos 60° = \dfrac{\pi r^2}{2}$

   Flux = $B \times$ normal area

   $= \dfrac{0.2 \times 0.2}{2} = 0.02\,\text{Wb}$

23. **(c)** $A = 200\,\text{cm}^2 = 200 \times 10^{-4}\,\text{m}^2$; $N = 100$; $R = 2\Omega$

   Initial magnetic flux linked with the coil is
   $\phi_i = BA\cos\theta = 0.1 \times 200 \times 10^{-4} \times \cos 0° = 2 \times 10^{-3}$ Wb

   Final magnetic flux linked with the coil is $\phi_f = 0$

   $\varepsilon = -\dfrac{N\Delta\phi}{\Delta t} = \dfrac{-N(\phi_f - \phi_i)}{\Delta t} = \dfrac{-100(0 - 2 \times 10^{-3})}{1} = 0.2V$

   Induced current $I = \dfrac{\varepsilon}{R} = \dfrac{0.2V}{2\Omega} = 0.1A$

   Induced charge $q = It = 0.1 \times 1 = 0.1$ C

24. **(c)** Self inductance, $L = \mu_r\mu_0 N^2 Al$

25. **(d)** Self inductance of a solenoid $= \dfrac{\mu n^2 A}{\ell}$

   So, self induction $\propto n^2$
   So, inductance becomes 4 times when n is doubled.

26. **(d)** The self inductance of a long solenoid is given by

   $L = \mu_r\mu_0 n^2 Al$

Self inductance of a long solenoid is independent of the current flowing through it.

27. **(c)** $E = \dfrac{1}{2}Li^2 = \dfrac{1}{2} \times (100 \times 10^{-3}) \times 1^2 = 0.05\,J$

28. **(c)** According to faraday law of electro magnetic induction,

$$e = \left| L\frac{dI}{dt} \right| = 0.4 \times \frac{500}{1} = 200\,\text{volts.}$$

29. **(a)** Given : $e = 10\,V$ and $\dfrac{dI}{dt} = \dfrac{1 - 0.5}{0.2} = \dfrac{0.5}{0.2} = 2.5\,A/s$

Self inductance of coil $L = \dfrac{e}{dI/dt} = \dfrac{10}{2.5} = 4\,H$

30. **(c)** $L = 2mH,\ i = t^2 e^{-t}$

$$E = -L\frac{di}{dt} = -L[-t^2 e^{-t} + 2te^{-t}]$$

when $E = 0$,

$-e^{-t} t^2 + 2te^{-t} = 0$ or, $2t\,e^{-t} = e^{-t} t^2$ $\Rightarrow t = 2$ sec.

31. **(a)** $e = L\dfrac{di}{dt}$

Given that $L = 40 \times 10^{-3}\,H$,

di $= 11\,A - 1\,A = 10\,A$

and dt $= 4 \times 10^{-3}\,s$

$$\therefore \quad e = 40 \times 10^{-3} \times \left(\frac{10}{4 \times 10^{-3}} \right) = 100V$$

32. **(d)** $\Delta I = 6A,\ \Delta t = 0.3s,\ E = 30\,V$

$$E = L\frac{dI}{dt} \quad \therefore\ L = \frac{30 \times 0.3}{6} = 1.5\,H.$$

33. **(a)** According to Faraday's law of electro-magnetic inductions,

$$e = \left| L\frac{dI}{dt} \right| \Rightarrow 2 = L\,\frac{(8-2)}{3 \times 10^{-2}} \Rightarrow L = 10\,mH$$

34. **(d)** $e = -\dfrac{\Delta\phi}{\Delta t} = \dfrac{-\Delta(LI)}{\Delta t} = -L\dfrac{\Delta I}{\Delta t} \quad \therefore\ |e| = L\dfrac{\Delta I}{\Delta t}$

$$\Rightarrow 8 = L \times \frac{4}{0.05} \quad \Rightarrow L = \frac{8 \times 0.05}{4} = 0.1H$$

35. **(b)** Mutual inductance depends on the relative position and orientation of the two coils.

36. **(b)** Induction furnace is based on the heating effect of eddy current. The furnace is used to prepare alloys by melting the constituent metals. It produces very high temperature.

37. **(b)** $e \propto \omega$

38. **(a)** The back e.m.f. in a motor is induced e.m.f., which is maximum, when speed of rotation of the coil is maximum.

39. **(a)**   **40. (b)**

Chapter Test

1. **(d)** $\varphi = BA\cos\theta = 2.0 \times 0.5 \times \cos 60°$

$$= \frac{2.0 \times 0.5}{2} = 0.5\ \text{weber.}$$

2. **(b)** Length of conductor $(l) = 0.4\,m$; Speed $(v) = 7\,m/s$ and magnetic field $(B) = 0.9\,Wb/m^2$. Induced e.m.f. $(\varepsilon) = Blv\cos\theta = 0.9 \times 0.4 \times 7 \times \cos 0° = 2.52\,V$.

3. **(b)**

4. **(d)** $e = -\dfrac{d\phi}{dt} = -\dfrac{d(N\vec{B}.\vec{A})}{dt}$

$$= -N\frac{d}{dt}(BA\cos\omega t) = NBA\omega\sin\omega t \ \Rightarrow e_{max} = NBA\omega$$

5. **(d)**

6. **(c)** In purely resistive circuit, the current and emf are in the same phase.

7. **(a)** If a wire, 1 meter in length, moves perpendicular to a magnetic field of B weber/meter^2 with a velocity of v meter/second, then the e.m.f. induced in the wire is given by $V = B\,v\ell$ volt.

Here, $B = 0.30 \times 10^{-4}$ weber/meter^2,

$v = 5.0$ meter/second and $\ell = 10$ meter.

$\therefore\ B = 0.30 \times 10^{-4} \times 5.0 \times 10 = 0.0015$ volt.

8. **(a)** $\vec{\ell}, \vec{v},$ and $\vec{B}$ are coplanar.

9. **(b)** Till front side of the loop moves into the field the emf induced $e = Bvl$ across it. When rear side comes in the field, the emf is induced across it.

10. **(b)** The e.m.f. induced is directly proportional to rate at which flux is intercepted which in turn varies directly as the speed of rotation of the generator.

11. **(c)** E.m.f. will remain same because change in area per unit time will be same in both cases.

12. No, because magnetic flux $\phi = NBA = $ constant

$$e = \frac{d\phi}{dt} = 0 \Rightarrow i = 0$$

13. The e.m.f induced across the spokes are parallel.

$\therefore$ The number of spokes does not affect the net e.m.f.

14. Faraday's laws of electromagnetic induction:

1st law: Whenever there is a change in magnetic flux associated with a coil, an e.m.f is induced in the coil. It lasts as long as the change in magnetic flux continues.

2nd law: The magnitude of induced e.m.f is directly proportional to the rate of change of magnetic flux and directed opposite to the change of magnetic flux,

$$e = -\frac{d\phi}{dt}$$

15. Eddy currents are induced currents produced in the body of a conductor.

Advantage- The eddy current produced in the non-magnetic metallic core of the coil of a galvanometer brings it back to rest quickly. This is called dead beat galvanometer.

Disadvantage- The heat produced due to eddy current in the soft iron core of a transformer leads to heat loss.

7 | Alternating Current

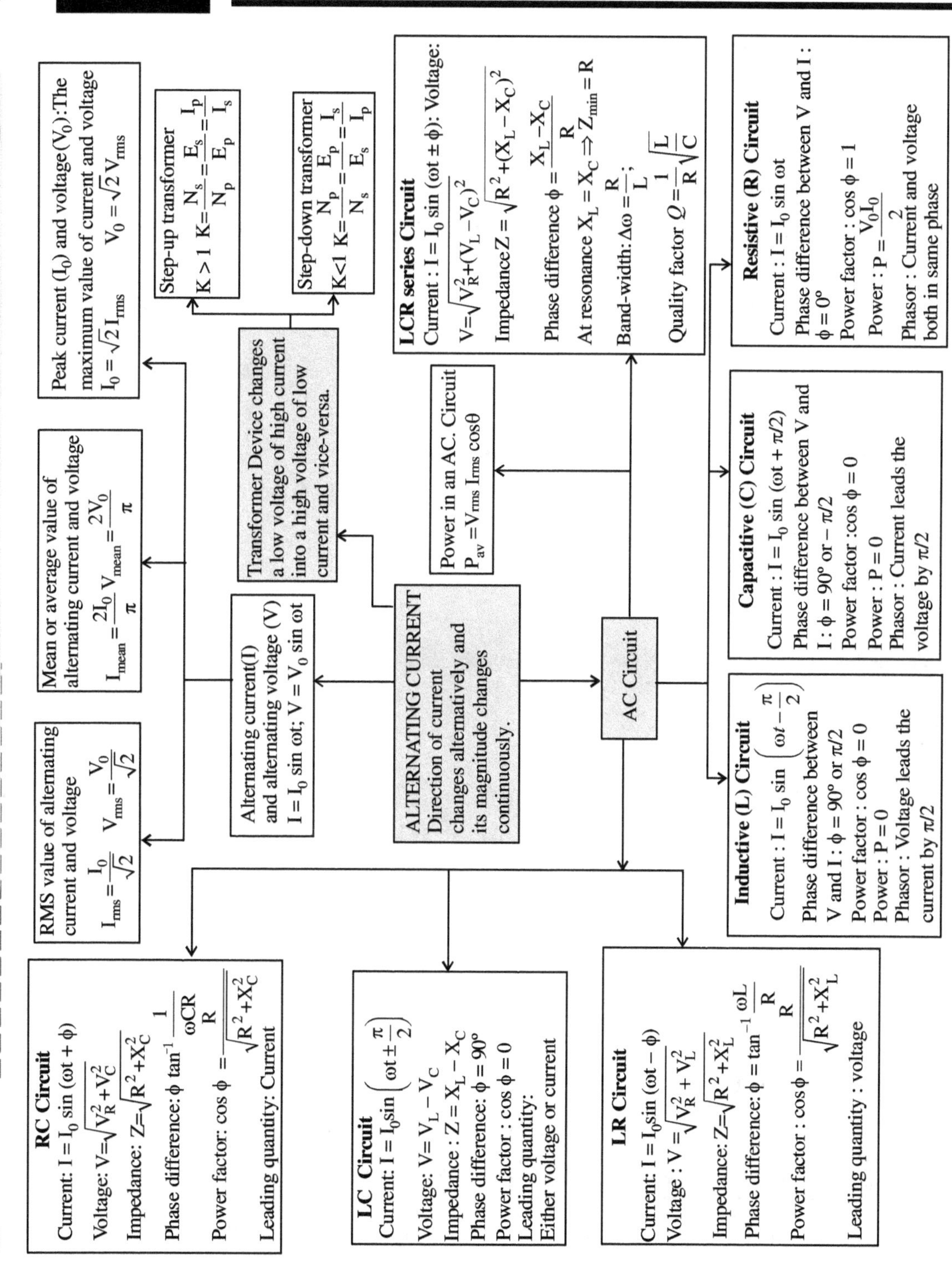

Topic 1	Alternating Current, Average, RMS & Peak Value of  Alternating Current and Alternating Voltage

ALTERNATING CURRENT

Alternating current (A.C.) is the current whose magnitude changes with time and direction reverses periodically.
Instantaneous value of alternating current is given by

$$I = I_0 \sin \omega t \text{ or } I = I_0 \cos \omega t$$

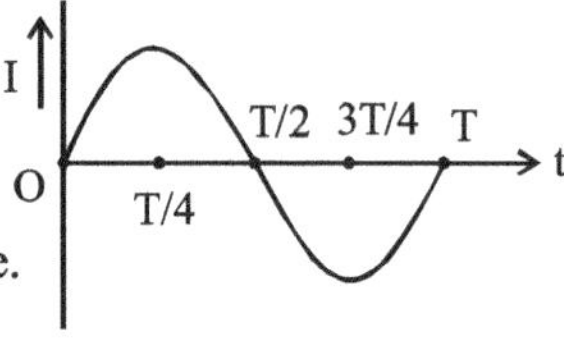

where I_0 = peak or maximum value of A.C. or amplitude of A.C.; I = value of current at an instant t.

$$\omega = \frac{2\pi}{T} = 2\pi v = \text{angular frequency of A.C.}; T = \text{Time period i.e. time to complete one full cycle.}$$

v = frequency of A.C.

Similarly, alternating e.m.f. changes in magnitude continuously with time and reverses its direction periodically.

Instantataneous value of alternating e.m.f. is given by $E = E_0 \sin \omega t$ or $E = E_0 \cos \omega t$

THE AVERAGE, RMS AND PEAK VALUE OF ALTERNATING CURRENT AND ALTERNATING VOLTAGE

Mean or Average Value of an Alternating Current and Voltage

It is defined as that value of steady current which would sent same amount of charge through a circuit in the time of half cycle ($\pi/2$) as is sent by the a.c. through the same circuit in the same time.

$$I_{mean} = \frac{2I_0}{\pi}, E_{mean} = \frac{2E_0}{\pi}$$

Here, I_0 and E_0 are Peak current and voltage.

Root Mean Square or Effective Value of an Alternating Current and Voltage

It is the steady current which when passed through a given resistor for a certain time, shall produce the same heat as the given A.C. shall do when passed for the same time.

$$I_{rms} = \frac{I_0}{\sqrt{2}} = 0.707 I_0, E_{rms} = \frac{E_0}{\sqrt{2}} = 0.707 E_0$$

Illustration 1 :

If a domestic appliance draws 2.5 A from a 220-V, 60- Hz power supply, find

(a) the average current
(b) the average of the square of the current
(c) the current amplitude
(d) the supply voltage amplitude.

Sol. (a) The average of sinusoidal AC values over any whole number of cycles is zero.

(b) RMS value of current $= I_{rms} = 2.5$ A $\quad\quad \therefore (I_{av})^2 = (I_{rms})^2 = 6.25 A^2$

(c) $I_{rms} = \dfrac{I_m}{\sqrt{2}}$

$\therefore$ Current amplitude $= \sqrt{2} I_{rms} = \sqrt{2}(2.5 A) = 3.5 A$

(d) $V_{rms} = 220V = \dfrac{V_m}{\sqrt{2}}$

$\therefore$ Supply voltage amplitude $V_m = \sqrt{2}(V_{rms}) = \sqrt{2}(220V) = 311$ V.

Illustration 2 :

Find out the rms value of the alternating emf E = 8 sin ωt + 6 sin 2 ωt volt.

Sol. The mean square value of given e.m.f. E (i.e., $\bar{E}^2$) over a complete cycle is calculated as follows:

$$\bar{E}^2 = \frac{\int_0^T E^2 dt}{\int_0^T dt} = \frac{\int_0^T (8\sin \omega t + 6\sin 2\omega t)^2 dt}{\int_0^T dt} = \frac{\int_0^T (64\sin^2 \omega t + 36\sin^2 2\omega t + 96\sin \omega t \sin 2\omega t) dt}{\int_0^T dt}$$

$$= \overline{64\sin^2 \omega t} + \overline{36\sin^2 2\omega t} + \overline{96 \sin \omega t \sin 2\omega t} \text{ where bars indicate the average values over a complete cycle.}$$

Now, $\overline{\sin^2 \omega t} = \dfrac{\int_0^T \sin^2 \omega t \, dt}{\int_0^T dt} = \dfrac{1}{2}$

Similarly, $\overline{\sin^2 2\omega t} = \dfrac{\int_0^T \sin^2 2\omega t \, dt}{\int_0^T dt} = \dfrac{1}{2}$ and $\overline{\sin \omega t \sin 2\omega t} = \dfrac{\int_0^T \sin \omega t \sin 2\omega t \, dt}{\int_0^T dt} = 0$

$\therefore \quad \overline{E}^2 = 64 \times (1/2) + 36 \times (1/2) + 96 \times 0 = 50; \qquad \therefore \quad E_{rms} = \sqrt{\overline{E}^2} = \sqrt{50} = 7.07 \text{volt.}$

Practice Exercise-1

Multiple Choice Questions

1. The average value of alternating current for one complete cycle is
   (a) zero
   (b) 1
   (c) $\sqrt{2}$
   (d) None of these

2. The ratio of mean value over half cycle to r.m.s. value of A.C. is
   (a) $2 : \pi$
   (b) $2\sqrt{2} : \pi$
   (c) $\sqrt{2} : \pi$
   (d) $\sqrt{2} : 1$

3. The instantaneous voltage through a device of impedance $20\,\Omega$ is $e = 80 \sin 100\,\pi t$. The effective value of the current is
   (a) 3 A
   (b) 2.828 A
   (c) 1.732 A
   (d) 4 A

4. If instantaneous current is given by $i = 4 \cos(\omega t + \phi)$ ampere, then the r.m.s value of current is,
   (a) 4 amperes
   (b) $4\sqrt{2}$ amperes
   (c) $2\sqrt{2}$ amperes
   (d) zero amperes

5. The average value of alternating current for one complete cycle is
   (a) zero
   (b) 1
   (c) $\sqrt{2}$
   (d) None of these

6. The r.m.s. value of potential difference V shown in the figure is

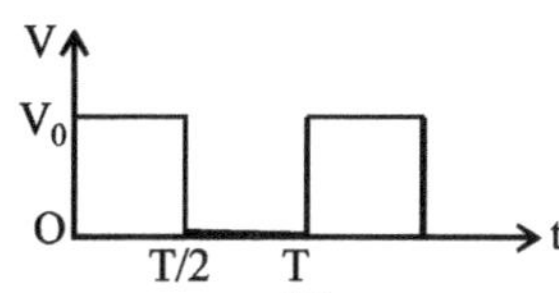

   (a) V_0
   (b) $V_0 / \sqrt{2}$
   (c) $V_0 / 2$
   (d) $V_0 / \sqrt{3}$

Assertion & Reason Question

DIRECTIONS (Q. 7) : *Each of these questions contains an assertion followed by reason. Read them carefully and answer the question on the basis of following options. You have to select the one that best describes the two statements.*

(a) If both Assertion and Reason are correct and the Reason is a correct explanation of the Assertion.

(b) If both Assertion and Reason are correct but Reason is not a correct explanation of the Assertion.

(c) If the Assertion is correct but Reason is incorrect.

(d) If the Assertion is incorrect but the Reason is correct.

7. **Assertion :** 200V AC is more dangerous than 200V D.C.

   Reason : For 200V AC, the corresponding peak value is $200\sqrt{2}$. But for 200V DC, peak value is 200V only.

Case / Passage Based Questions

Mean value of alternating current is defined as that value of steady current which would sent same amount of charge through a circuit in the time of half cycle ($\pi/2$) as is sent by the a.c. through the same circuit in the same time.

$$I_{mean} = \frac{2I_0}{\pi}, \; E_{mean} = \frac{2E_0}{\pi}$$

Here, I_0 and E_0 are Peak current and voltage.

R.M.S value of alternating current is the steady current which when passed through a given resistor for a certain time, shall produce the same heat as the given A.C. shall do when passed for the same time.

$$I_{rms} = \frac{I_0}{\sqrt{2}} = 0.707 I_0, \; E_{rms} = \frac{E_0}{\sqrt{2}} = 0.707 E_0$$

8. The alternating current of equivalent value of $\dfrac{I_0}{\sqrt{2}}$ is
   (a) peak current
   (b) r.m.s. current
   (c) D.C. current
   (d) all of these

9. The r.m.s value of an a.c. of 50 Hz is 10 amp. The time taken by the alternating current in reaching from zero to maximum value and the peak value of current will be
   (a) 2×10^{-2} sec and 14.14 amp
   (b) 1×10^{-2} sec and 7.07 amp
   (c) 5×10^{-3} sec and 7.07 amp
   (d) 5×10^{-3} sec and 14.14 amp

10. The instantaneous voltage through a device of impedance $20\,\Omega$ is $e = 80 \sin 100\,\pi t$. The effective value of the current is
    (a) 3 A
    (b) 2.828 A
    (c) 1.732 A
    (d) 4 A

11. The voltage of an ac supply varies with time (t) as $V = 120 \sin 100\,\pi t \cos 100\,\pi t$. The maximum voltage and frequency respectively are
    (a) 120 volt, 100 Hz
    (b) $\dfrac{120}{\sqrt{2}}$ volt, 100 Hz
    (c) 60 volt, 200 Hz
    (d) 60 volt, 100 Hz

12. The equation of alternating current is :

$I = 50\sqrt{2} \sin 400\pi t$ amp. Then the frequency and root mean square of current are respectively

(a) $200\,Hz$, $50\,amp$ (b) $400\pi\,Hz$, $50\sqrt{2}\,amp$

(c) $200\,Hz$, $50\sqrt{2}\,amp$ (d) $50\,Hz$, $200\,amp$

Very Short Answer Questions

13. The instantaneous current in an inducting circuit is $I = 14\cos 300\,t$ ampere. What is the value of average current over half cycle?

14. What is the frequency of domestic alternating current supply ? How many times does it become zero in one second?

Short Answer Questions

15. Derive an expression for the mean or average value of alternating current. What is the mean value of a.c. over a complete cycle?

16. Derive an expression for the root mean square value (R.M.S.) of an alternating current.

17. The instantaneous voltage from an a.c. source is given by $V = 300 \sin 314\,t$. What is the rms value of the voltage?

18. Explain why an ordinary moving coil ammeter used for d.c. cannot be used to measure a.c. ?

19. A sinusoidal voltage $V = 200 \sin 314\,t$ is applied to a resistor of $10\,\Omega$ resistance. Calculate

(i) rms value of voltage, (ii) rms value of current (iii) power dissipated as heat in watt.

Topic 2 — Phasor Diagram, Reactance & Impedance, A.C. through Resistor, Inductor & Capacitor, Series LR and RC Circuit, LCR Series Circuit, Resonance for Series Resonant Circuit, Power in an A.C. Circuit

REPRESENTATION OF AC CURRENT AND VOLTAGE BY ROTATING VECTORS – PHASOR DIAGRAM

In order to show phase relationship between voltage and current in an ac circuit, we use *phasors*. The analysis of an ac circuit is facilitated by the use of a phasor diagram. A phasor is a vector which rotates about the origin with angular speed ω, as shown in Fig. The vertical components of phasors V and I represent the sinusoidally varying quantities v and i. The magnitudes of phasors V and I represent the amplitudes or the peak values v_m and i_m of these oscillating quantities. From Fig. (a) we see that phasors V and I for the case of a resistor are in the same direction. This is so for all times. This means that the phase angle between the voltage and the current is zero.

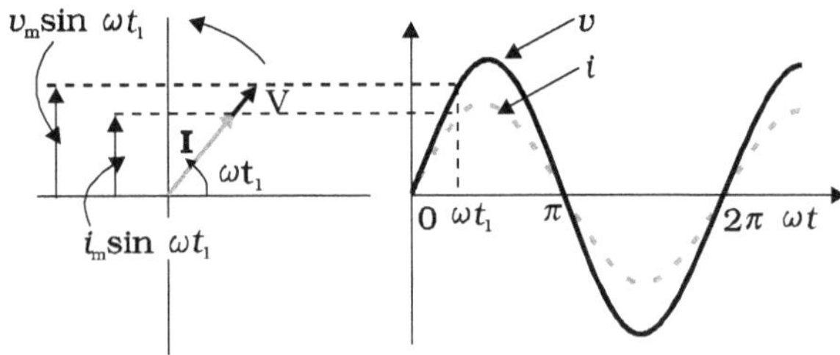

(a) A phasor diagram   (b) Graph of v and i versus ωt

REACTANCE AND IMPEDANCE

Reactance

Reactance is the opposition offered by inductor or capacitor or both to the flow of A.C. through it.

(i) **Inductive reactance** – Opposition offered by inductive circuit.

$X_L = \omega L = 2\pi f L$

(ii) **Capacitive reactance** – Opposition offered by capacitive circuit.

$$X_c = \frac{1}{\omega c} = \frac{1}{2\pi f c}$$

Impedance (Z)

Impedance is the opposition offered by A.C. circuits to the flow of A.C. through it.

A.C. THROUGH RESISTOR, INDUCTOR & CAPACITOR

A.C. Voltage Applied to a Resistor

Let the applied voltage across a pure resistor (R) is given by $V = V_0 \sin \omega t$.

The current through the resistor is given by $I = I_0 \sin \omega t$ or, $I = \dfrac{E}{R} = \dfrac{E_0 \sin \omega t}{R}$

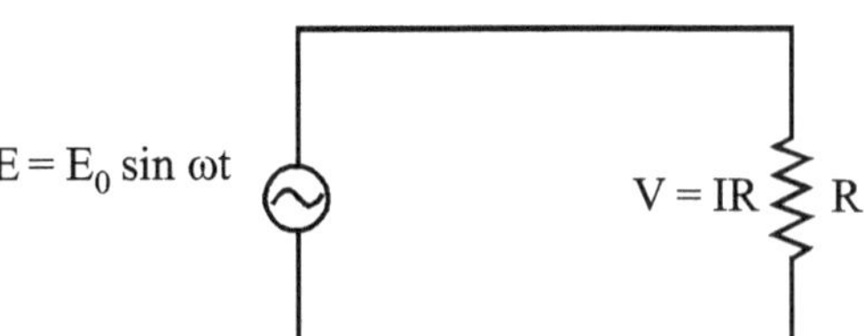

Thus, the voltage and current are in phase with each other.

A phasor diagram for the AC voltage applied to a resistor

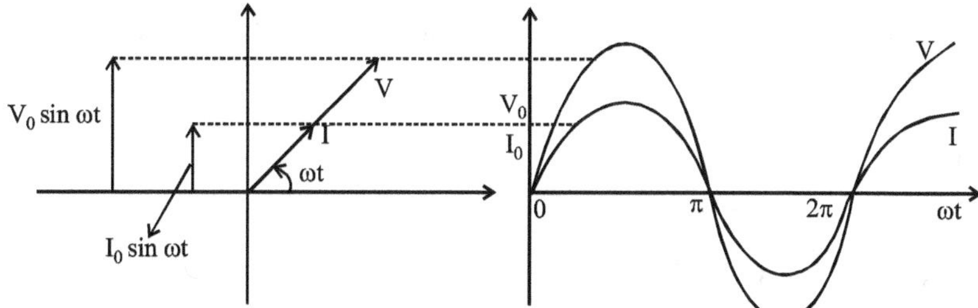

A.C. Voltage Applied to an Inductor

Let the voltage across a pure inductance L is given by, $V = V_0 \sin \omega t$
The current through the inductor is given by $I = I_0 \sin(\omega t - \pi/2)$
Thus, the current in an inductor lags the voltage by $\pi/2$

or, the alternating emf leads the a.c. by a phase angle of $\dfrac{\pi}{2}$.

A phasor diagram for the AC voltage applied to an inductor.

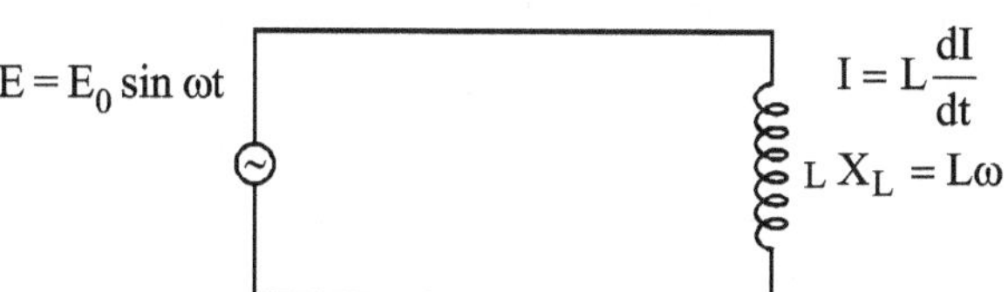

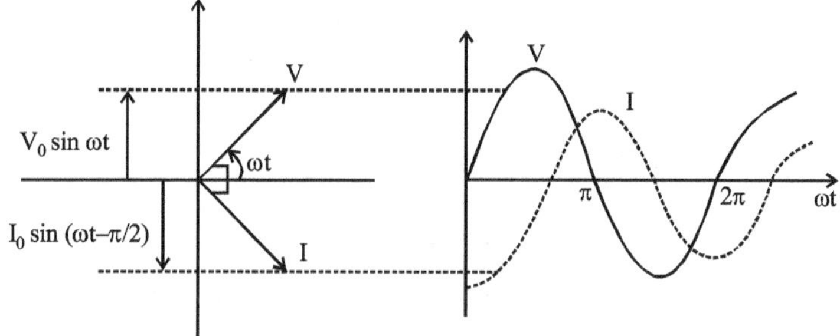

AC Voltage Applied to a Capacitor

Let the applied voltage across a pure capacitor C is given by, $V = V_0 \sin \omega t$

The current through the capacitor is given by, $I = I_0 \sin(\omega t + \pi/2)$

Thus, the current through a capacitor is ahead of voltage by $\pi/2$ or, the alternating emf lags behind the alternating current by a

phase angle of $\dfrac{\pi}{2}$.

A phasor diagram for the AC voltage applied to a capacitor.

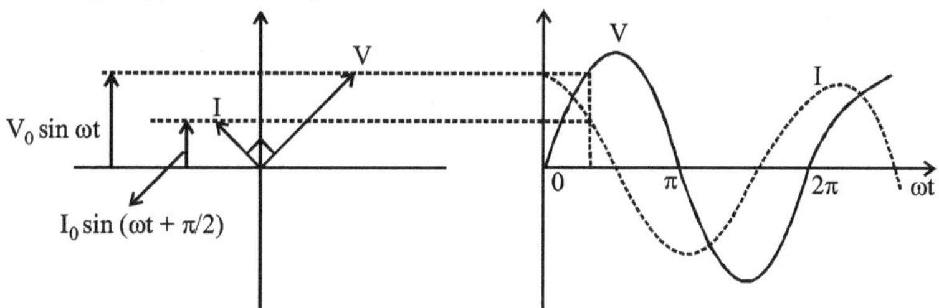

SERIES LR AND RC CIRCUIT

Resistance and Inductance in Series - LR Circuit

In series LR circuit the applied emf E leads the current I or conversely the current I lags behind the emf by a phase angle ϕ

$$\tan\phi = \frac{V_L}{V_R} = \frac{IX_L}{IR} = \frac{X_L}{R} = \frac{\omega L}{R} \qquad \tan\phi = \frac{\omega L}{R} \ \text{ or, } \ \phi = \tan^{-1}\left(\frac{\omega L}{R}\right)$$

In LR circuit the maximum value of current $I_0 = \dfrac{E_0}{\sqrt{R^2 + \omega^2 L^2}}$

Impedance of L.R. circuit, $Z_L = \sqrt{R^2 + \omega^2 L^2} = \sqrt{R^2 + (2\pi f L)^2}$

Resistance and Capacitance in Series – RC Circuit

In RC circuit the applied e.m.f. lags behind the current I or the current I leads the e.m.f. E by a phase angle ϕ given by

$$\tan\phi = \frac{V_C}{R} = \frac{X_C}{R} = \frac{\frac{1}{\omega C}}{R} = \frac{1}{\omega CR} \quad \text{or,} \quad \tan\phi = \frac{X_C}{R} = \frac{1}{\omega CR} \quad \text{or,} \quad \phi = \tan^{-1}\left(\frac{1}{\omega CR}\right)$$

Capacitive impedance $Z_C = \sqrt{R^2 + X_C^2} = \sqrt{R^2 + \left(\frac{1}{\omega C}\right)^2}$

LCR SERIES CIRCUIT (INDUCTANCE, CAPACITANCE AND RESISTANCE IN SERIES)

A circuit containing a series combination of a resistance R, a coil of inductance L and a capacitor of capacitance C, connected with a source of alternating e.m.f. of peak value of E_0, as shown in fig.

Let in series LCR circuit applied alternating emf is $E = E_0 \sin \omega t$.

As L, C and R are joined in series, therefore, current at any instant through the three elements has the same amplitude and phase.

However voltage across each element bears a different phase relationship with the current.

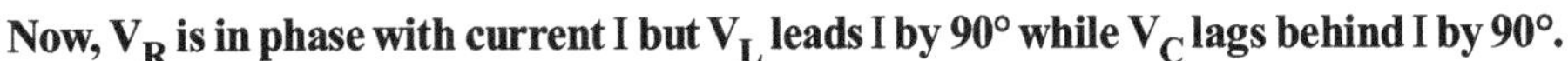

Phasor digram

Let at any instant of time t the current in the circuit is I

Let at this time t the potential differences across L, C, and R

$V_L = I X_L$, $V_C = I X_C$ and $V_R = I R$

Now, V_R is in phase with current I but V_L leads I by 90° while V_C lags behind I by 90°.

The vector $\overrightarrow{OP}$ represents V_R which is in phase with I, the vector $\overrightarrow{OQ}$ represent V_L which leads I by 90° and the vector OS represents V_C which lags behind I by 90°. V_L and V_C are opposite to each other. If $V_L > V_C$ (as shown in figure) then their resultant will be $(V_L - V_C)$ which is represented by OT. Finally, the vector OK represents the resultant of V_R and $(V_L - V_C)$, that is, the resultant of all the three = applied e.m.f.

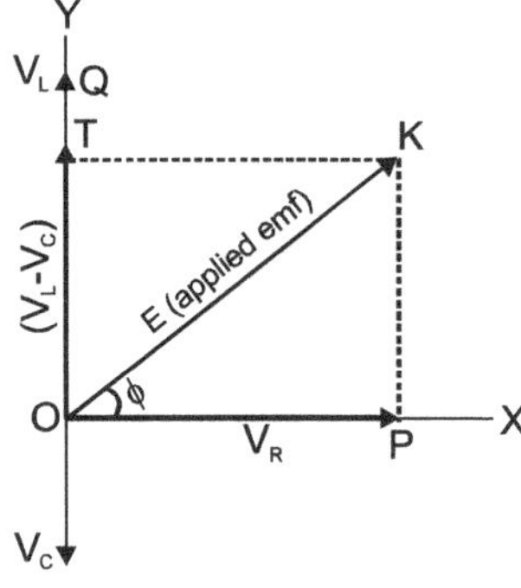

Thus, $E = \sqrt{V_R^2 + (V_L - V_C)^2}$

$$E^2 = V_R^2 + (V_L - V_C)^2 \quad \text{or} \quad E^2 = I^2\,[R^2 + (X_L - X_C)^2] \quad \text{or} \quad I = \frac{E}{\sqrt{R^2 + (X_L - X_C)^2}}$$

It is clear that the term $\sqrt{R^2 + (X_L - X_C)^2}$ represents the "**effective resistance**" of the circuit and is called **impedance Z** of the circuit.

Thus, $Z = \sqrt{R^2 + (X_L - X_C)^2} = \sqrt{R^2 + \left(\omega L - \frac{1}{\omega C}\right)^2}$

The phasor diagram also shows that in LCR circuit the applied e.m.f. leads the current I by a phase angle ϕ

Special Cases:

(a)   When $\omega L > \dfrac{1}{\omega C}$, then $\tan\phi$ is +ve i.e., ϕ is positive. In this case, the alternating emf leads the current I by a phase angle ϕ. The a.c. circuit is then inductance dominated circuit.

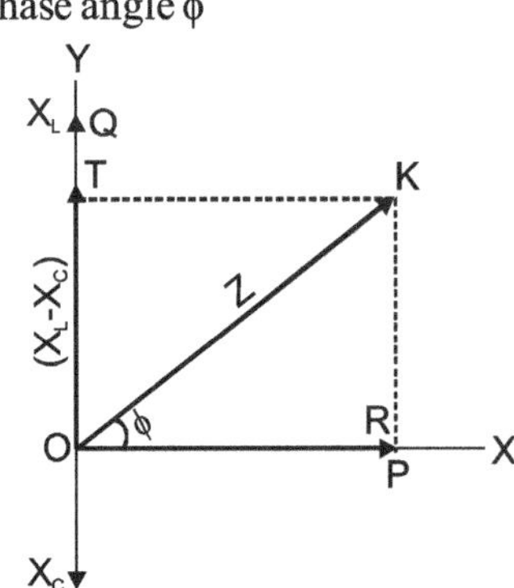

(b)   When $\omega L < \dfrac{1}{\omega C}$, then $\tan\phi$ is –ve i.e., ϕ is negative. In this case, the alternating e.m.f. lags behind the current I by a phase angle ϕ. The a.c. circuit is then capacitance dominated circuit.

(c)   When $\omega L = \dfrac{1}{\omega C}$, then $\tan\phi = 0$ i.e., $\phi = 0$. In the case, the alternating e.m.f. and current I are in phase. The a.c. circuit is then non-inductive.

RESONANCE FOR SERIES LCR CIRCUIT

Series Resonant Circuit

For an A.C. circuit with resistance R, inductance L and capacitance C, in series. The impedance of the circuit

$$Z = \sqrt{R^2 + \left(\omega L - \frac{1}{\omega C}\right)^2} \quad \text{and} \quad I_{rms} = \frac{E_{rms}}{Z} = \frac{E_{rms}}{\sqrt{R^2 + \left(\omega L - \frac{1}{\omega C}\right)^2}}$$

It is clear that both the impedance and current depend on the frequency of the applied e.m.f.

At very low frequency

Inductive reactance $X_L = \omega L$ is negligible but capacitive reactance ($X_C = 1/\omega C$) is very high. As frequency of alternating emf applied to the circuit is increased, X_L goes on increasing and X_C goes on decreasing.

For a particular value of $f = f_r$, $X_L = X_C$ 'inductive reactance' is equal to capacitive reactance.

$X = X_L - X_C = 0$ i.e., 'reactance' of the circuit is zero.

$$Z = \sqrt{R^2 + X^2} = R$$

The impedance of the circuit becomes minimum, $Z_{min} = R$. At frequency f_r the current becomes maximum. This particular frequency f_r at which the impedance of the circuit becomes minimum and therefore current becomes maximum, is called **resonance frequency of the circuit.**

$$I_0 = \frac{E_0}{Z} = \frac{E_0}{R} = \text{max.}, \text{ i.e., current in the circuit is maximum}$$

Before resonance ($f < f_r$) : Current in the circuit lags in phase by the applied voltage ($X_L > X_C$)

After resonance ($f > f_r$) : Current leads in phase by the applied voltage ($X_C > X_L$)

At resonance ($f = f_r$): $\phi = \tan^{-1}\frac{X}{R} = \tan^{-1}\frac{0}{R} = 0$,

i.e., current is in 'phase' with applied voltage. Current through L and C are same but voltage across these two 180° out of phase with respect to each other so that net PD across reactance is zero.

i.e., $V_X = V_L - V_C = 0$ with $V = V_R$

At this frequency f_r or angular frequency ω_r circuit is known as series resonant circuit.

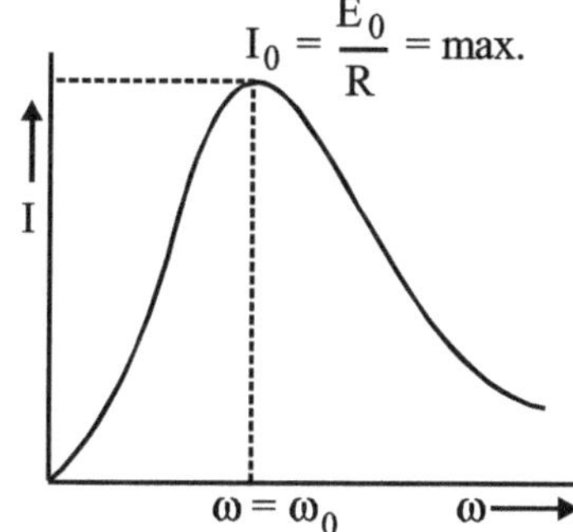

Quality Factor (Q-factor) and Sharpness of Resonance

From the current versus frequency graph, curve is quite flat for a larger value of resistance and becomes more and more sharp as the value of the resistance is decreased.

A slight change in angular frequency produces comparatively a large change in current, when the resistance in the circuit is low than in the case, when the resistance is high.

If the value of resistance in the LCR series circuit is very low; then a large current flows, when the angular frequency of a.c. source is near the resonance frequency ω_r. Such an LCR-series circuit is said to be more sharp or more selective.

The sharpness of a resonance circuit : The sharpness of the circuit is measured by quality-factor (Q-factor).

The Q-factor of series resonant circuit is defined as the ratio of the voltage developed across the inductance or capacitance at resonance to the applied voltage (the voltage applied across R)

$$Q = \frac{\text{Voltage across } L \text{ or } C}{\text{Applied voltage} \left(= \text{voltage across } R\right)} \quad \text{or} \quad Q = \frac{(\omega_0 L) I}{RI} \quad \text{or} \quad Q = \frac{\omega_r L}{R}$$

Hence $Q = \dfrac{1}{\sqrt{LC}} \times \dfrac{L}{R} = \dfrac{1}{R}\sqrt{\dfrac{L}{C}}$ or, $Q = \dfrac{1}{R}\sqrt{\dfrac{L}{C}}$ $\left(\because \omega_0 = \dfrac{1}{\sqrt{LC}}\right)$

At resonance, $I_0 = \dfrac{E_0}{R}$

so, $V_L = I_0 X_L = \dfrac{\omega L}{R} E_0 = Q E_0 \left[\because \dfrac{\omega L}{R} = Q\right]$

At resonance, the voltage drop across inductance (or capacitance) is Q times the applied voltage.

The chief characteristic of series resonant circuit is 'voltage magnification'.

Illustration 3 :

In LR series circuit, a sinusoidal $V = V_0 \sin\omega t$ is applied.

It is given that $L = 35\ mH$, $R = 11\ \Omega$, $V_{rms} = 220\ V$, $\dfrac{\omega}{2\pi} = 50\,Hz$ and $\pi = \dfrac{22}{7}$.

Find the amplitude of current in steady state and obtain the phase difference between the current and the voltage. Also plot the variation of current for one cycle on the given graph.

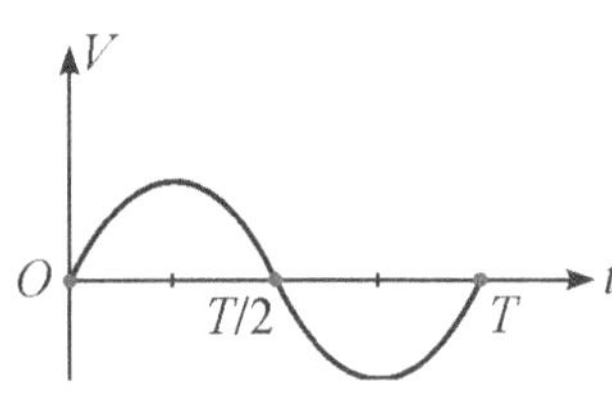

Sol. The impedance of the circuit is given by

$$Z = \sqrt{R^2 + X_L{}^2}$$

where $\qquad X_L = \omega L = 2\pi \times 50 \times 35 \times 10^{-3} = 11\Omega$

$\therefore \qquad Z = \sqrt{11^2 + 11^2} = 11\sqrt{2}\ \Omega$

Variation of V and i with time

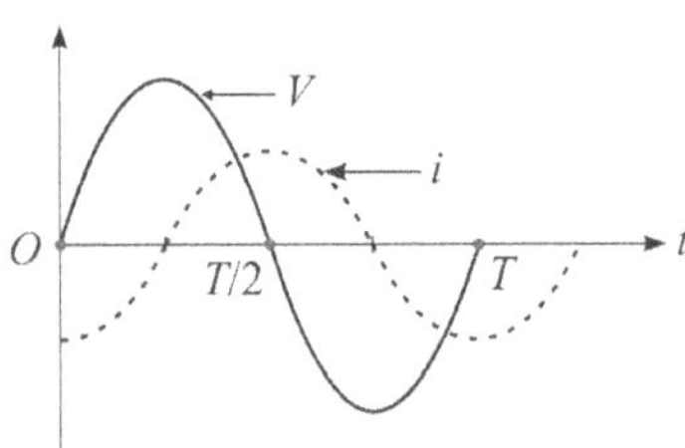

Voltage amplitude $V_0 = \sqrt{2}\ V_{rms} = \sqrt{2} \times 220\ V$.

Current amplitude $i_0 = \dfrac{V_0}{Z} = \dfrac{\sqrt{2} \times 220}{11\sqrt{2}} = 20\ A$

If ϕ is the phase between V and i, then

$\tan\phi = \dfrac{\omega L}{R} = \dfrac{11}{11} = 1 \qquad \therefore\ \phi = \dfrac{\pi}{4}\ rad.$

Thus we can write $\quad V = 220\sqrt{2}\ \sin\omega t$ and $i = 20\sin\left(\omega t - \dfrac{\pi}{4}\right)$

Illustration 4 :

A series circuit contains a resistance of 4Ω, an inductance of $0.5\ H$ and a variable capacitor across a $100\ V$, $50\ Hz$ supply. Find

(a)   the capacitance for getting resonance,

(b)   p.d. across inductance and capacitance

(c)   the Q-factor of the series circuit.

Sol. (a) For resonance $X_L = X_C$ or $\omega L = \dfrac{1}{\omega C}$ $\quad \therefore\ C = \dfrac{1}{\omega^2 L} = \dfrac{1}{(2\pi f)^2 L} = \dfrac{1}{(2 \times \pi \times 50)^2 \times 0.5} = 20.3 \times 10^{-6}\ F$

(b) Current at resonance $= \dfrac{100}{4} = 25\ A$

P.d. across inductor or capacitor $V_L = V_C = iX_L = 25\,(2\pi \times 50 \times 0.5) = 3925\ V$

(c) Q-factor $= \dfrac{\omega_0 L}{R} = \dfrac{(2\pi \times 50) \times 0.5}{4} = 39.25$

Illustration 5 :

A box contains L, C and R. When 250 dc is applied to the terminals of the box, a current of 1.0 A flows in the circuit. When an ac source of 250 V rms at 2250 rad/s is connected, a current of 1.25 A rms flows. It is observed that the current rises with frequency and becomes maximum at 4500 rad/s. Find the values of L, C and R.

Sol. When dc is used in the circuit, only resistor remain effective

$\therefore \qquad R = \dfrac{V}{i} = \dfrac{250}{1} = 250\ \Omega$ $\hspace{4cm}$ ...(i)

When dc is used, there is current in the circuit it means capacitor must not be in series. It may be in parallel to resistor together with inductor.

When ac source is used in the circuit, all the circuit element remain effective.

$\therefore \qquad Z = \dfrac{V}{i} = \dfrac{250}{1.25} = 200\ \Omega$ or $\dfrac{1}{R^2} + \dfrac{1}{\left(\omega L - \dfrac{1}{\omega C}\right)^2} = \dfrac{1}{Z^2} = \dfrac{1}{200^2}$ $\hspace{2cm}$ ...(ii)

With increase of frequency, current increases and becomes maximum at $\omega = 4500$ rad/s.
It means Z must be minimum. It will when

$$\omega L - \frac{1}{\omega C} = 0 \text{ or } \omega^2 = \frac{1}{LC} \quad \text{or} \quad LC = \frac{1}{\omega^2} = \frac{1}{(4500)^2} \qquad \text{...(iii)}$$

After solving equations (i), (ii) and (iii), we get $L = \frac{4}{81}H$ and $C = 1\,\mu F$

POWER IN AN A.C. CIRCUIT

Power in D.C. circuits P = voltage E × current I.

If current is measured in ampere and voltage in volt, the power is measured in watt.

The instantaneous power P of an a.c. circuit :

The instantaneous power P = Instantaneous e.m.f. E × instantaneous current I

Let the instantaneous alternating e.m.f. $E = E_0 \sin \omega t$ and the instantaneous current in an a.c. circuit $I = I_0 \sin(\omega t \pm \phi)$

Instantaneous power in the circuit

$$P = EI = E_0 \sin \omega t . I_0 \sin(\omega t \pm \phi) = E_0 I_0 (\sin \omega t \sin \omega t \cos \phi \pm \cos \omega t \sin \phi) = E_0 I_0 \sin^2 \omega t \cos \phi \pm E_0 I_0 \sin \omega t \cos \omega t \sin \phi$$

or $\quad P = P_1 + P_2$

$P_1 = E_0 I_0 \sin^2 \omega t \cos \phi$ and $P_2 = E_0 I_0 \sin \omega t \cos \omega t \sin \phi$

First part of power is $P_1 = (E_0 \sin \omega t)(I_0 \sin \omega t) \cos \phi$

In this part of power emf $(E_0 \sin \omega t)$ and current $(I_0 \cos \phi \sin \omega t)$ both are in same phase.

In this part amplitude of current $= (I_0 \cos \phi)$

Average of first part $\overline{P_1} = E_0 . I_0 \,\overline{\sin^2 \omega t}\, \cos \phi$ (average of $\sin^2 \omega t = \overline{\sin^2 \omega t} = 1/2) = \frac{1}{2} E_0 I_0 \cos \phi\ = \frac{E_0}{\sqrt{2}} \times \frac{I_0}{\sqrt{2}} \times \cos \phi$

or $\quad \overline{P_1} = E_{rms} \times I_{rms} \times \cos \phi$

Second part of power is $P_2 = (E_0 \sin \omega t)(I_0 \cos \omega t) \sin \phi = (E_0 \sin \omega t)[(I_0 \sin \phi) \sin(\omega t + \pi/2)]$

In this part of power emf and current are in phase difference of $\pi/2$

In this part amplitude of current $= (I_0 \sin \phi)$

Average of second part of power $P_2 = \overline{P_2}$

$$\overline{P_2} = \overline{E_0 I_0 \sin \omega t . \cos \omega t . \cos \phi} = \overline{E_0 I_0 \sin \omega t \cos \omega t} . \overline{\cos \phi} = \frac{1}{2} E_0 I_0 \overline{\sin 2\omega t}$$

or $\overline{P_2} = 0 \quad (\because \overline{\sin 2\omega t} = 0)$

Hence, average power over one complete cycle $\overline{P} = \overline{P_1} + \overline{P_2} = E_{rms} \times I_{rms} \times \cos \phi + 0$ or $P_{av} = E_{rms} . I_{rms} . \cos \phi$

Average power is also known as True power.

The quantity $E_{rms} I_{rms}$ is known as the apparent power or virtual power.

Practice Exercise-2

Multiple Choice Questions

1. Which of the following graphs represents the correct variation of capacitive reactance X_C with frequency f ?

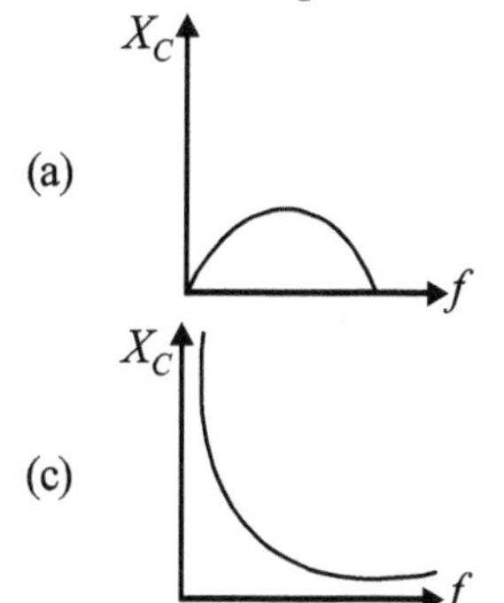

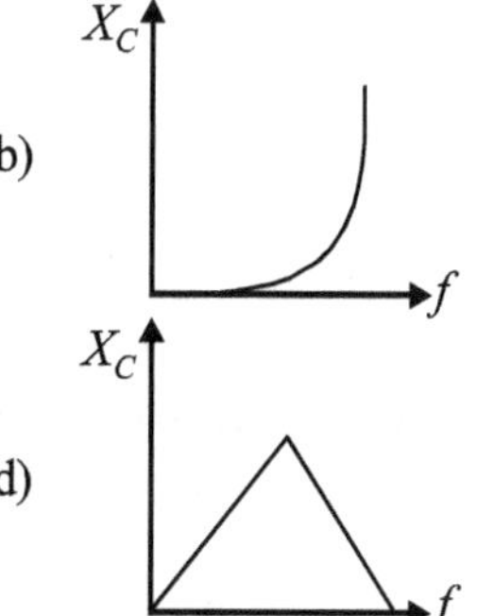

2. Which of the following graphs represents the correct variation of inductive reactance X_L with frequency f ?

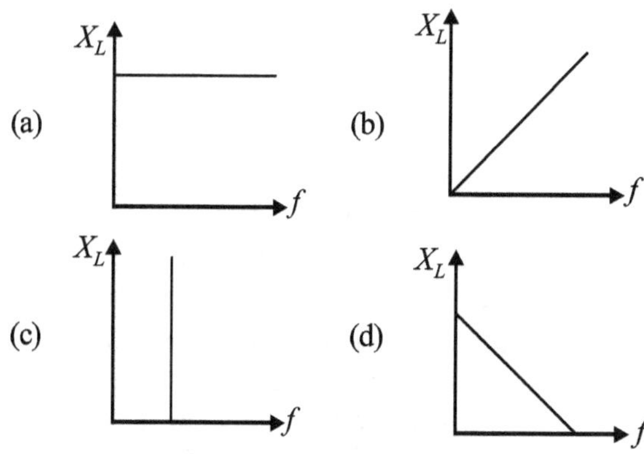

3. Match Columns I and II.

Column I		Column II	
(A)	RL circuit	(1)	Leading quantity - current
(B)	RC circuit	(2)	Leading quantity - voltage
(C)	Inductive circuit	(3)	Phase difference between voltage and current $0°$
(D)	Resistive circuit	(4)	Phase difference between voltage and current $90°$

   (a) (A) → (2); (B) → (3); (C) → (1); (D) → (4)
   (b) (A) → (2); (B) → (2); (C) → (4); (D) → (3)
   (c) (A) → (4); (B) → (3); (C) → (2); (D) → (1)
   (d) (A) → (2); (B) → (1); (C) → (4); (D) → (3)

4. In a series LCR circuit at resonance. Match columns I and II.

Column I		Column II	
(A)	Net Impedance is Z_{min} means	(1)	Circuit behaves as a resistive circuit
(B)	$V_L = V_C \Rightarrow V$ means	(2)	Whole voltage appears across the resistance
(C)	Power consumption $P = V_{rms} i_{rms}$	(3)	$0°$
(D)	Phase difference	(4)	$\frac{1}{2} V_0 i_0$

   (a) (A) → (2); (B) → (1); (C) → (3); (D) → (4)
   (b) (A) → (1); (B) → (2); (C) → (4); (D) → (3)
   (c) (A) → (1); (B) → (3); (C) → (2); (D) → (4)
   (d) (A) → (2); (B) → (3); (C) → (4); (D) → (1)

5. In a series LCR circuit which of the following statements is/are true/false?

   I. At resonance impedance becomes minimum and current becomes maximum.

   II. At resonance current is in phase with applied voltage

   III. Resonant frequency depends upon the resistance of the circuit.

   (a) T,F,F   (b) F,T,F
   (c) T,F,T   (d) T,T,F

6. If the frequency of an A.C. is made 4 times of its initial value, the inductive reactance will
   (a) be 4 times   (b) be 2 times
   (c) be half   (d) remain the same

7. In an ac circuit an alternating voltage $e = 200 \sqrt{2} \sin 100$ t volts is connected to a capacitor of capacity 1 μF. The r.m.s. value of the current in the circuit is
   (a) 10 mA   (b) 100 mA   (c) 200 mA   (d) 20 mA

DIRECTIONS (Qs. 8-14) : *Each of these questions contains an assertion followed by reason. Read them carefully and answer the question on the basis of following options. You have to select the one that best describes the two statements.*

(a) If both Assertion and Reason are correct and the Reason is a correct explanation of the Assertion.

(b) If both Assertion and Reason are correct but Reason is not a correct explanation of the Assertion.

(c) If the Assertion is correct but Reason is incorrect.

(d) If the Assertion is incorrect but the Reason is correct.

8. **Assertion :** The alternating current lags behind the emf by a phase angle of $\frac{\pi}{2}$, when AC flows through an inductor.

   Reason : The inductive reactance increases as the frequency of AC source increases.

9. **Assertion :** The inductive reactance limits amplitude of the current in a purely inductive circuit.

   Reason: The inductive reactance is independent of the frequency of the current.

10. **Assertion :** A capacitor is connected to a direct current source. Its reactance is infinite.

    Reason : Reactance of a capacitor is given by $X_c = \frac{1}{\omega C}$.

11. **Assertion :** In series LCR resonance circuit, the impedance is equal to the ohmic resistance.

    Reason: At resonance, the inductive reactance exceeds the capacitive reactance.

12. **Assertion :** The electrostatic energy stored in capacitor plus magnetic energy stored in inductor will always be zero in a series LCR circuit driven by ac voltage source under condition of resonance.

    Reason : The voltage of ac source appears partially across the resistor in a series LCR circuit driven by ac voltage source under condition of resonance.

13. **Assertion :** In a series R, L, C circuit if V_R, V_L, and V_C denote rms voltage across R, L and C respectively and V_S is the rms voltage across the source, then
    $$V_S = V_R + V_L + V_C.$$

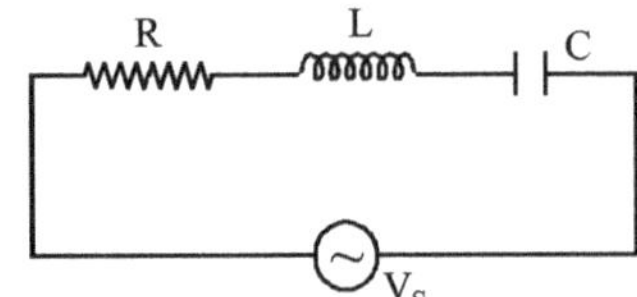

    Reason : In AC circuits, Kirchhoff voltage law is not valid at every instant of time.

Case / Passage Based Questions

In a series LCR circuit with an ideal ac source of peak voltage E_0 = 50V, frequency $v = \dfrac{50}{\pi}$ Hz and $R = 300\,\Omega$. The average electric field energy stored in the capacitor and average magnetic energy stored in the coil are 25 mJ and 5 mJ respectively. The value of RMS current in the circuit is 0.1 A. Then find :

14. Capacitance (C) of the capacitor is
(a) $10\mu F$ (b) $15\mu F$
(c) $20\mu F$ (d) None of these

15. Inductance (L) of inductor is
(a) 0.25 henry   (b) 0.5 henry
(c) 1 henry   (d) 2 henry

16. The sum of rms potential difference across each of the three elements is
(a) 50 volt   (b) $50\sqrt{2}$ volt
(c) $\dfrac{50}{\sqrt{2}}$ volt   (d) None of these

17. In a LCR circuit at resonance which of these will effect the current in circuit
(a) R only   (b) L and R only
(c) R and C only   (d) all L, C and R

18. In a series combination of R, L and C to an A.C. source at resonance, if R = 20 ohm, then impedance Z of the combination is
(a) 20 ohm   (b) Zero
(c) 1 ohm   (d) 400 ohm

Very Short Answer Questions

19. On what principle does a metal detector work?

20. In LCR series ac circuit $X_C < X_L$, how does the current vary with source voltage?

21. The divisions marked on the scale of an a.c. ammeter are not equally spaced. Why?

Short Answer Questions

22. A bulb is connected in alternating current circuit. The frequency of a.c. source is 50 Hz. The current becomes zero 100 times in a second, then why does the bulb not lit intermittently?

23. A pure inductance is connected to an a.c. source of 220 V, 50 Hz. What will be the phase difference and applied emf in the circuit ?

24. A pure capacitor is connected to an ac source of 220 V, 50 Hz. What will be the phase difference between current and applied emf in the circuit ?

25. A bulb and a capacitor are connected in series to a source of alternating current. What will happen on increasing the frequency of ac source?

26. What will be the effect on inductive reactance X_L and capacitive reactance X_C, if frequency of a.c. source is increased?

27. In an inductor of inductance L, current passed is I_0 and energy stored in it is U. The current is now reduced to $\dfrac{I_0}{2}$. What will be the new energy stored in the inductor?

28. Derive an expression for the average power cunsumed in an a.c circuit containing pure inductance over a complete cycle.

29. A coil of inductance L, a capacitor of capacitance C and a resistor of resistance R are connected in series with an alternating source of emf $E = E_0 \sin \omega t$. Write expressions for
(i) Total impedance of circuit
(ii) Frequency of source emf for which circuit will show resonance.

30. The series LCR circuit shown in the figure is in resonance. Calculate the voltage across the inductor in terms of the source voltage and frequency.

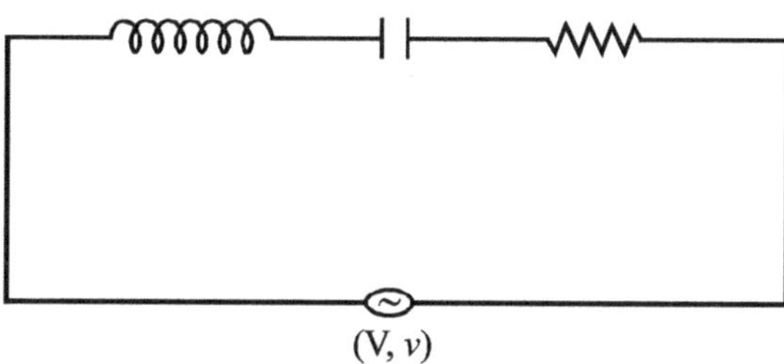

31. A capacitor, a resistor, and a 40 mH inductor are connected in series to an a.c. source of frequency 60 Hz. Calculate the capacitance of the capacitor, if the current is in phase with the applied voltage.

32. A 25 µF capacitor, a 0.1 H inductor and a 25 Ω resistor are connected in series with an a.c. source of emf given by $E = 310 \sin 314\,t$
(a) What is the frequency of emf?
(b) Calculate (i) the reactance of circuit, (ii) the impedance of circuit and (iii) the current in circuit.

33. A 50 mH inductor, a capacitor of capacitance 20 µF and a 10 Ω resistor are connected in series acros a 220 V a.c. source of variable frequency. Calculate (i) the resonant frequency of the circuit, (ii) current amplitude at resonance and (iii) maximum power dissipation.

34. Derive an expression for the a.c. across a resistance R connected to an alternating source of e.m.f. $E = E_0 \sin \omega\, t$. Explain the variations of e.m.f. and current graphically and with a phasor diagram.

35. Derive an expression for the average power consumed in a pure resistive circuit over a complete cycle.

36. Derive an expression for the alternating current across a pure inductor L connected to an alternating source of e.m.f $E = E_0 \sin \omega t$. Explain the variation of e.m.f and current graphically and with a phasor diagram.

37. Derive an expression for the alternating current across a pure capacitor C connected to an alternating ource of e.m.f. $E = E_0 \sin \omega t$. Explain the variation of e.m.f and current graphically and with a phasor diagram.

38. Derive an expression for the energy stored in an inductor.

39. An electric lamp connected in series with a capacitor and an a.c. source is glowing with certain brightness. How does the brightness of the lamp change on reducing the capacitance?

40. A choke coil and a bulb are connected in series to an a.c source. The bulb shines brightly. How does the brightness change when an iron core is inserted in the choke coil?

41. When a capacitor is connected in series LR circuit, the alternating current flowing in the circuit increases. Explain why?

42. A radio frequency choke is air cored whereas an audio frequency choke is iron cored coil.

Give reason for this difference.

43. A 12 ohm resistance and an inductance of $\dfrac{0.05}{\pi}$ H are connected in series. Across the ends of this circuit an alternating voltage of 130 V and frequency 50 cycles/s is connected. Calculate the current in the circuit and the potential difference across the inductance.

44. A bulb of resistance 10 Ω, connected to an inductor of inductance L is in series with an a.c. source marked 100V, 50 Hz. If the phase angle between the voltage and current is $\pi/4$ radian, calculate new voltage of L.

45. In a series RC circuit, R = 30 Ω, C = 0.25 μF, V = 100V, ω = 1,00,000 rad/s. Find the current in the circuit and calculate the voltage across the resistor and the capacitor.

46. In the given circuit, the potential difference across the inductor L and resistor R are 200 V and 150 V respectively and the r.m.s value of current is 5 A.

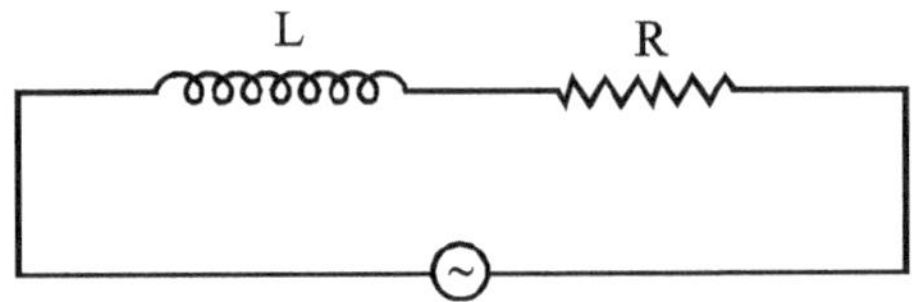

Calculate the angle between the voltage and the current.

47. An a.c. source of frequency 50 Hz is connected to a 50 mH inductor and a bulb. The bulb glows with some brightness. Calculate the capacitance of the capacitor to be connected in series with the circuit, so that the bulb glows with maximum brightness.

48. An inductor L of reactance X_L is connected in series with a bulb B to an a.c. source as shown in the figure.

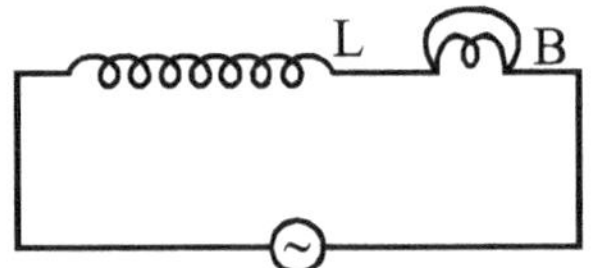

Explain briefly how does the brightness of the bulb changes when

(i) number of turns of the inductor is reduced and

(ii) a capacitor of reactance $X_C = X_L$ is introduced in the circuit.

Topic 3   LC Oscillations and Transformer

LC OSCILLATIONS

A capacitor and an inductor can store electrical and magnetic energy respectively. A circuit containing an inductor L and a capacitor C (initially charged) with no ac source and no resistance exhibit the phenomenon of electrical oscillations.

The charge q of the capacitor is given by the equation, $\dfrac{d^2q}{dt^2} + \dfrac{1}{LC}q = 0$

This equation has the form of a simple harmonic oscillator.

The charge, therefore, oscillates with a natural frequency $\omega_0 = \dfrac{1}{\sqrt{LC}}$.

The energy in the system oscillates between the capacitor and the inductor but the total energy is constant in time.

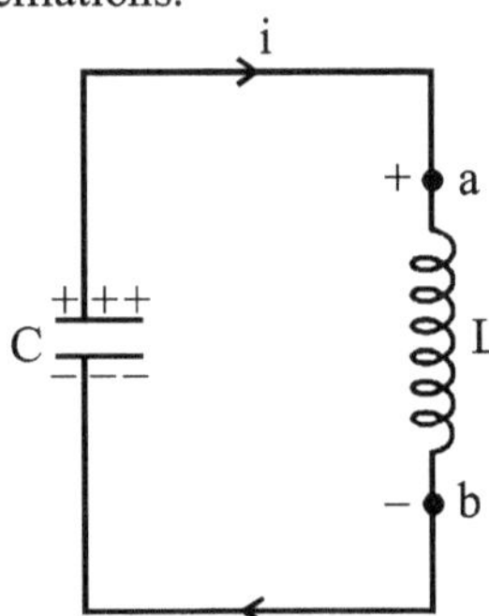

Wattless Current

Since average of the second part of power (P_2) is zero $(\overline{P_2} = 0)$

Current related with second part of power (P_2) in which emf and current having phase difference of $\pi/2$ in known as wattless current. Amplitude of wattless current $= I_0 \sin \phi$

If the resistance of an a.c. circuit is zero, although current flows in the circuit but the average power consumed in the circuit remains zero. The current in such a circuit is called wattless current.

Let E_{rms} leads I_{rms} by phase angle ϕ, as shown in fig. It can be assumed i general that I_{rms} is the vector sum of two perpendicular components $I_{rms} \cos \phi$ and $I_{rms} \sin \phi$.

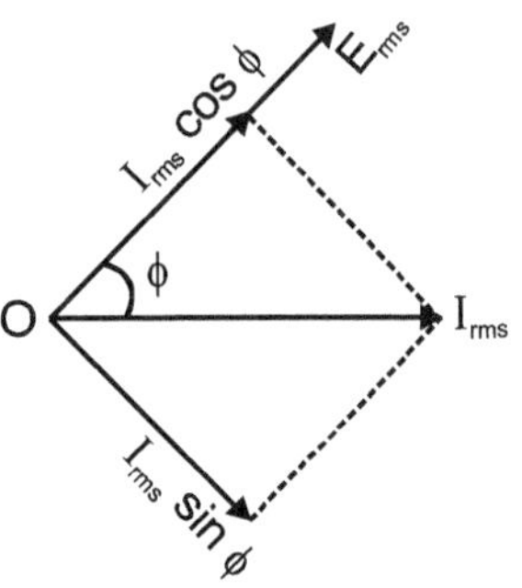

Since phase angle between E_{rms} and $I_{rms} \sin \phi$ is $\pi/2$, average power consumed in the circuit due to component $I_{rms} \sin \phi$ is zero.

Only the component $I_{rms} \cos \phi$ is actually responsible for consumption of power in an a.c. circuit.

TRANSFORMER

It is a device used for transforming a low alternating voltage of high current into a high alternating voltage of low current and vice versa, without increasing power or changing frequency.

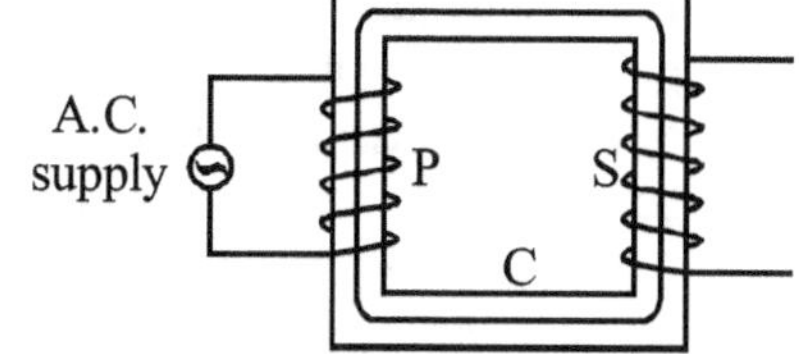

Principle : It works on the phenomenon of mutual induction.

If a low voltage is to be transformed into a high voltage, then the number of turns in secondary is more than those in primary. The transformer is called a **step up transformer.**

If a high voltage is to be transformed into a low voltage, then the number of turns in secondary is less than those in primary. The transformer is called a **step-down transformer.**

Transformation ratio of the transformer,

$$K = \frac{\text{Number of turns in secondary } (N_s)}{\text{Number of turns in primary } (N_p)}$$

$K > 1$, for step-up transformer.

$K < 1$, for step-down transformer.

The whole arrangement is kept immersed in a special oil called transformer oil, taken in metallic cans. The oil provides insulation as well as cooling.

Theory and working : An alternating e.m.f. E_p is applied across the primary which produces current I_p in the primary circuit and a current I_s in the secondary circuit. The currents in the coils produce a magnetization in the soft-iron core and there is a corresponding magnetic field B inside the core. The field due to magnetization of the core is large as compared to the field due to the current in the coils. We assume that the field is constant in magnitude everywhere in the core and hence, its flux (BA) through each turn is same for the primary as well as for the secondary coil.

Let the flux through each turn be Φ.

The emf induced in the primary, $E_P = -N_p \dfrac{d\Phi}{dt}$ and induced emf in the secondary, $E_S = -N_s \times \dfrac{d\Phi}{dt}$

If we neglect the resistance in the primary circuit, Kirchhoff's loop law applied to the primary circuit which gives,

$$E_p = N_p \frac{d\Phi}{dt} \qquad \text{......(i)} \qquad \text{Also,} \qquad E_s = -N_s \frac{d\Phi}{dt} \qquad \text{......(ii)}$$

From (i) and (ii), $\quad E_s = -\dfrac{N_s}{N_p} E_p$

The minus sign shows that E_s is $180°$ out of phase with E_p.

Equⁿs. (i) and (ii) are valid for all values of currents in the primary and the secondary circuits. If there is no loss of power in output and input circuit then, **input power = output power**

i.e., $\quad E_p \times I_p = E_s \times I_s \quad$ or, $\quad \dfrac{I_p}{I_s} = \dfrac{E_s}{E_p} = \dfrac{N_s}{N_p}$

But in practice there is always energy loss so, input power > output power.

Hence, $\quad E_p \times I_p > E_s \times I_s$

Efficiency of a Transformer

In an ordinary transformer, there is some loss of energy due to coil resistance, hysteresis in the core, eddy currents in the core etc. The percentage efficiency of a transformer is defined as

i.e., $\quad \eta\% = \dfrac{\text{Output power}}{\text{Input power}} \times 100 = \dfrac{V_S I_S}{V_P I_P} \times 100$

Efficiency for an ideal transformer is 100% but of practical transformer lies between 70% – 90%.

Step up transformer increases voltage and decreases current.

Step down transformer decreases voltage and increases current.

Uses of Transformer

A transformer is used in almost all ac operations.

(i)   In voltage regulators for TV, refrigerator, computer, air conditioner etc.

(ii)   In the induction furnaces.

(iii)   Step down transformer is used for welding purposes.

(iv)   In the transmission of ac over long distance.

(v)   Step down and step up transformers are used in electrical power distribution.

(vi)   Audio frequency transformers are used in radiography, television, radio, telephone etc.

(vii)   Radio frequency transformers are used in radio communication.

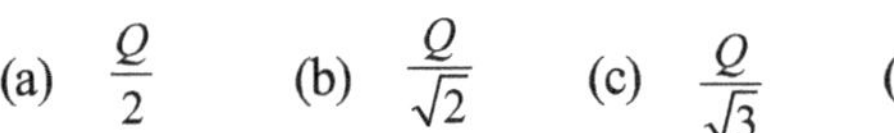

Illustration 6 :

A transformer having efficiency 90% is working on 100 V and at 2.0 kW power. If the current in the secondary coil is 5A, calculate (i) the current in the primary and (ii) voltage across the secondary coil.

Sol. Here, $\eta = 90\% = \dfrac{9}{10}$, $I_s = 5A$, $E_p = 100$ V. $E_p I_p = 2\,kW = 2000\,W$

(i) $E_p I_p = 2000\,W$ $\therefore$ $I_p = \dfrac{2000}{E_p}$ or $I_p = \dfrac{2000}{100} = 20\,A$

(ii) Efficiency $\eta = \dfrac{\text{output power}}{\text{input power}} = \dfrac{E_s I_s}{E_p I_p}$ or, $E_s I_s = \eta \times E_p I_p = \dfrac{9}{10} \times 2000 = 1800\,W$ $\therefore$ $E_S = \dfrac{1800}{I_s} = \dfrac{1800}{5} = 360$ Volt

Practice Exercise-3

Multiple Choice Questions

1.   A step up transformer operates on a 230 V line and supplies a current of 2 ampere. The ratio of primary and secondary winding is 1:25 . The current in primary is __________.
   (a) 25 A   (b) 50 A   (c) 15 A   (d) 12.5 A

2.   Consider the following statements and then select the true/false statements.
   I.   Most of the electrical device we use require AC voltage.
   II.   Most of the electrical energy sold by power companies is transmitted and distributed as alternating current.
   III.   AC voltage can be easily and efficiently converted from one to the other by means of transformers.
   (a) T,F,F   (b) T,F,T   (c) T,T,F   (d) T,T,T

3.   The __________ is the loss of energy in the form of heat in the iron core of a transformer.
   (a) iron loss   (b) copper loss
   (c) mechanical loss   (d) None of these

4.   The primary winding of a transformer has 100 turns and its secondary winding has 200 turns. The primary is connected to an A.C. supply of 120 V and the current flowing in it is 10 A. The voltage and the current in the secondary are
   (a) 240 V, 5 A   (b) 240 V, 10 A
   (c) 60 V, 20 A   (d) 120 V, 20 A

5.   A charged 30 µF capacitor is connected to a 27 mH inductor. The angular frequency of free oscillations of the circuit is
   (a) 1.1×10^3 rad s^{-1} (b) 2.1×10^3 rad s^{-1}
   (c) 3.1×10^3 rad s^{-1} (d) 4.1×10^3 rad s^{-1}

6.   In an oscillation of L–C circuit, the maximum charge on the capacitor is Q. The charge on the capacitor, when the energy is stored equally between the electric and magnetic field is

    (a) $\dfrac{Q}{2}$ (b) $\dfrac{Q}{\sqrt{2}}$ (c) $\dfrac{Q}{\sqrt{3}}$ (d) $\dfrac{Q}{3}$

Assertion & Reason Questions

DIRECTIONS (Qs. 7-8) : *Each of these questions contains an assertion followed by reason. Read them carefully and answer the question on the basis of following options. You have to select the one that best describes the two statements.*

(a) If both Assertion and Reason are correct and the Reason is a correct explanation of the Assertion.

(b) If both Assertion and Reason are correct but Reason is not a correct explanation of the Assertion.

(c) If the Assertion is correct but Reason is incorrect.

(d) If the Assertion is incorrect but the Reason is correct.

7.   **Assertion :** Transformer can transfer power from primary to secondary coil.
   Reason : In an ideal transformer VI = varries.

8.   **Assertion :** A laminated core is used in transformers to increase eddy currents.
   Reason : The efficiency of a transformer increases with increase in eddy currents.

Case / Passage Based Questions

A thermal power plant produces electric power of 600 kW at 4000 V, which is to be transported to a place 20 km away from the power plant for consumers' usage. It can be transported either directly with a cable of large current carrying capacity or by using a combination of step-up and step-down transformers at the two ends. The drawback of the direct transmission is the large energy dissipation. In the method using transformers, the dissipation is much smaller. In this method , a step-up transformer is used at the plant side so that the current is reduced to a smaller value. At the consumers' end, a step-down transformer is used to supply power to the consumers at the specified lower voltage. It is reasonable to assume that the power cable is purely resistive and the transformers are ideal with power factor unity. All the currents and voltages mentioned are rms values.

9. In the method using the transformers, assume that the ratio of the number of turns in the primary to that in the secondary in the step-up transformer is 1 : 10. If the power to the consumers has to be supplied at 200 V, the ratio of the number of turns in the primary to that in the secondary in the step-down transformer is
   (a) 200 : 1 (b) 150 : 1 (c) 100 : 1 (d) 50 : 1

10. If the direct transmission method with a cable of resistance $0.4\ \Omega\ km^{-1}$ is used, the power dissipation| (in %) during transmission is
    (a) 20 (b) 30 (c) 40 (d) 50

11. Transformers are used
    (a) in DC circuit only
    (b) in AC circuits only
    (c) in both DC and AC circuits
    (d) neither in DC nor in AC circuits

12. A transformer is employed to
    (a) convert A.C. into D.C.
    (b) convert D.C. into A.C.
    (c) obtain a suitable A.C. voltage
    (d) obtain a suitable D.C. voltage

13. The transformer voltage induced in the secondary coil of a transformer is mainly due to
    (a) a varying electric field
    (b) a varying magnetic field
    (c) the vibrations of the primary coil
    (d) the iron core of the transformer

Very Short Answer Questions

14. How can the flux leakage in a transformer be reduced?

15. What is the cause of hysteresis loss in a transformer?

16. Why can't transformer be used to step up or step down dc voltage?

17. In an L.C. circuit name any physical quantity that oscillates in (i) the inductor (ii) the capacitor.

Short Answer Questions

18. In a transformer $\dfrac{V_S}{V_P} = \dfrac{N_S}{N_P}$. What are the assumption made in obtaining the relation?

19. The output voltage of an ideal transformer connected to a 240 V, a.c. mains in 24 V. When this transformer is used to light a bulb with rating 24 V, 24 W. Calculate the current in primary coil of circuit.

20. In an ideal transformer, the number of turns in the primary and secondary are 200 and 1000 respectively. If the power input to the primary is 10 kW at 200 V, calculate (i) output voltage and (ii) current in primary.

Important Tips & Formulae

▶ Alternating current in electric wires, bulbs etc., flows 50 times in one direction and 50 times in the opposite direction in 1 second.

▶ A direct current flows over the cross-section of the conductor. But an alternating current flows mainly along the surface of the conductor.

▶ AC equipments such as electric motors are more durable as compared to DC equipments.

▶ AC ammeter and AC voltmeter always measure r.m.s. value.

▶ AC is more dangerous than DC. It is because peak value of AC for 220 V AC is $220\sqrt{2} = 311\ V$. Thus, 311 V can cause more harm to the human body than 220 V DC.

▶ Average value of AC over a complete cycle is zero.

▶ All AC measuring instruments is based on heating effect of current.

▶ Phase is a dimensionless quantity. It is used to represents both the instantaneous value and direction of alternating quantity.

▶ The parallel resonance circuit is used as rejector circuit.

▶ The series resonance circuit is used as acceptor circuit.

▶ More the quality factor, more the sharpness of resonance.

▶ The power factor is a unitless and dimensionless quantity. Its value lies between 0 and 1.

▶ Impedance triangle is a right angled triangle whose base represents ohmic resistance R, perpendicular represents reactance and hypotenuse represents impedance Z of LCR circuit.

▶ The AC supply in our country is 220 volt, 50 c/s.

▶ While drawing phasor diagram for combination of elements the quantity which is constant should be plotted along X-axis.
   (i) In series circuit, current should be plotted along X-axis.
   (ii) In parallel circuit, voltage should be plotted along X-axis.

▶ The equation for growth and decay of current in R-L circuit is given by
$$I = I_0(1 - e^{-Rt/L})$$
Here, $\dfrac{L}{R} = \tau$ = time constant of the circuit.

▶ The equation for charging and discharging of a condenser through resistance R is given by
$$q = q_0(1 - e^{-t/RL})$$
Here, RC = τ = time constant of the circuit.

▶ The inductor and capacitor have different behaviour in ac and dc circuit.
For DC supply, $v = 0$ Therefore, $X_L = 2\pi v L = 0$
Thus, we can say an inductor act as conductor for DC current.
$$X_C = \frac{1}{2\pi v C} = \frac{1}{0} = \infty$$
Thus, condenser just block dc and allows ac current to pass through.

▶ In RLC circuit, impedance is infinite for $\omega = 0$ and also for $\omega = \infty$. The impedance is minimum (Z = R), when $\omega L = \dfrac{1}{\omega C}$ or $\omega = \dfrac{1}{\sqrt{LC}}$. At this frequency, resonance occur.

NCERT Questions

7.1 A 100 Ω resistor is connected to a 220 V, 50Hz ac supply.
 (a) What is the rms value of current in the circuit?
 (b) What is the net power consumed over a full cycle?

Sol. **Given:** Resistance R = 100 Ω
Voltage E_v = 220 V
frequency v = 50 Hz
To find: (a) rms current (b) net power.

Formula: (a) $I_v = \dfrac{E_v}{R}$ (b) $P = I_v^2 R$

(a) $I_v = \dfrac{E_v}{R} = \dfrac{220}{100} = 2.2$ A

(b) $P_{av} = I_v^2 R = (2.2)^2 \times 100 = 484$ W

7.2. (a) The peak voltage of an ac supply is 300 V. What is the rms voltage?
 (b) The rms value of current in an ac circuit is 10 A. What is the peak current?

Sol. **Given:** max voltage E_0 = 300 V
rms current I_v = 10 A
To find: (1) rms voltage E_v (2) max. current I_0

Formula : (a) $E_v = \dfrac{E_0}{\sqrt{2}} = \dfrac{300}{\sqrt{2}} = 212.1$ V

(b) $I_0 = \sqrt{2}\, I_v = \sqrt{2} \times 10 = 14.14$ A

7.3. A 44 mH inductor is connected to 220 V, 50 Hz ac supply. Determine the rms value of the current in the circuit.

Sol. **Given:** inductance L = 44 mH
voltage E_v = 220 V   frequency v = 50 Hz
To find: rms current

Formula: $I_v = \dfrac{E_v}{X_L}$ $I_v = \dfrac{E_v}{X_L} = \dfrac{E_v}{2\pi v L}$

$\Rightarrow I_v = \dfrac{220}{2 \times 3.14 \times 50 \times 44 \times 10^{-3}}$

$= \dfrac{10}{100 \times 2 \times 3.14 \times 10^{-3}} = \dfrac{100}{6.28} = 15.9$ A

7.4. A 60 μF capacitor is connected to a 110 V, 60 Hz ac supply. Determine the rms value of the current in the circuit.

Sol. **Given:** capacitance C = 60 μF
voltage E_v = 110 V   frequency v = 60 Hz
To find: rms current

Formula: $I_v = \dfrac{E_v}{X_c} = \dfrac{E_v}{1/\omega C} = E_v \times \omega C$

$= E_v \times 2\pi v\, C = 110 \times 2 \times 3.14 \times 60 \times 60 \times 10^{-6}$
$= 1.1 \times 6.28 \times 36 \times 10^{-2} = 2.49$ A

7.5. In Qs. 7.3 and 7.4, what is the net power absorbed by each circuit over a complete cycle. Explain your answer.

Sol. **To find:** net power in Q. 7.3 and 7.4
Formula: power $P_{av} = E_v I_v \cos \phi$

For Q7.3 (inductive circuit) current lags behind emf by $\pi/2$
Hence, $P_{av} = E_v I_v \cos \phi = 220 \times 15.9 \times \cos 90° = 0$
In Q. 7.4 (pure capacitative circuit) current leads emf by phase $\pi/2$
hence $P_{av} = E_v I_v \cos \phi = E_v I_v \cos \pi/2 = E_v I_v \cos 90° = 0$

7.6. Obtain the resonant frequency ω_r of a series LCR circuit with L = 2.0H, C = 32 μF and R = 10 Ω What is the Q-value of this circuit?

Sol. **Given:** L = 2H, C = 32 μF, R = 10 Ω
To find: Resonant frequency w_r, Q-value.

Formula: $\omega_r = \dfrac{1}{\sqrt{LC}}$, Q-value $= \dfrac{1}{R}\sqrt{\dfrac{L}{C}}$

$\omega_r = \dfrac{1}{\sqrt{LC}} = \dfrac{1}{\sqrt{2 \times 32 \times 10^{-6}}}$

$\Rightarrow \omega_r = \dfrac{1}{\sqrt{64 \times 10^{-6}}} = \dfrac{1}{8 \times 10^{-3}} = \dfrac{1000}{8}$

$\Rightarrow \omega_r = 125$ rad/s

$\text{Q-value} = \dfrac{1}{R}\sqrt{\dfrac{L}{C}} = \dfrac{1}{10}\sqrt{\dfrac{2}{32 \times 10^{-6}}}$

$= \dfrac{1}{10}\sqrt{\dfrac{1}{16 \times 10^{-6}}} = \dfrac{1}{10 \times 4 \times 10^{-3}} = \dfrac{1000}{40} = 25$

7.7. A charged 30 μF capacitor is connected to a 27 mH inductor. What is the angular frequency of free oscillations of the circuit?

Sol. **Given:** capacitance C = 30 μF
inductance L = 27 mH
To find: Frequency of free oscillation ω_r
Formula: Angular frequency of free oscillation

$= \text{resonant frequency} = \omega_r = \dfrac{1}{\sqrt{LC}}$

$= \dfrac{1}{\sqrt{27 \times 10^{-3} \times 30 \times 10^{-6}}} = \dfrac{1}{\sqrt{81 \times 10^{-8}}} = \dfrac{1}{9 \times 10^{-4}}$

$= \dfrac{10}{9} \times 10^3 = 1.1 \times 10^3$ rad/s

7.8. Suppose the initial charge on the capacitor in q_n. 7.7 is 6 mC. What is the total energy stored in the circuit initially? What is the total energy at later time?

Sol. **Given:** Capacity = 30 μF, charge q = 6 mC
To find: Total energy U

Formula: $U = \dfrac{q^2}{2C}$

For a capacitor, energy stored U

$= \dfrac{q^2}{2C} = \dfrac{(6 \times 10^{-3})^2}{2 \times 30 \times 10^{-6}}$ $U = \dfrac{36 \times 10^{-6}}{60 \times 10^{-6}} = 0.6$ J

This initial energy of capacitor is shared by inductance during oscillation (capacitor charges and discharges through the inductor) but the total energy of the LC tank circuit remains same.

7.9. A series LCR circuit with $R = 20\ \Omega$, $L = 1.5$ H and $C = 35\ \mu$F is connected to a variable-frequency of 200 V ac supply. When the frequency of the supply equals the natural frequency of the circuit, what is the average power transferred to the circuit in one complete cycle?

Sol. **Given:** $R = 20\ \Omega$, $L = 1.5$ H, $C = 35\ \mu$F, average emf $E_v = 200$

To find: Average power at resonance P_{av}

Formula: $P_{av} = I_v E_v$

When supply frequency equals natural frequency of circuit it is resonance and $X_L = X_C$ hence

$$I_v = \frac{E_v}{R} = \frac{200}{20} = 10\ \text{A}$$

$\therefore \cos\phi = 1$ at resonance and $P_{av} = E_v I_v = 200 \times 10 = 2000$ W

7.10. A radio can tune over the frequency range of a portion of MW broadcast band: (800 kHz to 1200 kHz). If its LC circuit has an effective inductance of 200 μH, what must be the range of its variable capacitor?

[Hint: For tuning, the natural frequency i.e., the frequency of free oscillations of the LC circuit should be equal to the frequency of the radiowave.]

Sol. **Given:** Max. frequency $v_1 = 1200$ kHz

min. frequency $v_2 = 800$ kHz

inductance $L = 200\ \mu$F

To find: Range of capacitor C_1 and C_2

Formula: $v = \dfrac{1}{2\pi\sqrt{LC}}$

Tuning of radio means natural frequency of LC circuit matches broadcast frequency.

For lower limit $v_2 = 800\ \text{kHz} = 800 \times 10^3\ \text{Hz} = 8 \times 10^5\ \text{Hz}$

$$\Rightarrow C_2 = \frac{1}{4\pi^2 L v_2^2} = \frac{1}{4 \times (3.14)^2 \times 200 \times 10^{-6} \times (8 \times 10^5)^2}$$

$$= \frac{1}{4 \times (3.14)^2 \times 2 \times 64 \times 10^{-4+10}}$$

$$= \frac{10^{-6}}{8 \times 64 \times 3.14} = 197.9 \times 10^{-12} = 198\ \text{pF}$$

For upper limit $v_1 = 1200\ \text{kHz} = 12 \times 10^5\ \text{Hz}$

$$C_1 = \frac{1}{4\pi^2 v_1^2 L} = \frac{1}{4 \times (3.14)^2 \times (12 \times 10^5)^2 \times 200 \times 10^{-6}}$$

$$= \frac{1}{8 \times (3.14)^2 \times 144 \times 200 \times 10^{10-4}}$$

$$= \frac{10^{-6}}{8 \times (3.14)^2 \times 144} = 87.9 \times 10^{-12}\ \text{F} \qquad C_1 \approx 88\ \text{pF}$$

$\therefore$ Range of capacitor is 88 to 198 pF

7.11. Figure shows a series LCR circuit connected to a variable frequency 230 V source. $L = 5.0$ H, $C = 80\mu$F, $R = 40\ \Omega$

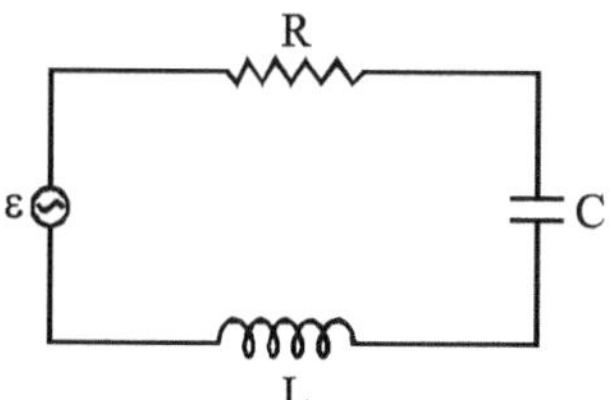

(a) Determine the source frequency which drives the circuit in resonance.

(b) Obtain the impedance of the circuit and the amplitude of current at the resonating frequency.

(c) Determine the rms potential drops across the three elements of the circuit. Show that the potential drop across the LC combination is zero at the resonating frequency.

Sol. **Given:** voltage $e_v = 230$ V $\quad L = 5$H, $C = 80\ \mu$F, $R = 40\ \Omega$

To find: (a) Resonant frequency ω_r

(b) impedance at amplitude of current at resonance Z, I_0

(c) rms voltage E_v across L, C, R.

Formula: $\omega_r = \dfrac{1}{\sqrt{LC}}$, $Z = R$, $I_0 = \sqrt{2}\, I_v$, $E_v = \dfrac{I_v}{Z_{L,C,R}}$

(a) $\omega_r = \dfrac{1}{\sqrt{LC}} = \dfrac{1}{\sqrt{5 \times 80 \times 10^{-6}}} = \dfrac{1}{\sqrt{400} \times 10^{-3}} = 50\ \text{rad/s}$

(b) At resonance $Z = R = 40\ \Omega$

$\therefore$ rms current $I_v = \dfrac{E_v}{R} = \dfrac{230}{40} \Rightarrow I_v = 5.75$ A

$\therefore$ max. current at resonance is

$I_0 = \sqrt{2}\, I_v = 1.414 \times 5.75 = 8.13$ A

(c) rms voltage across R

$E_v(R) = I_v R = 5.75 \times 40 = 230$ V

rms voltage across L

$E_v(L) = I_v X_L = I_v \omega_0 L = 5.75 \times 50 \times 5 = 1437.5$ V

rms voltage across C

$E_v(C) = I_v X_c = \dfrac{I_v}{\omega_0 C} = \dfrac{5.75}{50 \times 80 \times 10^{-6}} = 1437.5$ V

rms voltage across LC

$E_v(LC) = I_v \left(\omega_0 L - \dfrac{1}{\omega_0 C} \right) = 5.75$

$\left(\omega_0 L - \dfrac{1}{\omega_0 C} \right) = 1437.5 - 1437.5 = 0$

ADDITIONAL EXERCISES

7.12 An *LC* circuit contains a 20 mH inductor and a 50 μF capacitor with initial charge of 10 mC. The resistance of the circuit is negligible. Let the instant the circuit is closed be $t = 0$.

(a) What is the total energy stored initially? Is it conserved during *LC* oscillations?

(b) What is the natural frequency of the circuit?

(c) At what time is the energy stored

(i) completely electrical (i.e. stored in the capacitor)?

(ii) completely magnetic (i.e. stored in the inductor)?

(d) At what times is the total energy shared equally between the inductor and capacitor?

(e) If a resistor is inserted in the circuit, how much energy is eventually dissipated as heat?

Sol.

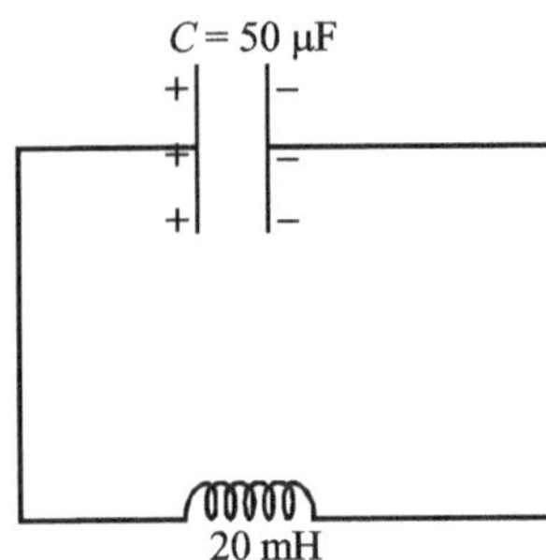

(a) Total energy is initially in the form of electric field within the plates of charged capacitor.

$$U_E = \frac{Q^2}{2C} = \frac{\left(10 \times 10^{-3}\right)^2}{2 \times 50 \times 10^{-6}} = 1J$$

If we neglect the losses due to resistance of connecting wires, the total energy remain consumed during LC oscillations.

(b) Natural frequency of the circuit

$$f = \frac{1}{2\pi \sqrt{LC}} = \frac{1}{2\pi \times \sqrt{20 \times 10^{-3} \times 50 \times 10^{-6}}} \text{ Hz}$$

$$= \frac{500}{\pi}$$

(c) Instantaneous electrical energy

$$U_E = \frac{q_0^2 \cos^2 \omega t}{2C}$$

(i) At $\omega t = 0,\ \pi,\ 2\pi,\ 3\pi...$ the energy is completely electrical.

$$t = \frac{n\pi}{2\pi f} = \frac{n}{2f} = \frac{n\pi}{1000} \text{ sec } n = 0, 1, 2, 3, 4...$$

or $t = 0, T/2, T, 3T/2 ...$

(ii) Instantaneous magnetic energy

$$U_B = \frac{1}{2} L q_0^2\ \omega^2 \sin^2 \omega t$$

or $U_B = \dfrac{q_0^2}{2C} \sin^2 \omega t$

so at $\omega t = \pi/2, 3\pi/2, 5\pi/2...$

The energy is completely magnetic

$$t = \frac{(2n+1)\pi}{2(2\pi f)} = \frac{(2n+1)}{4f} = \frac{(2n+1)\pi}{2000} \text{ sec}$$

where $n = 0, 1, 2, 3, 4...$ or $t = T/4, 3T/4, 5T/4...$

(d) timings for energy shared equally between inductor and capacitor.

$U_B = U_E$

$$\frac{q_0^2}{2C} \sin^2 \omega t = \frac{q_0^2}{2C} \cos^2 \omega t$$

$\tan^2 \omega t = 1$ or $\tan \omega t = \tan \pi/4$

$$t = \frac{\pi}{4\omega}, \frac{3\pi}{4\omega}, \frac{5\pi}{4\omega}... \text{ or } t = \frac{T}{8}, \frac{3T}{8}, \frac{5T}{8}...$$

(e) When a resistor in inserted in the circuit, eventually all the energy will be lost as heat across resistence. The oscillation will be damped.

7.13 A coil of inductance 0.50 H and resistance 100Ω is connected to a 240 V, 50 Hz ac supply.

(a) What is the maximum current in the coil?

(b) What is the time lag between the voltage maximum and the current maximum?

Sol.

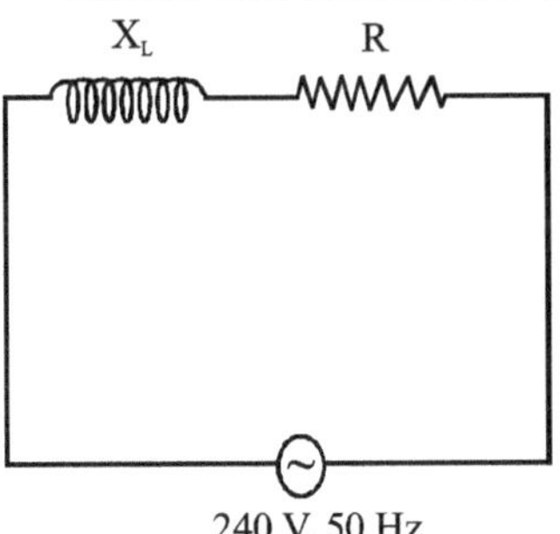

Inductive reactance $X_L = 2\pi f L = 2\pi \times 50 \times 0.5 = 157\ \Omega$

Impedence $Z = \sqrt{R^2 + X_L^2} = \sqrt{(100)^2 + (157)^2} = 186.14\ \Omega$

(a) Virtual current in the coil $I_v = \dfrac{E_v}{Z} = \dfrac{240}{186.14} = 1.29$ A

Maximum current, $I_0 = I_v \sqrt{2} = 1.82$ A

(b)

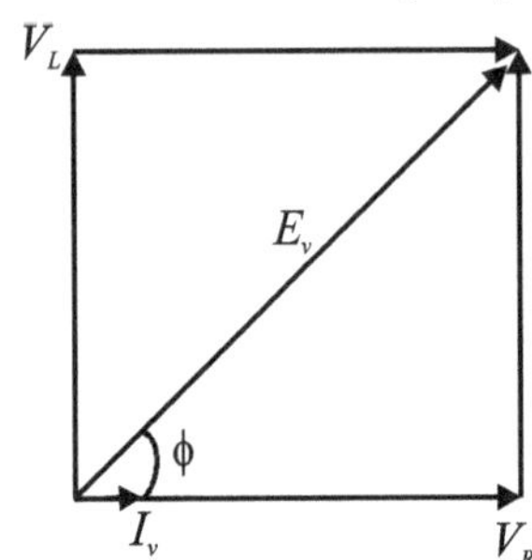

Phase lag, $\tan \phi = \dfrac{X_L}{R} = 1.57$

$\phi = \tan^{-1}(1.57) = 57.5°$ or $\phi = 0.32\pi$ radian

Time lag, $t = \phi/\omega = 3.2$ ms

7.14 Obtain the answers to (a) and (b) in Q. 7.13, if the circuit is connected to a high frequency supply (240 V, 10 kHz). Hence, explain the statement that at very high frequency, an inductor in a circuit nearly amounts to an open circuit. How does an inductor behave in a d.c circuit after the steady state?

Sol. (a) $I_0 = \dfrac{E_0}{\sqrt{R^2 + \omega^2 L^2}} = \dfrac{\sqrt{2} \times 240}{\sqrt{10^4 + 4\pi^2 \times 10^8 \times (0.5)^2}}$

$= 1.08 \times 10^{-2}$ A

(b) $\tan \phi = \dfrac{\omega L}{R} = \dfrac{2\pi \times 10^4 \times 0.5}{100} = 100\ \pi$

which is very large.

$\therefore$ $\phi \to$ tends to 90° or, $\pi/2$ radian.

At very high frequency, X_L increases to infinitely large, hence circuit behaves as open circuit.

$X_L = 2\pi f L = 2\pi (10 \times 10^3) \times 0.5 = 31400\ \Omega$

7.15 A 100 μF capacitor in series with a 40 Ω resistance is connected to a 110 V, 60 Hz supply.

(a) What is the maximum current in the circuit?

(b) What is the time lag between the current maximum and the voltage maximum?

Sol.

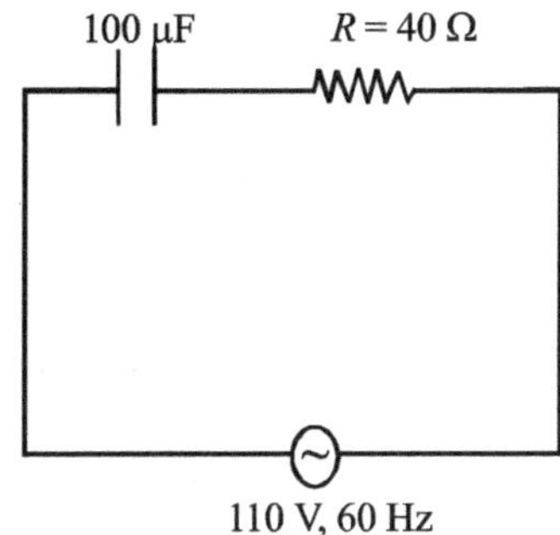

Capacitive reactance $X_C = \dfrac{1}{2\pi fC}$

$$X_C = \dfrac{1}{2\times\pi\times 60\times 100\times 10^{-6}} = 26.54\,\Omega$$

Impedence

$$Z = \sqrt{R^2 + X_C^2} = \sqrt{(40)^2 + (26.54)^2} = 48\,\Omega$$

(a) Virtual current in the circuit $I_v = \dfrac{E_v}{Z} = \dfrac{110}{48} = 2.29\,\text{A}$

Maximum current $I_0 = I_v\sqrt{2} = 3.24\,\text{A}$

(b) $\tan\phi = \dfrac{V_C}{V_R} = \dfrac{1}{\omega CR}$

Phase lag $\phi = \tan^{-1}\left(\dfrac{1}{\omega CR}\right)$

$= \tan^{-1}\left(\dfrac{26.54}{40}\right)$

$\phi = 33.56° = 0.186\pi$ radian

Time lag $t = \phi/\omega = \dfrac{0.18\pi}{2\pi(60)} = 1.5\,\text{ms}$

7.16 **Obtain the answers to (a) and (b) in Q. 7.15 if the circuit is connected to a 110 V, 12 kHz supply? Hence, explain the statement that a capacitor is a conductor at very high frequencies. Compare this behaviour with that of a capacitor in a dc circuit after the steady state.**

Sol. At very high frequency of 12 kHz the capacitive reactance

$$X_C = \dfrac{1}{2\pi fC} = \dfrac{1}{2\pi\left(12\times 10^3\right)\times 100\times 10^{-6}} = 0.13\,\Omega.$$

So, the capacitor offers negligible reactance at high frequency and behaves nearly a conductor.

For d.c circuit $X_C = \infty$, capacitor completely blocks d.c after the steady state.

7.17 **Keeping the source frequency equal to the resonating frequency of the series *LCR* circuit, if the three elements, *L*, *C* and *R* are arranged in parallel, show that the total current in the parallel *LCR* circuit is minimum at this frequency. Obtain the current rms value in each branch of the circuit for this frequency. Source has e.m.f. 230 V and L = 5.0 H, C = 80 μF, R = 40 Ω**

Sol.

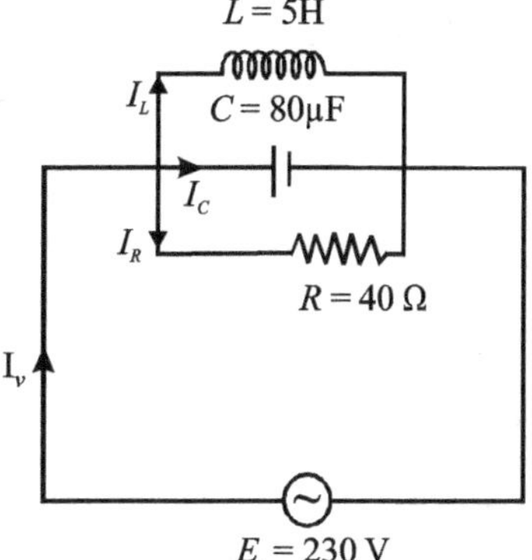

Resonating angular frequency

$$\omega = \dfrac{1}{\sqrt{LC}} = \dfrac{1}{\sqrt{5\times 80\times 10^{-6}}} = 50\,\dfrac{\text{rad}}{\text{sec}}$$

∴ Resonance of *L* and *C* in parallel can be calculated

$$\dfrac{1}{X} = \dfrac{1}{X_L} - \dfrac{1}{X_C} = \dfrac{1}{\omega L} - \omega C$$

Impedance of *R* and *X* in parallel is given by

$$\dfrac{1}{Z} = \sqrt{\dfrac{1}{R^2} + \dfrac{1}{X^2}}$$

At resonating frequency of series *LCR*,

$$X_L = X_C$$

So, $\dfrac{1}{X} = \dfrac{1}{X_L} - \dfrac{1}{X_C} = 0$

Thus impedances $Z = R$ and will be maximum. Hence in parallel resonant circuit current is minimum at resonant frequency.

$$I_R = \dfrac{E_v}{R} = \dfrac{230}{40} = 5.75\,\text{A}$$

$$I_L = \dfrac{E_v}{X_L} = \dfrac{230}{\omega L} = \dfrac{230}{50\times 5} = 0.92\,\text{A}$$

$$I_C = \dfrac{E_v}{X_C} = \dfrac{230}{(1/\omega C)} = 230\times 50\times 80\times 10^{-6} = 0.92\,\text{A}$$

Since I_L and I_C are opposite in phase, so net current I_v
$I_v = I_R + I_L + I_C$

$I_V = 5.75 + 0.92\sqrt{2}\ \sin\left(\omega t - \pi/2\right) + 0.92$

$\sqrt{2}\ \sin\left(\omega t + \pi/2\right)$

$I_v = 5.75 - 0.92\sqrt{2}\,\cos\omega t + 0.92\sqrt{2}\,\cos\omega t$

$I_v = 5.75\,\text{A}$

7.18 **A circuit containing a 80 mH inductor and a 60 μF capacitor in series is connected to a 230 V, 50 Hz supply. The resistance of the circuit is negligible.**
(a) Obtain the current amplitude and rms values.
(b) Obtain the rms values of potential drops across each element.
(c) What is the average power transferred to the inductor?
(d) What is the average power transferred to the capacitor.
(e) What is the total average power absorbed by the circuit? ['Average' implies 'averaged over one cycle'.]

Sol.

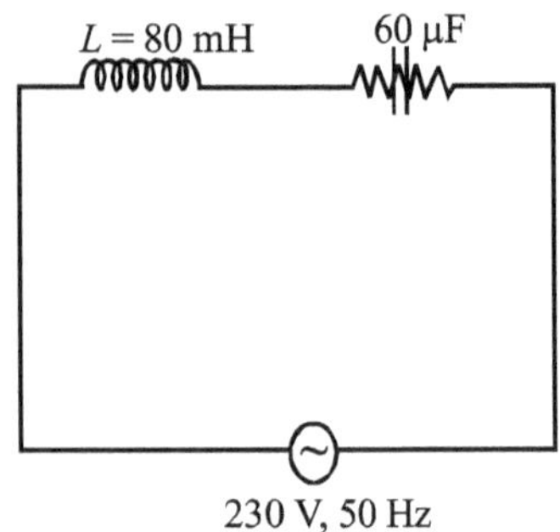

(a) Inductive reactance $X_L = 2\pi f L$

$X_L = 2\pi (50)\, 80 \times 10^{-3} = 25.12\,\Omega$

Capacitive reactance $X_C = \dfrac{1}{2\pi f C}$

$X_C = \dfrac{1}{2 \times 3.14 \times 50 \times 60 \times 10^{-6}} = 53.05\,\Omega$

Impedance $= X_C - X_L = 53.05 - 25.12 = 27.93\,\Omega$

rms value of current $I_v = \dfrac{E_v}{Z} = \dfrac{230}{27.93} = 8.235\,\text{A}$

Peak Value $I_0 = I_v \sqrt{2} = 11.644\,\text{A}$

(b) Potential drop across L, $V_L = I_L X_L = 206.68\,\text{V}$
Potential drop across C, $V_C = I_v \times X_C = 436.87\,\text{V}$

(c) Average power transferred to inductor is zero, because of phase difference $\pi/2$.
$P = E_v I_v \cos\phi.$ $\phi = \pi/2, \therefore P = 0$

(d) Average power transferred to capacitor is also zero, because of phase difference $\pi/2$.
$P = E_v I_v \cos\phi.$
$\phi = \pi/2, \therefore P = 0$

(c) Total power absorbed by the circuit

$P_{Total} = P_L + P_C = 0$

7.19. **Suppose the circuit in Q. 7.18 has a resistance of 15 Ω. Obtain the average power transferred to each element of the circuit and the total power absorbed.**

Sol. If the circuit has a resistance of 15 Ω, now it is LCR series resonant circuit.

Now the impedance

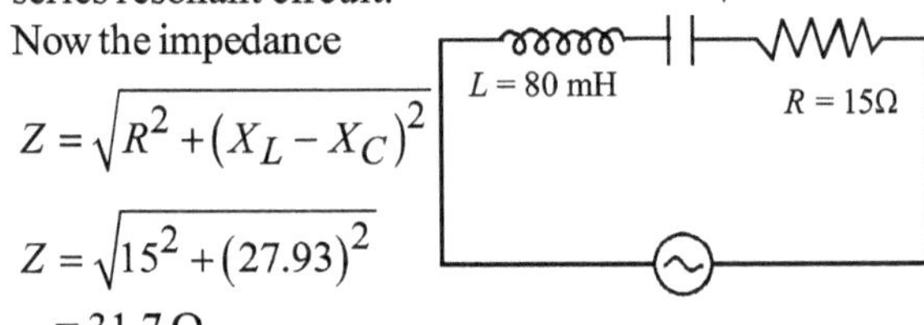

$Z = \sqrt{R^2 + \left(X_L - X_C\right)^2}$

$Z = \sqrt{15^2 + (27.93)^2}$

$\quad = 31.7\,\Omega$

Virtual current $I_v = \dfrac{E_v}{Z} = \dfrac{230}{31.7} = 7.255\,\text{A}$

Average power transferred to 'L',

$P_L = I_v E_v \cos\dfrac{\pi}{2} = 0$

Average power transferred to 'C',

$P_C = E_v I_v \cos\dfrac{\pi}{2} = 0$

Average power transferred to 'R'
$P_R = V_R I_v \cos 0°$
$P_R = \left(I_v R\right) I_v = I_v^2 R = (7.255)^2 \times 15 = 789.5\,\text{W}$

7.20 **A series LCR circuit with $L = 0.12$ H, $C = 480$ µF, $R = 23\,\Omega$ is connected to a 230 V variable frequency supply.**
(a) What is the source frequency for which current amplitude is maximum. Obtain this maximum value.
(b) What is the source frequency for which average power absorbed by the circuit is maximum. Obtain the value of this maximum power.
(c) For which frequencies of the source is the power transferred to the circuit half the power at resonant frequency? What is the current amplitude at these frequencies?
(d) What is the Q-factor of the given circuit?

Sol.

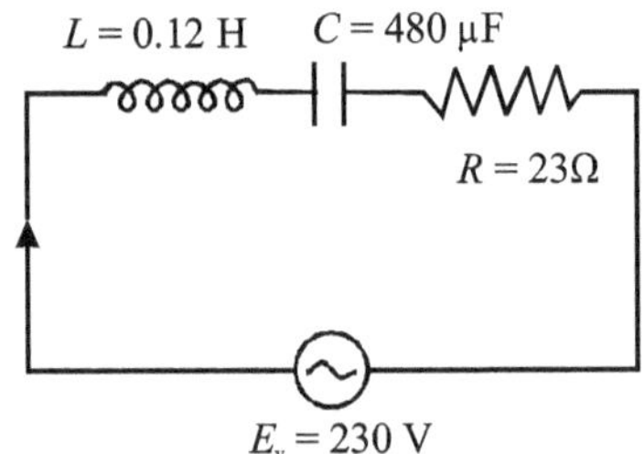

(a) At natural frequency the current amplitude is maximum.

$F = \dfrac{1}{2\pi\sqrt{LC}} = \dfrac{1}{2\pi\sqrt{0.12 \times 480 \times 10^{-6}}} = 663\,\text{Hz}$

$I_v = \dfrac{E_v}{R}, I_0 = I_v\sqrt{2} = \dfrac{E_v\sqrt{2}}{R} = \dfrac{230\sqrt{2}}{23} = 14.14\text{A}$

(b) Maximum power loss at resonant frequency,
$P = E_v I_v \cos\phi$

$P = E_v \dfrac{E_v}{R} \cos 0° = \dfrac{E_v^2}{R} = \dfrac{(230)^2}{23} = 2300\,\text{W}$

(c) Let at an angular frequency the source power is half the power at resonant frequency.
$P = E_v I_v \cos\phi$

$\dfrac{1}{2}\left[\dfrac{E_v^2}{R}\right] = \dfrac{E_v E_v}{Z}\dfrac{R}{Z}$

$Z^2 = 2R^2$
$R^2 + (X_L - X_C)^2 = 2R^2$
$X_L - X_C = R$

$\omega L - \dfrac{1}{\omega C} = R$ or $\omega^2 - \dfrac{1}{LC} = \dfrac{R}{L}\omega$

where resonant angular frequency

$\omega_r = \dfrac{1}{LC} = \dfrac{1}{0.12 \times 480 \times 10^{-6}}$

so, $\omega^2 - w_r^2 = \pm\dfrac{R}{L}\omega$

two quadratic equations can be formed

$\omega^2 - \dfrac{R}{L}\omega - \omega r^2 = 0$ and $\omega^2 + \dfrac{R}{L}\omega - \omega_r^2 = 0$

On solving, we get

$\omega_1 = \dfrac{R}{2L} + \left[\omega_r^2 + \dfrac{R^2}{4L^2}\right]^{\frac{1}{2}} = \omega_r + \Delta\omega$ and

$$\omega_2 = -\frac{R}{2L} + \left[\omega^2 + \frac{R^2}{4L^2}\right]^{\frac{1}{2}} = \omega_r - \Delta\omega$$

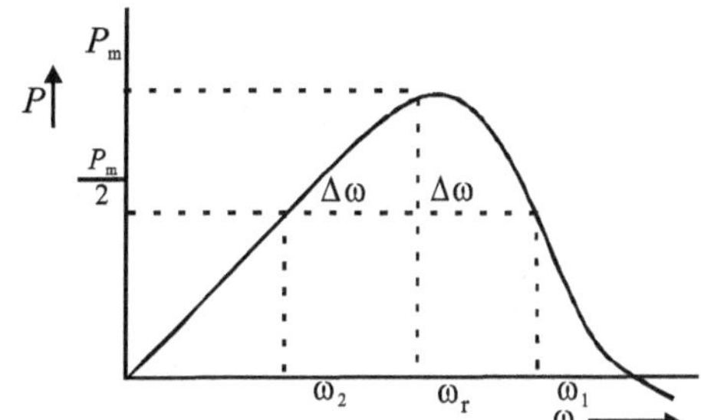

Now, $\omega_1 - \omega_2 = \dfrac{R}{L}$

$$[\omega_r + \Delta\omega] - [\omega_r - \Delta\omega] = \frac{R}{L} = \Delta\omega = \frac{R}{L}$$

$\Delta\omega = \dfrac{R}{2L}$ bandwidth of angular frequency

So, band width of frequency

$$\Delta f = \frac{\Delta\omega}{2\pi} = \frac{R}{4\pi L} = \frac{23}{4 \times 3.14 \times 0.12}$$

$\Delta f = 15.26\,\text{Hz}$

Hence the two frequencies for half power

$f_z = f_2 - \Delta f$ and $f_1 = f_r + \Delta f$

$f_z = 663 - 15.26 = 647.74\,\text{Hz}$

and $f_1 = 663 + 15.26 = 678.26\,\text{Hz}$

At these frequencies the current amplitude is

$$I = \frac{I_0}{\sqrt{2}} = 10\text{A}$$

(d) Q factor, $Q = \dfrac{1}{R}\sqrt{\dfrac{L}{C}}$ $Q = \dfrac{1}{23}\sqrt{\dfrac{0.12}{480 \times 10^{-6}}} = 21.7$

7.21. **Obtain the resonant frequency and Q-factor of a series LCR circuit with $L = 3.0\,\text{H}$, $C = 27\,\mu\text{F}$, and $R = 7.4\,\Omega$. It is desired to improve the sharpness of the resonance of the circuit by reducing its full width at half maximum by a factor of 2. Suggest a suitable way.**

Sol. Quality factor in the given resonant circuit.

$$Q = \frac{1}{R}\sqrt{\frac{L}{C}} = \frac{1}{7.4}\sqrt{\frac{3}{27 \times 10^{-6}}} = 45$$

We want to improve the quality factor to twice, without changing resonant frequency (without changing L and C).

$$Q' = 2Q = 90 = \frac{1}{R'}\sqrt{\frac{L}{C}} \text{ or } R' = \frac{1}{90}\sqrt{\frac{3}{27 \times 10^{-6}}} = 3.7\,\Omega$$

7.22. **Answer the following questions.**
  (a) **In any ac circuit, is the applied instantaneous voltage equal to the algebraic sum of the instantaneous voltages across the series elements of the circuit? Is the same true for rms voltage?**
  (b) **A capacitor is used in the primary circuit of an induction coil.**
  (c) **An applied voltage signal consists of a superposition of a dc voltage and an ac voltage of high frequency.**

The circuit consists of an inductor and a capacitor in series. Show that the dc signal will appear across C and the ac signal across L.
  (d) **A choke coil in series with a lamp is connected to a dc line. The lamp is seen to shine brightly. Insertion of an iron core in the choke causes no change in the lamp's brightness. Predict the corresponding observations if the connection is to an ac line.**
  (e) **Why is choke coil needed in the use of fluorescent tubes with ac mains? Why can we not use an ordinary resistor instead of the choke coil?**

Sol. (a) It is true that applied instantaneous voltage is equal to algebraic sum of instantaneous potential drop across each circuit element in series.

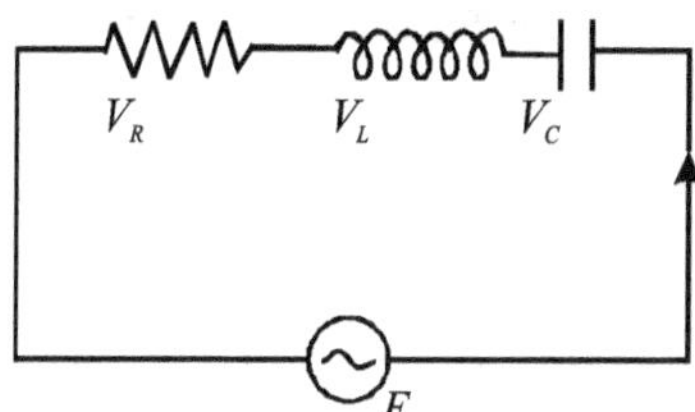

$$E = V_R + V_L + V_C$$

$$E_0\sin\omega t = \frac{E_0}{R}\sin\omega t + \frac{E_0}{X_L}\sin\left(\omega t - \frac{\pi}{2}\right) + \frac{E_0}{X_C}\sin\left(\omega t + \frac{\pi}{2}\right)$$

But the rms voltage applied is equal to vector sum of potential drop across each element, as voltage drops are in different phase.

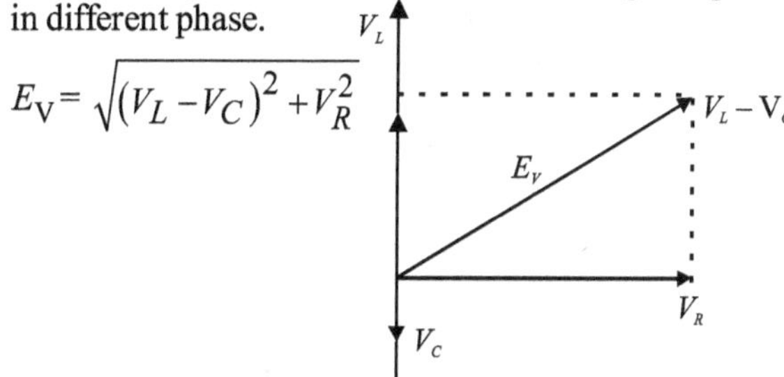

$$E_V = \sqrt{(V_L - V_C)^2 + V_R^2}$$

(b) At the time of broken circuit of the induction coil the high voltage induced charges the capacitor. This avoid sparking in the circuit.

(c) Inductive reactance $X_L = 2\pi fl$

  For a.c. $X_C \propto f$ For d.c. $f = 0, X_L = 0$

  Capacitive reactance $X_C = \dfrac{1}{2\pi fC}$

  For a.c. $X \propto \dfrac{1}{f}$ For d.c. $f = 0\ X_C = \infty$

So, superimpose applied voltage will have all d.c potential drop across X_C and will have most of a.c potential drop across X_L.

(d) Inductor offer no hinderance to d.c $X_L = 0$, so insertion of iron core does not effect the d.c. current or brightness of lamp connected.

But it definitely effect a.c. current as inserted of iron core increases 'L' $L = \mu_m\,nI$

thus increase X_L $(2\pi f L)$. a.c. current in the circuit

reduce $I_v = \dfrac{E_v}{X_L}$ and brightness of the bulb also reduce.

(e) A fluorescent tube is connected directly across a 220 V source, it would draw large current which may damage the filaments of the tube, so a choke coil which behaves as L-R circuit reduces the current to appropriate value, and that also which a lesser power loss.

$$I_v = \frac{E_v}{\sqrt{R^2 + X_L^2}}, \quad P = E_v I_v \cos\phi$$

An ordinary resistor used to control the current would have maximum power wastage as heat

$$I_v = \frac{E_v}{R}, \quad P_{max} = E_v I_v$$

7.23. **A power transmission line feeds input power at 2300 V to a step down transformer with its primary windings having 4000 turns. What should be the number of turns in the secondary in order to get output power at 230 V?**

Sol. Here $E_p = 2300$ V, $N_p = 400$ turns, $E_s = 230$ V, $N_s = ?$

We know in a transformer, $\dfrac{E_s}{E_p} = \dfrac{N_s}{N_p}$

$$N_s = \frac{E_s N_p}{E_p} = \frac{230 \times 4000}{2300} = 400 \text{ turns}$$

7.24. **At a hydroelectric power plant, the water pressure head is at a height of 300 m and the water flow available is $100 \text{ m}^3\text{s}^{-1}$. If the turbine generator efficiency is 60%, estimate the electric power available from the plant ($g = 9.8 \text{ ms}^2$).**

Sol. Work done by liquid pressure = pressure × volume shifted power of flowing water

$$\text{Hydro-power} = \frac{\text{work}}{\text{time}} = \text{pressure} \times \frac{\text{volume}}{\text{time}}$$

Hydro-power = $hdg \times (V/t)$
$= 300 \times 10^3 \times 9.8 \times 100 = 29.4 \times 10^7$ Watt

$$\text{Efficiency of turbine } \eta = \frac{\text{electric power}}{\text{hydro} - \text{power}}$$

$$0.6 = \frac{\text{electric power}}{29.4 \times 10^7}$$

Electric power $= 0.6 \times 29.4 \times 10^7 = 176.4 \times 10^6$ W
$= 176.4$ MW

7.25. **A small town with a demand of 800 kW of electric power at 220 V is situated 15 km away from an electric plant generating power at 440V. The resistance of the two wire line carrying power is 0.5 Ω per km. The town gets power from the line through a 4000-220 V step-down transformer at a sub station in the town.**
(a) Estimate the line power loss in the form of heat.
(b) How much power must the plant supply, assuming there is negligible power loss due to leakage?
(c) Characterise the step up transformer at the plant.

Sol.

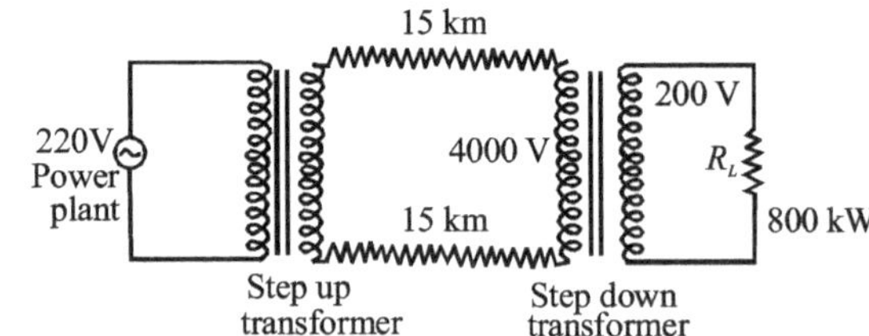

Line resistance = length of two wire line × resistance per unit length

Line resistance $(R) = 2 \times 15 \text{ km} \times 0.5 \dfrac{\Omega}{\text{km}} = 15\ \Omega$

Virtual a.c in the line, $P = E_v I_v$

$800 \times 10^3 = 4000\, I_V$ or $I_v = 200$ A

(a) Line power loss $P_{loss} = I_v^2 R = (200)^2 \times 15 = 600$ kW

(b) Assuming no power loss due to leakage, total power need to be supply by the power plant.

$$P_{total} = P_{loss} + P_{output} = 600 \text{ kW} + 800 \text{ kW} = 1400 \text{ kW}$$

(c) Potential drop in the line, $V = I_v R = 200 \times 15 = 3000$ V

So, the voltage output of step-up transformer at the plant should be $4000 + 3000 = 7000$ V.

hence at the plant the step-up transformer should be $440 - 7000$ V.

7.26. **Do the same exercise as above with the replacement of the earlier transformer by a 40,000 - 200 V step down transformer. (Neglect, as before, leakage losses through this may not be a good assumption any longer because of the very high voltage transmission involved) Hence, explain why high voltage transmission is preferred?**

Sol.

Virtual a.c in the time

$$I_v = \frac{P_{output}}{E_v} = \frac{800 \times 10^3}{40,000} = 20 \text{ A}$$

(a) Line power loss $P_{loss} = I_v^2 R = (20)^2 \times 15 = 6$ kW

(b) Power supplied by the plant
$$P_{Total} = P_{Loss} + P_{output} = 6 \text{ kW} + 800 \text{ kW} = 806 \text{ kW}$$

(c) Voltage drop in the line, $V = I_v R = 20 \times 15 = 300$ V.

Voltage output of step-up transformer at power station $Vf' = 40,000 + 300 = 40,300$ V

So, the step up transformer at the power plant is $220V - 40,300$ V.

Power loss in earlier arrangement,

$$P_1 = \frac{600 \times 10^3}{1400 \times 10^3} \times 100 = 43\%$$

Power loss in the arrangement,

$$P_2 = \frac{6 \times 10^3}{806 \times 10^3} \times 100 = 0.74\%$$

So, by supply of electricity at higher voltage, 40,000V instead by 4000 V the power loss is reduced greatly that is why the electric power is always transmitted at very high voltage.

Past year Exercise

Fill in the Blank

1. Laminated iron sheets are used to minimize _______ currents in the core of a transformer.

Very Short Answer Questions

2. A reactive element, in an AC circuit, causes the current flowing

   (i)   to lead in phase by $\pi/2$

   (ii) to lag in phase by $\pi/2$

with respect to the applied voltage. Identify the element in each case.

3. Define the term 'rms value of the current'. How is it related to the peak value?

4. The current flowing through a pure inductance 2 mH is, $I = 15 \cos 300t$ A. What is the (i) rms and (ii) average value of current for a complete cycle?

5. Define the term 'wattless current'.

6. Mention the two characteristic properties of the material suitable for making core of a transformer.

7. Why is the core of transformer laminated?

8. Why is the use of A.C. voltage preferred over D.C. voltage? Give two reasons.

9. Draw a graph to show variation of capacitive-reactance with frequency in an a.c. circuit.

10. Define capacitor reactance. Write its S.I. units.

Short Answer Questions

11. An AC voltage, $V = V_0 \sin \omega t$, is applied across a pure capacitor, C. Obtain an expression for the current, I in the circuit and hence, obtain the

   (i)   capacitive reactance of the circuit and

   (ii) the 'phase' of the current flowing with respect to the applied voltage.

12. Calculate the quality factor of a series L-C-R circuit with $L = 2.0$ H, $C = 2\mu F$ and $R = 10\Omega$. Mention the significance of quality factor in L-C-R circuit.

13. The graphs (i) and (ii) represent the variation of the opposition offered by the circuit element to the flow of alternating current with frequency of the applied emf. Identify the circuit element corresponding to each graph.

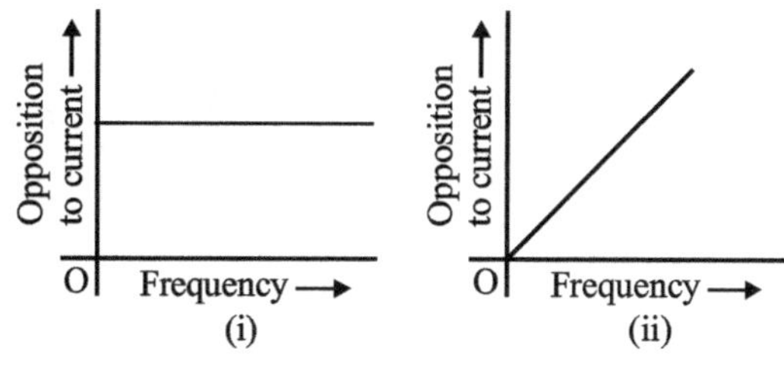

14. A light bulb is rated 150 W for 220 V AC supply of 60 Hz. Calculate

   (i)   the resistance of the bulb

   (ii) the rms current through the bulb.

15. An alternating voltage given by $V = 140 \sin 314\,t$ is connected across a pure resistor of 50 Ω. Find.

   (i)   the frequency of the source.

   (ii) the rms current through the resistor.

16. The figure shows a series L-C-R circuit with $L = 10.0$ H, $C = 40$ μF, $R = 60$ Ω connected to a variable frequency 240 V source, calculate

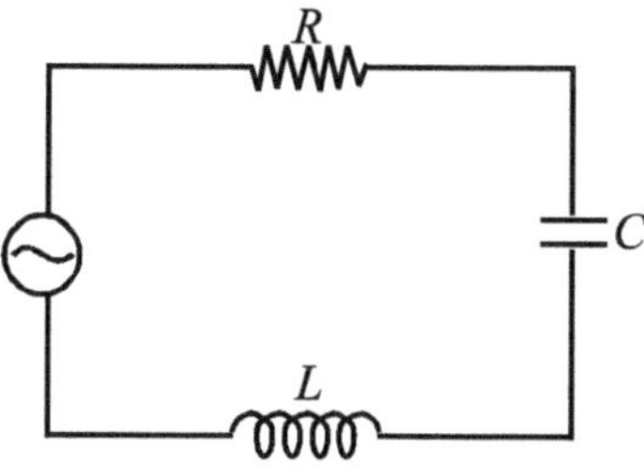

   (i)   the angular frequency of the source which drives the circuit at resonance.

   (ii) the current at the resonating frequency.

   (iii) the rms potential drop across the inductor at resonance.

17. A series L-C-R circuit is connected to an AC source. Using the phasor diagram, derive the expression for the impedance of the circuit. Plot a graph to show the variation of current with frequency of the source, explaining the nature of its variation.

18. (a) When an ac source is connected to an ideal capacitor show that the average power supplied by the source over a complete cycle is zero.

   (b) A lamp is connected in series with a capacitor. Predict your observations when the system is connected first across a dc and then an ac source. What happens in each case if the capacitance of the capacitor is reduced ?

19. In a series LCR circuit connected to an ac source of variable frequency and voltage $v = v_m \sin \omega t$, draw a plot showing the variation of current (I) with angular frequency (ω) for two different values of resistance R_1 and R_2 ($R_1 > R_2$). Write the condition under which the phenomenon of resonance occurs. For which value of the resistance out of the two curves, a sharper resonance is produced? Define Q-factor of the circuit and give its significance.

20. (a) For a given ac, $i = i_m \sin \omega t$, show that the average power dissipated in a resistor R over a complete cycle is $\dfrac{1}{2}i_m^2 R$.

   (b) A light bulb is rated at 100 W for a 220 V ac supply. Calculate the resistance of the bulb.

21. A voltage $V = V_0 \sin \omega t$ is applied to a series LCR circuit. Derive the expression for the average power dissipated over a cycle.

Under what condition (i) no power is dissipated even though the current flows through the circuit, (ii) maximum power is dissipated in the circuit?

22. A series LCR circuit is connected across an a.c. source of variable angular frequency 'ω'. Plot a graph showing variation of current 'i' as a function of 'ω' for two resistances R_1 and R_2 $(R_1 > R_2)$.

Answer the following questions using this graph.

(a) In which case is the resonance sharper and why?

(b) In which case is the power dissipation more and why?

23. An inductor L of inductance X_L is connected in series with a bulb B and an ac source. How would brightness of the bulb change when (i) number of turn in the inductor is reduced, (ii) an iron rod is inserted in the inductor and (iii) a capacitor of reactance $X_C = X_L$ is inserted in series in the circuit. Justify your answer in each case.

24. (i) When an AC source is connected to an ideal inductor show that the average power supplied by the source over a complete cycle is zero.

(ii) A lamp is conncected in series with an inductor and an AC source. What happens to the brightness of the lamp when the key is plugged in and an iron rod is inserted inside the inductor? Explain.

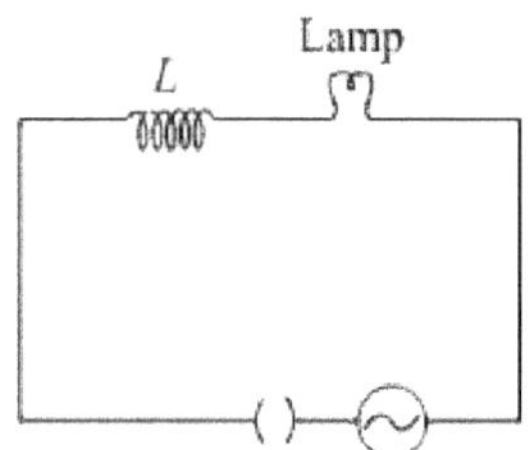

25. A resistance R and a capacitor C are connected in series to a source $V = V_0 \sin \omega t$.

Find:

(a) The peak value of the voltage across the (i) resistance and (ii) capacitor.

(b) The phase difference between the applied voltage and current. Which of them is ahead?

NCERT Exemplar

Multiple Choice Questions

1. If the rms current in a 50 Hz AC circuit is 5 A, the value of the current 1/300 s after its value becomes zero is

(a) $5\sqrt{2}$A   (b) $5\sqrt{3}/2$ A   (c) $5/6$ A   (d) $5/\sqrt{2}$A

2. An alternating current generator has an internal reactance R_g and an internal reactance X_g. It is used to supply power to a passive load consisting of a resistance R_g and a reactance X_L. For maximum power to be delivered from the generator to the load, the value of X_L is equal to

(a) zero   (b) X_g (c) $-X_g$ (d) R_g

3. When a voltage measuring device is connected to AC mains, the meter shows the steady input voltage of 220 V. This means

(a) input voltage cannot be AC voltage, but a DC voltage

(b) maximum input voltage is 220 V

(c) the meter reads not v but $< v^2 >$ and is calibrated to read $\sqrt{<v^2>}$

(d) The pointer of the meter is stuck by some mechanical defect

4. To reduce the resonant frequency in an L-C-R series circuit with a generator

(a) the generator frequency should be reduced

(b) another capacitor should be added in parallel to the first

(c) the iron core of the inductor should be removed

(d) dielectric in the capacitor should be removed

5. Which of the following combinations should be selected for better tuning of an L-C-R circuit used for communication?

(a) $R = 20\,\Omega, L = 1.5\,H, C = 35\,\mu F$

(b) $R = 25\,\Omega, L = 2.5\,H, C = 45\,\mu F$

(c) $R = 15\,\Omega, L = 3.5\,H, C = 30\,\mu F$

(d) $R = 25\,\Omega, L = 1.5\,H, C = 45\,\mu F$

6. An inductor of reactance $1\,\Omega$ and a resistor of $2\,\Omega$ are connected in series to the terminals of a 6 V (rms) AC source. The power dissipated in the circuit is

(a) 8 W   (b) 12 W   (c) 14.4 W   (d) 18 W

7. The output of a step-down transformer is measured to be 24 V when connected to a 12 W light bulb. The value of the peak current is

(a) $1/\sqrt{2}$ A   (b) $\sqrt{2}$ A   (c) 2 A   (d) $2\sqrt{2}$ A

Very Short Answer Questions

8. Draw the effective equivalent circuit of the circuit shown in Fig., at very high frequencies and find the effective impedance.

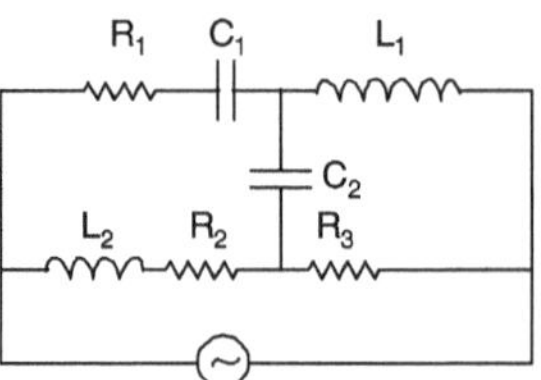

9. What will be the resonance point in $X_L - f$ and $X_C - f$ curves?

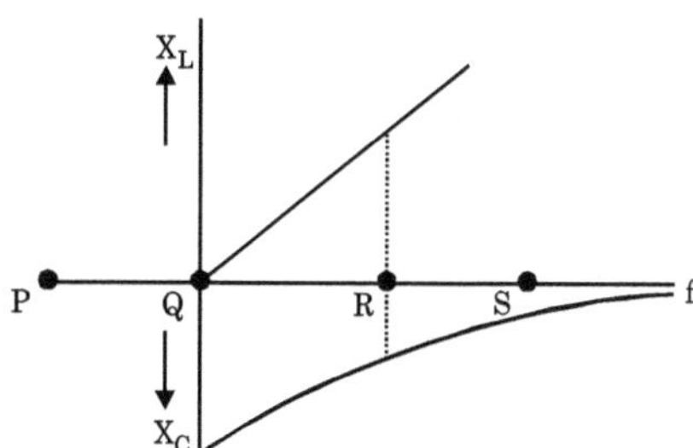

10. In a non-resonant ac circuit, what will be the nature of circuit for the frequencies higher than the resonant frequency?

Short Answer Questions

11. A device 'X' is connected to an a.c. source. The variation of voltage current and power in one complete cycle is shown in Fig.
    (a) Which curve shows power consumption over a full cycle?
    (b) What is the average power consumption over a cycle?
    (c) Identify the device 'X'.

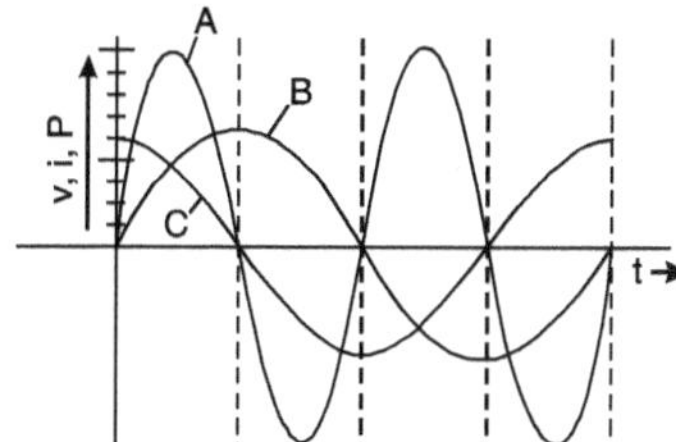

12. Explain why the reactance provided by a capacitor to an alternating current decreases with increasing frequency.

13. Three students X, Y and Z peformed an experiment for studying the variation of alternating currents with angular frequency in a series LCR circuit and obtained the graphs shown below. They all used a.c sources of the same r.m.s. value and inductances of the same value.

    What can we (qualitatively) conclude about the
    (i) capacitance value
    (ii) resistance values
    used by them. In which case will the quality factor be maximum?

    What can we conclude about nature of the impendance of the set up at frequency ω_0?

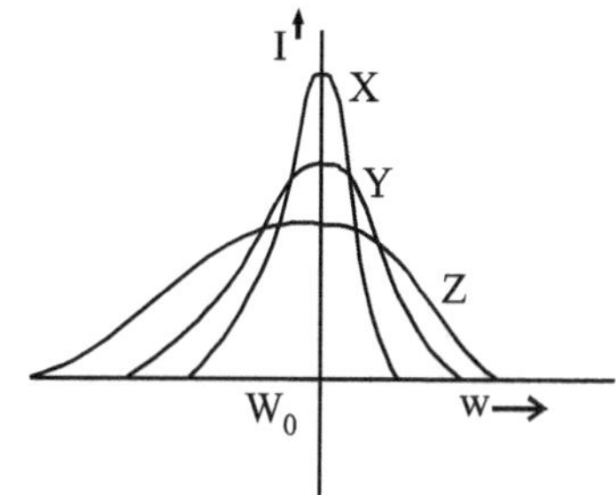

14. (a) If the current in a sinusoidally driven series RLC circuit leads the emf, would be increase or decrease the capacitance to increase the rate at which energy is supplied to the resistance?

    (b) Will this change bring the resonant angular frequency of the circuit closer to the angular frequency of the emf or put it farther away ?

Objective Practice Exercise

1. Alternating current cannot be measured by dc ammeter because
   (a) average value of complete cycle is zero
   (b) ac cannot pass through dc ammeter
   (c) ac is virtual
   (d) ac changes its direction

2. The r.m.s. value of current, I_{rms} is related to the peak current, I_0 by the relation

   (a) $I_{rms} = \sqrt{2}\, I_0$ (b) $I_{rms} = \pi I_0$

   (c) $I_{rms} = \dfrac{1}{\pi} I_0$ (d) $I_{rms} = \dfrac{1}{\sqrt{2}} I_0$

3. The instantaneous voltage through a device of impedance $20\,\Omega$ is $e = 80 \sin 100\,\pi t$. The effective value of the current is
   (a) 3 A   (b) 2.828 A
   (c) 1.732 A   (d) 4 A

4. A lamp consumes only 50% of peak power in an a.c. circuit. What is the phase difference between the applied voltage and the circuit current?

   (a) $\dfrac{\pi}{6}$ (b) $\dfrac{\pi}{3}$ (c) $\dfrac{\pi}{4}$ (d) $\dfrac{\pi}{2}$

5. When an ac voltage of 220 V is applied to the capacitor C, then
   (a) the maximum voltage between plates is 220 V.
   (b) the current is in phase with the applied voltage.
   (c) the charge on the plate is not in phase with the applied voltage.
   (d) power delivered to the capacitor per cycle is zero.

6. The voltage of an ac source varies with time according to the equation $V = 100 \sin 100\,\pi t \cos 100\,\pi t$ where t is in seconds and V is in volt. Then
   (a) the peak voltage of the source is 100 volt
   (b) the peak voltage of the source is 50 volt
   (c) the peak voltage of the source is $100/\sqrt{2}$ volt
   (d) the frequency of the source is 50 Hz

7. The voltage of an ac supply varies with time (t) as $V = 120 \sin 100\,\pi t \cos 100\,\pi t$. The maximum voltage and frequency respectively are

(a)   120 volt, 100 Hz (b) $\dfrac{120}{\sqrt{2}}$ volt, 100 Hz

(c)   60 volt, 200 Hz (d)   60 volt, 100 Hz

8. Determine the rms value of the emf given by
    E (in volt) = 8 sin (ω t) + 6sin (2 ω t)

    (a) $5\sqrt{2}$V (b) $7\sqrt{2}$V (c)   10V (d) $10\sqrt{2}$V

9. In an A.C. circuit with voltage V and current I the power dissipated is

    (a) $\dfrac{1}{\sqrt{2}}$VI

    (b) $\dfrac{1}{2}$VI

    (c)   VI

    (d)   dependent on the phase between V and I

10. The current I passed in any instrument in alternating current circuit is I = 2 sin ωt amp and potential difference applied is given by V = 5 cos ωt volt then power loss in instrument is
    (a)   2.5 watt (b)   5 watt (c)   10 watt (d)   zero

11. A resistance of 20 ohm is connected to a source of an alternating potential V = 200 cos(100 πt). The time taken by the current to change from its peak value to rms value, is
    (a) 2.5×10^{-3} s (b) 25×10^{-3} s
    (c)   0.25 s (d)   0.20 s

12. An alternating e.m.f. of angular frequency ω is applied across an inductance. The instantaneous power developed in the circuit has an angular frequency

    (a) $\dfrac{\omega}{4}$ (b) $\dfrac{\omega}{2}$ (c) ω (d)   2ω

13. A sinusoidal AC current flows through a resistor of resistance R. If the peak current is I_p, then power dissipated is

    (a) $I_p^2 R \cos\theta$ (b) $\dfrac{1}{2}I_p^2 R$

    (c) $\dfrac{4}{3}I_p^2 R$ (d) $\dfrac{1}{\pi^2}I_p^2 R$

14. A direct current of 5A is superimposed on an alternating current I = 10 sin ωt flowing through a wire. The effective value of the resulting current will be:

    (a)   15/2 amp (b) $5\sqrt{3}$ amp

    (c) $5\sqrt{5}$ amp (d)   15 amp

15. In an LCR circuit
    (a)   the impedance is equal to reactance
    (b)   the ratio between effective voltage to effective current is called reactance
    (c)   at resonance the resistance is equal to the resistance
    (d)   at resonance the net reactance is zero

16. The power factor in a circuit connected to an A.C.
    (a)   unity when the circuit contians an ideal inductance only
    (b)   unity when the circuit contians an ideal resistance only
    (c)   zero when the circuit contains an ideal resistance only
    (d)   unity when the circuit contains an ideal capacitance only

17. The time constant of C–R circuit is
    (a)   1/CR (b)   C/R (c)   CR (d)   R/C

18. In LCR circuit if resistance increases, quality factor
    (a)   increases finitely (b)   decreases finitely
    (c)   remains constant (d)   None of these

19. An inductor, a resistor and a capacitor are joined in series with an AC source. As the frequency of the source is slightly increased from a very low value, the reactance of the
    (a)   inductor increases (b)   resistor increases
    (c)   capacitor increases (d)   circuit increases

20. With increase in frequency of an A.C. supply, the impedance of an L-C-R series circuit
    (a)   remains constant
    (b)   increases
    (c)   decreases
    (d)   decreases at first, becomes minimum and then increases.

21. In an L.C.R. series a.c. circuit, the current
    (a)   is always in phase with the voltage
    (b)   always lags the generator voltage
    (c)   always leads the generator voltage
    (d)   None of these

22. A bulb and a capacitor are connected in series to a source of alternating current. If its frequency is increased, while keeping the voltage of the source constant, then bulb will
    (a)   give more intense light
    (b)   give less intense light
    (c)   give light of same intensity before
    (d)   stop radiating light

23. An LCR series circuit, connected to a source E, is at resonance. Then the voltage across
    (a)   R is zero (b)   R equals applied voltage
    (c)   C is zero (d)   L equals applied voltage

24. A capacitor in an ideal LC circuit is fully charged by a DC source, then it is disconnected from DC source, the current in the circuit
    (a)   becomes zero instantaneously
    (b)   grows , monotonically
    (c)   decays monotonically
    (d)   oscillate infinitely

25. Which one of the following curves represents the variation of impedance (Z) with frequency f in series LCR circuit?

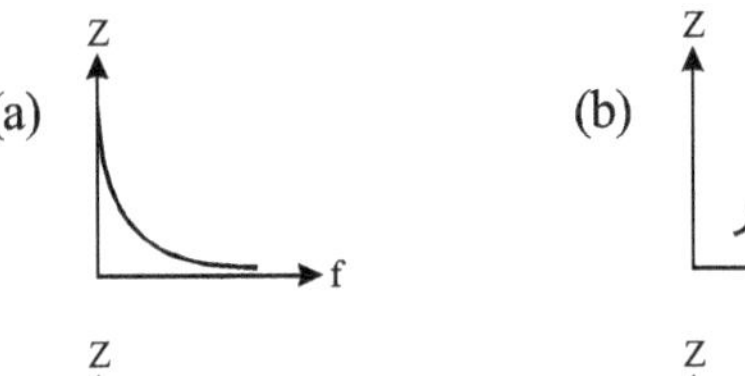

(a) 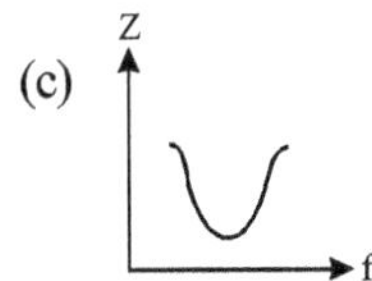 (b) 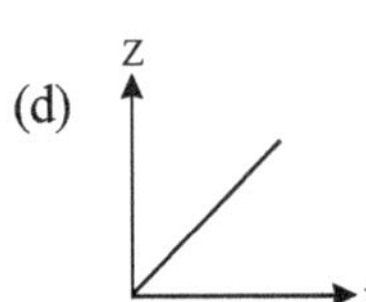

(c) (d)

26. An A.C. source is connected to a resistive circuit. Which of the following is true?
    (a)   Current leads ahead of voltage in phase
    (b)   Current lags behind voltage in phase
    (c)   Current and voltage are in same phase
    (d)   Any of the above may be true depending upon the value of resistance.

27. A resistance 'R' draws power 'P' when connected to an AC source. If an inductance is now placed in series with the resistance, such that the impedance of the circuit becomes 'Z', the power drawn will be

(a) $P\sqrt{\dfrac{R}{Z}}$ (b) $P\left(\dfrac{R}{Z}\right)$

(c) P (d) $P\left(\dfrac{R}{Z}\right)^2$

28. With increase in frequency of an A.C. supply, the inductive reactance

(a) decreases

(b) increases directly with frequency

(c) increases as square of frequency

(d) decreases inversely with frequency

29. The transformer voltage induced in the secondary coil of a transformer is mainly due to

(a) a varying electric field

(b) a varying magnetic field

(c) the vibrations of the primary coil

(d) the iron core of the transformer

30. A transformer is employed to

(a) convert A.C. into D.C.

(b) convert D.C. into A.C.

(c) obtain a suitable A.C. voltage

(d) obtain a suitable D.C. voltage

31. The loss of energy in the form of heat in the iron core of a transformer is

(a) iron loss   (b) copper loss

(c) mechanical loss   (d) None of these

32. Quantity that remains unchanged in a transformer is

(a) voltage   (b) current

(c) frequency   (d) None of these

33. The transformation ratio in the step-up transformer is

(a) one

(b) greater than one

(c) less than one

(d) the ratio greater or less than one depends on the other factor

34. A transistor-oscillator using a resonant circuit with an inductor L (of negligible resistance) and a capacitor C in series produce oscillations of frequency f. If L is doubled and C is changed to 4C, the frequency will be

(a) 8f   (b) $f/2\sqrt{2}$ (c) f/2   (d) f/4

35. A transformer has an efficiency of 80%. It works at 4 kW and 100 V. If secondary voltage is 240 V, the current in primary coil is

(a) 0.4 A   (b) 4 A   (c) 10 A   (d) 40 A

36. In an oscillating LC circuit the maximum charge on the capacitor is Q. The charge on the capacitor when the energy is stored equally between the electric and magnetic field is

(a) $\dfrac{Q}{2}$ (b) $\dfrac{Q}{\sqrt{3}}$ (c) $\dfrac{Q}{\sqrt{2}}$ (d) Q

37. In a transformer, number of turns in the primary coil are 140 and that in the secondary coil are 280. If current in primary coil is 4 A, then that in the secondary coil is

(a) 4 A   (b) 2 A   (c) 6 A   (d) 10 A.

38. A fully charged capacitor C with initial charge q_0 is connected to a coil of self inductance L at $t = 0$. The time at which the energy is stored equally between the electric and the magnetic fields is:

(a) $\dfrac{\pi}{4}\sqrt{LC}$ (b) $2\pi\sqrt{LC}$ (c) $\sqrt{LC}$ (d) $\pi\sqrt{LC}$

39. The primary winding of a transformer has 100 turns and its secondary winding has 200 turns. The primary is connected to an A.C. supply of 120 V and the current flowing in it is 10 A. The voltage and the current in the secondary are

(a) 240 V, 5 A   (b) 240 V, 10 A

(c) 60 V, 20 A   (d) 120 V, 20 A

40. An AC generator of 220 V having internal resistance r = 10Ω and external resistance R = 100Ω. What is the power developed in the external circuit?

(a) 484 W   (b) 400 W   (c) 441 W   (d) 369 W

41. A transformer is used to light a 100 W and 110 V lamp from a 220 V mains. If the main current is 0.5 amp, the efficiency of the transformer is approximately

(a) 50%   (b) 90%   (c) 10%   (d) 30%.

42. A treansformer is used to light a 140 watt, 24 volt lamp form 240 V AC mains. The current in the main cable is 0.4 4 amp. The efficiency of the transformer is:

(a) 48%   (b) 63.8%   (c) 83.3%   (d) 90%

43. A transformer reduces 220 V to 11 V. The primary draws 5 A of current and secondary 90 A. The efficiency of the transformer is

(a) 20%   (b) 40%   (c) 70%   (d) 90%

44. The current flowing in a step down transformer 220 V to 22 V having impedance 220 Ω, is

(a) 0.1 mA   (b) 1 mA   (c) 0.1 A   (d) 1 A

Chapter Test

Time : *30 minutes*   **Max. Marks : *15***

Direction :

Each question number **1-15** carry **1 mark** each.

1. Determine the rms value of the emf given by E(in volt) $= 8\sin(\omega t) + 6\sin(2\omega t)$
   (a) $5\sqrt{2}\,V$ (b) $7\sqrt{2}\,V$ (c) $10\,V$ (d) $10\sqrt{2}\,V$

2. In series combination of R, L and C with an A.C. source at resonance, if R = 20 ohm, then impedence Z of the combination is
   (a) 20 ohm (b) zero (c) 10 ohm (d) 400 ohm

3. Eddy currents in the core of transformer can't be developed by
   (a) increasing the number of turns in secondary coil
   (b) taking laminated transformer
   (c) making step down transformer
   (d) using a weak a.c. at high potential

4. A.C. power is transmitted from a power house at a high voltage as
   (a) the rate of transmission is faster at high voltages
   (b) it is more economical due to less power loss
   (c) power cannot be transmitted at low voltages
   (d) a precaution against theft of transmission lines

DIRECTIONS (Qs. 5-6) : *Each of these questions contains an assertion followed by reason. Read them carefully and answer the question on the basis of following options. You have to select the one that best describes the two statements.*
(a) If both Assertion and Reason are correct and the Reason is a correct explanation of the Assertion.
(b) If both Assertion and Reason are correct but Reason is not a correct explanation of the Assertion.
(c) If the Assertion is correct but Reason is incorrect.
(d) If the Assertion is incorrect but the Reason is correct.

5. **Assertion :** In the purely resistive element of a series LCR, AC circuit the maximum value of rms current increases with increase in the angular frequency of the applied emf.

   Reason : $\varepsilon_{max} = \dfrac{I_{max}}{z}$, $z = \sqrt{R^2 + \left(\omega L - \dfrac{1}{\omega C}\right)^2}$,

   where I_{max} is the peak current in a cycle.

6. **Assertion :** A capacitor blocks direct current in the steady state.

   Reason : The capacitive reactance of the capacitor is inversely proportional to frequency f of the source of emf.

DIRECTIONS : (Qs. 7-11) *are case based questions.*
A circuit containing a series combination of a resistance R, a coil of inductance L and a capacitor of capacitance C, connected with a source of alternating e.m.f. of peak value of E_0, as shown in fig.

Let in series LCR circuit applied alternating emf is $E = E_0 \sin \omega t$. As L, C and R are joined in series, therefore, current at any instant through the three elements has the same amplitude and phase. However voltage across each element bears a different phase relationship with the current.

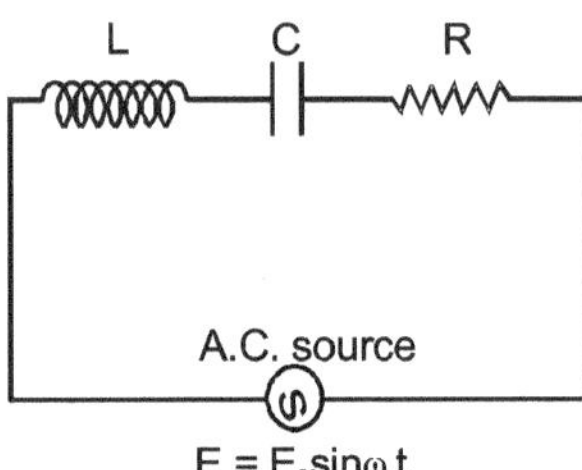

7. If an LCR series circuit is connected to an ac source, then at resonance the voltage across
   (a) R is zero
   (b) R equals the applied voltage
   (c) C is zero
   (d) L equals the applied voltage

8. At resonant frequency the current amplitude in series *LCR* circuit is
   (a) maximum (b) minimum (c) zero (d) infinity

9. Resonance frequency of LCR series a.c. circuit is f_0. Now the capacitance is made 4 times, then the new resonance frequency will become
   (a) $f_0/4$ (b) $2f_0$ (c) f_0 (d) $f_0/2$

10. If resistance of $100\,\Omega$, and inductance of 0.5 henry and capacitance of 10×10^6 farad are connected in series through 50 Hz A.C. supply, then impedance is
    (a) $1.8765\,\Omega$ (b) $18.76\,\Omega$
    (c) $187.6\,\Omega$ (d) $101.3\,\Omega$

11. In an L-C-R series circuit connected to an AC source, $V = V_0 \sin\left(100\pi t + \dfrac{\pi}{6}\right)$. Given $V_R = 40V$, $V_L = 40V$ and $V_C = 10V$. Resistance $R = 4\Omega$.
    Peak value of current in the circuit is
    (a) $10\sqrt{2}\,A$ (b) $15\sqrt{2}\,A$ (c) $20\sqrt{2}\,A$ (d) $25\sqrt{2}\,A$

Very Short Answer Type Questions

12. A capacitor of capacitive reactance $100\,\Omega$ is put across an alternating voltage $V = 200\sin 100t$ volts. Find the value of current in the circuit.

13. The frequency of a.c. is doubled. How do R_L, X_L and X_C get affected?

14. Show that a series LCR circuit driven by an a.c. source exhibits reronance at $\omega_r = \dfrac{1}{\sqrt{LC}}$

15. A series LCR circuit with $L = 0.12\,H$, $C = 4.8 \times 10^{-7}F$, $R = 23\Omega$ is connected to a variable frequency supply. At what frequency is the current maximum?

Solutions

1. **(a)**

2. **(b)** We know that, $I_{rms} = I_0 / \sqrt{2}$ and $I_m = 2I_0 / \pi$

$$\therefore \quad \frac{I_m}{I_{rms}} = \frac{2\sqrt{2}}{\pi}$$

3. **(b)** Given equation, $e = 80 \sin 100\pi t$ ...(i)
Standard equation of instantaneous voltage is given by
$e = e_m \sin\omega t$ ...(ii)
Compare (i) and (ii), we get $e_m = 80$ V
where e_m is the voltage amplitude.

Current amplitude, $I_m = \dfrac{e_m}{Z}$ where Z = impendence
$= 80/20 = 4$ A

$$I_{r.m.s} = \frac{4}{\sqrt{2}} = \frac{4\sqrt{2}}{2} = 2\sqrt{2} = 2.828 \text{ A}$$

4. **(c)** $i_{rms} = \dfrac{i_0}{\sqrt{2}} = \dfrac{4}{\sqrt{2}} = 2\sqrt{2}$ ampere

5. **(a)**

6. **(b)** $V_{rms} = \sqrt{\dfrac{(T/2)V_0^2 + 0}{T}} = \dfrac{V_0}{\sqrt{2}}$.

7. **(a)** DC is a constant current but AC varies sinusoidally.

8. **(b)** $\dfrac{I_0}{\sqrt{2}} = $ RMS current

9. **(d)**

10. **(b)** Given equation, $e = 80 \sin 100\pi t$ ...(i)
Standard equation of instantaneous voltage is given by
$e = e_m \sin\omega t$ ...(ii)
Compare (i) and (ii), we get $e_m = 80$ V
where e_m is the voltage amplitude.

Current amplitude $I_m = \dfrac{e_m}{Z}$ where Z = impendence
$= 80/20 = 4$ A.

$$I_{r.m.s} = \frac{4}{\sqrt{2}} = \frac{4\sqrt{2}}{2} = 2\sqrt{2} = 2.828 \text{ A}.$$

11. **(d)** $V = 120\sin100\pi t \cos100\pi t \Rightarrow V = 60 \sin200\pi t$
$V_{max} = 60 V$ and $v = 100$ Hz

12. **(a)** $2\pi n t = 400\pi t \quad \therefore n = 200$

$I_0 = 50\sqrt{2}$ amp.

r.m.s. current $= I_0 / \sqrt{2} = 50$ amp.

13. $I_{av} = \dfrac{2I_0}{\pi} = \dfrac{2 \times 14}{3.14} = 8.917$ A.

14. Frequency of domestic alternating current is 50 Hz.
It becomes zero twice in a complete cycle. So in one second it becomes zero 100 times.

15. Let the input alternating current is $I = I_0 \sin\omega t$.
If I remains constant for a small time dt, small amount of charge sent in time $dt = dq = Idt$
Total charge sent by a.c. in the first half cycle

$$= q = \int_0^{T/2} Idt = \int_0^{T/2} I_0 \sin\omega t = I_0 \left[-\frac{\cos\omega t}{\omega}\right]_0^{T/2}$$

$$= -\frac{I_0}{\omega}\left[\cos\frac{\omega t}{2} - \cos 0\right] = -\frac{I_0}{\omega}(\cos\pi - \cos 0°)$$

$$= -\frac{I_0}{\omega}(-1-1)$$

If I_m be the mean or average value of a.c. over first half cycle then

$$q = I_m \times \frac{I}{2} \text{ (by definition)}$$

$$\therefore \quad I_m \times \frac{T}{2} = \frac{2I_0}{\omega} = \frac{2I_0 \cdot T}{2\pi} \quad \therefore \quad I_m = \frac{2}{\pi}I_0 = 0.637\, I_0$$

Average value of a.c. over a complete cycle is zero.

$$I_{av} = \frac{\displaystyle\int_0^T I_0 \sin\omega t\, dt}{\displaystyle\int_0^T dt}$$

16. Let $I = I_0 \sin\omega t$ is the alternating current flowing through a resistance R in a small time dt.
$\therefore$ Heat produced $= dH = I^2Rdt$ ...(i)
If $I_{r.m.s}$ be the r.m.s value of current then by definition, heat produced in time t,

$$H = I_{r.m.s}^2 RT \qquad \text{...(ii)}$$

Comparing equations (i) and (ii),

$$I_{r.m.s}^2 RT = \int_0^T I^2 Rdt = R\int_0^T I^2 dt = R\int_0^T I_0^2 \sin^2 \omega t dt$$

$$I_{r.m.s}^2 T = \frac{I_0^2}{2}\int_0^T 2\sin^2 \omega t dt = \frac{I_0^2}{2}\int_0^T (1 - \cos 2\omega t)dt$$

$$= \frac{I_0^2}{2}\left[t - \frac{\sin 2\omega t}{2\omega}\right]_0^T = \frac{I_0^2}{2}\left[t - \frac{1}{2\omega}\left(\sin 2 \times \frac{2\pi}{T}t\right)\right]_0^T$$

$$= \frac{I_0^2}{2}\left[t - \frac{1}{2\omega}(\sin 4\pi - \sin 0)\right] = \frac{I_0^2 T}{2}$$

$$\therefore \quad I_{rms}^2 = \frac{I_0^2}{2} \qquad \therefore \quad I_{rms} = \frac{I_0}{\sqrt{2}}$$

17. As we know, $V = 300 \sin 313\, t$
Comparing this with the standard expression for the emf,
$V = V_0 \sin \omega t$, we get
$V_0 = 300$V
R.m.s value of voltage

$$V_{rms} = \frac{V_0}{\sqrt{2}} = \frac{300}{\sqrt{2}} = \frac{300\sqrt{2}}{2} = 150\sqrt{2} = 150 \times 1.414 = 212.1 \text{V}$$

18. Alternating current changes in magnitude and direction and the mean value of a.c. over a complete cycle is zero. Therefore moving coil ammeter will always read zero when cannected in an a.c. circuit of any frequency.

19. Here, $V = 200 \sin 314\,t$

Comparing this with the standard equation

$V = V_0 = \sin\omega t$, we get, $V_0 = 200\,V$, $R = 10\,\Omega$

(i) rms value of voltage $= V_{rms} = \dfrac{V_0}{\sqrt{2}} = \dfrac{200}{\sqrt{2}}$

$= 100\sqrt{2} = 100 \times 1.4.14 = 1414\,V.$

(ii) rms value of current $= I_{rms} = \dfrac{V_{rms}}{R} = \dfrac{141.4}{10} = 14.14\,A$

(iii) Average power dimipated as heat $= P = V_{rms} I_{rms} \cos\varphi$
For pure resistive circuit, $\varphi = 0 \Rightarrow \cos\varphi = 1$
$\therefore \quad P = V_{rms} I_{rms} = 141.4 \times 14.14 = 2000\,w = 2kW$

Practice Exercise-2

1. **(c)** Capacitive reactance, $X_C = \dfrac{1}{\omega C} = \dfrac{1}{2\pi f C}$

$\Rightarrow \ X_L \propto \dfrac{1}{f}$

With increases in frequency, X_C decreases.
Hence, option (c) represents the hyperbolic graph which is correct.

2. **(b)** Inductive reactance,
$X_L = \omega L = 2\pi f L$
$\Rightarrow \ X_L \propto f$
Hence, inductive reactance increases linearly with frequency.

3. **(d)** $(A) \to (2)$; $(B) \to (1)$; $(C) \to (4)$; $(D) \to (3)$
4. **(b)** $(A) \to (1)$; $(B) \to (2)$; $(C) \to (4)$; $(D) \to (3)$
5. **(d)** Resonant frequency does not depend upon the resistance of the circuit.
6. **(a)**

7. **(d)** $V_{rms} = \dfrac{200\sqrt{2}}{\sqrt{2}} = 200\,V$

$I_{rms} = \dfrac{V_{rms}}{X_C} = \dfrac{\dfrac{200}{1}}{100 \times 10^{-6}}$

$= 2 \times 10^{-2} = 20mA$

8. **(b)** In case of inductive circuit emf leads current by $\pi/2$ rad
9. **(c)** The inductive reactance limits the amplitude of current in a purely inductive circuit in the same way as the resistance limits the current in a purely resistive circuit.

i.e. $I_0 = \dfrac{\varepsilon_0}{X_L}$

10. **(a)** As $X_C = \dfrac{1}{\omega C}$, so for $\omega = 0$, $X_C \to \infty$.

11. **(c)** In series resonance circuit,

inductive reactance is equal to capacitive reactance.

i.e. $\omega L = \dfrac{1}{\omega C}$

$\therefore \ Z = \sqrt{R^2 + \left(\omega L = \dfrac{1}{\omega C}\right)^2} = R$

12. **(d)** In resonance condition when energy across capacitor is maximum, energy stored in inductor is zero, vice versa is also true.

13. **(d)** Assertion is false because the given relation is true if all voltages are instantaneous.

14. **(c)** Av. electric field energy $= \left(\dfrac{1}{2} CV_{rms}^2\right) = 25 \times 10^{-3}\,J$

$\therefore \quad \dfrac{1}{2} C \times (I_{rms} X_C)$

$\therefore \quad \dfrac{1}{2} \times C.I_{rms}^2 \times \dfrac{1}{4\pi^2 v^2 c^2} = 25 \times 10^{-3}\,J$

$\therefore \quad C = 20\mu F$

15. **(c)** Av. magnetic energy $\left(\dfrac{1}{2} LI_{rms}^2\right)$

$\therefore \quad L = \dfrac{2 \times 5 \times 10^{-3}}{(.10)^2} \Rightarrow L = 1\ \text{henry}$

16. **(d)** The sum for rms voltage across C, rms voltage across R and rms voltage across L is not equal to rms voltage across ideal ac source.

17. **(a)** At resonance, $\omega L = \dfrac{1}{\omega C}$

Hence the impedance of the circuit would be just equal to R (minimum). In other words, the LCR-series circuit will behave as a purely resistive circuit. Due to this the current is maximum. This condition is known as resonance

$\therefore \quad Z = R, \quad \text{Current} = \dfrac{V}{R}$

18. **(a)** At resonance inpedence $Z = R$
19. The metal detector works on the principle of resonance in ac circuits.
20. If $X_C < X_L$, the circuit is inductive and the current lags the source voltage.
21. A.C. ammeter works on the principle of heating effect. $(H \propto I^2 R)$
22. When the frequency of the input a.c. is 50 Hz the direction of current changes so rapidly that it can not be seen. Due to persistence of vision the bulb does not appear to lit intermittently but continuously.
23. In a pure inductor, the current lags behind the applied emf by $\pi/2$.
24. In a pure capacitive circuit, the current leads the voltage by $\pi/2$.
25. When frequency is increased, the impedance of the circuit

$Z = \sqrt{R^2 + \left(\dfrac{1}{\omega C}\right)^2}$ will decrease as $\omega = 2\pi f$ So the

current in the circuit $\left(I = \dfrac{E}{Z}\right)$ will increase, so the

brightness of the bulb will increase.

26. Inductive reactance $= X_L = \omega L = 2\pi fL$
If f increases, X_L will increase. Capacitive reactance $= X_C$
$$= \frac{1}{\omega C} = \frac{1}{2\pi fC}$$
If f increases, X_L will decrease.

27. Energy in the inductor $U \propto I^2$; $\quad \therefore U' = \dfrac{U}{4}$

28. Instantaneous power across a pure inductor $= P = EI = E_0 \sin\omega t\, I_0 \sin(\omega t - \pi/2)$
Average power over a full cycle of time period T

$$P = \frac{1}{T}\int_0^T EIdt = \frac{1}{T}\int_0^T E_0 I_0 \sin\omega t \sin(\omega t - \pi/2)dt$$

$$= -\frac{E_0 I_0}{2T}\int_0^T 2\sin\omega t \cos\omega t\, dt = -\frac{E_0 I_0}{2T}\int_0^T \sin\omega t\, dt$$

$$= \frac{E_0 I_0}{2T}\left[\frac{\cos 2\omega t}{2\omega}\right]_0^T = \frac{E_0 I_0}{2T.2\omega}$$

$\therefore$ Average power across a pure inductor over a complete cycle is zero.

29. Refer to Theory

30. Current at resonance $I = \dfrac{V}{R}$.

$\therefore$ Voltage across inductor, $V_L = I.X_L = \dfrac{V}{R}.\omega L = \dfrac{V}{R}.2\pi vL$

31. When current and voltage in LCR series circuit are in same phase, then $X_C = X_L =$ i.e. $\dfrac{1}{\omega C} = \omega L \Rightarrow \omega^2 = \dfrac{1}{LC}$

$$\therefore \quad C = \frac{1}{\omega^2 L} = \frac{1}{(2\pi f)^2 L} = \frac{1}{4\pi^2 f^2 L}$$

Here, $f = 60$ Hz, $L = 40$ mH $= 40 \times 10^{-3}$ H

$$\therefore \quad C = \frac{1}{4 \times (3.14)^2 \times (60)^2 \times 40 \times 10^{-3}} = 1.8 \times 10^{-4} \text{F}$$

32. Applied e.m.f. $= E = 310 \sin 314 t$
Comparing this with the standard equation of $E = E_0 \sin\omega t$, we get,

$E_0 = 310$, $\omega = 314$ sec^{-1} $\qquad E_{rms} = \dfrac{E_0}{\sqrt{2}} = \dfrac{310}{1.41} = 220$ V

Frequency $= f = \dfrac{\omega}{2\pi} = \dfrac{314}{2 \times 3.14}$ Hz.

$C = 25\,\mu F = 25 \times 10^{-6}$ F, $L = 0.1$H, $R = 25\,\Omega$

(i) $X_C = \dfrac{1}{314 \times 25 \times 10^{-6}} = 127.4\,\Omega$

$X_L = \omega L = 314 \times 0.1 = 31.4\,\Omega$

(ii) Impedance of the circuit,

$$Z = \sqrt{R^2 - (X_C - X_L)^2}$$

$$Z = \sqrt{R^2 - (X_C - X_L)^2} = \sqrt{(25)^2 + (96)^2}$$

$$= \sqrt{625 + 9216} = \sqrt{9841} = 99.2\,\Omega$$

(iii) Current in circuit $= I = \dfrac{E_{rms}}{Z} = \dfrac{220}{99.2} = 2.2$ A

33. $L = 50$ mH $= 50 \times 10^{-3}$H, $C = 20\,\mu F = 20 \times 10^{-6}$F, $R = 10\,\Omega$, $V = 220$ V

(i) resonant frequency $= \omega$

$$= \frac{1}{\sqrt{LC}} = \frac{1}{\sqrt{50 \times 10^{-3} \times 20 \times 10^{-6}}} = 10^3 \text{ rad/s.}$$

(ii) current at resonance $= I = \dfrac{V}{R} = \dfrac{220}{10} = 22$ A

(iii) Maximum power dissipated $= E_{rms}\, I_{rms}$

$$= 220 \times \frac{220}{10} = 4840 \text{ W}$$

34.

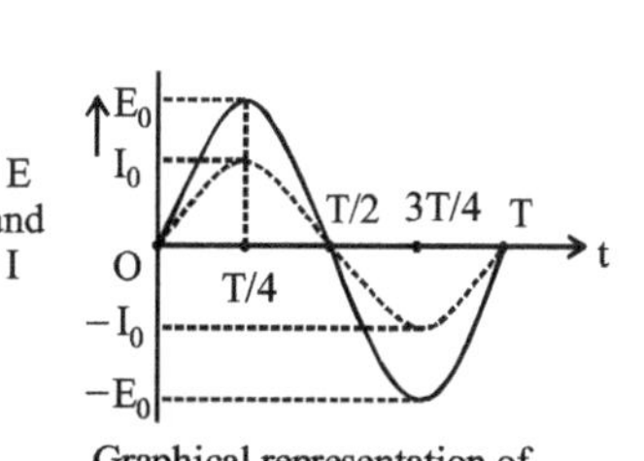

Let V_R be the instantaneous voltage drop across R.
E is the applied alternating e.m.f. to the circuit. E_0 is the maximum voltage.

$\therefore \qquad E = E_0 \sin\omega t = IR$

$\therefore \qquad I = \dfrac{E_0}{R}\sin\omega t = I_0 \sin\omega t$

where $I_0 = \dfrac{E_0}{R} =$ Maximum value of current.

$\therefore \qquad$ Current and voltage are in phase with each other.

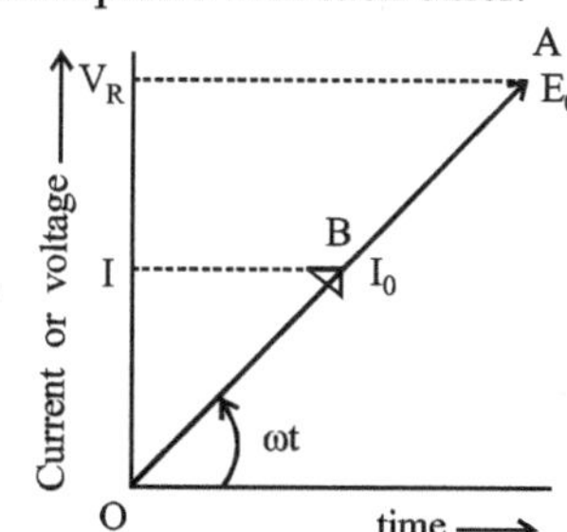

Graphical representation of voltage and current

Phasor Diagram

The reflections of E_0 and I_0 on y-axis gives the instantaneous voltage drop across R (V_R). ωt is called the phase angle.

35. Instantaneous power $= P = EI = E_0 \sin\omega t . I_0 \sin\omega t$
as current and voltage are in phase with each other in a pure resistive circuit.
Average power over a full cycle of period T

$$= P = \frac{1}{T}\int_0^T EIdt = \frac{E_0 I_0}{T}\int_0^T \sin^2\omega t\, dt$$

$$= \frac{E_0 I_0}{2T}\int_0^T (1 - \cos 2\omega t)dt$$

$$P = \frac{E_0 I_0}{2T}\left[\int_0^T dt - \int_0^T \cos 2\omega t\, dt\right] = \frac{E_0 I_0}{2T}\left[t\Big|_0^T - \frac{\sin 2\omega t}{2\omega}\Big|_0^T\right]$$

$$= \frac{E_0 I_0}{2T}\left[(T - 0) - \frac{1}{2\omega}(\sin 2\omega T - \sin 0)\right]$$

$$= \frac{E_0 I_0}{2T}\left[T - \frac{1}{2\omega}(\sin 4\pi - \sin 0)\right] \quad [\because \ \omega T = 2\pi]$$

$$= \frac{E_0 I_0}{2T}.T = \frac{E_0 I_0}{2} = \frac{E_0}{\sqrt{2}}.\frac{I_0}{\sqrt{2}} = E_{rms}.I_{rms}.$$

$$\therefore \ P = E_{rms}.I_{rms} = \frac{E_{rms}}{R}$$

36.

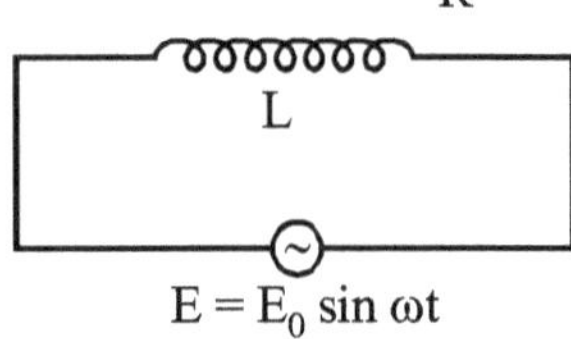

$$E = E_0 \sin \omega t$$

Consider a pure inductor across which an alternating e.m.f
$E = E_0 \sin \omega t$ is applied.

A pure inductor has no resistance.

$\therefore$ By Faraday's law of electromagnetic induction,

Instantaneous voltage across I = Induced e.m.f. across it (numerically)

$$E = L\frac{dI}{dt} = E_0 \sin \omega t$$

$$\therefore \ \int dI = \frac{E_0 / L}{\sin \omega t \, dt} \qquad \therefore \ dI = \frac{E_0}{L}\sin \omega t \, dt$$

Integrating,

$$I = \frac{E_0}{L}\left(-\frac{\cos \omega t}{\omega}\right) = -\frac{E_0}{\omega L}\sin\left(\frac{\pi}{2} - \omega t\right)$$

$$I = \frac{E_0}{\omega L}\sin\left(\omega t - \pi / 2\right) = I_0(\omega t - \pi / 2)$$

where $I_0 = \dfrac{E_0}{\omega L} = \dfrac{E_0}{X_L}$

$X_L = \omega L$ is called inductive reactance.

Current in inductor lags behind the voltage by $\pi / 2$.

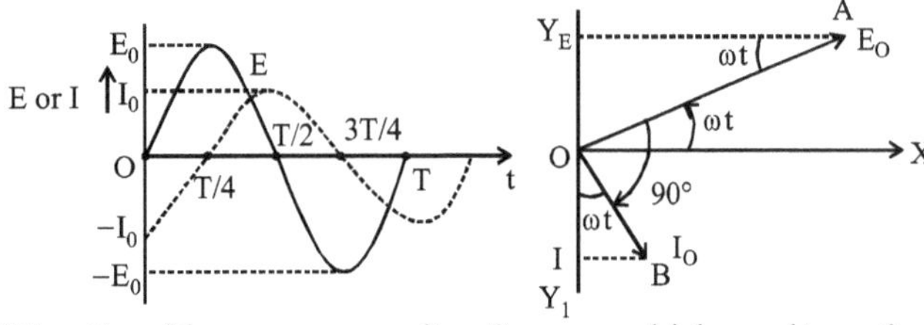

37. Consider a pure capacitor C across which an alternating emf $E = E_0 \sin \omega t$ is applied.

Instantaneous potential drop across the capacitor is equal to the instantaneous applied e.m.f.

$$\therefore \ V = \frac{q}{C} = E_0 \sin \omega t \ \Rightarrow \ q = CE_0 \sin \omega t$$

$$\therefore \ I = \frac{dq}{dt} = \frac{d}{dt}(CE_0 \sin \omega t) = CE_0\omega(\cos \omega t)$$

$$\Rightarrow \ I = \frac{E_0}{1 / \omega C}\sin \ (\omega t + \pi / 2) = I_0 \sin \ (\omega t + \pi / 2)$$

where $I_0 = \dfrac{E_0}{1 / \omega C} = \dfrac{E_0}{X_C}$ where X_C is called capacitive

reactance and $X_C = \dfrac{1}{\omega C} = \dfrac{1}{2\pi fC}$.

Current leads e.m.f in pure capacitor by $\pi / 2$

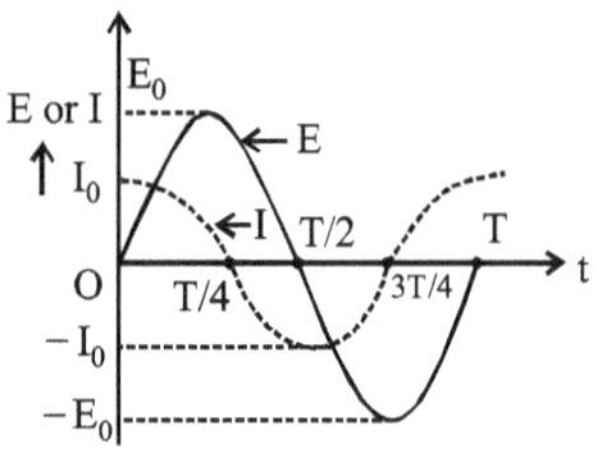

Graphical representation of E and I

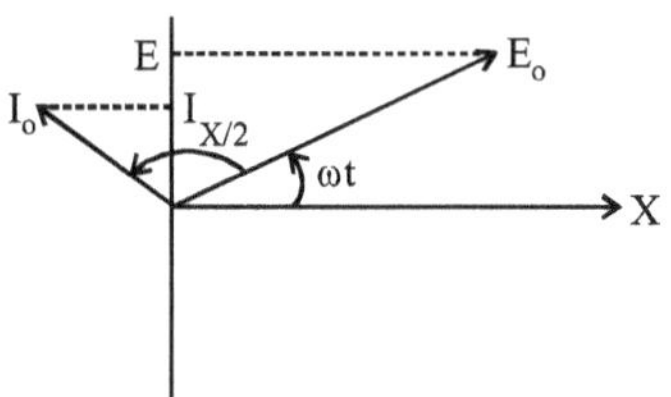

Phasor diagram showing that current
leads the voltage by $\pi/2$

38. Consider a pure inductor of inductance L.
The induced e.m.f at any instant of time is equal to the applied e.m.f across L at that instant.

$$\therefore \ E = -L\frac{dI}{dt}$$

This induced e.m.f tends to oppose the growth of current. To maintain this growth, power has to be supplied from external source. Total work done by a source to establish a current I from O is stored at any instant t,

$$\frac{d\omega}{dt} = EI = L\frac{dI}{dt}.I$$

$$\therefore \quad d\omega = LIdI$$

$\therefore$ Total work done to build up current from 0 to I_0

$$W = \int_0^{I_0} LIdI = L\left[\frac{I^2}{2}\right]_0^{I_0} = \frac{1}{2}LI_0^2$$

$\therefore$ Energy stored in an inductor $= \dfrac{1}{2}LI_0^2$

39. When capacitance is reduced, capacitive reactance,

$X_C = \dfrac{1}{\omega C}$ increases, hence impedance of circuit

$Z = \sqrt{R^2 + X_C^2}$ increases and hence current $I = \dfrac{V}{Z}$

decreases. As a result, brightness of the bulb is reduced.

40. When an iron core is inserted in the choke coil, the brightness of the bulb decreases. The room is, when the iron core is inserted into the choke coil, the inductance of the coil increases. So the inductive reactance $(X_L = \omega L)$

of the coil increases and impedance $\left(Z = \sqrt{R^2 + X_L^2}\right)$

also increases. Therefore, the current $I = \dfrac{V}{Z}$ decreases and

consequently the bulb becomes dim.

41. Impedance of series LR circuit $= Z = \sqrt{R^2 + X_L^2}$.

When capacitor is also connected in circuit, impedance,

$$Z' = \sqrt{R^2 + (X_L - X_C)^2}$$

Clearly $Z' < Z$, so value of current $\left(I = \dfrac{V}{Z}\right)$ increases.

42. The self inductance of iron cored choke is much greater than air cored choke. The resonant frequency $\omega_r = \dfrac{1}{\sqrt{LC}} \propto \dfrac{1}{\sqrt{L}}$ for same C. Radio frequency is higher than audio frequency. Therefore for resonance with radio frequency less inductance of air cored choke is required; whereas for resonance with audio frequency greater value of inductance or iron core choke is used.

43. Given : $R = 12\,\Omega$, $L = \dfrac{0.05}{\pi}\,H$, $f = 50$ cycles/s

Inductive reactance $= X_L = \omega L = 2\pi$

$fL = 2\pi \times 50 \times \dfrac{0.05}{\pi} = 5\,\Omega$

Impedance of the circuit

$$Z = \sqrt{R^2 + X_L^2} = \sqrt{12^2 + 5^2} = 12\,\Omega$$

Current in the circuit $= I_{rms} = \dfrac{V_{rms}}{Z} = \dfrac{130}{13} = 10\,A$

Potential difference across the inductor $= V_L = I\,X_L = 5 \times 10 = 50\,V$

44. Here, $R = 10\,\Omega$, $E = 100V$, $f = 50Hz$, $\varphi = \pi/4$

$$\tan\varphi = \dfrac{X_L}{R} = \dfrac{\omega L}{R} = \dfrac{2\pi f L}{R}$$

$$\therefore L = \dfrac{R\tan\varphi}{\pi f} = \dfrac{10 \times \tan\dfrac{\pi}{4}}{2 \times 3.14 \times 50} = \dfrac{10 \times 1}{314} = 0.03184\,H$$

45. Here, $R = 30\,\Omega$, $C = 0.25\,\mu F = 0.25 \times 10^{-6}\,F$, $V = 100\,V$, $\omega = 1,00,000$ rad/s $= 10^5$ rad/s

$$X_C = \dfrac{1}{\omega C} = \dfrac{1}{10^5 \times 0.25 \times 10^{-6}} = 40\,\Omega$$

$$Z = \sqrt{R^2 + X_C^2} = \sqrt{30^2 + 40^2} = 50\,\Omega$$

$$\text{Current} = \dfrac{V}{Z} = \dfrac{100}{50} = 2\,A$$

Voltage across resistance $= V_R = IR = 30 \times 2 = 60V$.

Voltage across capacitance $= V_C = I\,X_C = 40 \times 2 = 80V$.

The sum of the voltage across the resistance and capacitance is more than the applied voltage because of the phase difference $\pi/2$ between the voltages V_R and V_C.

46. Applied Voltage $= V$

$$= \sqrt{V_C^2 + V_R^2} = \sqrt{(200)^2 + (150)^2} = 250\,V$$

Impedance of circuit $= Z = \dfrac{V}{I} = \dfrac{250}{5} = 50\,\Omega$

Phase angle between voltage and current $= \tan\varphi$

$$= \dfrac{X_L}{R} = \dfrac{V_L}{V_R} = \dfrac{200}{150} = \dfrac{4}{3} \quad \therefore \varphi = \tan^{-1}\left(\dfrac{4}{3}\right) = 53°$$

47. Here, $f = 50$ Hz, $L = 50$ mH $= 50 \times 10^{-3}\,H$

For maximum brightness of the bulb, the impedance of the circuit should be minimum.

Condition for minimum impedance is $X_L = X_C$

$$\Rightarrow \omega L = \dfrac{1}{\omega C} \Rightarrow \omega^2 = \dfrac{1}{LC}$$

$$C = \dfrac{1}{\omega^2 L} = \dfrac{1}{(2\pi f)^2 L} = \dfrac{1}{4\pi^2 f^2 L}$$

$$= \dfrac{1}{4 \times (3.14)^2 \times (500)^2 \times 50 \times 10^{-3}}$$

$$C = 2 \times 10^{-4}\,F$$

48. (i) When the number of turns in the inductor is reduced, the self inductance of coil decreases; so impedance of circuit reduces and so current increases. Thus the brightness of the bulb increases.

(ii) When capacitor of reactance $X_C = X_L$ is introduced the net reactance of circuit becomes zero, so impedance of circuit decreases. Therefore $Z = R$, so current in the circuit increases, hence brightness of bulb increases. Thus brightness of bulb increases in both cases.

Practice Exercise-3 

1. **(b)** $\dfrac{n_p}{n_s} = \dfrac{E_p}{E_s} = \dfrac{1}{25}$

$\therefore E_s = 25\,E_p$

But $E_s I_s = E_p I_p \Rightarrow I_p = \dfrac{E_s \times I_s}{E_p} \Rightarrow I_p = 50A$

2. **(d)** Most of the electrical devices we use require AC voltage. This is mainly because most of the electrical energy sold by power companies is transmitted and distributed as alternating current. The main reason for preferring use of AC voltage over DC voltage is that AC voltage can be easily and efficiently converted from one voltage to the other by means of transformers.

3. **(a)** Iron loss is the energy loss in the form of heat due to the formation of eddy currents in the iron core of the transformer.

4. **(a)** $\dfrac{E_s}{E_p} = \dfrac{n_s}{n_p}$ or $E_s = E_p \times \left(\dfrac{n_s}{n_p}\right)$

$\therefore E_s = 120 \times \left(\dfrac{200}{100}\right) = 240\,V$

$\dfrac{I_p}{I_s} = \dfrac{n_s}{n_p}$ or $I_s = I_p \left(\dfrac{n_p}{n_s}\right)$ $\therefore I_s = 10\left(\dfrac{100}{200}\right) = 5$ amp

5. **(a)** Here, $C = 30\,\mu F = 30 \times 10^{-6}\,F$, $L = 27$ mH $= 27 \times 10^{-3}\,H$

$\therefore \omega = \dfrac{1}{\sqrt{LC}} = \dfrac{1}{\sqrt{27 \times 10^{-3} \times 30 \times 10^{-6}}} = \dfrac{1}{\sqrt{81 \times 10^{-8}}}$

$= \dfrac{10^4}{9} = 1.1 \times 10^3$ rad s^{-1}

6. **(b)** If q is the required charge, then

$$\dfrac{q^2}{2C} = \dfrac{1}{2}\dfrac{Q^2}{2C}$$

$$\therefore q = \dfrac{Q}{\sqrt{2}}.$$

7. **(c)** Transformer cannot produce power, but it transfer from primary to secondary.

8. **(d)** Large eddy currents are produced in non-laminated iron core of the transformer by the induced emf, as the resistance of bulk iron core is very small. By using thin iron sheets as core the resistance is increased. Laminating the core substantially reduces the eddy currents. Eddy current heats up the core of the transformer. More the eddy currents greater is the loss of energy and the efficiency goes down.

9. **(a)** Step up transformer

$$\frac{N_s}{N_p} = \frac{V_s}{V_p} \Rightarrow \frac{10}{1} = \frac{V_s}{4000}$$

$\therefore$ $V_s = 40,000\,V$

Step down transformer

$$\frac{N_p}{N_s} = \frac{V_p}{V_s} = \frac{40,000}{200} = \frac{200}{1}$$

10. **(b)** Power $P = V \times I$

$$\Rightarrow I = \frac{P}{V} = \frac{600 \times 1000}{4000} = 150\,A$$

Total resistance $= 0.4 \times 20 = 8\,\Omega$

$\therefore$ Power dissipated as heat $= I^2 R = (150)^2 \times 8$

$$= 180,000\,W = 180\,kW$$

$\therefore$ % loss $= \dfrac{180}{600} \times 100 = 30\%$

11. **(b)** Transformers are used in AC circuits only

12. **(c)** A transformer is employed to obtain a suitable AC voltage.

13. **(b)** Voltage induced in the secondary coil of a transformer is mainly due to a varying magnetic field.

14. The flux leakage in a transformer can be reduced by winding the primary and secondary coils one over the other.

15. The magnetisation of the core is repeatedly reversed by the alternating magnetic field which results in loss of energy as heat.

16. In steady current, the phenomenon of mutual induction does not take place.

17. (i) Magnetic energy (ii) Electrical energy.

18. There are three assumptions:–
(i) The primary resistance and current are small.
(ii) The same flux links both the primary and the secondary as very little flux escapes from the core.
(iii) The secondary current is small.

19. For an ideal transformer, output power = input power

$$E_s I_s = E_p I_p = 24\,W$$

$E_s = 24\,V.$ $\qquad \therefore I_s = \dfrac{24}{E_s} = \dfrac{24}{24} = 1\,A$

$E_p = 240\,V.$ $\qquad \therefore I_p = \dfrac{24}{240} = 0.1\,A$

20. Given $N_p = 200$, $N_s = 1000$, $P_{output} = 10\,kW = 10^4\,W$,

$E_p = 200\,V.$

For an ideal transformer $P_{output} = P_{input} = 10^4\,W$

$$\Rightarrow E_s I_s = E_p I_p \Rightarrow \frac{E_s}{E_p} = \frac{N_s}{N_p}$$

$$\therefore E_s = \frac{N_s}{N_p} \times E_p = \frac{1000}{200} \times 200 = 1000\,V.$$

Input power $= E_p I_p = 10^4 \Rightarrow I_p = \dfrac{10^4}{200} = 50\,A$

Past year Exercise

1. Eddy currents.

2. (i) In case of pure capacitive circuit, the current leads in phase by $\pi/2$ with respect to the applied voltage. So, the element will be a capacitor.
(ii) In case of pure inductive circuit, the current lags in phase by $\pi/2$ w.r.t the applied voltage. So, the element will be an inductor.

3. The rms value of alternating current is equal to that value of DC which produces same amount of heat in a given resistance as produced by the given AC, when passed for the same time (T).

$$I_{rms} = \frac{I_0}{\sqrt{2}} \qquad \text{where, } I_0 = \text{peak value of AC.}$$

4. Current flowing through the inductor

$$I = 15\cos(300t)$$

Comparing with $I = I_0 \sin \omega t$

Here, peak value of current, $I_0 = 15\,A$

(i) $\therefore$ $I_{rms} = \dfrac{I_0}{\sqrt{2}} = \dfrac{15}{\sqrt{2}}\,A$

(ii) For complete cycle, average value of current is zero i.e., $I_{av} = 0$

5. **Wattless current** – The current in an AC circuit, when average power consumption in AC circuit is zero, is referred as wattless current.

If, ϕ is the phase difference between voltage and current then, power associated with $I \sin \phi$ $I \sin \phi$ component of current, is termed as wattless current.

6. (i) Low retentivity or coercivity.
(ii) Low hysterisis loss

7. To reduce the effects of eddy currents.

8. The reasons of using A.C. voltage over D.C. voltage are,
(i) By using a transformer A.C. voltage can be stepped up and stepped down as per the requirement
(ii) A.C. voltage can be transmitted over long distances without loss of energy as compared to D.C. voltage.

9. As capacitive reactance

$$X_C = \frac{1}{\omega C} = \frac{1}{2\pi f C}$$

Hence, it is inversely proportional to frequency f.
Graph: X_C versus f

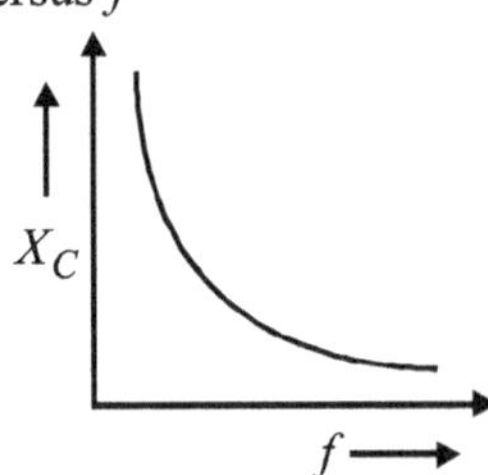

10. In a purely capacitive circuit the current leads the applied emf by an angle $\pi/2$ and the impedance of the circuit is $1/\omega C$ and this is known as capacitor or capacitive reactance $Z = X_C = \dfrac{1}{\omega C}$.

The SI unit of capacitor reactance is ohm (Ω).

11. (i) $V = V_0 \sin \omega t$ ...(i)

Let, alternating voltage, $V = V_0 \sin \omega t$ is applied across a capacitor, C. At any instant, the PD across the capacitor is equal to applied voltage.

$\therefore$ $V =$ Potential difference across the capacitor $= \dfrac{q}{C}$

$\Rightarrow$ $q = CV$ or $q = CV_0 \sin \omega t$

$\therefore$ $\dfrac{dq}{dt} = \omega C \, V_0 \cos \omega t$

or $I = \dfrac{V_0}{\left(\dfrac{1}{\omega C}\right)} \cos \omega t$ or $I = I_0 \sin\left(\omega t + \dfrac{\pi}{2}\right)$ ...(ii)

where, $I_0 = \dfrac{V_0}{\left(\dfrac{1}{\omega C}\right)} = \dfrac{V_0}{X_C}$

Capacitive reactant, $X_c = \dfrac{1}{\omega C}$

(ii) From Eqs. (i) and (ii), current leads the voltage by phase $\dfrac{\pi}{2}$.

12. Given,

$L = 2.0 \, \text{H}$

$C = 2\mu F = 2 \times 10^{-6} \, \text{F}$

$R = 10 \, \Omega$

Now, Q-factor $= \dfrac{1}{R}\sqrt{\dfrac{L}{C}} = \dfrac{1}{10}\sqrt{\dfrac{2}{2 \times 10^{-6}}}$

$= \dfrac{1}{10 \times 10^{-3}} = \dfrac{1}{10^{-2}} = 100$

Quality factor is also defined as $Q = 2\pi f \times \dfrac{\text{Energy stored}}{\text{Power loss}}$

So, higher the value of Q means the energy loss is at lower rate relative to the energy stored, i.e., the oscillations will die slowly and damping would be less.

13. (i) From graph (i), it is clear that resistance (opposition to current) is not changing with frequency, i.e., resistance does not depend on frequency of applied source, so the circuit element here is pure resistance (R)

From graph (ii), it is clear that resistance increases linearly with frequency, so the circuit element here is an inductor.

Inductive resistance $X_L = 2\pi f L \Rightarrow X_L \propto f$

14. (i) $P = 150 \, \text{W}, V = 220 \, \text{V}$

Resistance of the bulb,

$R = \dfrac{V^2}{P} = \dfrac{220 \times 220}{150} = 322.7 \, \Omega$

(ii) As $I_{rms} = \dfrac{V_{rms}}{R} = \dfrac{220}{322.7}$ $(V_{rms} = V = 220V)$

$\Rightarrow I_{rms} = 0.68 \, \Omega$

15. Given, $V = 140 \sin 314t, R = 50 \, \Omega$

Comparing it with $V = V_0 \sin \omega t$

(i) Here, $\omega = 314 \, \text{rad/s}$

i.e., $2\pi v = 314$ $[\because \omega = 2\pi v]$

$\Rightarrow$ $v = \dfrac{314}{2\pi} = \dfrac{31400}{2 \times 314} = 50 \, \text{Hz}$

Frequency of AC, $v = 50 \, \text{Hz}$

(ii) As, $I_{rms} = \dfrac{V_{rms}}{R}$ and $V_{rms} = \dfrac{V_0}{\sqrt{2}}$

Here, $V_0 = 140 \, \text{V} \Rightarrow V_{rms} = \dfrac{140}{\sqrt{2}} \times \dfrac{\sqrt{2}}{\sqrt{2}} = 70\sqrt{2} \, \text{V}$

$\therefore I_{rms} = \dfrac{70\sqrt{5}}{R} = \dfrac{70\sqrt{5}}{50} = 1.9 \, \text{A or } 2 \, \text{A}$

16. Given : $= L = 10 \, \text{H}, C = 40 \, \mu F, R = 60 \, \Omega, V_{rms} = 240 \, \text{V}$

(i) Resonating angular frequency,

$\omega_C = \dfrac{1}{\sqrt{LC}} = \dfrac{1}{\sqrt{10 \times 40 \times 10^{-6}}}$

$\dfrac{1}{20 \times 10^{-3}} = 50 \, \text{rad/s}$

(ii) Current at resonating frequency,

$I_{rms} = \dfrac{V_{rms}}{Z} = \dfrac{V_{rms}}{R}$ $(\because$ At resonance $Z = R)$

$= \dfrac{240}{60} = 4 \, \text{A}$

(iii) $\therefore$ Inductive reactance, $X_L = \omega L$

At resonance, $X_L = \omega_0 L = 50 \times 10 = 500 \, \Omega$

Potential drop to across inductor,

$V_{rms} = I_{rms} \times X_L = 4 \times 500$ $V_{rms} = 2000 \, \text{V}$

17. Refer to Theory

18. (a) When an ac source is connected to an ideal capacitor the instantaneous value of voltage and current are

$v = V_m \sin \omega t$ and

$i = I_m \sin(\omega t + \pi/2) = I_m \cos \omega t$

where $\pi/2$ is the phase angle by which voltage lags current when ac flows through a capacitor. Suppose the voltage and current remain constant for a small time dt.

Therefore, electrical energy consumed in the small time dt is $dW = v \, i \, dt$

The total electrical energy consumed in one time period of ac is given by

$$W = \int_0^T v \, i \, dt = \int_0^T V_m \sin \omega t \times I_m \cos \omega t \, dt$$

$$= V_m I_m \int_0^T \sin \omega t \cos \omega t \, dt$$

$$W = \dfrac{I_m V_m}{2} \int_0^T 2 \sin \omega t \cos \omega t \, dt$$

or $$W = \dfrac{I_m V_m}{2} \int_0^T \sin 2\omega t \, dt = \dfrac{I_m V_m}{2}\left[\dfrac{\cos(2\omega t)}{2\omega}\right]_0^T = 0$$

Hence, the total electrical energy consumed in an ac circuit by an ideal capacitor is zero.

Now, average power is defined as the ratio of the total electrical energy consumed over the entire cycle to the time period of the cycle, therefore,

$$P_{av} = \frac{W}{T} = 0$$

Hence, the average power consumed in an ac circuit by an ideal capacitor is zero.

(b) When the system is connected across the dc the total resistance of the circuit is infinite as capacitor blocks dc. Therefore, no current flows through the lamp. Hence, it does not glow. On the other hand, the lamp glows when system is connected to ac as the capacitor offers a low resistance to the flow of ac.

Now it is clear that, in case of dc there is no change if capacitance is reduced. In case of ac, on decreasing the capacitance, the capacitive reactance and hence the impedance increases. This decreases the current hence, the brightness of the lamp will decrease.

19. In a series LCR circuit, the impedance of the circuit is

given by $Z = \sqrt{\left(L\omega - \dfrac{1}{c\omega}\right)^2 + R^2}$, where ω is the angular

frequency. Clearly, as ω varies Z also varies and hence the current also varies. At a certain frequency (resonant frequency) $\omega = \omega_0$, Z becomes minimum and the current becomes maximum.

Plot showing variation of current with frequency:

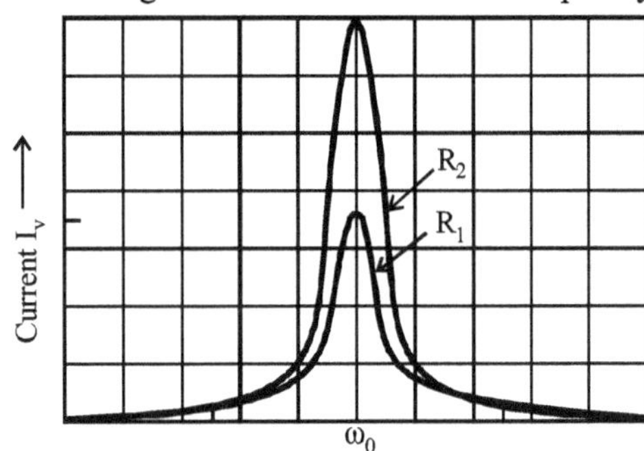

Current at resonance $\;i_v = \dfrac{E_v}{Z} = \dfrac{E_v}{R}\;\left(\text{as } L\omega_0 = \dfrac{1}{C\omega_0}\right)$

Smaller the value of R_2, sharper the resonance curve.

Q-factor of the circuit is defined as the ratio of inductive reactance at resonance to the resistance R in the circuit

i.e., $\;Q = \dfrac{L\omega_0}{R} = \dfrac{1}{C\omega_0 R}\;$ i.e., $\;Q \propto \dfrac{1}{R}$

Significance of Q-factor : The Q-factor of an LCR circuit is a measure of the sharpness of the resonance. Larger the value of Q-factor sharper is the resonance curve.

20. (a) Average power

$$P_a = \frac{1}{T}\int_0^T P_i\,dt = \frac{1}{T}\int_0^T i^2 R\,dt = \frac{1}{T}\int_0^T i_m^2 \sin^2 \omega t\, R\,dt$$

$$= \frac{1}{T} i_m^2 R \int_0^T \frac{(1-\cos 2\omega t)}{2}\,dt = \frac{1}{T}\frac{I_m^2}{2}R\left[T - \frac{\sin 2\omega t}{2\omega}\right]_0^T$$

$$= \frac{1}{T}\frac{I_m^2}{2}R\left[T - 0\right] = \frac{1}{2}I_m^2 R$$

(b) Given, P = 100 W, V = 220 V

As we know power, $\;P = \dfrac{V^2}{R}$, R is the resistance

$\therefore\quad R = \dfrac{V^2}{P} = \dfrac{220 \times 220}{100} = 484\;\Omega$

21. The power is defined as the rate of at which work is being done in the circuit.

When $V = V_0 \sin\omega t$ is applied to a series LCR circuit.

Current is $I = I_0 \sin(\omega t + \phi)$

$$I_0 = \frac{V_0}{Z}\;\text{ and }\;\phi = \tan^{-1}\left(\frac{X_C - X_L}{R}\right)$$

Instantaneous power supplied by the source is

$$P = VI = (V_0 \sin\omega t) \times (I_0 \sin(\omega t + \phi) = V_0 \sin\omega t\, I_0 \sin(\omega t + \phi)$$

The average power $P_{av} = V_{rms}\, I_{rms} \cos\phi = \dfrac{V_0}{\sqrt{2}} \cdot \dfrac{I_0}{\sqrt{2}} \cdot \cos\theta$

In this expression $\cos\phi$ is known as the power factor.

Case I : For pure inductive circuit or pure capacitive circuit,

the phase difference between current and voltage is $\dfrac{\pi}{2}$.

$$\therefore\; \phi = \frac{\pi}{2}\,,\; \cos\phi = 0$$

Therefore, $P_{av} = 0$. Thus no power is dissipated in the circuit. This current is sometimes referred to as wattless current and such a circuit is called wattless circuit.

Case II : For power dissipated at resonance in an LCR circuit,

$X_C - X_L = 0,\; \phi = 0\qquad \therefore \cos\phi = 1$

So, maximum power is dissipated in the circuit.

22. The variation of current with angular frequency for the two resistances R_1 and R_2 shown in the graph below.

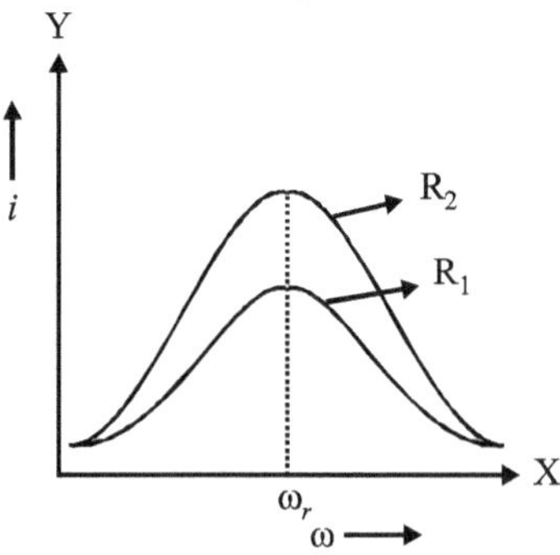

Here, ω_r = Resonance frequency

(a) From the graph, we can see that resonance for the resistance R_2 is sharper than for R_1 because resistance R_2 is less than resistance R_1. Therefore, at resonance, the value of peak current will rise more abruptly for a lower value of resistance.

(b) Power associated with the resistance is given by
$$P = E_v I_v$$
From the graph, we can say that the current in case of R_2 is more than the current in case of R_1. Hence, the power dissipation in case of the circuit with R_2 is more than that with R_1

23. (i) When the number of turns in the inductor is reduced, the self inductance of coil decreases; so impedance of circuit reduces and so current increases. Thus the brightness of the bulb increases.
(ii) If soft iron rod is inserted in the inductor, then the inductance L increases. Therefore, the current through the bulb will decrease, decreasing the brightness of the bulb.
(iii) When capacitor of reactance $X_C = X_L$ is introduced the net reactance of circuit becomes zero, so impedance of circuit decreases. Therefore $Z = R$, so current in the circuit increases, hence brightness of bulb increases. Thus brightness of bulb increases in both cases.

24. The average power supplied by the source over a complete cycle is given as
$$P = VI \cos \phi$$
where, $\cos \phi$ is called the power factor.
For pure inductive circuit, the phase difference between current and voltage is $\dfrac{\pi}{2}$.
$$\Rightarrow \cos\phi = \cos\frac{\pi}{2} = 0$$
Therefore, the average power dissipated is zero.
(ii) If an iron rod is inserted in the inductor, then the value of inductance L increases. As such, the current through the bulb will decrease, thus, decreasing the brightness of the bulb.

25. (a)

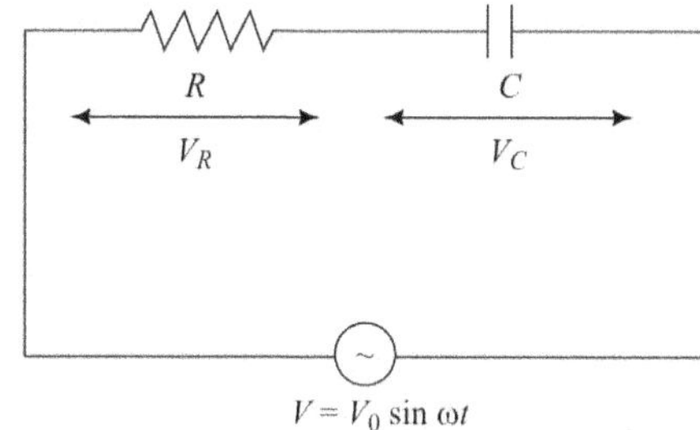

Total impedance of circuit
$$Z = \sqrt{R^2 + X_C^2}$$
$\therefore$ Current in circuit
$$I = \frac{V_0}{\sqrt{R^2 + X_C^2}}$$
Peak voltage across
(i) Resistance R
$$V_R = IR = \frac{V_0 R}{\sqrt{R^2 + X_C^2}}$$
(ii) Capacitor C
$$V_C = I X_C$$
$$= \frac{V_0 X_C}{\sqrt{R^2 + X_C^2}}$$

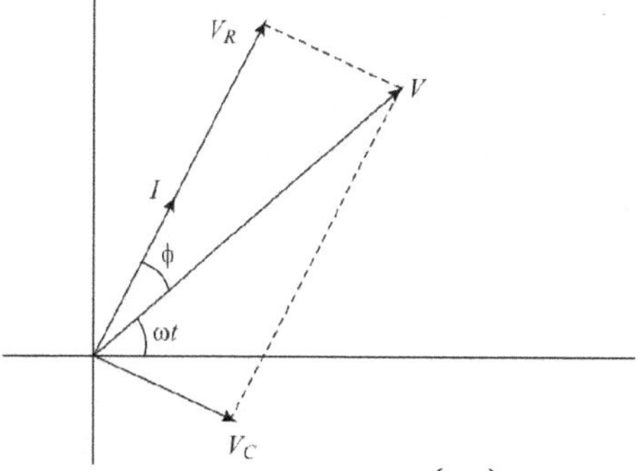

(b) $\tan \phi = \dfrac{V_C}{V_R} \Rightarrow \phi = \tan^{-1}\left(\dfrac{V_C}{V_R}\right) = \tan^{-1}\left(\dfrac{X_C}{R}\right)$

$\therefore$ Phase difference between V and I is $\tan^{-1}\left(\dfrac{X_C}{R}\right)$

NCERT Exemplar 

1. (b) As given that, $v = 50$ Hz, $I_{rms} = 5$A
$$t = \frac{1}{300}\text{s}$$
As we know that $I_{rms} = \dfrac{I_0}{\sqrt{2}}$

$I_0 = $ Peak value $= \sqrt{2}.I_{rms} = \sqrt{2} \times 5$

$I_0 = 5\sqrt{2}$A

at, $t = \dfrac{1}{300}$ sec , $I = I_0 \sin\omega t = 5\sqrt{2}\sin 2\pi vt$

$$= 5\sqrt{2}\sin 2\pi \times 50 \times \frac{1}{300}$$

$I = 5\sqrt{2}\sin\dfrac{\pi}{3} = 5\sqrt{2}\times\dfrac{\sqrt{3}}{2} = 5\sqrt{3/2}$ Amp

$$\left(\therefore \sin\frac{\pi}{3} = \frac{\sqrt{3}}{2}\right)$$

$I = \left(5\sqrt{\dfrac{3}{2}}\right)$ Amp

2. (c) To deliver maximum power from the generator to the load, total internal reactance must be equal to conjugate of total external reactance.
So, $X_{int} = X_{ext}$
$$X_g = (X_L) = -X_L$$
Hence, $X_L = -X_g$ (Reactance in external circuit)

3. (c) As we know that,
The voltmeter in AC reads rms values of voltage
$$I_{rms} = \sqrt{2}I_0 \text{ and } V_{rms} = \sqrt{2}v_0$$
The voltmeter in AC circuit connected to AC mains reads mean value ($<v^2>$) and is calibrated in such a way that it gives rms value of $<v^2>$, which is multiplied by form factor $\sqrt{2}$ to give rms value V_{rms}.

4. (b) As we know that,
The resonant frequency in an L-C-R series circuit is
$$v_0 = \frac{1}{2\pi\sqrt{LC}}$$

So, to reduce ν_0 either increase L or increase C.

To increase capacitance, another capacitor must be connect in parallel with the first capacitor.

5. **(c)** As we know that, Quality factor (Q) of an L-C-R circuit must be higher so Q is

$$Q = \frac{1}{R}\sqrt{\frac{L}{C}}$$

where R is resistance, L is inductance and C is capacitance of the circuit.

So, for higher Q, L must be large, and C and R should be low.

Hence, option (c) is verify.

6. **(c)** As given that,

$$X_L = 1\Omega, R = 2\Omega, E_{rms} = 6V, P_{av} = ?$$

The average power dissipated in the L, R, series circuit with AC source

Then $P_{av} = E_{rms}\, I_{rms} \cos\phi \qquad ...(i)$

$$I_{rms} = \frac{I_0}{\sqrt{2}} = \frac{E_{rms}}{Z}$$

$$Z = \sqrt{R^2 + X_L^2} = \sqrt{4+1} = \sqrt{5}$$

$$I_{rms} = \frac{6}{\sqrt{5}} A$$

$$\cos\phi = \frac{R}{Z} = \frac{2}{\sqrt{5}}$$

By putting the value of I_{rms}, E_{rms}, $\cos\phi$ in equation (i), then,

$$P_{av} = 6 \times \frac{6}{\sqrt{5}} \times \frac{2}{\sqrt{5}} = \frac{72}{\sqrt{5}\sqrt{5}}$$

$$= \frac{72}{5} = 14.4 \text{ watt}$$

7. **(a)** As given that,

Secondary voltage (V_S) is :

$$V_S = 24 \text{ Volt}$$

Power associated with secondary is :

$$P_S = 12 \text{ Watt}$$

As we know that $P_S = V_S I_S$

$$I_S = \frac{P_S}{V_S} = \frac{12}{24} = \frac{1}{2} A = 0.5 \text{ Amp}$$

Peak value of the current in the secondary

$$I_0 = I_S\sqrt{2} = 0.5\sqrt{2}$$

$$= \frac{5}{10}\sqrt{2}\left[I_0 = \frac{1}{\sqrt{2}} \text{ Amp} \right]$$

8. At high frequencies, capacitor $\approx$ short circuit (low reactance) and inductor $\approx$ open circuit (high reactance). Therefore, the equivalent circuit $Z \approx R_1 + R_3$ as shown in the Fig.

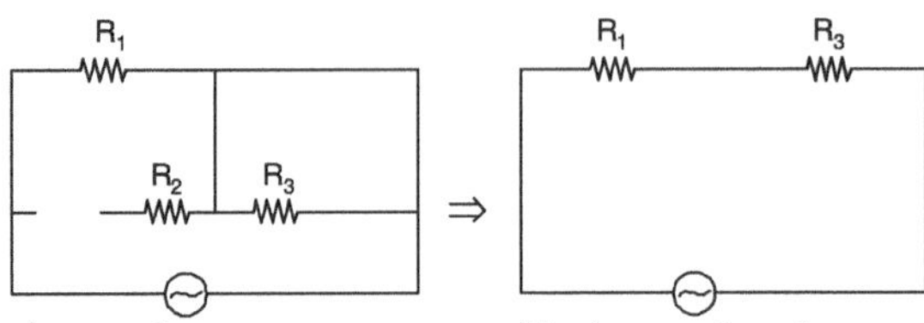

9. As we know at resonance, X_L is equal and opposite to X_C.

$\therefore$ Resonance point in the given question will be at R

10. For the frequencies higher than the resonant frequency $X_L > X_C$, i.e., the circuit will be more inductive than capacitive.

11. (a) A (b) Zero (c) L or C or LC

12. A capacitor does not allow flow of direct current through it as the resistance across the gap is infinite. When an alternating voltage is applied across the capacitor plates, the plates are alternately charged and discharged. The current through the capacitor is a result of this changing voltage (or charge). Thus, a capacitor will pass more current through it if the voltage is changing at a faster rate, i.e. if the frequency of supply is higher. This implies that the reactance offered by a capacitor is less with increasing frequency; it is given by $1/\omega C$.

13. (i) X has low capacitance value

(ii) X has low resistance value and Z has high resistance value.

The quality factor will be maximum in X.

The impedence will be maximum at frequency ω_0 when $X_L = X_C$ and impedence Z = resistance R.

14. (a) As the circuit is mainly capacitive, we would increase the capacitance inorder to decrease the capacitive reactance X_c to be closer to resonance for maximum power.

(b) This change would bring the resonant angular frequency closer to the angular frequency of the emf.

Objective Practice Exercise 

1. **(a)** Average value of complete cycle of ac is zero.

2. **(d)**

3. **(b)** Given equation, $e = 80 \sin 100\pi t$ ...(i)

Standard equation of instantaneous voltage is given by

$e = e_m \sin\omega t$ ...(ii)

Compare (i) and (ii), we get $e_m = 80$ V

where e_m is the voltage amplitude.

Current amplitude $I_m = \dfrac{e_m}{Z} = 80/20 = 4$ A.

$$I_{r.m.s} = \frac{4}{\sqrt{2}} = \frac{4\sqrt{2}}{2} = 2\sqrt{2} = 2.828 \text{ A.}$$

4. **(b)** $P = \dfrac{1}{2}V_0 i_0 \cos\phi \Rightarrow P = P_{peak} \cdot \cos\phi$

$$\Rightarrow \frac{1}{2}(P_{peak}) = P_{peak} \cos\phi \Rightarrow \cos\phi = \frac{1}{2} \Rightarrow \phi = \frac{\pi}{3}$$

5. **(d)** When an ac voltage of 220 V is applied to a capacitor C, the charge on the plates is in phase with the applied voltage.

As the circuit is pure capacitive so, the current developed leads the applied voltage by a phase angle of 90° Hence, power delivered to the capacitor per cycle is

$P = V_{rms}\, I_{rms} \cos 90° = 0.$

6. **(b)** $V = 50 \times 2 \sin 100\,\pi \cos 100\,\pi t = 50 \sin 200\,\pi t$

$\Rightarrow V_0 = 50\ Volts$ and $v = 100\ Hz$

7. **(d)** $V = 120 \sin 100\,\pi t \cos 100\,\pi t \Rightarrow V = 60 \sin 200\,\pi t$

$V_{max} = 60V$ and $v = 100 Hz$

8. **(a)** $E = 8 \sin \omega t + 6 \sin 2\omega t$

$\Rightarrow E_{peak} = \sqrt{8^2 + 6^2} = 10\ V$

$E_{rms} = \dfrac{10}{\sqrt{2}} = 5\sqrt{2}\ V$

9. **(d)** Power dissipated $= E_{rms}.\ I_{rms} = (E_{rms})\,(I_{rms})\cos\theta$

Hence, power dissipated depends upon phase difference.

10. **(d)** $I = 2 \sin \omega t$

$V = 5 \cos \omega t = 5 \sin\left(\dfrac{\pi}{2} - \omega t\right)$

Since, there is a phase difference of $\dfrac{\pi}{2}$ between the current and voltage

$\therefore$ Average power over a complete cycle is zero.

11. **(a)** The current and potential difference are in phase with the resistance. So, the time taken would be same as time for voltage to change from $(t = 0)$ that is peak value to rms value.

Time taken by voltage to achieve its rms value of $\dfrac{200}{\sqrt{2}}$.

$\dfrac{200}{\sqrt{2}} = 200 \cos(100\pi t)$

$\Rightarrow \cos(100\pi t) = \dfrac{1}{\sqrt{2}} = \cos\left(\dfrac{\pi}{4}\right)$

$t = \dfrac{1}{400}$ second $= 2.5 \times 10^{-3}$ sec.

12. **(d)** The instantaneous values of emf and current in inductive circuit are given by $E = E_0 \sin\omega t$ and i

$= i_0 \sin\left(\omega t - \dfrac{\pi}{2}\right)$ respectively.

$\therefore\ \ P_{inst} = E.i = E_0 \sin\omega t \times i_0 \sin\left(\omega t - \dfrac{\pi}{2}\right)$

$= -E_0 i_0 \sin\omega t \cos\omega t = -\dfrac{1}{2} E_0 i_0 \sin 2\omega t$

Hence, angular frequency of instantaneous power is 2ω

13. **(b)**   **14.** **(b)**

15. **(d)** At resonance, $X_C = X_L$

Reactance of circuit becomes zero and impedance become minimum and maximum current flows through the circuit.

16. **(b)** $\cos\phi = \dfrac{R}{Z}$, where Z is the impedance &

$Z = \sqrt{R^2 + (X_L - X_C)^2}$, if there is only resistance then

$Z = R \Rightarrow \cos\phi = 1$

17. **(c)** The time constant for resonance circuit, $= CR$

Growth of charge in a circuit containing capacitance and

resistance is given by the formula, $q = q_0(1 - e^{-t/CR})$

CR is known as time constant in this formula.

18. **(b)**

19. **(a)** The reactance of inductor, $X_L = \omega L$

The reactance of capacitor, $X_C = \dfrac{1}{\omega C}$

where $\omega = 2\pi n$ & n is the frequency of A.C source.

20. **(d)**

21. **(d)** $\tan\phi = \dfrac{V_C - V_L}{V_R}$ (if $V_C > V_L$)

$\qquad = \dfrac{V_L - V_C}{R}$ (if $V_L > V_C$)

where ϕ is angle between current & applied voltage.

22. **(a)**   **23.** **(b)**

24. **(a)** In ideal condition of LC circuit $R = 0$ and LC oscillation continue indefinitely. Energy being shunted back and forth between electric field of capacitor and magnetic field of inductor. As capacitor is fully charged

current in L is zero and $\dfrac{1}{2}\dfrac{q_0^2}{C}$ energy is stored in electric

field. Then capacitor begins to discharge through L causing a current to flow and build up a magnetic field, around L. Therefore, energy stored.

Now in $L = \dfrac{1}{2} L I_0^2$ when C is fully discharged, V across

the plate reduces to zero.

$\therefore$ Electric field energy is transferred to magnetic field and vice-versa.

25. **(c)** Impedance at resonant frequency is minimum in series LCR circuit.

So, $Z = \sqrt{R^2 + \left(2\pi fL - \dfrac{1}{2\pi fC}\right)^2}$

26. **(c)** When resistance is connected to A.C source, then current & voltage are in same phase.

27. **(d)**

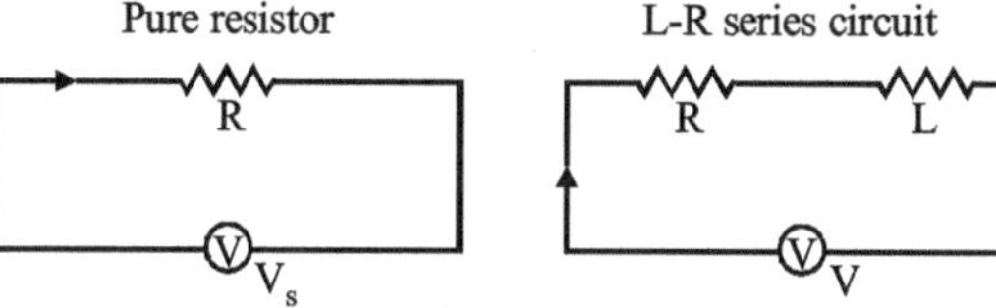

For pure resistor circuit, power

$P = \dfrac{V^2}{R} \Rightarrow V^2 = PR$

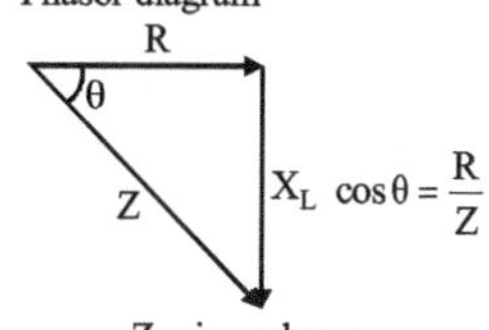

For L-R series circuit, power

$P^1 = \dfrac{V^2}{Z} \cos\theta = \dfrac{V^2}{Z}.\dfrac{R}{Z} = \dfrac{PR}{Z^2}.R = P\left(\dfrac{R}{Z}\right)^2$

28. **(b)** $X_L = \omega L \Rightarrow X_L \propto \omega$

29. **(b)**   **30.** **(c)**

31. **(a)** Iron loss is the energy loss in the form of heat due to the formation of eddy currents in the iron core of the transformer.

32. **(c)** A transformer does not change the frequency of ac.

33. **(b)**

34. **(b)** We know that frequency of electrical oscillation in L.C. circuit is

$$f = \frac{1}{2\pi}\sqrt{\frac{1}{LC}}\ ; \quad \text{Now, } L = 2L\ \&\ C = 4C$$

$$f' = \frac{1}{2\pi}\sqrt{\frac{1}{2L.4C}} = \frac{1}{2\pi}\sqrt{\frac{1}{LC}} \times \frac{1}{2\sqrt{2}} \Rightarrow f' = \frac{1}{2\sqrt{2}} \times f$$

35. **(d)** As $E_p I_p = P_i$ $\therefore\ I_p = \dfrac{P_i}{E_p} = \dfrac{4000}{100} = 40\,A.$

36. **(c)** When the capacitor is completely charged, the total energy in the L.C circuit is with the capacitor and that energy is $E = \dfrac{1}{2}\dfrac{Q^2}{C}$

When half energy is with the capacitor in the form of electric field between the plates of the capacitor we get

$\dfrac{E}{2} = \dfrac{1}{2}\dfrac{Q'^2}{C}$ where Q' is the charge on one plate of the capacitor

$$\therefore\ \frac{1}{2} \times \frac{1}{2}\frac{Q^2}{C} = \frac{1}{2}\frac{Q'^2}{C} \Rightarrow Q' = \frac{Q}{\sqrt{2}}$$

37. **(b)** $N_p = 140, N_s = 280, I_p = 4A, I_s = ?$

For a transformer $\dfrac{I_s}{I_p} = \dfrac{N_p}{N_s} \Rightarrow \dfrac{I_s}{4} = \dfrac{140}{280} \Rightarrow I_s = 2\,A$

38. **(a)** Energy stored in magnetic field $= \dfrac{1}{2}\,Li^2$

Energy stored in electric field $= \dfrac{1}{2}\dfrac{q^2}{C}$

$$\therefore\ \frac{1}{2}Li^2 = \frac{1}{2}\frac{q^2}{C}$$

Also $q = q_0 \cos \omega t$ and $\omega = \dfrac{1}{\sqrt{LC}}$

On solving $t = \dfrac{\pi}{4}\sqrt{LC}$

39. **(a)** $\dfrac{E_s}{E_p} = \dfrac{n_s}{n_p}$ or $E_s = E_p \times \left(\dfrac{n_s}{n_p}\right)$

$$\therefore\ E_s = 120 \times \left(\frac{200}{100}\right) = 240\,V$$

$\dfrac{I_p}{I_s} = \dfrac{n_s}{n_p}$ or $I_s = I_p\left(\dfrac{n_p}{n_s}\right)$ $\therefore\ I_s = 10\left(\dfrac{100}{200}\right) = 5\,amp$

40. **(b)** $V = 200V;\ r = 10\Omega$

$R' = 10 + 100\Omega = 110\Omega$

$$I = \frac{V}{R'} = \frac{220}{100} = 2A$$

$P = I^2R = 4 \times 100 = 400\,W$

41. **(b)** Efficiency of the transformer

$$\eta = \frac{P_{output}}{P_{input}} \times 100 = \frac{100}{220 \times 0.5} \times 100 = 90.9\%$$

42. **(c)**

43. **(d)** $\eta = \dfrac{E_s I_s}{E_p I_p} = \dfrac{11 \times 90}{220 \times 5} = 0.9 \times 100\% = 90\%$

44. **(c)** In a step down transformed voltage is 22 V. By ohm's law, $I = \dfrac{22V}{220\,ohm} = 0.1\,Amp$

1. **(a)** $E = 8\sin \omega t + 6 \sin 2\omega t$

$$\Rightarrow E_{peak} = \sqrt{8^2 + 6^2} = 10\,V$$

$$E_{rms} = \frac{10}{\sqrt{2}} = 5\sqrt{2}\,V$$

2. **(a)**   **3.** **(b)**   **4.** **(b)**   **5.** **(c)**   **6.** **(a)**

7. **(b)** In series RLC circuit,

Voltage, $V = \sqrt{V_R^2 + (V_L - V_C)^2}$

And, at resonance, $V_L = V_C$

Hence, $V = V_R$

8. **(a)**

9. **(d)** In LCR series circuit, resonance frequency f_0 is given by

$$L\omega = \frac{1}{C\omega} \Rightarrow \omega^2 = \frac{1}{LC} \quad \therefore\ \omega = \sqrt{\frac{1}{LC}} = 2\pi f_0$$

$$\therefore\ f_0 = \frac{1}{2\pi\sqrt{LC}} \quad \text{or} \quad f_0 \alpha \frac{1}{\sqrt{C}}$$

When the capacitance of the circuit is made 4 times, its resonant frequency become f_0'

$$\therefore\ \frac{f_0'}{f_0} = \frac{\sqrt{C}}{\sqrt{4C}} \quad \text{or} \quad f_0' = \frac{f_0}{2}$$

10. **(c)** $Z = \sqrt{R^2 + \left(\omega L - \dfrac{1}{\omega C}\right)^2}$

Here $R = 100\,W, L = 0.5$ henry, $C = 10 \times 10^6$ farad

$\omega = 2p\,\pi = 100\,\pi.$

11. **(a)**

12. Here, $X_C = 100\Omega, V_0 = 200$ volt.

$$\therefore\ \text{Current} = I = \frac{V_0}{X_C} = \frac{200}{100} = 2A$$

13. If the frequency of the source is doubled, R remains unchanged, but $X_L = \omega L = 2\pi fL$ becomes doubled and $X_C = \dfrac{1}{2\pi fC}$ becomes half.

14. In a series LCR circuit the instantaneons value of applied voltage of the current produced are given by $E = E_0 \sin\omega t$ and $I = I_0 \sin (\omega t - \varphi)$

The impedance of the circuit is given by

$Z = \sqrt{R^2 + (X_L - X_C)^2}$ provided $X_L = X_C$

$$\Rightarrow \omega_r L = \frac{1}{\omega_r C} \Rightarrow \omega_r^2 = \frac{1}{LC} \Rightarrow \omega_r = \frac{1}{\sqrt{LC}}$$

15. Here, $L = 0.12\,H, C = 4.85 \times 10^{-7}F, R = 23\,\Omega$

$\therefore\ Z = \sqrt{R^2 + (X_L - X_C)^2}$

Current will become maximum when $Z = \dfrac{V}{I}$ will be minimum.

i.e. $X_L = X_C$

$$\Rightarrow \omega L = \frac{1}{\omega C} \Rightarrow \omega = \frac{1}{\sqrt{LC}} = \frac{1}{\sqrt{0.12 \times 4.8 \times 10^{-7}}}$$

$\Rightarrow \omega = 66.3\,Hz.$